# SECOND EDITION

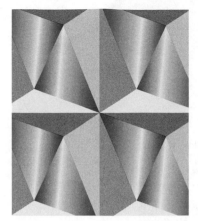

# Research Methods and Statistics
## A Critical Thinking Approach

# Sherri L. Jackson

**Jacksonville University**

**THOMSON**
━━━━━✦━━━━━ ™
**WADSWORTH**

Australia • Brazil • Canada • Mexico • Singapore • Spain
United Kingdom • United States

**THOMSON**
™
**WADSWORTH**

**Research Methods and Statistics: A Critical Thinking Approach,**
**Second Edition**
*Sherri L. Jackson*

Publisher/Executive Editor: *Vicki Knight*
Assistant Editor: *Dan Moneypenny*
Technology Project Manager: *Erik Fortier*
Editorial Assistants: *Lucy Faridany and Monica Sarmiento Arvin*
Marketing Manager: *Dory Schaeffer*
Marketing Assistant: *Nicole Morinon*
Executive Marketing Communications Manager: *Brian Chaffee*
Project Manager, Editorial Production: *Marti Paul*
Art Director: *Vernon Boes*
Print Buyer: *Judy Inouye*

Permissions Editor: *Joohee Lee*
Production Service: *Scratchgravel Publishing Services*
Text Designer: *Anne Draus, Scratchgravel Publishing Services*
Art Editor/Illustrator: *Greg Draus, Scratchgravel Publishing Services*
Copy Editor: *Carol Reitz*
Cover Designer: *Cheryl Carrington*
Cover Photo: *J. A. Kraulis/Masterfile*
Cover Printer: *R.R. Donnelley/Crawfordsville*
Compositor: *Cadmus*
Printer: *R.R. Donnelley/Crawfordsville*

**Thomson Higher Education**
**10 Davis Drive**
**Belmont, CA 94002-3098**
**USA**

For more information about our products, contact us at:
**Thomson Learning Academic Resource Center**
**1-800-423-0563**

For permission to use material from this text or product, submit a request online at
**http://www.thomsonrights.com.**
Any additional questions about permissions can be submitted by email to **thomsonrights@thomson.com.**

Library of Congress Control Number: 2005923117

ISBN 0-534-55660-4

To Rich

# About the Author

Sherri L. Jackson is Professor of Psychology at Jacksonville University, where she has taught since 1988. At JU, she has won Excellence in Scholarship and University Service Awards and also the university-wide Professor of the Year Award in 2004. She received her M.S. and Ph.D. in cognitive/experimental psychology from the University of Florida. Her research interests include human reasoning and the teaching of psychology. She has published numerous articles in both areas. In 1997, she received a research grant from the Office of Teaching Resources in Psychology (APA Division 2) to develop *A Compendium of Introductory Psychology Textbooks 1997–2000*. She is also the author of *Statistics: Plain and Simple* (Belmont, CA: Wadsworth, 2005).

# Brief Contents

# Contents

# 4  Descriptive Methods   68

**5** **Data Organization and Descriptive Statistics   89**

**6** **Correlational Methods and Statistics 122**

# 7 Hypothesis Testing and Inferential Statistics 143

# 8 The Logic of Experimental Design 174

# 9  Inferential Statistics: Two-Group Designs  195

# 10  Experimental Designs with More Than Two Levels of an Independent Variable  211

# 11  Complex Experimental Designs  241

# 12 Quasi-Experimental and Single-Case Designs   264

# 13 Nonparametric Procedures   282

**14**

# APA Communication Guidelines    296

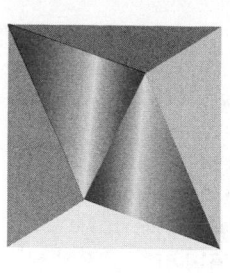

# Preface

When I first began teaching research methods 17 years ago, I did not include statistics in my class because my students took a separate statistics course as a prerequisite. However, as time passed, I began to integrate more and more statistical content so that students could understand more fully how methods and statistics relate to one another. Eventually I reached the point where I decided to adopt a textbook that integrated statistics and research methods. However, I was somewhat surprised to find that there were only a few integrated texts. In addition, these texts covered statistics in much greater detail than I needed or wanted. Thus, I wrote the present text to meet the market need for a brief, introductory-level, integrated text. My other writing goals were to be *concise yet comprehensive*, to use an *organization* that progresses for the most part from nonexperimental methods to experimental methods, to incorporate *critical thinking* throughout the text, and to use a simple, easy-to-understand *writing style.*

*Concise yet Comprehensive.*　　The present text is concise (it can be covered in a one-semester course) yet still integrates statistics with methods. To accomplish these twin goals, I chose to cover only those statistics most used by psychologists rather than to include all the statistics that might be covered in a regular statistics class. The result is a text that, in effect, integrates a brief statistical supplement within a methods text. The advantage of using this text rather than a statistical supplement with a methods text is that the statistics are integrated throughout the text. In other words, I have described the statistics that would be used with a particular research method in the same chapter or in a chapter immediately following the pertinent methods chapter.

I realize that some instructors may like the integrated approach but not want to cover inferential statistics in quite as much detail as I do. I have therefore structured the coverage of each inferential statistical test so that the calculations may be omitted if so desired. I have divided the section on each statistical test into four clear subsections. The first describes the statistical test and what it does for a researcher. The second subsection provides the formulas for the test and an example of how to apply the formulas. In the third subsection, I demonstrate how to interpret the results from the test; and in the final subsection, I list the assumptions that underlie the test. Instructors who simply want their students to understand the test, how to interpret it, and the assumptions behind it can omit (not assign) the subsection on statistical calculations without any problems of continuity. Thus, the text is appropriate both in methods classes for which statistics is not a prerequisite and in those classes for which statistics is a prerequisite. In the latter case, the calculation subsections may be omitted, or they may be used as a statistical review and as a means of demonstrating how statistics are used by psychologists.

*Organization.*   The text begins with chapters on science and getting started in research (Chapters 1 and 2). Measurement issues and descriptive methods and statistics are then covered, followed by correlational methods and statistics (Chapters 3–6). Hypothesis testing and inferential statistics are introduced in Chapter 7, followed by experimental design and the appropriate inferential statistics for analyzing such designs (Chapters 8–11). The final three chapters cover quasi-experiment and single-case designs (Chapter 12), nonparametric statistics (Chapter 13), and APA guidelines on writing (Chapter 14).

*Critical Thinking.*   Evaluation of any research design involves critical thinking, so this particular goal is not a novel one in research methods texts. However, I have made a special effort to incorporate a critical thinking mind-set into the text in the hopes of fostering this in students. I attempt to teach students to adopt a skeptical approach to research analysis through instructive examples and an explicit pedagogical aid incorporated within the text. At the end of each major section in each chapter, I have inserted a *Critical Thinking Check*. This feature varies in length and format but generally involves a series of application questions concerning the section information. The questions are designed to foster analytical/critical thinking skills in addition to reviewing the section information.

*Writing Style.*   I present the information in a simple, direct, easy-to-understand fashion. Because research methods is one of the more difficult courses for students, I also try to write in an engaging, conversational style, much as if the reader were a student seated in front of me in my classroom. I hope, through this writing style, to help students better understand some of the more troublesome concepts without losing their interest.

## Pedagogical Aids

The text incorporates several pedagogical aids at the chapter level. Each chapter begins with a *chapter outline*. Key terms are defined in a *running glossary* in the margins within each chapter. *In Review* summary matrices, at the end of major sections in each chapter, provide a review of the major concepts of the section in a tabular format. These summaries are immediately followed by the *Critical Thinking Checks* described above. Thus, students can use the In Review summary after reading a chapter section and then engage in the Critical Thinking Check on that information. *Chapter Exercises* are provided at the end of each chapter, so that students can further review and apply the knowledge in that chapter. Answers to the odd-numbered chapter exercises are provided in Appendix C. *Answers to the Critical Thinking Checks* appear at the end of each chapter.

## New to This Edition

The text has been expanded from 12 to 14 chapters, with coverage of ethics moved from Chapter 12 to Chapter 2. In addition, there is a new chapter on nonparametric statistics (Chapter 13). Lab resources and statistical software resources are noted at the end of each chapter where applicable. The chapter introducing experimental design has been expanded to include Latin square designs, increased coverage of counterbalancing, and developmental designs. Last, there is a new section on presenting papers and posters in the APA writing style chapter (Chapter 14).

## For the Instructor

An *Instructor's Manual/Test Bank* accompanies the text. The *Instructor's Manual* contains lecture outlines, transparency masters of most of the tables and figures from the text, resources to aid in the development of classroom exercises/demonstrations, and answers to all chapter exercises. A test bank, included in the instructor's manual and on disk, includes multiple-choice, short-answer, and essay questions.

## For the Student

In addition to the pedagogical aids built into the text, a *Study Guide* is available. The *Study Guide* provides a review of each chapter, a formula review for chapters with statistics, fill-in-the-blank questions, a multiple-choice self-test, and additional statistical exercises for those chapters in which statistics are covered. Web resources include practice quizzes for each chapter and statistics and research methods workshops at http://psychology.wadsworth.com/workshops.

## Acknowledgments

I must acknowledge many people for their help with this project. I thank the students in my research methods classes on which the text was pretested. Their comments were most valuable. I also thank my husband for his careful proofreading and insightful comments and Bennie and Henry for the encouragement of their ever-present wagging tails. In addition, I would like to thank those who reviewed the text in the first edition. They include: Patrick Ament, Central Missouri State University; Michele Breault, Truman State University; Stephen Levine, Georgian Court College; Patrick McKnight, University of Arizona; William Moyer, Millersville University; Michael Politano, The Citadel; Jeff Smith, Northern Kentucky University;

Bart Van Voorhis, University of Wisconsin, LaCrosse; Zoe Warwick, University of Maryland, Baltimore County; and Carolyn Weisz, University of Puget Sound. In this second edition, I was fortunate again to have reviewers who took their task seriously and provided very constructive suggestions for strengthening and improving the text. I am grateful for the suggestions and comments provided by Scott Bailey, Texas Lutheran University; James Ballard, California State University, Northridge; Stephen Blessing, University of Tampa; Amy Bohmann, Texas Lutheran University; Anne Cook, University of Utah; Julie Evey, University of Southern Indiana; Rob Mowrer, Angelo State University; Sandra Nicks, Christian Brothers University; Clare Porac, Pennsylvania State University, Erie, The Behrend College; and Diane Winn, Colby College.

Special thanks to the team at Wadsworth: Vicki Knight, Publisher, Psychology and Education, for her support and guidance; Marti Paul, Production Project Manager; Brian Chaffee, Executive Marketing Communications Manager; Dory Schaeffer, Marketing Manager; Vernon Boes, Art Director; Dan Moneypenny, Assistant Editor; Lucy Faridany and Monica Sarmiento Arvin, Editorial Assistants; and Joohee Lee, Permissions Editor. Finally, thanks to Anne and Greg Draus of Scratchgravel Publishing Services for their production expertise and to Carol Reitz for her excellent copyediting skills.

*Sherri L. Jackson*

# 1 Thinking Like a Scientist

**Areas of Psychological Research**
Psychobiology
Cognition
Human Development
Social Psychology
Psychotherapy

**Sources of Knowledge**
Superstition and Intuition
Authority
Tenacity
Rationalism
Empiricism
Science

**The Scientific (Critical Thinking) Approach and Psychology**
Systematic Empiricism
Public Verification
Solvable Problems

**Goals of Science**
Description
Prediction
Explanation

**Basic and Applied Research**

**An Introduction to Research Methods in Science**
Descriptive Methods
Predictive (Relational) Methods
Explanatory Method

**Doing Science**

**Proof and Disproof**

**The Research Process**

**Summary**

Welcome to what is most likely your first research methods class. If you are like most psychology students, you are probably wondering what in the world this class is about—and, more important, why you have to take it. Most psychologists and the American Psychological Association (APA) consider the research methods class especially important in the undergraduate curriculum. In fact, along with the introductory psychology class, the research methods class is one of the courses required by most psychology departments (Messer, Griggs, & Jackson, 1999). Why is this class considered so important, and what exactly is it all about?

Before answering these questions, I will ask you to complete a couple of exercises related to your knowledge of psychology. I usually begin my research methods class by asking my students to do them. I assume that you have had at least one other psychology class prior to this one. Thus, these exercises should not be too difficult.

Exercise 1: Try to name five psychologists. Make sure that your list does not include any "pop" psychologists such as Dr. Ruth or Dr. Laura. These individuals are considered by most psychologists to be "pop" psychologists because, although they are certified to do some sort of counseling, none actually completed a degree in psychology. Dr. Ruth has an Ed.D. in the Interdisciplinary Study of the Family, and Dr. Laura has a Ph.D. in Physiology and a Post-Doctoral Certification in Marriage, Family, and Child Counseling.

Okay, whom did you name first? If you are like most people, you named Sigmund Freud. In fact, if we were to stop 100 people on the street and ask the same question of them, we would probably find that, other than "pop" psychologists, Freud would be the most commonly named psychologist (Stanovich, 2001). What do you know about Freud? Do you believe that he is representative of all that psychology encompasses? Most people on the street believe so. In fact, most of them believe that psychologists "do" what they see "pop" psychologists doing and what they believe Freud did. That is, they believe that most psychologists listen to people's problems and try to help them solve those problems. If this represents your schema for psychology, this class should help you to see the discipline in a very different light.

Exercise 2 (taken from Bolt, 1998): Make two columns on a piece of paper, one labeled "Scientist" and one labeled "Psychologist." Now, write five descriptive terms for each. You may include terms or phrases that describe what you believe the "typical" scientist or psychologist looks like, dresses like, or acts like, as well as what personality characteristics you believe these individuals have. Once you have finished this task, evaluate your descriptions. Do they differ? Again, if you are like most students, even psychology majors, you have probably written very different terms to describe each of these categories.

First, consider your descriptions of a scientist. Most students see the scientist as a middle-aged man, usually wearing a white lab coat with a pocket protector on it. The terms for the scientist's personality usually describe someone who is analytical, committed, and introverted and has poor people/social skills. Are any of these similar to your descriptions?

Now let's turn to your descriptions of a typical psychologist. Once again, a majority of students tend to picture a man, although some picture a woman. They definitely do not see the psychologist in a white lab coat but instead in some sort of professional attire. The terms for personality characteristics tend to describe someone who is warm, caring, empathic, and concerned about others. Does this sound similar to what you have written?

What is the point behind these exercises? First, they illustrate that most people have misconceptions about what psychologists do and about what psychology is. In other words, most people believe that the majority of psychologists do what Freud did—try to help others with their problems. They also tend to see psychology as a discipline devoted to the mental health profession. As you will soon see, psychology includes many other areas of specialization, some of which may actually involve wearing a white lab coat and working with technical equipment.

Why did I ask you to describe a scientist versus a psychologist? Because I hoped that you would begin to realize that a psychologist *is* a scientist. Wait a minute, you may be saying. I decided to major in psychology because I don't like science. What you have failed to recognize is that what makes something a science is not *what* is studied but *how* it is studied. This is what we will be learning about in this course—how to use the scientific method to conduct research in psychology. This is also why you may have had to take statistics as a pre- or corequisite to this class and why statistics are covered in this text—because doing research requires an understanding of how to use statistics. In this text, you will learn about both research methods and the statistics most useful for these methods.

# Areas of Psychological Research

As we noted, psychology is not just about mental health. Psychology is a very diverse discipline that encompasses many areas of study. To illustrate this, examine Table 1.1, which lists the divisions of the American Psychological Association (APA). You will notice that the areas of study within psychology range from those that are closer to the so-called "hard" sciences (chemistry, physics, biology) to those that are closer to the so-called "soft" social sciences (sociology, anthropology, political science). The APA has 53 divisions, each representing an area of research or practice. To understand what psychology is, it is important that you have an appreciation of its diversity. In the following sections, we will briefly discuss some of the more popular research areas within the discipline of psychology.

## Psychobiology

One of the most popular research areas in psychology today is psychobiology. As the name implies, this research area combines biology and psychology. Researchers in this area typically study brain organization or the chemicals within the brain (neurotransmitters). Using the appropriate research methods, for example, psychobiologists have discovered links between illnesses such as schizophrenia and Parkinson's disease and various neurotransmitters in the brain—leading, in turn, to research on possible drug therapies for these illnesses.

**TABLE 1.1  Divisions of the American Psychological Association**

| | |
|---|---|
| 1. Society for General Psychology | 30. Society for Psychological Hypnosis |
| 2. Society for the Teaching of Psychology | 31. State Psychological Association Affairs |
| 3. Experimental Psychology | 32. Humanistic Psychology |
| 5. Evaluation, Measurement, and Statistics | 33. Mental Retardation and Developmental Disabilities |
| 6. Behavioral Neuroscience and Comparative Psychology | 34. Population and Environmental Psychology |
| 7. Developmental Psychology | 35. Society for the Psychology of Women |
| 8. Society for Personality and Social Psychology | 36. Psychology of Religion |
| 9. Society for Psychological Study of Social Issues | 37. Child, Youth, and Family Services |
| 10. Society for the Psychology of Aesthetics, Creativity and the Arts | 38. Health Psychology |
| 12. Society for Clinical Psychology | 39. Psychoanalysis |
| 13. Society for Consulting Psychology | 40. Clinical Neuropsychology |
| 14. Society for Industrial and Organizational Psychology | 41. American Psychology–Law Society |
| 15. Educational Psychology | 42. Psychologists in Independent Practice |
| 16. School Psychology | 43. Family Psychology |
| 17. Society for Counseling Psychology | 44. Society for the Psychological Study of Lesbian, Gay, and Bisexual Issues |
| 18. Psychologists in Public Service | 45. Society for the Psychological Study of Ethnic and Minority Issues |
| 19. Society for Military Psychology | 46. Media Psychology |
| 20. Adult Development and Aging | 47. Exercise and Sport Psychology |
| 21. Applied Experimental and Engineering Psychology | 48. Society for the Study of Peace, Conflict, and Violence: Peace Psychology Division |
| 22. Rehabilitation Psychology | 49. Group Psychology and Group Psychotherapy |
| 23. Society for Consumer Psychology | 50. Addictions |
| 24. Society for Theoretical and Philosophical Psychology | 51. Society for the Psychological Study of Men and Masculinity |
| 25. Behavior Analysis | 52. International Psychology |
| 26. Society for the History of Psychology | 53. Society of Clinical Child and Adolescent Psychology |
| 27. Society for Community Research and Action: Division of Community Psychology | 54. Society of Pediatric Psychology |
| 28. Psychopharmacology and Substance Abuse | 55. American Society for the Advancement of Pharmacotherapy |
| 29. Psychotherapy | |

NOTE: There is no Division 4 or 11.

## Cognition

Researchers who study cognition are interested in how humans process, store, and retrieve information, solve problems, use reasoning and logic, make decisions, and use language. Understanding and employing the appropriate research methods have enabled scientists in these areas to develop models of how memory works, ways to improve memory, methods to improve problem solving and intelligence, and theories of language acquisition. Whereas psychobiology researchers study the brain, cognitive scientists study the mind.

## Human Development

Psychologists in this area conduct research on the physical, social, and cognitive development of humans. This might involve research from the prenatal development period throughout the life span to research on the elderly (gerontology). Research on human development has led, for example, to better understanding of prenatal development and hence better prenatal care, knowledge of cognitive development and cognitive limitations in children, and greater awareness of the effects of peer pressure on adolescents.

## Social Psychology

Social psychologists are interested in how we view and affect one another. Research in this area combines the disciplines of psychology and sociology, in that social psychologists are typically interested in how being part of a group affects the individual. Some of the best-known studies in psychology represent work by social psychologists. For example, Milgram's (1963, 1974) classic experiments on obedience to authority and Zimbardo's (1972) classic prison simulation are social psychology studies.

## Psychotherapy

Psychologists also conduct research that attempts to evaluate psychotherapies. Research on psychotherapies is designed to assess whether a therapy is effective in helping individuals. Might patients have improved without the therapy, or did they improve simply because they thought the therapy was supposed to help? Given the widespread use of various therapies, it is important to have an estimate of the effectiveness of these therapies.

# Sources of Knowledge

There are many ways to gain knowledge, and some are better than others. As scientists, psychologists must be aware of each of these methods. Let's look at several ways of acquiring knowledge, beginning with sources that may not be as reliable or accurate as scientists might desire. We will then consider sources that offer greater reliability and ultimately discuss using science as a means of gaining knowledge.

## Superstition and Intuition

Gaining **knowledge via superstition** means acquiring knowledge that is based on subjective feelings, belief in chance, or belief in magic events. For example, you may have heard someone say "Bad things happen in threes." Where does

**knowledge via superstition**
Knowledge that is based on subjective feelings, belief in chance, or belief in magic events.

this idea come from? As far as I know, no study has ever verified that bad events occur in threes; yet you will frequently hear people say this and act as if they believe it. Some people believe that breaking a mirror brings seven years of bad luck or that the number 13 is unlucky. Once again, these are examples of superstitious beliefs that are not based on observation or hypothesis testing. As such, they represent a means of gaining knowledge that is neither reliable nor valid.

**knowledge via intuition**
Knowledge gained without being consciously aware of its source.

When we gain **knowledge via intuition**, it means that we have knowledge of something without being consciously aware of where the knowledge came from. You have probably heard people say things like "I don't know, it's just a gut feeling" or "I don't know, it just came to me, and I know it's true." These statements represent examples of intuition. Sometimes we intuit something based not on a "gut feeling" but on events we have observed. The problem is that the events may be misinterpreted and not representative of all events in that category. For example, many people believe that more babies are born during a full moon or that couples who have adopted a baby are more likely to conceive after the adoption. These are examples of *illusory correlation*—the perception of a relationship that does not exist. More babies are not born when the moon is full, nor are couples more likely to conceive after adopting (Gilovich, 1991). Instead, we are more likely to notice and pay attention to those couples who conceive after adopting, and not notice those who did not conceive after adopting.

## Authority

**knowledge via authority**
Knowledge gained from those viewed as authority figures.

When we accept what a respected or famous person tells us, we are gaining **knowledge via authority.** You may have gained much of your own knowledge through authority figures. As you were growing up, your parents provided you with information that, for the most part, you did not question, especially when you were very young. You believed that they knew what they were talking about, and thus you accepted the answers they gave you. You have probably also gained knowledge from teachers whom you viewed as authority figures, at times blindly accepting what they said as truth. Most people tend to accept information imparted by those they view as authority figures. Historically, authority figures have been a primary means of information. For example, in some time periods and cultures, the church and its leaders were responsible for providing much of the knowledge that individuals gained throughout the course of their lives.

Even today, many individuals gain much of their knowledge from authority figures. This may not be a problem if the perceived authority figure truly is an authority on the subject. However, problems may arise in situations where the perceived authority figure really is not knowledgeable about the material he or she is imparting. A good example is the information given in "infomercials." Celebrities are often used to deliver the message or a testimonial concerning a product. For example, Victoria Principal may tell us about a certain makeup product, or Christie Brinkley may provide a testimonial regarding a piece of gym equipment. Does Victoria Principal have a degree in dermatology? What does Christie Brinkley know about exercise physiology? These individuals may be experts on acting or modeling, but they are not authorities on the products they are advertising. Yet many individuals readily accept what they say.

In conclusion, accepting the word of an authority figure may be a reliable and valid means of gaining knowledge, but only if the individual is truly an authority on the subject. Thus, we need to question "authoritative" sources of knowledge and develop an attitude of skepticism so that we do not blindly accept whatever is presented to us.

## Tenacity

Gaining **knowledge via tenacity** involves hearing a piece of information so often that you begin to believe it is true and then, despite evidence to the contrary, clinging stubbornly to that belief. This method is often used in political campaigns, where a particular slogan is repeated so often that we begin to believe it. Advertisers also use the method of tenacity by repeating their slogan for a certain product over and over until people begin to associate the slogan with the product and believe that the product meets its claims. For example, the makers of Visine advertise that "It gets the red out." We have seen Visine commercials so many times, and heard this slogan so many times, that we probably now believe it. The problem with gaining knowledge through tenacity is that we do not know whether the claims are true. As far as we know, their accuracy may not have been evaluated in any valid way.

**knowledge via tenacity** Knowledge gained from repeated ideas and stubbornly clung to despite evidence to the contrary.

## Rationalism

Gaining **knowledge via rationalism** involves logical reasoning. With this approach, ideas are precisely stated and logical rules are applied in order to arrive at a logically sound conclusion. Rational ideas are often presented in the form of a syllogism. For example,

> All humans are mortal;
> I am a human;
> Therefore, I am mortal.

**knowledge via rationalism** Knowledge gained through logical reasoning.

This conclusion is logically derived from the major and minor premises in the syllogism. Consider, however, the following syllogism:

> Attractive people are good;
> Nellie is attractive;
> Therefore, Nellie is good.

This syllogism should identify for you the problem with gaining knowledge by logic. Although the syllogism is logically sound, the content of both premises is not necessarily true. If the content of the premises were true, then the conclusion would be true in addition to being logically sound. However, if the content of either of the premises is false (as is the premise "Attractive people are good"), then the conclusion is logically valid but empirically false and therefore of no use to a scientist. Logic deals with only the form of the syllogism and not its content. Obviously, researchers are interested in both form and content.

## Empiricism

**knowledge via empiricism**
Knowledge gained through objective observations of organisms and events in the real world.

**Knowledge via empiricism** involves gaining knowledge through objective observation and the experiences of one's senses. An individual who says "I believe nothing until I see it with my own eyes" is an empiricist. The empiricist gains knowledge by seeing, hearing, tasting, smelling, and touching. This method dates back to the age of Aristotle. Aristotle was an empiricist who made observations about the world in order to know it better. Plato, in contrast, preferred to theorize about the true nature of the world without gathering any data.

Empiricism alone is not enough, however. Empiricism represents a collection of facts. If, as scientists, we relied solely on empiricism, we would have nothing more than a long list of observations or facts. For these facts to be useful, we need to organize them, think about them, draw meaning from them, and use them to make predictions. In other words, we need to use rationalism together with empiricism to make sure that we are being logical about the observations that we make. As we will see, this is what science does.

## Science

**knowledge via science**
Knowledge gained through a combination of empirical methods and logical reasoning.

**hypothesis** A prediction regarding the outcome of a study, often involving the relationship between two variables.

**variable** An event or behavior that has at least two values.

**theory** An organized system of assumptions and principles that attempts to explain certain phenomena and how they are related.

Gaining **knowledge via science,** then, involves a merger of rationalism and empiricism. Scientists collect data (make empirical observations) and test hypotheses with these data (assess them using rationalism). A **hypothesis** is a prediction regarding the outcome of a study. Often, this prediction concerns the relationship between two variables (a **variable** is an event or behavior that has at least two values). By merging rationalism and empiricism, we have the advantage of using a logical argument based on observation. We may find that our hypothesis is not supported, and thus we have to reevaluate our position. On the other hand, our observations may support the hypothesis being tested.

In science, the goal of testing hypotheses is to arrive at or test a **theory**—an organized system of assumptions and principles that attempts to explain certain phenomena and how they are related. Theories help us to organize and explain the data gathered in research studies. In other words, theories allow us to develop a framework regarding the facts in a certain area. For example, Darwin's theory organizes and explains facts related to evolution. In order to develop his theory, Darwin tested many hypotheses. In addition to helping us organize and explain facts, theories help in producing new knowledge by steering researchers toward specific observations of the world.

Students are sometimes confused about the difference between a hypothesis and a theory. A hypothesis is a prediction regarding the outcome of a single study. Many hypotheses may be tested and several research studies conducted before a comprehensive theory on a topic is put forth. Once a theory is developed, it may aid in generating future hypotheses. In other words, researchers may have additional questions regarding the theory that help them to generate new hypotheses to test. If the results from these additional studies further support the theory, we are likely to have greater confidence in the theory. However, further research can also expose weaknesses in a theory that may lead to future revisions of the theory.

## Sources of Knowledge — IN REVIEW

| SOURCE | DESCRIPTION | ADVANTAGES/DISADVANTAGES |
| --- | --- | --- |
| Superstition | Gaining knowledge through subjective feelings, belief in chance, or belief in magic events | Not empirical or logical |
| Intuition | Gaining knowledge without being consciously aware of where the knowledge came from | Not empirical or logical |
| Authority | Gaining knowledge from those viewed as authority figures | Not empirical or logical; Authority figure may not be an expert in the area |
| Tenacity | Gaining knowledge by clinging stubbornly to repeated ideas, despite evidence to the contrary | Not empirical or logical |
| Rationalism | Gaining knowledge through logical reasoning | Logical but not empirical |
| Empiricism | Gaining knowledge through observations of organisms and events in the real world | Empirical but not necessarily logical/ systematic |
| Science | Gaining knowledge through empirical methods and logical reasoning | The only acceptable way for researchers/ scientists to gain knowledge |

Identify the source of knowledge in each of the following examples:

1. A celebrity is endorsing a new diet program, noting that she lost weight on the program and so will you.
2. Based on several observations that Pam has made, she feels sure that cell phone use does not adversely affect driving ability.
3. A friend tells you that she is not sure why but, because she has a feeling of dread, she thinks that you should not take the plane trip you were planning for next week.

CRITICAL
THINKING
CHECK
1.1

# The Scientific (Critical Thinking) Approach and Psychology

Now that we have briefly described what science is, let's discuss how this applies to the discipline of psychology. As mentioned earlier, many students believe that they are attracted to psychology because they think it is *not* a science. The error in their thinking is that they believe that subject matter alone defines what is and what is not science. Instead, what defines science is the manner in which something is studied. Science is a way of thinking about and observing events in order to achieve a deeper understanding of these events. Psychologists apply the scientific method to their study of human beings and other animals.

The scientific method involves invoking an attitude of skepticism. A **skeptic** is a person who questions the validity, authenticity, or truth of something

**skeptic** A person who questions the validity, authenticity, or truth of something purporting to be factual.

purporting to be factual. In our society, being described as a skeptic is not typically thought of as a compliment. However, for a scientist it is a compliment. It means that you do not blindly accept any new idea that comes down the pike. Instead, the skeptic needs data to support an idea and insists on proper testing procedures when the data were collected. Being a skeptic and using the scientific method involve applying three important criteria that help define science: systematic empiricism, public verification, and empirically solvable problems (Stanovich, 2001).

## Systematic Empiricism

**systematic empiricism**
Making observations in a systematic manner in order to test hypotheses and refute or develop a theory.

As we have seen, empiricism is the practice of relying on observation to draw conclusions. Most people today probably agree that the best way to learn about something is to observe it. This reliance on empiricism was not always a common practice. Before the 17th century, most people relied more on intuition, religious doctrine provided by authorities, and reason than they did on empiricism. Notice, however, that empiricism alone is not enough; it must be **systematic empiricism.** In other words, simply observing a series of events does not lead to scientific knowledge. The observations must be made in a systematic manner to test a hypothesis and refute or develop a theory. For example, if a researcher is interested in the relationship between vitamin C and the incidence of colds, she will not simply ask people haphazardly whether they take vitamin C and how many colds they have had. This approach involves empiricism, but not systematic empiricism. Instead, the researcher might design a study to assess the effects of vitamin C on colds. Her study will probably involve using a representative group of individuals, who are then randomly assigned to either take or not take vitamin C supplements. She will then observe whether the groups differ in the number of colds they report. We will go into more detail on designing such a study later in this chapter. By using systematic empiricism, researchers can draw more reliable and valid conclusions than they can from observation alone.

## Public Verification

**public verification** Presenting research to the public so that it can be observed, replicated, criticized, and tested.

Scientific research is research that is open to **public verification.** This means that the research is presented to the public in such a way that it can be observed, replicated, criticized, and tested for veracity by others. Most commonly, this involves submitting the research to a scientific journal for possible publication. Most journals are peer-reviewed—other scientists critique the research in order to decide whether it meets the standards for publication. If a study is published, other researchers can read about the findings, attempt to replicate them, and through this process demonstrate that the results are reliable. We should be suspicious of any claims made without the support of public verification. For example, many people have claimed that they were abducted by aliens. These claims do not fit the bill of public verification; they are simply the claims of individuals with no evidence to support them. Other people claim that they have lived past lives. Once again, there is no evidence to support such claims. These types of claims are unverifiable— there is no way that they are open to public verification.

## Solvable Problems

Science always investigates **solvable problems**—questions that are potentially answerable by means of currently available research techniques. If a theory cannot be tested using empirical techniques, then scientists are not interested in it. For example, the question "Is there life after death?" is not an empirical question and thus cannot be tested scientifically. However, the question "Does an intervention program minimize rearrests in juvenile delinquents?" can be empirically studied and thus is within the realm of science.

When solvable problems are studied, they are always open to the **principle of falsifiability**—the idea that a scientific theory must be stated in such a way that it is possible to refute or disconfirm it. In other words, the theory must predict not only what will happen but also what will not happen. A theory is not scientific if it is irrefutable. You may be thinking that if a theory is irrefutable, it must be really good. However, in science, this is not so. Read on to see why.

**solvable problems** Questions that are potentially answerable by means of currently available research techniques.

**principle of falsifiability** The idea that a scientific theory must be stated in such a way that it is possible to refute or disconfirm it.

© 2005 Sidney Harris, Reprinted with permission.

**Pseudoscience** (claims that appear to be scientific but that actually violate the criteria of science) is usually irrefutable and is also often confused with science. For example, those who believe in extrasensory perception (ESP, a pseudoscience) often argue with the fact that no publicly verifiable example of ESP has ever been documented through systematic empiricism. The reason they offer is that the conditions necessary for ESP to occur are violated under controlled laboratory conditions. This means that they have an answer for every situation. If ESP were ever demonstrated under empirical conditions, then they would say their belief is supported. However, when ESP repeatedly fails to be demonstrated in controlled laboratory conditions, they say their belief is not falsified because the conditions were not "right" for ESP to be demonstrated. Thus, because those who believe in ESP have set up a situation

**pseudoscience** Claims that appear to be scientific but that actually violate the criteria of science.

in which they claim falsifying data are not valid, the theory of ESP violates the principle of falsifiability.

You may be thinking that the explanation provided by the proponents of ESP makes some sense to you. Let me give you an analogous example from Stanovich (2001). Stanovich jokingly claims that he has found the underlying brain mechanism that controls behavior and that you will soon be able to read about it in the *National Enquirer*. According to him, two tiny green men reside in the left hemisphere of our brains. These little green men have the power to control the processes taking place in many areas of the brain. Why have we not heard about these little green men before? Well, that's easy to explain. According to Stanovich, the little green men have the ability to detect any intrusion into the brain, and when they do, they become invisible. You may feel that your intelligence has been insulted with this foolish explanation of brain functioning. However, you should see the analogy between this explanation and the one offered by proponents of ESP, despite any evidence to support it and much evidence to refute it.

| IN REVIEW | The Scientific Method | |
|---|---|---|
| **CRITERIA** | **DESCRIPTION** | **WHY NECESSARY** |
| Systematic empiricism | Making observations in a systematic manner | Aids in refuting or developing a theory in order to test hypotheses |
| Public verification | Presenting research to the public so that it can be observed, replicated, criticized, and tested | Aids in determining the veracity of a theory |
| Solvable problems | Stating questions in such a way that they are answerable by means of currently available research techniques | Aids in determining whether a theory can potentially be tested using empirical techniques and whether it is falsifiable |

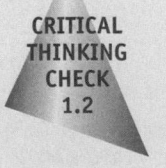

CRITICAL THINKING CHECK 1.2

1. Explain how a theory such as Freud's, which attributes much of personality and psychological disorders to unconscious drives, violates the principle of falsifiability.
2. Identify a currently popular pseudoscience and explain how it might violate each of the criteria identified above.

## Goals of Science

Scientific research has three basic goals: (1) to describe behavior, (2) to predict behavior, and (3) to explain behavior. All of these goals lead to a better understanding of behavior and mental processes.

## Description

**Description** begins with careful observation. Psychologists might describe patterns of behavior, thought, or emotions in humans. They might also describe the behavior(s) of other animals. For example, researchers might observe and describe the type of play behavior exhibited by children or the mating behavior of chimpanzees. Description allows us to learn about behavior and when it occurs. Let's say, for example, that you were interested in the channel-surfing behavior of men and women. Careful observation and description would be needed to determine whether or not there were any gender differences in channel-surfing. Description allows us to observe that two events are systematically related to one another. Without description as a first step, predictions cannot be made.

**description** Carefully observing behavior in order to describe it.

## Prediction

**Prediction** allows us to identify the factors that indicate when an event or events will occur. In other words, knowing the level of one variable allows us to predict the approximate level of the other variable. We know that if one variable is present at a certain level, then it is likely that the other variable will be present at a certain level. For example, if we observed that men channel-surf with greater frequency than women, we could then make predictions about how often men and women might change channels when given the chance.

**prediction** Identifying the factors that indicate when an event or events will occur.

## Explanation

Finally, **explanation** allows us to identify the causes that determine when and why a behavior occurs. In order to explain a behavior, we need to demonstrate that we can manipulate the factors needed to produce or eliminate the behavior. For example, in our channel-surfing example, if gender predicts channel-surfing, what might cause it? It could be genetic or environmental. Maybe men have less tolerance for commercials and thus channel-surf at a greater rate. Maybe women are more interested in the content of commercials and are thus less likely to change channels. Maybe the attention span of women is longer. Maybe something associated with having a Y chromosome increases channel-surfing, or something associated with having two X chromosomes leads to less channel-surfing. Obviously there are a wide variety of possible explanations. As scientists, we test these possibilities to identify the best explanation of why a behavior occurs. When we try to identify the best explanation for a behavior, we must systematically eliminate any alternative explanations. In order to eliminate alternative explanations, we must impose control over the research situation. We will discuss the concepts of control and alternative explanations shortly.

**explanation** Identifying the causes that determine when and why a behavior occurs.

# Basic and Applied Research

Some psychologists conduct research because they enjoy seeking knowledge and answering questions. This is referred to as **basic research**—the study of psychological issues in order to seek knowledge for its own sake. Most basic research is conducted in university or laboratory settings. The intent of basic

**basic research** The study of psychological issues in order to seek knowledge for its own sake.

research is not immediate application but the gaining of knowledge. However, many treatments and procedures that have been developed to help humans and other animals began with researchers asking basic research questions that later led to applications. Examples of basic research include identifying differences in capacity and duration in short-term memory and long-term memory, identifying whether cognitive maps can be mentally rotated, determining how various schedules of reinforcement affect learning, and determining how lesioning a certain area in the brains of rats affects their behavior.

**applied research** The study of psychological issues that have practical significance and potential solutions.

A second type of research is that which is applied. **Applied research** involves the study of psychological issues that have practical significance and potential solutions. Scientists who conduct applied research are interested in finding an answer to a question because the answer can be immediately applied to some situation. Much applied research is conducted by private businesses and the government. Examples of applied research include identifying how stress affects the immune system, determining the accuracy of eyewitness testimony, identifying therapies that are the most effective in treating depression, and identifying factors associated with weight gain. Some people think that most research should be directly relevant to a social problem or issue. In other words, some people favor *only* applied research. The problem with this approach is that much of what started out as basic research eventually led to some sort of application. If researchers stopped asking questions simply because they wanted to know the answer (stopped engaging in basic research), then many great ideas and eventual applications would undoubtedly be lost.

## An Introduction to Research Methods in Science

The goals of science map very closely onto the research methods scientists use. In other words, there are methods that are descriptive in nature, predictive in nature, and explanatory in nature. We will briefly introduce these methods here; the remainder of the text covers these methods in far greater detail. Descriptive methods are covered in Chapter 4 and descriptive statistics in Chapter 5; predictive methods and statistics are covered in Chapters 6 and 12; and explanatory methods are covered in Chapters 8–11. Thus, what follows will briefly introduce you to some of the concepts that we will be discussing in greater detail throughout the remainder of this text.

### Descriptive Methods

**observational method** Making observations of human or other animal behavior.
**naturalistic observation** Observing the behavior of humans or other animals in their natural habitat.

Psychologists use three types of descriptive methods. First is the **observational method**—simply observing human or other animal behavior. Psychologists approach observation in two ways. **Naturalistic observation** involves observing how humans or other animals behave in their natural habitat. Observing the mating behavior of chimpanzees in their natural setting is an example of this approach. **Laboratory observation** involves observing behavior in a more contrived and controlled situation, usually the laboratory. Bringing children to a laboratory playroom to observe play behavior is an example of this approach. Observation involves description at its most basic level. One advantage of the observational method, as well as other descriptive methods, is the flexibility to change what one is studying. A disadvantage of descriptive methods is that the researcher has little control. As we use more powerful methods, we gain control but lose flexibility.

A second descriptive method is the **case study method.** A case study is an in-depth study of one or more individuals. Freud used case studies to develop his theory of personality development. Similarly, Jean Piaget used case studies to develop his theory of cognitive development in children. This method is descriptive in nature because it involves simply describing the individual(s) being studied.

The third method that relies on description is the **survey method**—questioning individuals on a topic or topics and then describing their responses. Surveys can be administered by mail, over the phone, on the Internet, or in a personal interview. One advantage of the survey method over the other descriptive methods is that it allows researchers to study larger groups of individuals more easily. This method has disadvantages, however. One concern is whether the group of people who participate in the study (the **sample**) is representative of all of the people about whom the study is meant to generalize (the **population**). This concern can usually be overcome through random sampling. A **random sample** is achieved when, through random selection, each member of the population is equally likely to be chosen as part of the sample. Another concern has to do with the wording of questions. Are they easy to understand? Are they written in such a manner that they bias the respondents' answers? Such concerns relate to the validity of the data collected.

## Predictive (Relational) Methods

Two methods allow researchers not only to describe behaviors but also to predict from one variable to another. The first, the **correlational method,** assesses the degree of relationship between two measured variables. If two variables are correlated with each other, then we can predict from one variable to the other with a certain degree of accuracy. For example, height and weight are correlated. The relationship is such that an increase in one variable (height) is generally accompanied by an increase in the other variable (weight). Knowing this, we can predict an individual's approximate weight, with a certain degree of accuracy, based on knowing the person's height.

One problem with correlational research is that it is often misinterpreted. Frequently, people assume that because two variables are correlated, there must be some sort of causal relationship between the variables. This is not so. *Correlation does not imply causation.* Please remember that a correlation simply means that the two variables are related in some way. For example, being a certain height does not cause you also to be a certain weight. It would be nice if it did, because then we would not have to worry about

**laboratory observation**
Observing the behavior of humans or other animals in a more contrived and controlled situation, usually the laboratory.

**case study method** An in-depth study of one or more individuals.

**survey method** Questioning individuals on a topic or topics and then describing their responses.

**sample** The group of people who participate in a study.
**population** All of the people about whom a study is meant to generalize.
**random sample** A sample achieved through random selection in which each member of the population is equally likely to be chosen.

**correlational method** A method that assesses the degree of relationship between two variables.

being either under- or overweight. What if I told you that watching violent TV and displaying aggressive behavior were correlated? What could you conclude based on this correlation? Many people might conclude that watching violent TV causes one to act more aggressively. Based on the evidence given (a correlational study), however, we cannot draw this conclusion. All we can conclude is that those who watch more violent television programs also tend to act more aggressively. It is possible that violent TV causes aggression, but we cannot draw this conclusion based only on correlational data. It is also possible that those who are aggressive by nature are attracted to more violent television programs, or that some other "third" variable is causing both aggressive behavior and violent TV watching. The point is that observing a correlation between two variables means only that they are related to each other.

**positive relationship** A relationship between two variables in which an increase in one variable is accompanied by an increase in the other variable.

**negative relationship** A relationship between two variables in which an increase in one variable is accompanied by a decrease in the other variable.

**quasi-experimental method** Research that compares naturally occurring groups of individuals; the variable of interest cannot be manipulated.

**participant (subject) variable** A characteristic inherent in the participants that cannot be changed.

The correlation between height and weight, or violent TV and aggressive behavior, is a **positive relationship:** As one variable (height) increases, we observe an increase in the second variable (weight). Some correlations indicate a **negative relationship,** meaning that as one variable increases, the other variable systematically decreases. Can you think of an example of a negative relationship between two variables? Consider this: As mountain elevation increases, temperature decreases. Negative correlations also allow us to predict from one variable to another. If I know the mountain elevation, it will help me predict the approximate temperature.

Besides the correlational method, a second method that allows us to describe and predict is the quasi-experimental method. The **quasi-experimental method** allows us to compare naturally occurring groups of individuals. For example, we could examine whether alcohol consumption by students in a fraternity or sorority differs from that of students not in such organizations. You will see in a moment that this method differs from the experimental method, described below, in that the groups studied occur naturally. In other words, we do not control whether or not people join a Greek organization. They have chosen their groups on their own, and we are simply looking for differences (in this case, in the amount of alcohol typically consumed) between these naturally occurring groups. This is often referred to as a **subject** or **participant variable**—a characteristic inherent in the participants that cannot be changed. Because we are using groups that occur naturally, any differences that we find may be due to the variable of being or not being a Greek member, or they may be due to other factors that we were unable to control in this study. For example, maybe those who like to drink more are also more likely to join a Greek organization. Once again, if we find a difference between these groups in amount of alcohol consumed, we can use this finding to predict what type of student (Greek or non-Greek) is likely to drink more. However, we cannot conclude that belonging to a Greek organization *causes* one to drink more, because the participants came to us after choosing to belong to these organizations. In other words, what is missing when we use predictive methods such as the correlational and quasi-experimental methods is control.

When using predictive methods, we do not systematically manipulate the variables of interest; we only measure them. This means that, although we may observe a relationship between variables (such as that described between drinking and Greek membership), we cannot conclude that it is a causal relationship. Why? Because there could be other *alternative explanations* for this relationship. An **alternative explanation** is the idea that it is possible that some other, uncontrolled, extraneous variable may be responsible for the observed relationship. For example, maybe those who choose to join Greek organizations come from higher-income families and have more money to spend on such things as alcohol. Or maybe those who choose to join Greek organizations are more interested in socialization and drinking alcohol before they even join the organization. Thus, because these methods leave the possibility for alternative explanations, we cannot use them to establish cause-and-effect relationships.

**alternative explanation** The idea that it is possible that some other, uncontrolled, extraneous variable may be responsible for the observed relationship.

## Explanatory Method

When using the experimental method, researchers pay a great deal of attention to eliminating alternative explanations by using the proper controls. Because of this, the **experimental method** allows researchers not only to describe and predict but also to determine whether there is a cause-and-effect relationship between the variables of interest. In other words, this method enables researchers to know when and why a behavior occurs. Many preconditions must be met in order for a study to be experimental in nature; we will discuss many of these in detail in later chapters. Here, we will simply consider the basics—the minimum requirements needed for an experiment.

**experimental method** A research method that allows a researcher to establish a cause-and-effect relationship through manipulation of a variable and control of the situation.

The basic premise of experimentation is that the researcher controls as much as possible in order to determine whether there is a cause-and-effect relationship between the variables being studied. Let's say, for example, that a researcher is interested in whether taking vitamin C supplements leads to fewer colds. The idea behind experimentation is that the researcher manipulates at least one variable (known as the **independent variable**) and measures at least one variable (known as the **dependent variable**). In our study, what should the researcher manipulate? If you identified amount of vitamin C, then you are correct. If amount of vitamin C is the independent variable, then number of colds is the dependent variable. For comparative purposes, the independent variable has to have at least two groups or conditions. We typically refer to these two groups or conditions as the control group and the experimental group. The **control group** is the group that serves as the baseline or "standard" condition. In our vitamin C study, the control group is those who do not take vitamin C supplements. The **experimental group** is the group that receives the treatment—in this case, those who take vitamin C supplements. Thus, in an experiment, one thing that we control is the level of the independent variable that participants receive.

**independent variable** The variable in a study that is manipulated by the researcher.
**dependent variable** The variable in a study that is measured by the researcher.

**control group** The group of participants that does not receive any level of the independent variable and serves as the baseline in a study.
**experimental group** The group of participants that receives some level of the independent variable.

What else should we control to help eliminate alternative explanations? Well, we need to control the type of participants in each of the treatment conditions. We should begin by drawing a random sample of participants from the population. Once we have our sample of participants, we have to decide who will serve in the control group versus the experimental group. In order to gain as much control as possible, and eliminate as many alternative

**random assignment** Assigning participants to conditions in such a way that every participant has an equal probability of being placed in any condition.

explanations as possible, we should use **random assignment**—assigning participants to conditions in such a way that every participant has an equal probability of being placed in any condition. How does random assignment help us to gain control and eliminate alternative explanations? By using random assignment we should minimize or eliminate differences between the groups. In other words, we want the two groups of participants to be as alike as possible. The only difference we want between the groups is that of the independent variable we are manipulating—amount of vitamin C. Once participants are assigned to conditions, we keep track of the number of colds they have over a specified time period (the dependent variable).

Let's review some of the controls we have used in the present study. We have controlled who is in the study (we want a sample representative of the population about whom we are trying to generalize), who participates in each group (we should randomly assign participants to the two conditions), and the treatment each group receives as part of the study (some take vitamin C supplements and some do not). Can you identify other variables that we might need to consider controlling in the present study? How about amount of sleep received each day, type of diet, and amount of exercise (all variables that might contribute to general health and well-being)? There are undoubtedly other variables we would need to control if we were to complete this study. We will discuss control in greater detail in later chapters, but the basic idea is that when using the experimental method, we try to **control** as much as possible by manipulating the independent variable and controlling any other extraneous variables that could affect the results of the study. Randomly assigning participants also helps to control for participant differences between the groups. What does all of this control gain us? If, after completing this study with the proper controls, we found that those in the experimental group (those who took vitamin C supplements) did in fact have fewer colds than those in the control group, we would have evidence supporting a cause-and-effect relationship between these variables. In other words, we could conclude that taking vitamin C supplements reduces the frequency of colds.

**control** Manipulating the independent variable in an experiment or any other extraneous variables that could affect the results of a study.

| IN REVIEW | An Introduction to Research Methods | |
|---|---|---|
| **GOAL MET** | **RESEARCH METHODS** | **ADVANTAGES/DISADVANTAGES** |
| Description | Observational method | Allows description of behavior(s) |
| | Case study method | Does not support reliable predictions |
| | Survey method | Does not support cause-and-effect explanations |
| Prediction | Correlational method | Allows description of behavior(s) |
| | Quasi-experimental method | Supports reliable predictions from one variable to another |
| | | Does not support cause-and-effect explanations |
| Explanation | Experimental method | Allows description of behavior(s) |
| | | Supports reliable predictions from one variable to another |
| | | Supports cause-and-effect explanations |

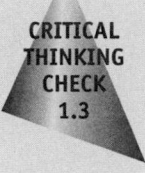

1. In a recent study, researchers found a negative correlation between income level and incidence of psychological disorders. Jim thinks that this means that being poor leads to psychological disorders. Is he correct in his conclusion? Why or why not?

2. In a study designed to assess the effects of exercise on life satisfaction, participants were assigned to groups based on whether or not they reported exercising. All participants then completed a life satisfaction inventory.
   a. What is the independent variable?
   b. What is the dependent variable?
   c. Is the independent variable a participant variable or a true manipulated variable?

3. What type of method would you recommend researchers use to answer the following questions?
   a. What percentage of cars run red lights?
   b. Do student athletes spend as much time studying as student nonathletes?
   c. Is there a relationship between type of punishment used by parents and aggressiveness in children?
   d. Do athletes who use imaging techniques perform better than those who do not use such techniques?

4. Your mother claims that she has found a wonderful new treatment for her arthritis. She read "somewhere" that rubbing vinegar into the affected area for 10 minutes twice a day would help. She tried this and is convinced that her arthritis has been lessened. She now thinks that the medical community should recommend this treatment. What alternative explanation(s) might you offer to your mother for why she feels better? How would you explain to her that her evidence is not sufficient for the medical/scientific community?

# Doing Science

Although the experimental method can establish a cause-and-effect relationship, most researchers would not wholeheartedly accept a conclusion from only one study. Why is that? Any one of a number of problems can occur in a study. For example, there may be control problems. Researchers may believe they have controlled everything but miss something, and the uncontrolled factor may affect the results. In other words, a researcher may believe that the manipulated independent variable caused the results when, in reality, it was something else.

Another reason for caution in interpreting experimental results is that a study may be limited by the technical equipment available at the time. For example, in the early part of the 19th century, many scientists believed that studying the bumps on a person's head allowed them to know something about the internal mind of the individual being studied. This movement, known as phrenology, was popularized through the writings of physician Joseph Gall (1758–1828). Based on what you have learned in this chapter, you can most likely see that phrenology is a pseudoscience. However, at the time it was popular, phrenology appeared very "scientific" and "technical." Obviously, with hindsight and with the technological advances that we have today, the idea of phrenology seems somewhat laughable to us now.

Finally, we cannot completely rely on the findings of one study because a single study cannot tell us everything about a theory. The idea of science is that it is not static; the theories generated through science change. For example, we often hear about new findings in the medical field, such as "Eggs are so high in cholesterol that you should eat no more than two a week." Then, a couple of years later, we might read "Eggs are not as bad for you as originally thought. New research shows that it is acceptable to eat them every day." People may complain when confronted with such contradictory findings: "Those doctors, they don't know what they're talking about. You can't believe any of them. First they say one thing, and then they say completely the opposite. It's best to just ignore all of them." The point is that when testing a theory scientifically, we may obtain contradictory results. These contradictions may lead to new, very valuable information that subsequently leads to a theoretical change. Theories evolve and change over time based on the consensus of the research. Just because a particular idea or theory is supported by data from one study does not mean that the research on that topic ends and that we just accept the theory as it currently stands and never do any more research on that topic.

# Proof and Disproof

When scientists test theories, they do not try to prove them true. Theories can be supported based on the data collected, but obtaining support for something does not mean it is true in all instances. Proof of a theory is logically impossible. As an example, consider the following problem, adapted from Griggs and Cox (1982). This is known as the Drinking Age Problem (the reason for the name will become readily apparent).

Imagine that you are a police officer responsible for making sure that the drinking age rule is being followed. The four cards on the next page represent information about four people sitting at a table. One side of a card indicates what the person is drinking, and the other side of the card indicates the person's age. The rule is: "If a person is drinking alcohol, then the person is 21 or over." In order to test whether the rule is true or false, which card or cards below would you turn over? Turn over only the card or cards that you need to check to be sure.

| Drinking a beer | 16 years old | Drinking a Coke | 22 years old |
|---|---|---|---|

Does turning over the beer card and finding that the person is 21 years of age or older prove that the rule is always true? No—the fact that one person is following the rule does not mean that it is always true. How, then, do we test a hypothesis? We test a hypothesis by attempting to falsify or disconfirm it. If it cannot be falsified, then we say we have support for it. Which cards would you choose in an attempt to falsify the rule in the Drinking Age Problem? If you identified the beer card as being able to falsify the rule, then you were correct. If we turn over the beer card and find that the individual is under 21 years of age, then the rule is false. Is there another card that could also falsify the rule? Yes, the 16 years of age card can. How? If we turn that card over and find that the individual is drinking alcohol, then the rule is false. These are the only two cards that can potentially falsify the rule. Thus, they are the only two cards that need to be turned over.

Even though disproof or disconfirmation is logically sound in terms of testing hypotheses, falsifying a hypothesis does not always mean that the hypothesis is false. Why? There may be design problems in the study, as described earlier. Thus, even when a theory is falsified, we need to be cautious in our interpretation. The point to be taken is that we do not want to completely discount a theory based on a single study.

## The Research Process

The actual process of conducting research involves several steps, the first of which is to identify a problem. Accomplishing this step is discussed more fully in Chapter 2. The other steps include reviewing the literature (Chapter 2), generating hypotheses (Chapter 7), designing and conducting the study (Chapters 4 and 8–12), analyzing the data and interpreting the results (Chapters 5–7, 9–11, and 13), and communicating the results (Chapter 14).

## Summary

We began the chapter by stressing the importance of research in psychology. We identified different areas within the discipline of psychology in which research is conducted, such as psychobiology, cognition, human development, social psychology, and psychotherapy. We discussed various sources of knowledge, including intuition, superstition, authority, tenacity, rationalism, empiricism, and science. We stressed the importance of using the scientific method to gain knowledge in psychology. The scientific method is a combination of empiricism and rationalism; it must meet the criteria of systematic empiricism, public verification, and empirically solvable problems.

We outlined the three goals of science (description, prediction, and explanation) and related them to the research methods used by psychologists. Descriptive methods include observation, case study, and survey methods. Predictive methods include correlational and quasi-experimental methods. The experimental method allows for explanation of cause-and-effect relationships. Finally, we introduced some practicalities of doing research, discussed proof and disproof in science, and noted that testing a hypothesis involves attempting to falsify it.

## KEY TERMS

knowledge via superstition
knowledge via intuition
knowledge via authority
knowledge via tenacity
knowledge via rationalism
knowledge via empiricism
knowledge via science
hypothesis
variable
theory
skeptic
systematic empiricism
public verification
solvable problems

principle of falsifiability
pseudoscience
description
prediction
explanation
basic research
applied research
observational method
naturalistic observation
laboratory observation
case study method
survey method
sample
population

random sample
correlational method
positive relationship
negative relationship
quasi-experimental method
participant (subject) variable
alternative explanation
experimental method
independent variable
dependent variable
control group
experimental group
random assignment
control

## CHAPTER EXERCISES

(Answers to odd-numbered exercises appear in Appendix C.)

1. Identify a piece of information that you have gained through each of the sources of knowledge discussed in the chapter (superstition and intuition, authority, tenacity, rationalism, empiricism, and science).
2. Provide an argument for the idea that basic research is as important as applied research.
3. Why is it a compliment for a scientist to be called a skeptic?
4. An infomercial asserts "A study proves that Fat-B-Gone works, and it will work for you also." What is wrong with this statement?
5. Many psychology students believe that they do not need to know about research methods because they plan to pursue careers in clinical/counseling psychology. What argument can you provide against this view?
6. In a study of the effects of type of study on exam performance, participants are randomly assigned to one of two conditions. In one condition, participants study alone using notes they took during class lectures. In a second condition, participants study in interactive groups with notes from class lectures. The amount of time spent studying is held constant. All students then take the same exam on the material.
   a. What is the independent variable in this study?
   b. What is the dependent variable in this study?

   c. Identify the control and experimental groups in this study.
   d. Is the independent variable manipulated, or is it a participant variable?
7. Researchers interested in the effects of caffeine on anxiety have randomly assigned participants to one of two conditions in a study—the no-caffeine condition or the caffeine condition. After drinking two cups of either regular or decaffeinated coffee, participants will take an anxiety inventory.
   a. What is the independent variable in this study?
   b. What is the dependent variable in this study?
   c. Identify the control and experimental groups in this study.
   d. Is the independent variable manipulated, or is it a participant variable?
8. Gerontologists interested in the effects of age on reaction time have two groups of participants take a test in which they must indicate as quickly as possible whether a probe word was a member of a previous set of words. One group of participants is between the ages of 25 and 45, and the other group is between the ages of 55 and 75. The time it takes to make the response is measured.
   a. What is the independent variable in this study?
   b. What is the dependent variable in this study?
   c. Identify the control and experimental groups in this study.
   d. Is the independent variable manipulated, or is it a participant variable?

## CRITICAL THINKING CHECK ANSWERS

### 1.1

1. Knowledge via authority
2. Knowledge via empiricism
3. Knowledge via superstition

### 1.2

1. A theory such as Freud's violates the principle of falsifiability because it is not possible to falsify or test the theory. The theory is irrefutable. Freud attributes much of personality to unconscious drives, and there is no way to test whether this is so—or, for that matter, whether there is such a thing as an unconscious drive.

2. Belief in paranormal events is a currently popular pseudoscience (based on the popularity of *The X-Files*). Belief in paranormal events violates all three criteria that define science. First, the ideas have not been supported by systematic empiricism. Most "authorities" in this area do not test hypotheses but rather offer demonstrations of their abilities. Second, there has been little or no public verification of these claims. There is little reliable and valid research on this topic, and what there is does not support the claims. Instead, most evidence tends to be testimonials. Third, many of the claims are stated in such a

way that they are not solvable problems. In other words, they do not open themselves to the principle of falsifiability ("My powers do not work in a controlled laboratory setting" or "My powers do not work when skeptics are present").

### 1.3

1. Jim is incorrect because he is inferring causation based on correlational evidence. He is assuming that because the two variables are correlated, one must be causing changes in the other. In addition, he is assuming the direction of the inferred causal relationship—that a lower income level causes psychological disorders, not that having a psychological disorder leads to a lower income level. The correlation simply indicates that these two variables are related in an inverse manner.

That is, those with psychological disorders also tend to have lower income levels.
2. a. The independent variable is exercise.
   b. The dependent variable is life satisfaction.
   c. The independent variable is a participant variable.
3. a. Naturalistic observation
   b. Quasi-experimental method
   c. Correlational method
   d. Experimental method
4. An alternative explanation might be that simply rubbing the affected area makes it feel better, regardless of whether she is rubbing in vinegar. Her evidence is not sufficient for the medical/scientific community because it was not gathered using the scientific method. Instead, it is simply a testimonial from one person.

## WEB RESOURCES

Check your knowledge of the content in this chapter by taking the practice quiz at www.Wadsworth.com. Or, for step-by-step practice and information, check out the Statistics and Research Methods Workshops at http://psychology.wadsworth.com/workshops.

# 2 Getting Started: Ideas, Resources, and Ethics

In the preceding chapter, we discussed the nature of science and how to think critically like a scientist. In addition, we offered a brief introduction to the various research methods used by psychologists. In this chapter, we will discuss some issues related to getting started on a research project, beginning with library research and moving on to conducting research ethically. We will discuss how to use some of the resources available through most libraries, and we will cover the guidelines set forth by the APA (American Psychological Association) for the ethical treatment of both human and nonhuman animals used in research. APA has very specific ethical guidelines for the treatment of humans used in research. These guidelines are set forth in the APA's *Ethical Principles of Psychologists and Code of Conduct* (2002). In discussing these guidelines, we will pay particular attention to several issues: how to obtain approval for a research project, the meaning of informed consent, how to minimize risk to participants, when it may be acceptable to use deception in a research study, debriefing your participants, and special considerations when using children as participants. We will also review the APA guidelines for using animals in research.

# Selecting a Problem

Getting started on a research project begins with selecting a problem. Some students find selecting a problem the most daunting task of the whole research process, whereas other students have so many ideas for research projects that they do not know where to begin. If you fall into the first category and are not sure what topic you might want to research, you can get an idea for a research project from a few different places.

If you are one of the people who have trouble generating research ideas, it is best to start with what others have already done. One place to start is with past research on a topic rather than just jumping in with a completely new idea of your own. For example, if you are interested in treatments for depression, you should begin by researching some of the treatments currently available. While reading about these treatments, you may find that one or more of the journal articles you read raise questions that have yet to be addressed. Thus, looking at the research already completed in an area gives you a firm foundation from which to begin your own research and may help suggest a hypothesis that your research project might address.

A second place from which to generate ideas is past theories on a topic. A good place to find a cursory review of theories on a particular topic is in your psychology textbooks. For example, when students tell me they are having trouble coming up with an idea for a research project, I begin by having them identify which psychology class they have found most interesting. I then have them look at the textbook from that class and identify which chapter they found most interesting. They then narrow it down to which topic within the chapter was most interesting, and the topical coverage within the chapter will usually provide details on several theories.

A third source of ideas for a research project is observation. We are all capable of observing behavior, and based on these observations, questions may arise. For example, you may have observed that some students at your institution cheat on exams or papers, whereas most students would never consider doing such a thing. Or you may have observed that certain individuals overindulge in alcohol, whereas others know their limits. Or maybe you believe, based on observation, that the type of music listened to affects one's mood. Any of these observations may lead to a future research project.

Last, ideas for research projects are often generated from practical problems encountered in daily life. This should sound familiar to you from Chapter 1 because research designed to find answers to practical problems is applied research. Thus, many students easily develop research ideas because they base them on practical problems that they or someone they know have encountered. For example, here are two ideas generated by my students based on practical problems they encountered: Do alcohol awareness programs lead to more responsible alcohol consumption by college students? Does art therapy improve the mood and general well-being of those recovering from surgery?

# Reviewing the Literature

Once you decide on a topic of interest, the next step is to conduct a literature review. A literature review involves searching the published studies on a topic to ensure that you have a grasp of all the research that has been conducted in that area that might be relevant to your intended study. This may sound like an overwhelming task, but several resources are available that help to simplify this process. Notice that I did not say the process is simple— only that these resources help to simplify it. A thorough literature review takes time, but the resources discussed here will help you make the best use of that time.

## Library Research

Usually, the best place to begin your research is at the library. Several resources available through most libraries are invaluable when conducting a literature review. One important resource, often overlooked by students, is the library staff. Reference librarians have been trained to find information—this is their job. Thus, if you provide them with sufficient information, they should be able to provide you with numerous resources. Do not expect them to do this on the spot, however. Plan ahead, and give the librarian sufficient time to help you.

## Journals

Most published research in psychology appears in the form of journal articles (see Table 2.1 for a list of major journals in psychology). Notice that the titles listed in Table 2.1 are journals, not magazines such as *Psychology Today*. The difference is that each paper published in these journals is first submitted to the editor of the journal, who sends the paper out for review by other scientists (specialists) in that area. This process is called *peer review,* and based on

**TABLE 2.1   Some journals whose articles are summarized in the *Psychological Abstracts***

**Applied Psychology**

Applied Cognitive Psychology

Educational and Psychological
Measurement

Educational Psychologist

Educational Psychology Review

Environment and Behavior

Health Psychology

Journal of Applied Behavior Analysis

Journal of Applied Developmental
Psychology

Journal of Applied Psychology

Journal of Educational Psychology

Journal of Environmental
Psychology

Journal of Sport Psychology

Law and Human Behavior

Law and Psychology Review

Psychological Assessment

Psychology, Public Policy, and Law

**Clinical/Counseling Psychology**

Counseling Psychologist

Journal of Abnormal Child
Psychology

Journal of Abnormal Psychology

Journal of Clinical Child Psychology

Journal of Clinical Psychology

Journal of Consulting and Clinical
Psychology

Journal of Contemporary
Psychotherapy

Journal of Counseling Psychology

Journal of Social and Clinical
Psychology

**Developmental Psychology**

Child Development

Developmental Psychobiology

Developmental Psychology

Developmental Review

Infant Behavior and Development

Journal of Experimental Child
Psychology

Psychology and Aging

**Experimental Psychology**

Animal Learning and Behavior

The Psychonomic Bulletin and Review

Cognition

Cognition and Emotion

Cognitive Psychology

Cognitive Science

Journal of Experimental Psychology:
Animal Behavior Processes

Journal of Experimental
Psychology: Applied

Journal of Experimental
Psychology: General

Journal of Experimental Psychology:
Human Perception and Performance

Journal of Experimental Psychology:
Learning, Memory, and Cognition

Journal of Memory and Language

Journal of the Experimental
Analysis of Behavior

Learning and Motivation

Memory and Cognition

Perception

Perception and Psychophysics

Quarterly Journal of Experimental
Psychology: Comparative and
Physiological Psychology

Quarterly Journal of Experimental
Psychology: Human Experimental
Psychology

Sensory Processes

Thinking and Reasoning

**Family Therapy**

American Journal of Family Therapy

Journal of Family Psychology

Journal of Marital and Family
Therapy

Journal of Marriage and the Family

**General Psychology**

American Psychologist

Contemporary Psychology

Psychological Bulletin

Psychological Bulletin and Review

Psychological Review

Psychological Science

**Personality and Social
Psychology**

Basic and Applied Social
Psychology

Journal of Applied Social
Psychology

Journal of Experimental Social
Psychology

Journal of Personality

Journal of Personality and Social
Psychology

Journal of Personality Assessment

Journal of Social and Personal
Relationships

Journal of Social Issues

Personality and Social Psychology
Bulletin

Personality and Social Psychology
Review

**Physiological Psychology**

Behavioral and Brain Sciences

Biological Psychology

Brain and Language

Genetic Psychology Monographs

Physiological Psychology

Physiology and Behavior

**Treatment**

Addictive Behaviors

Behavior Modification

Behavior Therapy

Journal of Anxiety Disorders

Journal of Behavioral Medicine

the reviews, the editor then decides whether to accept the paper for publication. Because of the limited space available in each journal, most papers that are submitted are ultimately rejected for publication. Thus, the research published in journals represents a fraction of the research conducted in an area, and because of the review process, it should be the best research in that area.

"THAT'S IT? THAT'S PEER REVIEW?"

As you can see in Table 2.1, a great many journals publish psychology papers. Obviously, it is not possible to keep up with all the research that is published in these journals. In fact, it would be very difficult to read all of the studies that are published in a given area. As a researcher, then, how can you identify those papers most relevant to your topic? It would take forever to browse through the psychology journals in your library to find articles of interest to you. Luckily for you, this is not necessary.

## Psychological Abstracts

Besides reference librarians, your other best friend in the library is *Psychological (Psych) Abstracts*. *Psych Abstracts* is a reference resource published by the American Psychological Association that contains abstracts, or brief summaries, of articles in psychology and related disciplines. *Psych Abstracts* is updated monthly and can be found in the reference section of your library. To use *Psych Abstracts*, begin with the index at the back of each monthly issue and look up the topic in which you are interested. Next to the topic you will find several numbers referencing abstracts in that issue. You can then refer to each of these abstracts to find where the full article is published, who wrote it, when it was published, the pages on which it appears, and a brief summary of the article.

## PsycINFO and PsycLIT

Most libraries now have *Psych Abstracts* in some electronic form. If your library has such a resource, you will probably find it easier to use than the hard copy of *Psych Abstracts* described above. PsycINFO is an electronic database that provides abstracts and citations to the scholarly literature in the behavioral sciences and mental health. The database, which is updated monthly, includes material of relevance to psychologists and professionals in related fields such as psychiatry, business, education, social science, neuroscience, law, and medicine. With the popularity of the Internet, most libraries now have access to PsycINFO. PyscLIT is the CD-ROM version of *Psych Abstracts*. Although PsycLIT is no longer published, the library at your school may still have copies of it available. PsycLIT was updated quarterly during its publication period.

To use either of these resources, you simply enter your topic of interest into the "Find" box, and the database will provide a listing of abstracts relevant to that topic. You will find when you use these resources that you do not want your topic to be either too broad or too narrow. In addition, it is helpful to try several different phrases when searching a particular topic. I frequently have students tell me that they typed in their topic and could not find anything on it. This means that the keyword they used may not be the word used by researchers in the field. To help you choose appropriate keywords, you might use the APA's *Thesaurus of Psychological Index Terms* (2001b). This resource is based on the vocabulary used in psychology and will direct you to the terms to use to locate articles on that topic. Ask your reference librarian for help in finding and using this resource. You will probably find, when using PsycINFO, that you need to complete several searches on a topic using different words and phrases. For example, if you selected the topic depression and entered this word into the "Find" box, you would find a very large number of articles because PsycINFO looks for the key word in the title of the article and in the abstract itself. Thus, you will need to limit your search by using some of the Boolean operators such as AND, OR, and NOT and also using some of the limiters available through PsycINFO.

For example, I conducted a search using the key word "depression" in the "Find" box and I limited the search to articles published in the year 2003. The search returned abstracts for 4,693 articles—obviously too many to review. I then limited my search further by using the Boolean operator AND by typing "depression AND college students" in the "Find" box and once again limiting it to articles published in 2003. This second search returned abstracts for 80 articles—a much more manageable number. I could further refine the search by using the Boolean operators NOT and OR. For example, some of the 80 journal articles returned in the second search were about scales used to measure depression. If I were not really interested in this aspect of depression, I could further limit my search by typing the following into the "Find" box: "depression AND college students NOT (measures OR scales)." When the search was conducted this way, it narrowed the number of journal articles published in 2003 to 35. Thus, with a little practice, PsycINFO should prove an invaluable resource to you in searching the literature.

## Social Science Citation Index and Science Citation Index

Other resources that are valuable when conducting a literature review are the *Social Science Citation Index* (SSCI) and the *Science Citation Index* (SCI). Whereas *Psych Abstracts* helps you to work backward in time (find articles published on a certain topic within a given year), the SSCI can help you to work from a given article (a "key article") and see what has been published on that topic since the key article was published. The SSCI includes the disciplines from the social and behavioral sciences, whereas the SCI includes disciplines such as biology, chemistry, and medicine. Both resources are used in a similar way. Imagine that you found a very interesting paper on the effects of music on mood that was published in 2000. Because this paper was published several years ago, you will need to know what has been published since then on this topic. The SSCI and the SCI enable you to search for subsequent articles that have cited the key article, and they also allow you to search for articles published by the author(s) of the key article. If a subsequent article cites your key article, the chances are good that it is on the same topic and will therefore be of interest to you. Moreover, if the author(s) of the key article have since published additional papers, those would also likely be of interest to you. Thus, the SSCI and the SCI allow you to fill in the gap between 2000 and the present. In this way, you can compile an up-to-date reference list and become familiar with most of the material published on a topic. When using the SSCI or the SCI, you may also find that one of the "new" articles you discover is another key article on your topic, and you can then look for subsequent articles that cite or were written by the author(s) of the new key article. The SSCI and the SCI are often available online through your library's home page.

## Other Resources

Another resource often overlooked by students is the set of references provided at the end of a journal article. If you have found a key article of interest to you, begin with the papers cited in the key article. The reference list provides information on where these cited papers were published, enabling you to obtain any of the cited articles that appear to be of interest.

In addition to the resources already described, several other resources and databases may be helpful to you.

- *PsyArticles* is an online database that provides full-text articles from many psychology journals and is available through many academic libraries.
- *ProQuest* is an online database that searches both scholarly journals and popular media sources. Full-text articles are often available. ProQuest is available through most academic libraries.
- *Sociological Abstracts* are similar to *Psych Abstracts*, except they summarize journal articles on sociological topics.

- The Educational Resources Information Center (ERIC) is a clearinghouse for research on educational psychology, testing, counseling, child development, evaluation research, and related areas. It is available online through most academic libraries.
- *Dissertation Abstracts International*, published monthly, includes abstracts of doctoral dissertations from hundreds of universities in the United States and Canada.

In addition to these resources, interlibrary loan (ILL) is a service provided by most libraries that allows you to borrow resources from other libraries if your library does not hold them. If, for example, you need a book that your library does not have or an article from a journal to which your library does not subscribe, you can use interlibrary loan to obtain it. Through this service, your library will borrow the resources needed from the closest library that holds them. See your reference librarian to use this service.

Finally, the World Wide Web may also be used as a resource. Many of the resources already described, such as PsycINFO, the SSCI, and ERIC, are available online through your library's home page. Be wary, however, of information you retrieve from the web through some source other than a library. Bear in mind that anyone can post anything on the web. Just because it looks scientific and appears to be written in the same form as a scientific journal article does not necessarily mean that it is. It is usually best to use the resources available through your library's home page. As with the resources available on the shelves of the library, these resources have been chosen by the librarians. This means that editors and other specialists have most likely reviewed them before they were published—unlike information on the web, which is frequently placed there by the author without any review by others.

| IN REVIEW | Library Research |

| TOOL | WHAT IT IS |
| --- | --- |
| *Psych Abstracts* | A reference resource published by the American Psychological Association that contains abstracts or brief summaries of articles in psychology and related disciplines |
| PsycINFO | The online version of *Psych Abstracts*, updated monthly |
| PsycLIT | The CD-ROM version of *Psych Abstracts*, updated quarterly |
| *Social Science Citation Index* (SSCI) | A resource that allows you to search for subsequent articles from the social and behavioral sciences that have cited a key article |
| *Science Citation Index* (SCI) | A resource that allows you to search for subsequent articles from disciplines such as biology, chemistry, or medicine that have cited a key article |
| Interlibrary loan (ILL) | A service provided by most libraries that allows you to borrow resources from other libraries if your library does not hold them |
| *Sociological Abstracts* | A reference that contains abstracts or brief summaries of articles in sociology and related disciplines |
| *PsyArticles* | An online database that contains full-text articles from many psychology journals |
| *ProQuest* | An online database that searches both scholarly journals and popular media sources; full-text articles are often available |

| TOOL | WHAT IT IS |
|------|-----------|
| ERIC | A clearinghouse for research on educational psychology, testing, counseling, child development, evaluation research, and related areas |
| *Dissertation Abstracts* | Abstracts of doctoral dissertations from hundreds of universities in the United States and Canada, published monthly |

# Reading a Journal Article: What to Expect

Your search for information in the library will undoubtedly provide you with many journal articles. Research articles have a very specific format. They usually have five main sections: Abstract, Introduction, Method, Results, and Discussion. Following is a brief description of what to expect from each of these sections.

## Abstract

The Abstract is a very brief description of the entire paper and typically discusses each section of the paper (Introduction, Method, Results, and Discussion). It should not exceed 120 words. The Abstract describes the problem under investigation and the purpose of the study, the participants and general methodology, the findings including statistical significance levels, and the conclusions and implications or applications of the study.

## Introduction

The Introduction has three basic components: an introduction to the problem under study; a review of relevant previous research, which cites works that are pertinent to the issue but not works of marginal or peripheral significance; and the purpose and rationale for the study.

## Method

The Method section describes exactly how the study was conducted, in sufficient detail that a person who reads the Method section could replicate the study. The Method section is generally divided into subsections. Although the subsections vary across papers, the most common subsections are Participants, Materials or Apparatus, and Procedure. The Participants subsection includes a description of the participants and how they were obtained. A Materials subsection usually describes any testing materials that were used, such as a particular test or inventory or a type of problem that participants were asked to solve. An Apparatus subsection describes any specific equipment that was used. The Procedure subsection summarizes each step in the execution of the research, including the groups used in the study, instructions given to the participants, the experimental manipulation, and specific control features in the design.

## Results

The Results section summarizes the data collected and the type of statistic used to analyze the data. In addition, the results of the statistical tests used are reported with respect to the variables measured and/or manipulated. This section should include a description of the results only, not an explanation of the results. In addition, the results are often depicted in tables and graphs or figures.

## Discussion

In the Discussion section, the results are evaluated and interpreted. Typically, this section begins with a restatement of the predictions of the study and tells whether or not the predictions were supported. It also typically includes a discussion of the relationship between the results and past research and theories. Last, criticisms of the study (such as possible confounds) and implications for future research are presented.

# Ethical Standards in Research with Human Participants

When conducting research with human (or nonhuman) participants, the researcher is ultimately responsible for the welfare of the participants. Thus, it is the researcher's responsibility to protect the participants from harm. What harm, you may be wondering, could a participant suffer in a simple research study? Let's consider some of the research studies that helped to initiate the implementation of ethical guidelines for using human participants in research.

The ethical guidelines we use today have their basis in the Nuremberg Code. This code lists 10 principles, developed in 1948, for the Nazi war crimes trials following World War II. The Nazis killed and abused millions of Jews, many of whom died in the name of "research." For example, Nazi doctors used many Jews for inhumane medical research projects that involved determining the effects on humans of viruses, poisons, toxins, and drugs.

The Nazis were not the only researchers who conducted ethically questionable research. For example, researchers who conducted the Tuskegee syphilis study, which began in 1932 and continued until 1972, examined the course of the disease in untreated individuals. The participants were approximately 400 black men living in and around Tuskegee, Alabama. The individuals, most of whom were poor and illiterate, were offered free meals, physical examinations, and money for their eventual burial for participating in the study (Jones, 1981). They were told that they were being treated for the disease by the U.S. Public Health Service (USPHS). In reality, they were never treated, nor were they ever told the real purpose of the study—to observe the progression of syphilis in an untreated population. Some of the participants realized that something was amiss and consulted other doctors in the area. Those who did so were eliminated from the study. In addition, the USPHS told doctors in the surrounding area not to treat any of the participants should they request treatment—even though an effective treatment for syphilis, penicillin, was discovered by the 1940s. The Tuskegee study continued until 1972, providing little new knowledge about syphilis but costing about 400 lives.

Obviously, the Nuremberg Code, established in 1948, had little effect on the researchers who conducted the Tuskegee study. In any case, the Nuremberg Code applied only to medical research. In 1953, therefore, the members of the APA decided to develop their own ethical guidelines for research with human participants.

In 1963, Stanley Milgram's paper detailing some of his research on obedience to authority brought ethical considerations to the forefront once again. In Milgram's study, each participant was assigned the role of "teacher" and given the responsibility for teaching a series of words to another individual, called the "learner." What the teachers did not realize was that the learner was really an accomplice of the experimenter. The teachers were told that the study was designed to investigate the effects of punishment on learning. Thus, they were instructed to deliver an electric shock each time the learner made a mistake. The shocks were not of a constant voltage level, but increased in voltage for each mistake made. Because the learner (who was located in a separate room from the teacher) was working for the experimenter, he purposely made mistakes. Milgram was interested in whether the teachers would continue to deliver stronger and stronger electric shocks given that (1) the learner appeared to be in moderate to extreme discomfort, depending on the level of shock administered, and (2) the experimenter repeatedly ordered the teachers to continue administering the electric shocks. In reality, the learner was not receiving electric shocks; however, the teachers believed that they were. Milgram found that nearly two-thirds of the teachers obeyed the experimenter and continued to deliver the supposed electric shocks up to the maximum level available.

"IT'S FROM THE PROTOZOA RIGHTS COMMITTEE. THEY WANT TO KNOW WHAT YOU'RE USING THEIR CLIENTS FOR."

Although the results of this experiment were valuable to society, the study was ethically questionable. Was it really an ethical use of human participants to place them in a situation where they were put under extreme psychological stress and where they may have learned things about themselves that they would have preferred not to know? This type of study would not be allowed today because the APA has continually revised and strengthened its ethical guidelines since 1953. The latest revision occurred in 2002. You can find the most recent information at http://www.apa.org/ethics. Some of the principles outlined in 2002 are provided in Table 2.2. In addition to the APA guidelines, federal guidelines (Federal Protection Regulations), developed in 1982, are enforced by Institutional Review Boards at most institutions.

## Institutional Review Boards

**Institutional Review Board (IRB)** A committee charged with evaluating research projects in which human participants are used.

An **Institutional Review Board (IRB)** is typically made up of several faculty members, usually from diverse backgrounds, and members of the community who are charged with evaluating research projects in which human participants are used. IRBs oversee all federally funded research involving human participants. Most academic institutions have either an IRB (if they receive federal funding) or some other committee responsible for evaluating research projects that use human participants. The evaluation process involves completing an application form in which the researcher details the method to be used in the study, the risks or benefits related to participating in the study, and the means of maintaining participants' confidentiality. In addition, the researcher should provide an informed consent form (discussed below). The purpose of the IRB is not necessarily to evaluate the scientific merit of the research study but rather to evaluate the treatment of participants to ensure that the study meets established ethical guidelines.

## Informed Consent

**informed consent form** A form given to individuals before they participate in a study to inform them of the general nature of the study and to obtain their consent to participate.

In studies where participants are at risk, an informed consent form is needed. (We will discuss exactly what "at risk" means later in the chapter.) The **informed consent form** is given to individuals before they participate in a research study to inform them of the general nature of the study and to obtain their consent to participate in the study. The informed consent form typically describes the nature and purpose of the study. However, to avoid compromising the outcome of the study, the researcher obviously cannot inform participants about the expected results. Thus, informed consent forms often offer only broad, general statements about the nature and purpose of a study. In cases where deception is used in the study, of course, the informed consent form tells participants nothing about the true nature and purpose of the study. (We will address the ethical ramifications of using deception later in the chapter.) The participants are also informed of what they will be asked to do as part of the study and that the researchers will make every effort to maintain confidentiality with respect to their performance

**TABLE 2.2    APA principles covering the treatment of human participants**

### 3.04 Avoiding Harm

Psychologists take reasonable steps to avoid harming their clients/patients, students, supervisees, research participants, organizational clients, and others with whom they work, and to minimize harm where it is foreseeable and unavoidable.

### 4. *Privacy and Confidentiality*

### 4.01 Maintaining Confidentiality

Psychologists have a primary obligation and take reasonable precautions to protect confidential information obtained through or stored in any medium, recognizing that the extent and limits of confidentiality may be regulated by law or established by institutional rules or professional or scientific relationship. (See also Standard 2.05, Delegation of Work to Others.)

### 4.02 Discussing the Limits of Confidentiality

(a) Psychologists discuss with persons (including, to the extent feasible, persons who are legally incapable of giving informed consent and their legal representatives) and organizations with whom they establish a scientific or professional relationship (1) the relevant limits of confidentiality and (2) the foreseeable uses of the information generated through their psychological activities. (See also Standard 3.10, Informed Consent.)

(b) Unless it is not feasible or is contraindicated, the discussion of confidentiality occurs at the outset of the relationship and thereafter as new circumstances may warrant.

(c) Psychologists who offer services, products, or information via electronic transmission inform clients/patients of the risks to privacy and limits of confidentiality.

### 4.03 Recording

Before recording the voices or images of individuals to whom they provide services, psychologists obtain permission from all such persons or their legal representatives. (See also Standards 8.03, Informed Consent for Recording Voices and Images in Research; 8.05, Dispensing with Informed Consent for Research; and 8.07, Deception in Research.)

### 4.04 Minimizing Intrusions on Privacy

(a) Psychologists include in written and oral reports and consultations, only information germane to the purpose for which the communication is made.

(b) Psychologists discuss confidential information obtained in their work only for appropriate scientific or professional purposes and only with persons clearly concerned with such matters.

### 4.05 Disclosures

(a) Psychologists may disclose confidential information with the appropriate consent of the organizational client, the individual client/patient, or another legally authorized person on behalf of the client/patient unless prohibited by law.

(b) Psychologists disclose confidential information without the consent of the individual only as mandated by law, or where permitted by law for a valid purpose such as to (1) provide needed professional services; (2) obtain appropriate professional consultations; (3) protect the client/patient, psychologist, or others from harm; or (4) obtain payment for services from a client/patient, in which instance disclosure is limited to the minimum that is necessary to achieve the purpose. (See also Standard 6.04e, Fees and Financial Arrangements.)

### 4.06 Consultations

When consulting with colleagues, (1) psychologists do not disclose confidential information that reasonably could lead to the identification of a client/patient, research participant, or other person or organization with whom they have a confidential relationship unless they have obtained the prior consent of the person or organization or the disclosure cannot be avoided, and (2) they disclose information only to the extent necessary to achieve the purposes of the consultation. (See also Standard 4.01, Maintaining Confidentiality.)

*(continued)*

**TABLE 2.2    APA principles covering the treatment of human participants (*continued*)**

### 4.07 Use of Confidential Information for Didactic or Other Purposes

Psychologists do not disclose in their writings, lectures, or other public media, confidential, personally identifiable information concerning their clients/patients, students, research participants, organizational clients, or other recipients of their services that they obtained during the course of their work, unless (1) they take reasonable steps to disguise the person or organization, (2) the person or organization has consented in writing, or (3) there is legal authorization for doing so.

### 8. *Research and Publication*

### 8.01 Institutional Approval

When institutional approval is required, psychologists provide accurate information about their research proposals and obtain approval prior to conducting the research. They conduct the research in accordance with the approved research protocol.

### 8.02 Informed Consent to Research

(a) When obtaining informed consent as required in Standard 3.10, Informed Consent, psychologists inform participants about (1) the purpose of the research, expected duration, and procedures; (2) their right to decline to participate and to withdraw from the research once participation has begun; (3) the foreseeable consequences of declining or withdrawing; (4) reasonably foreseeable factors that may be expected to influence their willingness to participate such as potential risks, discomfort, or adverse effects; (5) any prospective research benefits; (6) limits of confidentiality; (7) incentives for participation; and (8) whom to contact for questions about the research and research participants' rights. They provide opportunity for the prospective participants to ask questions and receive answers. (See also Standards 8.03, Informed Consent for Recording Voices and Images in Research; 8.05, Dispensing with Informed Consent for Research; and 8.07, Deception in Research.)

(b) Psychologists conducting intervention research involving the use of experimental treatments clarify to participants at the outset of the research (1) the experimental nature of the treatment; (2) the services that will or will not be available to the control group(s) if appropriate; (3) the means by which assignment to treatment and control groups will be made; (4) available treatment alternatives if an individual does not wish to participate in the research or wishes to withdraw once a study has begun; and (5) compensation for or monetary costs of participating including, if appropriate, whether reimbursement from the participant or a third-party payor will be sought. (See also Standard 8.02a, Informed Consent to Research.)

### 8.03 Informed Consent for Recording Voices and Images in Research

Psychologists obtain informed consent from research participants prior to recording their voices or images for data collection unless (1) the research consists solely of naturalistic observations in public places, and it is not anticipated that the recording will be used in a manner that could cause personal identification or harm, or (2) the research design includes deception, and consent for the use of the recording is obtained during debriefing. (See also Standard 8.07, Deception in Research.)

### 8.04 Client/Patient, Student, and Subordinate Research Participants

(a) When psychologists conduct research with clients/patients, students, or subordinates as participants, psychologists take steps to protect the prospective participants from adverse consequences of declining or withdrawing from participation.

(b) When research participation is a course requirement or an opportunity for extra credit, the prospective participant is given the choice of equitable alternative activities.

### 8.05 Dispensing with Informed Consent for Research

Psychologists may dispense with informed consent only (1) where research would not reasonably be assumed to create distress or harm and involves (a) the study of normal educational practices, curricula, or classroom management methods conducted in educational settings; (b) only anonymous questionnaires, naturalistic observations, or archival research for which disclosure of responses would not place participants at risk of criminal or civil liability or damage their financial standing, employability, or reputation, and confidentiality is protected; or (c) the study of factors

*(continued)*

**TABLE 2.2    APA principles covering the treatment of human participants (*continued*)**

related to job or organization effectiveness conducted in organizational settings for which there is no risk to participants' employability, and confidentiality is protected or (2) where otherwise permitted by law or federal or institutional regulations.

**8.06 Offering Inducements for Research Participation**

(a) Psychologists make reasonable efforts to avoid offering excessive or inappropriate financial or other inducements for research participation when such inducements are likely to coerce participation.

(b) When offering professional services as an inducement for research participation, psychologists clarify the nature of the services, as well as the risks, obligations, and limitations. (See also Standard 6.05, Barter with Clients/Patients.)

**8.07 Deception in Research**

(a) Psychologists do not conduct a study involving deception unless they have determined that the use of deceptive techniques is justified by the study's significant prospective scientific, educational, or applied value and that effective nondeceptive alternative procedures are not feasible.

(b) Psychologists do not deceive prospective participants about research that is reasonably expected to cause physical pain or severe emotional distress.

(c) Psychologists explain any deception that is an integral feature of the design and conduct of an experiment to participants as early as is feasible, preferably at the conclusion of their participation, but no later than at the conclusion of the data collection, and permit participants to withdraw their data. (See also Standard 8.08, Debriefing.)

**8.08 Debriefing**

(a) Psychologists provide a prompt opportunity for participants to obtain appropriate information about the nature, results, and conclusions of the research, and they take reasonable steps to correct any misconceptions that participants may have of which the psychologists are aware.

(b) If scientific or humane values justify delaying or withholding this information, psychologists take reasonable measures to reduce the risk of harm.

(c) When psychologists become aware that research procedures have harmed a participant, they take reasonable steps to minimize the harm.

**8.09 Humane Care and Use of Animals in Research**

(a) Psychologists acquire, care for, use, and dispose of animals in compliance with current federal, state, and local laws and regulations, and with professional standards.

(b) Psychologists trained in research methods and experienced in the care of laboratory animals supervise all procedures involving animals and are responsible for ensuring appropriate consideration of their comfort, health, and humane treatment.

(c) Psychologists ensure that all individuals under their supervision who are using animals have received instruction in research methods and in the care, maintenance, and handling of the species being used, to the extent appropriate to their role. (See also Standard 2.05, Delegation of Work to Others.)

(d) Psychologists make reasonable efforts to minimize the discomfort, infection, illness, and pain of animal subjects.

(e) Psychologists use a procedure subjecting animals to pain, stress, or privation only when an alternative procedure is unavailable and the goal is justified by its prospective scientific, educational, or applied value.

(f) Psychologists perform surgical procedures under appropriate anesthesia and follow techniques to avoid infection and minimize pain during and after surgery.

(g) When it is appropriate that an animal's life be terminated, psychologists proceed rapidly, with an effort to minimize pain and in accordance with accepted procedures.

**8.10 Reporting Research Results**

(a) Psychologists do not fabricate data. (See also Standard 5.01a, Avoidance of False or Deceptive Statements.)

(b) If psychologists discover significant errors in their published data, they take reasonable steps to correct such errors in a correction, retraction, erratum, or other appropriate publication means.

(continued)

**TABLE 2.2   APA principles covering the treatment of human participants (*continued*)**

### 8.11 Plagiarism

Psychologists do not present portions of another's work or data as their own, even if the other work or data source is cited occasionally.

### 8.12 Publication Credit

(a) Psychologists take responsibility and credit, including authorship credit, only for work they have actually performed or to which they have substantially contributed. (See also Standard 8.12b, Publication Credit.)

(b) Principal authorship and other publication credits accurately reflect the relative scientific or professional contributions of the individuals involved, regardless of their relative status. Mere possession of an institutional position, such as department chair, does not justify authorship credit. Minor contributions to the research or to the writing for publications are acknowledged appropriately, such as in footnotes or in an introductory statement.

(c) Except under exceptional circumstances, a student is listed as principal author on any multiple-authored article that is substantially based on the student's doctoral dissertation. Faculty advisors discuss publication credit with students as early as feasible and throughout the research and publication process as appropriate. (See also Standard 8.12b, Publication Credit.)

### 8.13 Duplicate Publication of Data

Psychologists do not publish, as original data, data that have been previously published. This does not preclude republishing data when they are accompanied by proper acknowledgment.

### 8.14 Sharing Research Data for Verification

(a) After research results are published, psychologists do not withhold the data on which their conclusions are based from other competent professionals who seek to verify the substantive claims through reanalysis and who intend to use such data only for that purpose, provided that the confidentiality of the participants can be protected and unless legal rights concerning proprietary data preclude their release. This does not preclude psychologists from requiring that such individuals or groups be responsible for costs associated with the provision of such information.

(b) Psychologists who request data from other psychologists to verify the substantive claims through reanalysis may use shared data only for the declared purpose. Requesting psychologists obtain prior written agreement for all other uses of the data.

### 8.15 Reviewers

Psychologists who review material submitted for presentation, publication, grant, or research proposal review respect the confidentiality of and the proprietary rights in such information of those who submitted it.

SOURCE: American Psychological Association. (2002). *Ethical principles of psychologists and code of conduct.* Copyright © 2002 by the American Psychological Association. Reprinted with permission.

in the study. Participants are told that they have the right to refuse to participate in the study and to change their mind about participation at any point during the study. Participants sign the form, indicating that they have given their informed consent to participate in the study. Typically, the form is also signed by a witness. Researchers should keep informed consent forms on file for two to three years after completion of a study and should also give a copy of the form to each participant. If participants in a study are under 18 years of age, then informed consent must be given by a parent or legal guardian. A sample informed consent form appears in Figure 2.1.

**FIGURE 2.1**
**A sample informed consent form**

### Informed Consent Form

You, _____, are being asked to participate in a research project titled
_____. This project is being conducted under the supervision of _____
and was approved by _____ University/College's IRB (or Committee on the Use of
Human Participants) on _____.

The investigators hope to learn _____ from this project.

While participating in this study, you will be asked to _____ for _____
period of time.

The nature of this study has been explained by _____. The anticipated benefits of
your participation are _____. The known risks of your participation in this study
are _____.

The researchers will make every effort to safeguard the confidentiality of the information that you
provide. Any information obtained from this study that can be identified with you will remain
confidential and will not be given to anyone without your permission.

If at any time you would like additional information about this project, you can contact
_____ at _____.

You have the right to refuse to participate in this study. If you do agree to participate, you have the
right to change your mind at any time and stop your participation. The grades and services you
receive from _____ University/College will not be negatively affected by your refusal
to participate or by your withdrawal from this project. Your signature below indicates that you
have given your informed consent to participate in the above-described project. Your signature
also indicates that:

➪ You have been given the opportunity to ask any and all questions about the described project
   and your participation and all of your questions have been answered to your satisfaction.
➪ You have been permitted to read this document and you have been given a signed copy of it.
➪ You are at least 18 years old.
➪ You are legally able to provide consent.
➪ To the best of your knowledge and belief, you have no physical or mental illness or weakness
   that would be adversely affected by your participation in the described project.


_____          _____
Signature of Participant             Date


_____          _____
Signature of Witness                 Date

## Risk

Typically, participants in a study are classified as being either "at risk" or "at minimal risk." Those at minimal risk are placed under no more physical or emotional risk than would be encountered in daily life or in routine physical or psychological examinations or tests (U.S. Department of Health and Human Services, 1981). In what types of studies might a participant be classified as being at minimal risk? Studies in which participants are asked to fill out paper-and-pencil tests such as personality inventories or depression inventories are classified as minimal risk. Other examples of studies in which participants are classified as at minimal risk are most research on memory processes, problem-solving abilities, and reasoning. If the participants in a study are classified as at minimal risk, then an informed consent is not mandatory. However, it is probably best to obtain informed consent anyway.

In contrast, the participants in the Tuskeegee study and in Milgram's (1963) obedience study would definitely be classified as at risk. Studies in which the participants are at risk for physical or emotional harm fit the definition of participants being at risk. When proposing a study in which participants are classified as at risk, the researcher and the members of the IRB must determine whether the benefits of the knowledge to be gained from the study outweigh the risk to participants. Clearly, Milgram believed that this was the case; members of IRBs today might not agree.

Participants are also often considered at risk if their privacy is compromised. Participants expect that researchers will protect their privacy and keep their participation in, and results from, the study confidential. In most research studies, there should be no need to tie data to individuals. Thus, in such cases, privacy and confidentiality are not issues because the participants have anonymity. However, in those situations in which it is necessary to tie data to an individual (for example, when data will be collected from the same participants over many sessions), every precaution should be made to safeguard the data and keep them separate from the identities of the participants. In other words, a coding system should be used that allows the researcher to identify the individual, but the information identifying them should be kept separate from the actual data so that if the data were seen by anyone, they could not be linked to any particular individual. In studies in which researchers need to be able to identify the participants, an informed consent form should be used because anonymity and confidentiality are at risk.

## Deception

**deception** Lying to the participants concerning the true nature of a study because knowing the true nature of the study might affect their performance.

Besides the risk of emotional harm, you may be wondering about another aspect of Milgram's (1963) study. Milgram deceived his participants by telling them that the experiment was about the effects of punishment on learning, not about obedience to authority. **Deception** in research involves lying to participants about the true nature of a study because knowing the true nature of the study might affect their performance. Clearly, in some research studies, it is not possible to fully inform participants of the nature of the study because this knowledge might affect their responses. How, then, do researchers obtain informed consent when deception is necessary? They give participants a general description of the study—not a detailed description of the hypothesis being tested. Remember that participants are also informed that they do not have to participate, that a refusal to participate will incur no penalties, and that they can stop participating in the study at any time. Given these precautions, deception can be used, when necessary, without violating ethical standards. After the study is completed, however, researchers should debrief (discussed below) the participants, informing them of the deception and the true intent of the study.

## Debriefing

One final ethical consideration concerns the debriefing of participants. **Debriefing** means providing information about the true purpose of the study as soon after the completion of data collection as possible. In the Milgram study, for example, debriefing entailed informing participants of the true nature of the study (obedience to authority) as soon after completion of the study as possible. Based on immediate debriefings and one-year follow-up interviews, Milgram (1977) found that only about 1% of the participants wished they had not participated in the study and that most were very glad they had participated. Debriefing is necessary in all research studies, not just those that involve deception. Through debriefing, participants learn more about the benefits of the research to them and to society in general, and the researcher has the opportunity to alleviate any discomfort the participants may be experiencing. During debriefing, the researcher should try to bring participants back to the same state of mind they were in before they participated in the study.

**debriefing** Providing information about the true purpose of a study as soon after the completion of data collection as possible.

# Ethical Standards in Research with Children

Special considerations arise in research studies that use children as participants. For example, how does informed consent work with children, and how do researchers properly debrief a child? Informed consent must be obtained from the parents or legal guardians for all persons under the age of 18. However, with children who are old enough to understand language, the researcher should also try to inform them of the nature of the study, explain what they will be asked to do during the study, and tell them that they do not have to participate and can request to end their participation at any time. The question remains, however, whether children really understand this information and whether they would feel comfortable exercising these rights. Thus, when doing research with children, the researcher must be especially careful to use good judgment when deciding whether to continue collecting data from an individual or whether to use a particular child in the research project.

# Ethical Standards in Research with Animals

Using animals in research has become a controversial issue. Some people believe that no research should be conducted on animals; others believe that research with animals is advantageous but that measures should be taken to ensure humane treatment. Taking the latter position, the APA has developed *Guidelines for Ethical Conduct in the Care and Use of Animals* (1996). These guidelines are presented in Table 2.3.

There is little argument that animal research has led to many advances for both human and nonhuman animals, especially in medical research. For example, research with animals has led to blood transfusions; advances in painkillers, antibiotics, behavioral medications, and drug treatments; and knowledge of the brain, nervous system, and psychopathology. However, animal rights activists believe that the cost of these advances is often too high.

**TABLE 2.3    APA guidelines for ethical conduct in the care and use of animals**

Developed by the American Psychological Association's Committee on Animal Research and Ethics (CARE)

### I. Justification of the Research

A. Research should be undertaken with a clear scientific purpose. There should be a reasonable expectation that the research will (a) increase knowledge of the processes underlying the evolution, development, maintenance, alteration, control, or biological significance of behavior; (b) determine the replicability and generality of prior research; (c) increase understanding of the species under study; or (d) provide results that benefit the health or welfare of humans or other animals.

B. The scientific purpose of the research should be of sufficient potential significance to justify the use of animals. Psychologists should act on the assumption that procedures that would produce pain in humans will also do so in other animals.

C. The species chosen for study should be best suited to answer the question(s) posed. The psychologist should always consider the possibility of using other species, nonanimal alternatives, or procedures that minimize the number of animals in research, and should be familiar with the appropriate literature.

D. Research on animals may not be conducted until the protocol has been reviewed by an appropriate animal care committee—for example, an institutional animal care and use committee (IACUC)—to ensure that the procedures are appropriate and humane.

E. The psychologist should monitor the research and the animals' welfare throughout the course of an investigation to ensure continued justification for the research.

### II. Personnel

A. Psychologists should ensure that personnel involved in their research with animals be familiar with these guidelines.

B. Animal use procedures must conform with federal regulations regarding personnel, supervision, record keeping, and veterinary care.[1]

C. Behavior is both the focus of study of many experiments as well as a primary source of information about an animal's health and well-being. It is therefore necessary that psychologists and their assistants be informed about the behavioral characteristics of their animal subjects, so as to be aware of normal, species-specific behaviors and unusual behaviors that could forewarn of health problems.

D. Psychologists should ensure that all individuals who use animals under their supervision receive explicit instruction in experimental methods and in the care, maintenance, and handling of the species being studied. Responsibilities and activities of all individuals dealing with animals should be consistent with their respective competencies, training, and experience in either the laboratory or the field setting.

*(continued)*

**TABLE 2.3   APA guidelines for ethical conduct in the care and use of animals (*continued*)**

### III. Care and Housing of Animals

The concept of psychological well-being of animals is of current concern and debate and is included in Federal Regulations (United States Department of Agriculture [USDA], 1991). As a scientific and professional organization, APA recognizes the complexities of defining psychological well-being. Procedures appropriate for a particular species may be inappropriate for others. Hence, APA does not presently stipulate specific guidelines regarding the maintenance of psychological well-being of research animals. Psychologists familiar with the species should be best qualified professionally to judge measures such as enrichment to maintain or improve psychological well-being of those species.

A. The facilities housing animals should meet or exceed current regulations and guidelines (USDA, 1990, 1991) and are required to be inspected twice a year (USDA, 1989).

B. All procedures carried out on animals are to be reviewed by a local animal care committee to ensure that the procedures are appropriate and humane. The committee should have representation from within the institution and from the local community. In the event that it is not possible to constitute an appropriate local animal care committee, psychologists are encouraged to seek advice from a corresponding committee of a cooperative institution.

C. Responsibilities for the conditions under which animals are kept, both within and outside of the context of active experimentation or teaching, rests with the psychologist under the supervision of the animal care committee (where required by federal regulations) and with individuals appointed by the institution to oversee animal care. Animals are to be provided with humane care and healthful conditions during their stay in the facility. In addition to the federal requirements to provide for the psychological well-being of nonhuman primates used in research, psychologists are encouraged to consider enriching the environments of their laboratory animals and should keep abreast of literature on well-being and enrichment for the species with which they work.

### IV. Acquisition of Animals

A. Animals not bred in the psychologist's facility are to be acquired lawfully. The USDA and local ordinances should be consulted for information regarding regulations and approved suppliers.

B. Psychologists should make every effort to ensure that those responsible for transporting the animals to the facility provide adequate food, water, ventilation, space, and impose no unnecessary stress on the animals.

C. Animals taken from the wild should be trapped in a humane manner and in accordance with applicable federal, state, and local regulations.

D. Endangered species or taxa should be used only with full attention to required permits and ethical concerns. Information and permit applications can be obtained from:
>Fish and Wildlife Service
>Office of Management Authority
>U.S. Dept. of the Interior
>4401 N. Fairfax Dr., Rm. 432
>Arlington, VA 22043
>703-358-2104

Similar caution should be used in work with threatened species or taxa.

### V. Experimental Procedures

Humane consideration for the well-being of the animal should be incorporated into the design and conduct of all procedures involving animals, while keeping in mind the primary goal of experimental procedures—the acquisition of sound, replicable data. The conduct of all procedures is governed by Guideline I.

A. Behavioral studies that involve no aversive stimulation to, or overt sign of distress from, the animal are acceptable. These include observational and other noninvasive forms of data collection.

B. When alternative behavioral procedures are available, those that minimize discomfort to the animal should be used. When using aversive conditions, psychologists should adjust the parameters of stimulation to levels that appear minimal, though compatible with the aims of the research. Psychologists are encouraged to test painful stimuli on themselves, whenever reasonable. Whenever consistent with the goals of the research, consideration should be given to providing the animals with control of the potentially aversive stimulation.

*(continued)*

**TABLE 2.3   APA guidelines for ethical conduct in the care and use of animals (*continued*)**

C. Procedures in which the animal is anesthetized and insensitive to pain throughout the procedure and is euthanized before regaining consciousness are generally acceptable.

D. Procedures involving more than momentary or slight aversive stimulation, which is not relieved by medication or other acceptable methods, should be undertaken only when the objectives of the research cannot be achieved by other methods.

E. Experimental procedures that require prolonged aversive conditions or produce tissue damage or metabolic disturbances require greater justification and surveillance. These include prolonged exposure to extreme environmental conditions, experimentally induced prey killing, or infliction of physical trauma or tissue damage. An animal observed to be in a state of severe distress or chronic pain that cannot be alleviated and is not essential to the purposes of the research should be euthanized immediately.

F. Procedures that use restraint must conform to federal regulations and guidelines.

G. Procedures involving the use of paralytic agents without reduction in pain sensation require particular prudence and humane concern. Use of muscle relaxants or paralytics alone during surgery, without general anesthesia, is unacceptable and should be avoided.

H. Surgical procedures, because of their invasive nature, require close supervision and attention to humane considerations by the psychologist. Aseptic (methods that minimize risks of infection) techniques must be used on laboratory animals whenever possible.

1. All surgical procedures and anesthetization should be conducted under the direct supervision of a person who is competent in the use of the procedures.

2. If the surgical procedure is likely to cause greater discomfort than that attending anesthetization, and unless there is specific justification for acting otherwise, animals should be maintained under anesthesia until the procedure is ended.

3. Sound postoperative monitoring and care, which may include the use of analgesics and antibiotics, should be provided to minimize discomfort and to prevent infection and other untoward consequences of the procedure.

4. Animals cannot be subjected to successive surgical procedures unless these are required by the nature of the research, the nature of the surgery, or for the well-being of the animal. Multiple surgeries on the same animal must receive special approval from the animal care committee.

I. When the use of an animal is no longer required by an experimental protocol or procedure, in order to minimize the number of animals used in research, alternative uses of the animals should be considered. Such uses should be compatible with the goals of research and the welfare of the animal. Care should be taken that such an action does not expose the animal to multiple surgeries.

J. The return of wild-caught animals to the field can carry substantial risks, both to the formerly captive animals and to the ecosystem. Animals reared in the laboratory should not be released because, in most cases, they cannot survive or they may survive by disrupting the natural ecology.

K. When euthanasia appears to be the appropriate alternative, either as a requirement of the research or because it constitutes the most humane form of disposition of an animal at the conclusion of the research:

1. Euthanasia shall be accomplished in a humane manner, appropriate for the species, and in such a way as to ensure immediate death, and in accordance with procedures outlined in the latest version of the American Veterinary Medical Association (AVMA) Panel on Euthanasia.[2]

2. Disposal of euthanized animals should be accomplished in a manner that is in accord with all relevant legislation, consistent with health, environmental, and aesthetic concerns, and approved by the animal care committee. No animal shall be discarded until its death is verified.

**VI. Field Research**

Field research, because of its potential to damage sensitive ecosystems and ethologies, should be subject to animal care committee approval. Field research, if strictly observational, may not require animal care committee approval (USDA, 1989, pg. 36126).

A. Psychologists conducting field research should disturb their populations as little as possible—consistent with the goals of the research. Every effort should be made to minimize potential harmful effects of the study on the population and on other plant and animal species in the area.

(continued)

**TABLE 2.3    APA guidelines for ethical conduct in the care and use of animals (*continued*)**

B.  Research conducted in populated areas should be done with respect for the property and privacy of the inhabitants of the area.
C.  Particular justification is required for the study of endangered species. Such research on endangered species should not be conducted unless animal care committee approval has been obtained and all requisite permits are obtained (see IV.D).

[1] U.S. Department of Agriculture. (1989, August 21). Animal welfare: Final rules. Federal Register. U.S. Department of Agriculture. (1990, July 16). Animal welfare: Guinea pigs, hamsters, and rabbits. Federal Register. U.S. Department of Agriculture. (1991, February 15). Animal welfare: Standards: Final rule. Federal Register.
[2] Write to AVMA, 1931 N. Meacham Road, Suite 100, Schaumburg, IL 60173, or call (708) 925-8070.
SOURCE: American Psychological Association. (1996). *Guidelines for ethical conduct in the care and use of animals.* Copyright © 1996 by the American Psychological Association. Reprinted with permission.

The APA guidelines address several issues with respect to animal welfare. For example, the researcher must provide a justification for the study, be sure that the personnel interacting with the animals are familiar with the guidelines and well trained, ensure that the care and housing of the animals meet federal regulations, and acquire the animals lawfully. The researcher must also ensure that all experimental procedures are humane, that treatments involving pain are used only when necessary, that alternative procedures that minimize discomfort are used when available, that surgical procedures use anesthesia and techniques to avoid pain and infection, and that all animals are treated in accordance with local, state, and federal laws. As an additional measure to make sure that animals are treated humanely, the U.S. Department of Agriculture is responsible for regulating and inspecting animal facilities. Finally, the Animal Welfare Act of 1985 requires that institutions establish Animal Care and Use Committees. These committees function in a manner similar to IRBs, reviewing all research proposals using nonhuman animals to determine whether the animals are being treated in an ethical manner.

1.  In what type of research might an investigator argue that deception is necessary? How can informed consent be provided in such a situation?
2.  What is the purpose of an IRB?
3.  When is it necessary and not necessary to obtain informed consent?

CRITICAL THINKING CHECK 2.1

# Summary

In the preceding sections, we discussed many elements relevant to getting started on a research project. We began with how to select a problem and conduct a literature search. This included discussion of several library resources, including *Psych Abstracts*, PsycINFO, the *Social Science Citation*

*Index*, and the *Science Citation Index*. In the second half of the chapter, we discussed the APA's ethical principles. In reviewing ethical guidelines for using humans for research purposes, we discussed the importance of IRBs and obtaining informed consent, which is a necessity when participants are at risk. We also considered the use of deception in research, along with the nature and intent of debriefing participants. Finally, we discussed special considerations when using children as research participants and presented the APA guidelines on the use of animals in research.

## KEY TERMS

Institutional Review Board (IRB)
informed consent form

debriefing
deception

## CHAPTER EXERCISES

(Answers to odd-numbered exercises appear in Appendix C.)

1. Select a topic of interest to you in psychology and use *Psych Abstracts*, PsycLIT, or PsycINFO to search for articles on this topic. Try to find at least five journal articles relevant to your topic.
2. What should be accomplished by debriefing participants?
3. Describe what is meant by "at risk" and "at minimal risk."
4. In addition to treating animals in a humane manner during a study, what other guidelines does APA provide concerning using animals for research purposes?
5. What special ethical considerations must be taken into account when conducting research with children?

## CRITICAL THINKING CHECK ANSWERS

### 2.1

1. The researcher could argue that deception is necessary in situations where, if the participants knew the true nature or hypothesis of the study, their behavior or responses might be altered. Informed consent is provided by giving participants a general description of the study, and also by informing them that they do not have to participate and can withdraw from the study at any time.

2. IRBs are charged with evaluating research projects in which humans participate to ensure the ethical treatment of participants.
3. In any study in which a participant is classified as "at risk," informed consent is necessary. Although it is not necessary when participants are classified as "at minimal risk," it is usually wise to obtain informed consent anyway.

## WEB RESOURCES

Check your knowledge of the content in this chapter by taking the practice quiz at www.Wadsworth.com. Or, for step-by-step practice and information, check out the Statistics and Research Methods Workshops at http://psychology.wadsworth.com/workshops.

# 3 Defining, Measuring, and Manipulating Variables

In the preceding chapter, we discussed library research, how to read journal articles, and ethics. In this chapter, we will discuss the definition, measurement, and manipulation of variables. As noted in Chapter 1, we typically refer to measured variables as dependent variables and manipulated variables as independent variables. Hence, some of the ideas addressed in this chapter are how we define independent and dependent variables, how we measure variables, the types of measures available to us, and finally, the reliability and validity of the measures.

## Defining Variables

An important step when beginning a research project is to define the variables in your study. Some variables are fairly easy to define, manipulate, and measure. For example, if a researcher were studying the effects of exercise on blood pressure, she could manipulate the amount of exercise by varying the length of time that individuals exercised or by varying the intensity of the exercise (as by monitoring target heart rates). She could also measure blood pressure periodically during the course of the study; a machine already exists that will take this measurement in a consistent and accurate manner. Does this mean that the measurement will always be accurate? No. We will discuss this issue later in the chapter when we address measurement error.

Now let's suppose that a researcher wants to study a variable that is not as concrete or easily measured as blood pressure. For example, many people study abstract concepts such as aggression, attraction, depression, hunger, or anxiety. How would we either manipulate or measure any of these variables? My definition of what it means to be hungry may be vastly different from yours. If I decided to measure hunger by simply asking participants in an experiment if they were hungry, the measure would not be accurate because each individual may define hunger in a different way. What we need is an **operational definition** of hunger—a definition of the variable in terms of the operations the researcher uses to measure or manipulate it. Because this is a somewhat circular definition, let's reword it in a way that may make more sense. An operational definition specifies the activities of the researcher in measuring and/or manipulating a variable (Kerlinger, 1986). In other words, we might define hunger in terms of specific activities, such as not having eaten for 12 hours. Thus, one operational definition of hunger could be that simple: Hunger occurs when 12 hours have passed with no food intake. Notice how much more concrete this definition is than simply saying hunger is that "gnawing feeling" that you get in your stomach. Specifying hunger in terms of the number of hours without food is an operational definition, whereas defining hunger as that "gnawing feeling" is not an operational definition.

Researchers must operationally define all variables—those measured (dependent variables) and those manipulated (independent variables). One reason for doing this is to ensure that the variables are measured consistently or manipulated in the same way during the course of the study.

**operational definition** A definition of a variable in terms of the operations (activities) a researcher uses to measure or manipulate it.

Another reason is to help us communicate our ideas to others. For example, what if a researcher said that he measured anxiety in his study. I would need to know how he operationally defined anxiety because it can be defined in many different ways. Thus, it can be measured in many different ways. Anxiety could be defined as the number of nervous actions displayed in a one-hour time period, a person's score on a GSR (galvanic skin response) machine, a person's heart rate, or a person's score on the Taylor Manifest Anxiety Scale. Some measures are better than others—*better* meaning more reliable and valid, concepts we will discuss later in this chapter. Once I understand how a researcher has operationally defined a variable, I can replicate the study if I desire. I can begin to have a better understanding of the study and whether or not it may have problems. I can also better design my own study based on how the variables were operationally defined in other research studies.

# Properties of Measurement

In addition to operationally defining independent and dependent variables, we must consider the level of measurement of the dependent variable. There are four levels of measurement, each based on the characteristics or properties of the data. These properties include identity, magnitude, equal unit size, and absolute zero. When a measure has the property of **identity**, objects that are different receive different scores. For example, if participants in a study had different political affiliations, they would receive different scores. Measurements have the property of **magnitude** (also called *ordinality*) when the ordering of the numbers reflects the ordering of the variable. In other words, numbers are assigned in order so that some numbers represent more or less of the variable being measured than others.

Measurements have an **equal unit size** when a difference of 1 is the same amount throughout the entire scale. For example, the difference between people who are 64 inches tall and 65 inches tall is the same as the difference between people who are 72 inches tall and 73 inches tall. The difference in each situation (1 inch) is identical. Notice how this differs from the property of magnitude. If we simply lined up and ranked a group of individuals based on their height, the scale would have the properties of identity and magnitude but not equal unit size. Can you think why this would be so? We would not actually measure people's height in inches but simply order them according to how tall they appear, from shortest (the person receiving a score of 1) to tallest (the person receiving the highest score). Thus, our scale would not meet the criterion of equal unit size. In other words, the difference in height between the two people receiving scores of 1 and 2 might not be the same as the difference in height between the two people receiving scores of 3 and 4.

Last, measures have an **absolute zero** when assigning a score of zero indicates an absence of the variable being measured. For example, time spent studying has the property of absolute zero because a score of zero on this measure means an individual spent no time studying. However, a score

**identity** A property of measurement in which objects that are different receive different scores.

**magnitude** A property of measurement in which the ordering of numbers reflects the ordering of the variable.

**equal unit size** A property of measurement in which a difference of 1 is the same amount throughout the entire scale.

**absolute zero** A property of measurement in which assigning a score of zero indicates an absence of the variable being measured.

of zero is not always equal to the property of absolute zero. As an example, think about the Fahrenheit temperature scale. That measurement scale has a score of zero (the thermometer can read 0 degrees), but does that score indicate an absence of temperature? No, it indicates a very cold temperature. Hence, it does not have the property of absolute zero.

# Scales of Measurement

As noted previously, the level or scale of measurement depends on the properties of the data. There are four scales of measurement (nominal, ordinal, interval, and ratio), and each of these scales has one or more of the properties described in the previous section. We will discuss the scales in order, from the one with the fewest properties to the one with the most properties—that is, from least to most sophisticated. As we will see in later chapters, it is important to establish the scale of measurement of your data in order to determine the appropriate statistical test to use when analyzing the data.

## Nominal Scale

**nominal scale** A scale in which objects or individuals are assigned to categories that have no numerical properties.

A **nominal scale** is one in which objects or individuals are assigned to categories that have no numerical properties. Nominal scales have the characteristic of identity but lack the other properties. Variables measured on a nominal scale are often referred to as *categorical variables* because the measuring scale involves dividing the data into categories. However, the categories carry no numerical weight. Some examples of categorical variables, or data measured on a nominal scale, are ethnicity, gender, and political affiliation. We can assign numerical values to the levels of a nominal variable. For example, for ethnicity, we could label Asian Americans as 1, African Americans as 2, Latin Americans as 3, and so on. However, these scores do not carry any numerical weight; they are simply names for the categories. In other words, the scores are used for identity but not for magnitude, equal unit size, or absolute value. We cannot order the data and claim that 1s are more than or less than 2s. We cannot analyze these data mathematically. It would not be appropriate, for example, to report that the mean ethnicity was 2.56. We cannot say that there is a true zero where someone would have no ethnicity. As we will see in later chapters, however, we can use certain statistics to analyze nominal data.

## Ordinal Scale

**ordinal scale** A scale in which objects or individuals are categorized and the categories form a rank order along a continuum.

An **ordinal scale** is one in which objects or individuals are categorized and the categories form a rank order along a continuum. Data measured on an ordinal scale have the properties of identity and magnitude but lack equal unit size and absolute zero. Ordinal data are often referred to as *ranked data* because the data are ordered from highest to lowest, or biggest to smallest.

For example, reporting how students did on an exam based simply on their rank (highest score, second highest, and so on) is an ordinal scale. This variable carries identity and magnitude because each individual receives a rank (a number) that carries identity, and that rank also conveys information about order or magnitude (how many students performed better or worse in the class). However, the ranking score does not have equal unit size (the difference in performance on the exam between the students ranked 1 and 2 is not necessarily the same as the difference between the students ranked 2 and 3) or an absolute zero.

## Interval Scale

An **interval scale** is one in which the units of measurement (intervals) between the numbers on the scale are all equal in size. When we use an interval scale, the criteria of identity, magnitude, and equal unit size are met. For example, the Fahrenheit temperature scale is an interval scale of measurement. A given temperature carries identity (days with different temperatures receive different scores on the scale), magnitude (cooler days receive lower scores and hotter days receive higher scores), and equal unit size (the difference between 50 and 51 degrees is the same as that between 90 and 91 degrees). However, the Fahrenheit scale does not have an absolute zero. Because of this, we are not able to form ratios based on this scale (for example, 100 degrees is not twice as hot as 50 degrees). We can still perform mathematical computations on interval data, as we will see in later chapters when we begin to cover statistical analysis.

**interval scale** A scale in which the units of measurement (intervals) between the numbers on the scale are all equal in size.

## Ratio Scale

A **ratio scale** is one in which, in addition to order and equal units of measurement, there is an absolute zero that indicates an absence of the variable being measured. Ratio data have all four properties of measurement—identity, magnitude, equal unit size, and absolute zero. Examples of ratio scales of measurement include weight, time, and height. Each of these scales has identity (individuals who weigh different amounts receive different scores), magnitude (those who weigh less receive lower scores than those who weigh more), and equal unit size (1 pound is the same weight anywhere along the scale and for any person using the scale). Ratio scales also have an absolute zero, which means that a score of zero reflects an absence of that variable. This also means that ratios can be formed. For example, a weight of 100 pounds is twice as much as a weight of 50 pounds. As with interval data, mathematical computations can be performed on ratio data. Because interval and ratio data are very similar, many psychologists simply refer to the category as *interval-ratio data* and typically do not distinguish between these two types of data. You should be familiar with the difference between interval and ratio data but aware that because they are so similar, they are often referred to as one type of data—interval-ratio.

**ratio scale** A scale in which, in addition to order and equal units of measurement, there is an absolute zero that indicates an absence of the variable being measured.

**Features of Scales of Measurement**

| | SCALES OF MEASUREMENT | | | |
|---|---|---|---|---|
| | **Nominal** | **Ordinal** | **Interval** | **Ratio** |
| Examples | Ethnicity<br>Religion<br>Sex | Class rank<br>Letter grade | Temperature<br>(Fahrenheit<br>and Celsius)<br>Many psychological<br>tests | Weight<br>Height<br>Time |
| Properties | Identity | Identity<br>Magnitude | Identity<br>Magnitude<br>Equal Unit Size | Identity<br>Magnitude<br>Equal unit size<br>Absolute zero |
| Mathematical Operations | None | Rank order | Add<br>Subtract | Add<br>Subtract |

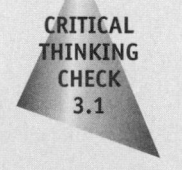

**CRITICAL THINKING CHECK 3.1**

1. Provide several operational definitions of *anxiety*. Include nonverbal measures and physiological measures. How would your operational definitions differ from a dictionary definition?
2. Identify the scale of measurement for each of the following variables:
   a. Zip code
   b. Grade of egg (large, medium, small)
   c. Reaction time
   d. Score on the SAT
   e. Class rank
   f. Number on a football jersey
   g. Miles per gallon

# Discrete and Continuous Variables

**discrete variables** Variables that usually consist of whole number units or categories and are made up of chunks or units that are detached and distinct from one another.

Another means of classifying variables is in terms of whether they are discrete or continuous in nature. **Discrete variables** usually consist of whole number units or categories. They are made up of chunks or units that are detached and distinct from one another. A change in value occurs a whole unit at a time, and decimals do not make sense with discrete scales. Most nominal and ordinal data are discrete. For example, gender, political party, and ethnicity are discrete scales. Some interval or ratio data can be discrete. For example, the number of children someone has is reported as a whole number (discrete data), yet it is also ratio data (you can have a true zero and form ratios).

**continuous variables** Variables that usually fall along a continuum and allow for fractional amounts.

**Continuous variables** usually fall along a continuum and allow for fractional amounts. The term *continuous* means that it "continues" between the whole number units. Examples of continuous variables are age (22.7 years), height (64.5 inches), and weight (113.25 pounds). Most interval and ratio data are continuous in nature. Discrete and continuous data will become more important in later chapters when we discuss research design and data presentation.

# Types of Measures

When psychology researchers collect data, the types of measures used can be classified into four basic categories: self-report measures, tests, behavioral measures, and physical measures. We will discuss each category, noting the advantages and possible disadvantages of each.

## Self-Report Measures

**Self-report measures** are typically administered as questionnaires or interviews to measure how people report that they act, think, or feel. Thus, self-report measures aid in collecting data on behavioral, cognitive, and affective events (Leary, 2001).

*Behavioral self-report measures* typically ask people to report how often they do something. This could be how often they eat a certain food, eat out at a restaurant, go to the gym, or have sex. The problem with this and the other self-report measures is that we are relying on the individuals to report on their own behaviors. When collecting data in this manner, we must be concerned with the veracity of the reports and also with the accuracy of the individual's memory. Researchers much prefer to collect data using a behavioral measure, but direct observation of some events is not always possible or ethical.

*Cognitive self-report measures* ask individuals to report what they think about something. You have probably participated in a cognitive self-report measure of some sort. For example, you may have been stopped on campus and asked what you think about parking, food services, or residence halls. Once again, we are relying on the individual to make an accurate and truthful report.

*Affective self-report measures* ask individuals to report how they feel about something. You may have participated in an affective self-report measure if you ever answered questions concerning emotional reactions such as happiness, depression, anxiety, or stress. Many psychological tests are affective self-report measures. These tests also fit into the category of measurement tests described below.

**self-report measures**
Usually questionnaires or interviews that measure how people report that they act, think, or feel.

## Tests

A **test** is a measurement instrument used to assess individual differences in various content areas. Psychologists frequently use two types of tests: personality tests and ability tests. Many personality tests are also affective self-report measures; they are designed to measure aspects of an individual's personality and feelings about certain things. Ability tests, however, are not self-report measures and generally fall into two different categories: aptitude tests and achievement tests. *Aptitude tests* measure an individual's potential to do something, whereas *achievement tests* measure an individual's competence in an area. In general, intelligence tests are aptitude tests, whereas school exams are achievement tests.

Most tests used by psychologists have been subjected to extensive testing themselves and are therefore considered objective, nonbiased means of

**test** A measurement instrument used to assess individual differences in various content areas.

collecting data. Keep in mind, however, that any measuring instrument always has the potential for problems. The problems may range from the state of the participant on a given day to the scoring and interpretation of the test.

## Behavioral Measures

**behavioral measures**
Measures taken by carefully observing and recording behavior.

Psychologists take **behavioral measures** by carefully observing and recording behavior. Behavioral measures are often referred to as *observational measures* because they involve observing anything that a participant does. Because we will discuss observational research studies in more detail in the next chapter, our discussion of behavioral measures will be brief here. Behavioral measures can be used to measure anything that a person or animal does—a pigeon pecking a disk, the way men and women carry their books, or how many cars actually stop at a stop sign. The observations can be direct (while the participant is engaging in the behavior) or indirect (via audio- or videotape).

When taking behavioral measures, a researcher will usually use some sort of coding system. A coding system is a means of converting the observations to numerical data. A very basic coding system involves simply counting the number of times that participants do something. For example, how many times does the pigeon peck the lighted disk, or how many cars stop at the stop sign? A more sophisticated coding system involves assigning behaviors to particular categories. For example, a researcher might watch children playing and classify their behavior into several categories of play (solitary, parallel, and cooperative). In the example of cars stopping at a stop sign, simply counting the number of stops might not be adequate. What is a stop? The researcher might operationally define a stop as the car stops moving for at least 3 seconds. Other categories might include a complete stop of less than 3 seconds, a rolling stop, and no stop. The researcher would then have a more complex coding system consisting of various categories.

You might also think about the problems of collecting data at a stop sign. If someone is standing there with a clipboard taking measures, how might this affect the behavior of drivers approaching the stop sign? Are we going to get a realistic estimate of how many cars actually stop at the sign? Probably not. For this reason, measures are sometimes taken in an unobtrusive manner. Observers may hide what they are doing, or hide themselves, or use a more indirect means of collecting the data (videotape). Using an unobtrusive means of collecting data reduces **reactivity**—participants reacting in an unnatural way to being observed. This issue will be discussed more fully in the next chapter.

**reactivity** A possible reaction by participants in which they act unnaturally because they know they are being observed.

Notice some of the possible problems with behavioral measures. First, they all rely on humans observing events. How do we know that they observed the events accurately? Second, the observers must then code the events into some numerical format. There is tremendous potential for error in this situation. Last, if the observers are visible, there is the possibility that participants may not be acting naturally because they know they are being observed.

## Physical Measures

Most **physical measures**, or measures of bodily activity, are not directly observable. Physical measures are usually taken with a piece of equipment. For example, weight is measured with a scale, blood pressure with a blood pressure cuff, and temperature with a thermometer. Sometimes the equipment used to take physical measures is more sophisticated. For example, psychologists frequently use the galvanic skin response (GSR) to measure emotional arousal, electromyography (EMG) recordings to measure muscle contractions, and electroencephalogram (EEG) recordings to measure electrical activity in the brain.

Notice that physical measures are much more objective than the previously described behavioral measures. A physical measure is not simply an observation (which may be subjective) of how a person or animal is acting. Instead, it is a measure of some physical activity that takes place in the brain or body. This is not to say that physical measures are problem-free. Keep in mind that humans are still responsible for running the equipment that takes the measures and, ultimately, for interpreting the data provided by the measuring instrument. Thus, even when using physical measures, a researcher needs to be concerned with the accuracy of the data.

**physical measures** Measures of bodily activity (such as pulse or blood pressure) that may be taken with a piece of equipment.

| Features of Types of Measures | | | | IN REVIEW |
|---|---|---|---|---|
| | **TYPES OF MEASURES** | | | |
| | **Self-Report** | **Tests** | **Behavioral** | **Physical** |
| Description | Questionnaires or interviews that measure how people report that they act, think, or feel | A measurement instrument used to assess individual differences | Careful observations and recordings of behavior | Measures of bodily activity |
| Examples | Behavioral self-report Cognitive self-report Affective self-report | Ability tests Personality tests | Counting behaviors Classifying behaviors | Weight EEG GSR Blood pressure |
| Considerations | Are participants being truthful? | Are participants being truthful? | Is there reactivity? How objective are observers? | Is the individual taking the measure skilled at using the equipment? |
| | How accurate are participants' memories? | How reliable and valid are the tests? | | How reliable and valid is the measuring instrument? |

1. Which types of measures are considered more subjective in nature? Which are more objective?
2. Why might there be measurement error even when using an objective measure such as a blood pressure cuff? How would you recommend trying to control for or minimize this type of measurement error?

**CRITICAL THINKING CHECK 3.2**

# Reliability

One means of determining whether the measure you are using is effective is to assess its reliability. **Reliability** refers to the consistency or stability of a measuring instrument. In other words, we want a measure to measure exactly the same way each time it is used. This means that individuals should receive a similar score each time they use the measuring instrument. For example, a bathroom scale needs to be reliable—it needs to measure the same way each time an individual uses it; otherwise, it is a useless measuring instrument.

## Error in Measurement

Consider some of the problems with the four types of measures discussed above. Some problems, known as *method error*, stem from the experimenter and the testing situation. Does the individual taking the measures know how to use the measuring instrument properly? Is the measuring equipment working correctly? Other problems, known as *trait error*, stem from the participants. Were the participants being truthful? Did they feel well on the day of the test? Both types of problems can lead to measurement error.

In effect, a measurement is a combination of the true score and an error score. The formula that follows represents the *observed score* for an individual on a measure—that is, the score recorded for a participant on the measuring instrument used. The observed score is the sum of the true score and measurement error. The true score is what the actual score on the measuring instrument would be if there were no error. The measurement error is any error (method or trait) that might be present (Leary, 2001; Salkind, 1997).

Observed score = True score + Measurement error

The observed score would be more reliable (more consistent) if we could minimize error and thus have a more accurate measure of the true score. True scores should not vary much over time, but error scores can vary tremendously from testing session to testing session. How, then, can we minimize error in measurement? We can make sure that all of the problems discussed for the four types of measures are minimized. This includes problems in recording or scoring data (method error) and problems in understanding instructions, motivation, fatigue, and the testing environment (trait error). The conceptual formula for reliability is

$$\text{Reliability} = \frac{\text{True score}}{\text{True Score} + \text{Error score}}$$

Based on this conceptual formula, a reduction in error would lead to an increase in reliability. Notice that if there were no error, reliability would be equal to 1.00; hence, 1.00 is the highest possible reliability score. You should also see that as error increases, reliability drops below 1.00. The greater the error, the lower the reliability of a measure.

## How to Measure Reliability: Correlation Coefficients

Reliability is measured using correlation coefficients. We will briefly discuss correlation coefficients here; a more comprehensive discussion, along with the appropriate formulas, appears in Chapter 6.

A **correlation coefficient** measures the degree of relationship between two sets of scores and can vary between −1.00 and +1.00. The stronger the relationship between the variables, the closer the coefficient will be to either −1.00 or +1.00. The weaker the relationship between the variables, the closer the coefficient will be to 0. For example, if we measured individuals on two variables and found that the top-scoring individual on variable 1 was also the top-scoring person on variable 2, the second-highest-scoring person on variable 1 was also the second-highest on variable 2, and so on down to the lowest-scoring person, there would be a perfect positive correlation (+1.00) between variables 1 and 2. If we observed a perfect negative correlation (−1.00), then the person having the highest score on variable 1 would have the lowest score on variable 2, the person with the second-highest score on variable 1 would have the second-lowest score on variable 2, and so on. In reality, variables are almost never perfectly correlated. Thus, most correlation coefficients are less than 1.

A correlation of 0 between two variables indicates the absence of any relationship, as might occur by chance. For example, if we were to draw a person's score on variable 1 out of a hat, do the same for the person's score on variable 2, and continue in this manner for each person in the group, we would expect no relationship between individuals' scores on the two variables. It would be impossible to predict a person's performance on variable 2 based on that person's score on variable 1 because there would be no relationship (a correlation of 0) between the variables.

The sign preceding the correlation coefficient indicates whether the observed relationship is positive or negative. The terms *positive* and *negative* do not refer to good and bad relationships but rather to how the variables are related. A **positive correlation** indicates a direct relationship between variables: In other words, when we see high scores on one variable, we tend to see high scores on the other variable; when we see low or moderate scores on one variable, we see similar scores on the second variable. Variables that are positively correlated include height with weight and high school GPA with college GPA. A **negative correlation** between two variables indicates an inverse or negative relationship: High scores on one variable go with low scores on the other variable, and vice versa. Examples of negative relationships are sometimes more difficult to generate and to think about. In adults, however, many variables are negatively correlated with age: As age increases, variables such as sight, hearing ability, strength, and energy level begin to decrease.

Correlation coefficients can be weak, moderate, or strong. Table 3.1 gives some guidelines for these categories. To establish the reliability (or consistency) of a measure, we expect a strong correlation coefficient—usually in the .80s or .90s—between the two variables or scores being measured (Anastasi & Urbina, 1997). We also expect that the coefficient will be positive. Why? A positive coefficient indicates that those who scored high on the

**correlation coefficient** A measure of the degree of relationship between two sets of scores. It can vary between −1.00 and +1.00.

**positive correlation** A direct relationship between two variables in which an increase in one is related to an increase in the other, and a decrease in one is related to a decrease in the other.

**negative correlation** An inverse relationship between two variables in which an increase in one variable is related to a decrease in the other, and vice versa.

**TABLE 3.1   Values for weak, moderate, and strong correlation coefficients**

| CORRELATION COEFFICIENT | STRENGTH OF RELATIONSHIP |
|---|---|
| ±.70–1.00 | Strong |
| ±.30–.69 | Moderate |
| ±.00–.29 | None (.00) to weak |

measuring instrument at one time also scored high at another time, those who scored low at one point scored low again, and those with intermediate scores the first time scored similarly the second time. If the coefficient measuring reliability were negative, this would indicate an inverse relationship between the scores taken at two different times. A measure would hardly be consistent if a person scored very high at one time and very low at another time. Thus, to establish that a measure is reliable, we need a positive correlation coefficient of around .80 or higher.

## Types of Reliability

Now that we have a basic understanding of reliability and how it is measured, let's talk about some specific types of reliability. We will discuss four different types: test/retest reliability, alternate-forms reliability, split-half reliability, and interrater reliability. Each type provides a measure of consistency, but the various types of reliability are used in different situations.

**test/retest reliability** A reliability coefficient determined by assessing the degree of relationship between scores on the same test administered on two different occasions.

*Test/Retest Reliability.* One of the most often used and obvious ways of establishing reliability is to repeat the same test on a second occasion—**test/retest reliability**. The obtained correlation coefficient is between the two scores of each individual on the same test administered on two different occasions. If the test is reliable, we expect the two scores for each individual to be similar, and thus the resulting correlation coefficient will be high (close to +1.00). This measure of reliability assesses the stability of a test over time. Naturally, some error will be present in each measurement (for example, an individual may not feel well at one testing or may have problems during the testing session such as a broken pencil). Thus, it is unusual for the correlation coefficient to be +1.00, but we expect it to be +.80 or higher. A problem related to test/retest measures is that on many tests there will be *practice effects*—some people will get better at the second testing, and this will lower the observed correlation. A second problem may occur if the interval between test times is short: Individuals may remember how they answered previously, both correctly and incorrectly. In this case, we may be testing their memories and not the reliability of the testing instrument, and we may observe a spuriously high correlation.

**alternate-forms reliability** A reliability coefficient determined by assessing the degree of relationship between scores on two equivalent tests.

*Alternate-Forms Reliability.* One means of controlling for test/retest problems is to use **alternate-forms reliability**—using alternate forms of the testing instrument and correlating the performance of individuals on the two different forms. In this case, the tests taken at times 1 and 2 are different but equivalent or parallel (hence, the terms *equivalent-forms reliability* and *parallel-forms reliability* are also used). As with test/retest reliability, alternate-forms reliability establishes the stability of the test over time and also the equivalency of the items from one test to another. One problem with alternate-forms reliability is making sure that the tests are truly parallel. To help ensure equivalency, the tests should have the same number of items, the items should be of the same difficulty level, and instructions, time limits, examples, and format should all be equal—often difficult if not impossible to accomplish. Second, if the tests are truly equivalent, there is the potential for practice, although not to the same extent as when exactly the same test is administered twice.

*Split-Half Reliability.* A third means of establishing reliability is by splitting the items on the test into equivalent halves and correlating scores on one half of the items with scores on the other half. This **split-half reliability** gives a measure of the equivalence of the content of the test but not of its stability over time as test/retest and alternate-forms reliability do. The biggest problem with split-half reliability is determining how to divide the items so that the two halves are in fact equivalent. For example, it would not be advisable to correlate scores on multiple-choice questions with scores on short-answer or essay questions. What is typically recommended is to correlate scores on even-numbered items with scores on odd-numbered items. Thus, if the items at the beginning of the test are easier or harder than those at the end of the test, the half scores will still be equivalent.

**split-half reliability** A reliability coefficient determined by correlating scores on one half of a measure with scores on the other half of the measure.

*Interrater Reliability.* Finally, to measure the reliability of observers rather than tests, you can use interrater reliability. **Interrater reliability** is a measure of consistency that assesses the agreement of observations made by two or more raters or judges. Let's say that you are observing play behavior in children. Rather than simply making observations on your own, it is advisable to have several independent observers collect data. The observers all watch the children playing but independently count the number and types of play behaviors they observe. Once the data are collected, interrater reliability needs to be established by examining the percentage of agreement between the raters. If the raters' data are reliable, then the percentage of agreement should be high. If the raters are not paying close attention to what they are doing, or if the measuring scale devised for the various play behaviors is unclear, the percentage of agreement among observers will not be high. Although interrater reliability is measured using a correlation coefficient, the following formula offers a quick means of estimating interrater reliability:

**interrater reliability** A reliability coefficient that assesses the agreement of observations made by two or more raters or judges.

$$\text{Interrater reliability} = \frac{\text{Number of agreements}}{\text{Number of possible agreements}} \times 100$$

Thus, if your observers agree 45 times out of a possible 50, the interrater reliability is 90%—fairly high. However, if they agree only 20 times out of 50, then the interrater reliability is low (40%). Such a low level of agreement indicates a problem with the measuring instrument or with the individuals using the instrument and should be of great concern to a researcher.

| IN REVIEW | Features of Types of Reliability | | | |
|---|---|---|---|---|
| | **TYPES OF RELIABILITY** | | | |
| | **Test/Retest** | **Alternate-Forms** | **Split-Half** | **Interrater** |
| What It Measures | Stability over time | Stability over time and equivalency of items | Equivalency of items | Agreement between raters |
| How It Is Accomplished | Administer the same test to the same people at two different times | Administer alternate but equivalent forms of the test to the same people at two different times | Correlate performance for a group of people on two equivalent halves of the same test | Have at least two people count or rate behaviors, and determine the percentage of agreement between them |

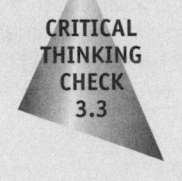

**CRITICAL THINKING CHECK 3.3**

1. Why does alternate-forms reliability provide a measure of both equivalency of items and stability over time?
2. Two people observe whether or not vehicles stop at a stop sign. They make 250 observations and disagree 38 times. What is the interrater reliability? Is this good, or should it be of concern to the researchers?

# Validity

**validity** A measure of the truthfulness of a measuring instrument. It indicates whether the instrument measures what it claims to measure.

In addition to being reliable, measures must also be valid. **Validity** refers to whether a measure is truthful or genuine. In other words, a measure that is valid is one that measures what it claims to measure. Several types of validity may be examined; we will discuss four types here. As with reliability, validity is measured by the use of correlation coefficients. For example, if researchers developed a new test to measure depression, they might establish the validity of the test by correlating scores on the new test with scores on an already established measure of depression, and as with reliability, we would expect the correlation to be positive. Unlike reliability coefficients, however, there is no established criterion for the strength of the validity coefficient. Coefficients as low as .20 or .30 may establish the validity of a measure (Anastasi & Urbina, 1997). What is important for validity coefficients is that they are *statistically significant* at the .05 or .01 level. We will explain this term in a later chapter, but in brief it means that the results are most likely not due to chance.

## Content Validity

**content validity** The extent to which a measuring instrument covers a representative sample of the domain of behaviors to be measured.

A systematic examination of the test content to determine whether it covers a representative sample of the domain of behaviors to be measured assesses **content validity**. In other words, a test with content validity has items that satisfactorily assess the content being examined. To determine whether a test has content validity, you should consult experts in the area being tested. For example, when designing the GRE subject exam for psychology, professors of psychology are asked to examine the questions to establish that they represent relevant information from the entire discipline of psychology as we know it today.

Sometimes face validity is confused with content validity. **Face validity** simply addresses whether or not a test looks valid on its surface. Does it appear to be an adequate measure of the conceptual variable? This is not really validity in the technical sense, as it refers not to what the test actually measures but to what it appears to measure. Face validity relates to whether or not the test looks valid to those who selected it and those who take it. For example, does the test selected by the school board to measure student achievement "appear" to be an actual measure of achievement? Face validity has more to do with rapport and public relations than with actual validity (Anastasi & Urbina, 1997).

**face validity** The extent to which a measuring instrument appears valid on its surface.

## Criterion Validity

The extent to which a measuring instrument accurately predicts behavior or ability in a given area establishes **criterion validity**. Two types of criterion validity may be used, depending on whether the test is used to estimate present performance (*concurrent validity*) or to predict future performance (*predictive validity*). The SAT and GRE are examples of tests that have predictive validity because performance on the tests correlates with later performance in college and graduate school, respectively. The tests can be used with some degree of accuracy to "predict" future behavior. A test used to determine whether or not someone qualifies as a pilot is a measure of concurrent validity. We are estimating the person's ability at the present time, not attempting to predict future outcomes. Thus, concurrent validation is used for diagnosis of existing status rather than prediction of future outcomes.

**criterion validity** The extent to which a measuring instrument accurately predicts behavior or ability in a given area.

## Construct Validity

Construct validity is considered by many to be the most important type of validity. The **construct validity** of a test assesses the extent to which a measuring instrument accurately measures a theoretical construct or trait that it is designed to measure. Some examples of theoretical constructs or traits are verbal fluency, neuroticism, depression, anxiety, intelligence, and scholastic aptitude. One means of establishing construct validity is by correlating performance on the test with performance on a test for which construct validity has already been determined. For example, performance on a newly developed intelligence test might be correlated with performance on an existing intelligence test for which construct validity has been previously established. Another means of establishing construct validity is to show that the scores on the new test differ across people with different levels of the trait being measured. For example, if you are measuring depression, you can compare scores on the test for those known to be suffering from depression with scores for those not suffering from depression. The new measure has construct validity if it measures the construct of depression accurately.

**construct validity** The degree to which a measuring instrument accurately measures a theoretical construct or trait that it is designed to measure.

# The Relationship Between Reliability and Validity

Obviously, a measure should be both reliable and valid. It is possible, however, to have a test or measure that meets one of these criteria and not the other. Think for a moment about how this might occur. Can a test be reliable without being valid? Can a test be valid without being reliable? To answer these questions, let's imagine that we are going to measure intelligence in a group of individuals with my "new" intelligence test. My test is based on my rather ridiculous theory of intelligence, which states that the larger your brain, the more intelligent you are. I also assume that the larger your brain, the larger your head is. Thus, I am going to measure intelligence by measuring head circumference. I gather a sample of individuals and measure the circumference of each person's head. Is this a reliable measure? Many people immediately say no, because head circumference seems like such a laughable way to measure intelligence. But remember, reliability is a measure of consistency, not truthfulness. Is this test going to consistently measure the same thing? Yes, it is consistently measuring head circumference, and this is not likely to change over time. Thus, your score at one time will be the same or very close to the same as your score at a later time. The test is therefore very reliable. Is it a valid measure of intelligence? No, the test in no way measures the construct of intelligence. Thus, we have established that a test can be reliable without being valid. However, because the test lacks validity, it is not a good measure. Can the reverse be true? In other words, can we have a valid test (a test that truly measures what it claims to measure) that is not reliable? If a test truly measured intelligence, individuals would score about the same each time they took it because intelligence does not vary much over time. Thus, if the test is valid, it must be reliable. Therefore, a test can be reliable and not valid, but if it is valid, it is by default reliable.

## IN REVIEW — Features of Types of Validity

| | Content | Criterion/Concurrent | Criterion/Predictive | Construct |
|---|---|---|---|---|
| What It Measures | Whether the test covers a representative sample of the domain of behaviors to be measured | The ability of the test to estimate present performance | The ability of the test to predict future performance | The extent to which the test measures a theoretical construct or trait |
| How It Is Accomplished | Ask experts to assess the test to establish that the items are representative of the trait being measured | Correlate performance on the test with a concurrent behavior | Correlate performance on the test with a behavior in the future | Correlate performance on the test with performance on an established test or with people who have different levels of the trait the test claims to measure |

CRITICAL THINKING CHECK 3.4

1. You have just developed a new comprehensive test for introductory psychology that covers all aspects of the course. What type(s) of validity would you recommend establishing for this measure?
2. Why is face validity not considered a true measure of validity?
3. How is it possible for a test to be reliable but not valid?
4. If on your next psychology exam you find that all of the questions are about American history rather than psychology, would you be more concerned about the reliability or validity of the test?

# Summary

In the preceding sections, we discussed many elements important to measuring and manipulating variables. We learned the importance of operationally defining both the independent and dependent variables in a study in terms of the activities involved in measuring or manipulating each variable. It is also important to determine the scale or level of measurement of a variable based on the properties (identity, magnitude, equal unit size, and absolute zero) of the particular variable. Once established, the level of measurement (nominal, ordinal, interval, or ratio) helps determine the appropriate statistics to be used with the data. Data can also be classified as discrete (whole number units) or continuous (allowing for fractional amounts).

We next described several types of measures, including self-report (reporting on how you act, think, or feel), test (ability or personality), behavioral (observing and recording behavior), and physical (measurements of bodily activity) measures. Finally, we examined various types of reliability (consistency) and validity (truthfulness) in measures. Here we discussed error in measurement, correlation coefficients used to assess reliability and validity, and the relationship between reliability and validity.

## KEY TERMS

| | | |
|---|---|---|
| operational definition | continuous variables | test/retest reliability |
| identity | self-report measures | alternate-forms reliability |
| magnitude | test | split-half reliability |
| equal unit size | behavioral measures | interrater reliability |
| absolute zero | reactivity | validity |
| nominal scale | physical measures | content validity |
| ordinal scale | reliability | face validity |
| interval scale | correlation coefficient | criterion validity |
| ratio scale | positive correlation | construct validity |
| discrete variables | negative correlation | |

## CHAPTER EXERCISES

(Answers to odd-numbered exercises appear in Appendix C.)

1. Which of the following is an operational definition of depression?
   a. Depression is defined as that low feeling you get sometimes.
   b. Depression is defined as what happens when a relationship ends.
   c. Depression is defined as your score on a 50-item depression inventory.
   d. Depression is defined as the number of boxes of tissues that you cry your way through.

2. Identify the type of measure used in each of the following situations:
   a. As you leave a restaurant, you are asked to answer a few questions regarding what you thought about the service you received.
   b. When you join a weight loss group, they ask that you keep a food journal noting everything that you eat each day.
   c. As part of a research study, you are asked to complete a 30-item anxiety inventory.
   d. When you visit your career services office, they give you a test that indicates professions to which you are best suited.
   e. While eating in the dining hall one day, you notice that food services has people tallying the number of patrons selecting each entrée.
   f. As part of a research study, your professor takes pulse and blood pressure measurements on students before and after completing a class exam.

3. Which of the following correlation coefficients represents the highest (best) reliability score?
   a. +.10
   b. −.95
   c. +.83
   d. .00

4. When you arrive for your psychology exam, you are flabbergasted to find that all of the questions are on calculus and not psychology. The next day in class, students complain so much that the professor agrees to give you all a makeup exam the following day. When you arrive to class the next day, you find that although the questions are different, they are once again on calculus. In this example, there should be high reliability of what type? What type(s) of validity is the test lacking? Explain your answers.

5. The librarians are interested in how the computers in the library are being used. They have three observers watch the terminals to see if students do research on the Internet, use e-mail, browse the Internet, play games, or do schoolwork (write papers, type homework, and so on). The three observers disagree 32 out of 75 times. What is the interrater reliability? How would you recommend that the librarians use the data?

## CRITICAL THINKING CHECK ANSWERS

### 3.1

1. Nonverbal measures:
   - Number of twitches per minute
   - Number of fingernails chewed to the quick

   Physiological measures:
   - Blood pressure
   - Heart rate
   - Respiration rate
   - Galvanic skin response

   These definitions are quantifiable and based on measurable events. They are not conceptual, as a dictionary definition would be.

2. a. Nominal     e. Ordinal
   b. Ordinal     f. Nominal
   c. Ratio       g. Ratio
   d. Interval

### 3.2

1. Self-report measures and behavioral measures are more subjective; tests and physical measures are more objective.

2. The machine may not be operating correctly, or the person using the machine may not be doing so correctly. Recommendations: proper training of individuals taking the measures; checks on equipment; multiple measuring instruments; multiple measures.

### 3.3

1. Because different questions on the same topic are used, alternative-forms reliability tells us whether the questions measure the same concepts (equivalency). Whether individuals perform similarly on equivalent tests at different times indicates the stability of a test.

2. If they disagreed 38 times out of 250 times, then they agreed 212 times out of 250 times. Thus, $212/250 = .85 \times 100 = 85\%$, which is very high interrater agreement.

### 3.4

1. Content and construct validity should be established for the new test.

2. Face validity has to do with only whether or not a test looks valid, not whether it truly is valid.

3. A test can consistently measure something other than what it claims to measure.

4. You should be more concerned about the validity of the test—it does not measure what it claims to measure.

## WEB RESOURCES

Check your knowledge of the content in this chapter by taking the practice quiz at www.Wadsworth.com. Or, for step-by-step practice and information, check out the Statistics and Research Methods Workshops at http://psychology.wadsworth.com/workshops.

# 4 Descriptive Methods

In the preceding chapters, we discussed certain aspects of getting started with a research project. We will now turn to a discussion of actual research methods—the nuts and bolts of conducting a research project—starting with various types of nonexperimental designs. In this chapter, we will discuss descriptive methods. These methods, as the name implies, allow us to describe a situation; however, they do not allow us to make accurate predictions or to establish a cause-and-effect relationship between variables. We will examine four different types of descriptive methods—observational methods, case studies, archival method, and surveys—providing an overview and examples of each method. In addition, we will note any special considerations that apply when using each of these methods.

# Observational Methods

As noted in Chapter 1, the observational method in its most basic form is as simple as it sounds—making observations of human or other animal behavior. This method is not used as widely in psychology as in other disciplines such as sociology, ethology, and anthropology, because most psychologists want to be able to do more than describe. However, this method is of great value in some situations. When we begin research in an area, it may be appropriate to start with an observational study before doing anything more complicated. In addition, certain behaviors that cannot be studied in experimental situations lend themselves quite nicely to observational research. We will discuss two types of observational studies—naturalistic or field observation and laboratory or systematic observation—along with the advantages and disadvantages of each type.

## Naturalistic Observation

Naturalistic observation (sometimes referred to as *field observation*) involves watching people or animals in their natural habitats. The greatest advantage of this type of observation is the potential for observing natural or true behaviors. The idea is that animals or people in their natural habitat, rather than an artificial laboratory setting, should display more realistic, natural behaviors. For this reason, naturalistic observation has greater ecological validity than most other research methods. **Ecological validity** refers to the extent to which research can be generalized to real-life situations (Aronson & Carlsmith, 1968). Both Jane Goodall and Dian Fossey engaged in naturalistic observation in their work with chimpanzees and gorillas, respectively. However, as we will see, they used the naturalistic method slightly differently.

**ecological validity** The extent to which research can be generalized to real-life situations.

"SHE'S BEEN WATCHING US FOR YEARS. WHEN THE HELL IS SHE GOING TO WRITE HER BOOK?"

## Options When Using Observation

**undisguised observation**
Studies in which the participants are aware that the researcher is observing their behavior.

**nonparticipant observation**
Studies in which the researcher does not participate in the situation in which the research participants are involved.

**participant observation**
Studies in which the researcher actively participates in the situation in which the research participants are involved.

Both Goodall and Fossey used **undisguised observation**—they made no attempt to disguise themselves while making observations. Goodall's initial approach was to observe the chimpanzees from a distance. Thus, she attempted to engage in **nonparticipant observation**—a study in which the researcher does not take part (participate) in the situation in which the research participants are involved. Fossey, on the other hand, attempted to infiltrate the group of gorillas that she was studying. She tried to act as they did in the hopes of being accepted as a member of the group so that she could observe as an insider. In **participant observation,** then, the researcher actively participates in the situation in which the research participants are involved.

Take a moment to think about the issues involved when using either of these methods. In nonparticipant observation, there is the issue of reactivity—participants reacting in an unnatural way to someone obviously watching them. Thus, Goodall's sitting back and watching the chimpanzees may have caused them to "react" to her presence, and she therefore may not have observed naturalistic or true behaviors from the chimpanzees. Fossey, on the other hand, claimed that the gorillas accepted her as a member of their group, thereby minimizing or eliminating reactivity. This claim is open to question, however, because no matter how much like a gorilla she acted, she was still human.

**disguised observation**
Studies in which the participants are unaware that the researcher is observing their behavior.

Imagine how much more effective both participant and nonparticipant observation might be if researchers used **disguised observation**—concealing the fact that they were observing and recording participants' behaviors. Disguised observation allows the researcher to make observations in a more unobtrusive manner. As a nonparticipant, a researcher can make observations by hiding or by videotaping participants. Reactivity is not an issue because participants are unaware that anyone is observing their behavior. Hiding or videotaping, however, may raise ethical problems if the participants are humans. This is one reason that all research, both human and animal, must be approved by an Institutional Review Board (IRB) or Animal Care and Use Committee, as described in Chapter 2, prior to beginning a study.

Disguised observation may also be used when one is acting as a participant in the study. Rosenhan (1973) demonstrated this in his classic study on the validity of psychiatric diagnoses. Rosenhan had 8 sane individuals seek admittance to 12 different mental hospitals. Each was asked to go to a hospital and complain of the same symptoms—hearing voices that said "empty," "hollow," and "thud." Once admitted to the mental ward, the individuals no longer reported hearing voices. If admitted, each individual was to make recordings of patient–staff interactions. Rosenhan was interested in how long it would take a "sane" person to be released from the mental hospital. He found that the length of stay varied from 7 to 52 days, although the hospital staff never detected that the individuals were "sane" and part of a disguised participant study.

As we have seen, one of the primary concerns of naturalistic studies is reactivity. Another concern for researchers who use this method is expectancy effects. **Expectancy effects** are the effect of the researcher's expectations on the outcome of the study. For example, the researcher may pay more attention to behaviors that they expect, or that support their hypotheses, while possibly ignoring behaviors that might not support their hypotheses. Because the only data in an observational study are the observations made by the researcher, expectancy effects can be a serious problem, leading to biased results.

**expectancy effects** The influence of the researcher's expectations on the outcome of the study.

Besides these potential problems, naturalistic observation can be costly—especially in studies like those conducted by Goodall and Fossey where travel to another continent is required—and are usually time-consuming. One reason is that often researchers are open to studying many different behaviors when conducting this type of study; anything of interest may be observed and recorded. This flexibility often means that the research can go on indefinitely and there is little control over what happens in the study.

## Laboratory Observation

An observational method that is usually less costly and time-consuming and affords more control is laboratory or systematic observation. In contrast to naturalistic observation, systematic or laboratory observation involves observing behavior in a more contrived setting, usually a laboratory, and focusing on a small number of carefully defined behaviors. The participants are more likely to know that they are participating in a research study in which they will be observed. However, as with naturalistic observation, the researcher can be either a participant or a nonparticipant and either disguised or undisguised. For example, in the classic "strange situation" study by Ainsworth and Bell (1970), mothers brought their children to a laboratory playroom. The mothers and children were then observed through a two-way mirror in various situations, such as when the child explored the room, was left alone in the room, was left with a stranger, and was reunited with the mother. This study used nonparticipant observation. In addition, it was conducted in an undisguised manner for the mothers (who were aware they were being observed) and disguised for the children (who were unaware they were being observed).

Laboratory observation may also be conducted with the researcher as a participant in the situation. For example, a developmental psychologist could observe play behavior in children as an undisguised participant by playing with the children or by posing as a teacher or daycare worker in the laboratory setting. In other studies involving laboratory observation, the participant is disguised. Research on helping behavior (altruism) often uses this method. For example, researchers might stage what appears to be an emergency while participants are supposedly waiting for an experiment to begin. The researcher participates in a disguised manner in the "emergency situation" and observes how the "real" participants act in this situation. Do they offer help right away, and does offering help depend on the number of people present?

In laboratory observation, as with naturalistic observation, we are concerned with reactivity and expectancy effects. In fact, reactivity may be a greater concern because most people will "react" simply to being in a laboratory. As noted, one way of attempting to control reactivity is by using a disguised type of design.

An advantage of systematic or laboratory settings is that they are contrived (not natural) and thus offer the researcher more control. The situation has been manufactured to some extent in order to observe a specific behavior or set of behaviors. Because the situation is contrived, the likelihood that the participants will actually engage in the behavior of interest is far greater than it would be in a natural setting. Most researchers view this control as advantageous because it reduces the length of time needed for the study. Notice, however, that as we increase control, we decrease flexibility. We are not free to observe whatever behavior we find of interest on any given day, as we would be with a naturalistic study. Researchers have to decide what is of greatest importance to them and then choose either the naturalistic or laboratory method.

## Data Collection

Another decision to be faced when conducting observational research is how to collect the data. In Chapter 3, we discussed several types of measures: self-report measures, tests, behavioral measures, and physical measures. Because observational research involves observing and recording behavior, data are most often collected through the use of behavioral measures. As noted in Chapter 3, behavioral measures can be taken in a direct (at the time the behavior occurs) or in an indirect manner (via audio- or videotape). In addition, researchers using the observational technique can collect data using narrative records or checklists.

*Narrative Records.* **Narrative records** are full narrative descriptions of a participant's behavior. These records may be created in a direct manner—writing notes by hand—or an indirect manner—audio- or videotaping the participants and then taking notes at a later time. The purpose of narrative records is to capture, in a complete manner, everything the participant said or did during a specified period of time.

One of the best examples of the use of narrative records is the work of Jean Piaget. Piaget studied cognitive development in children and kept extensive narrative records concerning everything a child did during the specified time period. His records were a running account of exactly what the child said and did.

Although narrative records provide a complete account of what took place with each participant in a study, they are a very subjective means of collecting data. In addition, narrative records cannot be analyzed quantitatively. To be analyzed, the data must be coded in some way, reducing the huge volume of narrative information to a more manageable quantitative form, such as the number of problems solved correctly by children in different age ranges. The data should be coded by more than one person in order to establish interrater reliability. You may recall from Chapter 3 that interrater reliability is a measure of reliability that assesses the agreement of observations made by two or more raters or judges.

*Checklists.* A more structured and objective method of collecting data involves using a **checklist**—a tally sheet on which the researcher records attributes of the participants and whether particular behaviors were observed. Checklists enable researchers to focus on a limited number of specific behaviors.

Researchers use two basic types of checklists. A **static checklist** is a means of collecting data on characteristics that will not change while the observations are being made. These static features may include how many people are present, the gender, race, and age of the participant, or what the weather is like (if relevant). Many different characteristics may be noted on the static checklist, depending on the nature of the study. For example, observations of hospital patients might include information on general health, whereas observations of driving behavior might include the make and type of vehicle driven.

The second type of checklist, an **action checklist,** is used to record whether specific behaviors were present or absent during the observational time period. An action checklist could be used to record the type of stop made at a stop sign (complete, rolling, or none) or the type of play behavior observed in children (solitary, cooperative, or parallel). Typically, an action checklist provides a means of tallying the frequency of different categories of behavior.

As discussed in Chapter 3, it is important that researchers who use the checklists understand the operational definition of each characteristic being measured in order to increase the reliability and validity of the measures. As you may recall, an operational definition of a variable is a definition of the variable in terms of the operations (activities) a researcher uses to measure or manipulate it. Thus, in order to use a checklist accurately, the person

**narrative records** Full narrative descriptions of a participant's behavior.

**checklist** A tally sheet on which the researcher records attributes of the participants and whether particular behaviors were observed.
**static checklist** A tally sheet on which attributes that will not change are recorded.

**action checklist** A tally sheet used to note the presence or absence of behaviors.

collecting the data must clearly understand what constitutes each category of behavior being observed.

The advantage of checklists over narrative records is that the data are already quantified and do not have to be reduced in any way. The disadvantage is that the behaviors and characteristics to be observed are determined when the checklist is devised. Thus, an interesting behavior that would have been included in a narrative record may be missed or not recorded because it is not part of the checklist.

| IN REVIEW | Features of Types of Observational Studies | |
|---|---|---|
| | **TYPES OF OBSERVATIONAL STUDIES** | |
| | **Naturalistic** | **Laboratory** |
| Description | Observing people or other animals in their natural habitats | Observing people or other animals in a contrived setting, usually a laboratory |
| Options | Participant versus nonparticipant Disguised versus nondisguised | Participant versus nonparticipant Disguised versus nondisguised |
| Means of Data Collection | Narrative records Checklists | Narrative records Checklists |
| Concerns | Reactivity Expectancy effects Time Money Lack of control | Reactivity Expectancy effects Lack of flexibility |

**CRITICAL THINKING CHECK 4.1**

1. Explain the differences in flexibility and control between naturalistic and laboratory observational research.
2. If reactivity were your greatest concern in an observational study, which method would you recommend using?
3. Why is data reduction of greater concern when using narrative records as opposed to checklists?

# Case Study Method

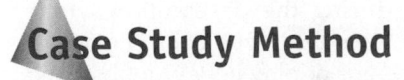

One of the oldest research methods, as we saw in Chapter 1, is the case study method—an in-depth study of one or more individuals in the hope of revealing things that are true of all of us. For example, Freud's theory of personality development was based on a small number of case studies. Piaget, whose research was used as an example of observational methods, began studying cognitive development by completing case studies on his own three children. This piqued his interest in cognitive development to such an extent that he then began to use observational methods to study hundreds of other children.

As another example, much of the research on split-brain patients and hemispheric specialization was conducted using case studies of the few individuals whose corpus callosum had been severed.

One advantage of case study research is that it often suggests hypotheses for future studies, as in Piaget's case. It also provides a method to study rare phenomena, such as rare brain disorders or diseases, as in the case of split-brain patients. Case studies may also offer tentative support for a psychological theory. Case study research also has problems, however. The individual being observed may be atypical, in which case any generalizations made to the general population would be erroneous. For example, Freud formulated a theory of personality development that he believed applied to everyone based on case studies of a few atypical individuals. Another potential problem is expectancy effects: Researchers may be biased in their interpretations of the observations made or in their data collection, paying more attention to data that support their theory and ignoring data that present problems for their theory. Because of these limitations, case study research should be used with caution, and the data should be interpreted for what they are—observations on one or a few possibly unrepresentative individuals.

# ◢ Archival Method

A third descriptive method is the archival method. The **archival method** involves describing data that existed before the time of the study. In other words, the data were not generated as part of the study. One of the biggest advantages of archival research is that the problem of reactivity is somewhat minimized because the data have already been collected and the researcher does not have to interact with the participants in any way. For example, let's assume that a researcher wants to study whether more babies are born when the moon is full. The researcher could use archival data from hospitals and count the number of babies born on days with full moons versus no full moons for as far back as he or she would like. You can see, based on this example, that another advantage of archival research is that it is usually less time-consuming than most other research methods because the data already exist. Thus, researchers are not confronted with the problems of getting participants for their study and taking the time to observe them—these tasks have already been done for them.

There are many sources for archival data. The most well known is the U.S. Census Bureau; however, any organization that collects data is a source for archival data. For example, the National Opinion Research Center, the Educational Testing Service, and local, state, and federal public records can all be sources for archival data. In addition to organizations that collect data, archival research may be conducted based on the content of newspapers or magazines, data in a library, or computer databases. Some data sources might be considered better than others. For example, reviewing letters to the editor at a local newspaper in order to gauge public sentiment on a topic might lead to biases in the data. In other words, there is a selection bias in who decided to write to the editor, and some opinions or viewpoints may be

**archival method** A descriptive research method that involves describing data that existed before the time of the study.

overlooked simply because the individuals who hold those viewpoints decided not to write to the editor. Moreover, in all archival research studies, the researcher is making conclusions on the basis of data collected by another person or organization. This means that the researcher can never be sure whether the data are reliable or valid. In addition, the researcher cannot be sure that what is currently in the archive represents everything that was originally collected. Some of the data may have been purged at some time and the researcher will not know this, nor will he or she know why data were purged or how the decision was made to purge some data and leave other data. Thus, as a research method, archival research typically provides a lot of flexibility in terms of what is studied, but no control in terms of who is studied or how they were studied.

# Survey Methods

Another means of collecting data for descriptive purposes is to use a survey. We will discuss several elements to consider when using surveys, including constructing the survey, administering the survey, and choosing sampling techniques.

## Survey Construction

We begin our coverage of the survey method by discussing survey construction. In order for the data collected to be both reliable and valid, the researcher must carefully plan the survey instrument. The type of questions used and the order in which they appear may vary depending on how the survey is ultimately administered (e.g., a mail survey versus a telephone survey).

*Writing the Questions.* The first task in designing a survey is to write the survey questions. Questions should be written in clear, simple language to minimize any possible confusion. Take a moment to think about surveys or exam questions you may have encountered where, because of poor wording, you misunderstood what was being asked of you. For example, consider the following questions:

- How long have you lived in Harborside?
- How many years have you lived in Harborside?

In both instances, the researcher is interested in determining the number of years the individual has resided in the area. Notice, however, that the first question does not actually ask this. An individual might answer "Since I was 8 years old" (meaningless unless the survey also asks for current age) or "I moved to Harborside right after I got married." In either case, the participant's interpretation of the question is different from the researcher's intent. It is important, therefore, to spend time thinking about the simplest wording that will elicit the specific information of interest to the researcher.

Another consideration when writing survey questions is whether to use open-ended, closed-ended, partially open-ended, or rating-scale questions.

**TABLE 4.1   Examples of types of survey questions**

---

*Open-ended*

Has your college experience been satisfying thus far?_____

_____

*Closed-ended*

Has your college experience been satisfying thus far?

Yes_____ No_____

*Partially open-ended*

With regard to your college experience, which of the following factors do you find satisfying?

Academics_____

Relationships_____

Residence halls_____

Residence life_____

Social life_____

Food service_____

Other_____

_____

*Likert Rating Scale*

I am very satisfied with my college experience.

| 1 | 2 | 3 | 4 | 5 |
|---|---|---|---|---|
| Strongly Disagree | Disagree | Neutral | Agree | Strongly Agree |

---

Table 4.1 provides examples of these types of questions. **Open-ended questions** ask participants to formulate their own responses. On written surveys, researchers can control the length of the response to some extent by the amount of room they leave for the respondent to answer the question. A single line encourages a short answer, whereas several lines indicate that a longer response is expected. **Closed-ended questions** ask the respondent to choose from a limited number of alternatives. Participants may be asked to choose the one answer that best represents their beliefs or to check as many answers as apply to them. When writing closed-ended questions, researchers must make sure that the alternatives provided include all possible answers. For example, suppose a question asks how many hours of television the respondent watched the previous day and provides the following alternatives: 0–1 hour, 2–3 hours, 4–5 hours, or 6 or more hours. What if an individual watched 1.5 hours? Should this respondent select the first or second alternative? Each participant would have to decide which alternative to choose. This, in turn, would compromise the data collected. In other words, the data would be less reliable and valid. **Partially open-ended questions** are similar to closed-ended questions, but one alternative is "Other" with a blank

**open-ended questions**
Questions for which participants formulate their own responses.

**closed-ended questions**
Questions for which participants choose from a limited number of alternatives.

**partially open-ended questions** Closed-ended questions with an open-ended "Other" option.

**rating scale**  A numerical scale on which survey respondents indicate the direction and strength of their response.

**Likert rating scale**  A type of numerical rating scale developed by Renis Likert in 1932.

space next to it. If none of the alternatives provided is appropriate, the respondent can mark "Other" and then write a short explanation.

Finally, researchers may use some sort of **rating scale** that asks participants to choose a number that represents the direction and strength of their response. One advantage of using a rating scale is that it is easy to convert the data to an ordinal or interval scale of measurement and proceed with statistical analysis. One popular version is the Likert rating scale, named after the researcher who developed the scale in 1932. A **Likert rating scale** presents a statement rather than a question, and respondents are asked to rate their level of agreement with the statement. The example in Table 4.1 uses a Likert scale with five alternatives. If you want to provide respondents with a neutral alternative, you should use a scale with an odd number of alternatives. If, however, you want to force respondents to lean in one direction or another, you should use an even number of alternatives.

Each type of question has advantages and disadvantages. Open-ended questions allow for a greater variety of responses from participants but are difficult to analyze statistically because the data must be coded or reduced in some manner. Closed-ended questions are easy to analyze statistically, but they seriously limit the responses that participants can give. Many researchers prefer to use a Likert-type scale because it is very easy to analyze statistically. Most psychologists view this scale as interval in nature, although there is some debate, and others see it as an ordinal scale. As we will see in later chapters, a wide variety of statistical tests can be used with interval data.

When researchers write survey items, it is very important that the wording not mislead the respondent. Several types of questions can mislead participants. A **loaded question** is one that includes nonneutral or emotionally laden terms. Consider this example: "Do you believe radical extremists should be allowed to burn the American flag?" The phrase *radical extremists* loads the question emotionally, conveying the opinion of the person who wrote the question. A **leading question** is one that sways the respondent to answer in a desired manner. For example: "Most people agree that conserving energy is important—do you agree?" The phrase *Most people agree* encourages the respondent to agree also. Finally, a **double-barreled question** asks more than one thing in a single item. Double-barreled questions often include the word *and* or *or*. For example, the following question is double-barreled: "Do you find using a cell phone to be convenient and time saving?" This question should be divided into two separate items, one addressing the convenience of cell phones and one addressing whether they save time.

**loaded question**  A question that includes nonneutral or emotionally laden terms.

**leading question**  A question that sways the respondent to answer in a desired manner.

**double-barreled question**  A question that asks more than one thing.

**response bias**  The tendency to consistently give the same answer to almost all of the items on a survey.

Finally, when writing a survey, the researcher should also be concerned with participants who employ a particular response set or **response bias**—the tendency to consistently give the same answer to almost all of the items on a survey. This is often referred to as "yea-saying" or "nay-saying." In other words, respondents might agree (or disagree) with one or two of the questions, but to make answering the survey easier on themselves, they simply respond yes (or no) to almost all of the questions. One way to minimize participants adopting such a response bias is to word the questions so that a positive (or negative) response to every question would be unlikely.

For example, an instrument designed to assess depression might phrase some of the questions so that agreement means the respondent is depressed ("I frequently feel sad") and other questions might have the meaning reversed so that disagreement indicates depression ("I am happy almost all of the time"). Although some individuals might legitimately agree to both of these items, when a respondent consistently agrees (or disagrees) with questions phrased in standard and reversed formats, it is reason to be concerned about "yea-saying" or "nay-saying."

*Arranging the Questions.* Another consideration is how to arrange questions on the survey. Writers of surveys sometimes assume that the questions should be randomized, but this is not the best arrangement to use. Dillman (1978) provides some tips for arranging questions on surveys. First, present related questions in subsets. This arrangement ensures that the general concept being investigated is made obvious to the respondents. It will also help the respondents to focus on one issue at a time. However, this suggestion should not be followed if you do not want the general concept being investigated to be obvious to the respondents. Second, place questions that deal with sensitive topics (such as drug use or sexual experiences) at the end of the subset of questions to which they apply. Respondents will be more likely to answer questions of a sensitive nature if they have already committed themselves to filling out the survey by answering questions of a less sensitive nature. Last, to prevent participants from losing interest in the survey, place **demographic questions**—questions that ask for basic information such as age, gender, ethnicity, or income—at the end of the survey. Although this information is important for the researcher, many respondents view it as boring, so avoid beginning your survey with these items.

**demographic questions** Questions that ask for basic information, such as age, gender, ethnicity, or income.

## Administering the Survey

We will examine three methods of surveying—mail surveys, telephone surveys, and personal interviews—along with the advantages and disadvantages of each.

*Mail Surveys.* **Mail surveys** are written surveys that are self-administered. They can be sent through the traditional mail system or by e-mail. It is especially important that a mail survey be clearly written and self-explanatory because no one will be available to answer questions regarding the survey once it has been mailed out.

**mail survey** A written survey that is self-administered.

Mail surveys have several advantages. Traditional mail surveys generally have less **sampling bias**—a tendency for one group to be overrepresented in a sample—than phone surveys or personal interviews. Can you identify why this might be so? Almost everyone has a mailing address and thus could receive a survey. Not everyone, however, has a phone or is available to spend time on a personal interview. Mail surveys also eliminate the problem of **interviewer bias**—the tendency for the person asking the questions (usually the researcher) to bias or influence the participants' answers. An interviewer might bias participants' answers by nodding and smiling

**sampling bias** A tendency for one group to be overrepresented in a sample.

**interviewer bias** The tendency for the person asking the questions to bias the participants' answers.

more when they answer as expected or frowning when they give unexpected answers. Interviewer bias is another example of an expectancy effect.

Mail surveys also have the advantage of allowing the researcher to collect data on more sensitive information. Participants who might be unwilling to discuss personal information with someone over the phone or face-to-face might be more willing to answer such questions on a written survey. A mail survey is also usually less expensive than a phone survey or personal interview in which the researcher has to pay workers to phone or canvas neighborhoods. Last, the answers provided on a mail survey are sometimes more complete because participants can take as much time as they need to think about the questions and formulate their responses without feeling the pressure of someone waiting for an answer.

Mail surveys also have some potential problems, however. One problem is that no one is available to answer questions if they arise. Thus, if an item is unclear to the respondent, it may be left blank or misinterpreted, which biases the results. Another problem with mail surveys is a generally low return rate. Typically, a single mailing produces a response rate of 25–30%—much lower than is typically achieved with phone surveys or personal interviews. Follow-up mailings may produce a response rate closer to 50% (Erdos, 1983). A good response rate is important in order to maintain a representative sample. If only a small portion of the original sample returns the survey, the final sample may be biased.

Shere Hite's (1987) work based on surveys completed by 4,500 women is a classic example of the problem of a biased survey sample. In her book *Women and Love*, Hite claimed, based on her survey, that 70% of women married five or more years were having affairs, 84% of them were dissatisfied with their intimate relationships with men, and 95% felt emotionally harassed by the men they loved. These results were widely covered by news programs and magazines and were even used as a cover story in *Time* (Wallis, 1987). Although Hite's book became a bestseller, largely because of the news coverage that her results received, researchers questioned her findings. It was discovered that the survey respondents came from one of two sources. Some surveys were mailed to women who were members of various women's organizations, such as professional groups, political groups, and women's rights organizations. Other women were solicited through talk show interviews given by Hite in which she publicized an address women could write to in order to request a copy of the survey. Both of these methods of gathering participants for a study should set off warning bells for you. In the first situation, women who are members of women's organizations are hardly representative of the average woman in the United States. The second situation represents a case of self-selection. Those who are interested in their relationships, and possibly having problems in their relationships, might be more likely to write for a copy of the survey and then participate in it.

After beginning with a biased sample, Hite had a return rate of only 4.5%. In other words, the 4,500 women who filled out the survey represented only 4.5% of those who received surveys. Doing the math, you can see that Hite sent out 100,000 surveys and received only 4,500 back. This represents a very poor and unacceptable return rate. How does a low return rate bias the results even further? Think about it. Who would be most likely to take the time to return a long (127-question) survey on which the questions were of a personal nature and often pertained to problems in their relationships with male partners? Most likely it would be women who had strong opinions on the topic—possibly women who were having problems in their relationships and wanted to tell someone about them. Thus, Hite's results were based on a specialized group of women, yet she attempted to generalize her results to all American women. The Hite survey has become a classic example of how a biased sample can lead to erroneous conclusions.

*Telephone Surveys.* **Telephone surveys** involve telephoning participants and reading the questions to them. This method can help to alleviate one of the problems with mail surveys because respondents can ask that the questions be clarified. In addition, the researchers can ask follow-up questions if they think they will provide more reliable data. Another advantage of telephone surveys is a generally higher response rate, 59–70% (Groves & Kahn, 1979). Individuals are less likely to hang up on a live person requesting help on a survey than they are to ignore a mail survey. This willingness to respond may have changed in recent years, however, with the tremendous increase in telemarketing. Individuals are now more suspicious of telephone interviews and often become angry or suspicious when interrupted by someone soliciting anything over the telephone (Jones, 1995).

Telephone surveys do have several disadvantages. First, they are more time-consuming than a mail survey because the researchers must read each of the questions and record the responses. Second, they can be costly. The researchers must call the individuals themselves or pay others to do the calling. If the calls are long-distance, then the cost is even greater. Third is the problem of interviewer bias. Finally, participants are more likely to give socially desirable responses over the phone than on a mail survey. A **socially desirable response** is one that is given because participants believe it is deemed appropriate by society, rather than because it truly reflects their own views or behaviors. For example, respondents may say that they attend church at least twice a month or read to their children several times a week because they believe this is what society expects them to do, not because they are true statements.

*Personal Interviews.* A **personal interview,** in which the questions are asked face-to-face, may be conducted anywhere—at the individual's home, on the street, or in a shopping mall. One advantage of personal interviews is that they allow the researcher to record not only verbal responses but also any facial or bodily expressions or movements such as grins, grimaces, or shrugs. These nonverbal responses may give the researcher greater insight into the respondents' true opinions and beliefs. A second advantage to personal interviews is that participants usually devote more time to answering the questions than they do in telephone surveys. As with telephone surveys, respondents can ask for question clarification. Finally, personal interviews usually have a fairly high response rate—typically around 80% (Dillman, 1978; Erdos, 1983).

**telephone survey** A survey in which the questions are read to participants over the telephone.

**socially desirable response** A response that is given because a respondent believes it is deemed appropriate by society.

**personal interview** A survey in which the questions are asked face-to-face.

Potential problems with personal interviews include many of those discussed in connection with telephone surveys—interviewer bias, socially desirable responses, and even greater time and expense than with telephone surveys. In addition, the lack of anonymity in a personal interview may affect the responses. Participants may not feel comfortable answering truthfully when someone is standing right there listening to them and writing down their responses.

A variation on the personal interview is the *focus group interview.* Focus group interviews involve interviewing 6 to 10 individuals at the same time. Focus groups usually meet once for 1–3 hours. The questions asked of the participants are usually open-ended and addressed to the whole group. This allows participants to answer in any way they choose and to respond to each other. Focus group interviews have many of the same problems that personal interviews do. One additional concern with focus group interviews is that one or two of the participants may dominate the conversation. Thus, it is important that the individual conducting the focus group is skilled at dealing with such problems.

In summary, the three survey methods offer different advantages and disadvantages. Mail surveys are usually less expensive but have very poor response rates. Telephone surveys have problems, too, but offer the opportunity for question clarification. Personal interviews are the most costly and time-consuming and may suffer the most from interviewer bias. However, they allow the researcher the greatest amount of flexibility in asking questions and far more leeway in interpreting responses. The researcher's choice will depend on the research question at hand.

## Sampling Techniques

Another concern for researchers using the survey method is who will participate in the survey. For the results to be meaningful, the individuals who take the survey should be representative of the population under investigation. As discussed in Chapter 1, the population consists of all of the people about whom a study is meant to generalize, whereas the sample represents the subset of people from the population who actually participate in the study. In almost all cases, it is not feasible to survey the entire population. Instead, we select a subgroup or sample from the population and give the survey to them. If we are to draw any reliable and valid conclusions concerning the population, it is imperative that the sample be "like" the population—a **representative sample.** When the sample is representative of the population, we can be fairly confident that the results we find based on the sample also hold for the population. In other words, we can generalize from the sample to the population. There are two ways to sample individuals from a population: probability and nonprobability sampling.

**representative sample**
A sample that is like the population.

*Probability Sampling.* When researchers use **probability sampling,** each member of the population has an equal likelihood of being selected to be part of the sample. We will discuss three types of probability sampling: random sampling, stratified random sampling, and cluster sampling.

**probability sampling**  A sampling technique in which each member of the population has an equal likelihood of being selected to be part of the sample.

A random sample is achieved through **random selection,** in which each member of the population is equally likely to be chosen as part of the sample. Let's say we start with a population of 300 students enrolled in introductory psychology classes at a university. Assuming we want to select a random sample of 30 students, how should we go about it? We do not want to get all of the students by simply going to one 30-person section of introductory psychology because, depending on the instructor and the time of day of the class, there could be biases in who registered for this section. For example, if it is an early morning class, it could represent students who like to get up early or those who registered for classes so late that nothing else was available. Thus, these students would not be representative of all students in introductory psychology.

Generating a random sample can be accomplished by using a table of random numbers, such as that provided in Appendix A (Table A.1). When using a random numbers table, the researcher chooses a starting place arbitrarily. Once the starting point is determined, the researcher looks at the number—say, a 6—counts down six people in the population, and chooses the sixth person to be in the sample. The researcher continues in this manner by looking at the next number in the table, counting down through the population, and including the appropriately numbered person in the sample. For our sample, we would continue this process until we had selected a sample of 30 people. A random sample can be generated in other ways—for example, by computer or by pulling names randomly out of a hat. The point is that in random sampling, each member of the population is equally likely to be chosen as part of the sample.

**random selection** A method of generating a random sample in which each member of the population is equally likely to be chosen as part of the sample.

BIZARRE SEQUENCE OF COMPUTER-GENERATED RANDOM NUMBERS

Sometimes a population is made up of members of different groups or categories. For example, both men and women make up the 300 students enrolled in introductory psychology, but maybe not in equal proportions. If we want to draw conclusions about the population of introductory psychology students based on our sample, then our sample must be representative of the strata within the population. For example, if the population consists of 70% women and 30% men, then we need to ensure that the sample is similar on this dimension.

**stratified random sampling**
A sampling technique designed to ensure that subgroups or strata are fairly represented.

One means of attaining such a sample is stratified random sampling. A **stratified random sample** allows us to take into account the different subgroups of people in the population and helps to guarantee that the sample accurately represents the population on specific characteristics. We begin by dividing the population into subsamples or strata. In our example, the strata would be based on gender—men and women. We would then randomly select 70% of our sample from the female stratum and 30% of our sample from the male stratum. In this manner, we ensure that the characteristic of gender in the sample is representative of the population.

**cluster sampling**   A sampling technique in which clusters of participants that represent the population are used.

Often the population is too large for random sampling of any sort. In these cases, it is common to use cluster sampling. As the name implies, **cluster sampling** involves using participants who are already part of a group or "cluster." For example, if you were interested in surveying students at a large university where it might not be possible to use true random sampling, you might sample from classes that are required of all students at the university, such as English composition. If the classes are required of all students, they should contain a good mix of students, and if you use several classes, the sample should represent the population.

**nonprobability sampling**
A sampling technique in which the individual members of the population do not have an equal likelihood of being selected to be a member of the sample.

*Nonprobability Sampling.*  **Nonprobability sampling** is used when the individual members of the population do not have an equal likelihood of being selected to be a member of the sample. Nonprobability sampling is typically used because it tends to be less expensive and it is easier to generate samples using this technique. We will discuss two types of nonprobability sampling: convenience sampling and quota sampling.

**convenience sampling**   A sampling technique in which participants are obtained wherever they can be found and typically wherever is convenient for the researcher.

**Convenience sampling** involves getting participants wherever you can find them and typically wherever is convenient. This is sometimes referred to as *haphazard sampling*. For example, if you wanted a sample of 100 college students, you could stand outside of the library and ask people who pass by to participate, or you could ask students in some of your classes to participate. This might sound somewhat similar to what I described earlier for cluster sampling; however, there is a difference. With cluster sampling, we try to identify clusters that are representative of the population. This is not the case with convenience sampling. We simply take whomever is convenient as a participant in the study.

**quota sampling**   A sampling technique that involves ensuring that the sample is like the population on certain characteristics but uses convenience sampling to obtain the participants.

A second type of nonprobability sampling is quota sampling. Quota sampling is to nonprobability sampling what stratified random sampling is to probability sampling. In other words, **quota sampling** involves ensuring that the sample is like the population on certain characteristics. However, even though we try to ensure similarity with the population on certain characteristics, we do not sample from the population randomly—we simply take participants wherever we find them, through whatever means is convenient. Thus, this method is slightly better than convenience sampling, but there is still not much effort devoted to creating a sample that is truly representative of the population, nor one in which all members of the population have an equal chance of being selected for the sample.

| Survey Methods | | IN REVIEW |
|---|---|---|
| Types of Survey Method | Mail survey | A written survey that is self-administered |
| | Telephone survey | A survey conducted by telephone in which the questions are read to the respondents |
| | Personal interview | A face-to-face interview of the respondent |
| Sampling Techniques | Random sampling | A sampling technique in which each member of the population is equally likely to be chosen as part of the sample |
| | Stratified random sampling | A sampling technique intended to guarantee that the sample represents specific subgroups or strata |
| | Cluster sampling | A sampling technique in which clusters of participants that represent the population are identified and included in the sample |
| Question Types | Open-ended questions | Questions for which respondents formulate their own responses |
| | Closed-ended questions | Questions on which respondents must choose from a limited number of alternatives |
| | Partially open-ended questions | Closed-ended questions with an open-ended "Other" option |
| | Rating scales (Likert scale) | Questions on which respondents must provide a rating on a numerical scale |
| Concerns | Sampling bias Interviewer bias Socially desirable responses Return rate Expense | |

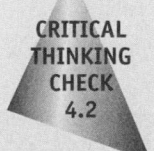

1. With which survey method(s) is interviewer bias of greatest concern?
2. Shere Hite had 4,500 surveys returned to her. This is a large sample (something desirable), so what was the problem with using all of the surveys returned?
3. How is stratified random sampling different from random sampling?
4. What are the problems with the following survey questions?
   a. Do you agree that school systems should be given more money for computers and recreational activities?
   b. Do you favor eliminating the wasteful excesses in the city budget?
   c. Most people feel that teachers are underpaid. Do you agree?

CRITICAL THINKING CHECK 4.2

# Summary

In this chapter, we discussed various ways of conducting a descriptive study. The four methods presented were the observational method (naturalistic versus laboratory), the case study method, the archival method, and the survey method (mail, telephone, or personal interview). Several advantages and disadvantages of each method were discussed. For observational methods, important issues include reactivity, experimenter expectancies, time, cost, control, and flexibility. The case study method is limited because it describes only one or a few people and is very subjective in nature, but it is often a good means of beginning a research project. The archival method is limited by the fact that the data already exist and were collected by someone other than the researcher. The various survey methods may have problems of biased samples, poor return rates, interviewer biases, socially desirable responses, and expense. Various methods of sampling participants for surveys were discussed, along with how best to write a survey and arrange the questions on the survey.

Keep in mind that all of the methods presented here are descriptive in nature. They allow researchers to describe what has been observed in a group of people or other animals, but they do not allow us to make accurate predictions or determine cause-and-effect relationships. In the next chapter, we will discuss descriptive statistics—statistics that can be used to summarize the data collected in a study. In later chapters, we will address methods that allow us to do more than simply describe—methods that allow us to make predictions and assess causality.

## KEY TERMS

| | | |
|---|---|---|
| ecological validity | closed-ended questions | telephone survey |
| undisguised observation | partially open-ended questions | socially desirable response |
| nonparticipant observation | rating scale | personal interview |
| participant observation | Likert rating scale | representative sample |
| disguised observation | loaded question | probability sampling |
| expectancy effects | leading question | random selection |
| narrative records | double-barreled question | stratified random sampling |
| checklist | response bias | cluster sampling |
| static checklist | demographic questions | nonprobability sampling |
| action checklist | mail survey | convenience sampling |
| archival method | sampling bias | quota sampling |
| open-ended questions | interviewer bias | |

## CHAPTER EXERCISES

(Answers to odd-numbered exercises appear in Appendix C.)

1. Imagine that you want to study cell phone use by drivers. You decide to conduct an observational study of drivers by making observations at three locations—a busy intersection, an entrance/exit to a shopping mall parking lot, and a residential intersection. You are interested in the number of

people who use cell phones while driving. How would you recommend conducting this study? How would you recommend collecting the data? What concerns do you need to take into consideration?

2. A student at your school wants to survey students regarding their credit card use. She decides to conduct the survey at the student center during lunch hour by interviewing every fifth person leaving the student center. What type of survey would you recommend she use? What type of sampling technique is being used? Can you identify a better way of sampling the student body?

3. Imagine that the questions below represent some of those from the survey described in Exercise 2. Can you identify any problems with these questions?
   a. Do you believe that capitalist bankers should charge such high interest rates on credit card balances?
   b. How much did you charge on your credit cards last month? $0–$400; $500–$900; $1,000–$1,400; $1,500–$1,900; $2,000 or more
   c. Most Americans believe that a credit card is a necessity—do you agree?

# CRITICAL THINKING CHECK ANSWERS

## 4.1

1. Naturalistic observation has more flexibility because researchers are free to observe any behavior they may find interesting. Laboratory observation has less flexibility because the behaviors to be observed are usually determined before the study begins. It is thus difficult to change what is being observed once the study has begun. Because naturalistic observation affords greater flexibility, it also has less control—the researcher does not control what happens during the study. Laboratory observation, having less flexibility, also has more control—the researcher determines more of the research situation.

2. If reactivity were your greatest concern, you might try using disguised observation. In addition, you might opt for a more naturalistic setting.

3. Data reduction is of greater concern when using narrative records because the narrative records must be interpreted and reduced to a quantitative form, using multiple individuals in order to establish interrater reliability. Checklists do not involve interpretation or data reduction because the individual collecting the data simply records whether a behavior is present or how often a behavior occurs.

## 4.2

1. Interviewer bias is of greatest concern with personal interviews because the interviewer is physically with the respondent. It is also of some concern with telephone interviews. However, because the telephone interviewer is not actually with the respondent, it is not as great a concern as it is with personal interviews.

2. The problem with using all 4,500 returned surveys was that Hite sent out 100,000 surveys. Thus, 4,500 represented a very small return rate (4.5%). If the 100,000 individuals who were sent surveys were a representative sample, it is doubtful that the 4,500 who returned them were representative of the population.

3. Stratified random sampling involves randomly selecting individuals from strata or groups. Using stratified random sampling ensures that subgroups, or strata, are fairly represented. This does not always happen when simple random sampling is used.

4. a. This is a double-barreled question. It should be divided into two questions, one pertaining to money for computers and one pertaining to money for recreational activities.
   b. This is a loaded question. The phrase *wasteful excesses* loads the question emotionally.
   c. This is a leading question. Using the phrase *Most people feel* sways the respondent.

## WEB RESOURCES

Check your knowledge of the content in this chapter by taking the practice quiz at www.Wadsworth.com. Or, for step-by-step practice and information, check out the Statistics and Research Methods Workshops at http://psychology.wadsworth.com/workshops.

## LAB RESOURCES

For hands-on experience using the research methods described in this chapter, see Chapters 1 and 2 ("Naturalistic Observation" and "Survey Research") in *Research Methods Laboratory Manual for Psychology*, 2nd ed., by William Langston (Belmont, CA: Wadsworth, 2005).

# 5 Data Organization and Descriptive Statistics

In this chapter, we will begin to discuss what to do with the observations made in the course of a study—namely, how to describe the data set through the use of descriptive statistics. First, we will consider ways of organizing the data by taking the large number of observations made during a study and presenting them in a manner that is easier to read and understand. Then we will discuss some simple descriptive statistics. These statistics allow us to do some "number crunching"—to condense a large number of observations into a summary statistic or set of statistics. The concepts and statistics we will describe in this chapter can be used to draw conclusions from data collected through descriptive, predictive, or explanatory methods. They do not come close to covering all that can be done with data gathered from a study. They do, however, provide a place to start.

# Organizing Data

We will discuss two methods of organizing data: frequency distributions and graphs.

## Frequency Distributions

To illustrate the processes of organizing and describing data, let's use the data set presented in Table 5.1. These data represent the scores of 30 students on an introductory psychology exam. One reason for organizing data and using statistics is so that we can draw meaningful conclusions. The list of exam scores in Table 5.1 is simply that—a list in no particular order. As shown here, the data are not especially meaningful. One of the first steps in organizing these data might be to rearrange them from highest to lowest or from lowest to highest.

Once the scores are ordered (see Table 5.2), we can condense the data into a **frequency distribution**—a table in which all of the scores are listed along with the frequency with which each occurs. We can also show the relative frequency, which is the proportion of the total observations included in each score. When a relative frequency is multiplied by 100, it is read as a percentage. A frequency distribution and a relative frequency distribution of our exam data are presented in Table 5.3.

The frequency distribution is a way of presenting data that makes the pattern of the data easier to see. We can make the data set even easier to read (especially desirable with large data sets) if we group the scores and create a class interval frequency distribution. In a **class interval frequency distribution,** we combine individual scores into categories, or intervals, and list them along with the frequency of scores in each interval. In our exam score example, the scores range from 45 to 95—a 50-point range. A rule of thumb when creating class intervals is to have between 10 and 20 categories (Hinkle, Wiersma, & Jurs, 1988). A quick method of calculating what the width of the interval should be is to subtract the lowest score from the highest score and then divide the result by the number of intervals we would like (Schweigert, 1994). If we want 10 intervals in our example, we proceed as follows:

**frequency distribution** A table in which all of the scores are listed along with the frequency with which each occurs.

**class interval frequency distribution** A table in which the scores are grouped into intervals and listed along with the frequency of scores in each interval.

**TABLE 5.1  Exam scores for 30 students**

| | |
|---|---|
| 56 | 74 |
| 69 | 70 |
| 78 | 90 |
| 80 · | 74 |
| 47 | 59 |
| 85 | 86 |
| 82 | 92 |
| 74 | 60 |
| 95 | 63 |
| 65 | 45 |
| 54 | 94 |
| 60 | 93 |
| 87 | 82 |
| 76 | 77 |
| 75 | 78 |

**TABLE 5.2  Exam scores ordered from lowest to highest**

| | |
|---|---|
| 45 | 76 |
| 47 | 77 |
| 54 | 78 |
| 56 | 78 |
| 59 | 80 |
| 60 | 82 |
| 60 | 82 |
| 63 | 85 |
| 65 | 86 |
| 69 | 87 |
| 70 | 90 |
| 74 | 92 |
| 74 | 93 |
| 74 | 94 |
| 75 | 95 |

**TABLE 5.3  Frequency and relative frequency distributions of exam data**

| SCORE | f (FREQUENCY) | rf (RELATIVE FREQUENCY) |
|---|---|---|
| 45 | 1 | .033 |
| 47 | 1 | .033 |
| 54 | 1 | .033 |
| 56 | 1 | .033 |
| 59 | 1 | .033 |
| 60 | 2 | .067 |
| 63 | 1 | .033 |
| 65 | 1 | .033 |
| 69 | 1 | .033 |
| 70 | 1 | .033 |
| 74 | 3 | .100 |
| 75 | 1 | .033 |
| 76 | 1 | .033 |
| 77 | 1 | .033 |
| 78 | 2 | .067 |
| 80 | 1 | .033 |
| 82 | 2 | .067 |
| 85 | 1 | .033 |
| 86 | 1 | .033 |
| 87 | 1 | .033 |
| 90 | 1 | .033 |
| 92 | 1 | .033 |
| 93 | 1 | .033 |
| 94 | 1 | .033 |
| 95 | 1 | .033 |
| | N = 30 | 1.00 |

$$\frac{95-45}{10} = \frac{50}{10} = 5$$

Table 5.4 is the frequency distribution using class intervals with a width of 5. Notice how much more compact the data appear when presented in a class interval frequency distribution. Although such distributions have the advantage of reducing the number of categories, they have the disadvantage of not providing as much information as a regular frequency distribution. For example, although we can see from the class interval frequency distribution that five people scored between 75 and 79, we do not know their exact scores within the interval.

**TABLE 5.4   A class interval distribution of the exam data**

| CLASS INTERVAL | f | rf |
|:---:|:---:|:---:|
| 45–49 | 2 | .067 |
| 50–54 | 1 | .033 |
| 55–59 | 2 | .067 |
| 60–64 | 3 | .100 |
| 65–69 | 2 | .067 |
| 70–74 | 4 | .133 |
| 75–79 | 5 | .166 |
| 80–84 | 3 | .100 |
| 85–89 | 3 | .100 |
| 90–94 | 4 | .133 |
| 95–99 | 1 | .033 |
| | N = 30 | 1.00 |

## Graphs

Frequency distributions provide valuable information, but sometimes a picture is of greater value. Several types of pictorial representations can be used to represent data. The choice depends on the type of data collected and what the researcher hopes to emphasize or illustrate. The most common graphs used by psychologists are bar graphs, histograms, and frequency polygons (line graphs). Graphs typically have two coordinate axes: the *x*-axis (the horizontal axis) and the *y*-axis (the vertical axis). Most commonly, the *y*-axis is shorter than the *x*-axis, typically 60–75% of the length of the *x*-axis.

*Bar Graphs and Histograms.* Bar graphs and histograms are frequently confused. If the data collected are on a nominal scale or if the variable is a **qualitative variable** (a categorical variable for which each value represents a discrete category), then a bar graph is most appropriate. A **bar graph** is a graphical representation of a frequency distribution in which vertical bars are centered above each category along the *x*-axis and are separated from each other by a space, indicating that the levels of the variable represent distinct, unrelated categories. If the variable is a **quantitative variable** (the scores represent a change in quantity) or if the data collected are ordinal, interval, or ratio in scale, then a histogram can be used.

A **histogram** is also a graphical representation of a frequency distribution in which vertical bars are centered above scores on the *x*-axis, but in a histogram the bars touch each other to indicate that the scores on the variable represent related, increasing values. In both a bar graph and a histogram, the height of each bar indicates the frequency for that level of the variable on the *x*-axis. The spaces between the bars on the bar graph indicate not only the qualitative differences among the categories but also that the order of the values of the

**qualitative variable** A categorical variable for which each value represents a discrete category.

**bar graph** A graphical representation of a frequency distribution in which vertical bars are centered above each category along the *x*-axis and are separated from each other by a space, indicating that the levels of the variable represent distinct, unrelated categories.

**quantitative variable** A variable for which the scores represent a change in quantity.

**histogram** A graphical representation of a frequency distribution in which vertical bars centered above scores on the *x*-axis touch each other to indicate that the scores on the variable represent related, increasing values.

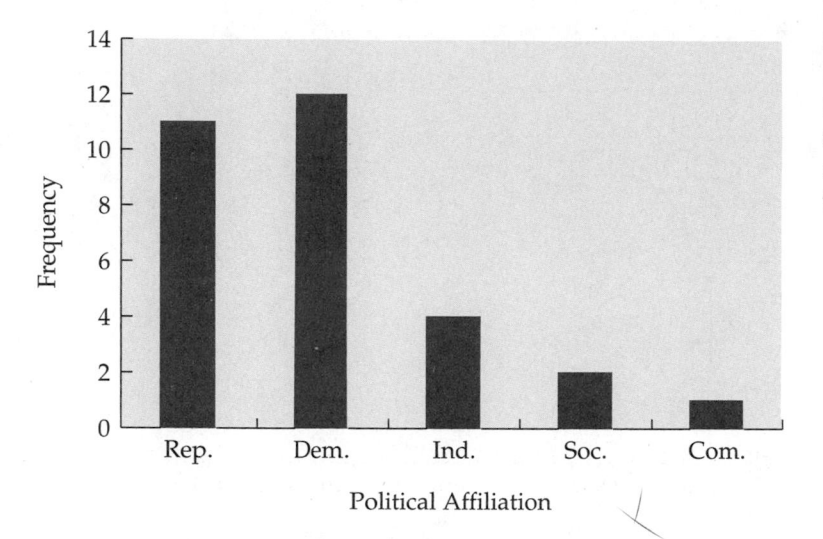

FIGURE 5.1
Bar graph repre-
senting political
affiliation for a
distribution of 30
individuals

variable on the *x*-axis is arbitrary. In other words, the categories on the *x*-axis in a bar graph can be placed in any order. The fact that the bars are contiguous in a histogram indicates not only the increasing quantity of the variable but also that the values of the variable have a definite order that cannot be changed.

A bar graph is illustrated in Figure 5.1. For a hypothetical distribution, the frequencies of individuals who affiliate with various political parties are indicated. Notice that the different political parties are listed on the *x*-axis, whereas frequency is recorded on the *y*-axis. Although the political parties are presented in a certain order, this order could be rearranged because the variable is qualitative.

Figure 5.2 illustrates a histogram. In this figure, the frequencies of intelligence test scores from a hypothetical distribution are indicated. A histogram is appropriate because the IQ score variable is quantitative. The values of the variable have a specific order that cannot be rearranged.

FIGURE 5.2
Histogram repre-
senting IQ score
data for 30
individuals

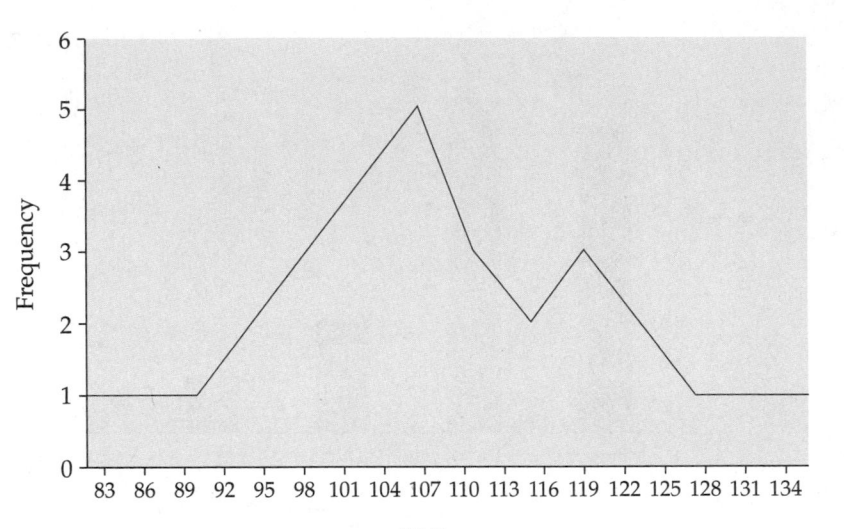

**FIGURE 5.3**
Frequency polygon
of IQ score data for
30 individuals

**frequency polygon** A line
graph of the frequencies of individual scores.

*Frequency Polygons.* We can also depict the data in a histogram as a **frequency polygon**—a line graph of the frequencies of individual scores or intervals. Again, scores (or intervals) are shown on the *x*-axis and frequencies on the *y*-axis. Once all the frequencies are plotted, the data points are connected. You can see the frequency polygon for the intelligence score data in Figure 5.3. Frequency polygons are appropriate when the variable is quantitative or the data are ordinal, interval, or ratio. In this respect, frequency polygons are similar to histograms. Frequency polygons are especially useful for continuous data (such as age, weight, or time) in which it is theoretically possible for values to fall anywhere along the continuum. For example, an individual may weigh 120.5 pounds or be 35.5 years old. Histograms are more appropriate when the data are discrete (measured in whole units)—for example, number of college classes taken or number of siblings.

## IN REVIEW    Data Organization

| | TYPES OF ORGANIZATIONAL TOOLS | | | |
| --- | --- | --- | --- | --- |
| | **Frequency Distribution** | **Bar Graph** | **Histogram** | **Frequency Polygon** |
| Description | A list of all scores occurring in the distribution along with the frequency of each | A pictorial graph with bars representing the frequency of occurrence of items for qualitative variables | A pictorial graph with bars representing the frequency of occurrence of items for quantitative variables | A line graph representing the frequency of occurrence of items for quantitative variables |
| Use with | Nominal, ordinal, interval, or ratio data | Nominal data | Typically ordinal, interval, or ratio data; most appropriate for discrete data | Typically ordinal, interval, or ratio data; most appropriate for continuous data |

CRITICAL
THINKING
CHECK
5.1

1. What do you think might be the advantage of a graphical representation of data over a frequency distribution?
2. A researcher observes driving behavior on a roadway, noting the gender of the drivers, the types of vehicle driven, and the speeds at which they are traveling. The researcher wants to organize the data in graphs but cannot remember when to use bar graphs, histograms, or frequency polygons. Which type of graph should be used to describe each variable?

# Descriptive Statistics

Organizing data into tables and graphs can help make a data set more meaningful. These methods, however, do not provide as much information as numerical measures. **Descriptive statistics** are numerical measures that describe a distribution by providing information on the central tendency of the distribution, the width of the distribution, and the distribution's shape.

**descriptive statistics**
Numerical measures that describe a distribution by providing information on the central tendency of the distribution, the width of the distribution, and the shape of the distribution.

## Measures of Central Tendency

A **measure of central tendency** is a representative number that characterizes the "middleness" of an entire set of data. The three measures of central tendency are the mean, the median, and the mode.

**measure of central tendency**
A number that characterizes the "middleness" of an entire distribution.

*Mean.* The most commonly used measure of central tendency is the **mean**—the arithmetic average of a group of scores. You are probably familiar with this idea. We can calculate the mean for our distribution of exam scores by adding all of the scores together and dividing the sum by the total number of scores. Mathematically, this is

**mean** A measure of central tendency; the arithmetic average of a distribution.

$$\mu = \frac{\Sigma X}{N}$$

where

$\mu$ (pronounced "mu") represents the symbol for the population mean;
$\Sigma$ represents the symbol for "the sum of";
$X$ represents the individual scores; and
$N$ represents the number of scores in the distribution.

To calculate the mean, then, we sum all of the $X$s, or scores, and divide by the total number of scores in the distribution ($N$). You may have also seen this formula represented as

$$\bar{X} = \frac{\Sigma X}{N}$$

In this formula, $\bar{X}$ represents the sample mean and $N$ represents the number of scores in the sample.

**TABLE 5.5** Frequency distribution of exam scores, including an *fX* column

| X | f | fX |
|---|---|---|
| 45 | 1 | 45 |
| 47 | 1 | 47 |
| 54 | 1 | 54 |
| 56 | 1 | 56 |
| 59 | 1 | 59 |
| 60 | 2 | 120 |
| 63 | 1 | 63 |
| 65 | 1 | 65 |
| 69 | 1 | 69 |
| 70 | 1 | 70 |
| 74 | 3 | 222 |
| 75 | 1 | 75 |
| 76 | 1 | 76 |
| 77 | 1 | 77 |
| 78 | 2 | 156 |
| 80 | 1 | 80 |
| 82 | 2 | 164 |
| 85 | 1 | 85 |
| 86 | 1 | 86 |
| 87 | 1 | 87 |
| 90 | 1 | 90 |
| 92 | 1 | 92 |
| 93 | 1 | 93 |
| 94 | 1 | 94 |
| 95 | 1 | 95 |
| | N = 30 | 2,220 = ΣX |

We can use either formula (they are the same) to calculate the mean for the distribution of exam scores. These scores are presented again in Table 5.5, along with a column showing the frequency (*f*) and another column showing the frequency of the score multiplied by the score (*f* times *X* or *fX*). The sum of all the values in the *fX* column is the sum of all the individual scores (ΣX). Using this sum in the formula for the mean, we have

$$\mu = \frac{\Sigma X}{N} = \frac{2,220}{30} = 74.00$$

The use of the mean is constrained by the nature of the data: The mean is appropriate for interval and ratio data, but not for ordinal or nominal data.

**TABLE 5.6    Yearly salaries for 25 employees**

| SALARY | FREQUENCY | fX |
|---|---|---|
| $  15,000 | 1 | 15,000 |
| 20,000 | 2 | 40,000 |
| 22,000 | 1 | 22,000 |
| 23,000 | 2 | 46,000 |
| 25,000 | 5 | 125,000 |
| 27,000 | 2 | 54,000 |
| 30,000 | 3 | 90,000 |
| 32,000 | 1 | 32,000 |
| 35,000 | 2 | 70,000 |
| 38,000 | 1 | 38,000 |
| 39,000 | 1 | 39,000 |
| 40,000 | 1 | 40,000 |
| 42,000 | 1 | 42,000 |
| 45,000 | 1 | 45,000 |
| 1,800,000 | 1 | 1,800,000 |
| | $N = 25$ | $\Sigma X = 2{,}498{,}000$ |

*Median.* Another measure of central tendency, the median, is used in situations in which the mean might not be representative of a distribution. Let's use a different distribution of scores to demonstrate when it is appropriate to use the median rather than the mean. Imagine that you are considering taking a job with a small computer company. When you interview for the position, the owner of the company informs you that the mean salary for employees at the company is approximately $100,000 and that the company has 25 employees. Most people would view this as good news. Having learned in a statistics class that the mean might be influenced by extreme scores, however, you ask to see the distribution of the 25 salaries. The distribution is shown in Table 5.6. The calculation of the mean for this distribution is

$$\frac{\Sigma X}{N} = \frac{2{,}498{,}000}{25} = 99{,}920$$

Notice that, as claimed, the mean salary of company employees is very close to $100,000. Notice also, however, that the mean in this case is not very representative of central tendency, or "middleness." The mean is thrown off center or inflated by one extreme score of $1,800,000 (the salary of the company's owner, needless to say). This extremely high salary pulls the mean toward it and thus increases or inflates the mean. Thus, in distributions that have one or a few extreme scores (either high or low), the mean is not a good indicator of central tendency. In such cases, a better measure of central tendency is the median.

**median** A measure of central tendency; the middle score in a distribution after the scores have been arranged from highest to lowest or lowest to highest.

The **median** is the middle score in a distribution after the scores have been arranged from highest to lowest or lowest to highest. The distribution of salaries in Table 5.6 is already ordered from lowest to highest. To determine the median, we simply have to find the middle score. In this situation, with 25 scores, that is the 13th score. You can see that the median of the distribution is a salary of $27,000, which is far more representative of the central tendency for this distribution of salaries.

Why is the median not as influenced as the mean by extreme scores? Think about the calculation of each of these measures. When calculating the mean, we must add in the atypical income of $1,800,000, thus distorting the calculation. When determining the median, however, we do not consider the size of the $1,800,000 income; it is only a score at one end of the distribution whose numerical value does not have to be considered in order to locate the middle score in the distribution. The point to remember is that the median is not affected by extreme scores in a distribution because it is only a positional value. The mean is affected because its value is determined by a calculation that has to include the extreme values.

In the salary example, the distribution has an odd number of scores ($N = 25$). Thus, the median is an actual score in the distribution (the 13th score). In distributions that have an even number of observations, the median is calculated by averaging the two middle scores. In other words, we determine the middle point between the two middle scores. Look back at the distribution of exam scores in Table 5.5. This distribution has 30 scores. The median is the average of the 15th and 16th scores (the two middle scores). Thus, the median is 75.5—not an actual score in the distribution, but the middle point nonetheless. Notice that in this distribution, the median (75.5) is very close to the mean (74.00). Why are they so similar? Because this distribution contains no extreme scores; both the mean and the median are representative of the central tendency of the distribution.

Like the mean, the median can be used with ratio and interval data and is inappropriate for use with nominal data, but unlike the mean, the median can be used with most ordinal data. In other words, it is appropriate to report the median for a distribution of ranked scores.

**mode** A measure of central tendency; the score in a distribution that occurs with the greatest frequency.

*Mode.* The third measure of central tendency is the **mode**—the score in a distribution that occurs with the greatest frequency. In the distribution of exam scores, the mode is 74 (similar to the mean and median). In the distribution of salaries, the mode is $25,000 (similar to the median, but not the mean). In some distributions, all scores occur with equal frequency; such a distribution has no mode. In other distributions, several scores occur with equal frequency. Thus, a distribution may have two modes (bimodal), three modes (trimodal), or even more. The mode is the only indicator of central tendency that can be used with nominal data. Although it can also be used with ordinal, interval, or ratio data, the mean and median are more reliable indicators of the central tendency of a distribution, and the mode is seldom used.

| Measures of Central Tendency | | | IN REVIEW |
|---|---|---|---|
| **TYPES OF CENTRAL TENDENCY MEASURES** | | | |
| | **Mean** | **Median** | **Mode** |
| Definition | The arithmetic average | The middle score in a distribution of scores organized from highest to lowest or lowest to highest | The score occurring with greatest frequency |
| Use with | Interval and ratio data | Ordinal, interval, and ratio data | Nominal, ordinal, interval, or ratio data |
| Cautions | Not for use with distributions with a few extreme scores | | Not a reliable measure of central tendency |

1. In the example described in Critical Thinking Check 5.1, a researcher collected data on drivers' gender, type of vehicle, and speed of travel. What is an appropriate measure of central tendency to calculate for each type of data?
2. If one driver was traveling at 100 mph (25 mph faster than anyone else), which measure of central tendency would you recommend against using?

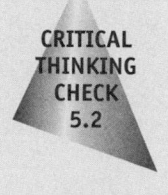

CRITICAL THINKING CHECK 5.2

## Measures of Variation

A measure of central tendency provides information about the "middleness" of a distribution of scores, but not about the width or spread of the distribution. To assess the width of a distribution, we need a measure of variation or dispersion. A **measure of variation** indicates the degree to which scores are either clustered or spread out in a distribution. As an illustration, consider the two very small distributions of exam scores shown in Table 5.7. Notice that the mean is the same for both distributions. If these data represented two very small classes of students, reporting that the two classes had the same mean on the exam might lead one to conclude that the classes performed essentially the same. Notice, however, how different the distributions are. Providing a measure of variation along with a measure of central tendency conveys the information that even though the distributions have the same mean, their spreads are very different.

We will discuss three measures of variation: the range, the average deviation, and the standard deviation. The range can be used with ordinal, interval, or ratio data; however, the standard deviation and average deviation are appropriate for only interval and ratio data.

**measure of variation**
A number that indicates the degree to which scores are either clustered or spread out in a distribution.

**TABLE 5.7  Two distributions of exam scores**

| CLASS 1 | CLASS 2 |
|---|---|
| 0 | 45 |
| 50 | 50 |
| 100 | 55 |
| $\Sigma = 150$ | $\Sigma = 150$ |
| $\mu = 50$ | $\mu = 50$ |

**range** A measure of variation; the difference between the
lowest and the highest scores
in a distribution.

*Range.* The simplest measure of variation is the **range**—the difference between
the lowest and the highest scores in a distribution. The range is usually
reported with the mean of the distribution. To find the range, we simply
subtract the lowest score from the highest score. In our hypothetical distributions of exam scores in Table 5.7, the range for Class 1 is 100 points, whereas
the range for Class 2 is 10 points. Thus, the range provides some information
concerning the difference in the spreads of the distributions. In this simple
measure of variation, however, only the highest and lowest scores enter the
calculation, and all other scores are ignored. For example, in the distribution
of 30 exam scores in Table 5.5, only 2 of the 30 scores are used in calculating
the range (95−45 = 50). Thus, the range is easily distorted by one unusually
high or low score in a distribution.

*Average Deviation and Standard Deviation.* More sophisticated measures
of variation use all of the scores in the distribution in their calculation. The
most commonly used measure of variation is the *standard deviation*. Most
people have heard this term before and may even have calculated a standard
deviation if they have taken a statistics class. However, many people who
know how to calculate a standard deviation do not really appreciate the
information it provides.

To begin, let's think about what the phrase *standard deviation* means.
Other words that might be substituted for the word *standard* include *average*,
*normal*, and *usual*. The word *deviation* means to *diverge, move away from*, or
*digress*. Putting these terms together, we see that the standard deviation
means the average movement away from something. But what? It is the
average movement away from the center of the distribution—the mean.

**standard deviation** A
measure of variation; the average difference between the
scores in the distribution and
the mean or central point of the
distribution, or more precisely,
the square root of the average
squared deviation from the
mean.

The **standard deviation,** then, is the average distance of all the scores in
the distribution from the mean or central point of the distribution—or, as
we will see shortly, the square root of the average squared deviation from the
mean. Think about how we would calculate the average distance of all the
scores from the mean of the distribution. First, we would have to determine
how far each score is from the mean; this is the deviation, or difference,
score. Then, we would have to average these scores. This is the basic idea
behind calculating the standard deviation.

The data in Table 5.5 are presented again in Table 5.8. Let's use these data
to calculate the average distance from the mean. We begin with a calculation
that is slightly simpler than the standard deviation, known as the *average
deviation*. The **average deviation** is essentially what the name implies—the
average distance of all the scores from the mean of the distribution.
Referring to Table 5.8, you can see that we begin by determining how much
each score deviates from the mean, or

**average deviation** An alternative measure of variation that,
like the standard deviation,
indicates the average difference
between the scores in a distribution and the mean of the
distribution.

$$X - \mu$$

Then we need to sum the deviation scores. Notice, however, that if we were
to sum these scores, they would add to zero. Therefore, we first take the
absolute value of the deviation scores (the distance from the mean, irrespec-
tive of direction), as shown in the third column of Table 5.8. The fourth column in the table shows the frequency with which each score appears in the

**TABLE 5.8** Calculations for the sum of the absolute values of the deviation scores ($\mu = 74$)

| X | $X - \mu$ | $|X - \mu|$ | f | $f|X - \mu|$ |
|---|---|---|---|---|
| 45 | −29.00 | 29.00 | 1 | 29.00 |
| 47 | −27.00 | 27.00 | 1 | 27.00 |
| 54 | −20.00 | 20.00 | 1 | 20.00 |
| 56 | −18.00 | 18.00 | 1 | 18.00 |
| 59 | −15.00 | 15.00 | 1 | 15.00 |
| 60 | −14.00 | 14.00 | 2 | 28.00 |
| 63 | −11.00 | 11.00 | 1 | 11.00 |
| 65 | −9.00 | 9.00 | 1 | 9.00 |
| 69 | −5.00 | 5.00 | 1 | 5.00 |
| 70 | −4.00 | 4.00 | 1 | 4.00 |
| 74 | 0.00 | 0.00 | 3 | 0.00 |
| 75 | 1.00 | 1.00 | 1 | 1.00 |
| 76 | 2.00 | 2.00 | 1 | 2.00 |
| 77 | 3.00 | 3.00 | 1 | 3.00 |
| 78 | 4.00 | 4.00 | 2 | 8.00 |
| 80 | 6.00 | 6.00 | 1 | 6.00 |
| 82 | 8.00 | 8.00 | 2 | 16.00 |
| 85 | 11.00 | 11.00 | 1 | 11.00 |
| 86 | 12.00 | 12.00 | 1 | 12.00 |
| 87 | 13.00 | 13.00 | 1 | 13.00 |
| 90 | 16.00 | 16.00 | 1 | 16.00 |
| 92 | 18.00 | 18.00 | 1 | 18.00 |
| 93 | 19.00 | 19.00 | 1 | 19.00 |
| 94 | 20.00 | 20.00 | 1 | 20.00 |
| 95 | 21.00 | 21.00 | 1 | 21.00 |
| | | | $N = 30$ | $332.00 = \Sigma|X - \mu|$ |

distribution, and the last column shows the frequency multiplied by the absolute value of the deviation score. To calculate the average deviation, we sum the absolute value of each deviation score (weighted by its frequency):

$$\Sigma|X - \mu|$$

Then we divide the sum by the total number of scores to find the average deviation:

$$AD = \frac{\Sigma|X - \mu|}{N}$$

Using the data from Table 5.8, we can calculate the average deviation as follows:

$$AD = \frac{\Sigma|X-\mu|}{N} = \frac{332}{30} = 11.07$$

For the exam score distribution, the scores fall an average of 11.07 points from the mean of 74.00.

Although the average deviation is fairly easy to compute, it is not as useful as the standard deviation because, as we will see in later chapters, the standard deviation is used in many other statistical procedures.

The standard deviation is very similar to the average deviation. The only difference is that rather than taking the absolute value of the deviation scores, we use another method to "get rid of" the negative deviation scores—we square them. This procedure is illustrated in Table 5.9. Notice that this table

**TABLE 5.9    Calculations for the sum of the squared deviation scores**

| X | $X-\mu$ | $(X-\mu)^2$ | f | $f(X-\mu)^2$ |
|---|---|---|---|---|
| 45 | −29.00 | 841.00 | 1 | 841.00 |
| 47 | −27.00 | 729.00 | 1 | 729.00 |
| 54 | −20.00 | 400.00 | 1 | 400.00 |
| 56 | −18.00 | 324.00 | 1 | 324.00 |
| 59 | −15.00 | 225.00 | 1 | 225.00 |
| 60 | −14.00 | 196.00 | 2 | 392.00 |
| 63 | −11.00 | 121.00 | 1 | 121.00 |
| 65 | −9.00 | 81.00 | 1 | 81.00 |
| 69 | −5.00 | 25.00 | 1 | 25.00 |
| 70 | −4.00 | 16.00 | 1 | 16.00 |
| 74 | 0.00 | 0.00 | 3 | 0.00 |
| 75 | 1.00 | 1.00 | 1 | 1.00 |
| 76 | 2.00 | 4.00 | 1 | 4.00 |
| 77 | 3.00 | 9.00 | 1 | 9.00 |
| 78 | 4.00 | 16.00 | 2 | 32.00 |
| 80 | 6.00 | 36.00 | 1 | 36.00 |
| 82 | 8.00 | 64.00 | 2 | 128.00 |
| 85 | 11.00 | 121.00 | 1 | 121.00 |
| 86 | 12.00 | 144.00 | 1 | 144.00 |
| 87 | 13.00 | 169.00 | 1 | 169.00 |
| 90 | 16.00 | 256.00 | 1 | 256.00 |
| 92 | 18.00 | 324.00 | 1 | 324.00 |
| 93 | 19.00 | 361.00 | 1 | 361.00 |
| 94 | 20.00 | 400.00 | 1 | 400.00 |
| 95 | 21.00 | 441.00 | 1 | 441.00 |
| | | | $N=30$ | $5,580.00 = \Sigma(X-\mu)^2$ |

is very similar to Table 5.8. It includes the distribution of exam scores, the deviation scores, the squared deviation scores, the score frequencies, and the product of each squared deviation and its frequency. The formula for the standard deviation is

$$\sigma = \sqrt{\frac{\Sigma(X-\mu)^2}{N}}$$

This formula represents the standard deviation for a population. The symbol for the population standard deviation is $\sigma$ (pronounced "sigma"). To derive the standard deviation for a sample, the calculation is the same, but the symbols differ. We will discuss this later in the chapter.

Notice that the formula for $\sigma$ is similar to that for the average deviation. We determine the deviation scores, square the deviation scores, sum the squared deviation scores, and divide by the number of scores in the distribution. Last, we take the square root of that number. Why? Squaring the deviation scores has inflated them. We now need to bring the squared deviation scores back to the same level of measurement as the mean so that the standard deviation is measured on the same scale as the mean.

Now, using the sum of the squared deviation scores (5,580.00) from Table 5.9, we can calculate the standard deviation:

$$\sigma = \sqrt{\frac{\Sigma(X-\mu)^2}{N}} = \sqrt{\frac{5,580.00}{30}} = \sqrt{186.00} = 13.64$$

We can compare this number with the average deviation calculated on the same data ($AD = 11.07$). The standard deviation tells us that the exam scores fall an average of 13.64 points from the mean of 74.00. The standard deviation is slightly larger than the average deviation of 11.07 and will always be larger whenever both of these measures of variation are calculated on the same distribution of scores. Can you see why? It is because we are squaring the deviation scores and thus giving more weight to those that are farther from the mean of the distribution. The scores that are lowest and highest have the largest deviation scores; squaring them exaggerates the difference. When all of the squared deviation scores are summed, these large scores necessarily lead to a larger numerator and, even after we divide by $N$ and take the square root, result in a larger number than what we find for the average deviation.

If you have taken a statistics class, you may have used the "raw-score (or computational) formula" to calculate the standard deviation. The raw-score formula is shown in Table 5.10, where it is used to calculate the standard deviation for the same distribution of exam scores. The numerator represents an algebraic transformation from the original formula that is somewhat shorter to use. Although the raw-score formula is slightly easier to use, it is more difficult to equate this formula with what the standard deviation actually is—the average deviation (or distance) from the mean for all the scores in the distribution. Thus, I prefer the definitional formula because it allows you not only to calculate the statistic but also to understand it better.

As mentioned previously, the formula for the standard deviation for a sample ($S$) differs from the formula for the standard deviation for a

**TABLE 5.10   Standard deviation raw-score formula**

$$\sigma = \sqrt{\frac{\Sigma X^2 - \frac{(\Sigma X)^2}{N}}{N}} = \sqrt{\frac{169,860 - \frac{(2,220)^2}{30}}{30}} = \sqrt{\frac{169,860 - \frac{4,928,400}{30}}{30}}$$

$$= \sqrt{\frac{169,860 - 164,280}{30}} = \sqrt{\frac{5,580}{30}} = \sqrt{186} = 13.64$$

population ($\sigma$) only in the symbols used to represent each term. The formula for a sample is

$$S = \sqrt{\frac{\Sigma(X - \bar{X})^2}{N}}$$

where

$X$ = each individual score
$\bar{X}$ = sample mean
$N$ = number of scores in the distribution
$S$ = sample standard deviation

Note that the main difference is in the symbol for the mean ($\bar{X}$ rather than $\mu$). This difference reflects the symbols for the population mean versus the sample mean. However, the calculation is exactly the same as for $\sigma$. Thus, if we used the data set in Table 5.9 to calculate $S$, we would arrive at exactly the same answer that we got for $\sigma$, 13.64.

If, however, we are using sample data to *estimate* the population standard deviation, then the standard deviation formula must be slightly modified. The modification provides what is called an "unbiased estimator" of the population standard deviation based on sample data. The modified formula is

$$s = \sqrt{\frac{\Sigma(X - \bar{X})^2}{N-1}}$$

Notice that the symbol for the unbiased estimator of the population standard deviation is $s$ (lowercase), whereas the symbol for the sample standard deviation is $S$ (uppercase). The main difference, however, is the denominator—$N-1$ rather than $N$. The reason is that the standard deviation within a small sample may not be representative of the population; that is, there may not be as much variability in the sample as there actually is in the population. We therefore divide by $N-1$ because dividing by a smaller number increases the standard deviation and thus provides a better estimate of the population standard deviation.

We can use the formula for $s$ to calculate the standard deviation on the same set of exam score data. Before we even begin the calculation, we know that because we are dividing by a smaller number ($N-1$), $s$ should be larger than either $\sigma$ or $S$ (which were both 13.64). Normally we would not compute

$\sigma$, $S$, and $s$ on the same distribution of scores because $\sigma$ is the standard deviation for the population, $S$ is the standard deviation for a sample, and $s$ is the unbiased estimator of the population standard deviation based on sample data. I am doing so here simply to illustrate the difference in the formulas.

$$s = \sqrt{\frac{\Sigma(X-\bar{X})^2}{N-1}} = \sqrt{\frac{5,580.00}{30-1}} = \sqrt{\frac{5,580.00}{29}} = \sqrt{192.41379} = 13.87$$

Note that $s$ (13.87) is slightly larger than $\sigma$ and $S$ (13.64).

One final measure of variability is called the variance. The **variance** is equal to the standard deviation squared. Thus, the variance for a population is $\sigma^2$, for a sample is $S^2$, and for the unbiased estimator of the population $s^2$. Because the variance is not measured in the same level of measurement as the mean (it is the standard deviation squared), it is not as useful a descriptive statistic as the standard deviation. Thus, we will not discuss it in great detail here. We will see, however, that it is used in more advanced statistical procedures presented later in the text.

**variance** The standard deviation squared

The formulas for the average deviation, standard deviation, and variance all use the mean. Thus, it is appropriate to use these measures with interval or ratio data, but not with ordinal or nominal data.

## Measures of Variation                                                   IN REVIEW

| | TYPES OF VARIATION MEASURES | | |
| | Range | Average Deviation | Standard Deviation |
| --- | --- | --- | --- |
| Definition | The difference between the lowest and highest scores in the distribution | The average distance of the scores from the mean of the distribution | The square root of the average squared deviation from the mean of a distribution |
| Use With | Primarily interval and ratio data | Primarily interval and ratio data | Primarily interval and ratio data |
| Cautions | A simple measure that does not use all scores in the distribution in its calculation | A more sophisticated measure in which all scores are used, but it may not weight extreme scores adequately | The most sophisticated and most frequently used measure of variation |

1. For a distribution of scores, what information does a measure of variation add that a measure of central tendency does not convey?
2. Today's weather report included information on the normal rainfall for this time of year. The amount of rain that fell today was 1.5 inches above normal. To decide whether this is an abnormally high amount of rain, you need to know that the standard deviation for rainfall is 0.75 of an inch. What would you conclude about how normal the amount of rainfall was today? Would your conclusion be different if the standard deviation were 2 inches rather than 0.75 of an inch?

CRITICAL THINKING CHECK 5.3

FIGURE 5.4
A normal
distribution

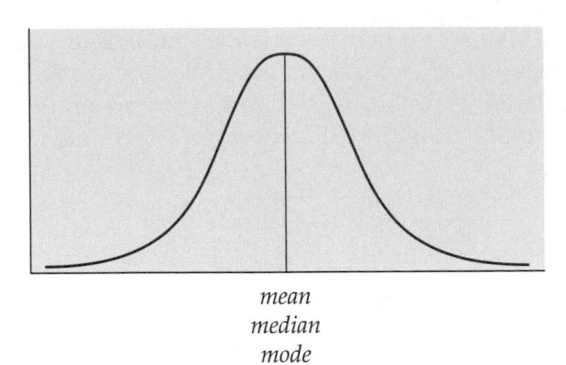

*mean*
*median*
*mode*

## Types of Distributions

In addition to knowing the central tendency and the width or spread of a distribution, it is important to know about the shape of the distribution.

*Normal Distributions.* When a distribution of scores is very large, it often tends to approximate a pattern called a *normal distribution*. When plotted as a frequency polygon, a normal distribution forms a symmetrical, bell-shaped pattern often called a **normal curve** (see Figure 5.4). We say that the pattern *approximates* a normal distribution because a true normal distribution is a theoretical construct not actually observed in the real world.

The **normal distribution** is a theoretical frequency distribution that has certain special characteristics. First, it is bell-shaped and symmetrical—the right half is a mirror image of the left half. Second, the mean, median, and mode are equal and are located at the center of the distribution. Third, the normal distribution is unimodal—it has only one mode. Fourth, most of the observations are clustered around the center of the distribution, with far fewer observations at the ends or "tails" of the distribution. Last, when standard deviations are plotted on the *x*-axis, the percentage of scores falling between the mean and any point on the *x*-axis is the same for all normal curves. This important property of the normal distribution will be discussed more fully later in the chapter.

*Kurtosis.* Although we typically think of the normal distribution as being similar to the curve depicted in Figure 5.4, there are variations in the shape of normal distributions. **Kurtosis** refers to how flat or peaked a normal distribution is. In other words, kurtosis refers to the degree of dispersion among the scores, or whether the distribution is tall and skinny or short and fat. The normal distribution depicted in Figure 5.4 is called mesokurtic—the term *meso* means middle. **Mesokurtic** curves have peaks of medium height and the distributions are moderate in breadth. Now look at the two distributions depicted in Figure 5.5. The normal distribution on the left is leptokurtic—the term *lepto* means thin. **Leptokurtic** curves are tall and thin, with only a few scores in the middle of the distribution having a high frequency. Last, see the curve on the right side of Figure 5.5. This is a platykurtic curve—*platy* means broad or flat. **Platykurtic** curves are short and more dispersed (broader).

**normal curve** A symmetrical, bell-shaped frequency polygon representing a normal distribution.

**normal distribution** A theoretical frequency distribution that has certain special characteristics.

**kurtosis** How flat or peaked a normal distribution is.

**mesokurtic** Normal curves that have peaks of medium height and distributions that are moderate in breadth.

**leptokurtic** Normal curves that are tall and thin, with only a few scores in the middle of the distribution having a high frequency.

**platykurtic** Normal curves that are short and more dispersed (broader).

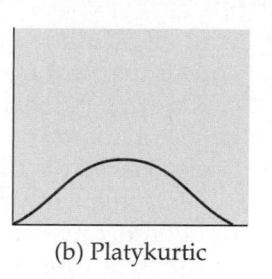

(a) Leptokurtic    (b) Platykurtic

**FIGURE 5.5**
**Types of distribu-tions: leptokurtic and platykurtic**

In a platykurtic curve, there are many scores around the middle score that all have a similar frequency.

*Positively Skewed Distributions.* Most distributions do not approximate a normal or bell-shaped curve. Instead they are skewed, or lopsided. In a skewed distribution, scores tend to cluster at one end or the other of the *x*-axis, with the tail of the distribution extending in the opposite direction. In a **positively skewed distribution,** the peak is to the left of the center point and the tail extends toward the right, or in the positive direction (see Figure 5.6).

Notice that what skews the distribution, or throws it off center, are the scores toward the right or positive direction. A few individuals have extremely high scores that pull the distribution in that direction. Notice also what this does to the mean, median, and mode. These three measures do not have the same value, nor are they all located at the center of the distribution as they are in a normal distribution. The mode—the score with the highest frequency—is the high point on the distribution. The median divides the distribution in half. The mean is pulled in the direction of the tail of the distribution; that is, the few extreme scores pull the mean toward them and inflate it.

*Negatively Skewed Distributions.* The opposite of a positively skewed distribution is a **negatively skewed distribution**—a distribution in which the peak is to the right of the center point and the tail extends toward the left, or in the negative direction. The term *negative* refers to the direction of the skew. As can be seen in Figure 5.6, in a negatively skewed distribution, the mean is pulled toward the left by the few extremely low scores in the distribution.

**positively skewed distribution** A distribution in which the peak is to the left of the center point and the tail extends toward the right, or in the positive direction.

**negatively skewed distribution** A distribution in which the peak is to the right of the center point and the tail extends toward the left, or in the negative direction.

 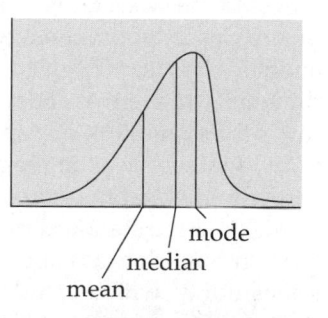

mode
median
mean

mode
median
mean

positively skewed distribution    negatively skewed distribution

**FIGURE 5.6**
**Positively and negatively skewed distributions**

As in all distributions, the median divides the distribution in half, and the mode is the most frequently occurring score in the distribution.

Knowing the shape of a distribution provides valuable information about the distribution. For example, would you prefer to have a negatively or positively skewed distribution of exam scores for an exam that you have taken? Students frequently answer that they would prefer a positively skewed distribution because they think the term *positive* means good. Keep in mind, though, that *positive* and *negative* describe the skew of the distribution, not whether the distribution is "good" or "bad." Assuming that the exam scores span the entire possible range (say, 0–100), you should prefer a negatively skewed distribution—meaning that most people have high scores and only a few have low scores.

Another example of the value of knowing the shape of a distribution is provided by Harvard paleontologist Stephen Jay Gould (1985). Gould was diagnosed in 1982 with a rare form of cancer. He immediately began researching the disease and learned that it was incurable and had a median mortality rate of only 8 months after discovery. Rather than immediately assuming that he would be dead in 8 months, Gould realized this meant that half of the patients lived longer than 8 months. Because he was diagnosed with the disease in its early stages and was receiving high-quality medical treatment, he reasoned that he could expect to be in the half of the distribution that lived beyond 8 months. The other piece of information that Gould found encouraging was the shape of the distribution. Look again at the two distributions in Figure 5.6 and decide which you would prefer in this situation. With a positively skewed distribution, the cases to the right of the median could stretch out for years; this is not true for a negatively skewed distribution. The distribution of life expectancy for Gould's disease was positively skewed, and Gould was obviously in the far right-hand tail of the distribution because he lived and remained professionally active for another 20 years.

## z-Scores

The descriptive statistics and types of distributions discussed so far are valuable for describing a sample or group of scores. Sometimes, however, we want information about a single score. For example, in our exam score distribution, we may want to know how one person's exam score compares with those of others in the class. Or we may want to know how an individual's exam score in one class, say psychology, compares with the same person's exam score in another class, say English. Because the two distributions of exam scores are different (different means and standard deviations), simply comparing the raw scores on the two exams does not provide this information. Let's say an individual who was in the psychology exam distribution used as an example earlier in the chapter scored 86 on the exam. Remember, the exam had a mean of 74.00 with a standard deviation ($S$) of 13.64. Assume that the same person took an English exam and made a score of 91, and that the English exam had a mean of 85 with a standard deviation of 9.58. On which exam did the student do better? Most people would immediately say the English exam because the score on this exam was higher. However, we are interested in how well this student did in comparison to everyone else who took the exams. In other words, how well did the individual do in comparison to those taking the psychology exam versus in comparison to those taking the English exam?

To answer this question, we need to convert the exam scores to a form we can use to make comparisons. A **z-score** or **standard score** is a measure of how many standard deviation units an individual raw score falls from the mean of the distribution. We can convert each exam score to a z-score and then compare the z-scores because they will be in the same unit of measurement. We can think of z-scores as a translation of raw scores into scores of the same language for comparative purposes. The formulas for a z-score transformation are

$$z = \frac{X - \bar{X}}{S}$$

and

$$z = \frac{X - \mu}{\sigma}$$

**z-score (standard score)**
A number that indicates how many standard deviation units a raw score is from the mean of a distribution.

where z is the symbol for the standard score. The difference between the two formulas is that the first is used when calculating a z-score for an individual in comparison to a sample, and the second is used when calculating a z-score for an individual in comparison to a population. Notice that the two formulas do exactly the same thing—indicate the number of standard deviations an individual score is from the mean of the distribution.

Conversion to a z-score is a statistical technique that is appropriate for use with data on an interval or ratio scale of measurement (scales for which means are calculated). Let's use the formula to calculate the z-scores for the previously mentioned student's psychology and English exam scores. The necessary information is summarized in Table 5.11.

To calculate the z-score for the English test, we first calculate the difference between the score and the mean, and then divide by the standard deviation. We use the same process to calculate the z-score for the psychology exam. These calculations are as follows:

$$z_{English} = \frac{X - \bar{X}}{S} = \frac{91 - 85}{9.58} = \frac{6}{9.58} = +0.626$$

$$z_{Psychology} = \frac{X - \bar{X}}{S} = \frac{86 - 74}{13.64} = \frac{12}{13.64} = +0.880$$

The individual's z-score for the English test is 0.626 standard deviation above the mean, and the z-score for the psychology test is 0.880 standard

**TABLE 5.11   Raw score ($X$), sample mean ($\bar{X}$), and standard deviation ($S$) for English and psychology exams**

|  | $X$ | $\bar{X}$ | $S$ |
|---|---|---|---|
| English | 91 | 85 | 9.58 |
| Psychology | 86 | 74 | 13.64 |

deviation above the mean. Thus, even though the student answered more questions correctly on the English exam (had a higher raw score) than on the psychology exam, the student performed better on the psychology exam relative to other students in the psychology class than on the English exam in comparison to other students in the English class.

The z-scores calculated in the previous example were both positive, indicating that the individual's scores were above the mean in both distributions. When a score is below the mean, the z-score is negative, indicating that the individual's score is lower than the mean of the distribution. Let's go over another example so that you can practice calculating both positive and negative z-scores.

Suppose you administered a test to a large sample of people and computed the mean and standard deviation of the raw scores, with the following results:

$$\bar{X} = 45$$
$$S = 4$$

Suppose also that four of the individuals who took the test had the following scores:

| Person | Score (X) |
|--------|-----------|
| Rich | 49 |
| Debbie | 45 |
| Pam | 41 |
| Henry | 39 |

Let's calculate the z-score equivalents for the raw scores of these individuals, beginning with Rich:

$$z_{Rich} = \frac{X_{Rich} - \bar{X}}{S} = \frac{49 - 45}{4} = \frac{4}{4} = +1$$

Notice that we substitute Rich's score ($X_{Rich}$) and then use the group mean ($\bar{X}$) and the group standard deviation ($S$). The positive sign ($+$) indicates that the z-score is positive, or above the mean. We find that Rich's score of 49 is 1 standard deviation above the group mean of 45.

Now let's calculate Debbie's z-score:

$$z_{Debbie} = \frac{X_{Debbie} - \bar{X}}{S} = \frac{45 - 45}{4} = \frac{0}{4} = 0$$

Debbie's score is the same as the mean of the distribution. Therefore, her z-score is 0, indicating that she scored neither above nor below the mean. Keep in mind that a z-score of 0 does not indicate a low score—it indicates a score right at the mean or average. See if you can calculate the z-scores for Pam and Henry on your own. Do you get $z_{Pam} = -1$ and $z_{Henry} = -1.5$? Good work!

In summary, the z-score tells whether an individual raw score is above the mean (a positive z-score) or below the mean (a negative z-score), and it tells how many standard deviations the raw score is above or below the mean. Thus, z-scores are a means of transforming raw scores to standard scores for purposes of comparison in both normal and skewed distributions.

## z-Scores, the Standard Normal Distribution, Probability, and Percentile Ranks

If the distribution of scores for which you are calculating transformations (z-scores) is normal (symmetrical and unimodal), then it is referred to as the **standard normal distribution**—a normal distribution with a mean of 0 and a standard deviation of 1. The standard normal distribution is actually a theoretical distribution defined by a specific mathematical formula. All other normal curves approximate the standard normal curve to a greater or lesser extent. The value of the standard normal curve is that it provides information about the proportion of scores that are higher or lower than any other score in the distribution. A researcher can also determine the probability of occurrence of a score that is higher or lower than any other score in the distribution. The proportions under the standard normal curve hold for only normal distributions—not for skewed distributions. Even though z-scores may be calculated on skewed distributions, the proportions under the standard normal curve do not hold for skewed distributions.

Take a look at Figure 5.7, which represents the area under the standard normal curve in terms of standard deviations. Based on this figure, we see that approximately 68% of the observations in the distribution fall between −1.0 and +1.0 standard deviations from the mean. This approximate percentage holds for all data that are normally distributed. Notice also that approximately 13.5% of the observations fall between −1.0 and −2.0 and another 13.5% between +1.0 and +2.0, and that approximately 2% of the observations fall between −2.0 and −3.0 and another 2% between +2.0 and +3.0. Only 0.13% of the scores are beyond a z-score of ±3.0. If we sum the percentages in Figure 5.7, we have 100%—all of the area under the curve, representing everybody in the distribution. If we sum half of the curve, we have 50%—half of the distribution.

With a curve that is normal or symmetrical, the mean, median, and mode are all at the center point; thus, 50% of the scores are above this number and 50% are below this number. This property helps us determine probabilities. A **probability** is defined as the expected relative frequency of a particular outcome. The outcome could be the result of an experiment or any situation

**standard normal distribution** A normal distribution with a mean of 0 and a standard deviation of 1.

**probability** The expected relative frequency of a particular outcome.

**FIGURE 5.7**
**Area under the standard normal curve**

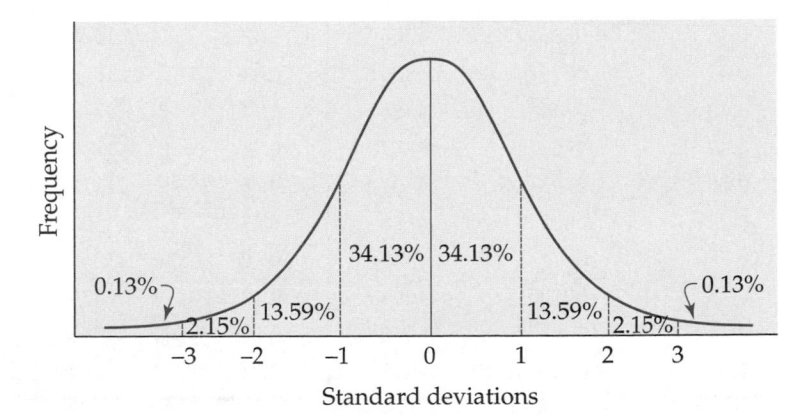

in which the result is not known in advance. For example, from the normal curve, what is the probability of randomly choosing a score that falls above the mean? The probability is equal to the proportion of scores in that area, or .50. Figure 5.7 gives a rough estimate of the proportions under the normal curve. Luckily for us, statisticians have determined the exact proportion of scores that will fall between any two z-scores—for example, between z-scores of +1.30 and +1.39. This information is provided in Table A.2 in Appendix A at the back of the text. A small portion of this table is shown in Table 5.12.

TABLE 5.12    A portion of the Standard Normal Curve table

| | AREAS UNDER THE STANDARD NORMAL CURVE FOR VALUES OF Z | | | | |
|---|---|---|---|---|---|
| z | Area Between Mean and z | Area Beyond z | z | Area Between Mean and z | Area Beyond z |
| 0.00 | .0000 | .5000 | 0.26 | .1026 | .3974 |
| 0.01 | .0040 | .4960 | 0.27 | .1064 | .3936 |
| 0.02 | .0080 | .4920 | 0.28 | .1103 | .3897 |
| 0.03 | .0120 | .4880 | 0.29 | .1141 | .3859 |
| 0.04 | .0160 | .4840 | 0.30 | .1179 | .3821 |
| 0.05 | .0199 | .4801 | 0.31 | .1217 | .3783 |
| 0.06 | .0239 | .4761 | 0.32 | .1255 | .3745 |
| 0.07 | .0279 | .4721 | 0.33 | .1293 | .3707 |
| 0.08 | .0319 | .4681 | 0.34 | .1331 | .3669 |
| 0.09 | .0359 | .4641 | 0.35 | .1368 | .3632 |
| 0.10 | .0398 | .4602 | 0.36 | .1406 | .3594 |
| 0.11 | .0438 | .4562 | 0.37 | .1443 | .3557 |
| 0.12 | .0478 | .4522 | 0.38 | .1480 | .3520 |
| 0.13 | .0517 | .4483 | 0.39 | .1517 | .3483 |
| 0.14 | .0557 | .4443 | 0.40 | .1554 | .3446 |
| 0.15 | .0596 | .4404 | 0.41 | .1591 | .3409 |
| 0.16 | .0636 | .4364 | 0.42 | .1628 | .3372 |
| 0.17 | .0675 | .4325 | 0.43 | .1664 | .3336 |
| 0.18 | .0714 | .4286 | 0.44 | .1770 | .3300 |
| 0.19 | .0753 | .4247 | 0.45 | .1736 | .3264 |
| 0.20 | .0793 | .4207 | 0.46 | .1772 | .3228 |
| 0.21 | .0832 | .4268 | 0.47 | .1808 | .3192 |
| 0.22 | .0871 | .4129 | 0.48 | .1844 | .3156 |
| 0.23 | .0910 | .4090 | 0.49 | .1879 | .3121 |
| 0.24 | .0948 | .4052 | 0.50 | .1915 | .3085 |
| 0.25 | .0987 | .4013 | 0.51 | .1950 | .3050 |

*(continued)*

**TABLE 5.12    A portion of the Standard Normal Curve table** *(continued)*

AREAS UNDER THE STANDARD NORMAL CURVE FOR VALUES OF $z$

| $z$ | Area Between Mean and $z$ | Area Beyond $z$ | $z$ | Area Between Mean and $z$ | Area Beyond $z$ |
|---|---|---|---|---|---|
| 0.52 | .1985 | .3015 | 0.68 | .2517 | .2483 |
| 0.53 | .2019 | .2981 | 0.69 | .2549 | .2451 |
| 0.54 | .2054 | .2946 | 0.70 | .2580 | .2420 |
| 0.55 | .2088 | .2912 | 0.71 | .2611 | .2389 |
| 0.56 | .2123 | .2877 | 0.72 | .2642 | .2358 |
| 0.57 | .2157 | .2843 | 0.73 | .2673 | .2327 |
| 0.58 | .2190 | .2810 | 0.74 | .2704 | .2296 |
| 0.59 | .2224 | .2776 | 0.75 | .2734 | .2266 |
| 0.60 | .2257 | .2743 | 0.76 | .2764 | .2236 |
| 0.61 | .2291 | .2709 | 0.77 | .2794 | .2206 |
| 0.62 | .2324 | .2676 | 0.78 | .2823 | .2177 |
| 0.63 | .2357 | .2643 | 0.79 | .2852 | .2148 |
| 0.64 | .2389 | .2611 | 0.80 | .2881 | .2119 |
| 0.65 | .2422 | .2578 | 0.81 | .2910 | .2090 |
| 0.66 | .2454 | .2546 | 0.82 | .2939 | .2061 |
| 0.67 | .2486 | .2514 | 0.83 | .2967 | .2033 |

The columns across the top of the table are labeled $z$, Area Between Mean and $z$, and Area Beyond $z$. There are also pictorial representations. The $z$ column refers to the $z$-score with which you are working. The Area Between Mean and $z$ is the area under the curve between the mean of the distribution (where $z = 0$) and the $z$-score with which you are working—that is, the proportion of scores between the mean and the $z$-score in column 1. The Area Beyond $z$ is the area under the curve from the $z$-score out to the tail end of the distribution. Notice that the entire table goes out to only a $z$-score of 4.00 because it is very unusual for a normally distributed population of scores to include scores larger than this. Notice also that the table provides information about only positive $z$-scores, even though the distribution of scores actually ranges from approximately $-4.00$ to $+4.00$. Because the distribution is symmetrical, the areas between the mean and $z$ and beyond the $z$-scores are the same whether the $z$-score is positive or negative.

Let's use some of the examples from earlier in the chapter to illustrate how to use these proportions under the normal curve. Assume that the test data described earlier (with $\bar{X} = 45$ and $S = 4$) are normally distributed, so that the proportions under the normal curve apply. We calculated $z$-scores for four individuals who took the test—Rich, Debbie, Pam, and Henry. Let's use Rich's $z$-score to illustrate the use of the normal curve table. Rich had a $z$-score equal to $+1.00$—1 standard deviation above the mean. I like to begin

FIGURE 5.8
Standard normal
curve with *z*-score
of +1.00 indicated

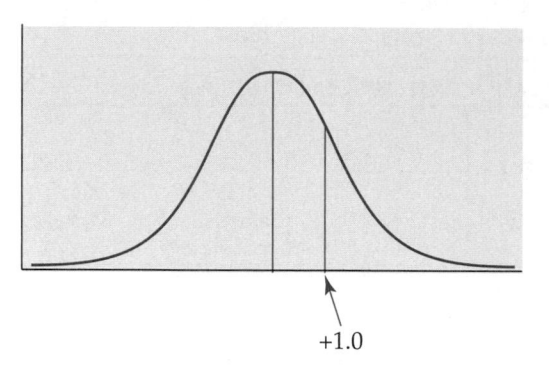

+1.0

by drawing a picture representing the normal curve and then sketch in the *z*-score with which I am working. Thus, Figure 5.8 shows a representation of the normal curve, with a line drawn at a *z*-score of +1.00.

Before we look at the proportions under the normal curve, we can begin to gather information from this picture. We see that Rich's score is above the mean. Using the information from Figure 5.7, we see that roughly 34% of the area under the curve falls between his *z*-score and the mean of the distribution, whereas approximately 16% of the area falls beyond his *z*-score. Using Table A.2 to get the exact proportions, we find (from the Area Beyond *z* column) that the proportion of scores falling above the *z*-score of +1.0 is .1587. This number can be interpreted to mean that 15.87% of the scores were higher than Rich's score, or that the probability of randomly choosing a score with a *z*-score greater than +1.00 is .1587. To determine the proportion of scores falling below Rich's *z*-score, we need to use the Area Between Mean and *z* column and add .50 to this proportion. According to the table, the area between the mean and the *z*-score is .3413. Why must we add .50 to this number? The table provides information about only one side of the standard normal distribution. We must add in the proportion of scores represented by the other half of the distribution, which is always .50. Look back at Figure 5.8. Rich's score is +1.00 above the mean, which means that he did better than those between the mean and his *z*-score (.3413) and also better than everybody below the mean (.50). Hence, 84.13% of the scores are below Rich's score.

Let's use Debbie's *z*-score to further illustrate the use of the *z* table. Debbie's *z*-score was 0.00—right at the mean. We know that if she is at the mean ($z = 0$), then half of the distribution is below her score and half is above her score. Does this match what Table A.2 tells us? According to the table, .5000 (50%) of scores are beyond this *z*-score, so the information in the table does agree with our reasoning.

Using the *z* table with Pam and Henry's *z*-scores is slightly more difficult because both Pam and Henry had negative *z*-scores. Remember, Pam had a *z*-score of −1.00, and Henry had a *z*-score of −1.50. Let's begin by drawing a normal distribution and then marking where both Pam and Henry fall on that distribution. This information is represented in Figure 5.9.

Before even looking at the *z* table, let's think about what we know from Figure 5.9. We know that both Pam and Henry scored below the mean, that they are in the lower 50% of the class, that the proportion of people scoring

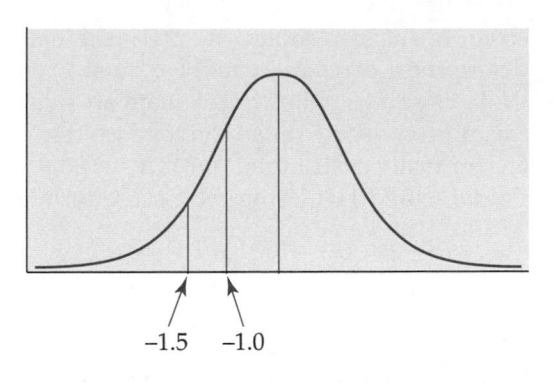

**FIGURE 5.9**
**Standard normal curve with *z*-scores of −1.0 and −1.5 indicated**

−1.5  −1.0

higher than them is greater than .50, and that the proportion of people scoring lower than them is less than .50. Keep this overview in mind as we use Table A.2. Using Pam's *z*-score of −1.0, see if you can determine the proportion of scores lying above and below her score. If you determine that the proportion of scores above hers is .8413 and that the proportion below is .1587, then you are correct! Why is the proportion above her score .8413? We begin by looking in the table at a *z*-score of 1.0 (remember, there are no negatives in the table). The Area Between Mean and *z* is .3413, and then we need to add the proportion of .50 in the top half of the curve. Adding these two proportions, we get .8413. The proportion below her score is represented by the area in the tail, the Area Beyond *z* of .1587. Note that the proportion above and the proportion below should sum to 1.0 (.8413 + .1587 = 1.0). Now see if you can compute the proportions above and below Henry's *z*-score of −1.5. Do you get .9332 above his score and .0668 below his score? Good work!

Now let's try something slightly more difficult by determining the proportion of scores that fall between Henry's *z*-score of −1.5 and Pam's *z*-score of −1.0. Referring back to Figure 5.9, we see that we are targeting the area between the two *z*-scores represented on the curve. Again, we use Table A.2 to provide the proportions. The area between the mean and Henry's *z*-score of −1.5 is .4332, whereas the area between the mean and Pam's *z*-score of −1.0 is .3413. To determine the proportion of scores that fall between the two, we subtract .3413 from .4332, obtaining a difference of .0919. This result is illustrated in Figure 5.10.

The standard normal curve can also be used to determine an individual's **percentile rank**—the percentage of scores equal to or below the given raw

**percentile rank** A score that indicates the percentage of people who scored at or below a given raw score.

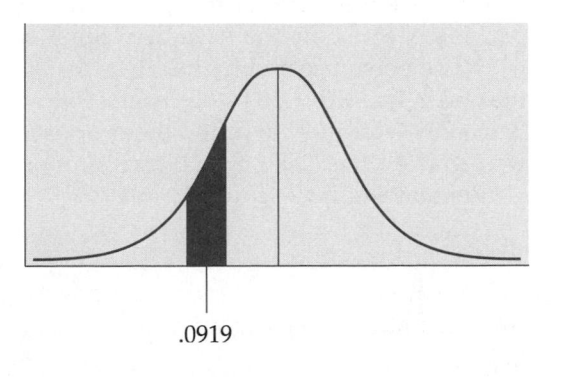

**FIGURE 5.10**
**Proportion of scores between *z*-scores of −1.0 and −1.5**

.0919

score, or the percentage of scores the individual's score is higher than. To determine a percentile rank, we must first know the individual's z-score.

Let's say we want to calculate an individual's percentile rank based on this person's score on an intelligence test. The scores on the intelligence test are normally distributed, with $\mu = 100$ and $\sigma = 15$. Let's suppose the individual scored 119. Using the z-score formula, we have

$$z = \frac{X - \mu}{\sigma} = \frac{119 - 100}{15} = \frac{19}{15} = +1.27$$

Looking at the Area Between Mean and z column for a score of $+1.27$, we find the proportion .3980. To determine all of the area below the score, we must add .50 to .3980; the entire area below a z-score of $+1.27$, then, is .8980. If we multiply this proportion by 100, we can describe the intelligence test score of 119 as being in the 89.80th percentile.

To practice calculating percentile ranks, see if you can calculate the percentile ranks for Rich, Debbie, Pam, and Henry from our previous examples. You should arrive at the following percentile ranks.

| Person | Score (X) | z-Score | Percentile Rank |
|--------|-----------|---------|-----------------|
| Rich | 49 | +1.0 | 84.13th |
| Debbie | 45 | 0.0 | 50.00th |
| Pam | 41 | −1.0 | 15.87th |
| Henry | 39 | −1.50 | 6.68th |

Students most often have trouble determining percentile ranks from negative z-scores. Always draw a figure representing the normal curve with the z-scores indicated; this will help you determine which column to use from the z table. When the z-score is negative, the proportion of the curve representing those who scored lower than the individual (the percentile rank) is found in the Area Beyond z. When the z-score is positive, the proportion of the curve representing those who scored lower than the individual (the percentile rank) is found by using the Area Between Mean and z and adding .50 (the bottom half of the distribution) to this proportion.

What if we know an individual's percentile rank and want to determine this person's raw score? Let's say we know that an individual scored at the 75th percentile on the intelligence test described previously. We want to know what score has 75% of the scores below it. We begin by using Table A.2 to determine the z-score for this percentile rank. If the individual is at the 75th percentile, we know the Area Between Mean and z is .25. How do we know this? The person scored higher than the 50% of people in the bottom half of the curve, and $.75 - .50 = .25$. Therefore, we look in the column labeled Area Between Mean and z and find the proportion that is closest to .25. The closest we come to .25 is .2486, which corresponds to a z-score of 0.67.

Remember, the z-score formula is

$$z = \frac{X - \mu}{\sigma}$$

We know that $\mu = 100$ and $\sigma = 15$, and now we know that $z = 0.67$. What we want to find is the person's raw score, X. So, let's solve the equation for X:

$$z = \frac{X - \mu}{\sigma}$$
$$z\sigma = X - \mu$$
$$z\sigma + \mu = X$$

Substituting the values we have for $\mu$, $\sigma$, and $z$, we find

$$X = z\sigma + \mu$$
$$X = 0.67(15) + 100$$
$$= 10.05 + 100$$
$$= 110.05$$

As you can see, the standard normal distribution is useful for determining how a single score compares with a population or sample of scores and also for determining probabilities and percentile ranks. Knowing how to use the proportions under the standard normal curve increases the information we can derive from a single score.

| Distributions | | | IN REVIEW |
|---|---|---|---|
| | **TYPES OF DISTRIBUTIONS** | | |
| | **Normal** | **Positively Skewed** | **Negatively Skewed** |
| Description | A symmetrical, bell shaped, unimodal curve | A lopsided curve with a tail extending toward the positive or right side | A lopsided curve with a tail extending toward the negative or left side |
| $z$-score transformations applicable? | Yes | Yes | Yes |
| Percentile ranks and proportions under standard normal curve applicable? | Yes | No | No |

1. On one graph draw two distributions with the same mean but different standard deviations. Draw a second set of distributions on another graph with different means but the same standard deviation.
2. Why is it not possible to use the proportions under the standard normal curve with skewed distributions?
3. Students in the psychology department at General State University consume an average of 7 sodas per day with a standard deviation of 2.5. The distribution is normal.
   a. What proportion of students consume an amount equal to or greater than 6 sodas per day?
   b. What proportion of students consume an amount equal to or greater than 8.5 sodas per day?
   c. What proportion of students consume an amount between 6 and 8.5 sodas per day?
   d. What is the percentile rank for an individual who consumes 5.5 sodas per day?
   e. How many sodas would an individual at the 75th percentile drink per day?

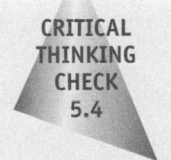

CRITICAL THINKING CHECK 5.4

4. Based on what you have learned about z-scores, percentile ranks, and the area under the standard normal curve, fill in the missing information in the following table representing performance on an exam that is normally distributed with $\bar{X} = 55$ and $S = 6$.

|       | X  | z-Score | Percentile Rank |
|-------|-----|---------|-----------------|
| John  | 63  |         |                 |
| Ray   |     | -1.66   |                 |
| Betty |     |         | 72              |

# Summary

In this chapter, we discussed data organization and descriptive statistics. We presented several methods of data organization, including a frequency distribution, a bar graph, a histogram, and a frequency polygon. We also discussed the types of data appropriate for each of these methods.

Descriptive statistics that summarize a large data set include measures of central tendency (mean, median, and mode) and measures of variation (range, average deviation, and standard deviation). These statistics provide information about the central tendency or "middleness" of a distribution of scores and about the spread or width of the distribution, respectively. A distribution may be normal, positively skewed, or negatively skewed. The shape of the distribution affects the relationships among the mean, median, and mode.

Finally, we discussed the calculation of z-score transformations as a means of standardizing raw scores for comparative purposes. Although z-scores may be used with either normal or skewed distributions, the proportions under the standard normal curve can be applied only to data that approximate a normal distribution.

Based on our discussion of these descriptive methods, you can begin to organize and summarize a large data set and also compare the scores of individuals to the entire sample or population.

# KEY TERMS

| | | |
|---|---|---|
| frequency distribution | mean | kurtosis |
| class interval frequency distribution | median | mesokurtic |
| | mode | leptokurtic |
| qualitative variable | measure of variation | platykurtic |
| bar graph | range | positively skewed distribution |
| quantitative variable | standard deviation | negatively skewed distribution |
| histogram | average deviation | z-score (standard score) |
| frequency polygon | variance | standard normal distribution |
| descriptive statistics | normal curve | probability |
| measure of central tendency | normal distribution | percentile rank |

# CHAPTER EXERCISES

(Answers to odd-numbered exercises appear in Appendix C.)

1. The following data represent a distribution of speeds (in miles per hour) at which individuals were traveling on a highway.

| 64 | 80 | 64 | 70 |
|----|----|----|----|
| 76 | 79 | 67 | 72 |
| 65 | 73 | 68 | 65 |
| 67 | 65 | 70 | 62 |
| 67 | 68 | 65 | 64 |

Organize these data into a frequency distribution with frequency ($f$) and relative frequency ($rf$) columns.

2. Organize the data in Exercise 1 into a class interval frequency distribution, using 10 intervals, with frequency ($f$) and relative frequency ($rf$) columns.

3. Which type of figure should be used to represent the data in Exercise 1—a bar graph, histogram, or frequency polygon? Why? Draw the appropriate figure for these data.

4. Calculate the mean, median, and mode for the data set in Exercise 1. Is the distribution normal or skewed? If it is skewed, what type of skew is it? Which measure of central tendency is most appropriate for this distribution, and why?

5. Calculate the mean, median, and mode for the following four distributions (a–d):

| a | b | c | d |
|----|----|----|----|
| 2 | 1 | 1 | 2 |
| 2 | 2 | 3 | 3 |
| 4 | 3 | 3 | 4 |
| 5 | 4 | 3 | 5 |
| 8 | 4 | 5 | 6 |
| 9 | 5 | 5 | 6 |
| 10 | 5 | 8 | 6 |
| 11 | 5 | 8 | 7 |
| 11 | 6 | 8 | 8 |
| 11 | 6 | 9 | 8 |
| | 8 | 10 | |
| | 9 | 11 | |

6. Calculate the range, average deviation, and standard deviation for the following five distributions:
   a. 1, 2, 3, 4, 5, 6, 7, 8, 9
   b. −4, −3, −2, −1, 0, 1, 2, 3, 4
   c. 10, 20, 30, 40, 50, 60, 70, 80, 90
   d. 0.1, 0.2, 0.3, 0.4, 0.5, 0.6, 0.7, 0.8, 0.9
   e. 100, 200, 300, 400, 500, 600, 700, 800, 900

7. The results of a recent survey indicate that the average new car costs $23,000 with a standard deviation of $3,500. The prices of cars are normally distributed.
   a. If someone bought a car for $32,000, what proportion of cars cost an equal amount or more than this?
   b. If someone bought a car for $16,000, what proportion of cars cost an equal amount or more than this?
   c. At what percentile rank is a car that sold for $30,000?
   d. At what percentile rank is a car that sold for $12,000?
   e. What proportion of cars were sold for an amount between $12,000 and $30,000?
   f. For what price would a car at the 16th percentile have sold?

8. A survey of college students was conducted during final exam week to assess the number of cups of coffee consumed each day. The mean number of cups was 5 with a standard deviation of 1.5 cups. The distribution was normal.
   a. What proportion of students drank 7 or more cups of coffee per day?
   b. What proportion of students drank 4 or more cups of coffee per day?
   c. What proportion of students drank between 2 and 7 cups of coffee per day?
   d. How many cups of coffee would an individual at the 60th percentile rank drink?
   e. What is the percentile rank for an individual who drinks 4 cups of coffee a day?
   f. What is the percentile rank for an individual who drinks 7.5 cups of coffee a day?

9. Fill in the missing information in the following table representing performance on an exam that is normally distributed with $\bar{X} = 75$ and $S = 9$.

| | X | z-Score | Percentile Rank |
|-------|----|---------|-----------------|
| Ken | 73 | — | — |
| Drew | — | 1.55 | — |
| Cecil | — | — | 82 |

## CRITICAL THINKING CHECK ANSWERS

### 5.1

1. One advantage is that it is easier to "see" the data set in a graphical representation. A picture makes it easier to determine where the majority of the scores are in the distribution. A frequency distribution requires more reading before a judgment can be made about the shape of the distribution.

2. Gender and type of vehicle driven are qualitative variables, measured on a nominal scale; thus, a bar graph should be used. The speed at which the drivers are traveling is a quantitative variable, measured on a ratio scale. Either a histogram or a frequency polygon could be used. A frequency polygon might be better because of the continuous nature of the variable.

### 5.2

1. Because gender and type of vehicle driven are nominal data, only the mode can be determined; it is inappropriate to use the median or the mean with these data. Speed of travel is ratio in scale, so the mean, median, or mode could be used. Both the mean and median are better indicators of central tendency than the mode. If the distribution is skewed, however, the mean should not be used.

2. In this case, the mean should not be used because of the single outlier (extreme score) in the distribution.

### 5.3

1. A measure of variation tells us about the spread of the distribution. In other words, are the scores clustered closely about the mean, or are they spread over a wide range?

2. The amount of rainfall for the indicated day is 2 standard deviations above the mean. I would therefore conclude that the amount of rainfall was well above average. If the standard deviation were 2 rather than 0.75, then the amount of rainfall for the indicated day would be less than

1 standard deviation above the mean—above average, but not greatly so.

### 5.4

1.

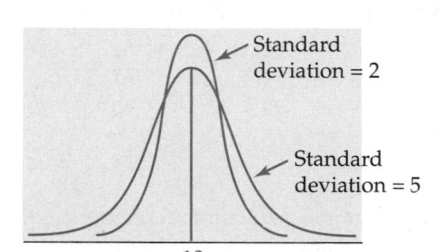

Same Mean, Different Standard Deviations

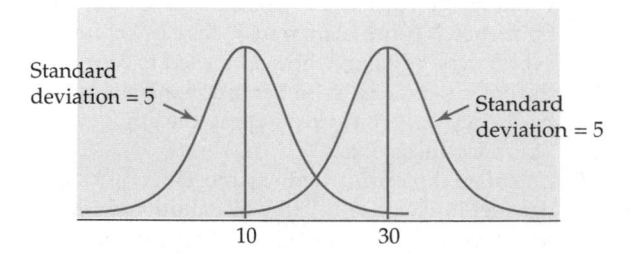

Same Standard Deviation, Different Means

2. The proportions hold for only normal (symmetrical) distributions where one half of the distribution is equal to the other. If the distribution were skewed, this condition would be violated.

3. a. .6554
   b. .2743
   c. .3811
   d. 27.43rd
   e. 8.68

4.

|  | X | z-Score | Percentile Rank |
|---|---|---|---|
| John | 63 | +1.33 | 90.82 |
| Ray | 45.05 | −1.66 | 4.85 |
| Betty | 58.48 | +.58 | 72 |

## WEB RESOURCES

Check your knowledge of the content in this chapter by taking the practice quiz at www.Wadsworth.com. Or, for step-by-step practice and information, check out the Statistics and Research Methods Workshops at http://psychology.wadsworth.com/workshops.

## STATISTICAL SOFTWARE RESOURCES

For hands-on experience using the statistical software to conduct the analyses described in this chapter, see Chapter 1 ("Describing Data, Frequency Distributions, and Making Charts") in *The Excel Statistics Companion* by Kenneth M. Rosenberg (Belmont, CA: Wadsworth, 2003).

# 6 Correlational Methods and Statistics

I n this chapter, we will discuss correlational research methods and correlational statistics. As a research method, correlational designs allow us to describe the relationship between two measured variables. A correlation coefficient (descriptive statistic) aids us by assigning a numerical value to the observed relationship. We will begin with a discussion of how to conduct correlational research, the magnitude and the direction of correlations, and graphical representations of correlations. We will then turn to special considerations when interpreting correlations, how to use correlations for predictive purposes, and how to calculate correlation coefficients. Last, we will discuss an advanced correlational technique, regression analysis.

# Conducting Correlational Research

When conducting correlational studies, researchers determine whether two naturally occurring variables (for example, height and weight, or smoking and cancer) are related to each other. Such studies assess whether the variables are "co-related" in some way: Do people who are taller tend to weigh more, or do those who smoke tend to have a higher incidence of cancer? As we saw in Chapter 1, the correlational method is a type of nonexperimental method that describes the relationship between two measured variables. In addition to describing a relationship, correlations allow us to make predictions from one variable to another. If two variables are correlated, we can predict from one variable to the other with a certain degree of accuracy. For example, knowing that height and weight are correlated allows us to estimate, within a certain range, an individual's weight based on knowing that person's height.

Correlational studies are conducted for a variety of reasons. Sometimes it is impractical or ethically impossible to do an experimental study. For example, it would be ethically impossible to manipulate smoking and assess whether it causes cancer in humans. How would you, as a participant in an experiment, like to be randomly assigned to the smoking condition and be told that you have to smoke a pack of cigarettes a day? Obviously, this is not a viable experiment, so one means of assessing the relationship between smoking and cancer is through correlational studies. In this type of study, we can examine people who have already chosen to smoke and assess the degree of relationship between smoking and cancer.

Sometimes researchers choose to conduct correlational research because they are interested in measuring many variables and assessing the relationships between them. For example, they might measure various aspects of personality and assess the relationship between dimensions of personality.

# Magnitude, Scatterplots, and Types of Relationships

Correlations vary in their **magnitude**—the strength of the relationship. Sometimes there is no relationship between variables, or the relationship may be weak; other relationships are moderate or strong. Correlations

**magnitude** An indication of the strength of the relationship between two variables.

**TABLE 6.1   Estimates for weak, moderate, and strong correlation coefficients**

| CORRELATION COEFFICIENT | STRENGTH OF RELATIONSHIP |
| --- | --- |
| ±.70–1.00 | Strong |
| ±.30–.69 | Moderate |
| ±.00–.29 | None (.00) to weak |

can also be represented graphically, in a scatterplot or scattergram. In addition, relationships are of different types—positive, negative, none, or curvilinear.

## Magnitude

The magnitude or strength of a relationship is determined by the correlation coefficient describing the relationship. As we saw in Chapter 3, a correlation coefficient is a measure of the degree of relationship between two variables; it can vary between –1.00 and +1.00. The stronger the relationship between the variables, the closer the coefficient is to either –1.00 or +1.00. The weaker the relationship between the variables, the closer the coefficient is to 0. You may recall from Chapter 3 that we typically discuss correlation coefficients as assessing a strong, moderate, or weak relationship, or no relationship. Table 6.1 provides general guidelines for assessing the magnitude of a relationship, but these do not necessarily hold for all variables and all relationships.

A correlation coefficient of either –1.00 or +1.00 indicates a perfect correlation—the strongest relationship possible. For example, if height and weight were perfectly correlated (+1.00) in a group of 20 people, this would mean that the person with the highest weight was also the tallest person, the person with the second-highest weight was the second-tallest person, and so on down the line. If height and weight had a perfect negative correlation (–1.00), this would mean that the person with the highest weight was the shortest, the person with the second-highest weight was the second shortest, and so on. It is very unlikely that you will ever observe a perfect correlation between two variables, but you may observe some very strong relationships between variables (±.70–.99). Whereas a correlation coefficient of ±1.00 represents a perfect relationship, a coefficient of 0.00 indicates no relationship between the variables.

## Scatterplots

**scatterplot** A figure that graphically represents the relationship between two variables.

A **scatterplot** or scattergram, a figure showing the relationship between two variables, graphically represents a correlation coefficient. Figure 6.1 presents a scatterplot of the height and weight relationship for 20 adults.

In a scatterplot, two measurements are represented for each participant by the placement of a marker. In Figure 6.1, the horizontal *x*-axis shows the participant's weight, and the vertical *y*-axis shows height. The two variables

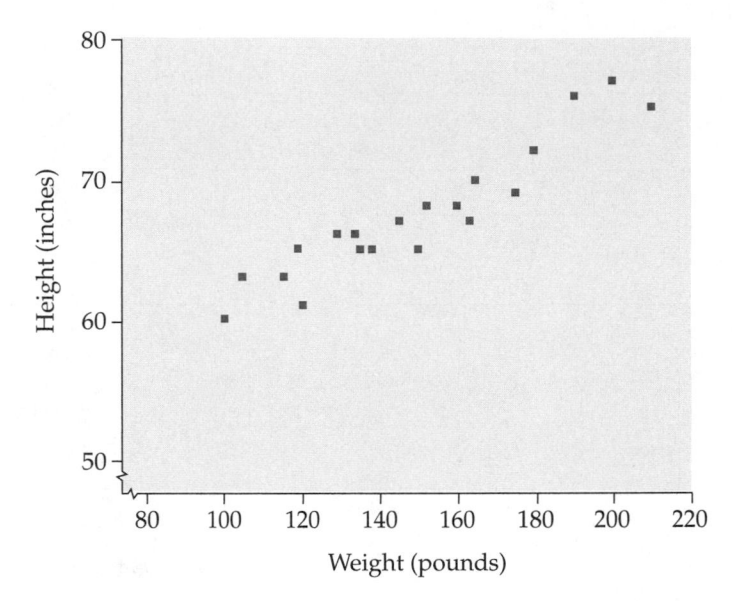

FIGURE 6.1
Scatterplot for
height and weight

could be reversed on the axes, and it would make no difference in the scatterplot. This scatterplot shows an upward trend, and the points cluster in a linear fashion. The stronger the correlation, the more tightly the data points cluster around an imaginary line through their center. When there is a perfect correlation ($\pm 1.00$), the data points all fall on a straight line. In general, a scatterplot may show four basic patterns: a positive relationship, a negative relationship, no relationship, or a curvilinear relationship.

## Positive Relationships

The relationship represented in Figure 6.2a shows a positive correlation, one in which there is a direct relationship between the two variables: This means that an increase in one variable is related to an increase in the other, and a decrease in one is related to a decrease in the other. Notice that this scatterplot is similar to the one in Figure 6.1. The majority of the data points fall along an upward angle (from the lower left corner to the upper right corner). In this example, a person who scored low on one variable also scored low on the other; an individual with a mediocre score on one variable had a mediocre score on the other; and those who scored high on one variable also scored high on the other. In other words, an increase (decrease) in one variable is accompanied by an increase (decrease) in the other variable—as variable $x$ increases (or decreases), variable $y$ does the same. If the data in Figure 6.2a represented height and weight measurements, we could say that those who are taller also tend to weigh more, whereas those who are shorter tend to weigh less. Notice also that the relationship is linear: We could draw a straight line representing the relationship between the variables, and the data points would all fall fairly close to that line.

FIGURE 6.2
Possible types of cor-
relational relation-
ships: (a) positive;
(b) negative;
(c) none;
(d) curvilinear

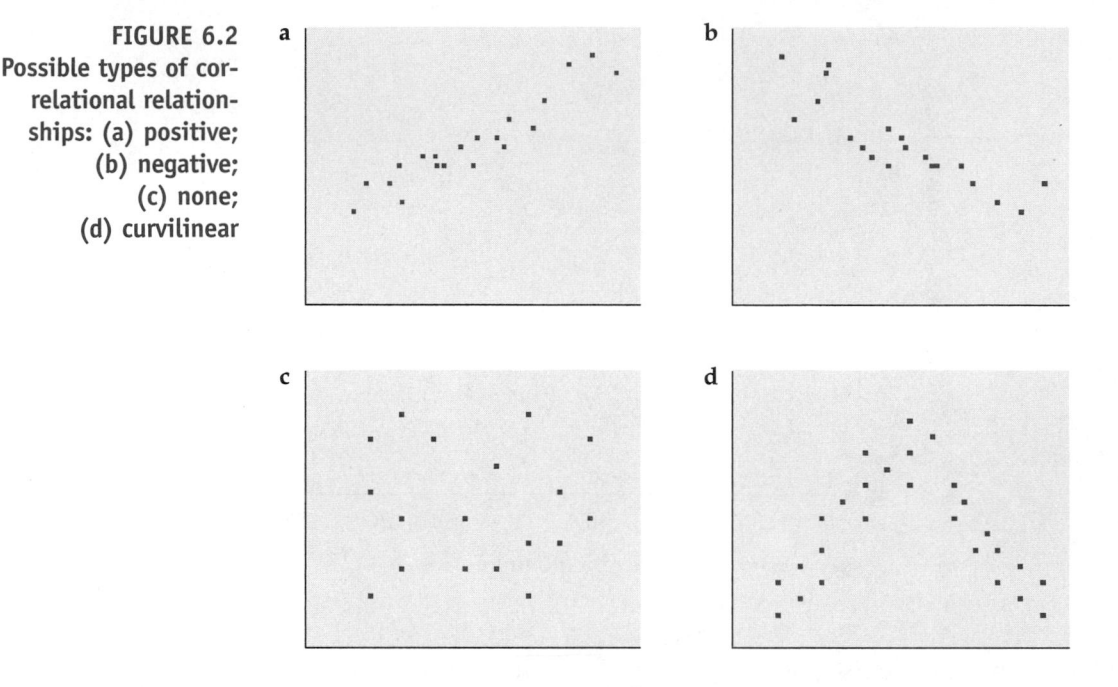

## Negative Relationships

Figure 6.2b represents a negative relationship between two variables. Notice that in this scatterplot the data points extend from the upper left to the lower right. This negative correlation indicates that an increase in one variable is accompanied by a *decrease* in the other variable. This represents an inverse relationship: The more of variable $x$ that we have, the less we have of variable $y$. Assume that this scatterplot represents the relationship between age and eyesight. As age increases, the ability to see clearly tends to decrease—a negative relationship.

## No Relationship

As shown in Figure 6.2c, it is also possible to observe no meaningful relationship between two variables. In this scatterplot, the data points are scattered in a random fashion. As you would expect, the correlation coefficient for these data is very close to 0 (–.09).

## Curvilinear Relationships

A correlation coefficient of 0 indicates no meaningful relationship between two variables. However, it is also possible for a correlation coefficient of 0 to indicate a curvilinear relationship, as illustrated in Figure 6.2d. Imagine that this graph represents the relationship between psychological arousal (the $x$-axis) and performance (the $y$-axis). Individuals perform better when they are moderately aroused than when arousal is either very low or very high. The correlation coefficient for these data is also very close to 0 (–.05). Think about why this would be so. The strong positive relationship depicted in the left half of the graph essentially cancels out the strong negative relationship in the right half of the graph. Although the correlation coefficient is very low, we would not conclude that there is no relationship between the two variables. As the figure shows, the variables are very strongly related to each other in a curvilinear manner—the points are tightly clustered in an inverted U shape.

Correlation coefficients tell us about only linear relationships. Thus, even though there is a strong relationship between the two variables in Figure 6.2d, the correlation coefficient does not indicate this because the relationship is curvilinear. For this reason, it is important to examine a scatterplot of the data in addition to calculating a correlation coefficient. Alternative statistics (beyond the scope of this text) can be used to assess the degree of curvilinear relationship between two variables.

| Relationships Between Variables | | | IN REVIEW |
|---|---|---|---|
| **TYPES OF RELATIONSHIPS** | | | |
| | **Positive** | **Negative** | **None** | **Curvilinear** |
| Description of Relationship | Variables increase and decrease together | As one variable increases, the other decreases—an inverse relationship | Variables are unrelated and do not move together in any way | Variables increase together up to a point and then as one continues to increase, the other decreases |
| Description of Scatterplot | Data points are clustered in a linear pattern extending from lower left to upper right | Data points are clustered in a linear pattern extending from upper left to lower right | There is no pattern to the data points—they are scattered all over the graph | Data points are clustered in a curved linear pattern forming a U shape or an inverted U shape |
| Example of Variables Related in This Manner | Smoking and cancer | Mountain elevation and temperature | Intelligence and weight | Memory and age |

1. Which of the following correlation coefficients represents the weakest relationship between two variables?

   −.59    +.10    −1.00    +.76

2. Explain why a correlation coefficient of 0.00 or close to 0.00 may not mean that there is no relationship between the variables.

3. Draw a scatterplot representing a strong negative correlation between depression and self-esteem. Make sure you label the axes correctly.

CRITICAL THINKING CHECK 6.1

# Misinterpreting Correlations

Correlational data are frequently misinterpreted, especially when presented by newspaper reporters, talk show hosts, and television newscasters. Here we discuss some of the most common problems in interpreting correlations. Remember, a correlation simply indicates that there is a weak, moderate, or strong relationship (either positive or negative), or no relationship, between two variables.

## The Assumptions of Causality and Directionality

The most common error made when interpreting correlations is assuming that the relationship observed is causal in nature—that a change in variable A *causes* a change in variable B. Correlations simply identify relationships— they do not indicate causality. For example, I recently saw a commercial on television sponsored by an organization promoting literacy. The statement was made at the beginning of the commercial that a strong positive correlation has been observed between illiteracy and drug use in high school students (those high on the illiteracy variable also tended to be high on the drug use variable). The commercial concluded with a statement like "Let's stop drug use in high school students by making sure they can all read." Can you see the flaw in this conclusion? The commercial did not air for very long, and I suspect someone pointed out the error in the conclusion.

**causality** The assumption that a correlation indicates a causal relationship between the two variables.

**directionality** The inference made with respect to the direction of a causal relationship between two variables.

This commercial made the error of assuming causality and also the error of assuming directionality. **Causality** refers to the assumption that the correlation indicates a causal relationship between two variables, whereas **directionality** refers to the inference made with respect to the direction of a causal relationship between two variables. For example, the commercial assumed that illiteracy was causing drug use; it claimed that if illiteracy were lowered, then drug use would be lowered also. As previously discussed, a correlation between two variables indicates only that they are related—they vary together. Although it is possible that one variable causes changes in the other, we cannot draw this conclusion from correlational data.

Research on smoking and cancer illustrates this limitation of correlational data. For research with humans, we have only correlational data indicating a positive correlation between smoking and cancer. Because these data are correlational, we cannot conclude that there is a causal relationship. In this situation, it is probable that the relationship is causal. However, based solely on correlational data, we cannot conclude that it is causal, nor can we assume the direction of the relationship. For example, the tobacco industry could argue that, yes, there is a correlation between smoking and cancer, but maybe cancer causes smoking—maybe those individuals predisposed to cancer are more attracted to smoking cigarettes. Experimental data based on research with laboratory animals do indicate that smoking causes cancer. The tobacco industry, however, frequently denies that this research is applicable to humans and continues to insist that no research has produced evidence of a causal link between smoking and cancer in humans.

A classic example of the assumption of causality and directionality with correlational data occurred when researchers observed a strong negative correlation between eye movement patterns and reading ability in children. Poorer readers tended to make more erratic eye movements, more movements from right to left, and more stops per line of text. Based on this correlation, some researchers assumed causality and directionality: They assumed that poor oculomotor skills caused poor reading and proposed programs for "eye movement training." Many elementary school students who were poor readers spent time in such training, supposedly developing oculomotor skills in the hope that this would improve their reading ability. Experimental research later provided evidence that the relationship between eye movement patterns and reading ability is indeed causal, but that the direction of the relationship is the reverse—poor reading causes more erratic eye movements! Children who are having trouble reading need to go back over the information more and stop and think about it more. When children improve their reading skills (improve recognition and comprehension), their eye movements become smoother (Olson & Forsberg, 1993). Because of the errors of assuming causality and directionality, many children never received the appropriate training to improve their reading ability.

## The Third-Variable Problem

When we interpret a correlation, it is also important to remember that although the correlation between the variables may be very strong, it may also be that the relationship is the result of some third variable that influences both of the measured variables. The **third-variable problem** results when a correlation between two variables is dependent on another (third) variable.

A good example of the third-variable problem is a well-cited study conducted by social scientists and physicians in Taiwan (Li, 1975). The researchers attempted to identify the variables that best predicted the use of birth control—a question of interest to the researchers because of overpopulation problems in Taiwan. They collected data on various behavioral and environmental variables and found that the variable most strongly correlated with contraceptive use was the number of electrical appliances (yes, electrical appliances—stereos, toasters, televisions, and so on) in the home. If we take this correlation at face value, it means that individuals with more electrical appliances tend to use contraceptives more, whereas those with fewer electrical appliances tend to use contraceptives less.

It should be obvious to you that this is not a causal relationship (buying electrical appliances does not cause individuals to use birth control, nor does using birth control cause individuals to buy electrical appliances). Thus, we probably do not have to worry about people assuming either causality or directionality when interpreting this correlation. The problem here is a third variable. In other words, the relationship between electrical appliances and contraceptive use is not really a meaningful relationship—other variables are tying these two together. Can you think of other dimensions on which individuals who use contraceptives and who have a large number of appliances might be similar? If you thought of education, you are beginning to

**third-variable problem** The problem of a correlation between two variables being dependent on another (third) variable.

understand what is meant by third variables. Individuals with a higher education level tend to be better informed about contraceptives and also tend to have a higher socioeconomic status (they get better-paying jobs). Their higher socioeconomic status allows them to buy more "things," including electrical appliances.

It is possible statistically to determine the effects of a third variable by using a correlational procedure known as *partial correlation*. **Partial correlation** involves measuring all three variables and then statistically removing the effect of the third variable from the correlation of the remaining two variables. If the third variable (in this case, education) is responsible for the relationship between electrical appliances and contraceptive use, then the correlation should disappear when the effect of education is removed, or partialed out.

**partial correlation** A correlational technique that involves measuring three variables and then statistically removing the effect of the third variable from the correlation of the remaining two variables.

## Restrictive Range

**restrictive range** A variable that is truncated and has limited variability.

The idea behind measuring a correlation is that we assess the degree of relationship between two variables. Variables, by definition, must vary. When a variable is truncated, we say that it has a **restrictive range**—the variable does not vary enough. Look at Figure 6.3a, which represents a scatterplot of SAT scores and college GPAs for a group of students. SAT scores and GPAs are positively correlated. Neither of these variables is restricted in range (for this group of students, SAT scores vary from 400 to 1600 and GPAs vary from 1.5 to 4.0), so we have the opportunity to observe a relationship between the variables. Now look at Figure 6.3b, which represents the correlation between the same two variables, except that here the range on the SAT variable is restricted to those who scored between 1000 and 1150. The variable has been restricted or truncated and does not "vary" very much. As a result, the

**FIGURE 6.3**
**Restricted range and correlation**

opportunity to observe a correlation has been diminished. Even if there were a strong relationship between these variables, we could not observe it because of the restricted range of one of the variables. Thus, when interpreting and using correlations, beware of variables with restricted ranges.

## Curvilinear Relationships

Curvilinear relationships and the caution in interpreting them were discussed earlier in the chapter. Remember, correlations are a measure of linear relationships. When a relationship is curvilinear, a correlation coefficient does not adequately indicate the degree of relationship between the variables. If necessary, look back over the previous section on curvilinear relationships to refresh your memory concerning them.

| Misinterpreting Correlations | | | IN REVIEW |
|---|---|---|---|
| **TYPES OF MISINTERPRETATIONS** | | | |
| | Causality and Directionality | Third Variable | Restrictive Range | Curvilinear Relationship |
| Description of Misinterpretation | We assume the correlation is causal and that one variable causes changes in the other | Other variables are responsible for the observed correlation | One or more of the variables is truncated or restricted and the opportunity to observe a relationship is minimized | The curved nature of the relationship decreases the observed correlation coefficient |
| Examples | We assume that smoking causes cancer or that illiteracy causes drug abuse because a correlation has been observed | We find a strong positive relationship between birth control and number of electrical appliances | If SAT scores are restricted (limited in range), the correlation between SAT and GPA appears to decrease | As arousal increases, performance increases up to a point; as arousal continues to increase, performance decreases |

1. I have recently observed a strong negative correlation between depression and self-esteem. Explain what this means. Make sure you avoid the misinterpretations described in the text.
2. General State University recently investigated the relationship between SAT scores and GPAs (at graduation) for its senior class. They were surprised to find a weak correlation between these two variables. They know they have a grade inflation problem (the whole senior class graduated with GPAs of 3.0 or higher), but they are unsure how this might help account for the low correlation observed. Can you explain?

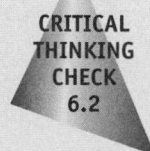

CRITICAL THINKING CHECK 6.2

# Prediction and Correlation

Correlation coefficients not only describe the relationship between variables; they also allow us to make predictions from one variable to another. Correlations between variables indicate that when one variable is present at a certain level, the other also tends to be present at a certain level. Notice the wording used. The statement is qualified by the phrase "tends to." We are not saying that a prediction is guaranteed or that the relationship is causal—but simply that the variables seem to occur together at specific levels. Think about some of the examples used in this chapter. Height and weight are positively correlated. One is not causing the other; nor can we predict exactly what an individual's weight will be based on height (or vice versa). But because the two variables are correlated, we can predict with a certain degree of accuracy what an individual's approximate weight might be if we know the person's height.

Let's take another example. We have noted a correlation between SAT scores and college freshman GPAs. Think about what the purpose of the SAT is. College admissions committees use the test as part of the admissions procedure. Why? Because there is a positive correlation between SAT scores and college GPAs. Individuals who score high on the SAT tend to have higher college freshman GPAs; those who score lower on the SAT tend to have lower college freshman GPAs. This means that knowing students' SAT scores can help predict, with a certain degree of accuracy, their freshman GPAs and thus their potential for success in college. At this point, some of you are probably saying "But that isn't true for me—I scored poorly (or very well) on the SAT and my GPA is great (or not so good)." Statistics tell us only what the trend is for most people in the population or sample. There will always be outliers—the few individuals who do not fit the trend. Most people, however, are going to fit the pattern.

Think about another example. We know there is a strong positive correlation between smoking and cancer, but you may know someone who has smoked for 30 or 40 years and does not have cancer or any other health problems. Does this one individual negate the fact that there is a strong relationship between smoking and cancer? No. To claim that it does would be a classic **person-who argument**—arguing that a well-established statistical trend is invalid because we know a "person who" went against the trend (Stanovich, 2001). A counterexample does not change the fact of a strong statistical relationship between the variables and that you are increasing your chance of getting cancer if you smoke. Because of the correlation between the variables, we can predict (with a fairly high degree of accuracy) who might get cancer based on knowing a person's smoking history.

**person-who argument**
Arguing that a well-established statistical trend is invalid because we know a "person who" went against the trend.

# Statistical Analysis: Correlation Coefficients

Now that you understand how to interpret a correlation coefficient, let's turn to the actual calculation of correlation coefficients. The type of correlation coefficient used depends on the type of data (nominal, ordinal, interval, or ratio) that were collected.

## Pearson's Product-Moment Correlation Coefficient: What It Is and What It Does

The most commonly used correlation coefficient is the **Pearson product-moment correlation coefficient**, usually referred to as **Pearson's r** (*r* is the statistical notation we use to report this correlation coefficient). Pearson's *r* is used for data measured on an interval or ratio scale of measurement. Refer back to Figure 6.1, which presents a scatterplot of height and weight data for 20 individuals. Because height and weight are both measured on a ratio scale, Pearson's *r* is applicable to these data.

The development of this correlation coefficient is typically credited to Karl Pearson (hence the name), who published his formula for calculating *r* in 1895. Actually, Francis Edgeworth published a similar formula for calculating *r* in 1892. Not realizing the significance of his work, however, Edgeworth embedded the formula in a statistical paper that was very difficult to follow, and it was not noted until years later. Thus, although Edgeworth had published the formula 3 years earlier, Pearson received the recognition (Cowles, 1989).

*Calculations for the Pearson Product-Moment Correlation.* Table 6.2 presents the raw scores from which the scatterplot in Figure 6.1 was derived, along with the mean and standard deviation for each distribution. Height is presented in inches, and weight in pounds. Let's use these data to demonstrate the calculation of Pearson's *r*.

To calculate Pearson's *r*, we begin by converting the raw scores on the two different variables to the same unit of measurement. This should sound familiar to you from an earlier chapter. In Chapter 5, we used z-scores to convert data measured on different scales to standard scores measured on the same scale (a z-score represents the number of standard deviation units a raw score is above or below the mean). High raw scores are always above the mean and have positive z-scores; low raw scores are always below the mean and thus have negative z-scores.

Think about what happens if we convert our raw scores on height and weight to z-scores. If the correlation is strong and positive, we should find that positive z-scores on one variable go with positive z-scores on the other variable, and negative z-scores on one variable go with negative z-scores on the other variable. After we calculate z-scores, the next step in calculating Pearson's *r* is to calculate what is called a *cross-product*—the z-score on one variable multiplied by the z-score on the other variable. This is also sometimes referred to as a *cross-product of z-scores*. Once again, think about what happens if both z-scores used to calculate the cross-product are positive—the cross-product is positive. What if both z-scores are negative? The cross-product is again positive (a negative number multiplied by a negative number results in a positive number). If we sum all of these positive cross-products and divide by the total number of cases (to obtain the average of the cross-products), we end up with a large positive correlation coefficient.

What if we find that, when we convert our raw scores to z-scores, positive z-scores on one variable go with negative z-scores on the other variable? These cross-products are negative and, when averaged (i.e., summed and divided by the total number of cases), result in a large negative correlation coefficient.

**Pearson product-moment correlation coefficient (Pearson's r)** The most commonly used correlation coefficient when both variables are measured on an interval or ratio scale.

**TABLE 6.2 Weight and height data for 20 individuals**

| WEIGHT (IN POUNDS) | HEIGHT (IN INCHES) |
|---|---|
| 100 | 60 |
| 120 | 61 |
| 105 | 63 |
| 115 | 63 |
| 119 | 65 |
| 134 | 65 |
| 129 | 66 |
| 143 | 67 |
| 151 | 65 |
| 163 | 67 |
| 160 | 68 |
| 176 | 69 |
| 165 | 70 |
| 181 | 72 |
| 192 | 76 |
| 208 | 75 |
| 200 | 77 |
| 152 | 68 |
| 134 | 66 |
| 138 | 65 |
| $\mu = 149.25$ | $\mu = 67.4$ |
| $\sigma = 30.42$ | $\sigma = 4.57$ |

Last, imagine what happens if there is no linear relationship between the variables being measured. In other words, some individuals who score high on one variable also score high on the other, and some individuals who score low on one variable score low on the other. Each of these situations results in positive cross-products. However, we also find that some individuals with high scores on one variable have low scores on the other variable, and vice versa. These situations result in negative cross-products. When all of the cross-products are summed and divided by the total number of cases, the positive and negative cross-products essentially cancel each other out and the result is a correlation coefficient close to 0.

Now that you have a basic understanding of the logic behind calculating Pearson's $r$, let's look at the formula for Pearson's $r$:

$$r = \frac{\sum z_X z_Y}{N}$$

Thus, we begin by calculating the z-scores for $X$ (weight) and $Y$ (height). They are shown in Table 6.3. Remember, the formula for a z-score is

$$z = \frac{X - \mu}{\sigma}$$

The first two columns list the weight and height raw scores for the 20 individuals. As a general rule of thumb, when calculating a correlation coefficient, we should have at least 10 participants per variable. Thus, with two variables, we need a minimum of 20 individuals, which we have. Following the raw scores for variable $X$ (weight) and variable $Y$ (height) are columns representing $z_X$, $z_Y$, and $z_X z_Y$ (the cross-product of z-scores). The cross-products column has been summed ($\Sigma$) at the bottom of the table. Now, let's use the information from the table to calculate $r$:

$$r = \frac{\sum z_X z_Y}{N} = \frac{18.82}{20} = +.94$$

There are alternative formulas to calculate Pearson's $r$, one of which is the computational formula. If your instructor prefers that you use this formula, it is presented in Table 6.4.

*Interpreting the Pearson Product-Moment Correlation.* The obtained correlation between height and weight for the 20 individuals represented in Table 6.3 is +.94. Can you interpret this correlation coefficient? The positive sign tells us that the variables increase and decrease together. The large magnitude (close to 1.00) tells us that there is a strong positive relationship between height and weight: Those who are taller tend to weigh more, whereas those who are shorter tend to weigh less.

In addition to interpreting the correlation coefficient, it is important to calculate the coefficient of determination. Calculated by squaring the correlation coefficient, the **coefficient of determination ($r^2$)** is a measure of the proportion of the variance in one variable that is accounted for by another variable. In our group of 20 individuals, there is variation in both the

**coefficient of determination ($r^2$)** A measure of the proportion of the variance in one variable that is accounted for by another variable; calculated by squaring the correlation coefficient.

**TABLE 6.3   Calculating the Pearson correlation coefficient**

| X (WEIGHT IN POUNDS) | Y (HEIGHT IN INCHES) | $z_X$ | $z_Y$ | $z_X z_Y$ |
|---|---|---|---|---|
| 100 | 60 | −1.62 | −1.62 | 2.62 |
| 120 | 61 | −0.96 | −1.40 | 1.34 |
| 105 | 63 | −1.45 | −0.96 | 1.39 |
| 115 | 63 | −1.13 | −0.96 | 1.08 |
| 119 | 65 | −0.99 | −0.53 | 0.52 |
| 134 | 65 | −0.50 | −0.53 | 0.27 |
| 129 | 66 | −0.67 | −0.31 | 0.21 |
| 143 | 67 | −0.21 | −0.09 | 0.02 |
| 151 | 65 | 0.06 | −0.53 | −0.03 |
| 163 | 67 | 0.45 | −0.09 | −0.04 |
| 160 | 68 | 0.35 | 0.13 | 0.05 |
| 176 | 69 | 0.88 | 0.35 | 0.31 |
| 165 | 70 | 0.52 | 0.57 | 0.30 |
| 181 | 72 | 1.04 | 1.01 | 1.05 |
| 192 | 76 | 1.41 | 1.88 | 2.65 |
| 208 | 75 | 1.93 | 1.66 | 3.20 |
| 200 | 77 | 1.67 | 2.10 | 3.51 |
| 152 | 68 | 0.09 | 0.13 | 0.01 |
| 134 | 66 | −0.50 | −0.31 | 0.16 |
| 138 | 65 | −0.37 | −0.53 | 0.20 |
| | | | | $\Sigma = +18.82$ |

**TABLE 6.4   Computational formula for Pearson's Product-Moment Correlation Coefficient**

$$r = \frac{\sum XY - \dfrac{(\sum X)(\sum Y)}{N}}{\sqrt{\left(\sum X^2 - \dfrac{(\sum X)^2}{N}\right)\left(\sum Y^2 - \dfrac{(\sum Y)^2}{N}\right)}}$$

height and weight variables, and some of the variation in one variable can be accounted for by the other variable. We could say that some of the variation in the weights of these 20 individuals can be explained by the variation in their heights. Some of the variation in their weights, however, cannot be explained by the variation in height. It might be explained by other factors such as genetic predisposition, age, fitness level, or eating habits. The coefficient of determination tells us how much of the variation in weight is accounted for by the variation in height. Squaring the obtained coefficient of $+.94$, we have $r^2 = .8836$. We typically report $r^2$ as a percentage. Hence, 88.36% of the variance in weight can be accounted for by the variance in height—a very high coefficient of determination. Depending on the research area, the coefficient of determination may be much lower and still be important. It is up to the researcher to interpret the coefficient of determination.

## Alternative Correlation Coefficients

As noted previously, the type of correlation coefficient used depends on the type of data collected in the research study. Pearson's correlation coefficient is used when both variables are measured on an interval or ratio scale. Alternative correlation coefficients can be used with ordinal and nominal scales of measurement. We will mention three such correlation coefficients, but we will not present the formulas because our coverage of statistics is necessarily selective. All of the formulas are based on Pearson's formula and can be found in a more comprehensive statistics text. Each of these coefficients is reported on a scale of $-1.00$ to $+1.00$. Thus, each is interpreted in a fashion similar to Pearson's $r$. Last, like Pearson's $r$, the coefficient of determination ($r^2$) can be calculated for each of these correlation coefficients to determine the proportion of variance in one variable accounted for by the other variable.

When one or more of the variables is measured on an ordinal (ranking) scale, the appropriate correlation coefficient is **Spearman's rank-order correlation coefficient**. If one of the variables is interval or ratio in nature, it must be ranked (converted to an ordinal scale) before the calculations are done. If one of the variables is measured on a dichotomous (having only two possible values, such as gender) nominal scale and the other is measured on an interval or ratio scale, the appropriate correlation coefficient is the **point-biserial correlation coefficient**. Last, if both variables are dichotomous and nominal, the **phi coefficient** is used.

Although both the point-biserial and phi coefficients are used to calculate correlations with dichotomous nominal variables, you should refer back to one of the cautions mentioned earlier in the chapter concerning potential problems when interpreting correlation coefficients—specifically, the caution regarding restricted ranges. Clearly, a variable with only two levels has

**Spearman's rank-order correlation coefficient** The correlation coefficient used when one or more of the variables is measured on an ordinal (ranking) scale.

**point-biserial correlation coefficient** The correlation coefficient used when one of the variables is measured on a dichotomous nominal scale and the other is measured on an interval or ratio scale.

**phi coefficient** The correlation coefficient used when both measured variables are dichotomous and nominal.

| IN REVIEW | Correlation Coefficients | | | |
|---|---|---|---|---|
| | **TYPES OF COEFFICIENTS** | | | |
| | **Pearson** | **Spearman** | **Point-Biserial** | **Phi** |
| Type of Data | Both variables must be interval or ratio | Both variables are ordinal (ranked) | One variable is interval or ratio and one variable is nominal and dichotomous | Both variables are nominal and dichotomous |
| Correlation Reported | ±0.0–1.0 | ±0.0–1.0 | ±0.0–1.0 | ±0.0–1.0 |
| $r^2$ Applicable? | Yes | Yes | Yes | Yes |

> 1. In a recent study, researchers were interested in determining the relationship between gender and amount of time spent studying for a group of college students. Which correlation coefficient should be used to assess this relationship?
>
> **CRITICAL THINKING CHECK 6.3**

a restricted range. What would the scatterplot for such a correlation look like? The points would have to be clustered in columns or groups, depending on whether one or both of the variables were dichotomous.

# Advanced Correlational Techniques: Regression Analysis

As we have seen, the correlational procedure allows us to predict from one variable to another, and the degree of accuracy with which we can predict depends on the strength of the correlation. A tool that enables us to predict an individual's score on one variable based on knowing one or more other variables is **regression analysis**. For example, imagine that you are an admissions counselor at a university and you want to predict how well a prospective student might do at your school based on both SAT scores and high school GPA. Or imagine that you work in a human resources office and you want to predict how well future employees might perform based on test scores and performance measures. Regression analysis allows you to make such predictions by developing a regression equation.

To illustrate regression analysis, let's use the height and weight data presented in Figure 6.1 and Table 6.2. When we used these data to calculate Pearson's *r*, we determined that the correlation coefficient was +.94. Also, we can see in Figure 6.1 that the relationship between the variables is *linear*, meaning that a straight line can be drawn through the data to represent the relationship between the variables. This **regression line** is shown in Figure 6.4; it

**regression analysis** A procedure that allows us to predict an individual's score on one variable based on knowing one or more other variables.

**regression line** The best-fitting straight line drawn through the center of a scatterplot that indicates the relationship between the variables.

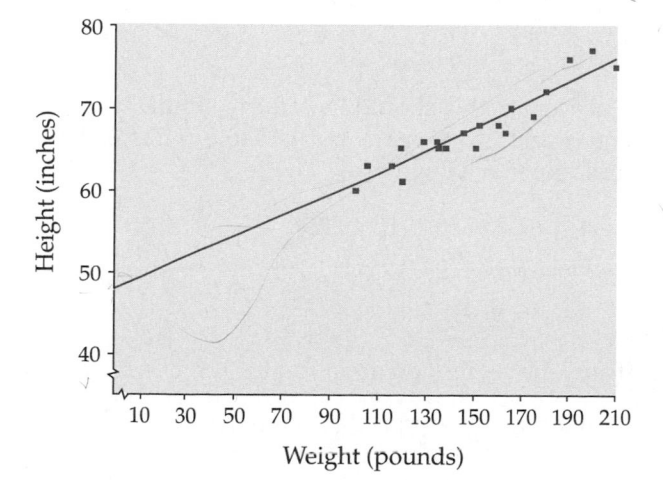

**FIGURE 6.4 The relationship between height and weight with the regression line indicated**

is the best-fitting straight line drawn through the center of the scatterplot that indicates the relationship between the variables height and weight for this group of individuals.

Regression analysis involves determining the equation for the best-fitting line for a data set. This equation is based on the equation for representing a line that you may remember from algebra class: $y = mx + b$, where $m$ is the slope of the line and $b$ is the $y$-intercept (the point where the line crosses the $y$-axis). For a linear regression analysis, the formula is essentially the same, although the symbols differ:

$$Y' = bX + a$$

where $Y'$ is the predicted value on the $Y$ variable, $b$ is the slope of the line, $X$ represents an individual's score on the $X$ variable, and $a$ is the $y$-intercept. Using this formula, then, we can predict an individual's approximate score on variable $Y$ based on that person's score on variable $X$. With the height and weight data, for example, we can predict an individual's approximate height based on knowing that person's weight. You can picture what we are talking about by looking at Figure 6.4. Given the regression line in Figure 6.4, if we know an individual's weight (read from the $x$-axis), we can predict the person's height (by finding the corresponding value on the $y$-axis).

To use the regression line formula, we need to determine both $b$ and $a$. Let's begin with the slope ($b$). The formula for computing $b$ is

$$b = r\left(\frac{\sigma_Y}{\sigma_X}\right)$$

This should look fairly simple to you. We have already calculated $r$ and the standard deviations ($\sigma$) for both height and weight (see Table 6.2). Using these calculations, we can compute $b$ as follows:

$$b = .94\left(\frac{4.57}{30.42}\right) = .94(0.150) = 0.141$$

Now that we have computed $b$, we can compute $a$. The formula for $a$ is

$$a = \bar{Y} - b(\bar{X})$$

Once again, this should look fairly simple because we have just calculated $b$, and $\bar{Y}$ and $\bar{X}$ are presented in Table 6.2 as $\mu$. Using these values in the formula for $a$, we have

$$a = 67.40 - 0.141(149.25)$$
$$= 67.40 - 21.04$$
$$= 46.36$$

Thus, the regression equation for the line for the data in Figure 6.4 is

$$Y' \text{ (height)} = 0.141X \text{ (weight)} + 46.36$$

where 0.141 is the slope and 46.36 is the y-intercept. Thus, if we know that an individual weighs 110 pounds, we can predict the person's height using this equation:

$$Y' = 0.141(110) + 46.36$$
$$= 15.51 + 46.36$$
$$= 61.87 \text{ inches}$$

Determining the regression equation for a set of data thus allows us to predict from one variable to the other.

A more advanced use of regression analysis is known as *multiple regression analysis*. Multiple regression analysis involves combining several predictor variables in a single regression equation. With multiple regression analysis, we can assess the effects of multiple predictor variables (rather than a single predictor variable) on the dependent measure. In our height and weight example, we attempted to predict an individual's height based on knowing the person's weight. We might be able to add other variables to the equation that would increase our predictive ability. For example, if, in addition to the individual's weight, we knew the height of the biological parents, this might increase our ability to accurately predict the person's height.

When we use multiple regression, the predicted value of $Y'$ represents the linear combination of all the predictor variables used in the equation. The rationale behind using this more advanced form of regression analysis is that in the real world it is unlikely that one variable is affected by only one other variable. In other words, real life involves the interaction of many variables on other variables. Thus, in order to more accurately predict variable A, it makes sense to consider all possible variables that might influence variable A. In our example, it is doubtful that height is influenced by weight alone. There are many other variables that might help us to predict height, such as the variable mentioned above—the height of each biological parent. The calculation of multiple regression is beyond the scope of this book. For further information on it, consult a more advanced statistics text.

# Summary

After reading this chapter, you should have an understanding of the correlational research method, which allows researchers to observe relationships between variables, and of correlation coefficients, the statistics that assess that relationship. Correlations vary in type (positive, negative, none, or curvilinear) and magnitude (weak, moderate, or strong). The pictorial representation of a correlation is a scatterplot. A scatterplot allows us to see the relationship, facilitating its interpretation.

Several errors are commonly made when interpreting correlations, including assuming causality and directionality, overlooking a third variable, having a restrictive range on one or both variables, and assessing a curvilinear relationship. Knowing that two variables are correlated allows researchers to make predictions from one variable to the other.

We introduced four different correlation coefficients (Pearson's, Spearman's, point-biserial, and phi) along with when each should be used. Also discussed were the coefficient of determination and regression analysis, which provides a tool for predicting from one variable to another.

## KEY TERMS

| | | |
|---|---|---|
| magnitude | person-who argument | point-biserial correlation |
| scatterplot | Pearson product-moment | coefficient |
| causality | correlation coefficient | phi coefficient |
| directionality | (Pearson's $r$) | regression analysis |
| third-variable problem | coefficient of determination ($r^2$) | regression line |
| partial correlation | Spearman's rank-order | |
| restrictive range | correlation coefficient | |

## CHAPTER EXERCISES

(Answers to odd-numbered exercises appear in Appendix C.)

1. A health club recently conducted a study of its members and found a positive relationship between exercise and health. It was claimed that the correlation coefficient between the variables of exercise and health was +1.25. What is wrong with this statement? In addition, it was stated that this proved that an increase in exercise increases health. What is wrong with this statement?

2. Draw a scatterplot indicating a strong negative relationship between the variables of income and mental illness. Be sure to label the axes correctly.

3. We have mentioned several times that there is a fairly strong positive correlation between SAT scores and freshman GPAs. The admissions process for graduate school is based on a similar test, the GRE, which also has a potential 400 to 1600 total point range. If graduate schools do not accept anyone who scores below 1000 and if a GPA below 3.00 represents failing work in graduate school, what would we expect the correlation between GRE scores and graduate school GPAs to be like in comparison to the correlation between SAT scores and college GPAs? Why would we expect this?

4. In a study on caffeine and stress, college students indicated how many cups of coffee they drink per day and their stress level on a scale of 1 to 10. The data appear below.

| Number of Cups of Coffee | Stress Level |
|---|---|
| 3 | 5 |
| 2 | 3 |
| 4 | 3 |
| 6 | 9 |
| 5 | 4 |
| 1 | 2 |
| 7 | 10 |
| 3 | 5 |

Calculate a Pearson's $r$ to determine the type and strength of the relationship between caffeine and stress level. How much of the variability in stress scores is accounted for by the number of cups of coffee consumed per day?

5. Given the data below, determine the correlation between IQ scores and psychology exam scores, between IQ scores and statistics exam scores, and between psychology exam scores and statistics exam scores.

| Student | IQ Score | Psychology Exam Score | Statistics Exam Score |
|---|---|---|---|
| 1 | 140 | 48 | 47 |
| 2 | 98 | 35 | 32 |
| 3 | 105 | 36 | 38 |
| 4 | 120 | 43 | 40 |
| 5 | 119 | 30 | 40 |
| 6 | 114 | 45 | 43 |
| 7 | 102 | 37 | 33 |
| 8 | 112 | 44 | 47 |
| 9 | 111 | 38 | 46 |
| 10 | 116 | 46 | 44 |

Calculate the coefficient of determination for each of these correlation coefficients, and explain what it means. In addition, calculate the regression equation for each pair of variables.

6. Assuming that the regression equation for the relationship between IQ score and psychology exam score is $y = 9 + 0.274x$, what would you expect the psychology exam scores to be for the following individuals given their IQ exam scores?

| Individual | IQ Score (x) | Psychology Exam Score (y) |
|---|---|---|
| Tim | 118 | |
| Tom | 98 | |
| Tina | 107 | |
| Tory | 103 | |

# CRITICAL THINKING CHECK ANSWERS

## 6.1

1. +.10
2. A correlation coefficient of 0.00 or close to 0.00 may indicate no relationship or a weak relationship. However, if the relationship is curvilinear, the correlation coefficient could also be 0.00 or close to this. In this case, there is a relationship between the two variables, but because the relationship is curvilinear, the correlation coefficient does not truly represent the strength of the relationship.

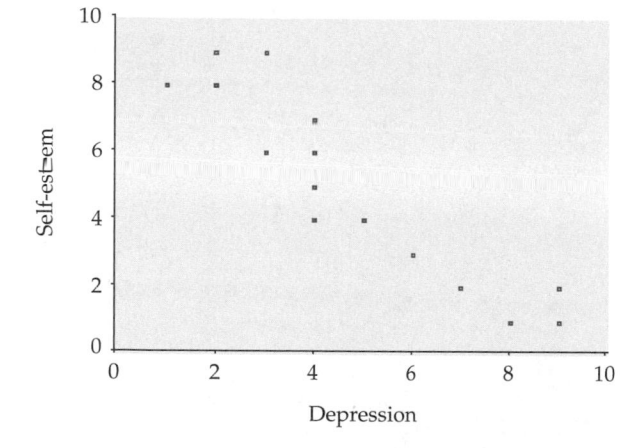

## 6.2

1. A strong negative correlation between depression and self-esteem means that individuals who are more depressed also tend to have lower self-esteem, whereas individuals who are less depressed tend to have higher self-esteem. It does not mean that one variable causes changes in the other, but simply that the variables tend to move together in a certain manner.
2. General State University observed such a weak correlation between GPAs and SAT scores because of a restrictive range on the GPA variable. Because of grade inflation, the whole senior class graduated with a GPA of 3.0 or higher. This restriction on one of the variables lessens the opportunity to observe a correlation.

## 6.3

1. In this study, gender is nominal in scale and the amount of time spent studying is ratio in scale. Thus, a point-biserial correlation coefficient is appropriate.

# WEB RESOURCES

Check your knowledge of the content in this chapter by taking the practice quiz at www.Wadsworth.com. Or, for step-by-step practice and information, check out the Statistics and Research Methods Workshops at http://psychology.wadsworth.com/workshops.

## LAB RESOURCES

For hands-on experience using the research methods described in this chapter, see Chapter 3 ("Correlation Research") in *Research Methods Laboratory Manual for* *Psychology*, 2nd ed., by William Langston (Belmont, CA: Wadsworth, 2005).

## STATISTICAL SOFTWARE RESOURCES

For hands-on experience using statistical software to complete the analyses described in this chapter, see Chapter 3 ("Correlation and Regression") in *The* *Excel Statistics Companion* by Kenneth M. Rosenberg (Belmont, CA: Wadsworth, 2003).

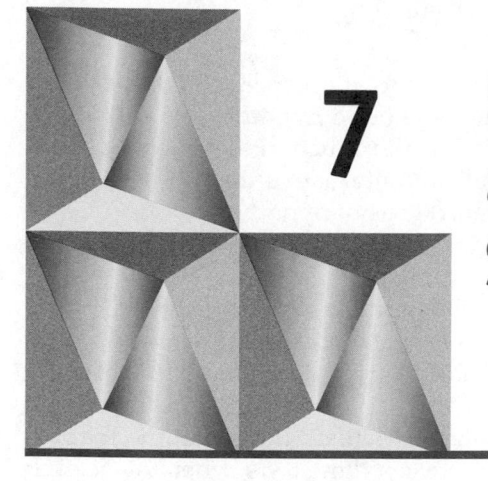

# 7 Hypothesis Testing and Inferential Statistics

**hypothesis testing** The process of determining whether a hypothesis is supported by the results of a research study.

**inferential statistics** Procedures for drawing conclusions about a population based on data collected from a sample.

In this chapter, you will be introduced to the concept of **hypothesis testing**—the process of determining whether a hypothesis is supported by the results of a research project. Our introduction to hypothesis testing will include a discussion of the null and alternative hypotheses, Type I and Type II errors, and one- and two-tailed tests of hypotheses, as well as an introduction to statistical significance and probability as they relate to inferential statistics.

In the remainder of this chapter, we will begin our discussion of **inferential statistics**—procedures for drawing conclusions about a population based on data collected from a sample. We will address two different statistical tests: the $z$ test and the $t$ test. After reading this chapter, engaging in the critical thinking checks, and working through the problems at the end of the chapter, you should understand the differences between these tests, when to use each test, how to use each to test a hypothesis, and the assumptions of each test.

## Hypothesis Testing

Research is usually designed to answer a specific question—for example, Do science majors score higher on tests of intelligence than students in the general population? The process of determining whether this statement is supported by the results of the research project is referred to as *hypothesis testing*.

© 2005 Sidney Harris, Reprinted with permission.

Suppose a researcher wants to examine the relationship between the type of after-school program attended by a child and the child's intelligence level. The researcher is interested in whether students who attend after-school programs that are academically oriented (math, writing, computer use) score higher on an intelligence test than students who do not attend such programs. The researcher will form a hypothesis. The hypothesis might be that children in academic after-school programs have higher IQ scores than children in the general population. Because most intelligence tests are standardized with a mean score ($\mu$) of 100 and a standard deviation ($\sigma$) of 15, the students in academic after-school programs must score higher than 100 for the hypothesis to be supported.

## Null and Alternative Hypotheses

Most of the time, researchers are interested in demonstrating the truth of some statement. In other words, they are interested in supporting their hypothesis. It is impossible statistically, however, to demonstrate that something is true. In fact, statistical techniques are much better at demonstrating that something is not true. This presents a dilemma for researchers. They want to support their hypotheses, but the techniques available to them are better for showing that something is false. What are they to do? The logical route is to propose exactly the opposite of what they want to demonstrate to be true, and then disprove or falsify that hypothesis. What is left (the initial hypothesis) must then be true (Kranzler & Moursund, 1995).

Let's use our sample hypothesis to demonstrate what we mean. We want to show that children who attend academic after-school programs have different (higher) IQ scores than those who do not. We understand that statistics cannot demonstrate the truth of this statement. We therefore construct what is known as a *null hypothesis* ($H_0$). Whatever the research topic, the **null hypothesis** always predicts that there is no difference between the groups being compared. This is typically what the researcher does not expect to find. Think about the meaning of *null*—nothing or zero. The null hypothesis means we have found nothing—no difference between the groups.

For the sample study, the null hypothesis is that children who attend academic after-school programs have the same intelligence level as other children. Remember, we said that statistics allow us to disprove or falsify a hypothesis. Therefore, if the null hypothesis is not supported, then our original hypothesis—that children who attend academic after-school programs have different IQs than other children—is all that is left. In statistical notation, the null hypothesis for this study is

$$H_0: \mu_0 = \mu_1, \text{ or } \mu_{\text{academic program}} = \mu_{\text{general population}}$$

The purpose of the study, then, is to decide whether $H_0$ is probably true or probably false.

The hypothesis that the researcher wants to support is known as the **alternative hypothesis ($H_a$)**, or the **research hypothesis ($H_1$)**. The statistical notation for $H_a$ is

$$H_a: \mu_0 > \mu_1, \text{ or } \mu_{\text{academic program}} > \mu_{\text{general population}}$$

When we use inferential statistics, we are trying to reject $H_0$, which means that $H_a$ is supported.

**null hypothesis ($H_0$)** The hypothesis predicting that no difference exists between the groups being compared.

**alternative hypothesis ($H_a$), or research hypothesis ($H_1$)** The hypothesis that the researcher wants to support, predicting that a significant difference exists between the groups being compared.

## One- and Two-Tailed Hypothesis Tests

**one-tailed hypothesis
(directional hypothesis)**
An alternative hypothesis in
which the researcher predicts
the direction of the expected
difference between the groups.

The manner in which the previous research hypothesis ($H_a$) was stated reflects what is known statistically as a **one-tailed hypothesis**, or a **directional hypothesis**—an alternative hypothesis in which the researcher predicts the direction of the expected difference between the groups. In this case, the researcher predicted the direction of the difference—namely, that children in academic after-school programs will be more intelligent than children in the general population. When we use a directional alternative hypothesis, the null hypothesis is also, in some sense, directional. If the alternative hypothesis is that children in academic after-school programs will have higher intelligence test scores, then the null hypothesis is that being in academic after-school programs either will have no effect on intelligence test scores or will decrease intelligence test scores. Thus, the null hypothesis for the one-tailed directional test might more appropriately be written as

$$H_0: \mu_0 \leq \mu_1, \text{ or } \mu_{\text{academic program}} \leq \mu_{\text{general population}}$$

In other words, if the alternative hypothesis for a one-tailed test is $\mu_0 > \mu$ then the null hypothesis is $\mu_0 \leq \mu_1$, and in order to reject $H_0$, the children in academic after-school programs have to have intelligence test scores higher than those in the general population.

**two-tailed hypothesis
(nondirectional hypothesis)**
An alternative hypothesis in
which the researcher predicts
that the groups being compared
differ, but does not predict the
direction of the difference.

The alternative to a one-tailed or directional test is a **two-tailed hypothesis**, or a **nondirectional hypothesis**—an alternative hypothesis in which the researcher expects to find differences between the groups but is unsure what the differences will be. In our example, the researcher would predict a difference in IQ scores between children in academic after-school programs and those in the general population, but the direction of the difference would not be predicted. Those in academic programs would be expected to have either higher or lower IQs, but not the same IQs as the general population of children. The statistical notation for a two-tailed test is

$$H_0: \mu_0 = \mu_1, \text{ or } \mu_{\text{academic program}} = \mu_{\text{general population}}$$
$$H_a: \mu_0 \neq \mu_1, \text{ or } \mu_{\text{academic program}} \neq \mu_{\text{general population}}$$

In our example, a two-tailed hypothesis does not really make sense.

Assume that the researcher has selected a random sample of children from academic after-school programs in order to compare their IQs with the IQs of children in the general population (as noted above, we know that the mean IQ for the population is 100). If we collected data and found that the mean intelligence level of the children in academic after-school programs is "significantly" (a term that will be discussed shortly) higher than the mean intelligence level for the population, we could reject the null hypothesis. Remember that the null hypothesis states that there is no difference between the sample and the population. Thus, the researcher concludes that the null hypothesis—that there is no difference—is not supported. When the null hypothesis is rejected, the alternative hypothesis—that those in academic programs have higher IQ scores than those in the general population—is supported. We can say that the evidence suggests that the sample of children in academic after-school programs represents a specific population that scores higher on the IQ test than the general population.

If, on the other hand, the mean IQ score of the children in academic after-school programs is not significantly different from the population mean score, then the researcher has failed to reject the null hypothesis and, by default, has failed to support the alternative hypothesis. In this case, the alternative hypothesis—that the children in academic programs have higher IQs than the general population—is not supported.

## Type I and II Errors in Hypothesis Testing

Anytime we make a decision using statistics, there are four possible outcomes (see Table 7.1). Two of the outcomes represent correct decisions, whereas two represent errors. Let's use our example to illustrate these possibilities.

If we reject the null hypothesis (that there is no IQ difference between groups), we may be correct in our decision or we may be incorrect. If our decision to reject $H_0$ is correct, that means there truly is a difference in IQ between children in academic after-school programs and the general population. However, our decision could be incorrect. The result may have been due to chance. Even though we observed a significant difference in IQs between the children in our study and the general population, the result might have been a fluke—maybe the children in our sample just happened to guess correctly on a lot of the questions. In this case, we have made what is known as a **Type I error**—we rejected $H_0$ when in reality we should have failed to reject it (it is true that there really is no IQ difference between the sample and the population). Type I errors can be thought of as false alarms—we said there was a difference, but in reality there is no difference.

**Type I error** An error in hypothesis testing in which the null hypothesis is rejected when it is true.

What if our decision is to not reject $H_0$, meaning we conclude that there is no difference in IQs between the children in academic after-school programs and children in the general population? This decision could be correct, meaning that in reality there is no IQ difference between the sample and the population. However, it could also be incorrect. In this case, we would be making a **Type II error**—saying there is no difference between groups when in reality there is a difference. Somehow we have missed the difference that really exists and have failed to reject the null hypothesis when it is false. These possibilities are summarized in Table 7.1.

**Type II error** An error in hypothesis testing in which there is a failure to reject the null hypothesis when it is false.

**TABLE 7.1  The four possible outcomes in statistical decision making**

| | THE TRUTH (UNKNOWN TO THE RESEARCHER) | |
|---|---|---|
| **The Researcher's Decision** | $H_0$ **Is True** | $H_0$ **Is False** |
| **Reject $H_0$** (say it is false) | Type I error | Correct decision |
| **Fail to reject $H_0$** (say it is true) | Correct decision | Type II error |

## Statistical Significance and Errors

Suppose we actually do the study on IQ levels and academic after-school programs. In addition, suppose we find that there is a difference between the IQ levels of children in academic after-school programs and children in the general population (those in academic programs score higher). Last, suppose this difference is statistically significant at the .05 (or the 5%) level (also known as the .05 alpha level). To say that a result has **statistical significance** at the .05 level means that a difference as large as or larger than what we observed between the sample and the population could have occurred by chance only 5 times or less out of 100. In other words, the likelihood that this result is due to chance is small. If the result is not due to chance, then it is most likely due to a true or real difference between the groups. If our result is statistically significant, we can reject the null hypothesis and conclude that we have observed a significant difference in IQ scores between the sample and the population.

**statistical significance** An observed difference between two descriptive statistics (such as means) that is unlikely to have occurred by chance.

Remember, however, that when we reject the null hypothesis, we could be correct in our decision or we could be making a Type I error. Maybe the null hypothesis is true, and this is one of those 5 or less times out of 100 when the observed differences between the sample and the population did occur by chance. This means that when we adopt the .05 level of significance (the .05 alpha level), as often as 5 times out of 100 we could make a Type I error. The .05 level, then, is the probability of making a Type I error. In the social and behavioral sciences, alpha is typically set at .05 (as opposed to .01 or .08 or anything else). This means that researchers in these areas are willing to accept up to a 5% risk of making a Type I error.

What if you want to reduce your risk of making a Type I error and decide to use the .01 alpha level—reducing the risk of a Type I error to 1 out of 100 times? This seems simple enough: Simply reduce alpha to .01, and you have reduced your chance of making a Type I error. By doing this, however, you have now increased your chance of making a Type II error. Do you see why? If I reduce my risk of making a false alarm—saying a difference is there when it really is not—I increase my risk of missing a difference that really is there. When we reduce the alpha level, we are insisting on more stringent conditions for accepting our research hypothesis, making it more likely that we could miss a significant difference when it is present. We will return to Type I and II errors later in this chapter when we cover statistical power and discuss alternative ways of addressing this problem.

Which type of error, Type I or Type II, do you think is considered more serious by researchers? Most researchers consider a Type I error more serious. They would rather miss a result (Type II error) than conclude that there is a meaningful difference when there really is not (Type I error). What about in other arenas—for example, in the courtroom? A jury could make a correct decision in a case (find guilty when truly guilty or find innocent when truly innocent). They could also make either a Type I error (say guilty when innocent) or a Type II error (say innocent when guilty). Which is more serious here? Most people believe that a Type I error is worse in this situation also. How about in the medical profession? Imagine a doctor attempting to determine whether or not a patient has cancer. Here again, the doctor could make one of the two correct decisions or one of the two types of errors. What would the Type I error be? This would be saying that cancer is present when in fact it is not. What about the Type II error? This would be saying that there is no cancer when in fact there is. In this situation, most people would consider a Type II error to be more serious.

| Hypothesis Testing | | IN REVIEW |
|---|---|---|
| **CONCEPT** | **DESCRIPTION** | **EXAMPLE** |
| Null Hypothesis | The hypothesis stating that the independent variable has no effect and that there will be no difference between the two groups | $H_0: \mu_0 = \mu_1$ |
| Alternative Hypothesis or Research Hypothesis | The hypothesis stating that the independent variable has an effect and that there will be a difference between the two groups | $H_a: \mu_0 \neq \mu_1$ (two-tailed) $H_a: \mu_0 < \mu_1$ (one-tailed) $H_a: \mu_0 > \mu_1$ (one-tailed) |
| Two-Tailed or Nondirectional Test | An alternative hypothesis stating that a difference is expected between the groups, but there is no prediction as to which group will perform better or worse | The mean of the sample will be different from or unequal to the mean of the general population |
| One-Tailed or Directional Test | An alternative hypothesis stating that a difference is expected between the groups, and it is expected to occur in a specific direction | The mean of the sample will be greater than the mean of the population, or the mean of the sample will be less than the mean of the population |
| Type I Error | The error of rejecting $H_0$ when we should have failed to reject it | This error in hypothesis testing is equivalent to a "false alarm," saying that there is a difference when in reality there is no difference between the groups |
| Type II Error | The error of failing to reject $H_0$ when we should have rejected it | This error in hypothesis testing is equivalent to a "miss," saying that there is not a difference between the groups when in reality there is |
| Statistical Significance | When the probability of a Type I error is low (less than .05) | The difference between the groups is so large that we conclude it is due to something other than chance |

1. A researcher hypothesizes that children in the South weigh less (because they spend more time outside) than the national average. Identify $H_0$ and $H_a$. Is this a one- or two-tailed test?
2. A researcher collects data on children's weights from a random sample of children in the South and concludes that children in the South weigh less than the national average. The researcher, however, does not realize that the sample includes many children who are small for their age and that in reality there is no difference in weight between

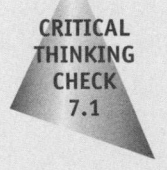

CRITICAL THINKING CHECK 7.1

children in the South and the national average. What type of error is the researcher making?

3. If a researcher decides to use the .10 level rather than the conventional .05 level of significance, what type of error is more likely to be made? Why? If the .01 level is used, what type of error is more likely? Why?

# Single-Sample Research and Inferential Statistics

**single-group design** A research study in which there is only one group of participants.

Now that we have an understanding of the concept of hypothesis testing, we can begin to discuss how hypothesis testing can be applied to research. The simplest type of study involves only one group and is known as a **single-group design.** The single-group design lacks a comparison group—there is no control group of any sort. We can, however, compare the performance of the group (the sample) with the performance of the population (assuming that population data are available).

Earlier in the chapter, we illustrated hypothesis testing using a single-group design—comparing the IQ scores of children in academic after-school programs (the sample) with the IQ scores of children in the general population. The null and alternative hypotheses for this study were

$$H_0: \mu_0 \leq \mu_1, \text{ or } \mu_{\text{academic program}} \leq \mu_{\text{general population}}$$
$$H_a: \mu_0 > \mu_1, \text{ or } \mu_{\text{academic program}} > \mu_{\text{general population}}$$

To compare the performance of the sample with that of the population, we need to know the population mean ($\mu$) and the population standard deviation ($\sigma$). We know that for IQ tests, $\mu = 100$ and $\sigma = 15$. We also need to decide who will be in the sample. As noted in previous chapters, random selection increases our chances of getting a representative sample of children enrolled in academic after-school programs. How many children do we need in the sample? We will see later in this chapter that the larger the sample, the greater the power of the study. We will also see that one of the assumptions of the statistical procedure we will be using to test our hypothesis is a sample size of 30 or more.

Once we have chosen our sample, we need to collect the data. We have discussed data collection in several earlier chapters. It is important to make sure that the data are collected in a nonreactive manner as discussed in Chapter 4. To collect IQ score data, we could either administer an intelligence test to the children or look at their academic files to see whether they had already taken such a test.

After the data are collected, we can begin to analyze them using inferential statistics. As noted previously, inferential statistics involve the use of procedures for drawing conclusions based on the scores collected in a research study and going beyond them to make inferences about a population. In this chapter, we will describe two inferential statistical tests. They are both **parametric tests**—tests that require us to make certain assumptions about estimates of population characteristics, or parameters. These assumptions typically involve knowing the mean ($\mu$) and standard deviation ($\sigma$) of the population and that the population distribution is normal. Parametric tests are generally used with interval or ratio data. The alternative to a parametric test is a **nonparametric test**—that is, a test that does not involve the use of any population parameters. In other words, $\mu$ and $\sigma$ are not needed, and the underlying distribution does not have to be normal. Nonparametric tests are most often used with ordinal or nominal data. Nonparametric tests will be covered in Chapter 12.

**parametric test** A statistical test that involves making assumptions about estimates of population characteristics, or parameters.

**nonparametric test** A statistical test that does not involve the use of any population parameters—$\mu$ and $\sigma$ are not needed, and the underlying distribution does not have to be normal.

| Inferential Statistical Tests | | IN REVIEW |
|---|---|---|
| **CONCEPT** | **DESCRIPTION** | **EXAMPLE** |
| Parametric Inferential Statistics | Inferential statistical procedures that require certain assumptions about the parameters of the population represented by the sample data, such as knowing $\mu$ and $\sigma$ and that the distribution is normal<br>Most often used with interval or ratio data | z test<br>t test |
| Nonparametric Inferential Statistics | Inferential procedures that do not require assumptions about the parameters of the population represented by the sample data; $\mu$ and $\sigma$ are not needed, and the underlying distribution does not have to be normal<br>Most often used with ordinal or nominal data | Chi-square tests<br>Wilcoxon tests<br>(Both discussed in Chapter 13) |

1. How do inferential statistics differ from descriptive statistics?
2. How does single-sample research involve the use of hypothesis testing? In other words, in a single-group design, what hypothesis is tested?

CRITICAL THINKING CHECK 7.2

# The z Test: What It Is and What It Does

The **z test** is a parametric statistical test that allows us to test the null hypothesis for a single sample when the population variance is known. This procedure allows us to compare a sample with a population in order to assess whether the sample differs significantly from the population. If the sample was drawn randomly from a certain population (children in academic after-school

**z test** A parametric inferential statistical test of the null hypothesis for a single sample where the population variance is known.

programs) and we observe a difference between the sample and a broader population (all children), we can then conclude that the population represented by the sample differs significantly from the comparison population. Let's return to our previous example and assume that we have actually collected IQ scores from 75 students enrolled in academic after-school programs. We want to determine whether the sample of children in academic after-school programs represents a population with a mean IQ higher than the mean IQ of the general population of children. We already know $\mu$ (100) and $\sigma$ (15) for the general population of children. The null and alternative hypotheses for a one-tailed test are

$$H_0: \mu_0 \leq \mu_1, \text{ or } \mu_{\text{academic program}} \leq \mu_{\text{general population}}$$

$$H_a: \mu_0 > \mu_1, \text{ or } \mu_{\text{academic program}} > \mu_{\text{general population}}$$

In Chapter 5, we learned how to calculate a $z$-score for a single data point (or a single individual's score). To review, the formula for a $z$-score is

$$z = \frac{X - \mu}{\sigma}$$

Remember that a $z$-score tells us how many standard deviations above or below the mean of the distribution an individual score falls. When using the $z$ test, however, we are not comparing an individual score with the population mean. Instead, we are comparing a sample mean with the population mean. We therefore cannot compare the sample mean with a population distribution of individual scores. We must compare it instead with a distribution of sample means, known as the sampling distribution.

## The Sampling Distribution

**sampling distribution** A distribution of sample means based on random samples of a fixed size from a population.

If you are becoming confused, think about it this way: A **sampling distribution** is a distribution of sample means based on random samples of a fixed size from a population. Imagine that we have drawn many different samples of the same size (say, 75) from the population (children on whom we can measure IQ). For each sample that we draw, we calculate the mean; then we plot the means of all the samples. What do you think the distribution will look like? Well, most of the sample means will probably be similar to the population mean of 100. Some of the sample means will be slightly lower than 100; some will be slightly higher than 100; and others will be right at 100. A few of the sample means, however, will not be similar to the population mean. Why? Based on chance, some samples will contain some of the rare individuals with either very high IQ scores or very low IQ scores. Thus, the means for these samples will be much higher than 100 or much lower than 100. Such samples, however, will be few in number. Thus, the sampling distribution (the distribution of sample means) will be normal (bell-shaped), with most of the sample means clustered around 100 and a few sample means in the tails or the extremes. Therefore, the mean for the sampling distribution will be the same as the mean for the distribution of individual scores (100).

## The Standard Error of the Mean

Here is a more difficult question: Will the standard deviation of the sampling distribution, known as the **standard error of the mean**, be the same as that for a distribution of individual scores? We know that $\sigma = 15$ for the distribution of individual IQ test scores. Will the variability in the sampling distribution be as great as it is in a distribution of individual scores? Let's think about it. The sampling distribution is a distribution of sample means. In our example, each sample has 75 people in it. Now, the mean for a sample of 75 people can never be as low or as high as the lowest or highest individual score. Why? Most people have IQ scores around 100. This means that in each of the samples, most people will have scores around 100. A few people will have very low scores, and when they are included in the sample, they will pull down the mean for that sample. A few others will have very high scores, and these scores will raise the mean for the sample in which they are included. A few people in a sample of 75, however, can never pull the mean for the sample as low as a single individual's score might be or as high as a single individual's score might be. For this reason, the standard error of the mean (the standard deviation of the sampling distribution) can never be as large as $\sigma$ (the standard deviation for the distribution of individual scores).

**standard error of the mean**
The standard deviation of the sampling distribution.

How does this relate to the $z$ test? A $z$ test uses the mean and standard deviation of the sampling distribution to determine whether the sample mean is significantly different from the population mean. Thus, we need to know the mean ($\mu$) and the standard error of the mean ($\sigma_{\bar{X}}$) for the sampling distribution. We have already said that $\mu$ for the sampling distribution is the same as $\mu$ for the distribution of individual scores—100. How will we determine what $\sigma_{\bar{X}}$ is? To find the standard error of the mean, we would need to draw a number of samples from the population, determine the mean for each sample, and then calculate the standard deviation for this distribution of sample means. This is hardly feasible. Luckily for us, there is a means of finding the standard error of the mean without doing all of this. We take the standard deviation for the population ($\sigma$) and divide by the square root of the sample size ($\sqrt{N}$):

$$\sigma_{\bar{X}} = \frac{\sigma}{\sqrt{N}}$$

We can now use this information to calculate $z$. The formula for $z$ is

$$z = \frac{\bar{X} - \mu}{\sigma_{\bar{X}}}$$

where

$\bar{X}$ = sample mean
$\mu$ = mean of the sampling distribution
$\sigma_{\bar{X}}$ = standard deviation of the sampling distribution, or standard error of the mean

| IN REVIEW | The z Test (Part I) | |
|---|---|---|
| CONCEPT | DESCRIPTION | USE |
| Sampling Distribution | A distribution of sample means where each sample is the same size (N) | Used for comparative purposes for z tests—a sample mean is compared with the sampling distribution to assess the likelihood that the sample is part of the sampling distribution |
| Standard Error of the Mean ($\sigma_{\bar{X}}$) | The standard deviation of a sampling distribution, determined by dividing $\sigma$ by $\sqrt{N}$ | Used in the calculation of z |
| z Test | Indication of the number of standard deviation units the sample mean is from the mean of the sampling distribution | An inferential test that compares a sample mean with the sampling distribution in order to determine the likelihood that the sample is part of the sampling distribution |

> **CRITICAL THINKING CHECK 7.3**
>
> 1. Explain how a sampling distribution differs from a distribution of individual scores.
> 2. Explain the difference between $\sigma_{\bar{X}}$ and $\sigma$.
> 3. How is a z test different from a z-score?

## Calculations for the One-Tailed z Test

You can see that the formula for a z test represents finding the difference between the sample mean ($\bar{X}$) and the population mean ($\mu$) and then dividing by the standard error of the mean ($\sigma_{\bar{X}}$). This will tell us how many standard deviation units a sample mean is from the population mean, or the likelihood that the sample is from that population. We already know $\mu$ and $\sigma$, so we need to find the mean for the sample ($\bar{X}$) and to calculate $\sigma_{\bar{X}}$ based on a sample size of 75.

Suppose we find that the mean IQ score for the sample of 75 children enrolled in academic after-school programs is 103.5. We can calculate $\sigma_{\bar{X}}$ based on knowing the sample size and $\sigma$:

$$\sigma_{\bar{X}} = \frac{\sigma}{\sqrt{N}} = \frac{15}{\sqrt{75}} = \frac{15}{8.66} = 1.73$$

We now use $\sigma_{\bar{X}}$ (1.73) in the z-test formula:

$$z = \frac{\bar{X} - \mu}{\sigma_{\bar{X}}} = \frac{103.5 - 100}{1.73} = \frac{3.5}{1.73} = +2.02$$

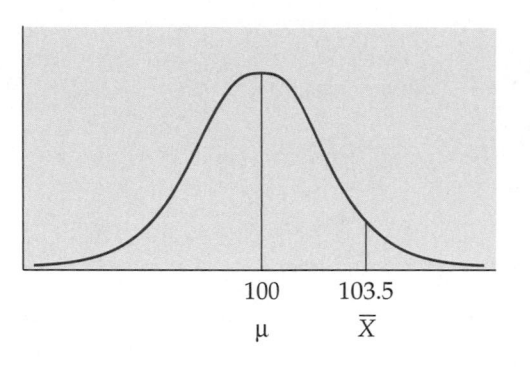

**FIGURE 7.1
The obtained mean
in relation to the
population mean**

## Interpreting the One-Tailed $z$ Test

Figure 7.1 shows where the sample mean of 103.5 lies with respect to the population mean of 100. The $z$-test score of 2.02 can be used to test our hypothesis that the sample of children in academic after-school programs represents a population with a mean IQ higher than the mean IQ for the general population. To do this, we need to determine whether the probability is high or low that a sample mean as large as 103.5 would be found from this sampling distribution. In other words, is a sample mean IQ score of 103.5 far enough away from, or different enough from, the population mean of 100 for us to say that it represents a significant difference with an alpha level of .05 or less?

How do we determine whether a $z$-score of 2.02 is statistically significant? Because the sampling distribution is normally distributed, we can use the area under the normal curve (Table A.2 in Appendix A). When we discussed $z$-scores in Chapter 5, we saw that Table A.2 provides information on the proportion of scores falling between μ and the $z$-score and the proportion of scores beyond the $z$-score. To determine whether a $z$ test is significant, we can use the area under the curve to determine whether the chance of a given score occurring is 5% or less. In other words, is the score far enough away from (above or below) the mean that only 5% or less of the scores are as far or farther away?

Using Table A.2, we find that the $z$-score that marks off the top 5% of the distribution is 1.645. This is referred to as the $z$ **critical value,** or $z_{cv}$—the value of a test statistic that marks the edge of the region of rejection in a sampling distribution. For us to conclude that the sample mean is significantly different from the population mean, then, the sample mean must be at least ±1.645 standard deviations ($z$ units) from the mean. The critical value of 1.645 is illustrated in Figure 7.2. The $z$ we obtained for our sample mean ($z_{obt}$) is 2.02, and this value falls within the region of rejection for the null hypothesis. We therefore reject $H_0$ that the sample mean represents the general population mean and support our alternative hypothesis that the sample mean represents a population of children in academic after-school programs whose mean IQ is higher than 100. We make this decision because the $z$-test score for the sample is greater than (farther out in the tail than) the critical value of ±1.645.

**critical value** The value of a test statistic that marks the edge of the region of rejection in a sampling distribution, where values equal to it or beyond it fall in the region of rejection.

FIGURE 7.2
The *z* critical value
and the *z* obtained
for the *z*-test
example

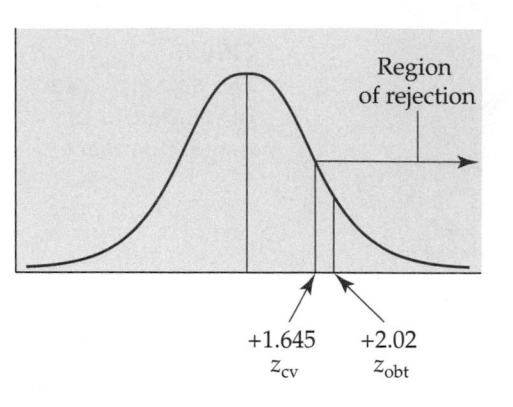

+1.645    +2.02
$z_{cv}$      $z_{obt}$

The test just conducted was a one-tailed test because we predicted that the sample would score higher than the population. What if this were reversed? For example, imagine I am conducting a study to see whether children in athletic after-school programs weigh less than children in the general population. What are $H_0$ and $H_a$ for this example?

$H_0: \mu_0 \geq \mu_1$, or $\mu_{\text{athletic programs}} \geq \mu_{\text{general population}}$

$H_a: \mu_0 < \mu_1$, or $\mu_{\text{athletic programs}} < \mu_{\text{general population}}$

Assume that the mean weight of children in the general population ($\mu$) is 90 pounds, with a standard deviation ($\sigma$) of 17 pounds. You take a random sample ($N = 50$) of children in athletic after-school programs and find a mean weight ($\bar{X}$) of 86 pounds. Given this information, you can test the hypothesis that the sample of children in athletic after-school programs represents a population with a mean weight that is lower than the mean weight for the general population of children.

First, we calculate the standard error of the mean ($\sigma_{\bar{X}}$):

$$\sigma_{\bar{X}} = \frac{\sigma}{\sqrt{N}} = \frac{17}{\sqrt{50}} = \frac{17}{7.07} = 2.40$$

Now, we enter $\sigma_{\bar{X}}$ into the z-test formula:

$$z = \frac{\bar{X} - \mu}{\sigma_{\bar{X}}} = \frac{86 - 90}{2.40} = \frac{-4}{2.4} = -1.67$$

The z-score for this sample mean is −1.67, meaning that it falls 1.67 standard deviations below the mean. The critical value for a one-tailed test is 1.645 standard deviations. This means the z-score has to be at least 1.645 standard deviations away from (above *or* below) the mean in order to fall in the region of rejection. In other words, the critical value for a one-tailed z test is ±1.645. Is our z-score at least that far away from the mean? It is, but just barely. Therefore, we reject $H_0$ and accept $H_a$—that children in athletic after-school programs weigh significantly less than children in the general population and hence represent a population of children who weigh less.

## Calculations for the Two-Tailed $z$ Test

So far, we have completed two $z$ tests, both one-tailed. Let's turn now to a two-tailed $z$ test. Remember that a two-tailed test is also known as a nondirectional test—a test in which the prediction is simply that the sample will perform differently than the population, with no prediction as to whether the sample mean will be lower or higher than the population mean.

Suppose that in the previous example, we used a two-tailed rather than a one-tailed test. We expect the weight of children in athletic after-school programs to differ from the weight of children in the general population, but we are not sure whether they will weigh less (because of the activity) or more (because of greater muscle mass). $H_0$ and $H_a$ for this two-tailed test appear below. See if you can determine what they would be before you continue reading.

$$H_0: \mu_0 = \mu_1, \text{ or } \mu_{\text{athletic programs}} = \mu_{\text{general population}}$$

$$H_a: \mu_0 \neq \mu_1, \text{ or } \mu_{\text{athletic programs}} \neq \mu_{\text{general population}}$$

Let's use the same data as before: The mean weight of children in the general population ($\mu$) is 90 pounds, with a standard deviation ($\sigma$) of 17 pounds; for children in the sample ($N = 50$), the mean weight ($\overline{X}$) is 86 pounds. Using this information, we can now test the hypothesis that children in athletic after-school programs differ in weight from those in the general population. Notice that the calculations will be exactly the same for this $z$ test; that is, $\sigma_{\overline{X}}$ and the $z$-score will be exactly the same as before. Why? All of the measurements are exactly the same. To review:

$$\sigma_{\overline{X}} = \frac{\sigma}{\sqrt{N}} = \frac{17}{\sqrt{50}} = \frac{17}{7.07} = 2.40$$

$$z = \frac{\overline{X} - \mu}{\sigma_{\overline{X}}} = \frac{86 - 90}{2.40} = \frac{-4}{2.4} = -1.67$$

## Interpreting the Two-Tailed $z$ Test

If we end up with the same $z$-score, how does a two-tailed test differ from a one-tailed test? The difference is in the $z$ critical value ($z_{cv}$). In a two-tailed test, both halves of the normal distribution have to be taken into account. Remember that with a one-tailed test, $z_{cv}$ was $\pm 1.645$; this $z$-score was so far away from the mean (*either* above *or* below) that only 5% of the scores were beyond it. How does the $z_{cv}$ for a two-tailed test differ? With a two-tailed test, $z_{cv}$ has to be so far away from the mean that a total of only 5% of the scores are beyond it (*both* above *and* below the mean). A $z_{cv}$ of $\pm 1.645$ leaves 5% of the scores above the positive $z_{cv}$ and 5% below the negative $z_{cv}$. If we take both sides of the normal distribution into account (which we do with a two-tailed test because we do not predict whether the sample mean will be above or below the population mean), then 10% of the distribution will fall beyond the two critical values. Thus, $\pm 1.645$ cannot be the critical value for a two-tailed test because this leaves too much chance (10%) operating.

To determine $z_{cv}$ for a two-tailed test, then, we need to find the $z$-score that is far enough away from the population mean that only 5% of the distribution—taking into account both halves of the distribution—is beyond the score. Because Table A.2 represents only half of the distribution, we need to look for the $z$-score that leaves only 2.5% of the distribution beyond it. Then, when we take into account both halves of the distribution, 5% of the distribution will be accounted for (2.5% + 2.5% = 5%). Can you determine this $z$-score using Table A.2? If you find that it is ±1.96, you are correct. This is the $z$-score that is far enough away from the population mean (using both halves of the distribution) that only 5% of the distribution is beyond it. The critical values for both one- and two-tailed tests are illustrated in Figure 7.3.

Okay, what do we do with this critical value? We use it exactly the same way we used $z_{cv}$ for a one-tailed test. In other words, $z_{obt}$ has to be as large as or larger than $z_{cv}$ in order for us to reject $H_0$. Is our $z_{obt}$ as large as or larger than ±1.96? No, our $z_{obt}$ is −1.67. We therefore fail to reject $H_0$ and conclude that the weight of children in athletic after-school programs does not differ significantly from the weight of children in the general population.

With exactly the same data (sample size, $\mu$, $\sigma$, $\bar{X}$, and $\sigma_{\bar{X}}$), we rejected $H_0$ using a one-tailed test and failed to reject $H_0$ with a two-tailed test. How can this be? The answer is that a one-tailed test is statistically a more powerful test than a two-tailed test. **Statistical power** refers to the probability that we can reject $H_0$ and find significant differences. With a one-tailed test, we are more likely to reject $H_0$ because $z_{obt}$ does not have to be as large (as far away from the population mean) to be considered significantly different from the population mean. (Remember, $z_{cv}$ for a one-tailed test is ±1.645, but for a two-tailed test, it is ±1.96.)

**statistical power**   The ability to find significant differences when they truly exist.

**FIGURE 7.3**
**Regions of rejection and critical values for one-tailed versus two-tailed tests**

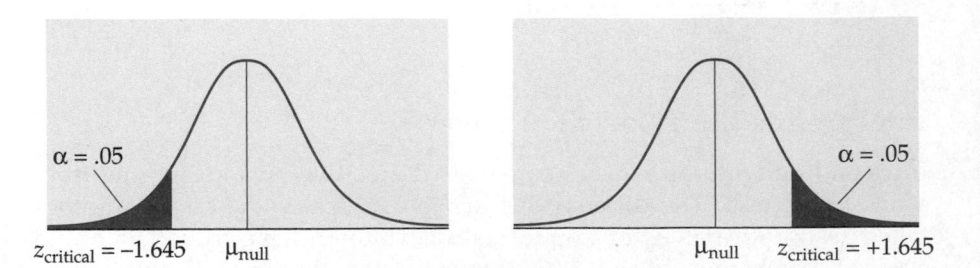

$\alpha = .05$

$z_{critical} = -1.645$    $\mu_{null}$

$\alpha = .05$

$\mu_{null}$    $z_{critical} = +1.645$

.025

.025

$z_{critical} = -1.96$    $\mu_{null}$    $z_{critical} = +1.96$

## Statistical Power

Let's think back to the discussion of Type I and II errors. We said that in order to reduce the risk of a Type I error, we need to lower the alpha level—for example, from .05 to .01. We also noted, however, that lowering the alpha level increases the risk of a Type II error. How, then, can we reduce the risk of a Type I error but not increase the risk of a Type II error? As we just noted, a one-tailed test is more powerful—we do not need as large a $z_{cv}$ in order to reject $H_0$. Here, then, is one way to maintain an alpha level of .05 but increase our chances of rejecting $H_0$. Of course, ethically we cannot simply choose to adopt a one-tailed test for this reason. The one-tailed test should be adopted only because we truly believe that the sample will perform above (or below) the mean.

By what other means can we increase statistical power? Look back at the z-test formula. We know that the larger $z_{obt}$ is, the greater the chance that it will be significant (as large as or larger than $z_{cv}$) and we can therefore reject $H_0$. What could we change in our study that might increase $z_{obt}$? Well, if the denominator in the z formula were a smaller number, then $z_{obt}$ would be larger and more likely to fall in the region of rejection. How can we make the denominator smaller? The denominator is $\sigma_{\bar{X}}$. Do you remember the formula for $\sigma_{\bar{X}}$?

$$\sigma_{\bar{X}} = \frac{\sigma}{\sqrt{N}}$$

It is very unlikely that we can change or influence the standard deviation of the population ($\sigma$). What part of the $\sigma_{\bar{X}}$ formula can we influence? The sample size ($N$).

If we increase the sample size, what will happen to $\sigma_{\bar{X}}$? Let's see. We can use the same example as before: a two-tailed test with all of the same measurements. The only difference will be the sample size. Thus, the null and alternative hypotheses are:

$H_0$: $\mu_0 = \mu_1$, or $\mu_{\text{athletic programs}} = \mu_{\text{general population}}$

$H_a$: $\mu_0 \neq \mu_1$, or $\mu_{\text{athletic programs}} \neq \mu_{\text{general population}}$

The mean weight ($\mu$) of children in the general population is once again 90 pounds, with a standard deviation ($\sigma$) of 17 pounds, and the sample of children in after-school programs again has a mean weight ($\bar{X}$) of 86 pounds. The only difference is the sample size. In this case, our sample has 100 children in it. Let's test the hypothesis (conduct the z test) for these data:

$$\sigma_{\bar{X}} = \frac{17}{\sqrt{100}} = \frac{17}{10} = 1.7$$

$$z = \frac{86 - 90}{1.7} = \frac{-4}{1.7} = -2.35$$

Do you see what happened when we increased the sample size? The standard error of the mean ($\sigma_{\bar{X}}$) decreased (we will discuss why in a minute) and

$z_{obt}$ increased—in fact, it increased to the extent that we can now reject $H_0$ with this two-tailed test because our $z_{obt}$ of $-2.35$ is larger than the $z_{cv}$ of $-1.96$. Therefore, another way to increase statistical power is to increase the sample size.

Why does increasing the sample size decrease $\sigma_{\bar{X}}$? Well, you can see why based on the formula, but let's think back to our earlier discussion about $\sigma_{\bar{X}}$. We said that it is the standard deviation of a sampling distribution—a distribution of sample means. If you recall the IQ example we used in our discussion of $\sigma_{\bar{X}}$ and the sampling distribution, we said that $\mu = 100$ and $\sigma = 15$. We discussed what $\sigma_{\bar{X}}$ is for a sampling distribution in which each sample mean is based on a sample size of 75. We further noted that $\sigma_{\bar{X}}$ is always smaller (has less variability) than $\sigma$ because it represents the standard deviation of a distribution of sample means, not a distribution of individual scores. What, then, does increasing the sample size do to $\sigma_{\bar{X}}$? If each sample in the sampling distribution has 100 people in it rather than 75, what do you think this will do to the distribution of sample means? As we noted earlier, most people in a sample will be close to the mean (100), with only a few people in each sample representing the tails of the distribution. If we increase the sample size to 100, we will have 25 more people in each sample. Most of them will probably be close to the population mean of 100; therefore, each sample mean will probably be closer to the population mean of 100. Thus, a sampling distribution based on samples of $N = 100$ rather than $N = 75$ will have less variability, which means that $\sigma_{\bar{X}}$ will be smaller. In sum, as the sample size increases, the standard error of the mean decreases.

## Assumptions and Appropriate Use of the *z* Test

As noted earlier in the chapter, the *z* test is a parametric inferential statistical test for hypothesis testing. Parametric tests involve the use of parameters, or population characteristics. With a *z* test, the parameters, such as $\mu$ and $\sigma$, are known. If they are not known, the *z* test is not appropriate. Because the *z* test involves the calculation and use of a sample mean, it is appropriate for use with interval or ratio data. In addition, because we use the area under the normal curve (see Table A.2), we are assuming that the distribution of random samples is normal. Small samples often fail to form a normal distribution. Therefore, if the sample size is small ($N < 30$), the *z* test may not be appropriate. In cases where the sample size is small, or where $\sigma$ is not known, the appropriate test is the *t* test, discussed in the next section.

| IN REVIEW | The *z* Test (Part II) | |
|---|---|---|
| **CONCEPT** | **DESCRIPTION** | **EXAMPLE** |
| One-Tailed *z* Test | A directional inferential test in which a prediction is made that the population represented by the sample will be either above or below the general population | $H_a$: $\mu_0 < \mu_1$ or $H_a$: $\mu_0 > \mu_1$ |
| Two-Tailed *z* Test | A nondirectional inferential test in which the prediction is made that the population represented by the sample | $H_a$: $\mu_0 \neq \mu_1$ |

| CONCEPT | DESCRIPTION | EXAMPLE |
|---------|-------------|---------|
| | will differ from the general population, but the direction of the difference is not predicted | |
| Statistical Power | The probability that the study will yield a significant result if the alternative hypothesis is true | One-tailed tests are more powerful; increasing sample size increases power |

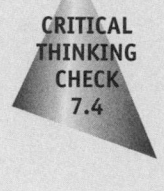

1. Imagine that I want to compare the intelligence level of psychology majors with the intelligence level of the general population of college students. I predict that psychology majors will have higher IQ scores. Is this a one- or two-tailed test? Identify $H_0$ and $H_a$.
2. Conduct the $z$ test for the example above. Assume that $\mu = 100$, $\sigma = 15$, $\bar{X} = 102.75$, and $N = 60$. Should we reject $H_0$ or fail to reject $H_0$?

CRITICAL THINKING CHECK 7.4

# Confidence Intervals

In this text, hypothesis tests such as the previously described $z$ test are the main focus. However, sometimes social and behavioral scientists use estimation of population means based on confidence intervals rather than statistical hypothesis tests. For example, imagine that you want to estimate a population mean based on sample data (a sample mean). This differs from the previously described $z$ test in that we are not determining whether the sample mean differs significantly from the population mean; rather, we are estimating the population mean based on knowing the sample mean. We can still use the area under the normal curve to accomplish this—we simply use it in a slightly different way.

Let's use the previous example in which we know the sample mean weight of children enrolled in athletic after-school programs ($\bar{X} = 86$), $\sigma$ (17), and the sample size ($N = 100$). However, imagine that we do not know the population mean ($\mu$). In this case, we can calculate a confidence interval based on knowing the sample mean and $\sigma$. A **confidence interval** is an interval of a certain width, which we feel "confident" will contain $\mu$. We want a confidence interval wide enough that we feel fairly certain it contains the population mean. For example, if we want to be 95% confident, we want a 95% confidence interval.

**confidence interval** An interval of a certain width, which we feel confident will contain $\mu$.

How can we use the area under the standard normal curve to determine a confidence interval of 95%? We use the area under the normal curve to determine the $z$ scores that mark off the area representing 95% of the scores under the curve. If you consult Table A.2, you will find that 95% of the scores will fall between ±1.96 standard deviations above and below the mean. Thus, we could determine which scores represent ±1.96 standard deviations from the mean of 86. This seems fairly simple, but we must remember that we are dealing with a distribution of sample means (the sampling distribution) and not with a distribution of individual scores. Thus, we must convert the standard deviation ($\sigma$) to the standard error of the mean ($\sigma_{\bar{X}}$, the standard deviation for a sampling distribution) and use the standard error of the mean in the calculation of a confidence interval. Remember, we calculate $\sigma_{\bar{X}}$ by dividing $\sigma$ by the square root of $N$.

$$\sigma_{\bar{X}} = \frac{17}{\sqrt{100}} = \frac{17}{10} = 1.7$$

We can now calculate the 95% confidence interval using the following formula:

$$CI = \bar{X} \pm z\left(\sigma_{\bar{X}}\right)$$

where

$\bar{X}$ = the sample mean
$\sigma_{\bar{X}}$ = the standard error of the mean
$z$ = the $z$-score representing the desired confidence interval
$CI = 86 \pm 1.96(1.7)$
$= 86 \pm 3.332$
$= 82.668 - 89.332$

Thus, the 95% confidence interval ranges from 82.67 to 89.33. We would conclude, based on this calculation, that we are 95% confident that the population mean lies within this interval.

What if we want to have greater confidence that our population mean is contained in the confidence interval? In other words, what if we want to be 99% confident? We would have to construct a 99% confidence interval. How would we go about doing this? We would do exactly what we did for the 95% confidence interval. First, we would consult Table A.2 to determine what $z$ scores mark off 99% of the area under the normal curve. We find that $z$ scores of ±2.58 mark off 99% of the area under the curve. We then apply the same formula for a confidence interval used previously.

$$CI = \bar{X} \pm z\left(\sigma_{\bar{X}}\right)$$
$$CI = 86 \pm 2.58(1.7)$$
$$= 86 \pm 4.386$$
$$= 81.614 - 90.386$$

Thus, the 99% confidence interval ranges from 81.61 to 90.39. We would conclude, based on this calculation, that we are 99% confident that the population mean lies within this interval.

Typically, statisticians recommend using a 95% or a 99% confidence interval. However, using Table A.2 (the area under the normal curve), you could construct a confidence interval of 55%, 70%, or any percentage you desire.

It is also possible to do hypothesis testing with confidence intervals. For example, if you construct a 95% confidence interval based on knowing a sample mean and then determine that the population mean is not in the confidence interval, the result is significant. For example, the 95% confidence interval we constructed earlier of 82.67–89.33 did not include the actual population mean reported earlier in the chapter ($\mu = 90$). Thus, there is less than a 5% chance that this sample mean could have come from this population— the same conclusion we reached when using the z test earlier in the chapter.

# The *t* Test: What It Is and What It Does

The *t* test for a single sample is similar to the z test in that it is also a parametric statistical test of the null hypothesis for a single sample. As such, it is a means of determining the number of standard deviation units a score is from the mean ($\mu$) of a distribution. With a *t* test, however, the population variance is not known. Another difference is that *t* distributions, although symmetrical and bell-shaped, do *not* fit the standard normal distribution. This means that the areas under the normal curve that apply for the z test do not apply for the *t* test.

**t test** A parametric inferential statistical test of the null hypothesis for a single sample where the population variance is not known.

## Student's *t* Distribution

The *t* distribution, known as **Student's *t* distribution**, was developed by William Sealey Gosset, a chemist who worked for the Guinness Brewing Company of Dublin, Ireland, at the beginning of the 20th century. Gosset noticed that for small samples of beer ($N < 30$) chosen for quality-control testing, the sampling distribution of the means was symmetrical and bell-shaped but not normal. In other words, with small samples, the curve was symmetrical, but it was not the standard normal curve; therefore, the proportions under the standard normal curve did not apply. As the size of the samples in the sampling distribution increased, the sampling distribution approached the normal distribution and the proportions under the curve became more similar to those under the standard normal curve. He eventually published his findings under the pseudonym "Student," and with the help of Karl Pearson, a mathematician, he developed a general formula for the *t* distributions (Peters, 1987; Stigler, 1986; Tankard, 1984; all cited in Aron & Aron, 1999).

**Student's *t* distribution** A set of distributions that, although symmetrical and bell-shaped, are not normally distributed.

We refer to *t* distributions in the plural because unlike the z distribution, of which there is only one, the *t* distributions are a family of symmetrical distributions that differ for each sample size. As a result, the critical value indicating the region of rejection changes for samples of different sizes. As the size of the samples increases, the *t* distribution approaches the z or normal distribution. Table A.3 in Appendix A at the back of the book provides the critical values ($t_{cv}$) for both one- and two-tailed tests for various sample sizes and alpha levels. Notice, however, that although we have said that the

**degrees of freedom (df)**
The number of scores in a sample that are free to vary.

critical value depends on sample size, there is no column in the table labeled $N$ for sample size. Instead, there is a column labeled **df**, which stands for **degrees of freedom**—the number of scores in a sample that are free to vary. The degrees of freedom are related to the sample size. For example, assume that you are given six numbers: 2, 5, 6, 9, 11, and 15. The mean of these numbers is 8. If you are told that you can change the numbers as you like but that the mean of the distribution must remain 8, how many numbers can you change arbitrarily? You can change five of the six numbers arbitrarily. Once you have changed five of the numbers arbitrarily, the sixth number is determined by the qualification that the mean of the distribution must equal 8. Therefore, in this distribution of six numbers, five are free to vary. Thus, there are five degrees of freedom. For any single distribution then, $df = N - 1$.

Look again at Table A.3 and notice what happens to the critical values as the degrees of freedom increase. Look at the column for a one-tailed test with alpha equal to .05 and degrees of freedom equal to 10. The critical value is ±1.812. This is larger than the critical value for a one-tailed z test, which was ±1.645. Because we are dealing with smaller, nonnormal distributions when using the $t$ test, the $t$-score must be farther away from the mean in order for us to conclude that it is significantly different from the mean. What happens as the degrees of freedom increase? Look in the same column—one-tailed test, alpha = .05—for 20 degrees of freedom. The critical value is ±1.725, smaller than the critical value for 10 degrees of freedom. Continue to scan down the same column, one-tailed test and alpha = .05, until you reach the bottom where $df = \infty$. Notice that the critical value is ±1.645, the same as it is for a one-tailed z test. Thus, when the sample size is large, the $t$ distribution is the same as the z distribution.

## Calculations for the One-Tailed $t$ Test

Let's illustrate the use of the single-sample $t$ test to test a hypothesis. Assume the mean SAT score of students admitted to General University is 1090. Thus, the university mean of 1090 is the population mean ($\mu$). The population standard deviation is unknown. The members of the biology department believe that students who decide to major in biology have higher SAT scores than the general population of students at the university. The null and alternative hypotheses are thus

$H_0$: $\mu_0 \leq \mu_1$, or $\mu_{\text{biology students}} \leq \mu_{\text{general population}}$

$H_a$: $\mu_0 > \mu_1$, or $\mu_{\text{biology students}} > \mu_{\text{general population}}$

Notice that this is a one-tailed test because the researchers predict that the biology students have higher SAT scores than the general population of students at the university. The researchers now need to obtain the SAT scores for a sample of biology majors. SAT scores for 10 biology majors are provided in Table 7.2, which shows that the mean SAT score for the sample is 1176. This represents our estimate of the population mean SAT score for biology majors.

**TABLE 7.2  SAT scores for a sample of 10 biology majors**

| X |
|---|
| 1010 |
| 1200 |
| 1310 |
| 1075 |
| 1149 |
| 1078 |
| 1129 |
| 1069 |
| 1350 |
| 1390 |
| $\Sigma X = 11{,}760$ |

$$\bar{X} = \frac{\Sigma X}{N} = \frac{11{,}760}{10} = 1176.00$$

## The Estimated Standard Error of the Mean

The $t$ test will tell us whether this mean differs significantly from the university mean of 1090. Because we have a small sample ($N = 10$) and because we do not know $\sigma$, we must conduct a $t$ test rather than a $z$ test. The formula for the $t$ test is

$$t = \frac{\bar{X} - \mu}{s_{\bar{X}}}$$

This looks very similar to the formula for the $z$ test that we used earlier in the chapter. The only difference is the denominator, where $s_{\bar{X}}$ (the **estimated standard error of the mean**—an estimate of the standard deviation of the sampling distribution based on sample data—has been substituted for $\sigma_{\bar{X}}$. We use $s_{\bar{X}}$ rather than $\sigma_{\bar{X}}$ because we do not know $\sigma$ (the standard deviation for the population) and thus cannot calculate $\sigma_{\bar{X}}$. We can, however, determine $s$ (the unbiased estimator of the population standard deviation) and, based on this, we can determine $s_{\bar{X}}$. The formula for $s_{\bar{X}}$ is

**estimated standard error of the mean** An estimate of the standard deviation of the sampling distribution.

$$s_{\bar{X}} = \frac{s}{\sqrt{N}}$$

We must first calculate $s$ (the estimated standard deviation for a population, based on sample data) and then use $s$ to calculate the estimated standard error of the mean ($s_{\bar{X}}$). The formula for $s$, which we learned in Chapter 5, is

$$s = \sqrt{\frac{\Sigma\left(X - \bar{X}\right)^2}{N - 1}}$$

Using the information in Table 7.2, we can use this formula to calculate $s$:

$$s = \sqrt{\frac{156,352}{9}} = \sqrt{17,372.44} = 131.80$$

Thus, the unbiased estimator of the standard deviation ($s$) is 131.80. We can now use this value to calculate $s_{\bar{X}}$, the estimated standard error of the sampling distribution:

$$s_{\bar{X}} = \frac{s}{\sqrt{N}} = \frac{131.80}{\sqrt{10}} = \frac{131.80}{3.16} = 41.71$$

Finally, we can use this value for $s_{\bar{X}}$ to calculate $t$:

$$t = \frac{\bar{X} - \mu}{s_{\bar{X}}} = \frac{1176 - 1090}{41.71} = \frac{86}{41.71} = +2.06$$

## Interpreting the One-Tailed $t$ Test

Our sample mean falls 2.06 standard deviations above the population mean of 1090. We must now determine whether this is far enough away from the population mean to be considered significantly different. In other words, is our sample mean far enough away from the population mean that it lies in the region of rejection? Because the alternative hypothesis is one-tailed, the region of rejection is in only one tail of the sampling distribution. Consulting Table A.3 for a one-tailed test with alpha = .05 and $df = N - 1 = 9$, we see that $t_{cv} = 1.833$. The $t_{obt}$ of 2.06 is therefore within the region of rejection. We reject $H_0$ and support $H_a$. In other words, we have sufficient evidence to allow us to conclude that biology majors have significantly higher SAT scores than the rest of the students at General University. Figure 7.4 illustrates the obtained $t$ in relation to the region of rejection.

**FIGURE 7.4**
**The $t$ critical value and the $t$ obtained for the single-sample one-tailed $t$-test example**

Region of rejection

+1.833   +2.06
$t_{cv}$     $t_{obt}$

## Calculations for the Two-Tailed $t$ Test

What if the biology department made no directional prediction concerning the SAT scores of its students? In other words, suppose the members of the department are unsure whether their students' SAT scores are higher or lower than those of the general population of students and are simply interested in whether biology students differ from the population. In this case, the test of the alternative hypothesis is two-tailed, and the null and alternative hypotheses are

$H_0$: $\mu_0 = \mu_1$, or $\mu_{\text{biology students}} = \mu_{\text{general population}}$

$H_a$: $\mu_0 \neq \mu_1$, or $\mu_{\text{biology students}} \neq \mu_{\text{general population}}$

If we assume that the sample of biology students is the same, then $\bar{X}$, $s$, and $s_{\bar{X}}$ are all the same. The population at General University is also the same, so $\mu$ is still 1090. Using all of this information to conduct the $t$ test, we end up with exactly the same $t$-test score of $+2.06$. What, then, is the difference for the two-tailed $t$ test? It is the same as the difference between the one- and two-tailed $z$ test—the critical values differ.

## Interpreting the Two-Tailed $t$ Test

Remember that with a two-tailed alternative hypothesis, the region of rejection is divided evenly between the two tails (the positive and negative ends) of the sampling distribution. Consulting Table A.3 for a two-tailed test with alpha = .05 and $df = N - 1 = 9$, we see that $t_{cv} = 2.262$. The $t_{obt}$ of 2.06 is therefore not within the region of rejection. We do not reject $H_0$ and thus cannot support $H_a$. In other words, we do not have sufficient evidence to allow us to conclude that the population of biology majors differs significantly on SAT scores from the rest of the students at General University. Thus, with exactly the same data, we rejected $H_0$ with a one-tailed test but failed to reject $H_0$ with a two-tailed test, illustrating once again that one-tailed tests are more powerful than two-tailed tests. Figure 7.5 illustrates the obtained $t$ for the two-tailed test in relation to the region of rejection.

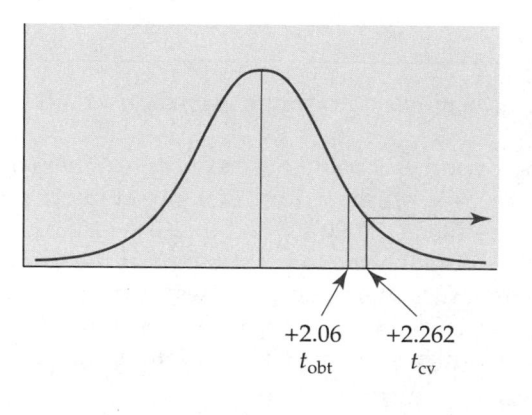

**FIGURE 7.5**
**The $t$ critical value and the $t$ obtained for the single-sample two-tailed $t$-test example**

$+2.06$     $+2.262$
$t_{obt}$        $t_{cv}$

## Assumptions and Appropriate Use of the Single-Sample *t* Test

The *t* test is a parametric test, as is the *z* test. As a parametric test, the *t* test must meet certain assumptions. These assumptions include that the data are interval or ratio and that the population distribution of scores is normally distributed. The *t* test is used in situations that meet these assumptions and in which the population mean is known but the population standard deviation ($\sigma$) is not known. In cases where these criteria are not met, a nonparametric test such as a chi-square test or Wilcoxon test is more appropriate. These nonparametric tests will be covered in Chapter 13.

### IN REVIEW    The *t* Test

| CONCEPT | DESCRIPTION | USE/EXAMPLE |
|---|---|---|
| Estimated standard error of the mean ($s_{\bar{x}}$) | The estimated standard deviation of a sampling distribution, calculated by dividing $s$ by $\sqrt{N}$ | Used in the calculation of a *t* test |
| *t* test | Indicator of the number of standard deviation units the sample mean is from the mean of the sampling distribution | An inferential statistical test that differs from the *z* test in that the sample size is small (usually < 30) and $\sigma$ is not known |
| One-tailed *t* test | A directional inferential test in which a prediction is made that the population represented by the sample will be either above or below the general population | $H_a: \mu_0 < \mu_1$ or $H_a: \mu_0 > \mu_1$ |
| Two-tailed *t* test | A nondirectional inferential test in which the prediction is made that the population represented by the sample will differ from the general population, but the direction of the difference is not predicted | $H_a: \mu_0 \neq \mu_1$ |

**CRITICAL THINKING CHECK 7.5**

1. Explain the difference in use and computation between the *z* test and the *t* test.
2. Test the following hypothesis using the *t* test: Researchers are interested in whether the pulses of long-distance runners differ from those of other athletes. They suspect that the runners' pulses will be slower. They obtain a random sample ($N = 8$) of long-distance runners, measure their resting pulses, and obtain the following data: 45, 42, 64, 54, 58, 49, 47, 55 beats per minute. The average resting pulse of athletes in the general population is 60 beats per minute.

# Correlation Coefficients and Statistical Significance

You may remember from Chapter 6 that correlation coefficients are used to describe the strength of a relationship between two variables. For example, we learned how to calculate the Pearson product-moment correlation coefficient, which is used when the variables are of interval or ratio scale. At that time, however, we did not discuss the idea of statistical significance. In this case, the null hypothesis ($H_0$) is that the true population correlation is 0.00—the variables are not related. The alternative hypothesis ($H_a$) is that the observed correlation is not equal to 0.00—the variables are related. But what if we obtain a rather weak correlation coefficient, such as $+0.33$? Determining the statistical significance of the correlation coefficient will allow us to decide whether or not to reject $H_0$.

To test the null hypothesis that the population correlation coefficient is 0.00, we must consult a table of critical values for $r$ (the Pearson product-moment correlation coefficient) as we have done for the other statistics discussed in this chapter. Table A.4 in Appendix A shows critical values for both one- and two-tailed tests of $r$. A one-tailed test of a correlation coefficient means that we have predicted the expected direction of the correlation coefficient (i.e., predicted either a positive or negative correlation), whereas a two-tailed test means that we have not predicted the direction of the correlation coefficient.

To use this table, we first need to determine the degrees of freedom, which for the Pearson product-moment correlation are equal to $N - 2$, where $N$ represents the total number of pairs of observations. If the correlation coefficient of $+.33$ is based on 20 pairs of observations, then the degrees of freedom are $20 - 2 = 18$. Once the degrees of freedom are determined, we can consult the critical values table. For 18 degrees of freedom and a two-tailed test at alpha $= .05$, $r_{cv}$ is $\pm.4438$. This means that $r_{obt}$ must be that large or larger in order to be statistically significant at the .05 level. Because our $r_{obt}$ is not that large, we fail to reject $H_0$. In other words, the observed correlation coefficient is not statistically significant.

# Summary

In this chapter, we introduced hypothesis testing and inferential statistics. The discussion of hypothesis testing included the null and alternative hypotheses, one- and two-tailed hypothesis tests, and Type I and Type II errors in hypothesis testing. In addition, we defined the concept of statistical significance. The simplest type of hypothesis testing—a single-group design in which the performance of a sample is compared with that of the general population—was used to illustrate the use of inferential statistics in hypothesis testing.

We described two parametric statistical tests: the $z$ test and the $t$ test. Each compares a sample mean with the general population. Because both are parametric tests, the distributions should be bell-shaped and certain parameters should be known (in the case of the $z$ test, $\mu$ and $\sigma$ must be known; for the $t$ test, only $\mu$ is needed). In addition, because the tests are parametric, the data should be interval or ratio in scale. These tests use the sampling distribution (the distribution of sample means). They also use the standard error of the mean (or estimated standard error of the mean for the $t$ test), which is the standard deviation of the sampling distribution. Both $z$ and $t$ tests can test one- or two-tailed alternative hypotheses, but one-tailed tests are more powerful statistically.

Nonparametric tests are those for which population parameters ($\mu$ and $\sigma$) are not known. In addition, the underlying distribution of scores is not assumed to be normal, and the data are most commonly nominal (categorical) in nature. Nonparametric tests will be covered in Chapter 13.

Last, we revisited correlation coefficients with respect to significance testing. We learned how to determine whether an observed correlation coefficient is statistically significant by using a critical values table.

In Chapters 9–11 and 13, we will continue our discussion of inferential statistics, looking at statistical procedures appropriate for experimental designs with two or more equivalent groups, those appropriate for designs with more than one independent variable, and nonparametric procedures.

## KEY TERMS

| | | |
|---|---|---|
| hypothesis testing | Type I error | critical value |
| inferential statistics | Type II error | statistical power |
| null hypothesis ($H_0$) | statistical significance | confidence interval |
| alternative hypothesis ($H_a$), or research hypothesis ($H_1$) | single-group design | $t$ test |
| | parametric test | Student's $t$ distribution |
| one-tailed hypothesis (directional hypothesis) | nonparametric test | degrees of freedom |
| | $z$ test | estimated standard error of the |
| two-tailed hypothesis (nondirectional hypothesis) | sampling distribution | mean |
| | standard error of the mean | |

## CHAPTER EXERCISES

(Answers to odd-numbered exercises appear in Appendix C.)

1. The admissions counselors at Brainy University believe that the freshman class they have just recruited is the brightest yet. If they want to test this belief (that the freshmen are brighter than the other classes), what are the null and alternative hypotheses? Is this a one- or two-tailed hypothesis test?

2. To test the hypothesis in Exercise 1, the admissions counselors select a random sample of freshmen and compare their scores on the SAT with those of the population of upper classmen. They find that the freshmen do in fact have a higher mean SAT score. However, they are unaware that the sample of freshmen was not representative of all freshmen at Brainy University. In fact, the sample overrepresented those with high scores and underrepresented those with low scores. What type of error (Type I or Type II) did the counselors make?

3. A researcher believes that family size has increased in the last decade in comparison to the previous decade—that is, people are now having more children than they were before. What are the null and alternative hypotheses in a study designed to assess this? Is this a one- or two-tailed hypothesis test?

4. What are the appropriate $H_0$ and $H_a$ for each of the following research studies? In addition,

note whether the hypothesis test is one- or two-tailed.

a. A study in which researchers want to test whether there is a difference in spatial ability between left- and right-handed people

b. A study in which researchers want to test whether nurses who work 8-hour shifts deliver higher-quality care than those who work 12-hour shifts

c. A study in which researchers want to determine whether crate-training puppies is superior to training without a crate

5. Assume that each of the following conclusions represents an error in hypothesis testing. Indicate whether each of the statements is a Type I or II error.

a. Based on the data, the null hypothesis is rejected.

b. There is no significant difference in quality of care between nurses who work 8- and 12-hour shifts.

c. There is a significant difference between right- and left-handers in their ability to perform a spatial task.

d. The researcher fails to reject the null hypothesis based on these data.

6. How do inferential statistics differ from descriptive statistics?

7. A researcher is interested in whether students who attend private high schools have higher average SAT scores than students in the general population. A random sample of 90 students at a private high school is tested and has a mean SAT score of 1050. The average score for public high school students is 1000 ($\sigma = 200$).

a. Is this a one- or two-tailed test?

b. What are $H_0$ and $H_a$ for this study?

c. Compute $z_{obt}$.

d. What is $z_{cv}$?

e. Should $H_0$ be rejected? What should the researcher conclude?

f. Determine the 95% confidence interval for the population mean, based on the sample mean.

8. The producers of a new toothpaste claim that it prevents more cavities than other brands of toothpaste. A random sample of 60 people use the new toothpaste for 6 months. The mean

number of cavities at their next checkup is 1.5. In the general population, the mean number of cavities at a 6-month checkup is 1.73 ($\sigma = 1.12$).

a. Is this a one- or two-tailed test?

b. What are $H_0$ and $H_a$ for this study?

c. Compute $z_{obt}$.

d. What is $z_{cv}$?

e. Should $H_0$ be rejected? What should the researcher conclude?

f. Determine the 95% confidence interval for the population mean, based on the sample mean.

9. Why does $t_{cv}$ change when the sample size changes? What must be computed in order to determine $t_{cv}$?

10. Henry performed a two-tailed test for an experiment in which $N = 24$. He could not find his table of $t$ critical values, but he remembered the $t_{cv}$ at $df = 13$. He decided to compare his $t_{obt}$ with this $t_{cv}$. Is he more likely to make a Type I or a Type II error in this situation?

11. A researcher hypothesizes that people who listen to music via headphones have greater hearing loss and will thus score lower on a hearing test than those in the general population. On a standard hearing test, the overall mean is 22.5. The researcher gives this same test to a random sample of 12 individuals who regularly use headphones. Their scores on the test are 16, 14, 20, 12, 25, 22, 23, 19, 17, 17, 21, 20.

a. Is this a one- or two-tailed test?

b. What are $H_0$ and $H_a$ for this study?

c. Compute $t_{obt}$.

d. What is $t_{cv}$?

e. Should $H_0$ be rejected? What should the researcher conclude?

12. A researcher hypothesizes that individuals who listen to classical music will score differently from the general population on a test of spatial ability. On a standardized test of spatial ability, $\mu = 58$. A random sample of 14 individuals who listen to classical music is given the same test. Their scores on the test are 52, 59, 63, 65, 58, 55, 62, 63, 53, 59, 57, 61, 60, 59.

a. Is this a one- or two-tailed test?

b. What are $H_0$ and $H_a$ for this study?

c. Compute $t_{obt}$.

d. What is $t_{cv}$?

e. Should $H_0$ be rejected? What should the researcher conclude?

## CRITICAL THINKING CHECK ANSWERS

### 7.1

1. $H_0$: $\mu_{southern\ children} \geq \mu_{children\ in\ general}$
   $H_a$: $\mu_{southern\ children} < \mu_{children\ in\ general}$

   This is a one-tailed test.
2. The researcher concluded that there was a difference when in reality there was no difference between the sample and the population. This is a Type I error.
3. With the .10 level of significance, the researcher is willing to accept a higher probability that the result may be due to chance. Therefore, a Type I error is more likely to be made than if the researcher used the more traditional .05 level of significance. With a .01 level of significance, the researcher is willing to accept only a .01 probability that the result may be due to chance. In this case, a true result is more likely to be missed, meaning that a Type II error is more likely.

### 7.2

1. Inferential statistics allow researchers to make inferences about a population based on sample data. Descriptive statistics simply describe a data set.
2. Single-sample research allows researchers to compare sample data with population data. The hypothesis tested is whether the sample performs similarly to the population or whether the sample differs significantly from the population and thus represents a different population.

### 7.3

1. A sampling distribution is a distribution of sample means. Thus, rather than representing scores for individuals, the sampling distribution plots the means of samples of a set size.
2. $\sigma_{\overline{X}}$ is the standard deviation for a sampling distribution. It therefore represents the standard deviation for a distribution of sample means. $\sigma$ is the standard deviation for a population of individual scores rather than sample means.
3. A z test compares the performance of a sample with the performance of the population by indicating the number of standard deviation units the sample mean is from the population mean. A

z-score indicates how many standard deviation units an individual score is from the population mean.

### 7.4

1. Predicting that psychology majors will have higher IQ scores makes this a one-tailed test.

   $H_0$: $\mu_{psychology\ majors} \leq \mu_{general\ population}$
   $H_a$: $\mu_{psychology\ majors} > \mu_{general\ population}$

2. 
$$\sigma_{\overline{X}} = \frac{15}{\sqrt{60}} = \frac{15}{7.75} = 1.94$$
$$z = \frac{102.75 - 100}{1.94} = \frac{2.75}{1.94} = 1.42$$

Because this is a one-tailed test, $z_{cv} = \pm 1.645$. The $z_{obt} = +1.42$. We therefore fail to reject $H_0$ and conclude that psychology majors do not differ significantly on IQ scores from the general population of college students.

### 7.5

1. The z test is used when the sample size is greater than 30, normally distributed, and $\sigma$ is known. The t test is used when the sample size is smaller than 30 and bell-shaped but not normal, and $\sigma$ is not known.
2. $H_0$: $\mu_{runners} \geq \mu_{other\ athletes}$
   $H_a$: $\mu_{runners} < \mu_{other\ athletes}$
   $\overline{X} = 51.75$
   $s = 7.32$
   $\mu = 60$

$$s_{\overline{X}} = \frac{7.32}{\sqrt{8}} = \frac{7.32}{2.83} = 2.59$$

$$t = \frac{51.75 - 60}{2.59} = \frac{-8.25}{2.59} = -3.19$$
$$df = 8 - 1 = 7$$
$$t_{cv} = \pm 1.895$$
$$t_{obt} = -3.19$$

Reject $H_0$. The runners' pulses are significantly slower than the pulses of athletes in general.

## WEB RESOURCES

Check your knowledge of the content in this chapter by taking the practice quiz at www.Wadsworth.com. Or, for step-by-step practice and information, check out the Statistics and Research Methods Workshops at http://psychology.wadsworth.com/workshops.

## STATISTICAL SOFTWARE RESOURCES

For hands-on experience using statistical software to complete the analyses described in this chapter, see Chapters 2 ("The z Statistic"), 4 ("Sampling Distributions"), 5 ("Probability"), and 6 ("The t Statistic—One Sample") in *The Excel Statistics Companion* by Kenneth M. Rosenberg (Belmont, CA: Wadsworth, 2003).

# 8 The Logic of Experimental Design

In this chapter, we will discuss the logic of the simple well-designed experiment. Pick up any newspaper or watch any news program, and you will be confronted with results and claims based on scientific research. Some people dismiss or ignore many of the claims because they do not understand how a study or a series of studies can lead to a single conclusion. In other words, they do not understand the concept of control in experiments and that when control is maximized, the conclusion is most likely reliable and valid. Other people accept everything they read, assuming that whatever is presented in a newspaper must be true. They too are not able to assess whether the research was conducted in a reliable and valid manner. This chapter will enable you to understand how to do so.

In previous chapters, we looked at nonexperimental designs. Most recently, in Chapter 6, we discussed correlational designs and the problems and limitations associated with using this type of design. We now turn to experimental designs, noting advantages of the true experimental design over the methods discussed previously.

# Between-Participants Experimental Designs

In a **between-participants design,** the participants in each group are different; that is, different people serve in the control and experimental groups. The idea behind experimentation, you should recall from Chapter 1, is that the researcher manipulates at least one variable (the *independent variable*) and measures at least one variable (the *dependent variable*). The independent variable has at least two groups or conditions. In other words, one of the most basic ideas behind an experiment is that there are at least two groups to compare. We typically refer to these two groups or conditions as the *control group* and the *experimental group.* The control group is the group that serves as the baseline or "standard" condition. The experimental group is the group that receives some level of the independent variable. Although we describe the two groups in an experiment as the experimental and control groups, an experiment may involve the use of two experimental groups with no control group. As we will see in later chapters, an experiment can also have more than two groups. In other words, there can be multiple experimental groups in an experiment.

Experimentation involves control. First, we have to control who is in the study. We want to have a sample that is representative of the population about whom we are trying to generalize. Ideally, we accomplish this through the use of random sampling. We also need to control who participates in each condition, so we should use random assignment of participants to the two conditions. By randomly assigning participants to conditions, we are trying to make the two groups as equivalent as possible. In addition to controlling who serves in the study and in each condition, we need to control what happens during the experiment, so that the only difference between conditions is in the level of the independent variable that participants receive. If, after controlling all of this, we observe behavioral changes when the independent variable is manipulated, we can then conclude that the independent variable caused these changes in the dependent variable.

**between-participants design** An experiment in which different participants are assigned to each group.

Let's consider the example from Chapter 6 on smoking and cancer to examine the difference between correlational research and experimental research. Remember, we said that there was a positive correlation between smoking and cancer. We also noted that no experimental evidence with humans supported a causal relationship between smoking and cancer. Why is this the case? Let's think about actually trying to design an experiment to determine whether smoking causes cancer in humans. Keep in mind potential ethical problems that might arise as we design this experiment.

Let's first determine what the independent variable would be. If you identified smoking behavior as the independent variable, you are correct. The control group would be the group that does not smoke, and the experimental group would be the group that does smoke. To prevent confounding of our study by previous smoking behavior, we could use only nonsmokers. We would then randomly assign them to either the smoking or the nonsmoking group. In addition to assigning participants to one of the two conditions, we would control all other aspects of their lives. This means that all participants in the study must be treated exactly the same for the duration of the study, except that half of them would smoke on a regular basis (we would decide when and how much) and half of them would not smoke at all. We would then determine the length of time for which the study should run. In this case, participants would have to smoke for many years in order to assess any potential differences between groups. During this time, all aspects of their lives that might contribute to cancer would have to be controlled—held constant between the groups.

What would the dependent variable be? The dependent variable would be the incidence of cancer. After several years had passed, we would begin to take measures on the two groups to determine whether there were any differences in cancer rates. Thus, the cancer rate would be the dependent variable. If control was maximized and the experimental group and control group were treated exactly the same except for the level of the independent variable that they received, then any difference observed between the groups in cancer rate would have to be due to the only difference that existed between the groups—the independent variable of smoking.

You should begin to appreciate the problems associated with designing a true experiment to test the effects of smoking on cancer. First, it is not ethical to determine for people whether or not they smoke. Second, it is not feasible to control all aspects of these individuals' lives for the period of time that is needed to conduct this study. It is for these reasons that there is no experimental study indicating that smoking causes cancer in humans.

It is perfectly feasible, however, to conduct experimental studies on other topics. For example, if we wanted to study the effects of a certain type of mnemonic device (a study strategy) on memory, we could have one group use the device while studying and another group not use the device while studying. We could then give each person a memory test and look for a difference in performance between the two groups. Assuming that everything else was held constant (controlled), any difference observed would have to be due to the independent variable. If the mnemonic group performed better, we could conclude that the mnemonic device caused memory to improve.

This memory study is what is known as a simple **posttest-only control group design.** We start with a control group and an experimental group made up of equivalent participants; we administer the treatment (mnemonic or no mnemonic); and we take a posttest (after-treatment) measure. It is very important that the experimental and control groups are equivalent because we want to be able to conclude that any differences observed between the two groups are due to the independent variable and not to some other difference between the groups. We help to ensure equivalency of groups by using random assignment.

When we manipulate the independent variable, we must ensure that the manipulation is valid—in other words, that there really is a difference in the manner in which the two groups are treated. This appears fairly easy for the study described above—either the participants use the prescribed mnemonic device, or they do no. However, how do we actually know that those in the mnemonic group truly are using the device and that those in the control group are not using any type of mnemonic device? These are questions the researcher would need to address before beginning the study so that the instructions given to participants leave no doubt as to what the participants in each condition should be doing during the study.

Last, the research must measure the dependent variable (memory) in order to assess any effects of the independent variable. To be able to compare performance across the two groups, the same measurement device must be used for both groups. If the groups were equivalent at the beginning of the study, and if the independent variable was adequately manipulated and the only difference between the two groups, then any differences observed on the dependent variable must be attributable to the independent variable.

We could make the above-described design slightly more sophisticated by using a **pretest/posttest control group design,** which involves adding a pretest to the design. This new design has the added advantage of ensuring that the participants are equivalent at the beginning of the study. This precaution is usually not considered necessary if participants are randomly assigned and if the researcher uses a sufficiently large sample of participants. The issue of how many participants is sufficient will be discussed in greater detail in Chapter 9; however, as a general rule, 20–30 participants per condition is considered adequate. There are disadvantages to pretest/posttest control groups designs, including the possibility of increasing demand characteristics and experimenter effects (both discussed later in the chapter). The participants might guess before the posttest what is being measured in the study. If the participants make an assumption (either correct or incorrect) about the intent of the study, their behavior during the study may be changed from what would "normally" happen. With multiple testings, there is also more opportunity for an experimenter to influence the participants. It is up to the researchers to decide which of these designs best suits their needs.

**posttest-only control group design** An experimental design in which the dependent variable is measured after the manipulation of the independent variable.

**protect/posttest control group design** An experimental design in which the dependent variable is measured both before and after manipulation of the independent variable.

## Control and Confounds

Obviously, one of the most critical elements of an experiment is control. It is imperative that control be maximized. If a researcher fails to control for something, then the study is open to confounds. A **confound** is an uncontrolled extraneous variable or flaw in an experiment. If a study is confounded, then it is impossible to say whether changes in the dependent variable were caused by the independent variable or by the uncontrolled variable.

The problem for most psychologists is that maximizing control with human participants can be very difficult. In other disciplines, control is not as difficult. For example, marine biologists do not need to be as concerned about preexisting differences between the sea snails they may be studying because sea snails do not vary on as many dimensions as do humans (personality, intelligence, and rearing issues, for example, are not relevant as they are for humans). Because of the great variability among humans on all dimensions, psychologists need to be very concerned about preexisting differences. Consider the previously described study on memory and mnemonic devices. A problem could occur if the differences in performance on the memory test resulted from the fact that, based on chance, the more educated participants made up the experimental group and the less educated participants made up the control group. In this case, we might have observed a difference in memory performance even if the experimental group had not used the mnemonic strategy.

Even when we use random assignment as a means of minimizing differences between the experimental and control groups, we still need to think about control in the study. For example, if we were to conduct the study on memory and mnemonic devices, we should consider administering some pretests as a means of assuring that the participants in the two groups are equivalent on any dimension (variable) that might affect memory performance. It is imperative that psychologists working with humans understand control and potential confounds due to human variability. If the basis of experimentation is that the control group and the experimental group (or the two experimental groups being compared) are as similar as possible except for differences in the independent variable, then it is up to the researcher to make sure that this is indeed the case. In short, the researcher needs to maximize the **internal validity** of the study—the extent to which the results can be attributed to the manipulation of the independent variable rather than to some confounding variable. A study with good internal validity has no confounds and offers only one explanation for the results.

## Threats to Internal Validity

We will now consider several potential threats to the internal validity of a study. The confounds described here are those most commonly encountered in psychological research; depending on the nature of the study, other confounds more specific to the type of research being conducted may arise. The confounds presented here will give you an overview of some potential problems and an opportunity to begin developing the critical thinking skills

**confound** An uncontrolled extraneous variable or flaw in an experiment.

**internal validity** The extent to which the results of an experiment can be attributed to the manipulation of the independent variable rather than to some confounding variable.

involved in designing a sound study. These confounds are most problematic for nonexperimental designs but may also pose a threat to experimental designs. Taking the precautions described should indicate whether or not the confound is present in a study.

*Nonequivalent Control Group.* One of the most basic concerns in an experiment is that the participants in the control and experimental groups are equivalent at the beginning of the study. Using random sampling and random assignment is typically considered sufficient to address the potential problem of a nonequivalent control group. When random sampling and random assignment are not used, participant selection or assignment problems may result. In this case, we would have a quasi-experimental design (discussed in Chapter 12), not a true experiment.

*History.* Changes in the dependent variable may be due to historical events that occur outside of the study, leading to the confound known as a **history effect.** These events are most likely unrelated to the study but may nonetheless affect the dependent variable. Imagine that you are conducting a study on the effects of a certain program on stress reduction in college students. The study covers a 2-month period during which students participate in your stress reduction program. If your posttest measure were taken during midterm or final exams, you might notice an increase in stress even though participants were involved in a program that was intended to reduce stress. Not taking the historical point in the semester into account might lead you to an erroneous conclusion concerning the stress reduction program. Notice also that a control group of equivalent participants would have helped reveal the confound in this study.

**history effect** A threat to internal validity in which an outside event that is not a part of the manipulation of the experiment could be responsible for the results.

*Maturation.* In research in which participants are studied over a period of time, a **maturation effect** can frequently be a problem. Participants mature physically, socially, and cognitively during the course of the study. Any changes in the dependent variable that occur across the course of the study, therefore, may be due to maturation and not to the independent variable of the study. Using a control group with equivalent participants will indicate whether changes in the dependent variable are due to maturation; if they are, the participants in the control group will change on the dependent variable during the course of the study even though they did not receive the treatment.

**maturation effect** A threat to internal validity in which naturally occurring changes within the participants could be responsible for the observed results.

*Testing.* In studies in which participants are measured numerous times, a **testing effect** may be a problem—repeated testing may lead to better or worse performance. Many studies involve pretest and posttest measures. Other studies involve taking measures on an hourly, daily, weekly, or monthly basis. In these cases, participants are exposed to the same or similar "tests" numerous times. As a result, changes in performance on the test may be due to prior experience with the test, and not to the independent variable. If, for example, participants took the same math test before and after participating in a special math course, the improvement observed in scores might be due to participants' familiarity with and practice on the test

**testing effect** A threat to internal validity in which repeated testing leads to better or worse scores.

items. This type of testing confound is sometimes referred to as a *practice effect*. Testing can also result in the opposite of a practice effect, a *fatigue effect* (sometimes referred to as a *negative practice effect*). Repeated testing fatigues the participants, and their performance declines as a result. Once again, having a control group of equivalent participants will help to control for testing confounds because researchers will be able to see practice or fatigue effects in the control group.

*Regression to the Mean.* Statistical regression occurs when individuals are selected for a study because their scores on some measure were extreme—either extremely high or extremely low. If we were studying students who scored in the top 10% on the SAT and we retested them on the SAT, then we would expect them to do well again. Not all students, however, would score as well as they did originally because of *statistical regression*, often referred to as **regression to the mean**—a threat to internal validity in which extreme scores, upon retesting, tend to be less extreme, moving toward the mean. In other words, some of the students did well the first time due to chance or luck. What is going to happen when they take the test a second time? They will not be as lucky, and their scores will regress toward the mean.

**regression to the mean**
A threat to internal validity in which extreme scores, upon retesting, tend to be less extreme, moving toward the mean.

Regression to the mean occurs in many situations other than research studies. Many people think that a hex is associated with being on the cover of *Sports Illustrated* and that an athlete's performance will decline after appearing on the cover. This can be explained by regression to the mean. When would athletes most likely appear on the cover of *Sports Illustrated*? After a very successful season or at the peak of their careers. What is most likely to happen after you have been performing exceptionally well over a period of time? You are likely to regress toward the mean and perform in a more average manner (Cozby, 2001). In a research study, having an equivalent control group of participants with extreme scores will indicate whether changes in the dependent measure are due to regression to the mean or to the effects of the independent variable.

**instrumentation effect**
A threat to internal validity in which changes in the dependent variable may be due to changes in the measuring device.

*Instrumentation.* An **instrumentation effect** occurs when the measuring device is faulty. Problems of consistency in measuring the dependent variable are most likely to occur when the measuring instrument is a human observer. The observer may become better at taking measures during the course of the study, or may become fatigued with taking measures. If the measures taken during the study are not done consistently, then any change in the dependent variable may be due to these measurement changes and not to the independent variable. Once again, having a control group of equivalent participants will help to identify this confound.

**mortality (attrition)**
A threat to internal validity in which differential dropout rates may be observed in the experimental and control groups, leading to inequality between the groups.

*Mortality or Attrition.* Most research studies encounter a certain amount of **mortality** or **attrition** (dropout). Most of the time, the attrition is equal across experimental and control groups. It is of concern to researchers, however, when attrition is not equal across the groups. Assume that we begin a study with two equivalent groups of participants. If more participants leave one group than the other, then the two groups of participants are most likely no longer equivalent, meaning that comparisons cannot be made between the groups. Why might we have differential attrition between the groups? Imagine we are conducting a study to test the effects of a program aimed at reducing smoking. We randomly select a group of smokers and then randomly assign half to the control group and half to the experimental group. The experimental group participates in our program to reduce smoking, but the heaviest smokers just cannot take the demands of the program and thus quit the program. When we take a posttest measure on smoking, only those participants who were originally light to moderate smokers are left in the experimental group. Comparing them to the control group would be pointless because the groups are no longer equivalent. Having a control group allows us to determine whether there is differential attrition across groups.

*Diffusion of Treatment.* When participants in a study are in close proximity to one another, a potential threat to internal validity is **diffusion of treatment**— observed changes in the behaviors of participants may be due to information received from other participants. For example, college students are frequently used as participants in research studies. Because many students live near one another and share classes, some students may discuss an experiment in which they participated. If other students were planning to participate in the study in the future, the treatment has now been compromised because they know how some of the participants were treated during the study. They know what is involved in one or more of the conditions in the study, and this knowledge may affect how they respond in the study regardless of the condition to which they are assigned. To control for this confound, researchers might try to test the participants in a study in large groups, or within a short time span, so that they do not have time to communicate with one another. In addition, researchers should stress to participants the importance of not discussing the experiment with anyone until it has ended.

**diffusion of treatment**
A threat to internal validity in which observed changes in the behaviors or responses of participants may be due to information received from other participants in the study.

*Experimenter and Participant Effects.* When researchers design experiments, they invest considerable time and effort in the endeavor. Often this investment leads the researcher to consciously or unconsciously affect or bias the results of the study. For example, a researcher may unknowingly smile more when participants are behaving in the predicted manner and frown or grimace when participants are behaving in a manner undesirable to the researcher. This type of **experimenter effect** is also referred to as *experimenter bias* because the results of the study are biased by the experimenter's expectations.

**experimenter effect**
A threat to internal validity in which the experimenter, consciously or unconsciously, affects the results of the study.

One of the most famous cases of experimenter effects is Clever Hans. Clever Hans was a horse that was purported to be able to do mathematical computations. Pfungst (1911) demonstrated that Hans's answers were based on experimenter effects. Hans supposedly solved mathematical problems by tapping out the answers with his hoof. A committee of experts who claimed Hans was receiving no cues from his questioners verified Hans's abilities. Pfungst later demonstrated that this was not so and that tiny head and eye movements were Hans's signals to begin and to end his tapping. When Hans was asked a question, the questioner would look at Hans's hoof as he tapped out the answer. When Hans approached the correct number of taps, the questioner would unknowingly make a subtle head or eye movement in an upward direction. This was a cue to Hans to stop tapping. If a horse was clever enough to pick up on cues as subtle as these, imagine how human participants might respond to similar subtle cues provided by an experimenter. For this reason, many researchers choose to combat experimenter effects by conducting blind experiments. There are two types of blind experiments, a single-blind experiment and a double-blind experiment. In a **single-blind experiment** either the experimenter or the participants are blind to the manipulation being made. The experimenter being blind in a single-blind experiment would help to combat experimenter effects. In a **double-blind experiment,** neither the experimenter nor the participant knows the condition in which the participant is serving—both parties are blind. Obviously, the coordinator of the study has this information; however, the researcher responsible for interacting with the participants does not know and therefore cannot provide any cues.

**single-blind experiment**
An experimental procedure in which either the participants or the experimenters are blind to the manipulation being made.

**double-blind experiment**
An experimental procedure in which neither the experimenter nor the participant knows the condition to which each participant has been assigned—both parties are blind to the manipulation.

"IT WAS MORE OF A 'TRIPLE-BLIND' TEST. THE PATIENTS DIDN'T KNOW WHICH ONES WERE GETTING THE REAL DRUG, THE DOCTORS DIDN'T KNOW, AND, I'M AFRAID, NOBODY KNEW."

Sometimes participants in a study bias the results based on their own expectations. They know they are being observed and hence may not behave naturally, or they may simply behave differently than when they are in more familiar situations. This type of confound is referred to as a **participant effect.** Sometimes participant effects are of a specific type. For example, many participants try to be "good participants," meaning that they try to

**participant effect** A threat to internal validity in which the participant, consciously or unconsciously, affects the results of the study.

determine what the researcher wants and to adjust their behavior accordingly. Such participants may be very sensitive to real or imagined cues from the researcher, referred to as *demand characteristics*. The participants are trying to guess what characteristics the experimenter is in effect "demanding." In this case, using a single-blind experiment in which the participants are blind or using a double-blind experiment would help to combat participant effects.

A special type of participant effect is often present in research on the effects of drugs and medical treatments. Most people report improvement when they are receiving a drug or other medical treatment. Some of this improvement may be caused by a *placebo effect;* that is, the improvement may be due not to the effects of the treatment but to the participant's expectation that the treatment will have an effect. For this reason, drug and medical research must use a special placebo condition, or **placebo group**—a group of participants who believe they are receiving treatment but in reality are not. Instead they are given an inert pill or substance called a **placebo.** The placebo condition helps to distinguish between the actual effects of the drug and placebo effects. For example, in a study on the effects of "ionized" wrist bracelets on musculoskeletal pain, researchers at Mayo Clinic used a double-blind procedure in which half of the participants wore an "ionized" bracelet and half of the participants wore a placebo bracelet. Both groups were told that they were wearing "ionized" bracelets intended to help with musculoskeletal pain. At the end of 4 weeks of treatment, both groups showed significant improvement in pain scores in comparison to baseline scores. No significant differences were observed between the groups. In other words, those wearing the placebo bracelet reported as much relief from pain as those wearing the "ionized" bracelet (Bratton et al., 2002).

**placebo group** A group or condition in which participants believe they are receiving treatment but are not.

**placebo** An inert substance that participants believe is a treatment.

*Floor and Ceiling Effects.* When conducting research, researchers must choose a measure for the dependent variable that is sensitive enough to detect differences between groups. If the measure is not sensitive enough, real differences may be missed. Although this confound does not involve an uncontrolled extraneous variable, it does represent a flaw in the experiment. For example, measuring the weights of rats in an experiment in pounds rather than ounces or grams is not advisable because no differences will be found. In this case, the insensitivity of the dependent variable is called a **floor effect.** All of the rats would be at the bottom of the measurement scale because the measurement scale is not sensitive enough to differentiate between scores at the bottom. Similarly, attempting to weigh elephants on a bathroom scale would also lead to sensitivity problems; however, this is a **ceiling effect.** All of the elephants would weigh at the top of the scale (300 or 350 pounds, depending on the bathroom scale used), and any changes that might occur in weight as a result of the treatment variable would not be reflected in the dependent variable. The use of a pretest can help to identify whether a measurement scale is sensitive enough. Participants should receive different scores on the dependent measure on the pretest. If all participants are scoring about the same (either very low or very high), then a floor or ceiling effect may be present.

**floor effect** A limitation of the measuring instrument that decreases its ability to differentiate between scores at the bottom of the scale.

**ceiling effect** A limitation of the measuring instrument that decreases its ability to differentiate between scores at the top of the scale.

## IN REVIEW　　Threats to Internal Validity

### MAJOR CONFOUNDING VARIABLES

| Type of Confound | Description | Means of Controlling/Minimizing |
|---|---|---|
| Nonequivalent Control Group | Problems in participant selection assignment may lead to important differences between the participants assigned to the experimental and control groups | Use random sampling and random assignment of participants |
| History Effect | Changes in the dependent variable may be due to outside events that take place during the course of the study | Use an equivalent control group |
| Maturation Effect | Changes in the dependent variable may be due to participants maturing (growing older) during the course of the study | Use an equivalent control group |
| Testing Effect | Changes in the dependent variable may be due to participants being tested repeatedly and getting either better or worse because of these repeated testings | Use an equivalent control group |
| Regression to the Mean | Participants who are selected for a study because they are extreme (either high or low) on some variable may regress toward the mean and be less extreme at a later testing | Use an equivalent group of participants with extreme scores |
| Instrumentation Effect | Changes in the dependent variable may be due to changes in the measuring device, either human or machine | Use an equivalent control group |
| Mortality or Attrition | Differential attrition or dropout in the experimental and control groups may lead to inequality between the groups | Monitor for differential loss of participants in experimental and control groups |
| Diffusion of Treatment | Changes in the behaviors or responses of participants may be due to information they have received from others participating in the study | Attempt to minimize by testing participants all at once or as close together in time as possible |
| Experimenter and Participant Effects | Either experimenters or participants consciously or unconsciously affect the results of the study | Use a double-blind or single-blind procedure |
| Floor and Ceiling Effects | The measuring instrument used is not sensitive enough to detect differences | Ensure that the measuring instrument is reliable and valid before beginning the study |

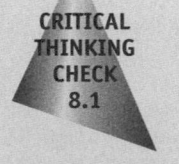

**CRITICAL THINKING CHECK 8.1**

1. We discussed the history effect with respect to a study on stress reduction. Review that section and explain how having a control group of equivalent participants would help to reveal the confound of history.
2. Imagine that a husband and wife who are very tall (well above the mean for their respective height distributions) have a son. Would you expect the child to be as tall as his father? Why or why not?
3. While grading a large stack of essay exams, Professor Hyatt becomes tired and hence more lax in her grading standards. Which confound is relevant in this example? Why?

## Threats to External Validity

A study must have internal validity in order for the results to be meaningful. However, it is also important that the study have external validity. **External validity** is the extent to which the results can be generalized beyond the participants used in the experiment and beyond the laboratory in which the experiment was conducted.

**external validity** The extent to which the results of an experiment can be generalized.

*Generalization to Populations.* Generalization to the population being studied can be accomplished by randomly sampling participants from the population. Generalization to other populations is problematic, however. Most psychology research is conducted on college students, especially freshmen and sophomores—hardly a representative sample from the population at large. This problem—sometimes referred to as the **college sophomore problem** (Stanovich, 2001)—means that most conclusions are based on studies of young people with a late adolescent mentality who are still developing self-identities and attitudes (Cozby, 2001).

**college sophomore problem** An external validity problem that results from using mainly college sophomores as participants in research studies.

Does using college students as participants in most research compromise our research ideals? There are three responses to the college sophomore criticism (Stanovich, 2001). First, using college sophomores as participants in a study does not negate the findings of the study. It simply means that the study needs to be replicated with participants from other populations to aid in overcoming this problem. Second, in the research conducted in many areas of psychology (for example, sensory research), the college sophomore problem is not an issue. The auditory and visual systems of college sophomores, for example, function in the same manner as do those of the rest of the population. Third, the population of college students today is varied. They come from different socioeconomic backgrounds and geographic areas. They have varied family histories and educational experiences. Hence, in terms of the previously mentioned variables, it is likely that college sophomores may be fairly representative of the general population.

*Generalization from Laboratory Settings.* Conducting research in a laboratory setting enables us to maximize control. We have discussed at several points the advantages of maximizing control, but control also has the potential disadvantage of creating an artificial environment. This means that we need to exercise some caution when generalizing from the laboratory setting to the real world. This problem is often referred to in psychology as the *artificiality criticism* (Stanovich, 2001). Keep in mind, however, that the whole point of experimentation is to create a situation in which control is maximized in order to determine cause-and-effect relationships. Obviously, we cannot relax our control in an experiment in order to counter this criticism.

How, then, can we address the artificiality criticism and the generalization issue? One way is through replication of the experiment to demonstrate that the result is reliable. A researcher might begin with an **exact replication**— repeating the study in exactly the same manner. However, in order to more adequately address a problem such as the artificiality criticism, one should consider a conceptual or systematic replication (Mitchell & Jolley, 2001).

**exact replication** Repeating a study using the same means of manipulating and measuring the variables as in the original study.

**conceptual replication**
A study based on another study that uses different methods, a different manipulation, or a different measure.

**systematic replication**
A study that varies from an original study in one systematic way—for example, by using a different number or type of participants, a different setting, or more levels of the independent variable.

**correlated-groups design**
An experimental design in which the participants in the experimental and control groups are related in some way.

**within-participants design**
A type of correlated-groups design in which the same participants are used in each condition.

A **conceptual replication** tests the same concepts in a different way. For example, we could use a different manipulation to assess its effect on the same dependent variable, or we could use the same manipulation and a different measure (dependent variable). A conceptual replication might also involve using other research methods to test the result. For example, we might conduct an observational study (see Chapter 4) in addition to a true experiment to assess the generalizability of a finding. A **systematic replication** systematically changes one thing at a time and observes the effect, if any, on the results. For example, a study could be replicated with more or different participants, in a more realistic setting, or with more levels of the independent variable.

# Correlated-Groups Designs

The designs described so far have all been between-participants designs—the participants in each condition are different. We will now consider the use of **correlated-groups designs**—designs in which the participants in the experimental and control groups are related. There are two types of correlated-groups designs: within-participants designs and matched-participants designs.

## Within-Participants Experimental Designs

In a **within-participants design,** the same participants are used in all conditions. Within-participants designs are often referred to as *repeated-measures designs* because we are repeatedly taking measures on the same individuals. A random sample of participants is selected, but random assignment is not relevant or necessary because all participants serve in all conditions. Within-participants designs are popular in psychological research for several reasons.

First, within-participants designs typically require fewer participants than between-participants designs. For example, suppose we were conducting the study mentioned earlier in the chapter on the effects of mnemonic devices on memory. We could conduct this study using a between-participants design and randomly assign different people to the control condition (no mnemonic device) and the experimental condition (those using a mnemonic device). If we wanted 20 participants in each condition, we would need a minimum of 20 people to serve in the control condition and 20 people to serve in the experimental condition, for a total of 40 participants. If we conducted the experiment using a within-participants design, we would need only 20 participants who would serve in both the control and experimental conditions. Because participants for research studies are difficult to recruit, using a within-participants design to minimize the number of participants needed is advantageous.

Second, within-participants designs usually require less time to conduct than between-participants designs. The study is conducted more quickly because participants can usually participate in all conditions in one session; the experimenter does not test a participant in one condition and then wait around for the next person to participate in the next condition. In addition, the instructions need to be given to each participant only once. If there are 10 participants in a within-participants design and participants are tested individually, this means explaining the experiment only 10 times. If there are 10 participants in each condition in a between-participants design in which participants are tested individually, this means explaining the experiment 20 times.

Third, and most important, within-participants designs increase statistical power. When the same individuals participate in multiple conditions, individual differences between those conditions are minimized. This in turn reduces variability and increases the chances of achieving statistical significance. Think about it this way. In a between-participants design, the differences between the groups or conditions may be mainly due to the independent variable. Some of the difference in performance between the two groups, however, is due to the fact that the individuals in one group are different from the individuals in the other group. This is referred to as *variability due to individual differences*. In a within-participants design, however, most variability between the two conditions (groups) must come from the manipulation of the independent variable because both groups of scores are produced by the same participants. The differences between the groups cannot be caused by individual differences, because the scores in both conditions come from the same person. Because of the reduction in individual differences (variability), a within-participants design has greater statistical power than a between-participants design—it provides a purer measure of the true effects of the independent variable.

Although the within-participants design has advantages, it also has weaknesses. First, within-participants designs are open to most of the confounds described earlier in the chapter. As with between-participants designs, internal validity is a concern for within-participants designs. In fact, several of the confounds described earlier in the chapter are especially troublesome for within-participants designs. For example, testing effects—called **order effects** in a within-participants design—are more problematic because all participants are measured at least twice—in the control condition and in the experimental condition. Because of this multiple testing, both practice and fatigue effects are common. However, these effects can be equalized across conditions in a within-participants design by **counterbalancing**—systematically varying the order of conditions for participants in a within-participants experiment. For example, if our memory experiment were counterbalanced, half of the people would participate in the control condition first, whereas the other half would participate in the experimental condition first. In this manner, practice and fatigue effects would be evenly distributed across conditions. When experimental designs are more complicated (i.e., they have three, four, or more conditions), counterbalancing can become more cumbersome. For example, a design with three conditions has 6 possible orders ($3! = 3 \times 2 \times 1$) in which to present the conditions, a design with four conditions has 24 possible orderings for the conditions ($4! = 4 \times 3 \times 2 \times 1$), and a design with five conditions has 120 possible orderings ($5! = 5 \times 4 \times 3 \times 2 \times 1$). Given that most research studies use a limited number of participants in each condition (usually 20–30), it is not possible to use all of the orderings of conditions (called *complete counterbalancing*) in studies with four or more conditions. Luckily, there are alternatives to complete

**order effects** A problem for within-participants designs in which the order of the conditions has an effect on the dependent variable.

**counterbalancing** A mechanism for controlling order effects either by including all orders of treatment presentation or by randomly determining the order for each participant.

counterbalancing, known as partial counterbalancing. One partial counterbalancing alternative is to randomize the order of presentation of conditions for each participant. Another alternative is to randomly select the number of orders that matches the number of participants. For example, in a study with four conditions and 24 possible orderings, if we had 15 participants, we could randomly select 15 of the 24 possible orderings.

**Latin square** A counterbalancing technique to control for order effects without using all possible orders.

A more formal way to use partial counterbalancing is to construct a Latin square. A **Latin square** utilizes a limited number of orders. When using a Latin square, we have the same number of orders as we have conditions. Thus, a Latin square for a design with four conditions uses 4 orders rather than the 24 orders used in the complete counterbalancing of a design with four conditions. Another criterion that must be met when constructing a Latin square is that each condition should be presented at each order. In other words, for a study with four conditions, each condition should appear once in each ordinal position. In addition, in a Latin square, each condition should precede and follow every other condition once. A Latin square for a study with four conditions appears in Table 8.1. The conditions are designated A, B, C, and D so that you can see how the order of conditions changes in each of the four orders used; however, once the Latin square is constructed using the letter symbols, each of the four conditions is randomly assigned to one of the letters to determine which condition will be A, B, and so on. A more complete discussion of Latin square designs can be found in Keppel (1991).

Another type of testing effect often present in within-participants designs is known as a *carryover effect*; that is, participants "carry" something with them from one condition to another. As a result of participating in one condition, they experience a change that they now carry with them to the second condition. Some drug research may involve carryover effects. The effects of the drug received in one condition will be present for a while and may be carried to the next condition. Our memory experiment would probably also involve a carryover effect. If individuals participate in the control condition first and then the experimental condition (using a mnemonic device), there probably would not be a carryover effect. If some individuals participate in the experimental condition first, however, it will be difficult not to continue using the mnemonic device once they have learned it. What they learned in one condition is carried with them to the next condition and alters their performance in that condition. Counterbalancing enables the experimenter to assess the extent

**TABLE 8.1    A Latin square for a design with four conditions**

| ORDER OF CONDITIONS | | | |
|---|---|---|---|
| A | B | D | C |
| B | C | A | D |
| C | D | B | A |
| D | A | C | B |

NOTE: The four conditions in the above experiment were randomly given the letter designations A, B, C, and D.

of carryover effects by comparing performance in the experimental condition when presented first versus second. However, using a matched-participants design (to be discussed next) will eliminate carryover effects.

Finally, within-participants designs are more open to demand characteristics—the information the participant infers about what the researcher wants. Because individuals participate in all conditions, they know how the instructions vary by condition and how each condition differs from the previous ones. This gives them information about the study that a participant in a between-participants design would not have. This information, in turn, may enable them to determine the purpose of the investigation, which could lead to a change in their performance.

Not all research can be conducted using a within-participants design. For example, most drug research is conducted using different participants in each condition, because drugs often permanently affect or change an individual. Thus, participants cannot serve in more than one condition. In addition, researchers who study reasoning and problem solving often cannot use within-participants designs, because once a participant has solved a problem, that person cannot then serve in another condition and attempt to solve the same problem again. Where it is possible, however, many psychologists choose to use within-participants designs because they believe the added strengths of the design outweigh the weaknesses.

## Matched-Participants Experimental Designs

The second type of correlated-groups design is a **matched-participants design.** Matched-participants designs share certain characteristics with both between- and within-participants designs. As in a between-participants design, different participants are used in each condition. However, for each participant in one condition, there is a participant in the other condition(s) who matches him or her on some relevant variable or variables. For example, if weight is a concern in a study and the researchers want to ensure that for each participant in the control condition there is a participant in the experimental condition of the same weight, they match participants on weight. Matching the participants on one or more variables makes the matched-participants design similar to the within-participants design. A within-participants design has perfect matching because the same people serve in each condition; with the matched-participants design, we are attempting to achieve as much equivalence between the groups as we can.

Why, then, do we not simply use a within-participants design? The answer is usually carryover effects. Participating in one condition changes the participants to such an extent that they cannot also participate in the second condition. For example, drug research usually utilizes between-participants designs or matched-participants designs, but rarely a within-participants design. Participants cannot take both the placebo and the real drug as part of an experiment; hence, this type of research requires that different people serve in each condition. But to ensure equivalency between groups, the researcher may choose to use a matched-participants design.

**matched-participants design** A type of correlated-groups design in which participants are matched between conditions on variable(s) that the researcher believes is (are) relevant to the study.

The matched-participants design has advantages over both between-participants and within-participants designs. First, because there are different people in each group, testing effects and demand characteristics are minimized in comparison to a within-participants design. Second, the groups are more equivalent than those in a between-participants design and almost as equivalent as those in a within-participants design. Third, because participants have been matched on variables of importance to the study, the same types of statistics used for the within-participants designs are used for the matched-participants designs. In other words, data from a matched-participants design are treated like data from a within-participants design. This means that a matched-participants design is as powerful as a within-participants design because individual differences have been minimized.

Of course, matched-participants designs also have weaknesses. First, more participants are needed than in a within-participants design. Also, if one participant in a matched-participants design drops out, the entire pair is lost. Thus, mortality is even more of an issue in matched-participants designs. The biggest weakness of the matched-participants design, however, is the matching itself. Finding an individual willing to participate in an experiment who exactly (or very closely) matches another participant on a specific variable can be difficult. If the researcher is matching participants on more than one variable (for example, height and weight), it becomes even more difficult. Because participants are hard to find, it is very difficult to find enough participants who are matches to take part in a matched-participants study.

## IN REVIEW  Comparison of Designs

|  | BETWEEN-PARTICIPANTS DESIGN | WITHIN-PARTICIPANTS DESIGN | MATCHED-PARTICIPANTS DESIGN |
|---|---|---|---|
| Description | Different participants are randomly assigned to each condition | The same participants are used in all conditions | Participants are randomly assigned to each condition after they are matched on relevant variables |
| Strengths | Testing effects are minimized<br>Demand characteristics are minimized | Fewer participants are needed<br>Less time-consuming<br>Equivalency of groups is ensured<br>More powerful statistically | Testing effects are minimized<br>Demand characteristics are minimized<br>Groups are fairly equivalent<br>More powerful statistically |
| Weaknesses | More participants are needed<br>More time-consuming<br>Groups may not be equivalent<br>Less powerful statistically | Probability of testing effects is high<br>Probability of demand characteristics is high | Matching is very difficult<br>More participants are needed |

CRITICAL THINKING CHECK 8.2

1. If a researcher wants to conduct a study with four conditions and 15 participants in each condition, how many participants will be needed for a between-participants design? For a within-participants design? For a matched-participants design?
2. People with anxiety disorders are selected to participate in a study on a new drug for the treatment of this disorder. The researchers know that the drug is effective in treating the disorder, but they are concerned with possible side effects. In particular, they are concerned with the effects of the drug on cognitive abilities. Therefore, they ask each participant in the experiment to identify a family member or friend who is the same gender as the participant and who is of a similar age as the participant (within 5 years) but who does not have an anxiety disorder. The researchers then administer the drug to those with the disorder and measure cognitive functioning in both groups. What type of design is this? Would you suggest measuring cognitive functioning more than once? When and why?

# Developmental Designs

Developmental psychologists typically use a special group of designs known as *developmental designs*. These designs differ from those already described in that they use age as a variable. There are two basic developmental designs: the cross-sectional design and the longitudinal design. The cross-sectional design shares some characteristics with between-participants designs in that individuals of different ages are studied. The longitudinal design shares some characteristics with within-participants designs in that the same individuals are studied over time as they mature through different ages.

## Cross-Sectional Designs

When using the **cross-sectional design,** researchers study individuals of different ages at the same time. Thus, a researcher interested in differences across ages in cognitive abilities might study groups of 5-year-olds, 8-year-olds, 11-year-olds, and so on. The advantage of this design is that a wide variety of ages can be studied in a short period of time. In fact, in some studies it is possible to collect all of the data in one day. Even though ease of data collection is a great advantage for the cross-sectional method, this method does have disadvantages. The main issue is that the researcher is typically attempting to determine whether or not there are differences across different ages; however, the reality of the design is such that the researcher tests not only individuals of different ages but also individuals who were born at different times and raised in different generations or cohorts. A **cohort** is a group of individuals born at about the same time. Thus, in a cross-sectional study, the researcher wants to be able to conclude that any difference observed in the dependent variable (for example, cognitive abilities) is due to age; however,

**cross-sectional design** A type of developmental design in which participants of different ages are studied at the same time.

**cohort** A group of individuals born at about the same time.

**cohort effect** A generational effect in a study that occurs when the era in which individuals are born affects how they respond in the study.

because these individuals were also raised at different times, some or all of the observed differences in cognitive ability could be due to a **cohort effect**— a generational effect. How might a cohort effect affect cognitive abilities in a cross-sectional study? Individuals born in different generations went through different educational systems and they also had varying opportunities for education—those born earlier had less access to education.

## Longitudinal Designs

**longitudinal design** A type of developmental design in which the same participants are studied repeatedly over time as they age.

An alternative to a cross-sectional design is a longitudinal design. With a **longitudinal design,** the same participants are studied repeatedly over a period of time. Depending on the age range the researcher wants to study, a longitudinal design may span from a few years or months to decades. If the study described above were conducted longitudinally, the same participants would periodically (e.g., every 3 years) be tested on cognitive abilities. This type of study eliminates any cohort effects because the same participants are studied over a period of time. Thus, we do not have the confound of using participants of different ages who were born in different generations. However, longitudinal designs introduce their own unique problems into a research study. First, they are more expensive and time-consuming than cross-sectional studies. In addition, researchers using longitudinal studies need to be particularly cognizant of attrition problems over time because those who drop out of the study likely differ in some possibly meaningful way from those who remain in the study. For example, they may be healthier, wealthier, or more conscientious and in general have more stable lives.

## Sequential Designs

**sequential design** A developmental design that is a combination of the cross-sectional and longitudinal designs.

One way to overcome many of the problems with both cross-sectional and longitudinal designs is to use a design that is a combination of the two. The **sequential design** is a combined cross-sectional and longitudinal design in that a researcher begins with participants of different ages (a cross-sectional design) and tests or measures them. Then, either a number of months or years later, the researcher retests or measures the same individuals (a longitudinal design). Thus, a researcher could measure cognitive abilities in 5-, 8-, and 11-year-olds; then 3 years later measure the same individuals when they are 8, 11, and 14 years old; and last measure them again when they are 11, 14, and 17 years old. Sequential designs are more expensive and time-consuming than the previous two types of designs, but they have the advantage of allowing researchers to examine cohort effects, usually without taking as much time as a longitudinal design alone.

## Summary

Researchers need to consider several factors when designing and evaluating a true experiment. First, they need to address the issues of control and possible confounds. The study needs to be designed with strong control and no confounds in order to maximize internal validity. Second, researchers need to consider external validity in order to ensure that the study is as generalizable as possible while maintaining control. In addition, they should use the design most appropriate for the type of research they are conducting. Researchers should consider the strengths and weaknesses of each of the three types of designs (between-, within-, and matched-participants) when determining which would be best for their study. Finally, when conducting developmental studies, researchers have three designs from which to choose: a cross-sectional design, a longitudinal design, or a combination of the two called a sequential design.

## KEY TERMS

between-participants design
posttest-only control group
   design
pretest/posttest control group
   design
confound
internal validity
history effect
maturation effect
testing effect
regression to the mean
instrumentation effect
mortality (attrition)

diffusion of treatment
experimenter effect
single-blind experiment
double-blind experiment
participant effect
placebo group
placebo
floor effect
ceiling effect
external validity
college sophomore problem
exact replication
conceptual replication

systematic replication
correlated-groups design
within-participants design
order effects
counterbalancing
Latin square
matched-participants design
cross-sectional design
cohort
cohort effect
longitudinal design
sequential design

## CHAPTER EXERCISES

(Answers to odd-numbered exercises appear in Appendix C.)

1. A researcher is interested in whether listening to classical music improves spatial ability. She randomly assigns participants to either a classical music condition or a no-music condition. Is this a between-participants or a within-participants design?

2. You read in a health magazine about a study in which a new therapy technique for depression was examined. A group of depressed individuals volunteered to participate in the study, which lasted 9 months. There were 50 participants at the beginning of the study and 29 at the end of the 9 months. The researchers claimed that of those who completed the program, 85% improved. What possible confounds can you identify in this study?

3. On the most recent exam in your biology class, every student made an A. The professor claims that he must really be a good teacher for all of the students to have done so well. Given the confounds discussed in this chapter, what alternative explanation can you offer for this result?

4. What are internal validity and external validity, and why are they so important to researchers?

5. How does using a Latin square aid a researcher in counterbalancing a study?

6. What are the similarities and differences between within-participants and matched-participants designs?

7. What are the similarities and differences between cross-sectional, longitudinal, and sequential designs?

## CRITICAL THINKING CHECK ANSWERS

### 8.1

1. Having a control group in the stress-reduction study would help to reveal the confound of history because if this confound were present, we would expect the control group to also increase in stress level, possibly more so than the experimental group. Having a control group informs a researcher about the effects of treatment versus no treatment and about the effects of historical events.

2. Based on what we have learned about regression to the mean, the son would probably not be as tall as his father. Because the father represents an extreme score on height, the son would most likely regress toward the mean and not be as tall as his father. However, because his mother is also extremely tall, there is the possibility that genetics may overcome regression to the mean.

3. This example is similar to an instrumentation effect. The way the measuring device is used has changed over the course of the "study."

### 8.2

1. The researcher will need 60 participants for a between-participants design, 15 participants for a within-participants design, and 60 participants for a matched-participants design.

2. This is a matched-participants design. The researcher might consider measuring cognitive functioning before the study begins to ensure that there are no differences between the two groups of participants before the treatment. Obviously, the researchers would also measure cognitive functioning at the end of the study.

## WEB RESOURCES

Check your knowledge of the content in this chapter by taking the practice quiz at www.Wadsworth.com. Or, for step-by-step practice and information, check out the Statistics and Research Methods Workshops at http://psychology.wadsworth.com/workshops.

## LAB RESOURCES

For hands-on experience using the research methods described in this chapter, see Chapter 4 ("Two-Group Experiments") in *Research Methods Laboratory Manual* *for Psychology*, 2nd ed., by William Langston (Belmont, CA: Wadsworth, 2005).

# 9 Inferential Statistics: Two-Group Designs

In this chapter, we will discuss the common types of parametric statistical analyses used with simple two-group designs. Depending on the type of data collected and whether a between-participants or a correlated-groups design is used, the statistic used to analyze the data will vary. We will look at the typical parametric inferential statistics used to analyze interval-ratio data for between-participants and correlated-groups designs. For the statistics presented in this chapter, the experimental design is similar—a two-group between-participants or correlated-groups (within-participants or matched-participants) design. Remember that a matched-participants design is analyzed statistically the same way as a within-participants design. The inferential statistics discussed in Chapter 7 compared single samples with populations (z test and t test). The statistics discussed in this chapter are designed to test differences between two equivalent groups of participants.

## Parametric Statistics for Two-Group Designs

In the two-group design, two samples (representing two populations) are compared by having one group receive nothing (the control group) and the second group receive some level of the independent variable (the experimental group). As noted in Chapter 8, it is also possible to have two experimental groups and no control group. In this case, members of each group receive a different level of the independent variable. The null hypothesis tested in a two-group design using a two-tailed test is that the populations represented by the two groups do not differ:

$$H_0: \mu_1 = \mu_2$$

The alternative hypothesis is that we expect differences in performance between the two populations but we are unsure which group will perform better or worse:

$$H_a: \mu_1 \neq \mu_2$$

As discussed in Chapter 7, for a one-tailed test, the null hypothesis is either

$$H_0: \mu_1 \leq \mu_2 \text{ or } H_0: \mu_1 \geq \mu_2$$

depending on which alternative hypothesis is being tested:

$$H_a: \mu_1 > \mu_2 \text{ or } H_a: \mu_1 < \mu_2, \text{ respectively.}$$

A significant difference between the two groups (samples representing populations) depends on the critical value for the statistical test being conducted. As with the statistical tests described in Chapter 7, alpha is typically set at .05 ($\alpha = .05$).

Remember from Chapter 7 that parametric tests, such as the $t$ test, are inferential statistical tests designed for sets of data that meet certain requirements. The most basic requirement is that the data fit a bell-shaped distribution. In addition, parametric tests involve data for which certain parameters are known, such as the mean ($\mu$) and the standard deviation ($\sigma$). Finally, parametric tests use interval-ratio data.

# $t$ Test for Independent Groups (Samples): What It Is and What It Does

The **independent-groups $t$ test** is a parametric statistical test that compares the means of two different samples of participants. It indicates whether the two samples perform so similarly that we conclude they are likely from the same population, or whether they perform so differently that we conclude they represent two different populations.

Imagine, for example, that a researcher wants to study the effects on exam performance of massed versus spaced study. All participants in the experiment study the same material for the same amount of time. The difference between the groups is that one group studies for 6 hours all at once (massed study), whereas the other group studies for 6 hours broken into three 2-hour blocks (spaced study). Because the researcher believes that the spaced study method will lead to better performance, the null and alternative hypotheses are

$H_0$: Spaced study $\leq$ Massed study, or $\mu_1 \leq \mu_2$
$H_a$: Spaced study $>$ Massed study, or $\mu_1 > \mu_2$

The 20 participants are chosen by random sampling and assigned to the groups randomly. Because of the random assignment of participants, we are confident that there are no major differences between the two groups prior to the study. The dependent variable is the participants' scores on a 30-item test of the material; these scores are listed in Table 9.1.

Notice that the mean score of the spaced-study group ($\bar{X}_1 = 22$) is higher than the mean score of the massed-study group ($\bar{X}_2 = 16.9$). However, we want to be able to say more than this. We need to statistically analyze the data to determine whether the observed difference is statistically significant. As you may recall from Chapter 7, statistical significance indicates that an observed

**independent-groups $t$ test**
A parametric inferential test for comparing sample means of two independent groups of scores

**TABLE 9.1  Numbers of items answered correctly by each participant under spaced versus massed study conditions using a between-participants design ($N = 20$)**

| SPACED STUDY | MASSED STUDY |
|:---:|:---:|
| 23 | 15 |
| 18 | 20 |
| 25 | 21 |
| 22 | 15 |
| 20 | 14 |
| 24 | 16 |
| 21 | 18 |
| 24 | 19 |
| 21 | 14 |
| 22 | 17 |
| $\bar{X}_1 = 22$ | $\bar{X}_2 = 16.9$ |

difference between two descriptive statistics (such as means) is unlikely to have occurred by chance. For this analysis, we will use an independent-groups $t$ test.

*Calculations for the Independent-Groups* t *Test.* The formula for an independent-groups $t$ test is

$$t_{obt} = \frac{\bar{X}_1 - \bar{X}_2}{s_{\bar{X}_1 - \bar{X}_2}}$$

This formula resembles that for the single-sample $t$ test discussed in Chapter 7. However, rather than comparing a single sample mean to a population mean, we are comparing two sample means. The denominator in the equation represents the **standard error of the difference between means**—the estimated standard deviation of the sampling distribution of differences between the means of independent samples in a two-sample experiment. When conducting an independent-groups $t$ test, we are determining how far from the difference between the population means the difference between the sample means falls. Based on the null hypothesis, we expect the difference between the population means to be zero. If the difference between the sample means is large, it will fall in one of the tails of the distribution (far from the difference between the population means).

To determine how far the difference between the sample means is from the difference between the population means, we convert the mean differences to standard errors. The formula for this conversion is similar to the formula for the standard error of the mean, introduced in Chapter 7:

$$s_{\bar{X}_1 - \bar{X}_2} = \sqrt{\frac{s_1^2}{n_1} + \frac{s_2^2}{n_2}}$$

The standard error of the difference between the means does have a logical meaning. If we took thousands of pairs of samples from these two populations and found $\bar{X}_1 - \bar{X}_2$ for each pair, those differences between means would not all be the same. They would form a distribution. The mean of that distribution would be the difference between the means of the populations $(\mu_1 - \mu_2)$, and its standard deviation would be $s_{\bar{X}_1 - \bar{X}_2}$.

Putting all of this together, we see that the formula for determining $t$ is

$$t_{obt} = \frac{\bar{X}_1 - \bar{X}_2}{\sqrt{\dfrac{s_1^2}{n_1} + \dfrac{s_2^2}{n_2}}}$$

where

$$
\begin{aligned}
t_{obt} &= \text{value of } t \text{ obtained} \\
\bar{X}_1 \text{ and } \bar{X}_2 &= \text{means for the two groups} \\
s_1^2 \text{ and } s_2^2 &= \text{variances of the two groups} \\
n_1 \text{ and } n_2 &= \text{number of participants in each of the two groups (we use } n
\end{aligned}
$$

to refer to the subgroups and $N$ to refer to the total number of people in the study)

**standard error of the difference between means** The standard deviation of the sampling distribution of differences between the means of independent samples in a two-sample experiment.

Let's use this formula to determine whether there are any significant differences between the spaced and massed study groups. We use the formulas for the mean and variance that we learned in Chapter 5 to do the preliminary calculations:

$$\bar{X}_1 = \frac{\sum X_1}{n_1} = \frac{220}{10} = 22 \qquad\qquad \bar{X}_2 = \frac{\sum X_2}{n_2} = \frac{169}{10} = 16.9$$

$$s_1^2 = \frac{\sum\left(X_1 - \bar{X}_1\right)^2}{n_1 - 1} = \frac{40}{9} = 4.44 \qquad\qquad s_2^2 = \frac{\sum\left(X_2 - \bar{X}_2\right)^2}{n_2 - 1} = \frac{56.9}{9} = 6.32$$

$$t = \frac{\bar{X}_1 - \bar{X}_2}{\sqrt{\dfrac{s_1^2}{n_1} + \dfrac{s_2^2}{n_2}}} = \frac{22 - 16.9}{\sqrt{\dfrac{4.44}{10} + \dfrac{6.32}{10}}} = \frac{5.1}{\sqrt{1.076}} = \frac{5.1}{1.037} = 4.92$$

"THIS IS THE PART I ALWAYS HATE."

***Interpreting the t Test.*** We get $t_{\text{obt}} = 4.92$. We now consult Table A.3 in Appendix A to determine the critical value for $t$ ($t_{\text{cv}}$). First we need to determine the degrees of freedom, which for an independent-groups $t$ test are $(n_1 - 1) + (n_2 - 1)$ or $n_1 + n_2 - 2$. In the present study, with 10 participants in each group, there are 18 degrees of freedom ($10 + 10 - 2 = 18$). The alternative hypothesis was one-tailed, and $\alpha = .05$.

Consulting Table A.3, we find that for a one-tailed test with 18 degrees of freedom, the critical value of $t$ is 1.734. Our $t_{\text{obt}}$ falls beyond the critical value

FIGURE 9.1
The obtained *t*-score
in relation to the *t*
critical value

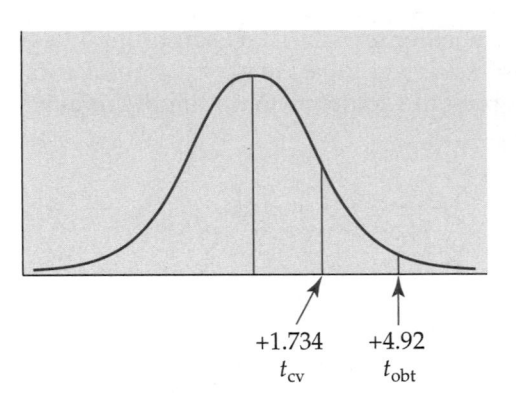

+1.734     +4.92
$t_{cv}$      $t_{obt}$

(is larger than the critical value). Thus, the null hypothesis is rejected, and the alternative hypothesis that participants in the spaced-study condition performed better on a test of the material than did participants in the massed-study condition is supported. This result is pictured in Figure 9.1. In APA style (discussed in detail in Chapter 14), the result is reported as

$$t(18) = 4.92, p < .05$$

This form conveys in a concise manner the *t*-score, the degrees of freedom, and that the results are significant at the .05 level. Keep in mind that when a result is significant, the *p* value is reported as less than (<) .05 (or some smaller probability), not greater than (>)—an error commonly made by students. Remember that the *p* value, or alpha level, indicates the probability of a Type I error. We want this probability to be small, meaning we are confident that there is only a small probability that our results were due to chance. This means it is highly probable that the observed difference between the groups is a meaningful difference—that it is actually due to the independent variable.

Look back at the formula for *t*, and think about what will affect the size of the *t*-score. We would like the *t*-score to be large in order to increase the chance that it will be significant. What will increase the size of the *t*-score? Anything that increases the numerator or decreases the denominator in the equation. What will increase the numerator? A larger difference between the means for the two groups (a greater difference produced by the independent variable). This difference is somewhat difficult to influence. However, if we minimize chance in our study and the independent variable truly does have an effect, then the means should be different. What will decrease the size of the denominator? Because the denominator is the standard error of the difference between the means ($s_{\bar{X}_1 - \bar{X}_2}$) and is derived by using *s* (the unbiased estimator of the population standard deviation), we can decrease $s_{\bar{X}_1 - \bar{X}_2}$ by decreasing the variability within each condition or group or by increasing the sample size. Look at the formula and think about why this would be so. In summary, then, three aspects of a study can increase power:

- Greater differences produced by the independent variable
- Less variability of raw scores in each condition
- Increased sample size

*Graphing the Means.* Typically, when a significant difference is found between two means, the means are graphed to provide a pictorial representation of the difference. In creating a graph, we place the independent variable on the *x*-axis and the dependent variable on the *y*-axis. As noted in Chapter 5, the *y*-axis should be 60–75% of the length of the *x*-axis. For a line graph, we plot each mean and connect them with a line. For a bar graph, we draw separate bars whose heights represent the means. Figure 9.2 shows a bar graph representing the data from the spaced versus massed study experiment. Recall that the mean number of items answered correctly by those in the spaced-study condition was 22, compared with a mean of 16.9 for those in the massed-study condition.

*Effect Size: Cohen's* **d.** In addition to the reported statistic, alpha level, and graph, the American Psychological Association (2001a) recommends that we also look at **effect size**—the proportion of variance in the dependent variable that is accounted for by the manipulation of the independent variable. Effect size indicates how big a role the conditions of the independent variable play in determining scores on the dependent variable. Thus, it is an estimate of the effect of the independent variable, regardless of sample size. The larger the effect size, the more consistent is the influence of the independent variable. In other words, the greater the effect size, the more knowing the conditions of the independent variable improves our accuracy in predicting participants' scores on the dependent variable. For the *t* test, the formula for effect size, know as **Cohen's** *d,* is

> **effect size** The proportion of variance in the dependent variable that is accounted for by the manipulation of the independent variable.

> **Cohen's** *d* An inferential statistic for measuring effect size.

$$d = \frac{\bar{X}_1 - \bar{X}_2}{\sqrt{\frac{s_1^2}{2} + \frac{s_2^2}{2}}}$$

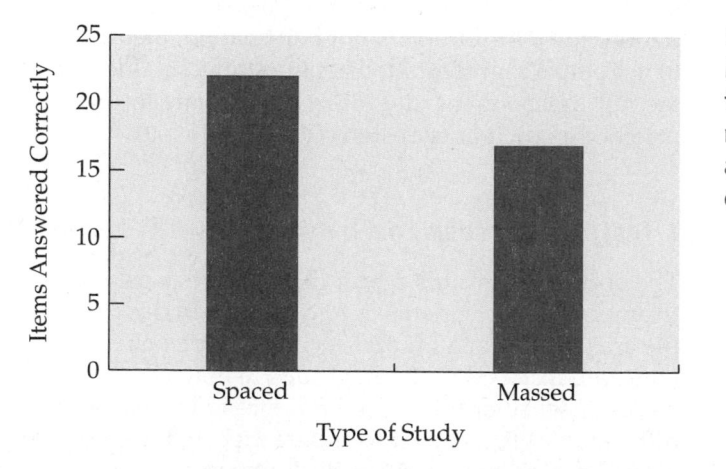

**FIGURE 9.2 Mean number of items answered correctly under spaced and massed study conditions**

Let's begin by working on the denominator, using the data from the spaced versus massed study experiment:

$$\sqrt{\frac{s_1^2}{2} + \frac{s_2^2}{2}} = \sqrt{\frac{4.44}{2} + \frac{6.32}{2}} = \sqrt{2.22 + 3.16} = \sqrt{5.38} = 2.32$$

We can now put this denominator into the formula for Cohen's $d$:

$$d = \frac{22 - 16.9}{2.32} = \frac{5.1}{2.32} = 2.198$$

According to Cohen (1988, 1992), a small effect size is one of at least 0.20, a medium effect size is at least 0.50, and a large effect size is at least 0.80. Obviously, our effect size of 2.198 is far greater than 0.80, indicating a very large effect size (most likely a result of using fabricated data). Using APA style, we report that the effect size estimated with Cohen's $d$ is 2.198.

The preceding example illustrates a $t$ test for independent groups with equal $n$ values (sample sizes). In situations where the $n$ values are unequal, a modified version of the previous formula is used. If you need this formula, you can find it in more advanced undergraduate statistics texts.

*Assumptions of the Independent-Groups* **t** *Test.* The assumptions of the independent-groups $t$ test are similar to those of the single-sample $t$ test. They are as follows:

- The data are interval-ratio scale.
- The underlying distributions are bell-shaped.
- The observations are independent.
- Homogeneity of variance: If we could compute the true variance of the population represented by each sample, the variances in each population would be the same.

If any of these assumptions is violated, it is appropriate to use another statistic. For example, if the scale of measurement is not interval-ratio or if the underlying distribution is not bell-shaped, then it may be more appropriate to use a nonparametric statistic (described in Chapter 13). If the observations are not independent, then it is appropriate to use a statistic for within- or matched-participants designs (described next).

## $t$ Test for Correlated Groups: What It Is and What It Does

**correlated-groups** $t$ **test**    A parametric inferential test used to compare the means of two related (within- or matched-participants) samples.

The **correlated-groups** $t$ **test,** like the previously discussed $t$ test, compares the means of participants in two groups. In this case, however, the same people are used in each group (a within-participants design) or different participants are matched between groups (a matched-participants design). The test indicates whether there is a difference in the sample means and whether this difference is greater than would be expected based on chance. In a correlated-groups design, the sample includes two scores for each person, instead of just one. To conduct the $t$ test for correlated groups (also called the $t$ test for dependent groups or samples), we must convert the two scores for each person into one score. That is, we compute a difference score for each person by subtracting one score from the other for that person (or for the two individuals in a matched pair). Although this may sound confusing, the dependent-groups $t$ test is actually easier to compute than the independent-groups $t$ test. Because the two samples are related, the analysis becomes easier because we work with pairs of scores. The null hypothesis is that there is no difference between the two scores; that is, a person's score in one condition is the same as that (or a matched) person's score in the second condition. The alternative hypothesis is that there is a difference between the paired scores—that the individuals (or matched pairs) performed differently in each condition.

To illustrate the use of the correlated-groups $t$ test, imagine that we conduct a study in which participants are asked to learn two lists of words. One list is composed of 20 concrete words (for example, *desk, lamp, bus*); the other is 20 abstract words (for example, *love, hate, deity*). Each participant is tested twice, once in each condition. (Think back to the discussion of weaknesses in within-participants designs from the previous chapter, and identify how you would control for practice and fatigue effects in this study.)

Because each participant provides one pair of scores, a correlated-groups $t$ test is the appropriate way to compare the means of the two conditions. We expect to find that recall performance is better for the concrete words. Thus, the null hypothesis is

$$H_0: \mu_1 - \mu_2 = 0$$

and the alternative hypothesis is

$$H_a: \mu_1 - \mu_2 > 0$$

representing a one-tailed test of the null hypothesis.

To better understand the correlated-groups $t$ test, consider the sampling distribution for the test. This is a sampling distribution of the differences between pairs of sample means. Imagine the population of people who must recall abstract words versus the population of people who must recall concrete words. Further, imagine that samples of eight participants are chosen (the eight participants in each individual sample come from one population), and each sample's mean score in the abstract condition is subtracted from the mean score in the concrete condition. We do this repeatedly until the entire population has been sampled. If the null hypothesis is true, the differences between the sample means should be zero, or very close to zero. If, as the researcher suspects, participants remember more concrete words than abstract words, the difference between the sample means should be significantly greater than zero.

The data representing each participant's performance are presented in Table 9.2. Notice that we have two sets of scores, one for the concrete word list and one for the abstract list. The calculations for the correlated-groups $t$ test involve transforming the two sets of scores into one set by determining difference scores. **Difference scores** represent the difference between participants' performance in one condition and their performance in the other condition. The difference scores for our study are shown in Table 9.3.

**difference scores** Scores representing the difference between participants' performance in one condition and their performance in a second condition.

**TABLE 9.2** Numbers of abstract and concrete words recalled by each participant using a correlated-groups (within-participants) design

| PARTICIPANT | CONCRETE | ABSTRACT |
|:---:|:---:|:---:|
| 1 | 13 | 10 |
| 2 | 11 | 9 |
| 3 | 19 | 13 |
| 4 | 13 | 12 |
| 5 | 15 | 11 |
| 6 | 10 | 8 |
| 7 | 12 | 10 |
| 8 | 13 | 13 |

**TABLE 9.3** Numbers of concrete and abstract words recalled by each participant, with difference scores

| PARTICIPANT | CONCRETE | ABSTRACT | d (DIFFERENCE SCORE) |
|:---:|:---:|:---:|:---:|
| 1 | 13 | 10 | 3 |
| 2 | 11 | 9 | 2 |
| 3 | 19 | 13 | 6 |
| 4 | 13 | 12 | 1 |
| 5 | 15 | 11 | 4 |
| 6 | 10 | 8 | 2 |
| 7 | 12 | 10 | 2 |
| 8 | 13 | 13 | 0 |
| | | | $\Sigma = 20$ |

*Calculations for the Correlated-Groups* t *Test.* After calculating the difference scores, we have one set of scores representing the performance of participants in both conditions. We can now compare the mean of the difference scores with zero (based on the null hypothesis stated previously). The computations from this point on for the dependent-groups $t$ test are similar to those for the single-sample $t$ test in Chapter 7:

$$t = \frac{\bar{D} - 0}{s_{\bar{D}}}$$

where

$\bar{D}$ = mean of the difference scores
$s_{\bar{D}}$ = standard error of the difference scores

**standard error of the difference scores** The standard deviation of the sampling distribution of mean differences between dependent samples in a two-group experiment.

The **standard error of the difference scores** ( $s_{\bar{D}}$) is the standard deviation of the sampling distribution of mean differences between dependent samples in a two-group experiment. It is calculated in a similar manner to the estimated standard error of the mean ($s_{\bar{X}}$) that we learned how to calculate in Chapter 7:

$$s_{\bar{D}} = \frac{s_D}{\sqrt{N}}$$

where $s_D$ is the unbiased estimator of the standard deviation of the difference scores. The standard deviation of the difference scores is calculated in the same manner as the standard deviation for any set of scores:

$$s_D = \sqrt{\frac{\sum(D - \bar{D})^2}{N-1}}$$

Or if you prefer, you may use the computational formula for the standard deviation:

$$s_D = \sqrt{\frac{\sum D^2 - \frac{(\sum D)^2}{N}}{N-1}}$$

Let's use the computational formula to determine $s_D$, $s_{\bar{D}}$, and the final $t$-score. We begin by squaring the difference scores, as shown in Table 9.4. We can now use the sum of the difference scores and the sum of the squared difference scores to calculate $s_D$:

$$s_D = \sqrt{\frac{74 - \frac{(20)^2}{8}}{8-1}} = \sqrt{\frac{74 - \frac{400}{8}}{7}} = \sqrt{\frac{74 - 50}{7}} = \sqrt{\frac{24}{7}} = \sqrt{3.429} = 1.85$$

**TABLE 9.4  Difference scores and squared difference scores for numbers of concrete and abstract words recalled**

| CONCRETE | ABSTRACT | d (DIFFERENCE SCORE) | d² |
|---|---|---|---|
| 13 | 10 | 3 | 9 |
| 11 | 9 | 2 | 4 |
| 19 | 13 | 6 | 36 |
| 13 | 12 | 1 | 1 |
| 15 | 11 | 4 | 16 |
| 10 | 8 | 2 | 4 |
| 12 | 10 | 2 | 4 |
| 13 | 13 | 0 | 0 |
| | | $\Sigma = 20$ | $\Sigma = 74$ |

FIGURE 9.3
The obtained *t*-score
in relation to the
*t* critical value

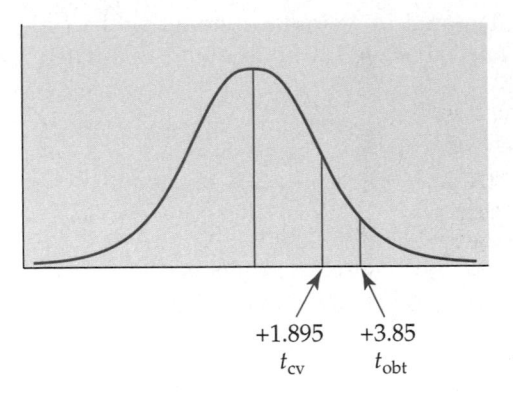

$$+1.895 \quad +3.85$$
$$t_{cv} \quad\quad t_{obt}$$

Next, we use the standard deviation ($s_D = 1.85$) to calculate the standard error of the difference scores ($s_{\bar{D}}$):

$$s_{\bar{D}} = \frac{s_D}{\sqrt{N}} = \frac{1.85}{\sqrt{8}} = \frac{1.85}{2.83} = 0.65$$

Finally, we use the standard error of the difference scores ($s_{\bar{D}} = 0.65$) and the mean of the difference scores ($\bar{D} = 20 \div 8 = 2.5$) in the *t*-test formula:

$$t = \frac{\bar{D} - 0}{s_{\bar{D}}} = \frac{2.5 - 0}{0.65} = \frac{2.5}{0.65} = 3.85$$

*Interpreting the Correlated-Groups* **t** *Test and Graphing the Means.* The degrees of freedom for a correlated-groups *t* test are equal to $N - 1$—in this case, $8 - 1 = 7$. We can use Table A.3 in Appendix A to determine $t_{cv}$ for a one-tailed test with $\alpha = .05$ and 7 *df*. We find that $t_{cv} = 1.895$. Our $t_{obt} = 3.85$ and therefore falls in the region of rejection. Figure 9.3 shows this $t_{obt}$ in relation to $t_{cv}$. In APA style, this is reported as $t(7) = 3.85$, $p < .05$, indicating that there is a significant difference in the number of words recalled in the two conditions.

This difference is illustrated in Figure 9.4, in which the mean numbers of concrete and abstract words recalled by the participants have been graphed. Thus, we can conclude that participants performed significantly better in the concrete word condition, which supports the alternative (research) hypothesis.

*Effect Size: Cohen's* **d.** As with the independent-groups *t* test, we should also compute Cohen's *d* (the proportion of variance in the dependent variable that is accounted for by the manipulation of the independent variable) for the correlated-groups *t* test. Remember, effect size indicates how big a role the conditions of the independent variable play in determining scores on the dependent variable. For the correlated-groups *t* test, the formula for Cohen's *d* is

$$d = \frac{\bar{D}}{s_D}$$

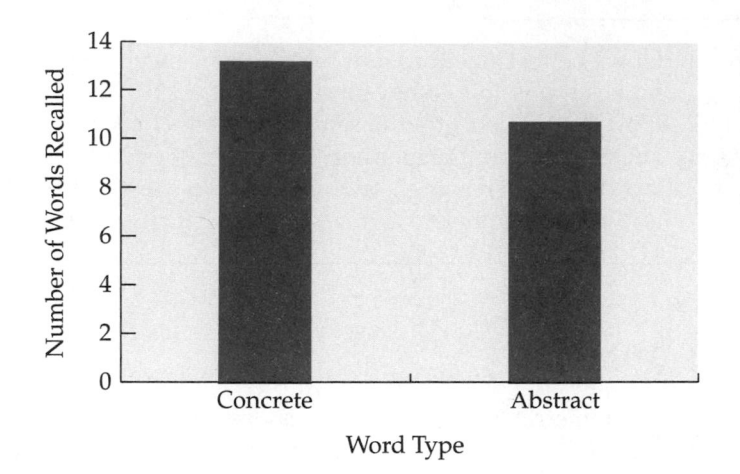

**FIGURE 9.4**
Mean number of words recalled correctly under concrete and abstract word conditions

where $\bar{D}$ is the mean of the difference scores and $s_D$ is the standard deviation of the difference scores. We have already calculated each of these as part of the $t$ test. Thus,

$$d = \frac{2.5}{1.85} = 1.35$$

Cohen's $d$ for a correlated-groups design is interpreted in the same manner as $d$ for an independent-groups design. That is, a small effect size is one of at least 0.20, a medium effect size is at least 0.50, and a large effect size is at least 0.80. Obviously, our effect size of 1.35 is far greater than 0.80, indicating a very large effect size.

*Assumptions of the Correlated-Groups t Test* The assumptions for the correlated-groups $t$ test are the same as those for the independent-groups $t$ test, except for the assumption that the observations are independent. In this case, the observations are not independent—they are correlated.

## Independent-Groups and Correlated-Groups *t* Tests                IN REVIEW

| | TYPE OF TEST | |
|---|---|---|
| | **Independent-Groups *t* Test** | **Correlated-Groups *t* Test** |
| What It Is | A parametric test for a two-group between-participants design | A parametric test for a two-group within-participants or matched-participants design |
| What It Does | Compares performance of the two groups to determine whether they represent the same population or different populations | Analyzes whether each individual performed in a similar or different manner across conditions |
| Assumptions | Interval-ratio data | Interval-ratio data |
| | Bell-shaped distribution | Bell-shaped distribution |
| | Independent observations | |
| | Homogeneity of variance | Homogeneity of variance |

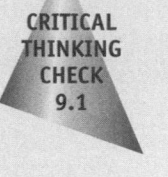

CRITICAL THINKING CHECK 9.1

1. How is effect size different from significance level? In other words, how is it possible to have a significant result yet a small effect size?
2. How does increasing the sample size affect a *t* test? Why does it affect a *t* test in this manner?
3. How does decreasing variability affect a *t* test? Why does it affect a *t* test in this manner?

# Summary

Two parametric inferential statistics used with two-group designs were presented in this chapter. The statistics vary based on whether the study is a between-participants or correlated-groups design. It is imperative that the appropriate statistic be used to analyze the data collected in an experiment. The first point to consider when determining which statistic to use is whether it should be a parametric or nonparametric statistic. This decision is based on the type of data collected, the type of distribution to which the data conform, and whether any parameters of the distribution are known. The second consideration is whether a between-participants or correlated-groups design has been used. This information enables us to select and conduct the statistical test most appropriate to the particular study's design and data.

## KEY TERMS

independent-groups *t* test
standard error of the difference
   between means

effect size
Cohen's *d*
correlated-groups *t* test

difference scores
standard error of the difference
   scores

## CHAPTER EXERCISES

(Answers to odd-numbered exercises appear in Appendix C.)

1. A college student is interested in whether there is a difference between male and female students in the amount of time they spend studying each week. The student gathers information from a random sample of male and female students on campus. The amounts of time spent studying are normally distributed. The data are:

| Males | Females | Males | Females |
|-------|---------|-------|---------|
| 27 | 25 | 16 | 20 |
| 25 | 29 | 22 | 15 |
| 19 | 18 | 14 | 19 |
| 10 | 23 | | |

a. What statistical test should be used to analyze these data?
b. Identify $H_0$ and $H_a$ for this study.
c. Conduct the appropriate analysis.
d. Should $H_0$ be rejected? What should the researcher conclude?
e. If significant, compute the effect size and interpret this.
f. If significant, draw a graph representing the data.

2. A student is interested in whether students who study with music playing devote as much attention to their studies as do students who study under quiet conditions. He randomly assigns participants to either the music or no-music

condition and has them read and study the same passage of information for the same amount of time. Participants are then all given the same 10-item test on the material. Their scores appear below. Scores on the test represent interval-ratio data and are normally distributed.

| Music | No Music |
|-------|----------|
| 6 | 10 |
| 5 | 9 |
| 6 | 7 |
| 5 | 7 |
| 6 | 6 |
| 6 | 6 |
| 7 | 8 |
| 8 | 6 |
| 5 | 9 |

a. What statistical test should be used to analyze these data?
b. Identify $H_0$ and $H_a$ for this study.
c. Conduct the appropriate analysis.
d. Should $H_0$ be rejected? What should the researcher conclude?
e. If significant, compute the effect size and interpret this.
f. If significant, draw a graph representing the data.

3. A researcher is interested in whether participating in sports positively influences self-esteem in young girls. She identifies a group of girls who have not played sports before but are now planning to begin participating in organized sports. She gives them a 50-item self-esteem inventory before they begin playing sports and administers the same test again after 6 months of playing sports. The self-esteem inventory is measured on an interval scale, with higher numbers indicating higher self-esteem. In addition, scores on the inventory are normally distributed. The scores appear below.

| Before | After |
|--------|-------|
| 44 | 46 |
| 40 | 41 |

| Before | After |
|--------|-------|
| 39 | 41 |
| 46 | 47 |
| 42 | 43 |
| 43 | 45 |

a. What statistical test should be used to analyze these data?
b. Identify $H_0$ and $H_a$ for this study.
c. Conduct the appropriate analysis.
d. Should $H_0$ be rejected? What should the researcher conclude?
e. If significant, compute the effect size and interpret this.
f. If significant, draw a graph representing the data.

4. The researcher in Exercise 2 decides to conduct the same study using a within-participants design in order to control for differences in cognitive ability. He selects a random sample of participants and has them study different material of equal difficulty in both the music and no-music conditions. The study is completely counterbalanced to control for order effects. The data appear below. As before, they are measured on an interval-ratio scale and are normally distributed.

| Music | No Music |
|-------|----------|
| 7 | 7 |
| 6 | 8 |
| 5 | 7 |
| 6 | 7 |
| 8 | 0 |
| 8 | 8 |

a. What statistical test should be used to analyze these data?
b. Identify $H_0$ and $H_a$ for this study.
c. Conduct the appropriate analysis.
d. Should $H_0$ be rejected? What should the researcher conclude?
e. If significant, compute the effect size and interpret this.
f. If significant, draw a graph representing the data.

## CRITICAL THINKING CHECK ANSWERS

### 9.1

1. Effect size indicates the magnitude of the influence of the experimental treatment, regardless of the sample size. A result can be statistically significant because the sample size is very large, even if the

effect of the independent variable is not so large. Effect size indicates whether this is the case, because in this situation effect size should be small.

2. In the long run, it means that the obtained $t$ is more likely to be significant. In terms of the

formula used to calculate $t$, increasing the sample size will decrease the standard error of the difference between means ($s_{\bar{X}_1 - \bar{X}_2}$). This, in turn, will increase the size of the obtained $t$. A larger obtained $t$ means that the obtained value is more likely to exceed the critical value and be significant.

3. Decreasing variability also makes a $t$ test more powerful (likely to be significant) because

decreasing variability also means that $s_{\bar{X}_1 - \bar{X}_2}$ (the standard error of the difference between means) will be smaller. Again, this increases the size of the obtained $t$, and a larger obtained $t$ means that the obtained value is more likely to exceed the critical value and be significant.

## WEB RESOURCES

Check your knowledge of the content in this chapter by taking the practice quiz at www.Wadsworth.com. Or, for step-by-step practice and information, check out the Statistics and Research Methods Workshops at http://psychology.wadsworth.com/workshops.

## STATISTICAL SOFTWARE RESOURCES

For hands-on experience using statistical software to complete the analyses described in this chapter, see Chapter 7 ("The $t$ Statistic—Two Samples") in *The* *Excel Statistics Companion* by Kenneth M. Rosenberg (Belmont, CA: Wadsworth, 2003).

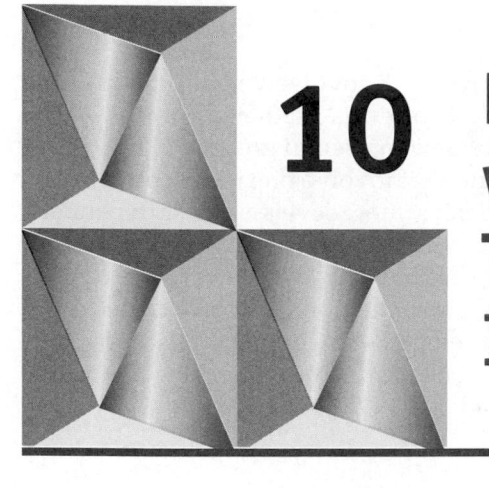

# 10 Experimental Designs with More Than Two Levels of an Independent Variable

The experiments described in Chapter 8 involved manipulating one independent variable with only two levels—either a control group and an experimental group or two experimental groups. In this chapter, we will discuss experimental designs that involve one independent variable with more than two levels. Examining more levels of an independent variable allows us to address more complicated and interesting questions. Often experiments begin as two-group designs and then develop into more complex designs as the questions asked become more elaborate and sophisticated. The same design principles presented in Chapter 8 also apply to these more complex designs; that is, we still need to be concerned about control, internal validity, and external validity.

# Using Designs with More Than Two Levels of an Independent Variable

Researchers may decide to use a design with more than two levels of an independent variable for three reasons. First, it allows them to compare multiple treatments. Second, it enables them to compare multiple treatments with no treatment (the control group). Third, more complex designs allow researchers to compare a placebo group with control and experimental groups (Mitchell & Jolley, 2001).

## Comparing More Than Two Kinds of Treatment in One Study

To illustrate this advantage of more complex experimental designs, imagine that we want to compare the effects of various types of rehearsal on memory. We have participants study a list of 10 words using either rote rehearsal (repetition) or some form of elaborative rehearsal. In addition, we specify the type of elaborative rehearsal to be used in the different experimental groups. Group 1 (the control group) uses rote rehearsal, group 2 uses an imagery mnemonic technique, and group 3 uses a story mnemonic device. You may be wondering why we don't simply conduct three studies or comparisons. Why don't we compare group 1 to group 2, group 2 to group 3, and group 1 to group 3 in three different experiments? There are several reasons this is not recommended.

You may remember from Chapter 9 that a *t* test is used to compare performance between two groups. If we do three experiments, we need to use three *t* tests to determine these differences. The problem is that using multiple tests inflates the Type I error rate. Remember, a Type I error means that we reject the null hypothesis when we should have failed to reject it; that is, we claim that the independent variable has an effect when it does not. For most statistical tests, we use the .05 alpha level, meaning that we are willing to accept a 5% risk of making a Type I error. Although the chance of making a Type I error on one *t* test is .05, the overall chance of making a Type I error increases as more tests are conducted.

Imagine that we conducted three *t* tests or comparisons among the three groups in the memory experiment. The probability of a Type I error on any single comparison is .05. The probability of a Type I error on at least one of the three tests, however, is considerably higher. To determine the chance of a Type I error when making multiple comparisons, we use the formula $1 - (1 - \alpha)^c$, where *c* equals the number of comparisons performed. Using this formula for the present example, we get

$$1-(1-.05)^3 = 1-(.95)^3 = 1-.86 = .14$$

Thus, the probability of a Type I error on at least one of the three tests is .14, or 14%.

One way of counteracting the increased chance of a Type I error is to use a more stringent alpha level. The **Bonferoni adjustment,** in which the desired alpha level is divided by the number of tests or comparisons, is typically used to accomplish this. For example, if we were using the *t* test to make the three comparisons described above, we would divide .05 by 3 and get .017. By not accepting the result as significant unless the alpha level is .017 or less, we minimize the chance of a Type I error when making multiple comparisons. We know from discussions in previous chapters, however, that although using a more stringent alpha level decreases the chance of a Type I error, it increases the chance of a Type II error (failing to reject the null hypothesis when it should have been rejected—missing an effect of an independent variable). Thus, the Bonferoni adjustment is not the best method of handling the problem. A better method is to use a single statistical test that compares all groups rather than using multiple comparisons and statistical tests. Luckily for us, there is a statistical technique that will do this—the analysis of variance (ANOVA), which will be discussed shortly.

**Bonferoni adjustment** Setting a more stringent alpha level for multiple tests in order to minimize Type I errors.

Another advantage of comparing more than two kinds of treatment in one experiment is that it reduces both the number of experiments conducted and the number of participants needed. Once again, refer back to the three-group memory experiment. If we do one comparison with three groups, we can conduct only one experiment and we need participants for only three groups. If, however, we conduct three comparisons, each with two groups, then we need to perform three experiments and we need participants for six groups or conditions.

## Comparing Two or More Kinds of Treatment with the Control Group (No Treatment)

Using more than two groups in an experiment also allows researchers to determine whether each treatment is more or less effective than no treatment (the control group). To illustrate this, imagine that we are interested in the effects of aerobic exercise on anxiety. We hypothesize that the more aerobic activity one engages in, the more anxiety will be reduced. We use a control group that does not engage in any aerobic activity and a high aerobic activity group that engages in 50 minutes per day of aerobic activity—a simple two-group design. Assume, however, that when using this design, we find that both those in the control group and those in the experimental group have high levels of anxiety at the end of the study—not what we expected to find. How could a design with more than two groups provide more information? Suppose we add another group to this study—a moderate aerobic activity group (25 minutes per day)—and get the following results:

| Control group | High anxiety |
| Moderate aerobic activity | Low anxiety |
| High aerobic activity | High anxiety |

Based on these data, we have a V-shaped function. Up to a certain point, aerobic activity reduces anxiety. However, when the aerobic activity exceeds a certain level, anxiety increases again. If we had conducted the original study with only two groups, we would have missed this relationship and erroneously concluded that there was no relationship between aerobic activity and anxiety. Using a design with multiple groups allows us to see more of the relationship between the variables.

Figure 10.1 illustrates the difference between the results obtained with the three-group and the two-group design in this hypothetical study. It also shows the other two-group comparisons—control compared to moderate aerobic activity, and moderate aerobic activity compared to high aerobic activity. This set of graphs illustrates how two-group designs limit our ability to see the complete relationship between variables.

Figure 10.1a shows clearly how the three-group design allows us to assess more fully the relationship between the variables. If we had conducted only

**FIGURE 10.1**
Determining relationships with three-group versus two-group designs: (a) three-group design; (b) two-group comparison of control to high aerobic activity; (c) two-group comparison of control to moderate aerobic activity; (d) two-group comparison of moderate aerobic activity to high aerobic activity

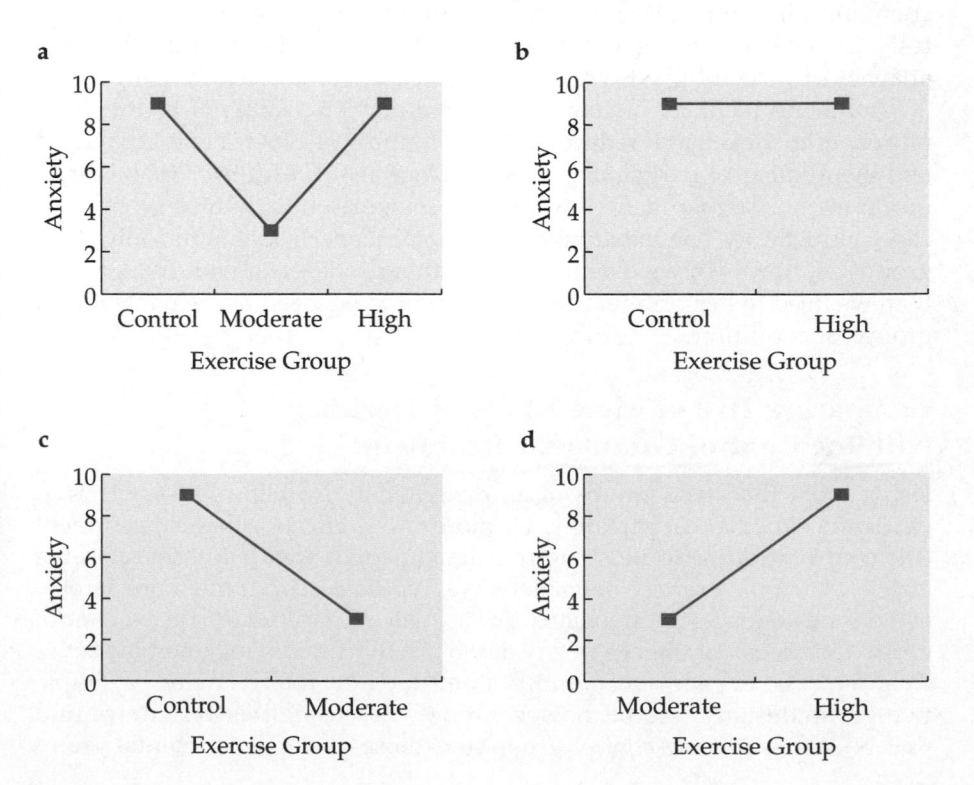

a two-group study, such as those illustrated in Figure 10.1b, c, or d, we would have drawn a much different conclusion than that drawn from the three-group design. Comparing only the control to the high aerobic activity group (Figure 10.1b) would have led us to conclude that aerobic activity does not affect anxiety. Comparing only the control and the moderate aerobic activity group (Figure 10.1c) would have led to the conclusion that increasing aerobic activity reduces anxiety. Comparing only the moderate aerobic activity group and the high aerobic activity group (Figure 10.1d) would have led to the conclusion that increasing aerobic activity increases anxiety.

Being able to assess the relationship between the variables means that we can determine the type of relationship that exists. In the preceding example, the variables produced a V-shaped function. Other variables may be related in a straight linear manner or in an alternative curvilinear manner (for example, a J-shaped or S-shaped function). In summary, adding levels to the independent variable allows us to determine more accurately the type of relationship that exists between the variables.

## Comparing a Placebo Group with the Control and Experimental Groups

A final advantage of designs with more than two groups is that they allow for the use of a *placebo group*. How can adding a placebo group improve an experiment? Consider an often cited study by Paul (1966, 1967) involving children who suffered from maladaptive anxiety in public speaking situations. Paul used a control group, which received no treatment; a placebo group, which received a placebo that they were told was a potent tranquilizer; and an experimental group, which received desensitization therapy. Of those in the experimental group, 85% showed improvement, compared with only 22% in the control condition. If the placebo group had not been included, the difference between the therapy and control groups (85% − 22% = 63%) would overestimate the effectiveness of the desensitization program. The placebo group showed 50% improvement, meaning that the therapy's true effectiveness is much less (85% − 50% = 35%). Thus, a placebo group allows for a more accurate assessment of a therapy's effectiveness because, in addition to spontaneous remission, it controls for participant expectation effects.

| Designs with More Than Two Levels of an Independent Variable | IN REVIEW |
|---|---|
| **ADVANTAGES** | **CONSIDERATIONS** |
| Allows comparisons of more than two types of treatment | Type of statistical analysis (e.g., multiple *t* tests or |
| Requires fewer participants | ANOVA) |
| Allows comparisons of all treatments with control condition | Multiple *t* tests increase chance of Type I error; |
| Allows for use of a placebo group with control and experimental groups | Bonferoni adjustment increases chance of Type II error |

| | |
|---|---|
| **CRITICAL THINKING CHECK 10.1** | 1. Imagine that a researcher wants to compare four different types of treatment. The researcher decides to conduct six individual studies to make these comparisons. What is the probability of a Type I error, with alpha = .05, across these six comparisons? Use the Bonferoni adjustment to determine the suggested alpha level for these six tests. |

# Analyzing the Multiple-Group Experiment

**ANOVA (analysis of variance)** An inferential statistical test for comparing the means of three or more groups.

As noted previously, *t* tests are not recommended for comparing performance across groups in a multiple-group design because of the increased probability of a Type I error. For multiple-group designs in which interval-ratio data are collected, the recommended statistical analysis is the **ANOVA (analysis of variance)**—an inferential parametric statistical test for comparing the means of three or more groups. As its name indicates, this procedure allows us to analyze the variance in a study. You should be familiar with variance from Chapter 5 on descriptive statistics. Nonparametric analyses are also available for designs in which ordinal data are collected (the Kruskal-Wallis analysis of variance) and for designs in which nominal data are collected (the chi-square test). Nonparametric statistics are covered in Chapter 13.

## Between-Participants Designs: One-Way Randomized ANOVA

**one-way randomized ANOVA** An inferential statistical test for comparing the means of three or more groups using a between-participants design and one independent variable.

We will begin our coverage of statistics appropriate for multiple-group designs by discussing those used with data collected from a between-participants design. Recall that a between-participants design is one in which different participants serve in each condition. Imagine that we conducted the experiment mentioned at the beginning of the chapter in which participants are asked to study a list of 10 words using rote rehearsal or one of two forms of elaborative rehearsal. A total of 24 participants are randomly assigned, 8 to each condition. Table 10.1 lists the number of words correctly recalled by each participant.

Because these data represent an interval-ratio scale of measurement and because there are more than two groups, an ANOVA is the appropriate statistical test to analyze the data. In addition, because this is a between-participants design, we use a **one-way randomized ANOVA.** The term *randomized* indicates that participants are randomly assigned to conditions in a between-participants design. The term *one-way* indicates that the design uses only one independent variable—in this case, type of rehearsal. We will discuss statistical tests appropriate for correlated-groups designs later in this chapter, and tests appropriate for designs with more than one independent variable in the next chapter. Please note that although all of the studies used to illustrate the ANOVA procedure in this chapter have an equal number of participants in each condition, this is not necessary to the procedure.

**TABLE 10.1** Numbers of words recalled correctly in rote rehearsal, imagery, and story conditions

| ROTE REHEARSAL | IMAGERY | STORY | |
|:---:|:---:|:---:|:---|
| 2 | 4 | 6 | |
| 4 | 5 | 5 | |
| 3 | 7 | 9 | |
| 5 | 6 | 10 | |
| 2 | 5 | 8 | |
| 7 | 4 | 7 | |
| 6 | 8 | 10 | |
| 3 | 5 | 9 | |
| $\overline{X} = 4$ | $\overline{X} = 5.5$ | $\overline{X} = 8$ | Grand mean = 5.833 |

*One-Way Randomized ANOVA: What It Is and What It Does.* The analysis of variance (ANOVA) is a parametric inferential statistical test for comparing the means of three or more groups. In addition to helping maintain an acceptable Type I error rate, the ANOVA has the advantage over using multiple $t$ tests of being more powerful and thus less susceptible to a Type II error. In this section, we will discuss the simplest use of ANOVA—a design with one independent variable with three levels.

Let's continue to use the experiment and data presented in Table 10.1. Remember that we are interested in the effects of rehearsal type on memory. The null hypothesis ($H_0$) for an ANOVA is that the sample means represent the same population ($H_0$: $\mu_1 = \mu_2 - \mu_3$). The alternative hypothesis ($H_a$) is that they represent **different** populations ($H_a$: at least one $\mu \neq$ another $\mu$). When a researcher rejects $H_0$ using an ANOVA, it means that the independent variable affected the dependent variable to the extent that at least one group mean differs from the others by more than would be expected based on chance. Failing to reject $H_0$ indicates that the means do not differ from each other more than would be expected based on chance. In other words, there is not enough evidence to suggest that the sample means represent at least two different populations.

In our example, the mean number of words recalled in the rote rehearsal condition is 4, for the imagery condition it is 5.5, and in the story condition it is 8. If you look at the data from each condition, you will notice that most participants in each condition did not score exactly at the mean for that condition. In other words, there is variability within each condition. The **grand mean**—the mean performance across all participants in all conditions—is 5.833. Because none of the participants in any condition recalled exactly 5.833 words, there is also variability between conditions. What we are interested in is whether this variability is due primarily to the independent variable (differences in rehearsal type) or to **error variance**—the amount of variability among the scores caused by chance or uncontrolled variables (such as individual differences between participants).

**grand mean** The mean performance across all participants in a study.

**error variance** The amount of variability among the scores caused by chance or uncontrolled variables.

The error variance can be estimated by looking at the amount of variability *within* each condition. How will this give us an estimate of error variance? Each participant in each condition was treated similarly; each was instructed to rehearse the words in the same manner. Because the participants in each condition were treated in the same manner, any differences observed in the number of words recalled are attributable only to error variance. In other words, some participants may have been more motivated, or more distracted, or better at memory tasks—all factors that would contribute to error variance in this case. Therefore, the **within-groups variance** (the variance within each condition or group) is an estimate of the population error variance.

Now we can compare the means between the groups. If the independent variable (rehearsal type) had an effect, we would expect some of the group means to differ from the grand mean. If the independent variable had no effect on the number of words recalled, we would still expect the group means to vary from the grand mean slightly, as a result of error variance attributable to individual differences. In other words, all participants in a study will not score exactly the same. Therefore, even when the independent variable has no effect, we do not expect that the group means will exactly equal the grand mean. If there were no effect of the independent variable, then the variance between groups would be due to error.

Between-groups variance may be attributed to several sources. There could be systematic differences between the groups, referred to as *systematic variance*. The systematic variance between the groups could be due to the effects of the independent variable (variance due to the experimental manipulation). However, it could also be due to the influence of uncontrolled confounding variables (variance due to extraneous variables). In addition, there is always some error variance in any between-groups variance estimate. In sum, **between-groups variance** is an estimate of systematic variance (the effect of the independent variable and any confounds) *and* error variance.

By looking at the ratio of between-groups variance to within-groups variance, known as the **F-ratio,** we can determine whether most of the variability is attributable to systematic variance (hopefully due to the independent variable and not to confounds) or to chance and random factors (error variance):

$$F = \frac{\text{Between-groups variance}}{\text{Within-groups varience}} = \frac{\text{Systematic variance} + \text{Error variance}}{\text{Error variance}}$$

Looking at the *F*-ratio, we can see that if the systematic variance (which we assume is due to the effect of the independent variable) is substantially greater than the error variance, the ratio will be substantially greater than 1. If there is no systematic variance, then the ratio will be approximately 1.00 (error variance divided by error variance). There are two points to remember regarding *F*-ratios. First, in order for an *F*-ratio to be significant (show a statistically meaningful effect of an independent variable), it must be substantially greater than 1 (we will discuss exactly how much greater than 1 later in the chapter). Second, if an *F*-ratio is approximately 1, then the between-groups variance

**within-groups variance** The variance within each condition; an estimate of the population error variance.

**between-groups variance** An estimate of the effect of the independent variable *and* error variance.

**F-ratio** The ratio of between-groups variance to within-groups variance.

equals the within-groups variance and there is no effect of the independent variable.

Refer back to Table 10.1, and think about the within-groups versus between-groups variance in this study. Notice that the amount of variance within the groups is small—the scores within each group vary from each individual group mean, but not by very much. The between-groups variance, on the other hand, is large—the scores across the three conditions vary to a greater extent. With these data, then, it appears that we have a relatively large between-groups variance and a smaller within-groups variance. Our $F$-ratio will therefore be greater than 1.00. To assess how large it is, we will need to conduct the appropriate calculations (described in the next section). At this point, however, you should have a general understanding of how an ANOVA analyzes variance to determine whether the independent variable has an effect.

---

1. Imagine that the data presented below are from the study just described (the effects of type of rehearsal on number of words recalled). Do you think that the between-groups and within-groups variances are large, moderate, or small? Will the corresponding $F$-ratio be greater than, equal to, or less than 1.00?

CRITICAL THINKING CHECK 10.2

| Rote Rehearsal | Imagery | Story |
|:---:|:---:|:---:|
| 2 | 4 | 5 |
| 4 | 2 | 2 |
| 3 | 5 | 4 |
| 5 | 3 | 2 |
| ? | 2 | 3 |
| 7 | 7 | 6 |
| 6 | 6 | 3 |
| 3 | 2 | 7 |
| $\bar{X} = 4$ | $\bar{X} = 3.88$ | $\bar{X} = 4$   Grand mean $= 3.96$ |

---

*Calculations for the One-Way Randomized ANOVA.* To see exactly how ANOVA works, we begin by calculating the sums of squares ($SS$). This should sound somewhat familiar to you because we calculated sums of squares as part of the calculation for standard deviation in Chapter 5. The sum of squares in that formula represented the sum of the squared deviations of each score from the overall mean. Determining the sums of squares is the first step in calculating the various types or sources of variance in an ANOVA.

Several types of sums of squares are used in the calculation of an ANOVA. In describing them in this section, I provide *definitional formulas* for each. The definitional formula follows the definition for each sum of squares and should give you the basic idea of how each $SS$ is calculated. When we are dealing with

"EVERY ONCE IN A WHILE I JUST LIKE TO UNWIND WITH A LITTLE ADDITION AND SUBTRACTION."

very large data sets, however, the definitional formulas can become somewhat cumbersome. Thus, statisticians have transformed the definitional formulas into *computational formulas*. A computational formula is easier to use in terms of the number of steps required. However, computational formulas do not follow the definition of the *SS* and thus do not necessarily make sense in terms of the definition of each *SS*. If your instructor prefers that you use the computational formulas, they are provided in Appendix B.

**total sum of squares** The sum of the squared deviations of each score from the grand mean.

The first sum of squares that we need to describe is the **total sum of squares** ($SS_{Total}$)—the sum of the squared deviations of each score from the grand mean. In a definitional formula, this is represented as $\sum(X - \bar{X}_G)^2$, where $X$ represents each individual score and $\bar{X}_G$ is the grand mean. In other words, we determine how much each individual participant varies from the grand mean, square that deviation score, and sum all of the squared deviation scores. For our study on the effects of rehearsal type on memory, the total sum of squares ($SS_{Total}$) = 127.32. To see where this number comes from, refer to Table 10.2. (For the computational formula, see Appendix B.) Once we have calculated the sum of squares within and between groups (see below), they should equal the total sum of squares when added together. In this way, we can check our calculations for accuracy. If the sums of squares within and between do not equal the sum of squares total, then you know that there is an error in at least one of the calculations.

**within-groups sum of squares** The sum of the squared deviations of each score from its group mean.

Because an ANOVA analyzes the variances between groups and within groups, we need to use different formulas to determine the variance attributable to these two factors. The **within-groups sum of squares** is the sum of the squared deviations of each score from its group or condition mean and is a reflection of the amount of error variance. In the definitional formula, it is $\sum(X - \bar{X}_g)^2$, where $X$ refers to each individual score and $\bar{X}_g$ is the mean for each group or condition. To determine this, we find the difference

**TABLE 10.2** Calculation of $SS_{Total}$ using the definitional formula

| ROTE REHEARSAL | | IMAGERY | | STORY | |
|---|---|---|---|---|---|
| $X$ | $(X-\bar{X}_G)^2$ | $X$ | $(X-\bar{X}_G)^2$ | $X$ | $(X-\bar{X}_G)^2$ |
| 2 | 14.69 | 4 | 3.36 | 6 | 0.03 |
| 4 | 3.36 | 5 | 0.69 | 5 | 0.69 |
| 3 | 8.03 | 7 | 1.36 | 9 | 10.03 |
| 5 | 0.69 | 6 | 0.03 | 10 | 17.36 |
| 2 | 14.69 | 5 | 0.69 | 8 | 4.70 |
| 7 | 1.36 | 4 | 3.36 | 7 | 1.36 |
| 6 | 0.03 | 8 | 4.70 | 10 | 17.36 |
| 3 | 8.03 | 5 | 0.69 | 9 | 10.03 |
| | $\Sigma = 50.88$ | | $\Sigma = 14.88$ | | $\Sigma = 61.56$ |

$SS_{Total} = 50.88 + 14.88 + 61.56 = 127.32$

NOTE: All numbers have been rounded to two decimal places.

between each score and its group mean, square these deviation scores, and then sum all of the squared deviation scores. The use of this definitional formula to calculate $SS_{Within}$ is illustrated in Table 10.3. The computational formula appears in Appendix B. Thus, rather than comparing every score in the entire study to the grand mean of the study (as is done for $SS_{Total}$), we compare each score in each condition to the mean of that condition. Thus, $SS_{Within}$ is a reflection of the amount of variability within each condition. Because the participants in each condition were treated in a similar manner, we would expect little variation among the scores within each group. This means that the within groups sum of squares ($SS_{Within}$) should be small, indicating a small amount of error variance in the study. For our memory study, the within-groups sum of squares ($SS_{Within}$) is 62.

**TABLE 10.3** Calculation of $SS_{Within}$ using the definitional formula

| ROTE REHEARSAL | | IMAGERY | | STORY | |
|---|---|---|---|---|---|
| $X$ | $(X-\bar{X}_g)^2$ | $X$ | $(X-\bar{X}_g)^2$ | $X$ | $(X-\bar{X}_g)^2$ |
| 2 | 4 | 4 | 2.25 | 6 | 4 |
| 4 | 0 | 5 | 0.25 | 5 | 9 |
| 3 | 1 | 7 | 2.25 | 9 | 1 |
| 5 | 1 | 6 | 0.25 | 10 | 4 |
| 2 | 4 | 5 | 0.25 | 8 | 0 |
| 7 | 9 | 4 | 2.25 | 7 | 1 |
| 6 | 4 | 8 | 6.25 | 10 | 4 |
| 3 | 1 | 5 | 0.25 | 9 | 1 |
| | $\Sigma = 24$ | | $\Sigma = 14$ | | $\Sigma = 24$ |

$SS_{Within} = 24 + 14 + 24 = 62$

NOTE: All numbers have been rounded to two decimal places.

**TABLE 10.4   Calculation of $SS_{Between}$ using the definitional formula**

| |
|---|
| **Rote Rehearsal** |
| $(\bar{X}_g - \bar{X}_G)^2 n = (4 - 5.833)^2 8 = (-1.833)^2 8 = (3.36)8 = 26.88$ |
| **Imagery** |
| $(\bar{X}_g - \bar{X}_G)^2 n = (5.5 - 5.833)^2 8 = (-0.333)^2 8 = (0.11)8 = 0.88$ |
| **Story** |
| $(\bar{X}_g - \bar{X}_G)^2 n = (8 - 5.833)^2 8 = (2.167)^2 8 = (4.696)8 = 37.57$ |
| $SS_{Between} = 26.88 + 0.88 + 37.57 = 65.33$ |

**between-groups sum of squares** The sum of the squared deviations of each group's mean from the grand mean, multiplied by the number of participants in each group.

The **between-groups sum of squares** is the sum of the squared deviations of each group's mean from the grand mean, multiplied by the number of participants in each group. In the definitional formula, this is $\Sigma[(\bar{X}_g - \bar{X}_G)^2 n]$, where $\bar{X}_g$ is the mean for each group, $\bar{X}_G$ is the grand mean, and $n$ is the number of participants in each group. The use of the definitional formula to calculate $SS_{Between}$ is illustrated in Table 10.4. The computational formula appears in Appendix B. The between-groups variance is an indication of the systematic variance across the groups (the variance due to the independent variable and any confounds) and error. The basic idea behind the between-groups sum of squares is that if the independent variable had no effect (if there were no differences between the groups), then we would expect all the group means to be about the same. If all the group means were similar, they would also be approximately equal to the grand mean and there would be little variance across conditions. If, however, the independent variable caused changes in the means of some conditions (caused them to be larger or smaller than other conditions), then the condition means would not only differ from each other but would also differ from the grand mean, indicating variance across conditions. In our memory study, $SS_{Between} = 65.33$.

We can check the accuracy of our calculations by adding $SS_{Within}$ and $SS_{Between}$. When added, these numbers should equal $SS_{Total}$. Thus, $SS_{Within}$ (62) + $SS_{Between}$ (65.33) = 127.33. The $SS_{Total}$ that we calculated earlier was 127.32 and is essentially equal to $SS_{Within} + SS_{Between}$, taking into account rounding errors.

Calculating the sums of squares is an important step in the ANOVA. It is not, however, the end. Now that we have determined $SS_{Total}$, $SS_{Within}$, and $SS_{Between}$, we must transform these scores into the mean squares. The term **mean square** (MS) is an abbreviation of mean squared deviation scores. The MS scores are estimates of variance between and within the groups. To calculate the MS for each group ($MS_{Within}$ and $MS_{Between}$), we divide each SS by the appropriate $df$ (degrees of freedom). The reason for this is that the MS scores are variance estimates. You may remember from Chapter 5 that when calculating standard deviation and variance, we divide the sum of squares by $N$ (or $N - 1$ for the unbiased estimator) to get the average deviation from the mean. In this same manner, we must divide the SS scores by their degrees of freedom (the number of scores that contributed to each SS minus 1).

**mean square** An estimate of either variance between groups or variance within groups.

In the present example, we first need to determine the degrees of freedom for each type of variance. Let's begin with $df_{Total}$, which we will use to check our accuracy when calculating $df_{Within}$ and $df_{Between}$. In other words, $df_{Within}$ and $df_{Between}$ should sum to $df_{Total}$. We determined $SS_{Total}$ by calculating the deviations around the grand mean. We therefore had one restriction on our data—the grand mean. This leaves us with $N - 1$ total degrees of freedom (the total number of participants in the study minus the one restriction). For our study on the effects of rehearsal type on memory,

$$df_{Total} = 24 - 1 = 23$$

If we use a similar logic, the degrees of freedom within each group would then be $n - 1$ (the number of participants in each condition minus 1). However, we have more than one group: We have $k$ groups, where $k$ refers to the number of groups or conditions in the study. The degrees of freedom within groups is therefore $k(n - 1)$ or $(N - k)$. For our example,

$$df_{Within} = 24 - 3 = 21$$

Last, the degrees of freedom between groups is the variability of $k$ means around the grand mean. Therefore, $df_{Between}$ equals the number of groups ($k$) minus 1 ($k - 1$). For our study, this is

$$df_{Between} = 3 - 1 = 2$$

Notice that the sum of $df_{Within}$ and $df_{Between}$ is $df_{Total}$: $21 + 2 - 23$. This allows us to check our calculations for accuracy. If the degrees of freedom between and within do not sum to the degrees of freedom total, we know there is a mistake somewhere.

Now that we have calculated the sums of squares and their degrees of freedom, we can use these numbers to calculate estimates of the variances between and within groups. As stated previously, the variance estimates are called mean squares and are determined by dividing each $SS$ by its corresponding $df$. In our example,

$$MS_{Within} = \frac{SS_{Within}}{df_{Within}} = \frac{62}{21} = 2.95$$

$$MS_{Between} = \frac{SS_{Between}}{df_{Between}} = \frac{65.33}{2} = 32.67$$

We can now use the estimates of between-groups and within-groups variances to determine the $F$-ratio:

$$F = \frac{MS_{Between}}{MS_{Within}} = \frac{32.67}{2.95} = 11.07$$

The definitional formulas for the sums of squares along with the formulas for the degrees of freedom, means squares, and the final $F$-ratio are summarized in Table 10.5. The ANOVA summary table for the $F$-ratio just calculated is presented in Table 10.6. This is a common format for summarizing ANOVA findings. You will often see ANOVA summary tables in journal

TABLE 10.5   ANOVA summary table: definitional formulas

| SOURCE | df | SS | MS | F |
|---|---|---|---|---|
| Between groups | $k - 1$ | $\Sigma[(\bar{X}_g - \bar{X}_G)^2 n]$ | $\dfrac{SS_{Between}}{df_{Between}}$ | $\dfrac{MS_{Between}}{MS_{Within}}$ |
| Within groups | $N - k$ | $\Sigma(X - \bar{X}_g)^2$ | $\dfrac{SS_{Within}}{df_{Within}}$ | |
| Total | $N - 1$ | $\Sigma(X - \bar{X}_G)^2$ | | |

TABLE 10.6   ANOVA summary table for the memory study

| SOURCE | df | SS | MS | F |
|---|---|---|---|---|
| Between groups | 2 | 65.33 | 32.67 | 11.07 |
| Within groups | 21 | 62 | 2.95 | |
| Total | 23 | 127.33 | | |

articles because they are a concise way of presenting the results from an analysis of variance.

***Interpreting the One-Way Randomized ANOVA.*** Our obtained $F$-ratio of 11.07 is obviously greater than 1.00. However, we do not know whether it is large enough to let us reject the null hypothesis. To make this decision, we need to compare the obtained $F$ ($F_{obt}$) of 11.07 with the $F_{cv}$—the critical value that determines the cutoff for statistical significance. The underlying $F$ distribution is actually a family of distributions, each based on the degrees of freedom between and within each group. Remember that the alternative hypothesis is that the population means represented by the sample means are not from the same population. Table A.5 in Appendix A provides the critical values for the family of $F$ distributions when $\alpha = .05$ and when $\alpha = .01$. To use the table, look at the $df_{Within}$ running down the left-hand side of the table and the $df_{Between}$ running across the top of the table. $F_{cv}$ is found where the row and column of these two numbers intersect. For our example, $df_{Within} = 21$ and $df_{Between} = 2$. Because there is no 21 in the $df_{Within}$ column, we use the next lower number, 20. According to Table A.5, $F_{cv}$ for the .05 level is 3.49. Because our $F_{obt}$ exceeds this, it is statistically significant at the .05 level. Let's check the .01 level also. The critical value for the .01 level is 5.85. Our $F_{obt}$ is greater than this critical value also. We can therefore conclude that $F_{obt}$ is significant at the .01 level. In APA publication format, this is written as $F(2, 21) = 11.07$, $p < .01$. This means that we reject $H_0$ and support $H_a$. In other words, at least one group mean differs significantly from the others.

Let's consider what factors might affect the size of the final $F_{obt}$. Because $F_{obt}$ is derived using the between-groups variance as the numerator and the within-groups variance as the denominator, anything that increases the numerator or decreases the denominator will increase $F_{obt}$. What might increase the numerator? Using stronger controls in the experiment could have this effect because it would make any differences between the groups more noticeable or larger. This means that $MS_{Between}$ (the numerator in the $F$-ratio) would be larger and therefore lead to a larger final $F$-ratio.

What would decrease the denominator? Once again, using better control to reduce the overall error variance would have this effect; so would increasing the sample size, which increases $df_{Within}$ and ultimately decreases $MS_{Within}$. Why would each of these affect the $F$-ratio in this manner? Each would decrease the size of $MS_{Within}$, which is the denominator in the $F$-ratio. Dividing by a smaller number would lead to a larger final $F$-ratio and, therefore, a greater chance that it would be significant.

*Graphing the Means and Effect Size.* As noted in Chapter 9, we usually graph the means when we find a significant difference between them. As in our previous graphs, the independent variable is placed on the $x$-axis and the dependent variable on the $y$-axis. A bar graph representing the mean performance of each group is shown in Figure 10.2. In this experiment, those in the rote rehearsal condition remembered an average of 4 words, those in the imagery condition remembered an average of 5.5 words, and those in the story condition remembered an average of 8 words.

In addition to graphing the data, we should assess effect size. Based on $F_{obt}$, we know that there was more variability between groups than within groups. In other words, the between-groups variance (the numerator in the $F$-ratio) was larger than the within-groups variance (the denominator in the $F$-ratio). However, it would be useful to know how much of the variability in the dependent variable can be attributed to the independent variable. In other words, it would be useful to have a measure of effect size. For an ANOVA, effect size can be estimated using **eta-squared** ($\eta^2$), which is calculated as follows:

$$\eta^2 = \frac{SS_{Between}}{SS_{Total}}$$

**eta-squared** ($\eta^2$)   An inferential statistic for measuring effect size with an ANOVA.

Because $SS_{Between}$ reflects the differences between the means from the various levels of an independent variable and $SS_{Total}$ reflects the total differences

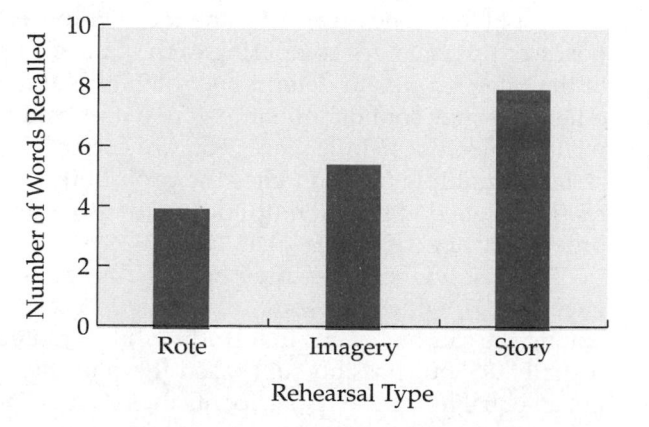

**FIGURE 10.2 Mean number of words recalled as a function of rehearsal type**

between all scores in the experiment, $\eta^2$ reflects the proportion of the total differences in the scores that is associated with differences between sample means, or how much of the variability in the dependent variable (memory) is attributable to the manipulation of the independent variable (rehearsal type).

Referring to the summary for our example in Table 10.6, we see that $\eta^2$ is calculated as follows:

$$\eta^2 = \frac{65.33}{127.33} = .51$$

In other words, approximately 51% of the variance among the scores can be attributed to the rehearsal condition to which the participant was assigned. In this example, the independent variable of rehearsal type is fairly important in determining the number of words recalled by participants because the $\eta^2$ of 51% represents a considerable effect.

*Assumptions of the One-Way Randomized ANOVA.* As with most statistical tests, certain conditions must be met to ensure that the statistic is being used properly. The assumptions for the randomized one-way ANOVA are similar to those for the *t* test for independent groups:

- The data are on an interval-ratio scale.
- The underlying distribution is normally distributed.
- The variances among the populations being compared are homogeneous.

Because the ANOVA is a robust statistical test, violations of some of these assumptions do not necessarily affect the results. Specifically, if the distributions are slightly skewed rather than normally distributed, it does not affect the results of the ANOVA. In addition, if the sample sizes are equal, the assumption of homogeneity of variances can be violated. However, it is not acceptable to violate the assumption of interval-ratio data. If the data collected in a study are ordinal or nominal in scale, other statistical procedures must be used. These procedures will be discussed in Chapter 13.

*Tukey's Post Hoc Test.* Because the results from our ANOVA indicate that at least one of the sample means differs significantly from the others (represents a different population from the others), we must now compute a post hoc test (a test conducted after the fact—in this case, after the ANOVA). A **post hoc test** involves comparing each of the groups in the study with each of the other groups to determine which ones differ significantly from each other. This may sound familiar to you. In fact, you may be thinking, isn't that what a *t* test does? In a sense, you are correct. However, remember that a series of multiple *t* tests inflates the probability of a Type I error. A post hoc test is designed to permit multiple comparisons and still maintain alpha (the probability of a Type I error) at .05.

The post hoc test presented here is **Tukey's honestly significant difference (HSD),** which allows a researcher to make all pairwise comparisons among the sample means in a study while maintaining an acceptable alpha (usually .05, but possibly .01) when the conditions have equal *n.* If there is not an equal number of participants in each condition, then another post hoc

**post hoc test** When used with an ANOVA, a means of comparing all possible pairs of groups to determine which ones differ significantly from each other.

**Tukey's honestly significant difference (HSD)** A post hoc test used with ANOVAs for making all pairwise comparisons when conditions have equal *n.*

test, such as Fisher's protected $t$ test, which can be used with equal or unequal $n$'s, is appropriate. Because the coverage of statistics in this text is necessarily selective, you will need to consult a more comprehensive statistics text regarding alternative post hoc tests if you need such a test.

Tukey's test identifies the smallest difference between any two means that is significant with alpha = .05 or alpha = .01. The formula for Tukey's HSD is

$$HSD_{.05} = Q(k, df_{Within})\sqrt{\frac{MS_{Within}}{n}}$$

Using this formula, we can determine the HSD for the .05 alpha level. This involves using Table A.6 in Appendix A to look up the value for $Q$. To look up $Q$, we need $k$ (the number of means being compared—in our study on memory, this is 3) and $df_{Within}$ (found in the ANOVA summary table, Table 10.6). Referring to Table A.6 for $k = 3$ and $df_{Within} = 21$ (because there is no 21 in the table, we use 20), we find that at the .05 level, $Q = 3.58$. In addition, we need $MS_{Within}$ from Table 10.6 and $n$ (the number of participants in each group). Using these numbers, we calculate HSD as follows:

$$HSD_{.05} = (3.58)\sqrt{\frac{2.95}{8}} = (3.58)\sqrt{0.369} = (3.58)(0.607) = 2.17$$

This tells us that a difference of 2.17 or greater for any pair of means is significant at the .05 level. In other words, the difference between the means is greater than what would be expected based on chance.

Table 10.7 summarizes the differences between the means for each pairwise comparison. Can you identify which comparisons are significant using Tukey's HSD?

If you identify the differences between the story condition and the rote rehearsal condition and between the story condition and the imagery condition as the two honestly significant differences, you are correct because the difference between the means is greater than 2.17. Because these differences are significant at alpha = .05, we should also check $HSD_{.01}$. To do this, we use the same formula, but we use $Q$ for the .01 alpha level from Table A.6. The calculations are as follows:

$$HSD_{.01} = (4.64)\sqrt{\frac{2.95}{8}} = (4.64)(0.607) = 2.82$$

**TABLE 10.7** **Differences between each pair of means in the memory study**

|  | ROTE REHEARSAL | IMAGERY | STORY |
|---|---|---|---|
| Rote Rehearsal | — | 1.5 | 4.0 |
| Imagery |  | — | 2.5 |
| Story |  |  | — |

The only difference significant at this level is between the rote rehearsal and the story conditions. Thus, based on these data, those in the story condition recalled significantly more words than those in the imagery condition ($p < .05$) and those in the rote rehearsal condition ($p < .01$).

| IN REVIEW | One-Way Randomized ANOVA |
|---|---|
| **CONCEPT** | **DESCRIPTION** |
| Null Hypothesis ($H_0$) | The independent variable had no effect—the samples all represent the same population |
| Alternative Hypothesis ($H_a$) | The independent variable had an effect—at least one of the samples represents a different population than the others |
| F-ratio | The ratio formed when the between-groups variance is divided by the within-groups variance |
| Between-groups Variance | An estimate of the variance of the group means about the grand mean; includes both systematic variance and error variance |
| Within-groups Variance | An estimate of the variance within each condition in the experiment; also known as error variance, or variance due to chance |
| Eta-squared ($\eta^2$) | A measure of effect size—the variability in the dependent variable attributable to the independent variable |
| Tukey's Post Hoc Test | A test conducted to determine which conditions in a study with more than two groups differ significantly from each other |

**CRITICAL THINKING CHECK 10.3**

1. Of the following four F-ratios, which appears to indicate that the independent variable had an effect on the dependent variable?

    1.25/1.11        0.91/1.25        1.95/0.26        0.52/1.01

2. The ANOVA summary table below represents the results from a study on the effects of exercise on stress. There were three conditions in the study: a control group, a moderate exercise group, and a high exercise group. Each group had 10 participants, and the mean stress levels for each group were control = 75.0, moderate exercise = 44.7, and high exercise = 63.7. Stress was measured using a 100-item stress scale, with 100 representing the highest level of stress. Complete the ANOVA summary table, and determine whether the F-ratio is significant. In addition, calculate eta-squared and Tukey's HSD if necessary.

*ANOVA Summary Table*

| Source | df | SS | MS | F |
|---|---|---|---|---|
| Between | | 4,689.27 | | |
| Within | | 82,604.20 | | |
| Total | | | | |

## Correlated-Groups Designs: One-Way Repeated Measures ANOVA

Like between-participants designs, correlated-groups designs may use more than two levels of an independent variable. You should remember from Chapter 8 that there are two types of correlated-groups designs: a within-participants design and a matched-participants design. The same statistical analyses are used for both designs. We will use a within-participants design to illustrate the statistical analysis appropriate for a correlated-groups design with more than two levels of an independent variable.

Imagine now that we want to conduct the same study as before, on the effects of rehearsal type on memory, but using a within-participants rather than a between-participants design. Why might we want to do this? As noted in Chapter 8, within-participants designs—in fact, all correlated-groups designs—are more powerful than between-participants designs. Therefore, one reason for this choice is to increase statistical power. In addition, the within-participants design uses fewer participants and provides almost perfect control across conditions. Because the same people participate in each condition, we know that the individuals in each condition are equivalent and that the only difference between conditions is the type of rehearsal used.

In this study, the same three conditions will be used—rote rehearsal, rehearsal with imagery, and rehearsal with a story. The only difference is that the same eight participants serve in every condition. Obviously, we cannot use the same list of words across conditions because there could be a large practice effect. We therefore have to use three lists of words that are equivalent in difficulty and that are counterbalanced across conditions. In other words, not all participants in each condition will receive the same list of words. Let's assume that we have taken the design problems into account and that the data in Table 10.8 represent the performance of the participants in this study. The number of words recalled in each condition is out of 10 words.

**TABLE 10.8  Numbers of words recalled in a within-participants study of the effects of rehearsal type on memory**

| ROTE REHEARSAL | IMAGERY | STORY | |
|---|---|---|---|
| 2 | 4 | 5 | |
| 3 | 2 | 3 | |
| 3 | 5 | 6 | |
| 3 | 7 | 6 | |
| 2 | 5 | 8 | |
| 5 | 4 | 7 | |
| 6 | 8 | 10 | |
| 4 | 5 | 9 | |
| $\bar{X} = 3.5$ | $\bar{X} = 5$ | $\bar{X} = 6.75$ | Grand mean = 5.083 |

**one-way repeated measures ANOVA** An inferential statistical test for comparing the means of three or more groups using a correlated-groups design and one independent variable.

You can see that the data are similar to those from the between-participants design described earlier in the chapter. Because of the similarity in the data, we will be able to see how the statistics used with a within-participants design are more powerful than those used with a between-participants design. Because we have interval-ratio data, we will once again use an ANOVA to analyze these data. The only difference will be that the ANOVA used in this case is a **one-way repeated measures ANOVA.** The phrase *repeated measures* refers to the fact that measures are taken repeatedly on the same individuals; that is, the same participants serve in all conditions. The difference between this ANOVA and the one-way randomized ANOVA is that the conditions are correlated (related); therefore, the ANOVA procedure must be modified to take this relationship into account.

*One-Way Repeated Measures ANOVA: What It Is and What It Does.* With a one-way repeated measures ANOVA, participants in different conditions are equated prior to the experimental manipulation because the same participants are used in each condition. This means that the single largest factor contributing to error variance (individual differences across participants) has been removed. This also means that the error variance will be smaller. What part of the *F*-ratio is the error variance? Remember that the denominator in the *F*-ratio is the error variance. Thus, if the error variance (the denominator) is smaller, the resulting *F*-ratio will be larger. The end result is that a repeated measures ANOVA is more sensitive to small differences between groups. The null and alternative hypotheses for the repeated measures ANOVA are the same as those for the randomized ANOVA. The null hypothesis is that the means from the conditions tested are similar or the same, and the alternative hypothesis is that the mean from at least one condition differs from the means of the other conditions:

$H_0$: $\mu_1 = \mu_2 = \mu_3$

$H_a$: At least one $\mu \neq$ another $\mu$

A repeated measures ANOVA is calculated in a manner similar to that for a randomized ANOVA. We first determine the sums of squares (*SS*), then the degrees of freedom (*df*) and mean squares (*MS*), and finally the *F*-ratio. The main difference lies in the calculation of the sums of squares. As with the randomized ANOVA, I will describe what the different sums of squares are, provide the definitional formulas, and show how to use these formulas with the data from Table 10.8. The computational formulas for the sums of squares for a repeated measures ANOVA are presented in Appendix B. If your instructor prefers that you use them (rather than the definitional formulas) with the experimental data from Table 10.8, please refer to this appendix.

*Calculations for the One-Way Repeated Measures ANOVA.* The total sum of squares is calculated for a repeated measures ANOVA in the same manner as it is for a randomized ANOVA. The total sum of squares ($SS_{\text{Total}}$) is the total amount of variability in the entire data set (across all the conditions). It is calculated by summing the squared deviations of each score from the grand mean, or $\Sigma(X - \bar{X}_G)^2$, where $X$ refers to each individual score and $\bar{X}_G$ is the grand mean. The total sum of squares for the present example is 115.82. The calculations for this are shown in Table 10.9.

Because there is only one group of participants, what was referred to as the between-groups sum of squares in a randomized ANOVA is now called a between-treatments, or simply a between, sum of squares. The between sum of squares is the sum of the differences between each condition or treatment mean and the grand mean, squared and multiplied by the number of scores in each treatment. It is calculated in the same manner as in the randomized ANOVA: $\Sigma[(\bar{X}_t - \bar{X}_G)^2 n]$, where $\bar{X}_t$ represents the mean for each treatment, $\bar{X}_G$ is the grand mean, and $n$ is the number of scores in each treatment. The between sum of squares in the present example is 42.34 and is calculated in Table 10.10.

Finally, what was the within-groups sum of squares in the randomized ANOVA is split into two sources of variance in the repeated measures

**TABLE 10.9** Calculation of $SS_{Total}$ using the definitional formula

| ROTE REHEARSAL | | IMAGERY | | STORY | |
|---|---|---|---|---|---|
| $X$ | $(X - \bar{X}_G)^2$ | $X$ | $(X - \bar{X}_G)^2$ | $X$ | $(X - \bar{X}_G)^2$ |
| 2 | 9.50 | 4 | 1.17 | 5 | 0.01 |
| 3 | 4.34 | 2 | 9.50 | 3 | 4.34 |
| 3 | 4.34 | 5 | 0.01 | 6 | 0.84 |
| 3 | 4.34 | 7 | 3.67 | 6 | 0.84 |
| 2 | 9.50 | 5 | 0.01 | 8 | 8.51 |
| 5 | 0.01 | 4 | 1.17 | 7 | 3.67 |
| 6 | 0.84 | 8 | 8.51 | 10 | 24.18 |
| 4 | 1.17 | 5 | 0.01 | 9 | 15.34 |
| $\Sigma = 34.04$ | | $\Sigma = 24.05$ | | $\Sigma = 57.73$ | |

$SS_{Total} = 34.04 + 24.05 + 57.73 = 115.82$

NOTE: All numbers have been rounded to two decimal places.

**TABLE 10.10** Calculation of $SS_{Between}$ using the definitional formula

**Rote Rehearsal**

$(\bar{X}_t - \bar{X}_G)^2 n = (3.5 - 5.083)^2 8 = (-1.583)^2 8 = (2.51)8 = 20.05$

**Imagery**

$(\bar{X}_t - \bar{X}_G)^2 n = (5 - 5.083)^2 8 = (-0.083)^2 8 = (0.007)8 = 0.06$

**Story**

$(\bar{X}_t - \bar{X}_G)^2 n = (6.75 - 5.083)^2 8 = (1.667)^2 8 = (2.779)8 = 22.23$

$SS_{Between} = 20.05 + 0.06 + 22.23 = 42.34$

ANOVA: participant (subject) variance and error (residual) variance. To calculate these sums of squares, we begin by calculating the within-groups sum of squares just as we did in the randomized ANOVA. In other words, we calculate the sum of the squared difference scores for each score and its treatment mean, or $\Sigma(X - \bar{X}_t)^2$, where $X$ represents each score and $\bar{X}_t$ represents each treatment mean. The within-groups sum of squares is 73.48. The calculation for this is shown in Table 10.11.

Once we have calculated the within-groups sum of squares, we can determine the participant sum of squares, which is a reflection of the amount of within-groups variance due to individual differences. It is the sum of the squared difference scores for the mean of each participant across conditions and the grand mean, multiplied by the number of conditions. In a definitional formula, it is $\Sigma[(\bar{X}_P - \bar{X}_G)^2 k]$, where $\bar{X}_P$ represents the mean across treatments for each participant, $\bar{X}_G$ is the grand mean, and $k$ is the number of treatments. The participant sum of squares is 52.40. The calculation for this is shown in Table 10.12.

After the variability due to individual differences ($SS_{Participant}$) has been removed from the within-groups sum of squares, what is left is the error sum of squares. In definitional form, this is $SS_{Within} - SS_{Participant}$, or in our example, $73.48 - 52.40 = 21.08$. We will soon see that the final $F$-ratio is computed by dividing $MS_{Between}$ by $MS_{Error}$. The main difference, then, between the repeated measures ANOVA and the randomized ANOVA is that the within-groups variance is divided into two sources of variance (that attributable to individual differences and that attributable to error variance) and only the variance attributable to error is used in the calculation of $MS_{Error}$.

The next step is to calculate the $MS$, or mean square, for each term. You may remember that the $MS$ for each term is calculated by dividing the $SS$ by the $df$. Therefore, in order to calculate the $MS$ for each term, we need to know the degrees of freedom for each term. Table 10.13 provides the definitional

**TABLE 10.11  Calculation of $SS_{Within}$ using the definitional formula**

| ROTE REHEARSAL | | IMAGERY | | STORY | |
|---|---|---|---|---|---|
| $X$ | $(X - \bar{X}_t)^2$ | $X$ | $(X - \bar{X}_t)^2$ | $X$ | $(X - \bar{X}_t)^2$ |
| 2 | 2.25 | 4 | 1 | 5 | 3.06 |
| 3 | 0.25 | 2 | 9 | 3 | 14.06 |
| 3 | 0.25 | 5 | 0 | 6 | 0.56 |
| 3 | 0.25 | 7 | 4 | 6 | 0.56 |
| 2 | 2.25 | 5 | 0 | 8 | 1.56 |
| 5 | 2.25 | 4 | 1 | 7 | 0.06 |
| 6 | 6.25 | 8 | 9 | 10 | 10.56 |
| 4 | 0.25 | 5 | 0 | 9 | 5.06 |
| $\Sigma = 14$ | | $\Sigma = 24$ | | $\Sigma = 35.48$ | |

$SS_{Within} = 14 + 24 + 35.48 = 73.48$

NOTE: All numbers have been rounded to two decimal places.

**TABLE 10.12  Calculation of $SS_{Participant}$ using the definitional formula**

| ROTE REHEARSAL X | IMAGERY X | STORY X | $\bar{X}_P$ | $(\bar{X}_P - \bar{X}_G)^2 3$ |
|---|---|---|---|---|
| 2 | 4 | 5 | 3.67 | 5.99 |
| 3 | 2 | 3 | 2.67 | 17.47 |
| 3 | 5 | 6 | 4.67 | 0.51 |
| 3 | 7 | 6 | 5.33 | 0.18 |
| 2 | 5 | 8 | 5.00 | 0.02 |
| 5 | 4 | 7 | 5.33 | 0.18 |
| 6 | 8 | 10 | 8.00 | 25.53 |
| 4 | 5 | 9 | 6.00 | 2.52 |
| | | | $SS_{Participant}$ | = 52.40 |

NOTE: All numbers have been rounded to two decimal places.

**TABLE 10.13  Repeated measures ANOVA summary table: definitional formulas**

| SOURCE | df | SS | MS | F |
|---|---|---|---|---|
| Participant | $n - 1$ | $\Sigma[(\bar{X}_P - \bar{X}_G)^2 k]$ | $\dfrac{SS_{Participant}}{df_{Participant}}$ | |
| Between | $k - 1$ | $\Sigma[(\bar{X}_t - \bar{X}_G)^2 n]$ | $\dfrac{SS_{Between}}{df_{Between}}$ | $\dfrac{MS_{Between}}{MS_{Error}}$ |
| Error | $(k - 1)(n - 1)$ | $[\Sigma(X - \bar{X}_t)^2] - SS_P$ | $\dfrac{SS_{Error}}{df_{Error}}$ | |
| Total | $N - 1$ | $\Sigma(X - \bar{X}_G)^2$ | | |

formulas for the sums of squares and the formulas for the degrees of freedom, the mean squares, and the $F$-ratio. The $df_{Total}$ is calculated the same way that it was for the randomized ANOVA, $N - 1$. In this case, large $N$ is the total number of scores in the study, not the total number of participants. Thus, the $df_{Total}$ is $24 - 1 = 23$. The $df_{Participants}$ is calculated by subtracting 1 from the number of participants $(n - 1)$ and is $8 - 1 = 7$. The $df_{Between}$ is once again calculated by subtracting 1 from the number of conditions $(k - 1)$, or $3 - 1 = 2$. Last, the $df_{Error}$ is calculated by multiplying $df_{Between}$ by $df_{Participants}$: $(k - 1)(n - 1) = 2 \times 7 = 14$. Once the $MS$ for each term is determined (see Tables 10.13 and 10.14), we can calculate the $F$-ratio. In the repeated measures ANOVA, we divide $MS_{Between}$ by $MS_{Error}$. The degrees of freedom, sums of squares, mean squares, and $F_{obt}$ calculated for these data are shown in Table 10.14.

**TABLE 10.14**   Repeated measures ANOVA summary table for the memory study

| SOURCE | df | SS | MS | F |
|--------|-----|--------|-------|-------|
| Participant | 7 | 52.40 | 7.49 | |
| Between | 2 | 42.34 | 21.17 | 14.02 |
| Error | 14 | 21.08 | 1.51 | |
| Total | 23 | 115.82 | | |

*Interpreting the One-Way Repeated Measures ANOVA.* The repeated measures ANOVA is interpreted in the same way as the randomized ANOVA. We use Table A.5 in Appendix A to determine the critical value for the *F*-ratio. Using the $df_{Between}$ of 2 and the $df_{Error}$ of 14 in Table A.5, we find that $F_{cv}$ for the .05 level is 3.74. Because our $F_{obt}$ is much larger than this, we know that it is significant at the .05 level. Let's also look at $F_{cv}$ for the .01 level, which is 6.51. Once again, our $F_{obt}$ is larger than this. In APA publication format, this is reported as $F(2, 14) = 14.02, p < .01$.

If you look back to Table 10.6—the ANOVA summary table for the one-way randomized ANOVA, with very similar data to the repeated measures ANOVA—you can see how much more powerful the repeated measures ANOVA is than the randomized ANOVA. Notice that although the total sums of squares are very similar, the resulting *F*-ratio for the repeated measures ANOVA is much larger (14.02 versus 11.07). If the $F_{obt}$ is larger, then there is a higher probability that it will be statistically significant. Notice also that although the data used to calculate the two ANOVAs are similar, the group means in the repeated measures ANOVA are more similar (closer together) than those from the randomized ANOVA, yet the $F_{obt}$ from the repeated measures ANOVA is larger. Thus, with somewhat similar data, the resulting *F*-ratio for the repeated measures ANOVA is larger and thus affords more statistical power.

*Graphing the Means and Effect Size.* As with the one-way randomized ANOVA discussed earlier in the chapter, we should graph the results of this ANOVA because of the significant difference between the means. The resulting graph appears in Figure 10.3. In addition, we should compute effect size using eta-squared. Eta-squared is calculated by dividing $SS_{Between}$ by $SS_{Total}$, or $42.34/115.82 = .366$. This tells us that 36.6% of the variability among the scores can be attributed to the different rehearsal conditions. Notice that even though a fairly large amount of the variability in the dependent variable is accounted for by knowing the condition to which a participant was assigned, the effect size is not as large as that from the randomized ANOVA we calculated earlier in the chapter. This shows the importance of determining effect size. Although the repeated measures ANOVA may lead to a larger final *F*-ratio and greater statistical significance, it does not necessarily mean that the independent variable explains more of the variability in the dependent variable.

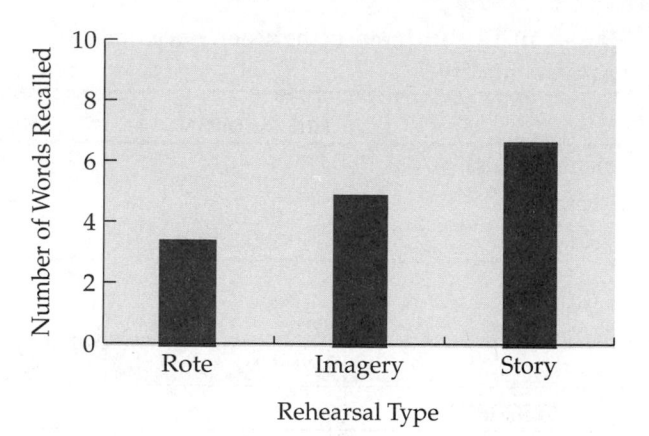

**FIGURE 10.3**
**Mean number of words recalled as a function of rehearsal type**

*Assumptions of the One-Way Repeated Measures ANOVA.* As with the randomized ANOVA, certain conditions must be met to ensure that the statistic is being used properly. The first three assumptions for the one-way repeated measures ANOVA are the same as those for the one-way randomized ANOVA:

- The data are on an interval-ratio scale.
- The underlying distribution is normally distributed.
- The variances among the populations being compared are homogeneous.
- The groups are correlated (within-participants or matched-participants).

*Tukey's Post Hoc Test.* As with the randomized ANOVA, we can perform post hoc tests when the resulting *F*-ratio is significant. Once again, we will use Tukey's HSD post hoc test:

$$\text{HSD} = Q(k, df_{\text{Error}})\sqrt{\frac{MS_{\text{Error}}}{n}}$$

Remember that we determine $Q$ by using Table A.6 in Appendix A. For our example, the honestly significant difference for the .05 level is

$$\text{HSD}_{.05} = 3.70\sqrt{\frac{1.51}{8}} = 3.70\sqrt{0.1887} = 3.70(0.434) = 1.61$$

To calculate HSD for the .01 level, we refer to Table A.6 once again and find that

$$\text{HSD}_{.01} = 4.89(0.434) = 2.12$$

Table 10.15 compares the means from the three conditions in the present study. We can see that the difference in means between the rote rehearsal and the story conditions is significant at the .01 level, and the difference between the imagery and the story conditions is significant at the .05 level. Thus, based on these data, those in the story condition recalled significantly more words than those in the imagery condition ($p < .05$) and those in the rote rehearsal condition ($p < .01$).

**TABLE 10.15** Differences between each pair of means in the within-participants study

| | ROTE REHEARSAL | IMAGERY | STORY |
|---|---|---|---|
| Rote Rehearsal | — | 1.5 | 3.25 |
| Imagery | | — | 1.75 |
| Story | | | — |

## IN REVIEW  One-Way Repeated Measures ANOVA

| CONCEPT | DESCRIPTION |
|---|---|
| Null Hypothesis ($H_0$) | The independent variable had no effect—the samples all represent the same population |
| Alternative Hypothesis ($H_a$) | The independent variable had an effect—at least one of the samples represents a different population than the others |
| $F$-ratio | The ratio formed when the between variance is divided by the error variance |
| Between Variance | An estimate of the variance of the treatment means about the grand mean; includes both systematic variance and error variance |
| Participant Variance | The variance due to individual differences; removed from the error variance |
| Error Variance | An estimate of the variance within each condition in the experiment after variance due to individual differences has been removed |
| Eta-squared ($\eta^2$) | A measure of effect size—the variability in the dependent variable attributable to the independent variable |
| Tukey's Post Hoc Test | A test conducted to determine which conditions in a study with more than two groups differ significantly from each other |

**CRITICAL THINKING CHECK 10.4**

1. Explain why a repeated measures ANOVA is statistically more powerful than a simple randomized one-way ANOVA.
2. Identify other advantage(s) associated with using a within-participants design.

## Summary

In this chapter, we discussed designs that use more than two levels of an independent variable. Advantages to such designs include being able to compare more than two kinds of treatment, to use fewer participants, to compare all treatments with a control group, and to use placebo groups. In addition, we discussed the statistical analyses most appropriate for use with these designs—most commonly, with interval-ratio data, an ANOVA. A randomized one-way ANOVA is used for between-participants designs, and a repeated measures one-way ANOVA for correlated-groups designs. Also discussed were appropriate post hoc tests (Tukey's HSD) and measures of effect size (eta-squared). After completing this chapter, you should appreciate the advantages of using more complicated designs and understand the basic statistics used to analyze such designs.

## KEY TERMS

Bonferoni adjustment
ANOVA (analysis of variance)
one-way randomized ANOVA
grand mean
error variance
within-groups variance

between-groups variance
F-ratio
total sum of squares
within-groups sum of squares
between-groups sum of squares
mean square

eta-squared ($\eta^2$)
post hoc test
Tukey's honestly significant
  difference (HSD)
one-way repeated measures
  ANOVA

## CHAPTER EXERCISES

(Answers to odd-numbered exercises appear in Appendix C.)

1. What is/are the advantage(s) of conducting a study with three or more levels of the independent variable?
2. What is the difference between a randomized ANOVA and a repeated measures ANOVA? What does the term *one way* mean with respect to an ANOVA?
3. Explain between-groups variance and within-groups variance.
4. If a researcher decides to use multiple comparisons in a study with three conditions, what is the probability of a Type I error across these comparisons? Use the Bonferoni adjustment to determine the suggested alpha level.
5. If $H_0$ is true, what should the F-ratio equal or be close to? If $H_a$ is supported, should the F-ratio be greater than, less than, or equal to 1?
6. When should post hoc comparisons be performed?
7. What information does eta-squared ($\eta^2$) provide?
8. Why is a repeated measures ANOVA statistically more powerful than a randomized ANOVA?
9. A researcher conducts a study on the effects of amount of sleep on creativity. The creativity scores for four levels of sleep (2 hours, 4 hours, 6 hours, and 8 hours) for $n = 5$ participants are presented below.

| *Amount of Sleep (in hours)* | | | |
|---|---|---|---|
| 2 | 4 | 6 | 8 |
| 3 | 4 | 10 | 10 |
| 5 | 7 | 11 | 13 |
| 6 | 8 | 13 | 10 |
| 4 | 3 | 9 | 9 |
| 2 | 2 | 10 | 10 |

a. Complete the ANOVA summary table below. (If your instructor wants you to calculate the sums of squares, use the above data to do so.)

| Source | df | SS | MS | F |
|---|---|---|---|---|
| Between groups | | 187.75 | | |
| Within groups | | 55.20 | | |
| Total | | 242.95 | | |

b. Is $F_{obt}$ significant at $\alpha = .05$?
c. Perform post hoc comparisons if necessary.
d. What conclusions can be drawn from the F-ratio and the post hoc comparisons?
e. What is the effect size, and what does this mean?
f. Graph the means.

10. In a study on the effects of stress on illness, a researcher tallied the number of colds people contracted during a 6-month period as a function of the amount of stress they reported during that same time period. There were three stress levels: minimal, moderate, and high stress. The sums of

squares appear in the ANOVA summary table below. The mean for each condition and the number of participants per condition are also noted.

| Source | df | SS | MS | F |
|---|---|---|---|---|
| Between groups | | 22.167 | | |
| Within groups | | 14.750 | | |
| Total | | 36.917 | | |

| Stress Level | Mean | n |
|---|---|---|
| Minimal | 3 | 4 |
| Moderate | 4 | 4 |
| High | 6 | 4 |

a. Complete the ANOVA summary table.
b. Is $F_{obt}$ significant at $\alpha = .05$?
c. Perform post hoc comparisons if necessary.
d. What conclusions can be drawn from the F-ratio and the post hoc comparisons?
e. What is the effect size, and what does this mean?
f. Graph the means.

11. A researcher interested in the effects of exercise on stress had participants exercise for 30, 60, or 90 minutes per day. The mean stress level on a 100-point stress scale (with 100 indicating high stress) for each condition appears below, along with the ANOVA summary table with the sums of squares indicated.

| Source | df | SS | MS | F |
|---|---|---|---|---|
| Between groups | | 4,689.27 | | |
| Within groups | | 82,604.20 | | |
| Total | | 87,293.47 | | |

| Exercise Level | Mean | n |
|---|---|---|
| 30 minutes | 75.0 | 10 |
| 60 minutes | 44.7 | 10 |
| 90 minutes | 63.7 | 10 |

a. Complete the ANOVA summary table.
b. Is $F_{obt}$ significant at $\alpha = .05$?
c. Perform post hoc comparisons if necessary.
d. What conclusions can be drawn from the F-ratio and the post hoc comparisons?
e. What is the effect size, and what does this mean?
f. Graph the means.

12. A researcher conducted an experiment on the effects of a new "drug" on depression. The researcher had a control group that received nothing, a placebo group, and an experimental group that received the "drug." A depression inventory that provided a measure of depression on a 50-point scale was used (50 indicates that an individual is very high on the depression variable). The ANOVA summary table appears below, along with the mean depression score for each condition.

| Source | df | SS | MS | F |
|---|---|---|---|---|
| Between groups | | 1,202.313 | | |
| Within groups | | 2,118.00 | | |
| Total | | 3,320.313 | | |

| "Drug" Condition | Mean | n |
|---|---|---|
| Control | 36.26 | 15 |
| Placebo | 33.33 | 15 |
| "Drug" | 24.13 | 15 |

a. Complete the ANOVA summary table.
b. Is $F_{obt}$ significant at $\alpha = .05$?
c. Perform post hoc comparisons if necessary.
d. What conclusions can be drawn from the F-ratio and the post hoc comparisons?
e. What is the effect size, and what does this mean?
f. Graph the means.

13. A researcher is interested in the effects of practice on accuracy in a signal-detection task. Participants are tested with no practice, after 1 hour of practice, and after 2 hours of practice. Each person participates in all three conditions. The data below indicate how many signals each participant detected accurately at each level of practice.

| | Amount of Practice | | |
|---|---|---|---|
| Participant | No Practice | 1 Hour | 2 Hours |
| 1 | 3 | 4 | 6 |
| 2 | 4 | 5 | 5 |
| 3 | 2 | 3 | 4 |
| 4 | 1 | 3 | 5 |
| 5 | 3 | 6 | 7 |
| 6 | 3 | 4 | 6 |
| 7 | 2 | 3 | 4 |

| Source | df | SS | MS | F |
|---|---|---|---|---|
| Participant | | 16.27 | | |
| Between | | 25.81 | | |
| Error | | 4.87 | | |
| Total | | 46.95 | | |

a. Complete the ANOVA summary table. (If your instructor wants you to calculate the sums of squares, use the above data to do so.)

b. Is $F_{obt}$ significant at $\alpha = .05$?

c. Perform post hoc comparisons if necessary.

d. What conclusions can be drawn from the F-ratio and the post hoc comparisons?

e. What is the effect size, and what does this mean?

f. Graph the means.

14. A researcher has been hired by a pizzeria to determine which type of crust customers prefer. The restaurant offers three types of crust: hand-tossed, thick, and thin. Following are the mean number of 1-inch pieces of pizza eaten for each condition from 10 participants who had the opportunity to eat as many pieces with each type of crust as they desired. The ANOVA summary table also follows.

| Source | df | SS | MS | F |
|---|---|---|---|---|
| Participant | | 2.75 | | |
| Between | | 180.05 | | |
| Error | | 21.65 | | |
| Total | | 204.45 | | |

| Crust Type | Mean | n |
|---|---|---|
| Hand-tossed | 2.73 | 10 |
| Thick | 4.20 | 10 |
| Thin | 8.50 | 10 |

a. Complete the ANOVA summary table.

b. Is $F_{obt}$ significant at $\alpha = .05$?

c. Perform post hoc comparisons if necessary.

d. What conclusions can be drawn from the F-ratio and the post hoc comparisons?

e. What is the effect size, and what does this mean?

f. Graph the means.

15. A researcher is interested in whether massed or spaced studying has a greater impact on grades in a course. The researcher has her class study for 6 hours all in one day for one exam (massed study condition). She has them study for 2 hours each day for 3 days for another exam (3-day spaced condition). Last, she has them study for 1 hour a day for 6 days for a third exam (6-day spaced condition). The mean exam score (out of a possible 100 points) for each condition appears below, along with the ANOVA summary table.

| Source | df | SS | MS | F |
|---|---|---|---|---|
| Participant | | 136.96 | | |
| Between | | 3,350.96 | | |
| Error | | 499.03 | | |
| Total | | 3,986.95 | | |

| Study Condition | Mean | n |
|---|---|---|
| Massed | 69.13 | 15 |
| 3-day spaced | 79.33 | 15 |
| 6-day spaced | 90.27 | 15 |

a. Complete the ANOVA summary table.

b. Is $F_{obt}$ significant at $\alpha = .05$?

c. Perform post hoc comparisons if necessary.

d. What conclusions can be drawn from the F-ratio and the post hoc comparisons?

e. What is the effect size, and what does this mean?

f. Graph the means.

## CRITICAL THINKING CHECK ANSWERS

### 10.1

1. The probability of a Type I error is 26.5%: $[1 - (1 - .05)^6] = [1 - (.95)^6] = [1 - .735] = 26.5\%$. With the Bonferoni adjustment, the alpha level is .008 for each comparison.

### 10.2

1. Both the within-groups and between-groups variances are moderate to small. This should lead to an F-ratio of approximately 1.

### 10.3

1. The F-ratio $1.95/0.26 = 7.5$ suggests that the independent variable had an effect on the dependent variable.

2. *ANOVA Summary Table*

| Source | df | SS | MS | F |
|---|---|---|---|---|
| Between | 2 | 4,689.27 | 2,344.64 | 0.766 |
| Within | 27 | 82,604.20 | 3,059.41 | |
| Total | 29 | 87,293.47 | | |

The resulting F-ratio is less than 1 and thus not significant. Although stress levels differ across some of the groups, the difference is not large enough to be significant.

### 10.4

1. A repeated measures ANOVA is statistically more powerful because the within-groups variance is

divided into two sources of variance: that due to individual differences (participant) and that left over (error). Only the error variance is used to calculate the *F*-ratio. We therefore divide by a smaller number, thus resulting in a larger *F*-ratio and a greater chance that it will be significant.

2. The within-participants design also has the advantages of requiring fewer participants, assuring equivalency of groups, and usually requiring less time to conduct the study. See Chapter 8 for a review of this information.

## WEB RESOURCES

Check your knowledge of the content in this chapter by taking the practice quiz at www.Wadsworth.com. Or, for step-by-step practice and information, check out the Statistics and Research Methods Workshops at http://psychology.wadsworth.com/workshops.

## LAB RESOURCES

For hands-on experience using the research methods described in this chapter, see Chapters 5 ("One-Way Designs I") and 6 ("One-Way Designs II") in *Research Methods Laboratory Manual for Psychology*, 2nd ed., by William Langston (Belmont, CA: Wadsworth, 2005).

## STATISTICAL SOFTWARE RESOURCES

For hands-on experience using statistical software to complete the analyses described in this chapter, see Chapter 8 ("Single-Factor ANOVA") in *The Excel Statistics Companion* by Kenneth M. Rosenberg (Belmont, CA: Wadsworth, 2003).

# 11 Complex Experimental Designs

In Chapter 10, we discussed designs with more than two levels of an independent variable. In this chapter, we will look at more complex designs—those with more than one independent variable. These are usually referred to as **factorial designs,** indicating that more than one factor or variable is being manipulated in the study. We will discuss the advantages of such designs over simpler designs. In addition, we will explain how to interpret the findings (called main effects and interaction effects) from such designs. Last, we will consider the statistical analysis of such designs.

**factorial design**   A design with more than one independent variable.

## Using Designs with More Than One Independent Variable

Remember the study discussed in Chapter 10 on the effects of rehearsal on memory. Participants used one of three types of rehearsal (rote, imagery, or story) in order to determine their effects on the number of words recalled. Imagine that upon further analysis of the data, we discovered that participants recalled concrete words (for example, *desk, bike, tree*) better than abstract words (for example, *love, truth, honesty*) in one rehearsal condition but not in another. Such a result is called an *interaction* between variables; this concept will be discussed in more detail later in the chapter. One advantage of using factorial designs is that they allow us to assess how variables interact. In the real world, it would be unusual to find that a certain behavior is produced by only one variable; behavior is usually contingent on many variables operating together in an interactive way. Designing experiments with more than one independent variable allows researchers to assess how multiple variables may affect behavior.

### Factorial Notation and Factorial Designs

A factorial design, then, is one with more than one factor or independent variable. A complete factorial design is one in which all levels of each independent variable are paired with all levels of every other independent variable. An incomplete factorial design also has more than one independent variable, but all levels of each variable are not paired with all levels of every other variable. The design illustrated in this chapter is a complete factorial design.

Remember that an independent variable must have at least two levels; if it does not vary, it is not a variable. Thus, the simplest complete factorial design is one with two independent variables, each with two levels. Let's consider an example. Suppose we manipulate two independent variables: word type (concrete versus abstract words) and rehearsal type (rote versus imagery). The independent variable Word Type has two levels: abstract and concrete; the independent variable Rehearsal Type also has two levels: rote and imagery. This is known as a $2 \times 2$ factorial design.

The factorial notation for a factorial design is determined as follows:

(Number of levels of independent variable 1) $\times$ (Number of levels of independent variable 2) $\times$ (Number of levels of independent variable 3) . . .

Thus, the **factorial notation** indicates how many independent variables are used in the study and how many levels are used for each independent variable. This is often confusing for students, who frequently think that in the factorial notation 2 × 2, the first number (2) indicates that there are two independent variables and the second number (2) indicates that each has two levels. This is *not* how to interpret factorial notation. Rather, each number in the notation specifies the number of levels of a single independent variable. Thus, a 3 × 6 factorial design is one with two independent variables; each of the two numbers in the factorial notation represents a single independent variable. In a 3 × 6 factorial design, one independent variable has three levels and the other has six levels.

Referring back to our 2 × 2 factorial design, we see that there are two independent variables, each with two levels. This factorial design has four conditions (2 × 2 = 4): abstract words with rote rehearsal, abstract words with imagery rehearsal, concrete words with rote rehearsal, and concrete words with imagery rehearsal. How many conditions would there be in a 3 × 6 factorial design? If you answer 18, you are correct. Is it possible to have a 1 × 3 factorial design? If you answer no, you are correct. It is not possible to have a factor (variable) with one level because then it does not vary.

## Main Effects and Interaction Effects

Two kinds of information can be gleaned from a factorial design. The first piece of information is whether there are any main effects. A **main effect** is an effect of a single independent variable. In our design with two independent variables, two main effects are possible: an effect of word type and an effect of rehearsal type. In other words, there can be as many main effects as there are independent variables. The second piece of information is whether there is an interaction effect. As the name implies, this is information regarding how the variables or factors interact. Specifically, an **interaction effect** is the effect of each independent variable across the levels of the other independent variable. When there is an interaction between two independent variables, the effect of one independent variable depends on the level of the other independent variable. If this makes no sense at this point, don't worry; it will become clearer as we work through our example.

Let's look at the data from our study on the effects of word type and rehearsal type on memory. Table 11.1 presents the mean performance for participants in each condition. This was a completely between-participants design—different participants served in each of the 4 conditions. There were 8 participants in each condition, for a total of 32 participants in the study. Each participant in each condition was given a list of 10 words (either abstract or concrete) to learn using the specified rehearsal technique (rote or imagery).

Typically, researchers begin by assessing whether there is an interaction effect because having an interaction effect indicates that the effect of one independent variable depends on the level of the other independent variable. However, when first beginning to interpret two-way designs, students usually find it easier to begin with the main effects and then move on to the interaction effect. What we need to keep in mind is that if we later find an

**factorial notation** The notation that indicates how many independent variables are used in a study and how many levels are used for each variable.

**main effect** An effect of a single independent variable.

**interaction effect** The effect of each independent variable across the levels of the other independent variable.

**TABLE 11.1   Results of the 2 × 2 factorial design: effects of word type and rehearsal type on memory**

| REHEARSAL TYPE (INDEPENDENT VARIABLE B) | WORD TYPE (INDEPENDENT VARIABLE A) | | ROW MEANS (MAIN EFFECT OF B) |
|---|---|---|---|
| | Concrete | Abstract | |
| Rote rehearsal | 5 | 5 | 5 |
| Imagery rehearsal | 10 | 5 | 7.5 |
| Column means (Main effect of A) | 7.5 | 5 | |

interaction effect, then any main effects will have to be qualified. Remember, because we have two independent variables, there is the possibility for two main effects: one for word type (variable A in the table) and one for rehearsal type (variable B in the table). The main effect of each independent variable tells us about the relationship between that single independent variable and the dependent variable. In other words, do different levels of one independent variable bring about changes in the dependent variable?

We can find the answer to this question by looking at the row and column means in Table 11.1. The column means tell us about the overall effect of variable A (word type). The column means indicate that there is a difference in the numbers of words recalled between the concrete and abstract word conditions. More concrete words were recalled (7.5) than abstract words (5). The column means represent the average performance for the concrete and abstract word conditions summarized across the rehearsal conditions. In other words, we obtained the column mean of 7.5 for the concrete word conditions by averaging the numbers of words recalled in the concrete word/rote rehearsal condition and the concrete word/imagery rehearsal condition [(5 + 10)/2 = 7.5]. Similarly, the column mean for the abstract word conditions (5) was obtained by averaging the data from the two abstract word conditions [(5 + 5)/2 = 5]. (Please note that determining the row and column means in this manner is possible only when the numbers of participants in each of the conditions are equal. If the numbers of participants in the conditions are unequal, then all individual scores in the single row or column must be used in the calculation of the row or column mean.)

The main effect for variable B (rehearsal type) can be assessed by looking at the row means. The row means indicate that there is a difference in the numbers of words recalled between the rote rehearsal and the imagery rehearsal conditions. More words were recalled when participants used the imagery rehearsal technique (7.5) than when they used the rote rehearsal technique (5). As with the column means, the row means represent the average performance in the rote and imagery rehearsal conditions, summarized across the word type conditions.

At face value, the main effects tell us that, overall, participants recall more words when they are concrete and when imagery rehearsal is used. However, we now need to assess whether there is an interaction between the variables. If so, the main effects noted previously will have to be qualified, because an interaction indicates that the effect of one independent variable depends on the level of the other independent variable. In other words, an interaction effect indicates that the effect of one independent variable is different at different levels of the other independent variable.

Look again at the data in Table 11.1. There appears to be an interaction in these results because when rote rehearsal is used, word type makes no difference (the means are the same—5 words recalled). However, when imagery rehearsal is used, word type makes a big difference. Specifically, when imagery is used with concrete words, participants do very well (recall an average of 10 words); yet when imagery is used with abstract words, participants perform the same as they did in both of the rote rehearsal conditions (recall an average of only 5 words). Think about what this means. When there is an interaction between the two variables, the effect of one independent variable differs at different levels of the other independent variable—there is a contrast or a difference in the way participants perform across the levels of the independent variables.

Another way to assess whether there is an interaction effect in a study is to graph the means. Figure 11.1 shows a line graph of the data presented in Table 11.1. The interaction may be easier for you to see here. First, when there is an interaction between variables, the lines are not parallel—they have different slopes. You can see in the figure that one line is flat (representing the data from the rote rehearsal conditions), whereas the other line has a positive slope (representing the data from the imagery rehearsal conditions). Look at the figure, and think about the interaction. The flat line indicates that when rote rehearsal was used, word type had no effect (the line is flat because the means are the same). The line with the positive slope indicates that when imagery rehearsal was used, word type had a big effect—participants remembered more concrete words than abstract words.

You are probably familiar with the concept of interaction in your own life. When we say "It depends," we are indicating that what we do in one situation depends on some other variable—there is an interaction. For example, whether you go to a party depends on whether you have to work and who is going to be at the party. If you have to work, you will not go to the party under any circumstance. However, if you do not have to work, you might go if a "certain person" is going to be there. If that person is not going to be there,

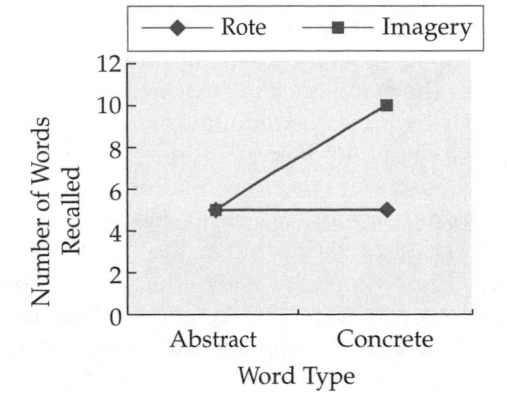

**FIGURE 11.1**
**Line graph representing interaction between rehearsal type and word type**

you will not go. See if you can graph this interaction. The dependent variable, which always goes on the y-axis, is the likelihood of going to the party. One independent variable is placed on the x-axis (whether or not you have to work), and the levels of the other independent variable are captioned in the graph (whether the certain person is or is not present at the party).

To determine whether main effects or an interaction effect are significant, we need to conduct statistical analyses. We will discuss the appropriate analysis later in this chapter.

## Possible Outcomes of a 2 × 2 Factorial Design

A 2 × 2 factorial design has several possible outcomes. Because there are two independent variables, there may or may not be a significant effect of each. In addition, there may or may not be a significant interaction effect. Thus, there are eight possible outcomes in all (possible combinations of significant and nonsignificant effects). Figure 11.2 illustrates these eight possible outcomes for a 2 × 2 factorial design, using the same study we have been discussing as an example. Obviously, only one of these outcomes is possible in a single study. All eight are graphed here to give you a concrete illustration of each possibility.

For each graph, the dependent variable (number of words recalled) is placed on the y-axis, and independent variable A (word type) is placed on the x-axis. The two means for one level of independent variable B (rehearsal type) are plotted, and a line is drawn to represent this level of independent variable B. In the same fashion, the means for the second level of independent variable B are plotted, and a second line is drawn to represent this level of independent variable B. Next to each graph is a matrix showing the means from the four conditions in the study. The graphs were derived by plotting the four means from each matrix. In addition, whether or not there are main effects and an interaction effect is indicated.

Can you tell from looking at the graphs which ones represent interaction effects? If you identify graphs a, b, c, and d as not having interaction effects and graphs e, f, g, and h as having interaction effects, you are correct. You should have a greater appreciation for interaction after looking at these graphs. Notice that in graphs a–d, there is no interaction because each level of independent variable A (word type) affects the levels of independent variable B (rehearsal type) in the same way. For example, look at graphs c and d. In graph c, the lines are parallel with no slope. This indicates that for both rote and imagery rehearsal, word type makes no difference. In graph d, the lines are parallel and sloped. This indicates that for both rote and imagery rehearsal, word type has the same effect: Performance is poorer for abstract words and then increases by the same amount for concrete words.

Now look at graphs e–h, which represent interaction effects. Sometimes there is an interaction because there is no relationship between the independent variable and the dependent variable at one level of the second independent variable, but a strong relationship at the other level of the second independent variable. Graphs e and f show this. In graph e, when rote rehearsal is used, word type makes no difference, whereas when imagery rehearsal is used, word type makes a big difference. In graph f, the interaction

## FIGURE 11.2
## Possible outcomes of a 2 × 2 factorial design with rehearsal type and word type as independent variables

**a. No Main Effects; No Interaction Effect**

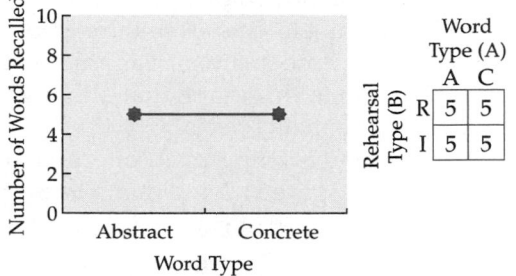

**e. Main Effect of A; Main Effect of B; Interaction Effect**

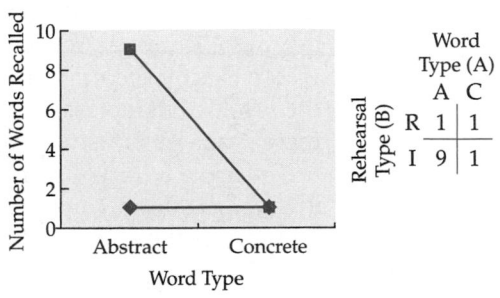

**b. Main Effect of A; No Main Effect of B; No Interaction Effect**

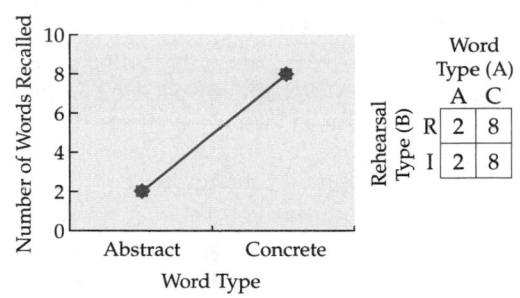

**f. Main Effect of A; No Main Effect of B; Interaction Effect**

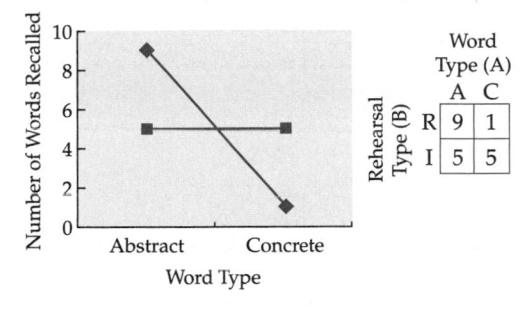

**c. No Main Effect of A; Main Effect of B; No Interaction Effect**

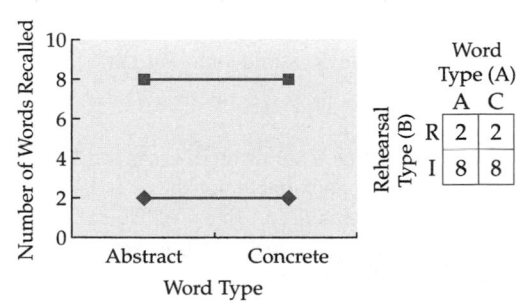

**g. No Main Effect of A; Main Effect of B; Interaction Effect**

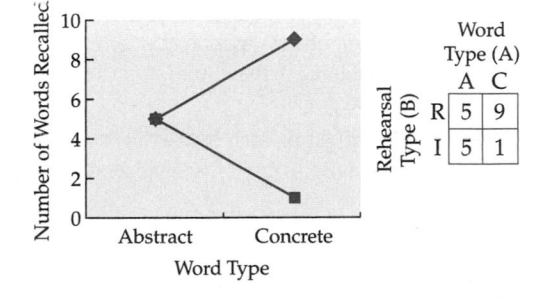

**d. Main Effect of A; Main Effect of B; No Interaction Effect**

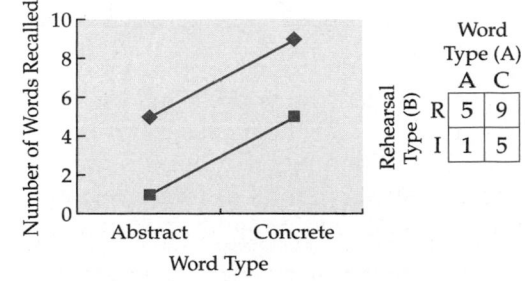

**h. No Main Effects; Interaction Effect**

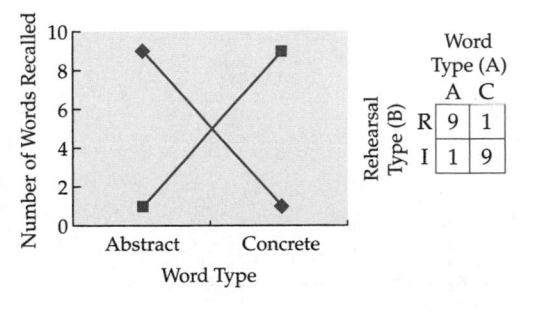

is due to a similar result. Sometimes, however, an interaction may indicate that an independent variable has an opposite effect on the dependent variable at different levels of the second independent variable. Graphs g and h illustrate this. In graph g, when rote rehearsal is used, performance improves for concrete words versus abstract words (a positive relationship). However, when imagery rehearsal is used, performance decreases for concrete words versus abstract words (a negative relationship). Finally, graph h shows similar but more dramatic results. Here there is a complete crossover interaction, where exactly the opposite result is occurring for independent variable B at the levels of independent variable A. Notice also in this graph that although there is a large crossover interaction, there are no main effects.

To make sure you completely understand interpreting main effects and interaction effects, cover the titles in each part of Figure 11.2 and quiz yourself on whether there are main effects and/or an interaction effect in each graph.

## IN REVIEW    Complex Designs

| | DESCRIPTION | ADVANTAGE OR EXAMPLE |
|---|---|---|
| Factorial Design | Any design with more than one independent variable. | In the example in this chapter, word type and rehearsal type were both manipulated to assess main effects and an interaction effect. The advantage is that it more closely resembles the real world because the results are due to more than one factor (variable). |
| Factorial Notation | The numerical notation corresponding to a factorial design. It indicates, in brief form, the number of independent variables and the number of levels of each variable. | A 3 × 4 design has two independent variables, one with three levels and one with four levels. |
| Main Effect | An effect of a single independent variable. A main effect describes the effect of a single variable as if there were no other variables in the study. | In a study with two independent variables, two main effects are possible—one for each variable. |
| Interaction Effect | The effect of each independent variable at the levels of the other independent variable. | Interaction effects allow us to assess whether the effect of one variable depends on the level of the other variable. In this way, we can more closely simulate the real world, where multiple variables often interact. |

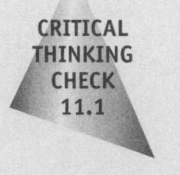

CRITICAL THINKING CHECK 11.1

1. What is the factorial notation for the following design? A pizza parlor owner is interested in what type of pizza is most preferred by his customers. He manipulates the type of crust for the pizzas by using thin, thick, and hand-tossed crusts. In addition, he manipulates the topping for the pizzas by offering cheese, pepperoni, sausage, veggie, and everything. He then has his customers sample the various

pizzas and rate them. After you have determined the factorial notation, indicate how many conditions are in this study.
2. How many main effect(s) and interaction effect(s) are possible in a
4 × 6 factorial design?
3. Draw a graph representing the following data from a study using the
same independent variables as in the chapter example. Determine
whether there are any main effects or an interaction effect.

Rote rehearsal/Concrete words: $\bar{X} = 10$
Rote rehearsal/Abstract words: $\bar{X} = 1$
Imagery rehearsal/Concrete words: $\bar{X} = 9$
Imagery rehearsal/Abstract words: $\bar{X} = 9$

# Statistical Analysis of Complex Designs

As discussed in Chapter 10, an ANOVA is the type of statistical analysis most
commonly used when interval-ratio data have been collected. For the factorial designs discussed in this chapter, a two-way ANOVA would be used.
The term *two-way* indicates that there are two independent variables in the
study. If a design has three independent variables, then we would use a
three-way ANOVA; if there were four independent variables, a four-way
ANOVA; and so on. With a between-participants design, a two-way randomized ANOVA is used. With a correlated-groups factorial design, a two-
way repeated measures ANOVA is used. If the data in a study are not
interval-ratio and the design is complex (more than one independent variable), then nonparametric statistics are appropriate. These will not be discussed in this chapter but can be found in more advanced statistics texts.

## Two-Way Randomized ANOVA: What It Is and What It Does

A two-way ANOVA is similar to a one-way ANOVA in that it analyzes the
variance between groups and within groups. The logic is the same: If either of
the variables has an effect, the variance between the groups should be greater
than the variance within the groups. As with the one-way ANOVA, an $F$-ratio
is formed by dividing the between-groups variance by the within-groups variance. The difference is that in the two-way ANOVA, between-groups variance
may be attributable to factor A (one of the independent variables in the study),
to factor B (the second independent variable in the study), and to the interaction of factors A and B. With two independent variables, there is a possibility
of a main effect for each variable, and an $F$-ratio is calculated to represent each
of these effects. In addition, there is the possibility of an interaction effect, and
an $F$-ratio is also needed to represent this effect. Thus, with a two-way
ANOVA, there are three $F$-ratios to calculate and ultimately to interpret.

In a 2 × 2 factorial design, such as the one we have been looking at in this
chapter, there are three null and alternative hypotheses. The null hypothesis

**TABLE 11.2   Numbers of words recalled as a function of word type and rehearsal type**

| REHEARSAL TYPE (INDEPENDENT VARIABLE B) | WORD TYPE (INDEPENDENT VARIABLE A) | | ROW MEANS (MAIN EFFECT OF B) |
| --- | --- | --- | --- |
| | Concrete | Abstract | |
| Rote Rehersal | 4 | 5 | |
| | 5 | 4 | |
| | 3 | 5 | |
| | 6 | 6 | 4.5 |
| | 2 | 4 | |
| | 2 | 5 | |
| | 6 | 6 | |
| Cell mean = 4 | 4 | 5 | Cell mean = 5 |
| Imagery rehearsal | 10 | 6 | |
| | 12 | 5 | |
| | 11 | 6 | |
| | 9 | 7 | 8 |
| | 8 | 6 | |
| | 10 | 6 | |
| | 10 | 7 | |
| Cell mean = 10 | 10 | 5 | Cell mean = 6 |
| Column means (Main effect of A) | 7 | 5.5 | Grand mean = 6.25 |

for factor A states that there is no main effect for factor A, and the alternative hypothesis states that there is an effect of factor A (the differences observed between the groups are greater than what would be expected based on chance). In other words, the null hypothesis states that the population means represented by the sample means are from the same population, and the alternative hypothesis states that the population means represented by the sample means are not from the same population. A second null hypothesis states that there is no main effect for factor B, and the alternative hypothesis states that there is an effect of factor B. The third null hypothesis states that there is no interaction of factors A and B, and the alternative hypothesis states that there is an interaction effect.

Table 11.2 presents the numbers of words recalled by the 32 participants in the memory study with 8 participants in each condition. We will use these data to illustrate the use of a two-way randomized ANOVA. As in Chapter 10, the definitional formulas for the various sums of squares (SS) will be provided and used to calculate each SS. The computational formulas are provided in Appendix B if your instructor prefers that you use them.

*Calculations for the Two-Way Randomized ANOVA.* In a two-way ANOVA, there are several sources of variance; therefore, several sums of

**TABLE 11.3  Calculation of $SS_{Total}$ using the definitional formula**

| ROTE/CONCRETE | | ROTE/ABSTRACT | | IMAGERY/CONCRETE | | IMAGERY/ABSTRACT | |
|---|---|---|---|---|---|---|---|
| $X$ | $(X - \bar{X}_G)^2$ | $X$ | $(X - \bar{X}_G)^2$ | $X$ | $(X - \bar{X}_G)^2$ | $X$ | $(X - \bar{X}_G)^2$ |
| 4 | 5.0625 | 5 | 1.5625 | 10 | 14.0625 | 6 | 0.0625 |
| 5 | 1.5625 | 4 | 5.0625 | 12 | 33.0625 | 5 | 1.5625 |
| 3 | 10.5625 | 5 | 1.5625 | 11 | 22.5625 | 6 | 0.0625 |
| 6 | 0.0625 | 6 | 0.0625 | 9 | 7.5625 | 7 | 0.5625 |
| 2 | 18.0625 | 4 | 5.0625 | 8 | 3.0625 | 6 | 0.0625 |
| 2 | 18.0625 | 5 | 1.5625 | 10 | 14.0625 | 6 | 0.0625 |
| 6 | 0.0625 | 6 | 0.0625 | 10 | 14.0625 | 7 | 0.5625 |
| 4 | 5.0625 | 5 | 1.5625 | 10 | 14.0625 | 5 | 1.5625 |
| $\Sigma =$ | 58.50 | | 16.50 | | 122.50 | | 4.50 |

$SS_{Total} = 58.50 + 16.50 + 122.50 + 4.50 = 202$

squares must be calculated. Let's begin with the total sum of squares ($SS_{Total}$), which represents the sum of the squared deviation scores for all participants in the study. This is calculated in the same manner as it was in Chapter 10. The definitional formula is $SS_{Total} = \Sigma(X - \bar{X}_G)^2$, where $X$ refers to each individual's score and $\bar{X}_G$ is the grand mean for the study. The use of this formula is illustrated in Table 11.3, where we see that $SS_{Total} = 202$. As in the one-way ANOVA, we can use $SS_{Total}$ as a check on the accuracy of our calculations. In other words, when we finish calculating all of the various other sums of squares, they should sum to equal the total sum of squares. The $df_{Total}$ is determined in the same manner as in the ANOVA examples in Chapter 10, $N - 1$. In this case, $df_{Total} = 31$.

In addition to total variance, there is variance due to factor A (word type). This will tell us whether the main effect of factor A is significant. Similarly, there is variance due to factor B (rehearsal type), which will tell us whether the main effect of factor B is significant. Both of these sources of variance are determined by first calculating the appropriate sums of squares for each term and then dividing by the corresponding degrees of freedom for each term in order to obtain the mean square for each factor. The **sum of squares factor A** ($SS_A$) represents the sum of the squared deviation scores of each group mean for factor A minus the grand mean times the number of scores in each factor A condition (column). The definitional formula is $SS_A = \Sigma[(\bar{X}_A - \bar{X}_G)^2 n_A]$, where $\bar{X}_A$ is the mean for each condition of factor A, $\bar{X}_G$ is the grand mean, and $n_A$ is the number of people in each of the factor A conditions. The use of this formula is illustrated in Table 11.4. Notice that $n_A = 16$. We use 16 because the column means for factor A are derived based on the 16 scores that make up the concrete word conditions (8 participants in the concrete/rote condition and 8 participants in the concrete/imagery condition) and the 16 scores that make up the abstract word conditions (8 participants in the abstract/rote condition and 8 participants in the abstract/imagery condition). As can be seen in Table 11.4, $SS_A = 18$. The

**sum of squares factor A** The sum of the squared deviation scores of each group mean for factor A minus the grand mean times the number of scores in each factor A condition.

**TABLE 11.4    Calculation of $SS_A$ using the definitional formula**

| |
|---|
| $SS_A = \Sigma[(\bar{X}_A - \bar{X}_G)^2 n_A]$ |
| $= [(7 - 6.25)^2 16] + [(5.5 - 6.25)^2 16]$ |
| $= [(0.75)^2 16] + [(-0.75)^2 16]$ |
| $= [(0.5625)16] + [(0.5625)16]$ |
| $= 9 + 9$ |
| $= 18$ |

**sum of squares factor B**
The sum of the squared deviation scores of each group mean for factor B minus the grand mean times the number of scores in each factor B condition.

**sum of squares interaction**
The sum of the squared difference of each condition mean minus the grand mean times the number of scores in each condition. $SS_A$ and $SS_B$ are then subtracted from this sum.

$df_A$ are equal to the number of levels of factor A minus 1. Because factor A has two levels, there is 1 degree of freedom. The mean square for factor A can now be calculated by dividing $SS_A$ by $df_A$. Thus, the mean square for factor A ($MS_A$) is $18/1 = 18$.

The **sum of squares factor B** ($SS_B$) is calculated in a similar manner. In other words, $SS_B$ is the sum of the squared deviation scores of each group mean for factor B minus the grand mean times the number of scores in each factor B condition. The definitional formula is $SS_B = \Sigma[(\bar{X}_B - \bar{X}_G)^2 n_B]$, where $\bar{X}_B$ is the mean for each condition of factor B, $\bar{X}_G$ is the grand mean, and $n_B$ is the number of people in each of the factor B conditions. The $SS_B$ calculated in Table 11.5 is 98. Notice that, as with factor A, $n_B$ is 16—the total number of scores that contribute to the row means. In addition, as with factor A, the mean square for factor B is calculated by dividing $SS_B$ by $df_B$. The $df_B$ is derived by taking the number of levels of factor B minus 1. This is $2 - 1 = 1$, and $MS_B$ is therefore $98/1 = 98$.

We also have to consider the variance due to the interaction of factors A and B, which will tell us whether or not there is a significant interaction effect. The **sum of squares interaction** ($SS_{A \times B}$) is the sum of the squared difference of each condition mean minus the grand mean times the number of scores in each condition. Because this gives us an estimate of the amount of variance of the scores about their respective condition means, it includes the amount of variance due to factor A, factor B, and the interaction. Thus, once this sum is calculated, we must subtract the variance due solely to factor A and the variance due solely to factor B. The definitional formula is thus $SS_{A \times B} = \Sigma[(\bar{X}_C - \bar{X}_G)^2 n_C] - SS_A - SS_B$, where $\bar{X}_C$ is the mean for each condition (cell), $\bar{X}_G$ is the grand mean, and $n_C$ is the number of scores in

**TABLE 11.5    Calculation of $SS_B$ using the definitional formula**

| |
|---|
| $SS_B = \Sigma[(\bar{X}_B - \bar{X}_G)^2 n_B]$ |
| $= [(4.5 - 6.25)^2 16] + [(8 - 6.25)^2 16]$ |
| $= [(-1.75)^2 16] + [(1.75)^2 16]$ |
| $= [(3.0625)16] + [(3.0625)16]$ |
| $= 49 + 49$ |
| $= 98$ |

**TABLE 11.6** Calculation of $SS_{A \times B}$ using the definitional formula

$$SS_{A \times B} = \Sigma[(\bar{X}_C - \bar{X}_G)^2 n_C] - SS_A - SS_B$$
$$= [(4 - 6.25)^2 8] + [(5 - 6.25)^2 8] + [(10 - 6.25)^2 8] + [(6 - 6.25)^2 8] - 18 - 98$$
$$= [(-2.25)^2 8] + [(-1.25)^2 8] + [(3.75)^2 8] + [(-0.25)^2 8] - 18 - 98$$
$$= [(5.0625)8] + [(1.5625)8] + [(14.0625)8] + [(0.0625)8] - 18 - 98$$
$$= 40.50 + 12.50 + 112.50 + 0.50 - 18 - 98$$
$$= 50$$

each condition. The calculation of $SS_{A \times B}$ is illustrated in Table 11.6. As can be seen, the sum of squares for the interaction term is 50. We must divide this number by its corresponding degrees of freedom. The degrees of freedom for the interaction are based on the number of conditions in the study. In the present study, there are four conditions. To determine the degrees of freedom across the conditions, we multiply the degrees of freedom for the factors involved in the interaction. In the present case, factor A has 1 degree of freedom, and factor B also has 1 degree of freedom. Thus, $df_{A \times B} = (A - 1)(B - 1) = 1$. Using this to determine $MS_{A \times B}$, we find that $50/1 = 50$.

Last, we have to determine the amount of variance due to error—the within-groups variance. As in a one-way ANOVA, the within-groups variance is an indication of the amount of variance of the scores within a cell or condition about that cell mean. The **sum of squares error** ($SS_{Error}$) is the sum of the squared deviations of each score from its condition (cell) mean. The definitional formula is $SS_{Error} = \Sigma(X - \bar{X}_C)^2$. The calculation of $SS_{Error}$ is illustrated in Table 11.7. In the present study, $SS_{Error}$ is 36. We can now check all of our calculations by summing $SS_A$, $SS_B$, $SS_{A \times B}$, and $SS_{Error}$: $18 + 98 + 50 + 36 = 202$. We previously found that $SS_{Total} = 202$, so we know that our calculations are correct.

**sum of squares error** The sum of the squared deviations of each score from its group (cell) mean; the within-groups sum of squares in a factorial design.

**TABLE 11.7** Calculation of $SS_{Error}$ using the definitional formula

| ROTE/CONCRETE | | ROTE/ABSTRACT | | IMAGERY/CONCRETE | | IMAGERY/ABSTRACT | |
|---|---|---|---|---|---|---|---|
| $X$ | $(X - \bar{X}_C)^2$ | $X$ | $(X - \bar{X}_C)^2$ | $X$ | $(X - \bar{X}_C)^2$ | $X$ | $(X - \bar{X}_C)^2$ |
| 4 | 0 | 5 | 0 | 10 | 0 | 6 | 0 |
| 5 | 1 | 4 | 1 | 12 | 4 | 5 | 1 |
| 3 | 1 | 5 | 0 | 11 | 1 | 6 | 0 |
| 6 | 4 | 6 | 1 | 9 | 1 | 7 | 1 |
| 2 | 4 | 4 | 1 | 8 | 4 | 6 | 0 |
| 2 | 4 | 5 | 0 | 10 | 0 | 6 | 0 |
| 6 | 4 | 6 | 1 | 10 | 0 | 7 | 1 |
| 4 | 0 | 5 | 0 | 10 | 0 | 5 | 1 |
| $\Sigma =$ | 18 | | 4 | | 10 | | 4 |

$SS_{Error} = 18 + 4 + 10 + 4 = 36$

The $df_{Error}$ is determined by assessing the degrees of freedom within each of the design's conditions. In other words, the number of conditions in the study is multiplied by the number of participants in each condition minus the one score not free to vary, or $AB(n - 1)$. In the present example, this is $4(8 - 1)$, or 28. As a check, when we total the degrees of freedom for A, B, A × B, and error, they should equal $df_{Total}$. In this case, $df_A = 1$, $df_B = 1$, $df_{AxB} = 1$, and $df_{Error} = 28$. They sum to 31, which is the $df_{Total}$ we calculated previously. To determine $MS_{Error}$, we divide $SS_{Error}$ by its degrees of freedom: $36/28 = 1.29$.

Now that we have calculated the sum of squares, degrees of freedom, and mean squares for each term, we can determine the corresponding $F$-ratios. In a two-way ANOVA, there are three $F$-ratios: one for factor A, one for factor B, and one for the interaction of factors A and B. Each of the $F$-ratios is determined by dividing the $MS$ for the appropriate term by the $MS_{Error}$. Thus, for factor A (word type), the $F$-ratio is $18/1.29 = 13.95$. For factor B (rehearsal type), the $F$-ratio is determined in the same manner: $98/1.29 = 75.97$. Last, for the interaction, the $F$-ratio is $50/1.29 = 38.76$. The definitional formulas for the sums of squares and the formulas for the degrees of freedom, mean squares, and $F$-ratios are summarized in Table 11.8. Table 11.9 shows the ANOVA summary table for the data from the present study.

*Interpreting the Two-Way Randomized ANOVA.* Our obtained $F$-ratios are all greater than 1.00. To determine whether they are large enough to let us reject the null hypotheses, however, we need to compare our obtained $F$-ratios with $F_{cv}$. As we learned in Chapter 10, the underlying $F$ distribution is actually a family of distributions, each based on the degrees of freedom between and within each group. Remember that the alternative hypotheses are that the population means represented by the sample means are not from the same population. Table A.5 in Appendix A provides the critical values for

**TABLE 11.8 ANOVA summary table: definitional formulas**

| SOURCE | df | SS | MS | F |
|---|---|---|---|---|
| Factor A (word type) | $A - 1$ | $\Sigma[(\bar{X}_A - \bar{X}_G)^2 n_A]$ | $\dfrac{SS_A}{df_A}$ | $\dfrac{MS_A}{MS_{Error}}$ |
| Factor B (rehearsal type) | $B - 1$ | $\Sigma[(\bar{X}_B - \bar{X}_G)^2 n_B]$ | $\dfrac{SS_B}{df_B}$ | $\dfrac{MS_B}{MS_{Error}}$ |
| A × B | $(A - 1)(B - 1)$ | $[\Sigma(\bar{X}_C - \bar{X}_G)^2 n_C] - SS_A - SS_B$ | $\dfrac{SS_{A\times B}}{df_{A\times B}}$ | $\dfrac{MS_{A\times B}}{MS_{Error}}$ |
| Error | $AB(n - 1)$ | $\Sigma(X - \bar{X}_C)^2$ | $\dfrac{SS_{Error}}{df_{Error}}$ | |
| Total | $N - 1$ | $\Sigma(X - \bar{X}_G)^2$ | | |

**TABLE 11.9  Two-way ANOVA summary table**

| SOURCE | df | SS | MS | F |
|---|---|---|---|---|
| Factor A (word type) | 1 | 18 | 18 | 13.95 |
| Factor B (rehearsal type) | 1 | 98 | 98 | 75.97 |
| A × B | 1 | 50 | 50 | 38.76 |
| Error | 28 | 36 | 1.29 | |
| Total | 31 | 202 | | |

the family of $F$ distributions when $\alpha = .05$ and when $\alpha = .01$. We use this table exactly as we did in the previous chapter. That is, we use the $df_{Error}$ (remember, $df_{Error}$ is the degrees of freedom within groups, or the degrees of freedom for error variance) running down the left-hand side of the table and the $df_{Between}$ running across the top of the table. $F_{cv}$ is found where the row and column corresponding to these two numbers intersect. You might be wondering what $df_{Between}$ is in the present example. It always represents the degrees of freedom between groups. However, in a two-way ANOVA, we have three values of $df_{Between}$: one for factor A, one for factor B, and one for the interaction term. Therefore, we need to determine three values of $F_{cv}$, one for each of the three terms in the study.

To determine $F_{cv}$ for factor A (word type), we look at the degrees of freedom for factor A ($df_A = 1$). This represents the degrees of freedom between groups for variable A, or the number running across the top of Table A.5. We move down the left-hand column to the $df_{Error}$ ($df_{Within}$), which is 28. Where 1 and 28 intersect, we find that $F_{cv}$ for the .05 level is 4.20 and $F_{cv}$ for the .01 level is 7.64. This means that in order for our $F_{obt}$ to be significant at either of these levels, it has to exceed the $F_{cv}$ for that alpha level. Because our $F_{obt}$ for factor A exceeds both these values of $F_{cv}$, it is significant at the .01 level. In APA publication format, this is written as $F(1, 28) = 13.95$, $p < .01$. This means that there was a significant main effect of factor A (word type). If we look at the column means from Table 11.2 for word type, we see that participants did better (remembered more words) when concrete words were used than when abstract words were used. I have initially interpreted the main effect of factor A at face value, but we will see when we interpret the interaction that participants did not remember concrete words better in both of the rehearsal type conditions.

We also need to determine $F_{cv}$ for variable B and for the interaction term. Because the degrees for freedom are the same for all of the terms in this study (1, 28), we use the same values of $F_{cv}$. In addition, because the values of $F_{obt}$ also exceed the $F_{cv}$ of 7.64 for the .01 level, we know that the $F_{obt}$ for factor B and for the interaction term are also significant at the .01 level. Thus, for factor B (rehearsal type), $F(1, 28) = 75.97$, $p < .01$, indicating a significant main effect of rehearsal type. Referring back to the row means from Table 11.2, we see that participants remembered substantially more words when imagery rehearsal was used than when rote rehearsal was used. Once again, I have interpreted the main effect of factor B at face value, but we will see that the interaction qualifies this interpretation. In other words, imagery rehearsal led to better performance overall, but not when we break it down by word type. Last, for the interaction term, $F(1, 28) = 38.76$, $p < .01$, indicating that there was a significant interaction effect. When rote rehearsal was used, word type made no difference; however, when imagery rehearsal was used, the performance for the two word types varied. With imagery rehearsal, participants remembered significantly more concrete words than abstract words. To aid in your interpretation, try to draw the graph representing the cell means for this $2 \times 2$ design.

***Assumptions of the Two-Way Randomized ANOVA.*** The two-way randomized ANOVA is used when you have a factorial design. The remaining assumptions are as follows:

- All conditions (cells) contain independent samples of participants (in other words, there are different participants in each condition).
- Interval or ratio data are collected.
- The populations represented by the data are roughly normally distributed.
- The populations represented by the data all have homogeneous variances.

***Post Hoc Tests and Effect Size.*** As with a one-way ANOVA, post hoc tests such as Tukey's HSD (honestly significant difference) test are recommended. For the present example, a $2 \times 2$ design, post hoc tests are not necessary

"I THINK YOU SHOULD BE MORE EXPLICIT HERE IN STEP TWO."

because any significant main effect indicates a significant difference between the two groups that make up that variable. In other words, because each independent variable in the present study has only two values, a significant main effect of that variable indicates significant differences between the two groups. If one or both of the independent variables in a factorial design have more than two levels and the main effect(s) is (are) significant, then Tukey's HSD test should be conducted to determine exactly which groups differ significantly from each other. In addition, it is also possible to use a variation of the Tukey HSD test to compare the means from a significant interaction effect. These calculations are beyond the scope of this book but can be found in a more advanced statistics text.

As noted in previous chapters, when a significant relationship is observed, we should also calculate the effect size—the proportion of variance in the dependent variable that is accounted for by the manipulation of the independent variables(s). In Chapter 10, we used eta-squared ($\eta^2$) as a measure of effect size with ANOVAs. You may remember that $\eta^2 = SS_{Between}/SS_{Total}$. When using a two-way ANOVA, we have three values of $SS_{Between}$: one for variable A, one for variable B, and one for the interaction term. Referring back to Table 11.9, we can obtain the $SS$ scores needed for these calculations. For factor A (word type), $\eta^2$ is calculated as

$$\eta^2 = \frac{18}{202} = .089$$

This means that factor A (word type) can account for 8.9% of the total variance in the number of words recalled. We can also calculate the effect sizes for factor B (rehearsal type) and the interaction term using the same formula. For factor B, $\eta^2$ is $98/202 = .485$. In other words, factor B (rehearsal type) can account for 48.5% of the total variance in the number of words recalled. Clearly, rehearsal type is very important in determining the number of words recalled; according to Cohen (1988), this effect size is meaningful. Last, for the interaction effect, $\eta^2 = 50/202 = .25$. Thus, the interaction of factors A and B can account for 25% of the variance in the number of words recalled. This means that knowing the individual cell or condition (in other words, the factor A by factor B condition) that the participants were in can account for 25% of the variance in the dependent variable. This is also a meaningful effect size.

| Two-Way Randomized ANOVA | IN REVIEW |
|---|---|

| CONCEPT | DESCRIPTION |
|---|---|
| Null Hypothesis ($H_0$) | The independent variable had no effect—the samples all represent the same population. In a two-way ANOVA, there are three null hypotheses: one for factor A, one for factor B, and one for the interaction of factors A and B. |
| Alternative Hypothesis ($H_a$) | The independent variable had an effect—at least one of the samples represents a different population than the others. In a two-way ANOVA, there are three alternative hypotheses: one for factor A, one for factor B, and one for the interaction of factors A and B. |
| F-ratio | The ratio formed when the between-groups variance is divided by the within-groups variance. In a two-way ANOVA, there are three F-ratios: one for factor A, one for factor B, and one for the interaction of factors A and B. |

| CONCEPT | DESCRIPTION |
|---|---|
| Between-Groups Variance | An estimate of the variance of the group means about the grand mean. In a two-way ANOVA, there are three types of between-groups variance: that attributable to factor A, that attributable to factor B, and that attributable to the interaction of factors A and B. |
| Within-Groups Variance | An estimate of the variance within each condition in the experiment—also known as error variance, or variance due to chance. |
| Eta-squared ($\eta^2$) | A measure of effect size—the variability in the dependent variable attributable to the independent variable. In a two-way ANOVA, eta-squared is calculated for factor A, for factor B, and for the interaction of factors A and B. |
| Tukey's Post Hoc Test | A test conducted to determine which conditions from a variable with more than two conditions differ significantly from each other. |

**CRITICAL THINKING CHECK 11.2**

1. Assuming that there were two significant main effects in a hypothetical 2 × 4 design, would Tukey's HSD need to be calculated for these main effects? Why or why not?
2. A researcher is attempting to determine the effects of practice and gender on a timed task. Participants in the experiment are given a computerized search task. They search a computer screen of various characters and attempt to find a particular character on each trial. When they find the designated character, they press a button to stop a timer. Their reaction time (in milliseconds) on each trial is recorded. Participants practice for 1, 2, or 3 hours and are either female or male. The ANOVA summary table appears below, along with the means for each condition and the number of participants in each condition.

*Two-Way ANOVA Summary Table*

| Source | df | SS | MS | F |
|---|---|---|---|---|
| Factor A (gender) | | 684,264 | | |
| Factor B (practice) | | 989,504 | | |
| A × B | | 489,104 | | |
| Error | | 2,967,768 | | |
| Total | | 5,130,640 | | |

| Condition | Mean | n |
|---|---|---|
| Female/1 hour | 1,778.125 | 8 |
| Female/2 hours | 1,512.375 | 8 |
| Female/3 hours | 1,182.75 | 8 |
| Male/1 hour | 1,763.375 | 8 |
| Male/2 hours | 1,764.25 | 8 |
| Male/3 hours | 1,662 | 8 |

a. Identify the factorial notation for the design.
b. Complete the ANOVA summary table.

c. Determine significance levels for any main or interaction effect(s).
d. Explain any significant main or interaction effect(s).
e. Calculate eta-squared for any significant effects.
f. Draw a graph representing the data.

## Two-Way Repeated Measures ANOVA

When a complex within-participants (the same participants are used in all conditions) or matched-participants (participants are matched across conditions) design is used, and the data collected are interval-ratio in scale, then the appropriate statistic is a two-way repeated measures ANOVA. This ANOVA is similar to the two-way randomized ANOVA in that it indicates whether there is a significant main effect of either independent variable in the study and whether the interaction effect is significant. However, a correlated-groups design requires slight modifications in the formulas applied. If you find yourself in a situation where it is necessary to use a two-way repeated measures ANOVA, you can find the calculations in a more advanced statistics text.

## Beyond the Two-Way ANOVA

In this and the previous chapter, we have discussed one- and two-way ANOVAs. It is possible to add more factors (independent variables) to a study and to analyze the data with an ANOVA. For example, if a study used three independent variables, then a three-way ANOVA would be used. In this situation, there would be three main effects, three two-way interactions, and one three-way interaction to interpret. This means that there would be seven $F$-ratios to calculate. Obviously, this complicates the interpretation of the data considerably. Because three-way interactions are so difficult to interpret, most researchers try to design studies that are not quite so complex.

All of the studies discussed so far have had only one dependent variable. Besides adding independent variables, it is also possible to add dependent variables to a study. With one dependent variable, we use *univariate* statistics to analyze the data. Thus, all of the statistics discussed thus far in this text have been univariate statistics. When we have more than one dependent variable, we must use *multivariate* statistics to analyze the data. Many types of multivariate statistics are available, including the multivariate $t$ test and the multivariate ANOVA, referred to as a MANOVA. These advanced statistics are beyond the scope of this book. If you encounter them in the literature, however, you can interpret them in a similar fashion to those statistics that we have covered. In other words, the larger the $t$-score or $F$-ratio, the more likely it is the samples represent different populations and that the test statistic is significant.

Finally, a *meta-analysis* is a statistical procedure (also beyond the scope of this book) that combines, tests, and describes the results from many different studies. Before this technique was developed, researchers had to rely on more subjective reviews of the literature to summarize the general findings from many studies. By allowing researchers to assess the results from a large number of studies through one statistical procedure, a meta-analysis enables us to draw more objective conclusions about the generalizability of research findings.

# Summary

In this chapter, we described experimental designs that use more than one independent variable. We discussed several advantages of using such designs and introduced the concepts of factorial notation, main effects, and interaction effects. After reading the section on main and interaction effects, you should be able to graph data from a factorial design and interpret what the graph means. We then discussed the statistical analysis of such designs, using a two-way randomized ANOVA. We presented the various calculations necessary to compute a two-way randomized ANOVA, along with the assumptions of the test and a description of how to interpret the results.

## KEY TERMS

factorial design
factorial notation
main effect

interaction effect
sum of squares factor A
sum of squares factor B

sum of squares interaction
sum of squares error

## CHAPTER EXERCISES

(Answers to odd-numbered exercises appear in Appendix C.)

1. What is the advantage of manipulating more than one independent variable in an experiment?

2. How many independent variables are in a 4 × 6 factorial design? How many conditions (cells) are in this design?

3. In a study, a researcher manipulated the number of hours that participants studied (either 4, 6, or 8), the type of study technique they used (shallow processing versus deep processing), and whether participants studied individually or in groups. What is the factorial notation for this design?

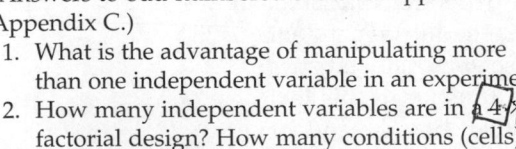

4. What is the difference between a cell (condition) mean and the means used to interpret a main effect?

5. How many main effects and interaction effects are possible in a 2 × 6 factorial design?

6. What is the difference between a complete factorial design and an incomplete factorial design?

7. The cell means for two experiments appear below. Determine whether there are any effects of factor A, factor B, and A × B for each experiment. In addition, draw a graph representing the data from each experiment.

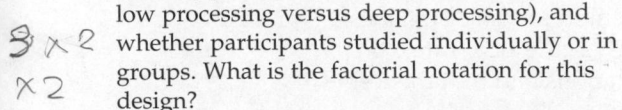

*Experiment 1*

|       | A₁ | A₂ |
|-------|----|----|
| B₁    | 3  | 5  |
| B₂    | 3  | 8  |

*Experiment 2*

|       | A₁ | A₂ |
|-------|----|----|
| B₁    | 12 | 4  |
| B₂    | 4  | 12 |

8. Explain the difference between a two-way ANOVA and a three-way ANOVA.

9. If you find two significant main effects in a 2 × 6 factorial design, should you compute Tukey's post hoc comparisons for both main effects?

10. Complete each of the ANOVA summary tables below. In addition, answer the following questions for each of the ANOVA summary tables:
   a. What is the factorial notation?
   b. How many conditions were in the study?
   c. How many participants were in the study?
   d. Identify significant main effects and interaction effects.

| Source | df | SS | MS | F |
|--------|----|----|----|----|
| A | 1 | 60 | | |
| B | 2 | 40 | | |
| A × B | 2 | 90 | | |
| Error | 30 | | | |
| Total | 35 | 390 | | |

| Source | df | SS | MS | F |
|--------|----|----|----|----|
| A | 2 | 40 | | |
| B | 3 | 60 | | |
| A × B | 6 | 150 | | |
| Error | 72 | | | |
| Total | 83 | 400 | | |

| Source | df | SS | MS | F |
|--------|----|----|----|----|
| A | 1 | 10 | | |
| B | 1 | 60 | | |
| A × B | 1 | 20 | | |
| Error | 36 | | | |
| Total | 39 | 150 | | |

11. In a study, a researcher measures the preference of men and women for two brands of frozen pizza (one low-fat and one regular) based on the number of 1-inch pieces of each type of pizza eaten when both types are available to the participants. The table below shows the number of pieces of each type of pizza eaten for each of the 24 participants in the study.

| | Women | Men |
|--------|-------|-----|
| Brand 1 | 3 | 9 |
| (low fat) | 4 | 7 |
| | 2 | 6 |
| | 2 | 8 |
| | 5 | 9 |
| | 3 | 7 |
| | | |
| Brand 2 | 8 | 4 |
| (regular) | 9 | 2 |
| | 7 | 5 |
| | 10 | 6 |
| | 9 | 2 |
| | 10 | 5 |

| Source | df | SS | MS | F |
|--------|----|----|----|----|
| Gender | | 0.167 | | |
| Pizza brand | | 6.00 | | |
| Gender × Pizza | | 130.67 | | |
| Error | | 35.00 | | |
| Total | | 171.83 | | |

a. Complete the ANOVA summary table. (If your instructor wants you to calculate the sums of squares, use the above data to do so.)
b. Are the values of $F_{obt}$ significant at $\alpha = .05$?
c. What conclusions can be drawn from the F-ratios?
d. What is the effect size, and what does this mean?
e. Graph the means.

12. A researcher is attempting to determine the effects of practice and gender on a timed task. Participants in an experiment are given a computerized search task. They search a computer screen of various characters and attempt to find a particular character on each trial. When they find the designated character, they press a button to stop a timer. Their reaction time (in seconds) on each trial is recorded. Participants practice for 2, 4, or 6 hours and are either female or male. The reaction time data for the 30 participants appear below.

| | Women | Men |
|---------|-------|-----|
| 2 Hours | 12 | 11 |
| | 13 | 12 |
| | 12 | 13 |
| | 11 | 12 |
| | 11 | 11 |
| | | |
| 4 Hours | 10 | 8 |
| | 10 | 8 |
| | 10 | 10 |
| | 8 | 10 |
| | 7 | 9 |
| | | |
| 6 Hours | 7 | 5 |
| | 5 | 6 |
| | 7 | 8 |
| | 6 | 6 |
| | 7 | 8 |

| Source | df | SS | MS | F |
|--------|----|----|----|----|
| Gender | | 0.027 | | |
| Practice | | 140.60 | | |
| Gender × Practice | | 0.073 | | |
| Error | | 28.00 | | |
| Total | | 168.70 | | |

a. Complete the ANOVA summary table. (If your instructor wants you to calculate the sums of squares, use the above data to do so.)
b. Are the values of $F_{obt}$ significant at $\alpha = .05$?
c. What conclusions can be drawn from the F-ratios?
d. What is the effect size, and what does this mean?
e. Graph the means.

## CRITICAL THINKING CHECK ANSWERS

### 11.1

1. This would be a 3 × 5 design. There are three types of crust and five types of toppings, so there are 15 conditions in this study.
2. A 4 × 6 factorial design has two independent variables. Thus, there is the possibility of two main effects (one for each independent variable) and one interaction effect (the interaction between the two independent variables).
3. There appears to be a main effect of word type, with concrete words recalled better than abstract words. There also appears to be a main effect of rehearsal type, with those who used imagery rehearsal remembering more words than those who used rote rehearsal. In addition, there appears to be an interaction effect. When imagery rehearsal is used, word type makes no difference; recall is very high for both types of words. When rote rehearsal is used, word type makes a large difference; concrete words are recalled very well and abstract words very poorly.

**Graph for Critical Thinking Check 11.1, item 3**

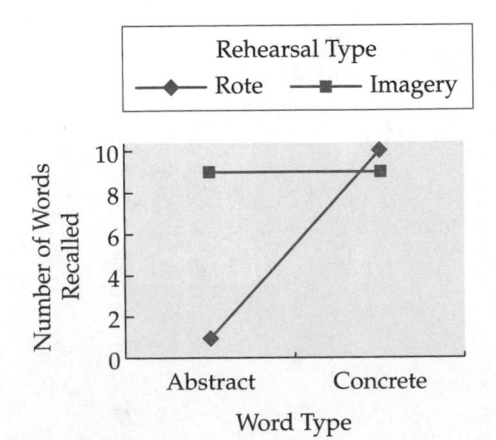

### 11.2

1. Tukey's HSD would not need to be calculated for the main effect of the variable with two levels because if there is a significant main effect for a variable with two levels, then we know that the difference between those two levels is significant. We would need to calculate Tukey's HSD for the variable with four levels in order to determine exactly which groups among the four differed significantly from each other.
2. a. This is a 2 × 3 design.

|  | Gender | | Row Means |
|---|---|---|---|
| Practice | Female | Male | (Practice) |
| 1 hour | 1,778.125 | 1,763.375 | 1,770.75 |
| 2 hours | 1,512.375 | 1,764.25 | 1,638.31 |
| 3 hours | 1,182.75 | 1,662 | 1,422.38 |
| Column means (gender) | 1,491.08 | 1,729.88 | |

b. *Two-Way ANOVA Summary Table*

| Source | df | SS | MS | F |
|---|---|---|---|---|
| Factor A (gender) | 1 | 684,264 | 684,264 | 9.68 |
| Factor B (practice) | 2 | 989,504 | 494,752 | 7.00 |
| A × B | 2 | 489,104 | 244,552 | 3.46 |
| Error | 42 | 2,967,768 | 70,661.143 | |
| Total | 47 | 5,130,640 | | |

c. Gender: $F(1, 42) = 9.68, p < .01$
Practice: $F(2, 42) = 7.00, p < .01$
Interaction: $F(2, 42) = 3.46, p < .05$
d. The significant main effect of gender indicates that females performed more quickly than males. The significant main effect of practice indicates that as the amount of time spent practicing increased, reaction time decreased. The

significant interaction effect indicates that practice affected only females; the more females practiced, the more quickly they responded. However, practice did not affect males; reaction times for males were consistent across the various practice conditions.

e. Eta-squared was .13 for gender, .19 for practice, and .095 for the interaction. Thus, overall, the proportion of variance in the dependent variable accounted for by the independent variables is .415, or 41.5%.

f.

## WEB RESOURCES

Check your knowledge of the content in this chapter by taking the practice quiz at www.Wadsworth.com. Or, for step-by-step practice and information, check out the Statistics and Research Methods Workshops at http://psychology.wadsworth.com/workshops.

## LAB RESOURCES

For hands-on experience using the research methods described in this chapter, see Chapters 7 ("Factorial Designs I") and 8 ("Factorial Designs II") in *Research Methods Laboratory Manual for Psychology*, 2nd ed., by William Langston (Belmont, CA: Wadsworth, 2005).

## STATISTICAL SOFTWARE RESOURCES

For hands-on experience using statistical software to complete the analyses described in this chapter, see Chapter 9 ("Two-Factor ANOVA") in *The Excel Statistics Companion* by Kenneth M. Rosenberg (Belmont, CA: Wadsworth, 2003).

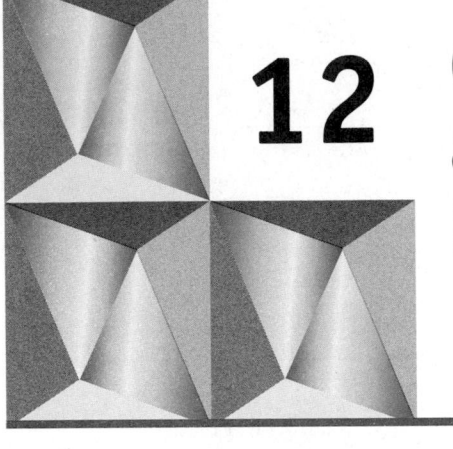

# 12 Quasi-Experimental and Single-Case Designs

Quasi-experimental research can be thought of as an intermediate point between correlational and true experimental research. As such, it allows us to draw slightly stronger conclusions than we might with correlational research. We can say there is more than a simple relationship between variables, but we cannot draw as strong a conclusion as we can with true experimental research. We cannot say that we have observed a causal relationship between variables. Quasi-experimental research frequently fits into the category of field research; that is, it often involves conducting research in more naturalistic settings. In this chapter, we will begin with a brief discussion of what quasi-experimental research is and how it differs from correlational and experimental research. We will then describe various types of quasi-experimental research designs and discuss how the quasi-experimental method limits internal validity in a study. Finally, we will discuss another type of field research, single-case research. As with quasi-experimental designs, we will discuss the value of single-case research and describe various types of single-case designs.

# Conducting Quasi-Experimental Research

The term *quasi* (meaning "having some but not all of the features") preceding the term *experimental* indicates that we are dealing with a design that resembles an experiment but is not exactly an experiment. How does a quasi-experimental design differ from an experimental design? Sometimes the difference is the lack of any control group or comparison group. In other words, only one group is given a treatment and then assessed. At other times, the independent variable is not a true manipulated independent variable; instead it is a participant variable or a nonmanipulated independent variable. Finally, there may be designs considered quasi-experimental because participants are not randomly assigned to conditions. In other words, they are already part of a group and the researcher attempts to manipulate a variable between pre-existing groups.

## Nonmanipulated Independent Variables

In some quasi-experiments, the researcher is interested in comparing groups of individuals (as is done in an experiment), but the groups occur naturally. In other words, participants are not assigned randomly to the groups. Notice the difference between this and correlational research. We are not simply looking for relationships between variables—such as between smoking and cancer. In quasi-experimental research, we are testing a hypothesis—for example: Individuals who have smoked for 20 years have a higher incidence of respiratory illness than nonsmokers. We would then randomly select a group of individuals who had smoked for 20 years and a group of individuals who had never smoked to serve as a control. Thus, rather than simply looking for a relationship between smoking and cancer/illness, we are comparing two groups in order to test a hypothesis.

**nonmanipulated indepen-
dent variable**   The independent variable in a quasi-
experimental design in which
participants are not randomly
assigned to conditions but
rather come to the study as
members of each condition.

The independent variable is referred to as a **nonmanipulated independent variable** because participants are not randomly assigned to the two groups. We are not truly manipulating smoking; participants come to the study as either smokers or nonsmokers. However, we do make comparisons between the groups. Thus, the study has the intent and "flavor" of an experiment without being a true experiment. Nonmanipulated independent variables are also known as *participant variables*. A participant variable, you may recall from Chapter 1, is a characteristic of the participant that cannot be changed, such as ethnicity, gender, age, or political affiliation. If a study is designed to assess differences in individuals on some participant variable, by default it is a quasi-experiment and not a true experiment because it uses a nonmanipulated independent variable; that is, participants are not randomly assigned to conditions.

## An Example: Snow and Cholera

In the 1850s in London, England, there were frequent outbreaks of cholera, an infection of the small intestine. The cause at the time was unknown, but the common theory was that cholera was somehow spread as people came in contact with cholera victims and shared or breathed the same air. This was known as the effluvia theory. John Snow, in his quest for the cause of cholera, had an alternative hypothesis (Goldstein & Goldstein, 1978). Snow thought that people contracted cholera by drinking contaminated water. He based his hypothesis on the observation that, of the several different water companies serving London, some provided water from upstream (it had not yet passed through the city and possibly become contaminated) whereas others used water from downstream (after it had passed through the city and possibly become contaminated).

To test this hypothesis, Snow used a quasi-experimental design. Obviously it was not feasible to use a true experimental design because it would have been impossible to randomly assign different houses to contract with a specific water company. Snow therefore had to look at houses that already received their water from a downstream company versus houses that received water from upstream. You should begin to see some of the problems inherent in quasi-experimental research. If people chose their water company, then there was most likely a reason for the choice. In most cases, the reason was socio-economic: The wealthier neighborhoods used upstream (more costly) companies, whereas the poorer neighborhoods used downstream (less costly) companies. This obviously presented a problem for Snow because he had no way of knowing whether differences in cholera incidence were due to the different water companies or to something else related to socioeconomic level, such as diet, living conditions, or medical care.

Luckily for Snow, he was able to find one neighborhood in which socio-economic status was stable but different houses received water from two different companies in an unsystematic manner. In other words, the choice of water companies in this neighborhood appeared to be random. It was so random, in fact, that in some cases the choice of water company varied from house to house on a single street. Here was a naturally occurring situation in which socioeconomic level was controlled and water company varied. It was important, however, to ensure that not only the water company but also the contamination level of the water varied. Snow was lucky in this respect, too, because one company had moved upstream after a previous cholera epidemic whereas the other company had stayed downstream. Snow calculated the number of deaths by cholera for individuals receiving water from upstream versus those receiving water from downstream. He found that there were 37 deaths per 10,000 households for the upstream company and 315 deaths per 10,000 households for the downstream company. Therefore, it appeared that water contamination was responsible for the spread of cholera.

As a review, the nonmanipulated independent variable in Snow's study was water company. This was a participant variable because individuals came to the study with their choice of water company already established. The dependent variable was number of deaths by cholera. Snow observed a difference in death rates between the two companies and concluded that the type of water (more contaminated versus less contaminated) appeared to be the cause. Snow was particularly lucky because of the naturally occurring situation in which socioeconomic level was controlled but water company varied. This type of control is often lacking in quasi-experimental research. However, even with such control, there is still not as much control as in an experiment because participants are not randomly assigned to conditions. Therefore, it is still possible for uncontrolled differences between the groups to affect the outcome of the study.

## Quasi-Experimental Versus Correlational Methods

**IN REVIEW**

| | VARIABLES | CONCLUSIONS | CAUTIONS |
|---|---|---|---|
| Correlational Method | Two measured variables | The variables may be related in some way. | We cannot conclude that the the relationship is causal. |
| Quasi-Experimental Method | Typically one non manipulated independent variable and one measured dependent variable | Systematic differences have been observed between two or more groups, but we cannot say that the nonmanipulated independent variable definitely caused the differences. | Due to confounds inherent in the use of nonmanipulated independent variables, there may be alternative explanations for the results. |

**CRITICAL THINKING CHECK 12.1**

1. Which of the following variables would be a participant variable if used as a nonmanipulated independent variable in a quasi-experiment?

   gender           ethnicity
   religious affiliation     visual acuity
   amount of time spent studying    amount of alcohol consumed

2. How does the quasi-experimental method allow us to draw slightly stronger conclusions than the correlational method? Why is it that the conclusions drawn from quasi-experimental studies cannot be stated in as strong a manner as those from a true experiment?

# Types of Quasi-Experimental Designs

The quasi-experimental design has several possible variations (Campbell & Stanley, 1963). One distinction is whether there are one or two groups of participants. A second distinction has to do with how often measurements are taken. We will begin by discussing quasi-experimental designs in which only one group of participants is observed. These designs include the single-group posttest-only design, the single-group pretest/posttest design, and the single-group time-series design. We will then consider designs that use two groups—referred to as *nonequivalent control group designs*. These include the nonequivalent control group posttest-only design, the nonequivalent control group pretest/posttest design, and the multiple-group time-series design.

## Single-Group Posttest-Only Design

**single-group posttest-only design** A design in which a single group of participants is given a treatment and then tested.

The **single-group posttest-only design** is the simplest quasi-experimental design. As the name implies, it involves the use of a single group of participants to whom some treatment is given. The participants are then assessed on the dependent variable. Research in education is frequently of this type. For example, some new educational technique—such as interactive learning, outcomes learning, or computer-assisted learning—is proposed, and school systems begin to adopt this new method. Posttest measures are then taken to determine the amount learned by students. However, there is neither a comparison group nor a comparison of the results to any previous measurements (usually because what is learned via the new method is so "different" from the old method that the claim is made that comparisons are not valid). You should see the problem with this type of design. How can we claim a method is better when we cannot compare the results for the group who participated with the results for any other group or standard? This design is open to so many criticisms and potential flaws that results based on this type of study should always be interpreted with caution.

Most frequently, you will see single-group posttest-only designs reported in popular literature, where they are frequently misinterpreted by those who read them. How many times have you read about people who lived through a certain experience or joined a particular group claiming that the experience or the group had an effect on their lives? These are examples of single-group posttest-only designs. Single-group posttest-only designs cannot be used to draw conclusions about how an experience has affected the individuals involved. The change in their lives could be due to any number of variables other than the experience they lived through or the program they went through.

## Single-Group Pretest/Posttest Design

**single-group pretest/posttest design** A design in which a single group of participants takes a pretest, then receives some treatment, and then takes a posttest measure.

The **single-group pretest/posttest design** is an improvement over the posttest-only design in that measures are taken twice—before the treatment and after the treatment. The two measures can then be compared, and any differences in the measures are assumed to be the result of the treatment.

For example, if we had a single group of depressed individuals who wanted to receive treatment (counseling) for their depression, we would measure their level of depression before the treatment, have them then participate in the counseling, and then measure their level of depression after the treatment. Can you think of possible problems with this design? The greatest problem is the lack of a comparison group. With no comparison group, we do not know whether any observed change in depression is due to the treatment or to something else that may have happened during the time of the study. For example, maybe the pretest depression measure was taken right after the holidays, when depression is higher for many people. Therefore, the participants might have scored lower on the posttest depression measure regardless of whether they received counseling or not.

## Single-Group Time-Series Design

The **single-group time-series design** involves using a single group of participants, taking multiple measures over a period of time before introducing the treatment, and then continuing to take several measures after the treatment. The advantage of this design is that the multiple measures allow us to see whether the behavior is stable before treatment and how, or if, it changes at the multiple points in time at which measures are taken after treatment.

**single-group time-series design** A design in which a single group of participants is measured repeatedly before and after a treatment.

An often cited good example of a time-series design, discussed by Campbell (1969), was used to evaluate the 1955 crackdown on speeding in Connecticut. The state found it necessary to institute the crackdown after a record-high number of traffic fatalities occurred in 1955. A pretest/posttest design would simply compare the number of fatalities before the crackdown with the number after the crackdown. The number of deaths fell from 324 in 1955 to 284 in 1956. However, alternative hypotheses, other than the crackdown, could be offered to explain this drop. For example, perhaps the number of deaths in 1955 was unusually high based on chance; in other words, it was just a "fluke." Campbell recommended a time-series design, examining traffic fatalities over an extended period of time. Figure 12.1 illustrates the results of this design, which includes traffic fatalities for the years 1951 through 1959. As can be seen in the figure, 1955 was a record-high year; after the crackdown, the number of fatalities declined not only in 1956 but also in the 3 following years. Using the time-series design, then, allowed for a clearer interpretation than was possible with data from only 1955 and 1956.

However, Campbell still saw a problem with attributing the decline to the crackdown. The problem is statistical regression, or regression to the mean, discussed in Chapter 8. To briefly review this concept, with the very high death rate in 1955, we would expect a drop in the death rate for several years, whether there was a speeding crackdown or not. Why? Because then the average death rate (calculated over several years) would remain the same. We will discuss Campbell's recommendation for an improved design shortly when we cover the multiple-group time-series design.

**FIGURE 12.1**
**Connecticut traffic**
**fatalities:**
**1951–1959**
SOURCE: Campbell, D. T. (1969).
Reforms as experiments.
*American Psychologist, 24,*
409–429. Copyright © 1969 by
the American Psychological
Association. Reprinted with
permission.

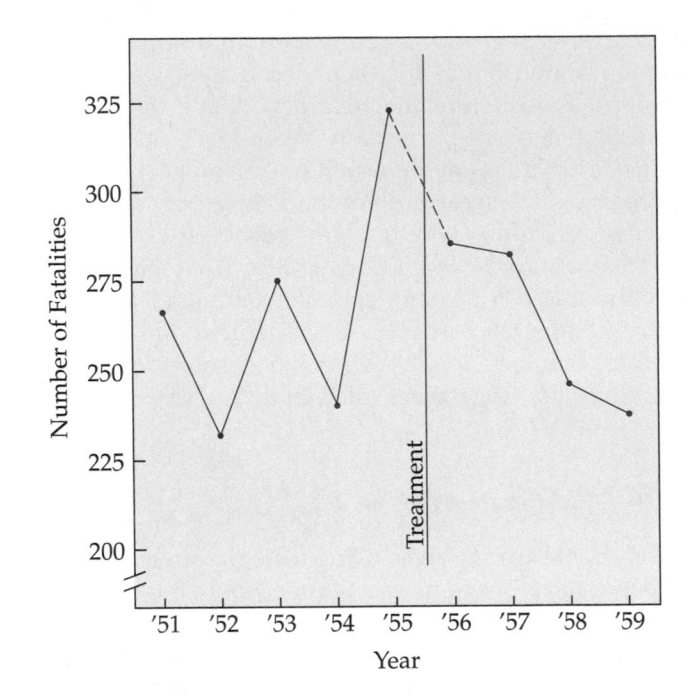

## Nonequivalent Control Group Posttest-Only Design

**nonequivalent control**
**group posttest-only design**
A design in which at least two
nonequivalent groups are given
a treatment and then a posttest
measure.

The **nonequivalent control group posttest-only design** is similar to the single-group posttest-only design; however, a nonequivalent control group is added as a comparison group. Notice that the control group is nonequivalent, meaning that participants are not assigned to either the experimental or the control group in a random manner. Instead, they are members of each group because of something that they chose or did—they come to the study already a member of one of the groups. This design is similar to the quasi-experimental study conducted by Snow on cholera, discussed earlier in this chapter. Participants selected either the upstream or the downstream water company and Snow took posttest measures on death rates by cholera. As noted earlier, Snow had some evidence that the two groups were somewhat equivalent on income level because they all lived in the same neighborhood. In many situations, however, there is no assurance that the two groups are at all equivalent on any variable prior to the study. For this reason, we cannot say definitively that the treatment is responsible for any observed changes in the groups. It could be that the groups were not equivalent at the beginning of the study; hence, the differences observed between the two groups on the dependent variable may be due to the nonequivalence of the groups and not to the treatment.

## Nonequivalent Control Group Pretest/Posttest Design

**nonequivalent control**
**group pretest/posttest**
**design** A design in which at
least two nonequivalent groups
are given a pretest, then a
treatment, and then a posttest
measure.

An improvement over the previous design involves the addition of a pretest measure, making it a **nonequivalent control group pretest/posttest design.** This is still not a true experimental design because, as with the previous designs, participants are not randomly assigned to the two conditions. However, a pretest allows us to assess whether the groups are equivalent on the dependent measure before the treatment is given to the experimental group. In addition, we can assess any changes that may have occurred in each group after treatment by comparing the pretest measures for each group with their posttest measures. Thus, not only can we compare performance between the two groups on both pretest and posttest measures, but we can compare performance within each group from the pretest to the posttest. If the treatment had some effect, then there should be a greater change from pretest to posttest for the experimental group than for the control group.

Williams (1986) and her colleagues used this design in a series of studies designed to assess the effects of television on communities. The researchers found a small Canadian town that had no television reception until 1973; they designated this town the Notel group. Life in Notel was then compared to life in two other communities: Unitel, which received only one station at the beginning of the study, and Multitel, which received four channels at the beginning of the study. A single channel was introduced to Notel at the beginning of the study. During the 2 years of the study, Unitel began receiving three additional stations. The researchers measured such factors as participation in community activities and aggressive behavior in children in all three groups both before and after the introduction of television in Notel. Results showed that after the introduction of television in Notel, there was a significant decline in participation in community activities and a significant increase in aggressive behavior in children.

## Multiple-Group Time-Series Design

The logical extension of the previous design is to take more than one pretest and posttest. In a **multiple-group time-series design,** several measures are taken on nonequivalent groups before and after treatment. Refer back to the study of the crackdown on speeding in Connecticut following a high number of traffic fatalities in 1955. Converting that single-group time-series design to a multiple-group time-series design would involve finding a comparison group—a state that did not crack down on speeding—during the same time period. Campbell (1969) found four other states that did not crack down on speeding at the same time as Connecticut. Figure 12.2 presents the data from this design. As can be seen, the fatality rates in the states used as the control group remained fairly stable, while the fatality rates in Connecticut decreased. Based on these data, Campbell concluded that the crackdown had the desired effect on fatality rates.

**multiple-group time-series design** A design in which a series of measures are taken on two or more groups both before and after a treatment.

# Internal Validity and Confounds in Quasi-Experimental Designs

As we have pointed out several times in our discussion of quasi-experimental research, the results need to be interpreted with caution because the design includes only one group or a nonequivalent control group. These results are always open to alternative explanations, or confounds—uncontrolled extraneous variables or flaws in an experiment. Because of the weaknesses in

**FIGURE 12.2**
**Multiple-group**
**time-series design**
**comparing**
**Connecticut fatality**
**rates (solid line)**
**with the fatality**
**rates of four other**
**states (dashed line)**
**used as a control**
**group**
SOURCE: Campbell, D. T. (1969).
Reforms as experiments.
*American Psychologist, 24,*
409–429. Copyright © 1969 by
the American Psychological
Association. Reprinted with
permission.

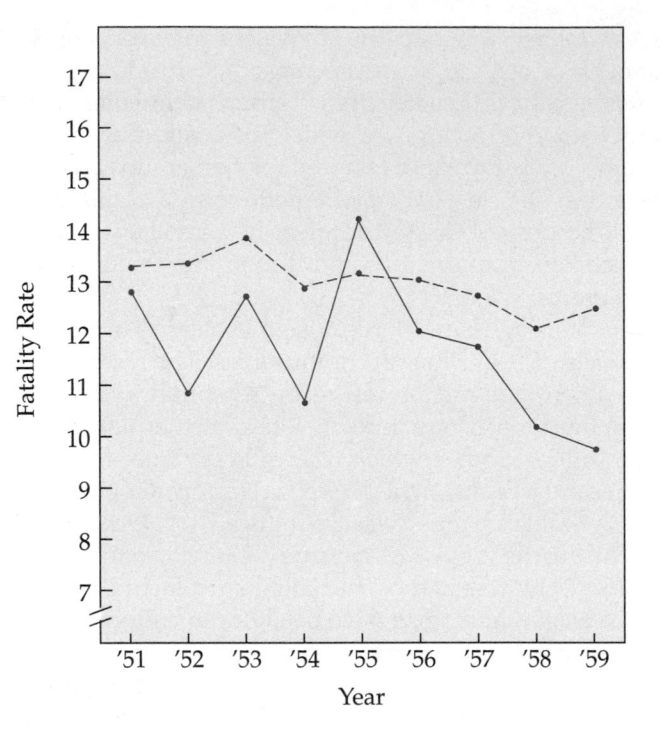

quasi-experimental designs, we can never conclude that the independent variable definitely caused any of the observed changes in the dependent variable. As you may recall from Chapter 8, internal validity is the extent to which the results of an experiment can be attributed to the manipulation of the independent variable, rather than to some confounding variable. Thus, quasi-experimental designs lack internal validity. You may want to review Chapter 8, where internal validity and confounds were discussed in some detail—including several of the confounds inherent in quasi-experimental designs and why a true experiment helps to control for these confounds.

# Statistical Analysis of Quasi-Experimental Designs

Data collected from a quasi-experimental design are analyzed in the same way as data collected through true experimental designs. Depending on the type of data (nominal, ordinal, or interval-ratio), the number of levels of the independent variable, the number of independent variables, and whether the design is between-participants or within-participants, we choose the appropriate statistic as we did for the experimental designs discussed in Chapters 9–11. Even though we use the same statistics, however, we are limited in the conclusions we can draw. Our conclusions must be tempered because of the confounds inherent in quasi-experimental designs.

| Quasi-Experimental Designs | | IN REVIEW |
|---|---|---|
| | **SINGLE-GROUP DESIGNS** | **NONEQUIVALENT CONTROL GROUP DESIGNS** |
| Posttest-Only | Open to many confounds | Control group is nonequivalent |
| | No comparison group | No pretest measures to establish equivalence of groups |
| | No equivalent control group | |
| | | Can compare groups on posttest measures, but differences may be due to treatment or confounds |
| Pretest/Posttest | Compare scores on pretest to those on posttest | Can compare between groups on pretest and posttest |
| | No equivalent control group for comparison | Can compare within groups from pretest to posttest |
| | If change is observed, may be due to treatment or confounds | Because participants are not randomly assigned to groups, cannot say that they are equivalent |
| | | If change is observed, may be due to treatment or confounds |
| Time Series | Because many measures taken, can see effect of treatment over time | Because many measures taken, can see effect of treatment over time |
| | No control group for comparison | Nonequivalent control group available for comparison |
| | If change is observed, may be due to treatment or confounds | Because participants are not randomly assigned to groups, cannot say that they are equivalent |
| | | If change is observed, may be due to treatment or confounds |

1. Imagine I randomly select a group of smokers and a group of non-smokers. I then measure lung disease in each group. What type of design is this? If I observe a difference between the groups in rate of lung disease, why can't I conclude that this difference is caused by smoking?
2. How are pretest/posttest designs an improvement over posttest-only designs?

**CRITICAL THINKING CHECK 12.2**

# Conducting Single-Case Research

Up to this point, the experiments we have discussed have all involved studying groups of people. In certain types of research, researchers use methods that minimize the number of participants in a study. This may sound contrary to the basic principles of design that we have discussed so far. However, these methods, often referred to as **single-case designs,** are versions of a within-participants experiment in which only one person is measured repeatedly.

**single-case design** A design in which only one participant is used.

**small-*n* design**  A design in which only a few participants are studied.

Often the research is replicated on one or two other participants. Thus, we sometimes refer to these studies as **small-*n* designs.** Such studies can also be thought of as a variation of the pretest/posttest quasi-experimental design discussed earlier in the chapter. However, in this case, pre- and posttest measures are taken on the single participant in the study.

A researcher may choose a single-case design for several reasons. The researcher may want information on only the single participant being studied. The researcher may not be interested in trying to generalize the results to a population, but only in how this one participant reacts to the manipulation. Single-case research is frequently used in clinical settings. In clinical studies, many researchers believe that it is unethical to use traditional experimental methods in which one group of participants receives the treatment and the other group serves as a control. They believe it is unethical to withhold treatment from one group—particularly when the participants may really need the treatment. In such cases, single-case or small-*n* designs are more ethically appealing because they involve providing treatment to all who participate in the study.

Sidman (1960) argues that of the several reasons for conducting single-case studies, each is based on a flaw in designs that use many participants (group designs). One problem with group designs, according to Sidman, is that they do not allow for adequate replication of results, whereas single-case designs do. Thus, single-case designs are better at demonstrating a reliable effect of an independent variable. Second, group designs contribute to error variance in a study. You may remember that error variance is the random differences in scores found within the conditions of an experiment. Using many people in a group design increases error variance resulting from individual differences. This increase in error variance may make it difficult to identify a relationship between the variables in the study. Third, Sidman notes that when using group designs, we typically look at the mean performance within each group. However, a mean score for a given condition may not accurately represent the performance of all of the participants in that condition. Once we have drawn conclusions based on the mean performance within each group, we then attempt to generalize the results to individuals. Psychologists thus draw conclusions about individual behavior based on studying the average performance of a group of people.

Single-case and small-*n* designs address each of these problems. To determine the reliability of the effect, we can repeatedly manipulate the independent variable with the same participant, or perform replications with a few other participants. Error variance resulting from individual differences is eliminated because only one participant is used. Finally, rather than looking at group means and conducting the appropriate statistical analyses, we look at only the performance of the single participant in the study to determine the relationship between the independent and dependent variables. Most commonly, we graph the performance of the single participant and examine the resulting graph. The effect of the independent variable is determined by how much the participant's behavior changes from one condition to another. Also, because the findings are based on individuals, it makes some sense to generalize the results to other individuals.

# Types of Single-Case Designs

Single-case designs are of several types. The basic distinction is between a reversal design and a multiple-baseline design. The reversal design typically involves studying a single behavior in a single participant in a single situation, whereas the multiple-baseline design may involve studying multiple people, behaviors, or situations.

## Reversal Designs

A **reversal design** is a within-participants design with only one participant in which the independent variable is introduced and removed one or more times. We typically begin the study by taking baseline measures—equivalent to a control condition in a group design. In other words, we need to assess how the participant performs before we introduce the independent variable. Once baseline measures have been taken, we can introduce the independent variable. At this point, we have a simple AB design, with A representing baseline performance and B representing the introduction of the independent variable. The problem with this simple pretest/posttest design is that if a change in behavior is observed, we do not know whether it is due to the introduction of the independent variable or to some extraneous variable (confound) that happened to occur at the same time. Thus, in order to improve on this design, it is typically recommended that some type of reversal be introduced.

**reversal design** A single-case design in which the independent variable is introduced and removed one or more times.

*ABA Reversal Designs.* An **ABA reversal design** involves taking baseline measures (A), introducing the independent variable (B) and measuring behavior again, and then removing the independent variable and retaking the baseline measures (A). In this manner, we can see whether the behavior changes with the introduction of the independent variable and then whether it changes back to baseline performance once the independent variable is removed. This combination of changes gives us a better indication of the effectiveness of the treatment. The problem with this design is an ethical one. If the treatment helped to improve the participant's life in some way, it is not ethical to end the experiment by removing the treatment and possibly return the participant to his or her original state. Thus, a further improvement over the ABA design is the ABAB design.

**ABA reversal design** A single-case design in which baseline measures are taken, the independent variable is introduced and behavior is measured, and the independent variable is then removed and baseline measures taken again.

*ABAB Reversal Designs.* The **ABAB reversal design** involves reintroducing the independent variable after the second baseline measurement. Thus, the experiment ends with the treatment, making it ethically more appealing. In addition, it allows us to further assess the effectiveness of the independent variable by introducing it a second time. A study by Hall, Axelrod, Foundopoulos, Shellman, Campbell, and Cranston (1971), assessing the effectiveness of punishment in reducing the aggressive behavior of a 7-year-old deaf girl, illustrates this design. The participant pinched and bit both herself and anyone else with whom she came in contact. The frequency of these behaviors averaged 72 occurrences per day, preventing normal classroom

**ABAB reversal design** A design in which baseline and independent variable conditions are reversed twice.

FIGURE 12.3
Number of bites and
pinches during the
school day
SOURCE: From "The Effective Use
of Punishment to Modify
Behavior in the Classroom"
by R. V. Hall, S. Axelrod,
M. Foundopoulos, J. Shellman,
R. A. Campbell, &
S. S. Cranston, 1971, in
K. D. O'Leary & S. O'Leary
(Eds.), Classroom Management:
The Successful Use of Behavior
Modification, p. 175. Copyright
© 1972 by Allyn & Bacon.
Reprinted with permission
of Pearson Education.

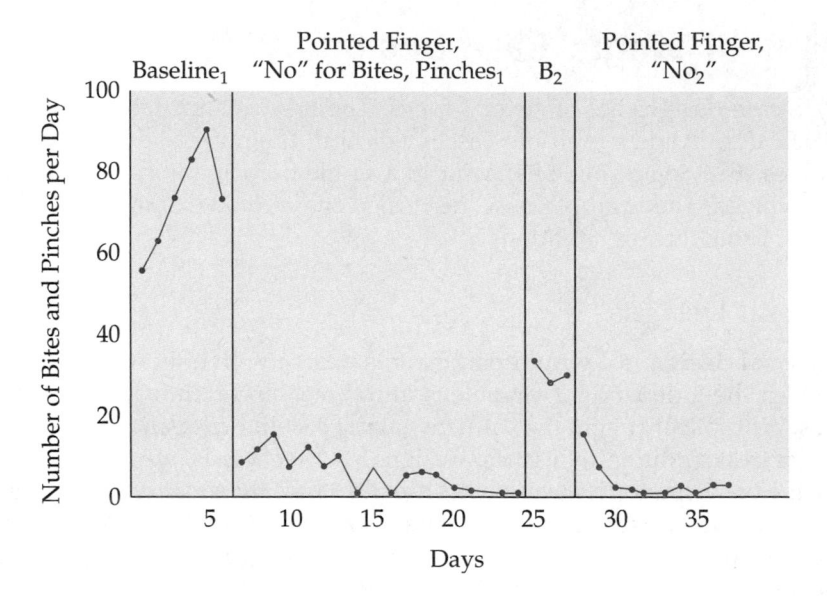

instruction. As can be seen in Figure 12.3, after a baseline measurement for 5 days, the experimenters introduced the treatment, in which the teacher pointed at the participant and shouted "NO!" after each bite or pinch. The change in the participant's behavior with the introduction of the treatment was quite dramatic even on the first day of treatment. Even though the participant was deaf, the treatment was still very effective. The number of bites and pinches per day dropped to zero by the end of the first treatment period. The researchers then returned to baseline for a few days to eliminate the possibility of an alternative explanation for the behavior change. As can be seen in the figure, the number of bites and pinches increased during this time. The treatment was then reintroduced on day 26, and once again the number of bites and pinches per day declined dramatically. Thus, the ABAB reversal design has the advantage of being more ethical than the ABA design and of offering two baseline measures and two treatment measures in order to eliminate alternative explanations of behavior change. This design could be further extended to an ABABA design or an ABABAB design.

## Multiple-Baseline Designs

Because single-case designs are a type of within-participants design, carry-over effects from one condition to another are of concern. For example, if the treatment in a reversal design permanently changes the participant, then it would not be possible to reverse back to a baseline condition after introducing the treatment. In other words, it would not be possible to use a reversal design. In addition, in some situations it would be unethical to treat people (improve their condition) and then remove the treatment to assess a baseline condition. In these situations, a multiple-baseline design is recommended. In a **multiple-baseline design,** rather than reversing the treatment and baseline

**multiple-baseline design**
A single-case or small-n design in which the effect of introducing the independent variable is assessed over multiple participants, behaviors, or situations.

conditions numerous times, we assess the effect of introducing the treatment over multiple participants, behaviors, or situations. We control for confounds not by reversing back to baseline after treatment, as in a reversal design, but by introducing the treatment at different times across different people, behaviors, or situations.

*Multiple Baselines Across Participants.* A **multiple-baseline design across participants** is a small-*n* design in which measures are taken at baseline and after the introduction of the independent variable at different times for different people. For example, Hall and his colleagues (1971) assessed the effectiveness of threatened punishment for low grades across three 10th-grade students. The three students were all failing their French class. The punishment was being kept after school for a half-hour of tutoring whenever they received a grade lower than C on their daily French quiz. Figure 12.4 shows the baseline and treatment results across the three students. Notice that the treatment was introduced at staggered times across the participants to help control for possible confounds. For the first participant, Dave, the threat of punishment was introduced on day 11, for Roy on day 16, and for Debbie on day 21. As shown in the graph, all participants immediately improved their quiz grades once the treatment was introduced. In fact, none of the three participants ever actually received extra tutoring because their grades improved immediately after the threat of punishment was introduced. By altering when the treatment is introduced to each participant, we minimize the

**multiple-baseline design across participants** A small-*n* design in which measures are taken at baseline and after the introduction of the independent variable at different times across multiple participants.

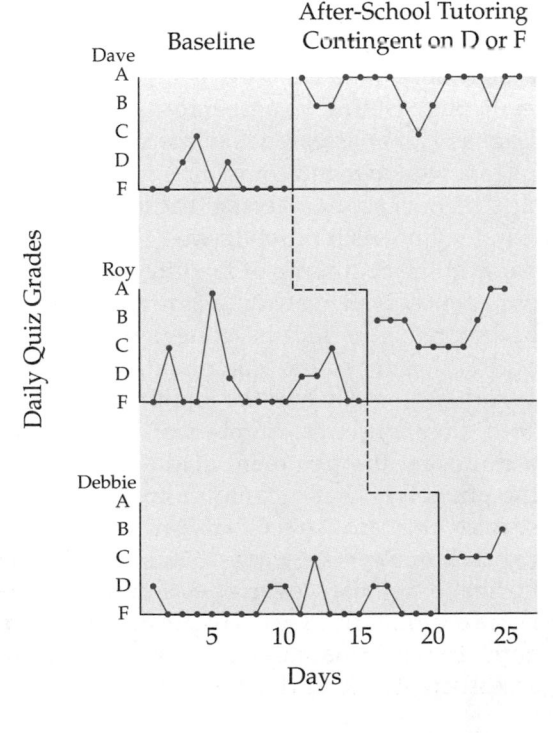

**FIGURE 12.4**
**Quiz grades for three high school French students**
SOURCE: From "The Effective Use of Punishment to Modify Behavior in the Classroom" by R. V. Hall, S. Axelrod, M. Foundopoulos, J. Shellman, R. A. Campbell, & S. S. Cranston, 1971, in K. D. O'Leary & S. O'Leary (Eds.), *Classroom Management: The Successful Use of Behavior Modification*, p. 177. Copyright © 1972 by Allyn & Bacon. Reprinted with permission of Pearson Education.

possibility that some other extraneous variable produced the results. In other words, because behavior changed for each participant right after the treatment was introduced and because the treatment was introduced at different times to each participant, we can feel fairly confident that it was the treatment and not some extraneous variable that caused the behavior change.

*Multiple Baselines Across Behaviors.* An alternative multiple-baseline design uses only one participant and assesses the effects of introducing a treatment over several behaviors. This design is referred to as a **multiple-baseline design across behaviors.** For example, imagine that a teacher wanted to minimize the number of problem behaviors emitted by a student during the school day. The teacher might begin by taking baseline measures on all of the problem behaviors (for example, aggressive behaviors, talking out of turn, and temper tantrums). The treatment would be introduced first for only aggressive behaviors. Several days after introducing the treatment for aggressive behaviors, the teacher would introduce the treatment for talking out of turn, and then several days later for temper tantrums. By introducing the treatment for different behaviors at different times, we can eliminate potential confounds. In other words, if all of the treatments were introduced at the same time and behavior changed, we would not know whether the change was due to the treatment or to some extraneous variable that also changed at the same time. If we see a systematic improvement across behaviors when the treatment is introduced at different times, we can feel fairly certain that it was the treatment that brought about the change.

**multiple-baseline design across behaviors** A single-case design in which measures are taken at baseline and after the introduction of the independent variable at different times across multiple behaviors.

*Multiple Baselines Across Situations.* A third way to use the multiple-baseline design is to assess the introduction of treatment across different situations—a **multiple-baseline design across situations.** For example, Hall and his colleagues (1971) assessed the effectiveness of punishment on a young boy's crying, whining, and complaining behavior during school. The child emitted these behaviors only during reading and math classes each day. Hall devised a system in which the child was given five slips of colored paper bearing his name at the beginning of reading and arithmetic periods each day. One slip of paper was taken away each time he cried, whined, or complained. As can be seen in Figure 12.5, baseline performance was established for the number of cries, whines, and complaints in each class. Then the treatment was introduced on day 6 in the reading class and on day 11 in the math class. In both situations, the number of cries, whines, and complaints declined. Introducing the treatment at different times in the two classes minimizes the possibility that a confounding variable is responsible for the behavior change. You can also see that Hall then reversed the treatment and went back to baseline. Reversal was possible in this situation because the treatment did not have any carryover effects and because reversing the treatment had no ethical ramifications. The treatment was then reintroduced on day 21 in both classes. Thus, this design is really a multiple-baseline reversal design across situations.

**multiple-baseline design across situations** A single-case design in which measures are taken at baseline and after the introduction of the independent variable at different times across multiple situations.

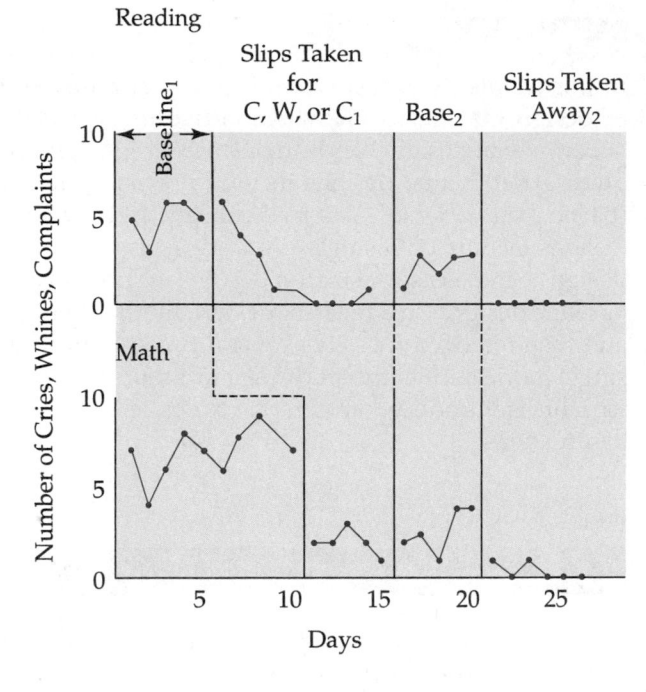

**FIGURE 12.5**
**Frequency of cries (C), whines (W), and complaints ($C_1$) during reading and math classes**

Source: From "The Effective Use of Punishment to Modify Behavior in the Classroom" by R. V. Hall, S. Axelrod, M. Foundopoulos, J. Shellman, R. A. Campbell, & S. S. Cranston, 1971, in K. D. O'Leary & S. O'Leary (Eds.), *Classroom Management: The Successful Use of Behavior Modification*, p. 180. Copyright © 1972 by Allyn & Bacon. Reprinted with permission of Pearson Education.

| Single-Case Designs | IN REVIEW |
| --- | --- |

### TYPES OF SINGLE-CASE DESIGNS

| Reversal Designs | Multiple-Baseline Designs |
| --- | --- |
| ABA design: Measures taken at baseline, after introduction of independent variable, and at baseline again | Across participants: Measures taken at baseline and after introduction of independent variable at different times across multiple participants |
| ABAB design: Measures taken at baseline, after introduction of independent variable, at baseline again, and after introduction of independent variable again | Across behaviors: Measures taken at baseline and after introduction of independent variable at different times across multiple behaviors |
| | Across situations: Measures taken at baseline and after introduction of independent variable at different times across multiple situations |

CRITICAL THINKING CHECK 12.3

1. Explain why single-case research is considered a variation of a within-participants design. Why might it also be considered a variation of a quasi-experimental design?
2. Why is an ABAB design considered more ethical than an ABA design?
3. How do reversal designs attempt to control for confounds?
4. How do multiple-baseline designs attempt to control for confounds?

# Summary

In this chapter, you were introduced to quasi-experimental designs—a type of design that falls somewhere between a correlational design and a true experimental design—and single-case designs. Important concepts related to quasi-experimental designs include nonmanipulated independent variables (participant variables), internal validity, and confounds. Quasi-experimental designs include both single-group designs and nonequivalent control group designs. Single-case or small-$n$ designs include reversal designs and multiple-baseline designs. In a reversal design, the independent variable is introduced and then removed (possibly several times) in order to assess its effect on the single participant in the study. In a multiple-baseline design, the independent variable is introduced at different times across a few participants, behaviors, or situations.

## KEY TERMS

nonmanipulated independent variable
single-group posttest-only design
single-group pretest/posttest design
single-group time-series design
nonequivalent control group posttest-only design

nonequivalent control group pretest/posttest design
multiple-group time-series design
single-case design
small-$n$ design
reversal design
ABA reversal design
ABAB reversal design

multiple-baseline design
multiple-baseline design across participants
multiple-baseline design across behaviors
multiple-baseline design across situations

## CHAPTER EXERCISES

(Answers to odd-numbered exercises appear in Appendix C.)

1. What is the difference between a true experimental design and a quasi-experimental design?
2. A psychology professor is interested in whether implementing weekly quizzes improves student learning. She decides to use the weekly quizzes in one section of her introductory psychology class and not to use them in another section of the same course. Which type of quasi-experimental design do you recommend for this study?
3. If the psychology professor in Exercise 2 had access to only one section of introductory psychology, describe how she might use a single-group design to assess the effectiveness of

weekly quizzes. Which of the three single-group designs would you recommend?
4. Identify some possible confounds in each of the studies you outlined in your answers to Exercises 2 and 3.
5. Give three reasons a researcher might choose to use a single-case design.
6. Explain what a reversal design is. Identify advantages and disadvantages to using reversal designs.
7. How does a multiple-baseline design differ from a reversal design?
8. When conducting single-case research, why do we look at graphs of data rather than statistically analyzing the data as with other designs?

## CRITICAL THINKING CHECK ANSWERS

### 12.1

1. Gender, religious affiliation, ethnicity, and visual acuity would all be participant variables.

2. We have slightly more control in a quasi-experimental study than in a correlational study because we typically introduce some sort of treatment. However, because participants come to us as members of either the control or the "experimental" group, we cannot conclude that the independent variable definitely caused changes in the dependent variable, as we can when using a true experimental design.

### 12.2

1. This is a nonequivalent control group posttest-only design. The participants came to the study as either smokers or nonsmokers. We then took posttest measures on them. We cannot conclude that any observed differences in lung disease are due to smoking because variables other than smoking may differ between the two groups.

2. Pretest/posttest designs are an improvement because they allow us to assess whether the groups are similar or different before we introduce the treatment and how much they change after the treatment is introduced. By this means,

we can determine whether the groups are in fact equivalent before the treatment.

### 12.3

1. Single-case research is considered a variation of a within-participants design because it involves studying one or a few participants in both the control and experimental conditions. It is also similar to the single-group pretest/posttest quasi-experimental design in that it involves taking pretest and posttest measures on a single participant rather than on a group of participants.

2. An ABAB design is considered more ethical than an ABA design because the final condition involves administering the treatment to the participant, rather than leaving the participant with no treatment (baseline).

3. Reversal designs attempt to control for confounds by reversing the baseline and treatment conditions one or more times in order to assess the impact on behavior.

4. Multiple-baseline designs attempt to control for confounds by introducing the treatment at differing time intervals to a few different people, to the same person in different situations, or to the same person across different behaviors.

## WEB RESOURCES

Check your knowledge of the content in this chapter by taking the practice quiz at www.Wadsworth.com. Or, for step-by-step practice and information, check out the Statistics and Research Methods Workshops at http://psychology.wadsworth.com/workshops.

## LAB RESOURCES

For hands-on experience using the research methods described in this chapter, see Chapter 9 ("Field Experiments") in *Research Methods Laboratory Manual* *for Psychology*, 2nd ed., by William Langston (Belmont, CA: Wadsworth, 2005).

# 13 Nonparametric Procedures

S tatistics used to analyze nominal and ordinal data are referred to as *nonparametric tests*. You may remember from Chapter 7 that a nonparametric test is a test that does not involve the use of any population parameters. In other words, $\mu$ and $\sigma$ are not needed, and the underlying distribution does not have to be normal. In addition, most nonparametric tests are based on fewer assumptions than parametric tests. Nonparametric tests are usually easier to compute than parametric tests. They are, however, less powerful than parametric tests, meaning that it is more difficult to reject the null hypothesis when it is false. In this chapter, we will look at two nonparametric tests for nominal data: the $\chi^2$ goodness-of-fit test and the $\chi^2$ test of independence. We will also discuss two tests for ordinal data: the Wilcoxon rank-sum test, used with between-participants designs, and the Wilcoxon matched-pairs signed-ranks $T$ test, used with correlated-groups designs.

# Chi-Square ($\chi^2$) Goodness-of-Fit Test: What It Is and What It Does

The **chi-square ($\chi^2$) goodness-of-fit test** is used for comparing categorical information against what we would expect based on previous knowledge. As such, it tests the **observed frequency** (the frequency with which participants fall into a category) against the **expected frequency** (the frequency expected in a category if the sample data represent the population). It is a nondirectional test, meaning that the alternative hypothesis is neither one-tailed nor two-tailed. The alternative hypothesis for a $\chi^2$ goodness-of-fit test is that the observed data do not fit the expected frequencies for the population, and the null hypothesis is that they do fit the expected frequencies for the population. There is no conventional way to write these hypotheses in symbols, as we have done with the previous statistical tests. To illustrate the $\chi^2$ goodness-of-fit test, let's look at a situation in which its use is appropriate.

**chi-square ($\chi^2$) goodness-of-fit test** A nonparametric inferential procedure that determines how well an observed frequency distribution fits an expected distribution.

**observed frequency** The frequency with which participants fall into a category.

**expected frequency** The frequency expected in a category if the sample data represent the population.

## Calculations for the $\chi^2$ Goodness-of-Fit Test

Suppose that a researcher is interested in determining whether the teenage pregnancy rate at a particular high school is different from the rate statewide. Assume that the rate statewide is 17%. A random sample of 80 female students is selected from the target high school. Seven of the students are either pregnant now or have been pregnant previously. The $\chi^2$ goodness-of-fit test measures the observed frequencies against the expected frequencies. The observed and expected frequencies are presented in Table 13.1.

As can be seen in the table, the observed frequencies represent the number of high school females in the sample of 80 who were pregnant versus not pregnant. The expected frequencies represent what we would expect based on chance, given what is known about the population. In this case, we would expect 17% of the females to be pregnant because this is the rate statewide. If we take 17% of 80 ($0.17 \times 80 = 14$), we would expect 14 of the students to be pregnant. By the same token, we would expect 83% of the students

**TABLE 13.1  Observed and expected frequencies for $\chi^2$ goodness-of-fit example**

| FREQUENCIES | PREGNANT | NOT PREGNANT |
|---|---|---|
| Observed | 7 | 73 |
| Expected | 14 | 66 |

$(0.83 \times 80 = 66)$ to be not pregnant. If the calculated expected frequencies are correct, when summed they should equal the sample size $(14 + 66 = 80)$.

Once the observed and expected frequencies have been determined, we can calculate $\chi^2$ using the following formula:

$$\chi^2 = \sum \frac{(O - E)^2}{E}$$

where $O$ is the observed frequency, $E$ is the expected frequency, and $\Sigma$ indicates that we must sum the indicated fractions for each category in the study (in this case, for the pregnant and not-pregnant groups). Using this formula with the present example, we have

$$\chi^2 = \frac{(7 - 14)^2}{14} + \frac{(73 - 66)^6}{66}$$

$$= \frac{(-7)^2}{14} + \frac{(7)^2}{66}$$

$$= \frac{49}{14} + \frac{49}{66}$$

$$= 3.5 + 0.74$$

$$= 4.24$$

## Interpreting the $\chi^2$ Goodness-of-Fit Test

The null hypothesis is rejected if $\chi^2_{obt}$ is greater than $\chi^2_{cv}$. The $\chi^2_{cv}$ is found in Table A.7 in Appendix A at the back of the book. To use the table, you need to know the degrees of freedom for the $\chi^2$ test. This is the number of categories minus 1. In our example, we have two categories (pregnant and not pregnant); thus, we have 1 degree of freedom. At alpha = .05, then, $\chi^2_{cv} = 3.84$. Our $\chi^2_{obt}$ of 4.24 is larger than the critical value, so we can reject the null hypothesis and conclude that the observed frequency of pregnancy is significantly lower than expected by chance. In other words, the female teens at the target high school have a significantly lower pregnancy rate than would be expected based on the statewide rate.

## Assumptions and Appropriate Use of the $\chi^2$ Goodness-of-Fit Test

Although the $\chi^2$ goodness-of-fit test is a nonparametric test and therefore less restrictive than a parametric test, it does have its own assumptions. First, the test is appropriate for nominal (categorical) data. If data are measured on a higher scale of measurement, they can be transformed to a nominal scale. Second, the frequencies in each cell should not be too small. If the frequency in any cell is too small (<5), then the $\chi^2$ test should not be conducted. Last, to be generalizable to the population, the sample should be randomly selected and the observations must be independent. In other words, each observation must be based on the score of a different participant.

# Chi-Square ($\chi^2$) Test of Independence: What It Is and What It Does

The logic of the **chi-square ($\chi^2$) test of independence** is the same as for any $\chi^2$ statistic—we are comparing how well an observed breakdown of people over various categories fits some expected breakdown (such as an equal breakdown). In other words, a $\chi^2$ test compares an observed frequency distribution to an expected frequency distribution. If we find a difference, we determine whether the difference is greater than what would be expected based on chance. The difference between the $\chi^2$ test of independence the $\chi^2$ goodness-of-fit test is that the goodness-of-fit test compares how well an observed frequency distribution of *one* nominal variable fits some expected pattern of frequencies, whereas the test of independence compares how well an observed frequency distribution of *two* nominal variables fits some expected pattern of frequencies. The formula we use is the same as for the $\chi^2$ goodness-of-fit test described previously:

$$\chi^2 = \sum \frac{(O-E)^2}{E}$$

The null hypothesis and the alternative hypothesis are similar to those used with the *t* tests. The null hypothesis is that there are no observed differences in frequency between the groups we are comparing; the alternative hypothesis is that there are differences in frequency between the groups and that the differences are greater than we would expect based on chance.

**chi-square ($\chi^2$) test of independence** A nonparametric inferential test used when frequency data have been collected to determine how well an observed breakdown of people over various categories fits some expected breakdown.

## Calculations for the $\chi^2$ Test of Independence

As a means of illustrating the $\chi^2$ test of independence, imagine that a sample of randomly chosen teenagers are categorized as having been employed as babysitters or never having been employed in this capacity. The teenagers are then asked whether they have ever taken a first aid course. In this case, we would like to determine whether babysitters are more likely to have taken first aid than those who have never worked as babysitters. Because we are examining the observed frequency distribution of two nominal variables (babysitting and taking a first aid class), the $\chi^2$ test of independence is appropriate. We find that 65 of the 100 babysitters have had a first aid course and 35 of the babysitters have not. In the non-babysitter group, 43 out of 90 have had a first aid course, and the remaining 47 have not. Table 13.2 is a contingency table showing the observed and expected frequencies.

**TABLE 13.2  Observed and expected frequencies for babysitters and non-babysitters having taken a first aid course**

| | | TAKEN FIRST AID COURSE | | |
| | | Yes | No | ROW TOTALS |
|---|---|---|---|---|
| Employed as | Yes | 65 (57) | 35 (43) | 100 |
| Babysitters | No | 43 (51) | 47 (39) | 90 |
| Column Totals | | 108 | 82 | 190 |

To determine the expected frequency for each cell, we use this formula:

$$E = \frac{(RT)(CT)}{N}$$

where $RT$ is the row total, $CT$ is the column total, and $N$ is the total number of observations. Thus, the expected frequency for the upper left cell is

$$E = \frac{(100)(108)}{190} = \frac{10,800}{190} = 56.8$$

The expected frequencies appear in parentheses in Table 13.2. Notice that the expected frequencies when summed equal 190, the $N$ in the study. Once we have the observed and expected frequencies, we can calculate $\chi^2$:

$$\chi^2 = \sum \frac{(O-E)^2}{E}$$

$$= \frac{(65-57)^2}{57} + \frac{(35-43)^2}{43} + \frac{(43-51)^2}{51} + \frac{(47-39)^2}{39}$$

$$= 1.123 + 1.488 + 1.255 + 1.641 = 5.507$$

## Interpreting the $\chi^2$ Test of Independence

The degrees of freedom for this $\chi^2$ test are equal to $(r-1)(c-1)$, where $r$ is the number of rows and $c$ is the number of columns. In our example, we have $(2-1)(2-1) = 1$. We now refer to Table A.7 in Appendix A to identify $\chi^2_{cv}$ for $df = 1$. At the .05 level, $\chi^2_{cv} = 3.841$. Our $\chi^2_{obt}$ of 5.507 exceeds the critical value, and we reject the null hypothesis. In other words, there is a significant difference between babysitters and non-babysitters in terms of their having taken a first aid class—significantly more babysitters have taken a first aid class. In APA style, this result is reported as $\chi^2(1, N = 190) = 5.507, p < .05$.

## Effect Size: Phi Coefficient

**phi coefficient** An inferential test used to determine effect size for a chi-square test.

As with many of the statistics discussed in previous chapters, we can also compute the effect size for a $\chi^2$ test of independence. For a $2 \times 2$ contingency table, we use the **phi coefficient** (ϕ), where

$$\phi = \sqrt{\frac{\chi^2}{N}}$$

In our example, this is

$$\phi = \sqrt{\frac{5.507}{190}} = \sqrt{0.02898} = 0.17$$

Cohen's (1988) specifications for the phi coefficient indicate that a phi coefficient of .10 is a small effect, .30 is a medium effect, and .50 is a large effect. Our effect size is small. Hence, even though the $\chi^2$ is significant, the effect size is not large. In other words, the difference observed in whether a teenager had taken a first aid class is not strongly accounted for by being a babysitter. Why do you think the $\chi^2$ was significant even though the effect size was small? If you attribute this to the large sample size, you are correct.

## Assumptions of the $\chi^2$ Test of Independence

The assumptions underlying the $\chi^2$ test of independence are the same as those noted previously for the $\chi^2$ goodness-of-fit test:

- The sample is random.
- The observations are independent.
- The data are nominal.

| $\chi^2$ Tests | | IN REVIEW |
|---|---|---|
| | **$\chi^2$ Goodness-of-Fit Test** | **$\chi^2$ Test of Independence** |
| What It Is | A nonparametric test comparing observed frequencies on one nominal variable to expected frequencies based on population data | A nonparametric test comparing observed to expected frequencies for a two-group between-participants design |
| What It Does | Will identify how well an observed frequency distribution of one nominal variable fits some expected pattern of frequencies | Will identify differences in frequency on two variables between groups |
| Assumptions | Random sample | Random sample |
| | Independent observations | Independent observations |

1. How do the $\chi^2$ tests differ in use from a $t$ test?
2. Why is the $\chi^2$ goodness-of-fit test a nonparametric test, and what does this mean?

CRITICAL THINKING CHECK 13.1

# Wilcoxon Rank-Sum Test: What It Is and What It Does

**Wilcoxon rank-sum test**
A nonparametric inferential test for comparing sample medians of two independent groups of scores.

The **Wilcoxon rank-sum test** is similar to the independent-groups $t$ test; however, it uses ordinal data rather than interval-ratio data and compares medians rather than means. Imagine that a teacher of fifth-grade students wants to compare the numbers of books read per term by female versus male students in her class. Rather than reporting the data as the actual number of books read (interval-ratio data), she ranks the female and male students, giving the student who read the fewest books a rank of 1 and the student who read the most books the highest rank. She does this because the distribution representing numbers of books read is skewed (not normal). She predicts that the girls will read more books than the boys. Thus, $H_0$ is that the median number of books read does not differ between girls and boys ($Md_{girls} = Md_{boys}$), and $H_a$ is that the median number of books read is greater for girls than for boys? ($Md_{girls} > Md_{boys}$). The numbers of books read by each group and the corresponding rankings are presented in Table 13.3. In our example none of the students read the same number of books, thus each student receives a different rank. However, if two students had read the same number of books (for example if there were two students who each read 10 books), these scores would take positions 1 and 2 in the ranking, each would be given a rank of 1.5 (halfway between the ranks of 1 and 2), and the next rank assigned would be 3.

## Calculations for the Wilcoxon Rank-Sum Test

As a check to confirm that the ranking has been done correctly, the highest rank should be equal to $n_1 + n_2$; in our example, $n_1 + n_2 = 12$ and the highest rank is also 12. In addition, the sum of the ranks should equal $N(N + 1)/2$, where $N$ is the total number of people in the study. In our example, $12(12 + 1)/2 = 78$. If we add the ranks ($1 + 2 + 3 + 4 + 5 + 6 + 7 + 8 + 9 + 10 + 11 + 12$), they also sum to 78. Thus, the ranking was done correctly.

**TABLE 13.3  Numbers of books read and corresponding ranks for female and male students**

| GIRLS | | BOYS | |
|---|---|---|---|
| X | Rank | X | Rank |
| 20 | 4 | 10 | 1 |
| 24 | 8 | 17 | 2 |
| 29 | 9 | 23 | 7 |
| 33 | 10 | 19 | 3 |
| 57 | 12 | 22 | 6 |
| 35 | 11 | 21 | 5 |
| | | | $\Sigma = 24$ |

The Wilcoxon test is completed by first summing the ranks for the group expected to have the smaller total. Because the teacher expects the boys to read less, she sums their ranks. This sum, as seen in the Table 13.3, is 24.

## Interpreting the Wilcoxon Rank-Sum Test

Using Table A.8 in Appendix A, we see that for a one-tailed test at the .05 level, if $n_1 = 6$ and $n_2 = 6$, the maximum sum of the ranks in the group expected to be lower is 28. If the sum of the ranks of the group expected to be lower (the boys in this situation) exceeds 28, then the result is not significant. Please note that this is the only statistic that we have discussed so far where the obtained value needs to be *equal to or less than* the critical value in order to be statistically significant. When we use this table, $n_1$ is always the smaller of the two groups; if the values of $n$ are equal, it does not matter which is $n_1$ and which is $n_2$. Moreover, Table A.8 presents the critical values for one-tailed tests only. If a two-tailed test is used, the table can be adapted by dividing the alpha level in half. In other words, we would use the critical values for the .025 level from the table to determine the critical value at the .05 level for a two-tailed test. We find that the sum of the ranks of the group predicted to have lower scores (24) is less than the cutoff for significance. Our conclusion is to reject the null hypothesis. In other words, we observed that the ranks in the two groups differed, there were not an equal number of high and low ranks in each group, and one group (the girls in this case) read significantly more books than the other. If we report this finding in APA style, it appears as $W_s (n_1 = 6, n_2 = 6) = 24, p < .05$.

## Assumptions of the Wilcoxon Rank-Sum Test

The Wilcoxon rank-sum test is a nonparametric procedure that is analogous to the independent-groups $t$ test. The assumptions of the test are as follows:

- The data are ratio, interval, or ordinal in scale, all of which must be converted to ranked (ordinal) data before conducting the test.
- The underlying distribution is not normal.
- The observations are independent.

If the observations are not independent (a correlated-groups design), then the Wilcoxon matched-pairs signed-ranks $T$ test should be used.

# Wilcoxon Matched-Pairs Signed-Ranks *T* Test: What It Is and What It Does

The **Wilcoxon matched-pairs signed-ranks *T* test** is similar to the correlated-groups $t$ test, except that it is nonparametric and compares medians rather than means. Imagine that the same teacher in the previous problem wants to compare the numbers of books read by all students (female and male) over two terms. During the first term, the teacher keeps track of how many books

**Wilcoxon matched-pairs signed-ranks *T* test** A nonparametric inferential test for comparing sample medians of two dependent or related groups of scores.

each student reads. During the second term, the teacher institutes a reading reinforcement program through which students can earn prizes based on the number of books they read. The numbers of books read by students are once again measured. As before, the distribution representing numbers of books read is skewed (not normal). Thus, a nonparametric statistic is necessary. However, in this case, the design is within-participants—two measures are taken on each student, one before the reading reinforcement program is instituted and one after the program is instituted.

Table 13.4 shows the numbers of books read by the students across the two terms. Notice that the numbers of books read during the first term are the data used in the previous Wilcoxon rank-sum test. The teacher uses a one-tailed test and predicts that students will read more books after the reinforcement program is instituted. Thus, $H_0$ is that the median numbers of books read do not differ between the two terms ($Md_{before} = Md_{after}$), and $H_a$ is that the median number of books read is greater after the reinforcement program is instituted ($Md_{before} < Md_{after}$).

## Calculations for the Wilcoxon Matched-Pairs Signed-Ranks $T$ Test

The first step in completing the Wilcoxon signed-ranks test is to compute a difference score for each individual. In this case, we have subtracted the number of books read in term 2 from the number of books read in term 1 for

**TABLE 13.4  Numbers of books read in each term**

| TERM 1 (NO REINFORCEMENT) | TERM 2 (REINFORCEMENT IMPLEMENTED) | DIFFERENCE SCORE ($D$) (TERM 1 − TERM 2) | RANK | SIGNED RANK |
|:---:|:---:|:---:|:---:|:---:|
| $X$ | $X$ | | | |
| 10 | 15 | −5 | 4.5 | −4.5 |
| 17 | 23 | −6 | 6 | −6 |
| 19 | 20 | −1 | 1.5 | −1.5 |
| 20 | 20 | 0 | — | — |
| 21 | 28 | −7 | 8 | −8 |
| 22 | 26 | −4 | 3 | −3 |
| 23 | 24 | −1 | 1.5 | −1.5 |
| 24 | 29 | −5 | 4.5 | −4.5 |
| 29 | 37 | −8 | 10 | −10 |
| 33 | 40 | −7 | 8 | −8 |
| 57 | 50 | 7 | 8 | 8 |
| 35 | 55 | −20 | 11 | −11 |
| | | | | $+\Sigma = 8$ |
| | | | | $-\Sigma = 58$ |

each student. Keep in mind the logic of a matched-pairs test. If the reinforcement program had no effect, we would expect all of the difference scores to be 0 or very close to 0. Columns 1–3 in Table 13.4 give the numbers of books read in each term and the difference scores. Next, we rank the absolute values of the difference scores. This is shown in column 4 of Table 13.4. Notice that the difference score of 0 is not ranked. Also note what happens when ranks are tied; for example, there are two difference scores of $-1$. These difference scores take positions 1 and 2 in the ranking; each is given a rank of 1.5 (halfway between the ranks of 1 and 2), and the next rank assigned is 3. As a check, the highest rank should equal the number of ranked scores. In our problem, we ranked 11 difference scores; thus, the highest rank should be 11, and it is.

Once the ranks have been determined, we attach to each rank the sign of the previously calculated difference score. This is represented in the last column of Table 13.4. The final step necessary to complete the Wilcoxon signed-ranks test is to sum the positive ranks and then sum the negative ranks. Once again, if there is no difference in the numbers of books read across the two terms, we would expect the sum of the positive ranks to equal or be very close to the sum of the negative ranks. The sums of the positive and negative ranks are shown at the bottom of the last column in Table 13.4.

For a two-tailed test, $T_{obt}$ is equal to the smaller of the summed ranks. Thus, if we were computing a two-tailed test, our $T_{obt}$ would equal 8. However, our test is one-tailed; the teacher predicted that the number of books read would increase during the reinforcement program. For a one-tailed test, we predict whether we expect more positive or negative difference scores. Because we subtracted term 2 (the term in which students were reinforced for reading) from term 1, we would expect more negative differences. The $T_{obt}$ for a one-tailed test is the sum of the signed ranks *predicted* to be smaller. In this case, we would predict the summed ranks for the positive differences to be smaller than that for negative differences. Thus, $T_{obt}$ for a one-tailed test is also 8.

## Interpreting the Wilcoxon Matched-Pairs Signed-Ranks $T$ Test

Using Table A.9 in Appendix A, we see that for a one-tailed test at the .05 level with $N = 11$ (we use $N = 11$ and not 12 because we ranked only 11 of the 12 difference scores), the maximum sum of the ranks in the group expected to be lower is 13. If the sum of the ranks for the group expected to be lower exceeds 13, then the result is not significant. Please note that, as with the Wilcoxon rank-sum test, the obtained value needs to be *equal to or less than* the critical value in order to be statistically significant. Our conclusion is to reject the null hypothesis. In other words, we observed that the sum of the positive versus the negative ranks differed, or the number of books read in the two conditions differed; significantly more books were read in the reinforcement condition than in the no reinforcement condition. If we report this in APA style, it appears as $T (N=11) = 8, p < .05$.

### Assumptions of the Wilcoxon Matched-Pairs Signed-Ranks *T* Test

The Wilcoxon matched-pairs signed-ranks *T* test is a nonparametric procedure that is analogous to the correlated-groups *t* test. The assumptions of the test are as follows:

- The data are ratio, interval, or ordinal in scale, all of which must be converted to ranked (ordinal) data before conducting the test.
- The underlying distribution is not normal.
- The observations are dependent or related (a correlated-groups design).

# Beyond the Wilcoxon Tests

Just as the ANOVA is an extension of a *t* test, the Wilcoxon tests have an analogous extension. For a between-participants design with more than two groups, the Kruskal-Wallis test is appropriate. Like the Wilcoxon tests, the Kruskal-Wallis is appropriate when the data are ordinal or if the involved populations are not normally distributed. The analogous test (more than two groups, ordinal data, and/or skewed distributions) for use with a within-participants design is the Friedman rank test. Each of these tests is beyond the scope of the present text. However, coverage of these tests can be found in more comprehensive statistics texts.

| IN REVIEW | Wilcoxon Tests | |
|---|---|---|
| | **TYPE OF TEST** | |
| | **Wilcoxon Rank-Sum Test** | **Wilcoxon Matched-Pairs Signed-Ranks *T* Test** |
| What It Is | A nonparametric test for a two-group between-participants design | A nonparametric test for a two-group correlated-groups (within- or matched-participants) design |
| What It Does | Will identify differences in ranks on a variable between groups | Will identify differences in signed ranks on a variable for correlated groups |
| Assumptions | Ordinal data | Ordinal data |
| | Distribution is not normal | Distribution is not normal |
| | Independent observations | Dependent or related observations |

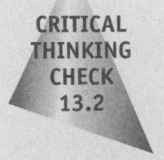

CRITICAL THINKING CHECK 13.2

1. I have recently conducted a study in which I ranked my participants (college students) on height and weight. I am interested in whether there are any differences in height and weight depending on whether the participant is an athlete (defined as being a member of a sports team) or not an athlete. Which statistic would you

recommend using to analyze these data? If the actual height (in inches) and weight (in pounds) data were available, what statistic would be appropriate?

2. Determine the difference scores and ranks for the set of matched-pairs data below. Finally, calculate $T$ for these data, and determine whether the $T$ score is significant for a two-tailed test.

| Participant | Score 1 | Score 2 |
|:-----------:|:-------:|:-------:|
| 1 | 12 | 15 |
| 2 | 10 | 9 |
| 3 | 15 | 14 |
| 4 | 17 | 23 |
| 5 | 17 | 16 |
| 6 | 22 | 19 |
| 7 | 20 | 30 |
| 8 | 22 | 25 |

# Summary

We discussed four different nonparametric statistics. The $\chi^2$ goodness-of-fit test examines how well an observed frequency distribution of one nominal variable fits some expected pattern of frequencies. The $\chi^2$ test of independence once again compares observed frequencies to expected frequencies. The difference here is that it compares how well an observed frequency distribution of two nominal variables fits some expected pattern of frequencies.

The final two nonparametric statistics covered were the Wilcoxon tests, which are used with ordinal data. The Wilcoxon rank-sum test compares ranked data for two groups of different participants—a between-participants design—in order to determine whether there are significant differences in the rankings in one group versus the other group. The Wilcoxon matched-pairs signed-ranks test compares ranked data for a single group of participants (or two groups of matched participants) on two measures. In other words, the Wilcoxon matched-pairs signed-ranks test is used with correlated groups designs to determine whether there are differences in participants' scores across the two conditions in which they served.

## KEY TERMS

chi-square ($\chi^2$) goodness-of-fit test
observed frequency
expected frequency

chi-square ($\chi^2$) test of
    independence
phi coefficient

Wilcoxon rank-sum test
Wilcoxon matched-pairs signed-ranks $T$ test

## CHAPTER EXERCISES

(Answers to odd-numbered exercises appear in Appendix C.)

1. When is it appropriate to use a $\chi^2$ test?
2. A researcher believes that the percentage of people who exercise in California is greater than the national exercise rate. The national rate is 20%. The researcher gathers a random sample of 120 individuals who live in California and finds that the number who exercise regularly is 31 out of 120.
   a. What is $\chi^2_{obt}$?
   b. What is $df$ for this test?
   c. What is $\chi^2_{cv}$?
   d. What conclusion should be drawn from these results?
3. A teacher believes that the percentage of students at her high school who go on to college is higher than the rate in the general population of high school students. The rate in the general population is 30%. In the most recent graduating class at her high school, the teacher found that 90 students graduated and that 40 of those went on to college.
   a. What is $\chi^2_{obt}$?
   b. What is $df$ for this test?
   c. What is $\chi^2_{cv}$?
   d. What conclusion should be drawn from these results?
4. You notice in your introductory psychology class that more women tend to sit up front and more men in the back. In order to determine whether this difference is significant, you collect data on the seating preferences for the students in your class. The data appear below.

| | Men | Women |
|---|---|---|
| Front of the Room | 15 | 27 |
| Back of the Room | 32 | 19 |

   a. What is $\chi^2_{obt}$?
   b. What is $df$ for this test?
   c. What is $\chi^2_{cv}$?
   d. What conclusion should be drawn from these results?
5. A researcher is interested in comparing the maturity level of students who volunteer for community service versus those who do not. The researcher assumes that those who perform community service will have higher maturity scores. Maturity scores tend to be skewed (not normally distributed). The maturity scores appear below. Higher scores indicate higher maturity levels.

| No Community Service | Community Service |
|---|---|
| 33 | 41 |
| 41 | 48 |
| 54 | 61 |
| 13 | 72 |
| 22 | 83 |
| 26 | 55 |

   a. What statistical test should be used to analyze these data?
   b. Identify $H_0$ and $H_a$ for this study.
   c. Conduct the appropriate analysis.
   d. Should $H_0$ be rejected? What should the researcher conclude?
6. Researchers at a food company are interested in how a new spaghetti sauce made from green tomatoes (and green in color) will compare to their traditional red spaghetti sauce. They are worried that the green color will adversely affect the tastiness scores. They randomly assign participants to either the green or red sauce condition. Participants indicate the tastiness of the sauce on a 10-point scale. Tastiness scores tend to be skewed. The scores appear below.

| Red Sauce | Green Sauce |
|---|---|
| 7 | 4 |
| 6 | 5 |
| 9 | 6 |
| 10 | 8 |
| 6 | 7 |
| 7 | 6 |
| 8 | 9 |

   a. What statistical test should be used to analyze these data?
   b. Identify $H_0$ and $H_a$ for this study.
   c. Conduct the appropriate analysis.
   d. Should $H_0$ be rejected? What should the researcher conclude?
7. Imagine that the researchers in Exercise 6 want to conduct the same study as a within-participants design. Participants rate both the green and red sauces by indicating the tastiness on a 10-point scale. As in Exercise 6, researchers are concerned that the color of the green sauce will adversely affect tastiness scores. Tastiness scores tend to be skewed. The scores appear below.

| Participant | Red Sauce | Green Sauce |
|---|---|---|
| 1 | 7 | 4 |
| 2 | 6 | 3 |
| 3 | 9 | 6 |
| 4 | 10 | 8 |
| 5 | 6 | 7 |
| 6 | 7 | 5 |
| 7 | 8 | 9 |

a. What statistical test should be used to analyze these data?
b. Identify $H_0$ and $H_a$ for this study.
c. Conduct the appropriate analysis.
d. Should $H_0$ be rejected? What should the researcher conclude?

## CRITICAL THINKING CHECK ANSWERS

### 13.1

1. The $\chi^2$ test is a nonparametric test used with nominal (categorical) data. It examines how well an observed frequency distribution of one or two nominal variables fits some expected pattern of frequencies. The $t$ test is a parametric test for use with interval and ratio data.

2. A nonparametric test is one that does not involve the use of any population parameters, such as the mean and standard deviation. In addition, a nonparametric test does not assume a bell-shaped distribution. The $\chi^2$ test is nonparametric because it fits this definition.

### 13.2

1. Because the participants have been ranked (ordinal data) on height and weight, the Wilcoxon rank-sum test is appropriate. If the actual height (in inches) and weight (in pounds) were reported, the data would be interval-ratio. In this case, the independent-groups $t$ test would be appropriate.

2.

| Difference Score | Rank | Signed Rank |
|---|---|---|
| −3 | 5 | −5 |
| 1 | 2 | 2 |
| 1 | 2 | 2 |
| −6 | 7 | −7 |
| 1 | 2 | 2 |
| 3 | 5 | 5 |
| −10 | 8 | −8 |
| −3 | 5 | −5 |
| | | $+\Sigma = 11$ |
| | | $-\Sigma = 25$ |

$T (N = 8) = 11$, not significant

## WEB RESOURCES

Check your knowledge of the content in this chapter by taking the practice quiz at www.wadsworth.com. For step-by-step practice and information, check out the Chi-Square Workshop at http://psychology.wadsworth.com/workshops.

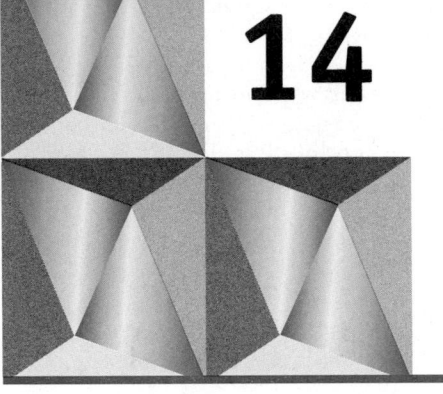

# 14 APA Communication Guidelines

In this final chapter, we will cover the guidelines set forth by the APA for writing style. APA has very specific writing style guidelines. The guidelines come from the fifth edition of the *Publication Manual of the American Psychological Association* (APA, 2001a). We will discuss general writing style, including clarity and grammar, how to cite others' work properly and avoid plagiarism, and basic typing or word processing configurations for your document. In addition, we will discuss the basic organization of an APA style paper and look at a sample paper. Last, we will briefly discuss guidelines for presenting your research at a conference.

# Writing Clearly

The APA style guidelines are intended to facilitate clear writing. First, the APA recommends an orderly and organized presentation of ideas in the paper. Toward this end, you should prepare an outline of the paper before you begin writing. Second, the APA guidelines stress smoothness of expression, or clear and logical communication. To help meet this goal, provide transitions from paragraph to paragraph and section to section, do not change topics suddenly, and make sure you have not omitted something that is necessary to understand the material being presented. Third, the APA recommends striving for economy of expression, avoiding wordiness and redundancy. Following are some examples of wordiness from the APA manual:

| *Wordy* | *Better* |
| --- | --- |
| at the present time | now |
| based on the fact that | because |
| the present study | this study |

In the following examples, again from the APA manual, the italicized words are redundant and can be omitted:

Six *different* groups saw
*a total of* 45 participants
in *close* proximity
*just* exactly
has been *previously* found

The APA manual provides several strategies to improve writing style and avoid potential problems, including writing from an outline; putting aside the first draft, then rereading it after a delay; and asking a colleague or peer to critique the draft for you.

# Avoiding Grammatical Problems

Clarity and smoothness also depend on grammatical correctness. Be sure to check for subject and verb agreement. If the subject is singular, then the verb in the sentence must be singular; if the subject is plural, then the verb should be plural.

*Incorrect:* Participant apathy as well as performance on the task decrease with practice.

*Correct:* Participant apathy as well as performance on the task decreases with practice.

A pronoun must agree with its antecedent. Pronouns replace nouns (antecedents). If the antecedent (noun) is singular, then the pronoun must be singular; if the antecedent is plural, then the pronoun should be plural.

*Incorrect:* The participant first entered their four-digit code.

*Correct:* The participants first entered their four-digit code.

*or:* The participant first entered his or her four-digit code.

Another common problem in student papers is the misuse of homophones. Homophones are words that sound the same or are pronounced the same but are spelled differently and have different meanings. For example, *to, too,* and *two* are homophones, as are *rite, write,* and *right* and *their, there,* and *they're.* Make sure you understand the proper use of each of these homophones.

Two other errors frequently made by students that resemble homophone errors are confusing *then* and *than* and *effect* and *affect.* The word *then* is an adverb meaning "at that time"; *than* is a conjunction meaning "in comparison with." The following examples illustrate correct usage:

*Then:* I was at work then.

I want to go to the gym first and then go to the store.

*Than:* She is a better dancer than I.

I would rather go to the game than study for my exam.

The word *effect* can be a noun or a verb. As a noun, it means "what is produced by a cause"; as a verb, it means "to bring about or accomplish."

*Effect* (noun): The amount of practice had a significant effect on reaction time.

*Effect* (verb): I effected a change in the grading policy.

The word *affect* can also be a noun or a verb. As a noun, it refers to emotion; as a verb, it means "to act on or to move."

*Affect* (noun): The participants in the placebo group maintained a flat affect.

*Affect* (verb): The amount of practice affected reaction time.

Other common problems include distinguishing between *that* and *which* and between *while* and *since.* *That* and *which* are relative pronouns that introduce an element that is subordinate to the main clause of the sentence. *That* clauses are restrictive; that is, they are essential to the meaning of the sentence.

*Example:* The animals that performed well in the first experiment were used in the second experiment.

In other words, only those animals that performed well were used in the second experiment. *Which* clauses are nonrestrictive and merely add further information.

*Example:* The animals, which performed well in the first experiment, were not proficient in the second experiment.

In other words, the second experiment was more difficult for all of the animals.

*While* and *since* are subordinate conjunctions that also introduce an element that is subordinate to the main clause of the sentence. Although some style authorities accept the use of *while* and *since* when they do not refer strictly to time, the APA manual calls for the use of *while* and *since* only when referring to time. *While* should be used to refer to simultaneous events; *since* should be used to refer to a subsequent event.

*While*: The participants performed well while listening to music.
*Since*: Since this original study, many others have been published.

When the writer is not referring to temporal events, the APA manual suggests using *although, whereas, and,* or *but* rather than *while,* and *because* rather than *since.*

Last, beware of misusing nouns of foreign origin such as *data,* which is a Latin plural noun (the singular is *datum*).

*Incorrect:* The data was analyzed using a two-way randomized ANOVA.
*Correct:* The data were analyzed using a two-way randomized ANOVA.

Other nouns of foreign origin with plural forms that are frequently misused include the following:

| *Singular* | *Plural* |
| --- | --- |
| phenomenon | phenomena |
| stimulus | stimuli |
| analysis | analyses |
| hypothesis | hypotheses |

# Reporting Numbers

You will most likely be reporting many numbers in your research paper, from the number of participants used to the statistics that you calculated. How should they be reported, as numbers or in words? The general rule for APA papers is to use words when expressing numbers below 10 that do not represent precise measurements and to use numerals for all numbers 10 and higher. This general rule has some exceptions, however:

- When starting a sentence with a number, use words.
  *Example:* Sixty students participated in the study.
- When reporting a percentage, use numerals followed by a percent sign.
  *Example:* The participants in the imagery practice condition improved by 40%, whereas those in the nonimagery practice condition improved by only 8%.
- When describing ages, use numerals.
  *Example:* The 10-year-olds performed better than the 8-year-olds.
- When describing sample size, use numerals.

**TABLE 14.1** Statistical abbreviations and examples of correct APA format for reporting test results

| STATISTICAL ABBREVIATION | STATISTICAL TEST | EXAMPLE OF CORRECT APA REPORTING FORMAT |
|---|---|---|
| $r$ | Pearson's product-moment correlation coefficient | $r(20) = .89, p < .01$ |
| $t$ | $t$ test | $t(18) = 3.95, p < .001$ |
| $\chi^2$ | $\chi^2$ test | $\chi^2(1) = 4.13, p < .05$ |
| $F$ | ANOVA | $F(2, 24) = 5.92, p < .01$ |

*Example:* There were 9 females and 9 males in each condition.
- When reporting statistics, use numerals.
*Example:* The mean score for the females was 6.
- When numbers above and below 10 are being compared in the same sentence, use numerals.
*Example:* Participants worked on either 5 or 10 logic problems.

One final consideration with respect to reporting numbers is how to report statistics. As noted above, they are reported as numbers. However, each statistical term is represented by an italicized abbreviation. The abbreviations for some of the more commonly used descriptive statistics are given here:

| | |
|---|---|
| $M$ | Mean |
| $SD$ | Standard deviation |
| $df$ | Degrees of freedom |
| $N$ | Total number of participants |

When we report the results of a statistical significance test, APA style is to report the abbreviation for the test, with the degrees of freedom in parentheses, the calculated value of the test statistic, and the probability level.

*Example:* The participants in the imagery rehearsal condition remembered more words ($M = 7.9$) than the participants in the rote rehearsal condition ($M = 4.5$), $t(18) = 4.86, p < .01$.

Table 14.1 provides examples of the correct APA format for reporting the results from several statistical significance tests.

# Citing and Referencing

Another important element of an APA style paper is citing and referencing properly. The most important general rule to keep in mind is that any information that you obtain from another source, whether quoted or simply reported, must be cited and referenced. The author's name and the publication date of the work are cited in the body of the paper. All sources cited within the paper must then appear in the references list, which in turn should contain entries only for those works cited within the text of the paper. This enables readers to identify the source of ideas and then to locate those published sources.

## Citation Style: One Author

APA journals use the author-date method of citation. This means that the surname of the author and the date of publication are inserted in the text at the appropriate point.

> Jones (1999) found that . . .
> A recent study of rehearsal type (Jones, 1999) suggests . . .
> According to one recent study (Jones, 1999), imagery rehearsal . . .
> Participants who used rote rehearsal remembered fewer words than those who used imagery rehearsal (Jones, 1999).

When the name of the author appears as part of the text, cite the year of publication in parentheses. When the name of the author is not part of the narrative, both the author and the date appear in parentheses, separated by a comma. This parenthetical citation may fall either within a sentence or at its end. Within a paragraph, there is no need to include the year of publication in subsequent citations of the same study as long as the study cannot be confused with other studies cited.

## Citation Style: Multiple Authors

When a work has two authors, always cite both authors every time the reference occurs. When a work has three to five authors, cite all authors the first time the reference occurs. After that, cite only the first author's surname followed by the abbreviation "et al." (and others).

> *First citation:* Burns, Menendez, Block, and Follows (2001) found . . .
> *Subsequent citation within the same paragraph:* Burns et al. found . . .
> *Subsequent first citation per paragraph thereafter:* Burns et al. (2001) found . . .

When a paper has six or more authors, cite only the surname of the first author followed by "et al." and the year of publication for the first and subsequent citations. When the paper appears in the references, however, include the names of all authors. Note that when two or more authors are cited in parentheses, the word *and* is replaced by an ampersand (&).

## Reference Style

APA reference style differs for journal articles, books, edited books, dissertations, magazines, newspaper articles, and information from the web. When in doubt about referencing format, it is best to consult the APA *Publication Manual* (2001a). References are typed in alphabetical order by the first author's last name. Each reference has several sections that are separated by periods—for example, author name(s), publication date, article title, and journal. The title of a journal (or book) and the volume number of the journal are italicized. The first line of each reference begins at the left margin, and all subsequent lines are indented—known as a hanging indent. The references, like the rest of the manuscript, are double-spaced. Following are the correct formats for some of the more commonly used types of references. If you are referencing a source that is not covered here, consult the *Publication Manual*.

*Journal Article*
Karau, S. J., & Williams, K. D. (1993). Social loafing: A meta-analytic review and theoretical integration. *Journal of Personality and Social Psychology, 65,* 681–706.

*Book: One Author, First Edition*
Hunt, M. (1993). *The story of psychology.* New York: Doubleday.

*Book: Multiple Authors, Second or Later Edition*
Bordens, K. S., & Abbott, B. B. (1999). *Research design and methods: A process approach* (4th ed.). Mountain View, CA: Mayfield.

*Edited Book*
Sternberg, R. J., & Barnes, M. L. (Eds.). (1988). *The psychology of love.* New Haven, CT: Yale University Press.

*Chapter or Article in an Edited Book*
Massaro, D. (1992). Broadening the domain of the fuzzy logical model of perception. In H. L. Pick, Jr., P. van den Broek, & D. C. Knill (Eds.), *Cognition: Conceptual and methodological issues* (pp. 51–84). Washington, DC: American Psychological Association.

*Magazine*
King, P. (1991, March 18). Bawl players. *Sports Illustrated,* 14–17.

*Diagnostic and Statistical Manual of Mental Disorders*
American Psychiatric Association. (1994). *Diagnostic and statistical manual of mental disorders* (4th ed.). Washington, DC: Author.

*Paper Presented at a Meeting*
Roediger, H. L., III. (1991, August). *Remembering, knowing, and reconstructing the past.* Paper presented at the annual meeting of the American Psychological Association, San Francisco.

*Poster Presented at a Meeting*
Griggs, R. A., Jackson, S. L., Christopher, A. N., & Marek, P. (1999, January). *Introductory psychology textbooks: An objective analysis and update.* Poster session presented at the annual meeting of the National Institute on the Teaching of Psychology, St. Pete Beach, FL.

*Internet Article Based on a Print Source*
Jacobson, J. W., Mulick, J. A., & Schwartz, A. A. (1995). A history of facilitated communication: Science, pseudoscience, and antiscience [Electronic version]. *American Psychologist, 50,* 750–765.

*Article in an Internet-Only Journal*
Fredrickson, B. L. (2000, March 7). Cultivating positive emotions to optimize health and well-being. *Prevention & Treatment, 3,* Article 0001a. Retrieved November 20, 2000, from http://journals.apa.org/prevention/volume3/pre0030001a.html.

# Typing and Word Processing

In APA style, the entire document is double-spaced. This means that even the title page, headings, footnotes, quotations, references, figure captions, and all parts of tables should be double-spaced. Use a 12-point font size in a serif style such as Courier, Palatino, or Times Roman. Margins should be set to at least 1 inch at the top, bottom, left, and right of every page. Justify the left margin, but leave the right margin uneven or ragged. Do not divide words at the end of a line, and do not use a hyphen to break words at the ends of lines. Use one space after punctuation marks, including commas, colons, semi-colons, punctuation at the ends of sentences, periods in citations, and all periods in the reference section. Begin numbering the manuscript on the title page and number all pages thereafter except the figure pages at the end of the manuscript. Page headers (the information at the top of each page) and page numbers should be about one-half inch from the top of the page. Paragraphs should be indented five to seven spaces. Last, type no more than 27 lines of text (not including any headers or footers) on a page.

# Organizing the Paper

An APA style manuscript has a specific organization. The proper order is title page, abstract, introduction, method, results, discussion, and references. Any appendixes, author notes, and footnotes follow the references. Finally, tables and figures appear at the very end of the manuscript. In the following sections, we will discuss the basic content for each of these parts of the manuscript. Refer to the sample paper in Appendix D as you read through the following material.

## Title Page

The title page in an APA style manuscript contains more information than simply the title of the paper. Refer to the title page in the sample manuscript in Appendix D. At the top of the page is a short title that consists of the first two or three meaningful words of the title of the paper. In the sample paper, the short title is "Effects of Salary." The short title is right-justified and appears about one-half inch from the top of the page. Thus, it is actually printed in the top margin of the page. Five spaces after the short title is the page number beginning with the title page as page 1. The short title and page number appear on every page of the manuscript except the figure page(s), if any. If you are using a word processing program, use the header/footer function to insert the short title and page number. Do not try to manually type the short title on each page. APA style requires the short title so that those reviewing the manuscript will have an easier time keeping the paper together and the pages in the correct order.

The first line on the title page, typed flush on the left margin, is the running head. First type the words "Running head," followed by a colon, and then the actual running head in all capital letters. The running head appears on only the title page in the manuscript version of your paper. However, if the paper is published in a journal, the running head will appear at the top of each page of the article. Thus, the running head should convey, in brief, what the paper is about. In other words, it is not simply the first two or three words of the title of the paper as is the short title. In our sample paper, the running head is "WILLINGNESS TO DATE." The running head should be no more than 50 characters, counting letters, punctuation, and spaces between words.

The title is centered below the running head. A title should be 10 to 12 words and should clearly and simply summarize the main idea of the paper. Notice that the title of the sample paper, "The Effects of Salary on Willingness to Date," states the effects of an independent variable on a dependent variable. Below the title of the paper is the author's name, and below that is his or her institutional affiliation. Please note that the title page is double-spaced, as is the entire manuscript.

## Abstract

Page 2 of the manuscript is the Abstract. Refer to the sample paper in Appendix D. Notice that the word "Abstract" is centered at the top of the page, that the Abstract is written as one block paragraph (no paragraph indent), and that the short title and page number are in the upper-right-hand margin of the page. The Abstract is a brief, comprehensive summary of the contents of the manuscript. It should not exceed 120 words. Although the Abstract appears at the beginning of the manuscript, it is usually easier to write the Abstract after you have written the entire paper because the Abstract is a very brief description of the entire paper. When writing the Abstract, you should generally try to describe each section of the paper (Introduction, Method, Results, and Discussion) in one or two concise sentences. You should describe the problem under investigation and the purpose of the study, the participants and general methodology, the findings including statistical significance levels, and the conclusions and implications or applications of the study. If your manuscript is published, the Abstract will appear in collections of abstracts such as those in the *Psychological Abstracts* described in Chapter 2.

## Introduction

The Introduction begins on page 3 of the manuscript. Notice that it is not labeled "Introduction"; instead, the title of the manuscript—exactly as it appears on the title page—is centered at the top of the page. The Introduction has three basic components. The first part introduces the problem under study. In the second part, you should review relevant previous research to provide an appropriate history, citing works that are pertinent to the issue but not works of marginal or peripheral significance. When summarizing earlier works, emphasize pertinent findings, relevant methodological issues, and major conclusions. Do not include nonessential details. The third part of the Introduction states the purpose and rationale for the study. You should explain your approach to solving the problem, define the variables, and state your hypotheses, along with the rationale for each hypothesis.

# Method

The Method section begins wherever the Introduction ends; it does not begin on a new page. The Method section describes exactly how the study was conducted, in sufficient detail that the study could be replicated by anyone who has read the Method section. The Method section is generally divided into subsections. Although the subsections vary across papers, the most common subsections are Participants, Materials or Apparatus, and Procedure. The Participants subsection should include a description of the participants and how they were obtained. Major demographic characteristics such as gender, age, and ethnicity should be described where appropriate, and the total number of participants should be indicated. A Materials subsection usually describes any testing materials that were used, such as a particular test or inventory or a type of problem that participants were asked to solve. An Apparatus subsection describes any specific equipment that was used. The Procedure subsection summarizes each step in the execution of the research, including the groups used in the study, instructions given to the participants, the experimental manipulation, any counterbalancing or randomization used, and specific control features in the design. If the design is particularly complex, you may want to consider having a separate Design subsection preceding the Procedure subsection.

# Results

The Results section begins right after the Method section. This section summarizes the data collected and the type of statistic used to analyze the data. It should include a description of the results only, not an explanation of the results. We discussed the APA format for presenting statistics earlier in the chapter. It is also common to use tables and figures when presenting the results. Tables usually provide exact values and can be used to present complex data and analyses in an easy-to-read format. Figures provide a visual impression and can be used to illustrate complex relationships, but they are generally not as precise as tables. Remember that tables and figures are used to supplement the text. When you use tables and figures, you must refer to them in the text, telling the reader what to look for. Although tables and figures are referred to in the Results section of the paper (and will be included here if the manuscript is published), the actual tables and figures appear at the end of the manuscript, after the references.

# Discussion

As with the previous two sections, the Discussion section begins immediately after the Results section. The Discussion allows you to evaluate and interpret the results. Typically, this section begins with a restatement of the predictions of the study. You then discuss whether or not the predictions were supported. Next comes a discussion of the relationship between the results and past research and theories. Last, you should include any criticisms of the study (such as possible confounds) and implications for future research. If the Discussion is relatively brief, it can be combined with the Results section as a Results and Discussion section or Results and Conclusions section.

## References

Earlier in the chapter, we discussed the correct format for references. The references begin on a new page after the end of the discussion. Center the word "References" at the top of the page. Remember to double-space the references, use a hanging indent, and include the short title and page number at the right-hand top of each page. Also remember that any works cited within the text must appear in the references, but that only works cited in the text should be included.

## Appendixes and Author Note

Appendixes are used to provide information that might be distracting if it were presented in the text. Some examples of material that might be included in an appendix are a computer program specifically designed for the research study, an unpublished test, a mathematical proof, and a survey instrument. The author note identifies the departmental affiliation of each author and the sources of financial support. It can also provide background information about the study, such as that it was based on the author's master's thesis or dissertation. The author note also provides acknowledgments to those colleagues who may have helped with the study. Last, the author note tells the reader whom to contact for further information concerning the article.

## Tables and Figures

As noted earlier, tables and figures are used, typically in the Results section, to supplement the text. Although they are referred to in the Results section, they appear at the end of the manuscript. Tables always precede figures at the end of the manuscript, no matter what order they were referred to in the text. Each table appears on a separate page. There are no specific rules for formatting tables, other than that they should not appear cramped, that horizontal lines should be used to define areas of the table, and that vertical lines may not be used. The columns and rows of the table should be labeled clearly. The short title and page number continue to be used on the pages with tables. In addition, each table should be numbered and have a brief explanatory title. Because the sample paper in Appendix D has no tables, the example in Table 14.2 illustrates the basic format for a table.

Figures are always placed after tables at the end of the manuscript. All figure captions are typed on a separate page that precedes the figures. The

**TABLE 14.2  Sample table**

**TABLE 1   Means of Personality Variables by Major and Gender**

|  | SCIENCE | | HUMANITIES | |
|---|---|---|---|---|
|  | Helping first | Mood first | Helping first | Mood first |
| Males | 22.22 | 23.00 | 45.40 | 61.11 |
| Females | 14.67 | 9.50 | 50.22 | 52.09 |

short title and page number appear on the figure caption page but not on the page(s) with the actual figure(s). If there is more than one figure in the manuscript, the figure captions all appear on the same figure caption page, but each figure appears on a separate page. Note the figure number in pencil on the back of each figure page. A figure has two axes—the horizontal $x$-axis and the vertical $y$-axis—and each should be clearly labeled. Several figures appear in Chapters 9, 10, and 11. You can use these or the figure that appears in the sample paper as guides. Usually, the levels of the independent variable are plotted on the $x$-axis and the values of the dependent variable are plotted on the $y$-axis. If a study has more than one independent variable, the levels of the second and successive independent variables are labeled within the figure. See Figure 11.1 for an example.

Figure 11.1 is an example of a line graph, one of two commonly used figures in psychology. The second commonly used figure is a bar graph. Figures 10.2 and 10.3 illustrate the use of bar graphs.

## The Use of Headings

APA style papers use one to five levels of headings. Level 1 and level 3 headings are those most commonly used. Sometimes you may find it necessary to use level 4 headings as well. Examples of these three types of headings follow:

(Level 1)                                  Centered Heading
          The heading is centered, and the first letter of each word is capitalized. The text begins indented on a new line.

(Level 3)     *Margin Heading*
          The heading is typed in italics, flush on the left margin. The first letter of each word is capitalized, and the text begins indented on a new line.

(Level 4)          *Paragraph heading.* The heading is indented, typed in italics, and has a period at the end. The first letter of the first word is capitalized, and the text begins on the same line.

Level 2 and level 5 headings are used only in more complex manuscripts in which more than one experiment was conducted. The sample paper in Appendix D uses only level 1 and level 3 headings.

Level 1 headings are used to head major sections such as the Abstract, the title of the paper, Method, Results, Discussion, and References. The heading is centered, and the first letter of each word is capitalized. Level 3 headings are used to divide the major sections into subsections. Thus, in the sample paper, level 3 headings divide the Method section into subsections. These headings are typed in italics, flush to the left margin, and the first letter of each word is capitalized. Level 4 headings may be used to organize material within a subsection. Thus, the Procedure subsection might be further subdivided into categories of instructions to participants, or the Materials subsection might be further divided into categories of tests. A level 4 heading begins on a new line, indented, and typed in italics. Only the first letter in the first word is capitalized. The heading ends with a period, and the text begins on the same line.

# ◢APA Formatting Checklist

The checklist in Table 14.3 itemizes some of the most common errors found in student papers. It is adapted from a paper published by Rewey, June, Weiser, and Davis (2000). Before finalizing a research paper, you should reread the manuscript and review this checklist for potential errors.

**TABLE 14.3   APA formatting checklist**

### General Formatting and Typing

- There are 1-inch margins on all four sides of each page of the manuscript.
- The font is the correct size (12 point on a word processor) and the correct style (a serif font such as Courier, Palatino, or Times Roman).
- The manuscript is double-spaced throughout, including title page, references, tables, figure captions, author notes, and appendixes.
- The page number appears on the same line with the short title and is five spaces to the right of the short title.
- The short title and page number are typed at the top of each page $1/2$ inch from the top of the page (in the top right margin).
- The figure number is handwritten on the back of all figures.
- There is only one space after punctuation marks, including commas, colons, semicolons, punctuation at the ends of sentences, periods in citations, and all periods in the reference section.
- Arabic numerals are used correctly to express numbers that are 10 or greater; numbers that immediately precede a unit of measurement; numbers that represent fractions and percentages; numbers that represent times, dates, ages, participants, samples, populations, scores, or points on a scale; and numbers less than 10 when those numbers are compared to a number greater than 10.
- Words are used correctly to express numbers less than 10 and numbers at the beginning of a title, sentence, or heading.

### Title Page

- The running head is aligned with the left margin and is less than 50 characters and spaces long.
- The author note does not appear on the title page; instead, the author note appears on a separate page after the appendixes and before the tables and figures.

### Abstract

- "Abstract" is centered at the top of the page.
- The first line of the abstract is even with the left margin (not indented).
- The abstract is 120 words or less.

### Body of the Manuscript

- There are no one-sentence paragraphs.
- The word *while* is used only to indicate events that take place simultaneously (alternatives: *although, whereas, but*).
- Terms that are abbreviated are written out completely the first time they are used and then always abbreviated thereafter.
- The word *and* is used in citations outside of parentheses.
- The ampersand (&) is used in citations within parentheses.
- Each and every citation used in the manuscript has a corresponding entry in the References section.
- The phrase *et al.* is used only when there are three or more authors.
- In the Method section, the word *participants* not *subjects* is consistently used.
- In the Results section, all test statistics ($F, t, \chi^2, p$) are italicized.

### References Section

- "References" is centered at the top of the first page.
- The first line of each reference is flush left, and subsequent lines are indented (a hanging indent).
- All entries are typed in alphabetical order.
- Authors' names are separated by commas.
- Authors' last names appear with first and (if provided) middle initials (do not type out first or middle names).
- The name of the journal and the volume number are italicized.
- Each and every entry is cited in the body of the manuscript.

1. What is the difference between the short title and the running head in an APA style manuscript?
2. Identify and briefly explain what the subsections in a Method section should be.
3. Explain what information should and should not appear in a Results section.

CRITICAL
THINKING
CHECK
14.1

# Conference Presentations

Psychologists conducting research frequently attend research conferences at which they present their finding. Their presentations typically take one of two forms: an oral presentation or a poster presentation. Brief descriptions of each of these methods of presenting research follow.

## Oral Presentations

Most oral presentations have one thing in common—you are limited in the amount of time you have to present. Typically you will have 10 to 15 minutes to present your research and answer questions. Thus, the first dilemma you must face is how to condense your entire paper down into a 10–15-minute presentation. According to the *Publication Manual*, the material you deliver verbally should differ in the level of detail from your written work. It is appropriate to omit many of the details of the scientific procedures because someone listening to your presentation cannot process at the same level of detail as someone reading a written paper. You should decide on a limited number of significant ideas you want the audience to process. In addition, you should use clear, simple language free of jargon to state what you studied, how you went about the research, what you discovered, and the implications of your results. It is appropriate to be redundant in order to emphasize important ideas. You might also consider using transparencies, slides, or PowerPoint slides as part of your presentation. It is also recommended that you write your presentation out and practice delivering it out loud in order to learn it and to determine the length of the presentation. You should also consider presenting your paper to a critical audience before you deliver it at a conference. When you actually deliver the paper, do not read it. Instead, try to speak directly to your audience and refer, when necessary, to an outline of key points. In addition, make sure you leave time for questions. Last, you should have copies of your paper ready for distribution (APA, 2001a).

## Poster Presentations

Poster presentations differ from oral paper presentations in that they provide the opportunity for the presenter and the audience to talk with one another. Typically, posters are presented in an exhibit area with many posters, often on a similar topic, being presented at the same time. In this manner, those interested in that topic can visit the exhibit area and wander about viewing the posters and speaking with the authors. Each presenter has a bulletin board, usually around 3.5 feet high by 3 feet wide, on which to display his or her poster. You should bring your own thumbtacks. In constructing the poster, here are a few simple guidelines. As with paper presentations, minimize jargon and try to use clear and simple language to describe what you studied, how you went about the research, what you discovered, and the implications of your results. Pictures, tables, and figures work very well in poster presentations. Make sure you use an appropriate font size when preparing the poster—you should be able to read it easily from a distance of 3 feet. As with oral paper presentations, you should have copies of your paper ready for distribution.

# Summary

After reading this chapter, you should have an understanding of APA's writing standards. We presented basic APA formatting and writing guidelines. We discussed how to write clearly, avoid grammatical problems, report numbers, and properly cite and reference the works of others. In addition, we described the organization of an APA style manuscript, with frequent references to the sample paper in Appendix D. Finally, we discussed presenting your research at conferences using either an oral paper presentation format or a poster presentation format.

## CHAPTER EXERCISES

(Answers to odd-numbered exercises appear in Appendix C.)

1. What information is contained on the title page of a manuscript?
2. Briefly describe the type of information that should be contained in an introduction.
3. Identify the grammatical or formatting errors in each of the following statements:

   a. 50 students participated in the study.
   b. The F-score was 6.54 with a p-value of .05 and 1 and 12 degrees of freedom.
   c. The data was analyzed using a one-way ANOVA.
   d. One group of participants took the medication while the other group did not.

## CRITICAL THINKING CHECK ANSWERS

### 14.1

1. The short title appears in the upper right-hand margin of an APA style manuscript (on all pages except the figure pages) and is usually the first two or three meaningful words of the title of the paper. The short title will not appear in the paper if it is ultimately published; it is simply used for organizational purposes during the review process. The running head appears only on the title page of the manuscript and briefly (50 characters or less) conveys the nature of the paper. If the paper is ultimately published, the running head will appear at the top of each page of the journal article.

2. The Participants subsection should be first. It provides a description of the participants, which may include gender, age, and ethnicity. Next comes a Materials or Apparatus subsection,

describing any testing materials or equipment used. The final subsection is usually a Procedure (or a Design and Procedure) subsection. It should describe the variables in the study and the procedure used to collect the data in sufficient detail that another researcher could replicate the study after reading this section.

3. The Results section should identify the statistics used to analyze the data and the results of those analyses. It should not include any explanation or qualification of the results, nor should it relate the results back to the hypothesis being tested. These matters will be covered in the Discussion section.

## WEB RESOURCES

Check your knowledge of the content in this chapter by taking the practice quiz at www.Wadsworth.com. Or, for step-by-step practice and information, check out the Statistics and Research Methods Workshops at http://psychology.wadsworth.com/workshops.

# Appendixes

313

# A Statistical Tables

## TABLE A.1    Random Numbers

|    | 1 | 2 | 3 | 4 | 5 | 6 | 7 | 8 | 9 | 10 |
|----|-------|-------|-------|-------|-------|-------|-------|-------|-------|-------|
| 1  | 39614 | 74819 | 23303 | 87516 | 18981 | 42314 | 89531 | 07870 | 12536 | 41222 |
| 2  | 02541 | 85748 | 56140 | 72328 | 54780 | 21638 | 30219 | 04220 | 69476 | 45002 |
| 3  | 87434 | 15686 | 74598 | 54299 | 92089 | 30832 | 30118 | 18505 | 67564 | 75455 |
| 4  | 69937 | 72720 | 06396 | 45725 | 93951 | 14151 | 03069 | 64938 | 81282 | 92018 |
| 5  | 30217 | 90732 | 03477 | 69920 | 05899 | 64950 | 96540 | 41121 | 73559 | 47139 |
| 6  | 74643 | 92005 | 05388 | 42797 | 34732 | 31463 | 27872 | 58056 | 98703 | 85255 |
| 7  | 17723 | 79504 | 30484 | 09868 | 38245 | 29772 | 19579 | 09007 | 79314 | 71295 |
| 8  | 09395 | 39991 | 23279 | 51552 | 18198 | 47560 | 09070 | 06643 | 68828 | 87934 |
| 9  | 21973 | 26112 | 67133 | 39727 | 85483 | 49720 | 28341 | 64165 | 90276 | 26897 |
| 10 | 85933 | 70911 | 43491 | 53764 | 43614 | 54764 | 63356 | 47404 | 78254 | 60403 |
| 11 | 42238 | 49831 | 20973 | 03463 | 40351 | 16448 | 58791 | 13781 | 68649 | 30077 |
| 12 | 11679 | 22530 | 97439 | 79312 | 50730 | 50080 | 59519 | 66892 | 71575 | 68744 |
| 13 | 58854 | 35870 | 07032 | 91644 | 63494 | 00611 | 26018 | 45269 | 14037 | 81753 |
| 14 | 21489 | 69392 | 25387 | 52044 | 48854 | 21681 | 56769 | 56484 | 56748 | 46908 |
| 15 | 06469 | 62608 | 95975 | 95649 | 95550 | 22440 | 05049 | 16259 | 06264 | 42268 |
| 16 | 38751 | 02296 | 73270 | 13029 | 86045 | 75368 | 19512 | 56590 | 98819 | 22963 |
| 17 | 44689 | 16095 | 95770 | 86491 | 51064 | 24154 | 44686 | 91832 | 09545 | 65321 |
| 18 | 38733 | 27628 | 56475 | 64890 | 14744 | 30022 | 70836 | 08636 | 42319 | 36704 |
| 19 | 91265 | 37053 | 27298 | 16684 | 75518 | 86499 | 33758 | 63366 | 40964 | 31788 |
| 20 | 12341 | 31819 | 18943 | 69025 | 18575 | 55021 | 86764 | 30701 | 35862 | 30606 |
| 21 | 02772 | 52994 | 83438 | 66689 | 77898 | 57471 | 51105 | 25160 | 21380 | 98977 |
| 22 | 83632 | 79155 | 07501 | 94003 | 33840 | 64639 | 49638 | 20189 | 01406 | 37403 |
| 23 | 60273 | 69879 | 05014 | 66353 | 82444 | 04590 | 01591 | 52172 | 11244 | 48747 |
| 24 | 72043 | 56215 | 15075 | 80363 | 69817 | 95706 | 53583 | 68622 | 64000 | 71738 |
| 25 | 62198 | 76663 | 33956 | 06407 | 46018 | 65251 | 55897 | 86686 | 72765 | 49192 |
| 26 | 44391 | 91384 | 10573 | 61162 | 97936 | 58620 | 28613 | 33529 | 15322 | 99018 |
| 27 | 81137 | 70046 | 51476 | 70815 | 99604 | 35304 | 45699 | 35201 | 35014 | 99538 |
| 28 | 88919 | 01999 | 59446 | 45609 | 48651 | 31870 | 21733 | 66319 | 46468 | 90205 |
| 29 | 28016 | 75902 | 55462 | 20746 | 70013 | 21517 | 46756 | 12227 | 12172 | 63905 |
| 30 | 32688 | 50818 | 09219 | 69417 | 67210 | 92271 | 22840 | 40948 | 74473 | 27807 |
| 31 | 21085 | 99986 | 90579 | 05026 | 84208 | 29442 | 78843 | 47748 | 56599 | 82832 |
| 32 | 20428 | 52337 | 29526 | 05211 | 99377 | 10956 | 26259 | 16837 | 83248 | 02443 |
| 33 | 16377 | 63587 | 18741 | 77267 | 60596 | 36977 | 74605 | 20893 | 19462 | 61136 |
| 34 | 43752 | 18312 | 70650 | 78635 | 04359 | 35347 | 66054 | 42705 | 31321 | 25522 |
| 35 | 74595 | 21172 | 56672 | 02362 | 24411 | 66963 | 68042 | 65596 | 46193 | 86219 |
| 36 | 78700 | 35203 | 59012 | 87472 | 90460 | 29115 | 60164 | 99859 | 37950 | 29774 |
| 37 | 37686 | 43145 | 48745 | 45825 | 70982 | 38692 | 24111 | 18725 | 19787 | 52035 |
| 38 | 62836 | 37190 | 64406 | 55495 | 38545 | 79690 | 65020 | 85005 | 63094 | 73190 |
| 39 | 28237 | 43483 | 72763 | 35049 | 46008 | 73602 | 71899 | 41478 | 79980 | 13053 |
| 40 | 17896 | 78913 | 34611 | 45389 | 87031 | 59593 | 89049 | 74395 | 58014 | 81329 |
| 41 | 61395 | 89603 | 15298 | 68711 | 36087 | 35310 | 03766 | 12297 | 96362 | 96068 |
| 42 | 13860 | 41531 | 99262 | 75077 | 59394 | 34074 | 63052 | 56053 | 26579 | 60969 |
| 43 | 99201 | 77070 | 30502 | 89537 | 64812 | 49188 | 97991 | 97408 | 69927 | 83253 |
| 44 | 50815 | 81403 | 80027 | 73638 | 20195 | 60928 | 95619 | 98857 | 99743 | 06373 |
| 45 | 12553 | 07045 | 19554 | 66426 | 91173 | 37564 | 45736 | 98952 | 29124 | 50288 |

*(continued)*

**TABLE A.1    Random Numbers** *(continued)*

| | 1 | 2 | 3 | 4 | 5 | 6 | 7 | 8 | 9 | 10 |
|---|---|---|---|---|---|---|---|---|---|---|
| 46 | 08202 | 76964 | 86354 | 04138 | 68315 | 45098 | 29731 | 00994 | 86391 | 76663 |
| 47 | 78681 | 49348 | 69232 | 49665 | 88576 | 31435 | 45445 | 45114 | 86855 | 30974 |
| 48 | 21523 | 02344 | 41744 | 91052 | 48033 | 55259 | 20070 | 35304 | 50175 | 39339 |
| 49 | 37052 | 10834 | 24631 | 22659 | 58300 | 96513 | 76076 | 72730 | 06103 | 58816 |
| 50 | 62268 | 63136 | 35899 | 35687 | 04210 | 75126 | 39473 | 89465 | 65075 | 29856 |
| 51 | 38277 | 46021 | 96399 | 69062 | 81152 | 13475 | 65337 | 93823 | 70135 | 15787 |
| 52 | 68620 | 46563 | 17963 | 40057 | 24590 | 22575 | 33124 | 45939 | 33238 | 11588 |
| 53 | 27711 | 75053 | 21842 | 41145 | 13065 | 40777 | 93404 | 51071 | 97728 | 13453 |
| 54 | 51423 | 93976 | 65864 | 79424 | 48966 | 20822 | 17848 | 11282 | 22393 | 46946 |
| 55 | 87111 | 40920 | 04568 | 85241 | 73261 | 17363 | 62151 | 11495 | 19426 | 04623 |
| 56 | 31457 | 69197 | 14273 | 52489 | 20250 | 04312 | 72765 | 55459 | 93634 | 08114 |
| 57 | 11275 | 57354 | 99108 | 67783 | 20867 | 57633 | 36529 | 79894 | 67442 | 78749 |
| 58 | 24738 | 81623 | 43339 | 62377 | 31994 | 36636 | 24127 | 79170 | 57644 | 43142 |
| 59 | 26063 | 90696 | 52743 | 10239 | 79951 | 29431 | 68850 | 06024 | 84278 | 17774 |
| 60 | 86890 | 70786 | 17291 | 39544 | 84737 | 26281 | 36076 | 26550 | 69395 | 56119 |
| 61 | 73325 | 46838 | 18946 | 92976 | 43299 | 66005 | 57006 | 80058 | 74934 | 49419 |
| 62 | 68557 | 22370 | 35913 | 30957 | 51765 | 10392 | 84551 | 00596 | 83520 | 71631 |
| 63 | 16866 | 67316 | 34663 | 48594 | 65436 | 75575 | 51737 | 33602 | 35529 | 58560 |
| 64 | 41298 | 17974 | 48171 | 13238 | 35468 | 58663 | 55432 | 25165 | 73844 | 52543 |
| 65 | 46178 | 44975 | 25344 | 31026 | 29358 | 49777 | 90658 | 80651 | 01983 | 02169 |
| 66 | 25930 | 87929 | 80510 | 15778 | 85107 | 58678 | 01983 | 97126 | 00564 | 61244 |
| 67 | 02526 | 32123 | 10916 | 34572 | 56443 | 43753 | 26536 | 33219 | 69122 | 74163 |
| 68 | 80622 | 16039 | 42225 | 14679 | 88050 | 62365 | 14983 | 27681 | 78312 | 31629 |
| 69 | 51091 | 87347 | 61458 | 08651 | 84822 | 64159 | 33320 | 59188 | 12526 | 42756 |
| 70 | 32032 | 13964 | 68743 | 50019 | 61049 | 87889 | 87827 | 71689 | 81379 | 45268 |
| 71 | 00484 | 82620 | 41074 | 13235 | 10252 | 13118 | 58967 | 39269 | 83221 | 40147 |
| 72 | 05746 | 52643 | 34139 | 09318 | 39429 | 54018 | 33098 | 85708 | 60355 | 75997 |
| 73 | 90147 | 64441 | 05184 | 41040 | 75236 | 14018 | 96502 | 70565 | 41085 | 18877 |
| 74 | 17112 | 86434 | 91901 | 81315 | 16663 | 75722 | 90165 | 38789 | 74615 | 19435 |
| 75 | 98138 | 35097 | 09900 | 58316 | 44812 | 25627 | 07634 | 94965 | 73637 | 12743 |
| 76 | 73340 | 00030 | 16175 | 79663 | 96139 | 09620 | 06533 | 85526 | 76017 | 92204 |
| 77 | 62739 | 84532 | 19307 | 38191 | 03080 | 73877 | 72350 | 80278 | 40811 | 35350 |
| 78 | 93650 | 63683 | 02908 | 80620 | 91836 | 45855 | 66053 | 31548 | 63180 | 17397 |
| 79 | 84818 | 18939 | 30581 | 59102 | 66185 | 28215 | 28117 | 62472 | 63920 | 82709 |
| 80 | 07087 | 27776 | 18856 | 08117 | 44135 | 72470 | 51614 | 23486 | 84133 | 95086 |
| 81 | 69759 | 29092 | 43043 | 52467 | 06441 | 85442 | 49094 | 77087 | 96653 | 59989 |
| 82 | 77457 | 31420 | 04997 | 97650 | 48963 | 93232 | 61394 | 76641 | 21065 | 07790 |
| 83 | 35642 | 68168 | 99463 | 53054 | 70143 | 98368 | 01507 | 24563 | 58748 | 93819 |
| 84 | 19616 | 74320 | 18093 | 14482 | 53798 | 80896 | 08118 | 48166 | 60022 | 97799 |
| 85 | 08824 | 87697 | 01286 | 55376 | 77956 | 27591 | 98054 | 17596 | 40841 | 21085 |
| 86 | 98876 | 87868 | 79050 | 76638 | 84380 | 17690 | 61811 | 70118 | 56245 | 09904 |
| 87 | 97436 | 44511 | 65629 | 71628 | 84806 | 07059 | 51058 | 67597 | 99117 | 52987 |
| 88 | 15029 | 29791 | 99460 | 26758 | 21267 | 84526 | 57465 | 85288 | 35734 | 69944 |
| 89 | 47481 | 35745 | 80478 | 97125 | 93401 | 18676 | 45882 | 28755 | 31805 | 78987 |
| 90 | 57727 | 63038 | 23891 | 60592 | 04956 | 00819 | 66778 | 54903 | 32145 | 21366 |

*(continued)*

**TABLE A.1  Random Numbers** *(continued)*

| | 1 | 2 | 3 | 4 | 5 | 6 | 7 | 8 | 9 | 10 |
|---|---|---|---|---|---|---|---|---|---|---|
| 91 | 59052 | 74855 | 74779 | 34359 | 62203 | 19150 | 94757 | 37866 | 08921 | 34590 |
| 92 | 31759 | 26526 | 36958 | 87795 | 56661 | 93495 | 40992 | 05477 | 12394 | 50493 |
| 93 | 13408 | 10419 | 47588 | 91004 | 71438 | 14162 | 15913 | 10582 | 53356 | 30935 |
| 94 | 40784 | 60942 | 35067 | 17352 | 35933 | 22404 | 54003 | 85497 | 91733 | 37114 |
| 95 | 25578 | 27194 | 01185 | 59301 | 22981 | 17753 | 80426 | 85534 | 52412 | 65731 |
| 96 | 67281 | 90510 | 24773 | 20692 | 45928 | 81741 | 07638 | 34250 | 00151 | 12611 |
| 97 | 75156 | 28476 | 85861 | 62232 | 06904 | 28497 | 98585 | 31225 | 88651 | 63209 |
| 98 | 00886 | 22699 | 53246 | 58311 | 95808 | 54463 | 04665 | 37063 | 72314 | 23986 |
| 99 | 93941 | 16409 | 78203 | 07727 | 10916 | 27584 | 29695 | 56751 | 80052 | 19454 |
| 100 | 37662 | 58023 | 67325 | 24651 | 18807 | 33435 | 88961 | 07716 | 09155 | 37966 |
| 101 | 87406 | 41154 | 03732 | 79059 | 60241 | 48157 | 77044 | 77070 | 28044 | 44254 |
| 102 | 42504 | 56673 | 03818 | 70240 | 54765 | 70672 | 95660 | 99951 | 46891 | 42404 |
| 103 | 75291 | 55474 | 38747 | 61321 | 65945 | 70604 | 28728 | 65794 | 87930 | 89340 |
| 104 | 36299 | 20993 | 99257 | 28539 | 04857 | 30763 | 53472 | 71252 | 95633 | 34483 |
| 105 | 84597 | 57437 | 16084 | 90543 | 44311 | 02420 | 92687 | 07700 | 52520 | 23447 |
| 106 | 01339 | 77912 | 98217 | 10354 | 13171 | 74500 | 90741 | 94559 | 86479 | 33587 |
| 107 | 84989 | 02220 | 32025 | 46312 | 60161 | 69590 | 67297 | 54002 | 77403 | 99503 |
| 108 | 49861 | 06783 | 45237 | 94178 | 50448 | 75576 | 53502 | 70408 | 03920 | 25679 |
| 109 | 20478 | 38323 | 96404 | 14624 | 43440 | 47789 | 62906 | 30155 | 82719 | 13838 |
| 110 | 25084 | 77112 | 46461 | 19607 | 88120 | 48998 | 39298 | 68961 | 94980 | 21665 |
| 111 | 99683 | 13728 | 46550 | 95970 | 42861 | 62645 | 64706 | 98971 | 15590 | 39086 |
| 112 | 88576 | 30968 | 62474 | 79066 | 35947 | 62261 | 91816 | 52373 | 85427 | 06401 |
| 113 | 87947 | 50767 | 13082 | 08535 | 50007 | 47251 | 79627 | 47161 | 90388 | 29648 |
| 114 | 97363 | 25452 | 91936 | 29043 | 54051 | 57839 | 66414 | 79440 | 04298 | 39566 |
| 115 | 07026 | 25551 | 62334 | 06898 | 68193 | 49025 | 04204 | 12642 | 86638 | 94295 |
| 116 | 94855 | 98806 | 94977 | 95905 | 05111 | 21859 | 99540 | 13110 | 34542 | 63316 |
| 117 | 54471 | 84019 | 78520 | 71743 | 15765 | 57428 | 22745 | 00065 | 61402 | 58077 |
| 118 | 95598 | 95449 | 30163 | 53934 | 15973 | 94787 | 29088 | 94468 | 92550 | 62199 |
| 119 | 79508 | 72698 | 93936 | 75445 | 67148 | 88316 | 72824 | 31091 | 70792 | 71189 |
| 120 | 69344 | 49406 | 45440 | 87520 | 55163 | 82209 | 00015 | 75305 | 94560 | 04186 |
| 121 | 40533 | 96074 | 72805 | 46226 | 06984 | 19928 | 36835 | 85262 | 80041 | 09725 |
| 122 | 32773 | 90316 | 22391 | 23971 | 42671 | 97667 | 10877 | 53548 | 16961 | 01869 |
| 123 | 84652 | 88429 | 89859 | 33272 | 94329 | 32874 | 78670 | 39467 | 34944 | 12929 |
| 124 | 06242 | 28165 | 30158 | 04448 | 08559 | 85133 | 12497 | 54417 | 57171 | 04664 |
| 125 | 31100 | 58358 | 56923 | 62643 | 47467 | 99735 | 20279 | 85524 | 59862 | 30169 |
| 126 | 19164 | 37522 | 32866 | 06495 | 10800 | 90370 | 45175 | 87631 | 52395 | 00920 |
| 127 | 62020 | 24007 | 98973 | 37366 | 94360 | 34991 | 70207 | 33776 | 44159 | 14853 |
| 128 | 99251 | 74203 | 71903 | 88835 | 73058 | 30061 | 54450 | 76256 | 36346 | 78890 |
| 129 | 04925 | 95455 | 94235 | 04948 | 21374 | 38608 | 00057 | 88482 | 04851 | 66123 |
| 130 | 16018 | 42290 | 56522 | 24473 | 70916 | 96268 | 70235 | 00728 | 74961 | 15370 |
| 131 | 77381 | 86478 | 27238 | 30733 | 53391 | 78252 | 43413 | 84165 | 12623 | 99856 |
| 132 | 16003 | 92042 | 66817 | 36298 | 03878 | 09742 | 05626 | 77638 | 11872 | 18914 |
| 133 | 79728 | 37849 | 45869 | 03904 | 68625 | 89163 | 96263 | 23888 | 25640 | 34053 |
| 134 | 62114 | 46023 | 17421 | 20212 | 27285 | 91385 | 15777 | 68808 | 88835 | 78987 |
| 135 | 54511 | 83298 | 99598 | 76251 | 88026 | 25910 | 89371 | 41611 | 86307 | 45995 |

*(continued)*

**TABLE A.1**   Random Numbers *(continued)*

|      | 1 | 2 | 3 | 4 | 5 | 6 | 7 | 8 | 9 | 10 |
|------|------|------|------|------|------|------|------|------|------|------|
| 136 | 39020 | 38705 | 44814 | 39677 | 97245 | 70233 | 82746 | 76238 | 58675 | 76171 |
| 137 | 00746 | 47633 | 33976 | 06011 | 63868 | 74571 | 85602 | 21805 | 73681 | 43811 |
| 138 | 96320 | 83130 | 41974 | 48664 | 59590 | 55024 | 12837 | 96231 | 10198 | 83482 |
| 139 | 03776 | 05966 | 21234 | 66527 | 83292 | 31998 | 74478 | 72815 | 46140 | 66065 |
| 140 | 53693 | 45801 | 35060 | 50247 | 04379 | 33108 | 83377 | 70812 | 69079 | 49249 |
| 141 | 04186 | 36371 | 25790 | 07918 | 89173 | 94202 | 81339 | 56386 | 97721 | 45273 |
| 142 | 52483 | 58626 | 93586 | 31781 | 50513 | 18920 | 43677 | 74414 | 42727 | 46413 |
| 143 | 49922 | 08374 | 68933 | 16398 | 69784 | 73560 | 57482 | 59586 | 21831 | 24220 |
| 144 | 88842 | 42747 | 41742 | 78893 | 31387 | 81376 | 21615 | 05030 | 20766 | 72671 |
| 145 | 24924 | 07377 | 73544 | 02921 | 13514 | 51621 | 99312 | 68729 | 08790 | 48673 |
| 146 | 38697 | 67357 | 41388 | 93283 | 56187 | 39093 | 60747 | 19652 | 24476 | 02488 |
| 147 | 65492 | 25507 | 31924 | 52593 | 40211 | 39907 | 54692 | 53553 | 68653 | 62542 |
| 148 | 46981 | 25733 | 51790 | 52181 | 99713 | 11791 | 22826 | 00439 | 37716 | 31124 |
| 149 | 92419 | 75268 | 32477 | 83407 | 67761 | 08239 | 38105 | 58212 | 27761 | 71403 |
| 150 | 78531 | 83192 | 50803 | 58800 | 02666 | 10611 | 33547 | 88029 | 59575 | 15901 |
| 151 | 87437 | 42161 | 88427 | 69610 | 62154 | 35744 | 63137 | 01001 | 52384 | 39931 |
| 152 | 35364 | 36300 | 28277 | 31799 | 25887 | 58083 | 62152 | 23623 | 23866 | 12418 |
| 153 | 78507 | 38711 | 04464 | 64415 | 44923 | 10182 | 26411 | 04577 | 79555 | 36987 |
| 154 | 74289 | 16564 | 00908 | 48107 | 81211 | 98003 | 14101 | 16451 | 86728 | 83127 |
| 155 | 19576 | 85966 | 99421 | 35398 | 66511 | 30070 | 46573 | 23475 | 69632 | 79835 |
| 156 | 83888 | 86715 | 53167 | 86628 | 98900 | 19323 | 01325 | 51333 | 77123 | 53643 |
| 157 | 52558 | 94886 | 04931 | 54523 | 00624 | 55637 | 34924 | 15361 | 87079 | 25507 |
| 158 | 30848 | 82175 | 66593 | 35466 | 37731 | 69025 | 23122 | 04826 | 20732 | 30385 |
| 159 | 34973 | 97296 | 74459 | 88391 | 10128 | 94123 | 06391 | 92267 | 75463 | 48468 |
| 160 | 27611 | 93970 | 06005 | 98616 | 28890 | 54076 | 11271 | 22845 | 90072 | 24261 |
| 161 | 92969 | 71154 | 26181 | 52033 | 39471 | 66386 | 98334 | 59917 | 68143 | 53807 |
| 162 | 65164 | 02318 | 89278 | 28928 | 25601 | 58202 | 31328 | 02889 | 00448 | 25801 |
| 163 | 13595 | 38529 | 16446 | 38407 | 22204 | 93038 | 48948 | 44041 | 51749 | 55322 |
| 164 | 45369 | 95706 | 53339 | 71707 | 58546 | 08168 | 45724 | 78256 | 79998 | 88561 |
| 165 | 87521 | 71220 | 75032 | 11141 | 39703 | 45972 | 18256 | 20494 | 94619 | 82744 |
| 166 | 57989 | 34739 | 98175 | 06613 | 75091 | 98872 | 48501 | 49961 | 95042 | 31934 |
| 167 | 52398 | 29427 | 23754 | 16681 | 51950 | 27962 | 40229 | 19272 | 92997 | 49047 |
| 168 | 17324 | 65519 | 92394 | 25938 | 62611 | 28707 | 58305 | 41235 | 98394 | 57274 |
| 169 | 11889 | 86230 | 95333 | 95371 | 64746 | 92052 | 69767 | 04007 | 81467 | 09769 |
| 170 | 63788 | 85653 | 25664 | 67469 | 39180 | 08755 | 05926 | 28259 | 54662 | 58646 |
| 171 | 92840 | 09580 | 15761 | 16788 | 98042 | 97741 | 38720 | 98341 | 36444 | 39095 |
| 172 | 82305 | 44880 | 93304 | 64691 | 56025 | 51409 | 14584 | 58225 | 49723 | 52991 |
| 173 | 49955 | 38728 | 69481 | 01323 | 17723 | 83157 | 11448 | 60597 | 51916 | 90819 |
| 174 | 58358 | 56847 | 19975 | 00370 | 58842 | 16104 | 83533 | 07008 | 56022 | 18152 |
| 175 | 92320 | 05584 | 63357 | 63593 | 76564 | 63939 | 69237 | 04346 | 09895 | 07589 |
| 176 | 62279 | 72652 | 44480 | 67863 | 09559 | 05803 | 17639 | 61096 | 47394 | 78575 |
| 177 | 11550 | 56073 | 14387 | 20361 | 95577 | 88556 | 30101 | 52452 | 57955 | 05884 |
| 178 | 12211 | 46742 | 79984 | 46120 | 65738 | 34460 | 54416 | 45960 | 02082 | 75050 |
| 179 | 89384 | 68977 | 51273 | 79285 | 80139 | 69109 | 43032 | 41572 | 99802 | 86265 |
| 180 | 29882 | 01181 | 29545 | 88598 | 46398 | 02495 | 28403 | 74115 | 13013 | 29574 |

*(continued)*

**TABLE A.1** **Random Numbers** *(continued)*

| | 1 | 2 | 3 | 4 | 5 | 6 | 7 | 8 | 9 | 10 |
|---|---|---|---|---|---|---|---|---|---|---|
| 181 | 75420 | 24581 | 34180 | 02933 | 28180 | 84180 | 55863 | 55840 | 32788 | 33225 |
| 182 | 31330 | 21475 | 29404 | 04200 | 77341 | 95351 | 65166 | 19097 | 76598 | 92505 |
| 183 | 12884 | 57531 | 42825 | 13240 | 53387 | 41705 | 06960 | 84919 | 15835 | 41466 |
| 184 | 64343 | 40221 | 34644 | 67312 | 97550 | 60273 | 69171 | 51882 | 59601 | 68260 |
| 185 | 05635 | 72277 | 57640 | 05453 | 81853 | 02426 | 48333 | 07194 | 82639 | 24739 |
| 186 | 84420 | 19310 | 66969 | 33379 | 46081 | 83319 | 00109 | 94211 | 67572 | 47230 |
| 187 | 71780 | 77359 | 64536 | 23169 | 65061 | 93813 | 66523 | 46301 | 51425 | 66324 |
| 188 | 95712 | 12537 | 51767 | 32514 | 45629 | 52188 | 67692 | 26389 | 90531 | 32632 |
| 189 | 04069 | 86663 | 47975 | 84019 | 75108 | 57378 | 30548 | 37394 | 75405 | 76086 |
| 190 | 69785 | 86331 | 79153 | 87718 | 02453 | 14194 | 23406 | 95085 | 51354 | 72282 |
| 191 | 11077 | 13740 | 64078 | 36461 | 07998 | 74833 | 65394 | 56414 | 70730 | 61476 |
| 192 | 84178 | 34007 | 09641 | 14986 | 06694 | 64621 | 68345 | 42105 | 39839 | 87089 |
| 193 | 28128 | 74988 | 84266 | 07257 | 92892 | 14904 | 96410 | 70228 | 30322 | 14319 |
| 194 | 55526 | 47006 | 75447 | 94935 | 78536 | 25446 | 29456 | 16446 | 39872 | 06648 |
| 195 | 16145 | 81233 | 16323 | 37456 | 85440 | 35355 | 47389 | 37981 | 40452 | 07443 |
| 196 | 27166 | 27857 | 04848 | 33880 | 57246 | 38181 | 05127 | 77578 | 21639 | 47405 |
| 197 | 92173 | 59159 | 21696 | 01258 | 80090 | 93765 | 91472 | 67657 | 82374 | 17086 |
| 198 | 27633 | 14604 | 56124 | 18439 | 14520 | 26787 | 02600 | 56703 | 02522 | 99362 |
| 199 | 59354 | 46227 | 21428 | 66633 | 26728 | 22227 | 21993 | 15473 | 86893 | 04117 |
| 200 | 60591 | 87491 | 71349 | 47470 | 24207 | 61775 | 21366 | 58257 | 72358 | 49467 |

Source: Lehman, R. S. (1995). *Statistics in the Behavioral Sciences: A Conceptual Introduction.* Pacific Grove, CA: Brooks/Cole Publishing. Reprinted by permission of the author.

## TABLE A.2 Areas Under the Normal Curve (z Table)

| z | Area Between Mean and z | Area Beyond z | z | Area Between Mean and z | Area Beyond z |
|---|---|---|---|---|---|
| 0.00 | 0.00000 | 0.50000 | 0.43 | 0.16641 | 0.33359 |
| 0.01 | 0.00400 | 0.49600 | 0.44 | 0.17003 | 0.32997 |
| 0.02 | 0.00798 | 0.49202 | 0.45 | 0.17366 | 0.32634 |
| 0.03 | 0.01198 | 0.48802 | 0.46 | 0.17724 | 0.32276 |
| 0.04 | 0.01595 | 0.48405 | 0.47 | 0.18083 | 0.31917 |
| 0.05 | 0.01995 | 0.48005 | 0.48 | 0.18439 | 0.31561 |
| 0.06 | 0.02392 | 0.47608 | 0.49 | 0.18794 | 0.31206 |
| 0.07 | 0.02791 | 0.47209 | 0.50 | 0.19146 | 0.30854 |
| 0.08 | 0.03188 | 0.46812 | 0.51 | 0.19498 | 0.30502 |
| 0.09 | 0.03587 | 0.46413 | 0.52 | 0.19847 | 0.30153 |
| 0.10 | 0.03983 | 0.46017 | 0.53 | 0.20195 | 0.29805 |
| 0.11 | 0.04381 | 0.45619 | 0.54 | 0.20540 | 0.29460 |
| 0.12 | 0.04776 | 0.45224 | 0.55 | 0.20885 | 0.29115 |
| 0.13 | 0.05173 | 0.44827 | 0.56 | 0.21226 | 0.28774 |
| 0.14 | 0.05567 | 0.44433 | 0.57 | 0.21567 | 0.28433 |
| 0.15 | 0.05963 | 0.44037 | 0.58 | 0.21904 | 0.28096 |
| 0.16 | 0.06356 | 0.43644 | 0.59 | 0.22242 | 0.27758 |
| 0.17 | 0.06751 | 0.43249 | 0.60 | 0.22575 | 0.27425 |
| 0.18 | 0.07142 | 0.42858 | 0.61 | 0.22908 | 0.27092 |
| 0.19 | 0.07536 | 0.42464 | 0.62 | 0.23237 | 0.26763 |
| 0.20 | 0.07926 | 0.42074 | 0.63 | 0.23566 | 0.26434 |
| 0.21 | 0.08318 | 0.41682 | 0.64 | 0.23891 | 0.26109 |
| 0.22 | 0.08706 | 0.41294 | 0.65 | 0.24216 | 0.25784 |
| 0.23 | 0.09096 | 0.40904 | 0.66 | 0.24537 | 0.25463 |
| 0.24 | 0.09483 | 0.40517 | 0.67 | 0.24858 | 0.25142 |
| 0.25 | 0.09872 | 0.40128 | 0.68 | 0.25175 | 0.24825 |
| 0.26 | 0.10257 | 0.39743 | 0.69 | 0.25491 | 0.24509 |
| 0.27 | 0.10643 | 0.39357 | 0.70 | 0.25804 | 0.24196 |
| 0.28 | 0.11026 | 0.38974 | 0.71 | 0.26116 | 0.23884 |
| 0.29 | 0.11410 | 0.38590 | 0.72 | 0.26424 | 0.23576 |
| 0.30 | 0.11791 | 0.38209 | 0.73 | 0.26732 | 0.23268 |
| 0.31 | 0.12173 | 0.37827 | 0.74 | 0.27035 | 0.22965 |
| 0.32 | 0.12552 | 0.37448 | 0.75 | 0.27338 | 0.22662 |
| 0.33 | 0.12931 | 0.37069 | 0.76 | 0.27637 | 0.22363 |
| 0.34 | 0.13307 | 0.36693 | 0.77 | 0.27936 | 0.22064 |
| 0.35 | 0.13684 | 0.36316 | 0.78 | 0.28230 | 0.21770 |
| 0.36 | 0.14058 | 0.35942 | 0.79 | 0.28525 | 0.21475 |
| 0.37 | 0.14432 | 0.35568 | 0.80 | 0.28814 | 0.21186 |
| 0.38 | 0.14803 | 0.35197 | 0.81 | 0.29104 | 0.20896 |
| 0.39 | 0.15174 | 0.34826 | 0.82 | 0.29389 | 0.20611 |
| 0.40 | 0.15542 | 0.34458 | 0.83 | 0.29674 | 0.20326 |
| 0.41 | 0.15911 | 0.34089 | 0.84 | 0.29955 | 0.20045 |
| 0.42 | 0.16276 | 0.33724 | 0.85 | 0.30235 | 0.19765 |

*(continued)*

## TABLE A.2 Areas Under the Normal Curve (z Table) (continued)

| z | Area Between Mean and z | Area Beyond z | z | Area Between Mean and z | Area Beyond z |
|---|---|---|---|---|---|
| 0.86 | 0.30511 | 0.19489 | 1.29 | 0.40149 | 0.09851 |
| 0.87 | 0.30786 | 0.19214 | 1.30 | 0.40320 | 0.09680 |
| 0.88 | 0.31057 | 0.18943 | 1.31 | 0.40491 | 0.09509 |
| 0.89 | 0.31328 | 0.18672 | 1.32 | 0.40658 | 0.09342 |
| 0.90 | 0.31594 | 0.18406 | 1.33 | 0.40825 | 0.09175 |
| 0.91 | 0.31860 | 0.18140 | 1.34 | 0.40988 | 0.09012 |
| 0.92 | 0.32121 | 0.17879 | 1.35 | 0.41150 | 0.08850 |
| 0.93 | 0.32383 | 0.17617 | 1.36 | 0.41309 | 0.08691 |
| 0.94 | 0.32639 | 0.17361 | 1.37 | 0.41467 | 0.08533 |
| 0.95 | 0.32895 | 0.17105 | 1.38 | 0.41621 | 0.08379 |
| 0.96 | 0.33147 | 0.16853 | 1.39 | 0.41775 | 0.08225 |
| 0.97 | 0.33399 | 0.16601 | 1.40 | 0.41924 | 0.08076 |
| 0.98 | 0.33646 | 0.16354 | 1.41 | 0.42074 | 0.07926 |
| 0.99 | 0.33892 | 0.16108 | 1.42 | 0.42220 | 0.07780 |
| 1.00 | 0.34134 | 0.15866 | 1.43 | 0.42365 | 0.07635 |
| 1.01 | 0.34376 | 0.15624 | 1.44 | 0.42507 | 0.07493 |
| 1.02 | 0.34614 | 0.15386 | 1.45 | 0.42648 | 0.07352 |
| 1.03 | 0.34851 | 0.15149 | 1.46 | 0.42785 | 0.07215 |
| 1.04 | 0.35083 | 0.14917 | 1.47 | 0.42923 | 0.07077 |
| 1.05 | 0.35315 | 0.14685 | 1.48 | 0.43056 | 0.06944 |
| 1.06 | 0.35543 | 0.14457 | 1.49 | 0.43190 | 0.06810 |
| 1.07 | 0.35770 | 0.14230 | 1.50 | 0.43319 | 0.06681 |
| 1.08 | 0.35993 | 0.14007 | 1.51 | 0.43449 | 0.06551 |
| 1.09 | 0.36215 | 0.13785 | 1.52 | 0.43574 | 0.06426 |
| 1.10 | 0.36433 | 0.13567 | 1.53 | 0.43700 | 0.06300 |
| 1.11 | 0.36651 | 0.13349 | 1.54 | 0.43822 | 0.06178 |
| 1.12 | 0.36864 | 0.13136 | 1.55 | 0.43944 | 0.06056 |
| 1.13 | 0.37077 | 0.12923 | 1.56 | 0.44062 | 0.05938 |
| 1.14 | 0.37286 | 0.12714 | 1.57 | 0.44180 | 0.05820 |
| 1.15 | 0.37494 | 0.12506 | 1.58 | 0.44295 | 0.05705 |
| 1.16 | 0.37698 | 0.12302 | 1.59 | 0.44409 | 0.05591 |
| 1.17 | 0.37901 | 0.12099 | 1.60 | 0.44520 | 0.05480 |
| 1.18 | 0.38100 | 0.11900 | 1.61 | 0.44631 | 0.05369 |
| 1.19 | 0.38299 | 0.11701 | 1.62 | 0.44738 | 0.05262 |
| 1.20 | 0.38493 | 0.11507 | 1.63 | 0.44846 | 0.05154 |
| 1.21 | 0.38687 | 0.11313 | 1.64 | 0.44950 | 0.05050 |
| 1.22 | 0.38877 | 0.11123 | 1.65 | 0.45054 | 0.04946 |
| 1.23 | 0.39066 | 0.10934 | 1.66 | 0.45154 | 0.04846 |
| 1.24 | 0.39251 | 0.10749 | 1.67 | 0.45255 | 0.04745 |
| 1.25 | 0.39436 | 0.10564 | 1.68 | 0.45352 | 0.04648 |
| 1.26 | 0.39617 | 0.10383 | 1.69 | 0.45450 | 0.04550 |
| 1.27 | 0.39797 | 0.10203 | 1.70 | 0.45543 | 0.04457 |
| 1.28 | 0.39973 | 0.10027 | 1.71 | 0.45638 | 0.04362 |

(continued)

**TABLE A.2   Areas Under the Normal Curve (*z* Table) (*continued*)**

| *z* | Area Between Mean and *z* | Area Beyond *z* | *z* | Area Between Mean and *z* | Area Beyond *z* |
|-----|---------------------------|------------------|-----|---------------------------|------------------|
| 1.72 | 0.45728 | 0.04272 | 2.15 | 0.48423 | 0.01577 |
| 1.73 | 0.45820 | 0.04180 | 2.16 | 0.48461 | 0.01539 |
| 1.74 | 0.45907 | 0.04093 | 2.17 | 0.48501 | 0.01499 |
| 1.75 | 0.45995 | 0.04005 | 2.18 | 0.48537 | 0.01463 |
| 1.76 | 0.46080 | 0.03920 | 2.19 | 0.48575 | 0.01425 |
| 1.77 | 0.46165 | 0.03835 | 2.20 | 0.48610 | 0.01390 |
| 1.78 | 0.46246 | 0.03754 | 2.21 | 0.48646 | 0.01354 |
| 1.79 | 0.46328 | 0.03672 | 2.22 | 0.48679 | 0.01321 |
| 1.80 | 0.46407 | 0.03593 | 2.23 | 0.48714 | 0.01286 |
| 1.81 | 0.46486 | 0.03514 | 2.24 | 0.48745 | 0.01255 |
| 1.82 | 0.46562 | 0.03438 | 2.25 | 0.48779 | 0.01221 |
| 1.83 | 0.46639 | 0.03361 | 2.26 | 0.48809 | 0.01191 |
| 1.84 | 0.46712 | 0.03288 | 2.27 | 0.48841 | 0.01159 |
| 1.85 | 0.46785 | 0.03215 | 2.28 | 0.48870 | 0.01130 |
| 1.86 | 0.46856 | 0.03144 | 2.29 | 0.48900 | 0.01100 |
| 1.87 | 0.46927 | 0.03073 | 2.30 | 0.48928 | 0.01072 |
| 1.88 | 0.46995 | 0.03005 | 2.31 | 0.48957 | 0.01043 |
| 1.89 | 0.47063 | 0.02937 | 2.32 | 0.48983 | 0.01017 |
| 1.90 | 0.47128 | 0.02872 | 2.33 | 0.49011 | 0.00989 |
| 1.91 | 0.47194 | 0.02806 | 2.34 | 0.49036 | 0.00964 |
| 1.92 | 0.47257 | 0.02743 | 2.35 | 0.49062 | 0.00938 |
| 1.93 | 0.47321 | 0.02679 | 2.36 | 0.49086 | 0.00914 |
| 1.94 | 0.47381 | 0.02619 | 2.37 | 0.49112 | 0.00888 |
| 1.95 | 0.47442 | 0.02558 | 2.38 | 0.49134 | 0.00866 |
| 1.96 | 0.47500 | 0.02500 | 2.39 | 0.49159 | 0.00841 |
| 1.97 | 0.47559 | 0.02441 | 2.40 | 0.49180 | 0.00820 |
| 1.98 | 0.47615 | 0.02385 | 2.41 | 0.49203 | 0.00797 |
| 1.99 | 0.47672 | 0.02328 | 2.42 | 0.49224 | 0.00776 |
| 2.00 | 0.47725 | 0.02275 | 2.43 | 0.49246 | 0.00754 |
| 2.01 | 0.47780 | 0.02220 | 2.44 | 0.49266 | 0.00734 |
| 2.02 | 0.47831 | 0.02169 | 2.45 | 0.49287 | 0.00713 |
| 2.03 | 0.47883 | 0.02117 | 2.46 | 0.49305 | 0.00695 |
| 2.04 | 0.47932 | 0.02068 | 2.47 | 0.49325 | 0.00675 |
| 2.05 | 0.47983 | 0.02017 | 2.48 | 0.49343 | 0.00657 |
| 2.06 | 0.48030 | 0.01970 | 2.49 | 0.49362 | 0.00638 |
| 2.07 | 0.48078 | 0.01922 | 2.50 | 0.49379 | 0.00621 |
| 2.08 | 0.48124 | 0.01876 | 2.51 | 0.49397 | 0.00603 |
| 2.09 | 0.48170 | 0.01830 | 2.52 | 0.49413 | 0.00587 |
| 2.10 | 0.48214 | 0.01786 | 2.53 | 0.49431 | 0.00569 |
| 2.11 | 0.48258 | 0.01742 | 2.54 | 0.49446 | 0.00554 |
| 2.12 | 0.48300 | 0.01700 | 2.55 | 0.49462 | 0.00538 |
| 2.13 | 0.48342 | 0.01658 | 2.56 | 0.49477 | 0.00523 |
| 2.14 | 0.48382 | 0.01618 | 2.57 | 0.49493 | 0.00507 |

(continued)

## TABLE A.2 Areas Under the Normal Curve (z Table) (continued)

| z | Area Between Mean and z | Area Beyond z | z | Area Between Mean and z | Area Beyond z |
|------|------|------|------|------|------|
| 2.58 | 0.49506 | 0.00494 | 2.90 | 0.49813 | 0.00187 |
| 2.59 | 0.49521 | 0.00479 | 2.91 | 0.49820 | 0.00180 |
| 2.60 | 0.49534 | 0.00466 | 2.92 | 0.49825 | 0.00175 |
| 2.61 | 0.49548 | 0.00452 | 2.93 | 0.49832 | 0.00168 |
| 2.62 | 0.49560 | 0.00440 | 2.94 | 0.49836 | 0.00164 |
| 2.63 | 0.49574 | 0.00426 | 2.95 | 0.49842 | 0.00158 |
| 2.64 | 0.49585 | 0.00415 | 2.96 | 0.49846 | 0.00154 |
| 2.65 | 0.49599 | 0.00401 | 2.97 | 0.49852 | 0.00148 |
| 2.66 | 0.49609 | 0.00391 | 2.98 | 0.49856 | 0.00144 |
| 2.67 | 0.49622 | 0.00378 | 2.99 | 0.49862 | 0.00138 |
| 2.68 | 0.49632 | 0.00368 | 3.00 | 0.49865 | 0.00135 |
| 2.69 | 0.49644 | 0.00356 | 3.02 | 0.49874 | 0.00126 |
| 2.70 | 0.49653 | 0.00347 | 3.04 | 0.49882 | 0.00118 |
| 2.71 | 0.49665 | 0.00335 | 3.06 | 0.49889 | 0.00111 |
| 2.72 | 0.49674 | 0.00326 | 3.08 | 0.49896 | 0.00104 |
| 2.73 | 0.49684 | 0.00316 | 3.10 | 0.49903 | 0.00097 |
| 2.74 | 0.49693 | 0.00307 | 3.12 | 0.49910 | 0.00090 |
| 2.75 | 0.49703 | 0.00297 | 3.14 | 0.49916 | 0.00084 |
| 2.76 | 0.49711 | 0.00289 | 3.16 | 0.49921 | 0.00079 |
| 2.77 | 0.49721 | 0.00279 | 3.18 | 0.49926 | 0.00074 |
| 2.78 | 0.49728 | 0.00272 | 3.20 | 0.49931 | 0.00069 |
| 2.79 | 0.49738 | 0.00262 | 3.25 | 0.49943 | 0.00057 |
| 2.80 | 0.49744 | 0.00256 | 3.30 | 0.49952 | 0.00048 |
| 2.81 | 0.49753 | 0.00247 | 3.35 | 0.49961 | 0.00039 |
| 2.82 | 0.49760 | 0.00240 | 3.40 | 0.49966 | 0.00034 |
| 2.83 | 0.49768 | 0.00232 | 3.45 | 0.49973 | 0.00027 |
| 2.84 | 0.49774 | 0.00226 | 3.50 | 0.49977 | 0.00023 |
| 2.85 | 0.49782 | 0.00218 | 3.60 | 0.49984 | 0.00016 |
| 2.86 | 0.49788 | 0.00212 | 3.70 | 0.49989 | 0.00011 |
| 2.87 | 0.49796 | 0.00204 | 3.80 | 0.49993 | 0.00007 |
| 2.88 | 0.49801 | 0.00199 | 3.90 | 0.49995 | 0.00005 |
| 2.89 | 0.49808 | 0.00192 | 4.00 | 0.49997 | 0.00003 |

SOURCE: Lehman, R. S. (1995). *Statistics in the Behavioral Sciences: A Conceptual Introduction.* Pacific Grove, CA: Brooks/Cole Publishing. Reprinted by permission of the author.

**TABLE A.3    Critical Values for the Student's *t* Distribution**

| | Level of Significance for One-Tailed Test | | | | | |
|---|---|---|---|---|---|---|
| | .10 | .05 | .025 | .01 | .005 | .0005 |
| | Level of Significance for Two-Tailed Test | | | | | |
| df | .20 | .10 | .05 | .02 | .01 | .001 |
| 1 | 3.078 | 6.314 | 12.706 | 31.821 | 63.657 | 636.619 |
| 2 | 1.886 | 2.920 | 4.303 | 6.965 | 9.925 | 31.598 |
| 3 | 1.638 | 2.353 | 3.182 | 4.541 | 5.841 | . 12.941 |
| 4 | 1.533 | 2.132 | 2.776 | 3.747 | 4.604 | 8.610 |
| 5 | 1.476 | 2.015 | 2.571 | 3.365 | 4.032 | 6.859 |
| 6 | 1.440 | 1.943 | 2.447 | 3.143 | 3.707 | 5.959 |
| 7 | 1.415 | 1.895 | 2.365 | 2.998 | 3.499 | 5.405 |
| 8 | 1.397 | 1.860 | 2.306 | 2.896 | 3.355 | 5.041 |
| 9 | 1.383 | 1.833 | 2.262 | 2.821 | 3.250 | 4.781 |
| 10 | 1.372 | 1.812 | 2.228 | 2.764 | 3.169 | 4.587 |
| 11 | 1.363 | 1.796 | 2.201 | 2.718 | 3.106 | 4.437 |
| 12 | 1.356 | 1.782 | 2.179 | 2.681 | 3.055 | 4.318 |
| 13 | 1.350 | 1.771 | 2.160 | 2.650 | 3.012 | 4.221 |
| 14 | 1.345 | 1.761 | 2.145 | 2.624 | 2.977 | 4.140 |
| 15 | 1.341 | 1.753 | 2.131 | 2.602 | 2.947 | 4.073 |
| 16 | 1.337 | 1.746 | 2.120 | 2.583 | 2.921 | 4.015 |
| 17 | 1.333 | 1.740 | 2.110 | 2.567 | 2.898 | 3.965 |
| 18 | 1.330 | 1.734 | 2.101 | 2.552 | 2.878 | 3.922 |
| 19 | 1.328 | 1.729 | 2.093 | 2.539 | 2.861 | 3.883 |
| 20 | 1.325 | 1.725 | 2.086 | 2.528 | 2.845 | 3.850 |
| 21 | 1.323 | 1.721 | 2.080 | 2.518 | 2.831 | 3.819 |
| 22 | 1.321 | 1.717 | 2.074 | 2.508 | 2.819 | 3.792 |
| 23 | 1.319 | 1.714 | 2.069 | 2.500 | 2.807 | 3.767 |
| 24 | 1.318 | 1.711 | 2.064 | 2.492 | 2.797 | 3.745 |
| 25 | 1.316 | 1.708 | 2.060 | 2.485 | 2.787 | 3.725 |
| 26 | 1.315 | 1.706 | 2.056 | 2.479 | 2.779 | 3.707 |
| 27 | 1.314 | 1.703 | 2.052 | 2.473 | 2.771 | 3.690 |
| 28 | 1.313 | 1.701 | 2.048 | 2.467 | 2.763 | 3.674 |
| 29 | 1.311 | 1.699 | 2.045 | 2.462 | 2.756 | 3.659 |
| 30 | 1.310 | 1.697 | 2.042 | 2.457 | 2.750 | 3.646 |
| 40 | 1.303 | 1.684 | 2.021 | 2.423 | 2.704 | 3.551 |
| 60 | 1.296 | 1.671 | 2.000 | 2.390 | 2.660 | 3.460 |
| 120 | 1.289 | 1.658 | 1.980 | 2.358 | 2.617 | 3.373 |
| ∞ | 1.282 | 1.645 | 1.960 | 2.326 | 2.576 | 3.291 |

Source: Lehman, R. S. (1995). *Statistics in the Behavioral Sciences: A Conceptual Introduction.* Pacific Grove, CA: Brooks/Cole Publishing. Reprinted by permission of the author.

**TABLE A.4   Critical Values of the Pearson *r***
**(Pearson Product-Moment Correlation Coefficient)**

| | Level of Significance for One-Tailed Test | | |
| | .05 | .025 | .005 |
| | Level of Significance for Two-Tailed Test | | |
| df | .10 | .05 | .01 |
|---|---|---|---|
| 1 | .98769 | .99692 | .999877 |
| 2 | .90000 | .95000 | .990000 |
| 3 | .8054 | .8783 | .95873 |
| 4 | .7293 | .8114 | .91720 |
| 5 | .6694 | .7545 | .8745 |
| 6 | .6215 | .7067 | .8343 |
| 7 | .5822 | .6664 | .7977 |
| 8 | .5494 | .6319 | .7646 |
| 9 | .5214 | .6021 | .7348 |
| 10 | .4973 | .5760 | .7079 |
| 11 | .4762 | .5529 | .6835 |
| 12 | .4575 | .5324 | .6614 |
| 13 | .4409 | .5139 | .6411 |
| 14 | .4259 | .4973 | .6226 |
| 15 | .4124 | .4821 | .6055 |
| 16 | .4000 | .4683 | .5897 |
| 17 | .3887 | .4555 | .5751 |
| 18 | .3783 | .4438 | .5614 |
| 19 | .3687 | .4329 | .5487 |
| 20 | .3598 | .4227 | .5368 |
| 25 | .3233 | .3809 | .4869 |
| 30 | .2960 | .3494 | .4487 |
| 35 | .2746 | .3246 | .4182 |
| 40 | .2573 | .3044 | .3932 |
| 45 | .2428 | .2875 | .3721 |
| 50 | .2306 | .2732 | .3541 |
| 60 | .2108 | .2500 | .3248 |
| 70 | .1954 | .2319 | .3017 |
| 80 | .1829 | .2172 | .2830 |
| 90 | .1726 | .2050 | .2673 |
| 100 | .1638 | .1946 | .2540 |

Source: Abridged from Table VII in R. A. Fisher and F. Yates, *Statistical Tables for Biological, Agricultural, and Medical Research,* 6th ed., 1974, p. 63. © 1963 R. A. Fisher and F. Yates, reprinted by permission of Pearson Education Limited.

TABLE A.5   Critical Values for the *F* Distribution

| *df* for Denominator (*df* within or error) | α | 1 | 2 | 3 | 4 | 5 | 6 | 7 | 8 | 9 | 10 | 11 | 12 |
|---|---|---|---|---|---|---|---|---|---|---|---|---|---|
| | | | | | | *df* for Numerator (*df* between) | | | | | | | |
| 1 | .05 | 161 | 200 | 216 | 225 | 230 | 234 | 237 | 239 | 241 | 242 | 243 | 244 |
| 2 | .05 | 18.5 | 19.0 | 19.2 | 19.2 | 19.3 | 19.3 | 19.4 | 19.4 | 19.4 | 19.4 | 19.4 | 19.4 |
| | .01 | 98.5 | 99.0 | 99.2 | 99.2 | 99.3 | 99.3 | 99.4 | 99.4 | 99.4 | 99.4 | 99.4 | 99.4 |
| 3 | .05 | 10.1 | 9.55 | 9.28 | 9.12 | 9.01 | 8.94 | 8.89 | 8.85 | 8.81 | 8.79 | 8.76 | 8.74 |
| | .01 | 34.1 | 30.8 | 29.5 | 28.7 | 28.2 | 27.9 | 27.7 | 27.5 | 27.3 | 27.2 | 27.1 | 27.1 |
| 4 | .05 | 7.71 | 6.94 | 6.59 | 6.39 | 6.26 | 6.16 | 6.09 | 6.04 | 6.00 | 5.96 | 5.94 | 5.91 |
| | .01 | 21.2 | 18.0 | 16.7 | 16.0 | 15.5 | 15.2 | 15.0 | 14.8 | 14.7 | 14.5 | 14.4 | 14.4 |
| 5 | .05 | 6.61 | 5.79 | 5.41 | 5.19 | 5.05 | 4.95 | 4.88 | 4.82 | 4.77 | 4.74 | 4.71 | 4.68 |
| | .01 | 16.3 | 13.3 | 12.1 | 11.4 | 11.0 | 10.7 | 10.5 | 10.3 | 10.2 | 10.1 | 9.96 | 9.89 |
| 6 | .05 | 5.99 | 5.14 | 4.76 | 4.53 | 4.39 | 4.28 | 4.21 | 4.15 | 4.10 | 4.06 | 4.03 | 4.00 |
| | .01 | 13.7 | 10.9 | 9.78 | 9.15 | 8.75 | 8.47 | 8.26 | 8.10 | 7.98 | 7.87 | 7.79 | 7.72 |
| 7 | .05 | 5.59 | 4.74 | 4.35 | 4.12 | 3.97 | 3.87 | 3.79 | 3.73 | 3.68 | 3.64 | 3.60 | 3.57 |
| | .01 | 12.2 | 9.55 | 8.45 | 7.85 | 7.46 | 7.19 | 6.99 | 6.84 | 6.72 | 6.62 | 6.54 | 6.47 |
| 8 | .05 | 5.32 | 4.46 | 4.07 | 3.84 | 3.69 | 3.58 | 3.50 | 3.44 | 3.39 | 3.35 | 3.31 | 3.28 |
| | .01 | 11.3 | 8.65 | 7.59 | 7.01 | 6.63 | 6.37 | 6.18 | 6.03 | 5.91 | 5.81 | 5.73 | 5.67 |
| 9 | .05 | 5.12 | 4.26 | 3.86 | 3.63 | 3.48 | 3.37 | 3.29 | 3.23 | 3.18 | 3.14 | 3.10 | 3.07 |
| | .01 | 10.6 | 8.02 | 6.99 | 6.42 | 6.06 | 5.80 | 5.61 | 5.47 | 5.35 | 5.26 | 5.18 | 5.11 |
| 10 | .05 | 4.96 | 4.10 | 3.71 | 3.48 | 3.33 | 3.22 | 3.14 | 3.07 | 3.02 | 2.98 | 2.94 | 2.91 |
| | .01 | 10.0 | 7.56 | 6.55 | 5.99 | 5.64 | 5.39 | 5.20 | 5.06 | 4.94 | 4.85 | 4.77 | 4.71 |
| 11 | .05 | 4.84 | 3.98 | 3.59 | 3.36 | 3.20 | 3.09 | 3.01 | 2.95 | 2.90 | 2.85 | 2.82 | 2.79 |
| | .01 | 9.65 | 7.21 | 6.22 | 5.67 | 5.32 | 5.07 | 4.89 | 4.74 | 4.63 | 4.54 | 4.46 | 4.40 |
| 12 | .05 | 4.75 | 3.89 | 3.49 | 3.26 | 3.11 | 3.00 | 2.91 | 2.85 | 2.80 | 2.75 | 2.72 | 2.69 |
| | .01 | 9.33 | 6.93 | 5.95 | 5.41 | 5.06 | 4.82 | 4.64 | 4.50 | 439 | 4.30 | 4.22 | 4.16 |
| 13 | .05 | 4.67 | 3.81 | 3.41 | 3.18 | 3.03 | 2.92 | 2.83 | 2.77 | 2.71 | 2.67 | 2.63 | 2.60 |
| | .01 | 9.07 | 6.70 | 5.74 | 5.21 | 4.86 | 4.62 | 4.44 | 4.30 | 4.19 | 4.10 | 4.02 | 3.96 |
| 14 | .05 | 4.60 | 3.74 | 3.34 | 3.11 | 2.96 | 2.85 | 2.76 | 2.70 | 2.65 | 2.60 | 2.57 | 2.53 |
| | .01 | 8.86 | 6.51 | 5.56 | 5.04 | 4.69 | 4.46 | 4.28 | 4.14 | 4.03 | 3.94 | 3.86 | 3.80 |
| 15 | .05 | 4.54 | 3.68 | 3.29 | 3.06 | 2.90 | 2.79 | 2.71 | 2.64 | 2.59 | 2.54 | 2.51 | 2.48 |
| | .01 | 8.68 | 6.36 | 5.42 | 4.89 | 4.56 | 4.32 | 4.14 | 4.00 | 3.89 | 3.80 | 3.73 | 3.67 |
| 16 | .05 | 4.49 | 3.63 | 3.24 | 3.01 | 2.85 | 2.74 | 2.66 | 2.59 | 2.54 | 2.49 | 2.46 | 2.42 |
| | .01 | 8.53 | 6.23 | 5.29 | 4.77 | 4.44 | 4.20 | 4.03 | 3.89 | 3.78 | 3.69 | 3.62 | 3.55 |
| 17 | .05 | 4.45 | 3.59 | 3.20 | 2.96 | 2.81 | 2.70 | 2.61 | 2.55 | 2.49 | 2.45 | 2.41 | 2.38 |
| | .01 | 8.40 | 6.11 | 5.18 | 4.67 | 4.34 | 4.10 | 3.93 | 3.79 | 3.68 | 3.59 | 3.52 | 3.46 |
| 18 | .05 | 4.41 | 3.55 | 3.16 | 2.93 | 2.77 | 2.66 | 2.58 | 2.51 | 2.46 | 2.41 | 2.37 | 2.34 |
| | .01 | 8.29 | 6.01 | 5.09 | 4.58 | 4.25 | 4.01 | 3.84 | 3.71 | 3.60 | 3.51 | 3.43 | 3.37 |
| 19 | .05 | 4.38 | 3.52 | 3.13 | 2.90 | 2.74 | 2.63 | 2.54 | 2.48 | 2.42 | 2.38 | 2.34 | 2.31 |
| | .01 | 8.18 | 5.93 | 5.01 | 4.50 | 4.17 | 3.94 | 3.77 | 3.63 | 3.52 | 3.43 | 3.36 | 3.30 |

*(continued)*

**TABLE A.5   Critical Values for the *F* Distribution** *(continued)*

| | | | | | *df* for Numerator (*df* between) | | | | | | | | | |
|---|---|---|---|---|---|---|---|---|---|---|---|---|---|---|
| **15** | **20** | **24** | **30** | **40** | **50** | **60** | **100** | **120** | **200** | **500** | **∞** | **α** | **df for Denominator (df within or error)** |
| 246 | 248 | 249 | 250 | 251 | 252 | 252 | 253 | 253 | 254 | 254 | 254 | .05 | 1 |
| 19.4 | 19.4 | 19.5 | 19.5 | 19.5 | 19.5 | 19.5 | 19.5 | 19.5 | 19.5 | 19.5 | 19.5 | .05 | 2 |
| 99.4 | 99.4 | 99.5 | 99.5 | 99.5 | 99.5 | 99.5 | 99.5 | 99.5 | 99.5 | 99.5 | 99.5 | .01 | |
| 8.70 | 8.66 | 8.64 | 8.62 | 8.59 | 8.58 | 8.57 | 8.55 | 8.55 | 8.54 | 8.53 | 8.53 | .05 | 3 |
| 26.9 | 26.7 | 26.6 | 26.5 | 26.4 | 26.4 | 26.3 | 26.2 | 26.2 | 26.2 | 26.1 | 26.1 | .01 | |
| 5.86 | 5.80 | 5.77 | 5.75 | 5.72 | 5.70 | 5.69 | 5.66 | 5.66 | 5.65 | 5.64 | 5.63 | .05 | 4 |
| 14.2 | 14.0 | 13.9 | 13.8 | 13.7 | 13.7 | 13.7 | 13.6 | 13.6 | 13.5 | 13.5 | 13.5 | .01 | |
| 4.62 | 4.56 | 4.53 | 4.50 | 4.46 | 4.44 | 4.43 | 4.41 | 4.40 | 4.39 | 4.37 | 4.36 | .05 | 5 |
| 9.72 | 9.55 | 9.47 | 9.38 | 9.29 | 9.24 | 9.20 | 9.13 | 9.11 | 9.08 | 9.04 | 9.02 | .01 | |
| 3.94 | 3.87 | 3.84 | 3.81 | 3.77 | 3.75 | 3.74 | 3.71 | 3.70 | 3.69 | 3.68 | 3.67 | .05 | 6 |
| 7.56 | 7.40 | 7.31 | 7.23 | 7.14 | 7.09 | 7.06 | 6.99 | 6.97 | 6.93 | 6.90 | 6.88 | .01 | |
| 3.51 | 3.44 | 3.41 | 3.38 | 3.34 | 3.32 | 3.30 | 3.27 | 3.27 | 3.25 | 3.24 | 3.23 | .05 | 7 |
| 6.31 | 6.16 | 6.07 | 5.99 | 5.91 | 5.86 | 5.82 | 5.75 | 5.74 | 5.70 | 5.67 | 5.65 | .01 | |
| 3.22 | 3.15 | 3.12 | 3.08 | 3.04 | 3.02 | 3.01 | 2.97 | 2.97 | 2.95 | 2.94 | 2.93 | .05 | 8 |
| 5.52 | 5.36 | 5.28 | 5.20 | 5.12 | 5.07 | 5.03 | 4.96 | 4.95 | 4.91 | 4.88 | 4.86 | .01 | |
| 3.01 | 2.94 | 2.90 | 2.86 | 2.83 | 2.80 | 2.79 | 2.76 | 2.75 | 2.73 | 2.72 | 2.71 | .05 | 9 |
| 4.96 | 4.81 | 4.73 | 4.65 | 4.57 | 4.52 | 4.48 | 4.42 | 4.40 | 4.36 | 4.33 | 4.31 | .01 | |
| 2.85 | 2.77 | 2.74 | 2.70 | 2.66 | 2.64 | 2.62 | 2.59 | 2.58 | 2.56 | 2.55 | 2.54 | .05 | 10 |
| 4.56 | 4.41 | 4.33 | 4.25 | 4.17 | 4.12 | 4.08 | 4.01 | 4.00 | 3.96 | 3.93 | 3.91 | .01 | |
| 2.72 | 2.65 | 2.61 | 2.57 | 2.53 | 2.51 | 2.49 | 2.46 | 2.45 | 2.43 | 2.42 | 2.40 | .05 | 11 |
| 4.25 | 4.10 | 4.02 | 3.94 | 3.86 | 3.81 | 3.78 | 3.71 | 3.69 | 3.66 | 3.62 | 3.60 | .01 | |
| 2.62 | 2.54 | 2.51 | 2.47 | 2.43 | 2.40 | 2.38 | 2.35 | 2.34 | 2.32 | 2.31 | 2.30 | .05 | 12 |
| 4.01 | 3.86 | 3.78 | 3.70 | 3.62 | 3.57 | 3.54 | 3.47 | 3.45 | 3.41 | 3.38 | 3.36 | .01 | |
| 2.53 | 2.46 | 2.42 | 2.38 | 2.34 | 2.31 | 2.30 | 2.26 | 2.25 | 2.23 | 2.22 | 2.21 | .05 | 13 |
| 3.82 | 3.66 | 3.59 | 3.51 | 3.43 | 3.38 | 3.34 | 3.27 | 3.25 | 3.22 | 3.19 | 3.17 | .01 | |
| 2.46 | 2.39 | 2.35 | 2.31 | 2.27 | 2.24 | 2.22 | 2.19 | 2.18 | 2.16 | 2.14 | 2.13 | .05 | 14 |
| 3.66 | 3.51 | 3.43 | 3.35 | 3.27 | 3.22 | 3.18 | 3.11 | 3.09 | 3.06 | 3.03 | 3.00 | .01 | |
| 2.40 | 2.33 | 2.29 | 2.25 | 2.20 | 2.18 | 2.16 | 2.12 | 2.11 | 2.10 | 2.08 | 2.07 | .05 | 15 |
| 3.52 | 3.37 | 3.29 | 3.21 | 3.13 | 3.08 | 3.05 | 2.98 | 2.96 | 2.92 | 2.89 | 2.87 | .01 | |
| 2.35 | 2.28 | 2.24 | 2.19 | 2.15 | 2.12 | 2.11 | 2.07 | 2.06 | 2.04 | 2.02 | 2.01 | .05 | 16 |
| 3.41 | 3.26 | 3.18 | 3.10 | 3.02 | 2.97 | 2.93 | 2.86 | 2.84 | 2.81 | 2.78 | 2.75 | .01 | |
| 2.31 | 2.23 | 2.19 | 2.15 | 2.10 | 2.08 | 2.06 | 2.02 | 2.01 | 1.99 | 1.97 | 1.96 | .05 | 17 |
| 3.31 | 3.16 | 3.08 | 3.00 | 2.92 | 2.87 | 2.83 | 2.76 | 2.75 | 2.71 | 2.68 | 2.65 | .01 | |
| 2.27 | 2.19 | 2.15 | 2.11 | 2.06 | 2.04 | 2.02 | 1.98 | 1.97 | 1.95 | 1.93 | 1.92 | .05 | 18 |
| 3.23 | 3.08 | 3.00 | 2.92 | 2.84 | 2.78 | 2.75 | 2.68 | 2.66 | 2.62 | 2.59 | 2.57 | .01 | |
| 2.23 | 2.16 | 2.11 | 2.07 | 2.03 | 2.00 | 1.98 | 1.94 | 1.93 | 1.91 | 1.89 | 1.88 | .05 | 19 |
| 3.15 | 3.00 | 2.92 | 2.84 | 2.76 | 2.71 | 2.67 | 2.60 | 2.58 | 2.55 | 2.51 | 2.49 | .01 | |

*(continued)*

TABLE A.5   Critical Values for the *F* Distribution *(continued)*

| *df* for Denominator (*df* within or error) | α | \multicolumn{12}{c}{*df* for Numerator (*df* between)} |
|---|---|---|---|---|---|---|---|---|---|---|---|---|---|
| | | 1 | 2 | 3 | 4 | 5 | 6 | 7 | 8 | 9 | 10 | 11 | 12 |
| 20 | .05 | 4.35 | 3.49 | 3.10 | 2.87 | 2.71 | 2.60 | 2.51 | 2.45 | 2.39 | 2.35 | 2.31 | 2.28 |
| | .01 | 8.10 | 5.85 | 4.94 | 4.43 | 4.10 | 3.87 | 3.70 | 3.56 | 3.46 | 3.37 | 3.29 | 3.23 |
| 22 | .05 | 4.30 | 3.44 | 3.05 | 2.82 | 2.66 | 2.55 | 2.46 | 2.40 | 2.34 | 2.30 | 2.26 | 2.23 |
| | .01 | 7.95 | 5.72 | 4.82 | 4.31 | 3.99 | 3.76 | 3.59 | 3.45 | 3.35 | 3.26 | 3.18 | 3.12 |
| 24 | .05 | 4.26 | 3.40 | 3.01 | 2.78 | 2.62 | 2.51 | 2.42 | 2.36 | 2.30 | 2.25 | 2.21 | 2.18 |
| | .01 | 7.82 | 5.61 | 4.72 | 4.22 | 3.90 | 3.67 | 3.50 | 3.36 | 3.26 | 3.17 | 3.09 | 3.03 |
| 26 | .05 | 4.23 | 3.37 | 2.98 | 2.74 | 2.59 | 2.47 | 2.39 | 2.32 | 2.27 | 2.22 | 2.18 | 2.15 |
| | .01 | 7.72 | 5.53 | 4.64 | 4.14 | 3.82 | 3.59 | 3.42 | 3.29 | 3.18 | 3.09 | 3.02 | 2.96 |
| 28 | .05 | 4.20 | 3.34 | 2.95 | 2.71 | 2.56 | 2.45 | 2.36 | 2.29 | 2.24 | 2.19 | 2.15 | 2.12 |
| | .01 | 7.64 | 5.45 | 4.57 | 4.07 | 3.75 | 3.53 | 3.36 | 3.23 | 3.12 | 3.03 | 2.96 | 2.90 |
| 30 | .05 | 4.17 | 3.32 | 2.92 | 2.69 | 2.53 | 2.42 | 2.33 | 2.27 | 2.21 | 2.16 | 2.13 | 2.09 |
| | .01 | 7.56 | 5.39 | 4.51 | 4.02 | 3.70 | 3.47 | 3.30 | 3.17 | 3.07 | 2.98 | 2.91 | 2.84 |
| 40 | .05 | 4.08 | 3.23 | 2.84 | 2.61 | 2.45 | 2.34 | 2.25 | 2.18 | 2.12 | 2.08 | 2.04 | 2.00 |
| | .01 | 7.31 | 5.18 | 4.31 | 3.83 | 3.51 | 3.29 | 3.12 | 2.99 | 2.89 | 2.80 | 2.73 | 2.66 |
| 60 | .05 | 4.00 | 3.15 | 2.76 | 2.53 | 2.37 | 2.25 | 2.17 | 2.10 | 2.04 | 1.99 | 1.95 | 1.92 |
| | .01 | 7.08 | 4.98 | 4.13 | 3.65 | 3.34 | 3.12 | 2.95 | 2.82 | 2.72 | 2.63 | 2.56 | 2.50 |
| 120 | .05 | 3.92 | 3.07 | 2.68 | 2.45 | 2.29 | 2.17 | 2.09 | 2.02 | 1.96 | 1.91 | 1.87 | 1.83 |
| | .01 | 6.85 | 4.79 | 3.95 | 3.48 | 3.17 | 2.96 | 2.79 | 2.66 | 2.56 | 2.47 | 2.40 | 2.34 |
| 200 | .05 | 3.89 | 3.04 | 2.65 | 2.42 | 2.26 | 2.14 | 2.06 | 1.98 | 1.93 | 1.88 | 1.84 | 1.80 |
| | .01 | 6.76 | 4.71 | 3.88 | 3.41 | 3.11 | 2.89 | 2.73 | 2.60 | 2.50 | 2.41 | 2.34 | 2.27 |
| ∞ | .05 | 3.84 | 3.00 | 2.60 | 2.37 | 2.21 | 2.10 | 2.01 | 1.94 | 1.88 | 1.83 | 1.79 | 1.75 |
| | .01 | 6.63 | 4.61 | 3.78 | 3.32 | 3.02 | 2.80 | 2.64 | 2.51 | 2.41 | 2.32 | 2.25 | 2.18 |

*(continued)*

**TABLE A.5** Critical Values for the *F* Distribution *(continued)*

| | | | | | | | *df* for Numerator (*df* between) | | | | | | | *df* for Denominator (*df* within or error) |
|---|---|---|---|---|---|---|---|---|---|---|---|---|---|---|
| 15 | 20 | 24 | 30 | 40 | 50 | 60 | 100 | 120 | 200 | 500 | ∞ | α | |
| 2.20 | 2.12 | 2.08 | 2.04 | 1.99 | 1.97 | 1.95 | 1.91 | 1.90 | 1.88 | 1.86 | 1.84 | .05 | 20 |
| 3.09 | 2.94 | 2.86 | 2.78 | 2.69 | 2.64 | 2.61 | 2.54 | 2.52 | 2.48 | 2.44 | 2.42 | .01 | |
| 2.15 | 2.07 | 2.03 | 1.98 | 1.94 | 1.91 | 1.89 | 1.85 | 1.84 | 1.82 | 1.80 | 1.78 | .05 | 22 |
| 2.98 | 2.83 | 2.75 | 2.67 | 2.58 | 2.53 | 2.50 | 2.42 | 2.40 | 2.36 | 2.33 | 2.31 | .01 | |
| 2.11 | 2.03 | 1.98 | 1.94 | 1.89 | 1.86 | 1.84 | 1.80 | 1.79 | 1.77 | 1.75 | 1.73 | .05 | 24 |
| 2.89 | 2.74 | 2.66 | 2.58 | 2.49 | 2.44 | 2.40 | 2.33 | 2.31 | 2.27 | 2.24 | 2.21 | .01 | |
| 2.07 | 1.99 | 1.95 | 1.90 | 1.85 | 1.82 | 1.80 | 1.76 | 1.75 | 1.73 | 1.71 | 1.69 | .05 | 26 |
| 2.81 | 2.66 | 2.58 | 2.50 | 2.42 | 2.36 | 2.33 | 2.25 | 2.23 | 2.19 | 2.16 | 2.13 | .01 | |
| 2.04 | 1.96 | 1.91 | 1.87 | 1.82 | 1.79 | 1.77 | 1.73 | 1.71 | 1.69 | 1.67 | 1.65 | .05 | 28 |
| 2.75 | 2.60 | 2.52 | 2.44 | 2.35 | 2.30 | 2.26 | 2.19 | 2.17 | 2.13 | 2.09 | 2.06 | .01 | |
| 2.01 | 1.93 | 1.89 | 1.84 | 1.79 | 1.76 | 1.74 | 1.70 | 1.68 | 1.66 | 1.64 | 1.62 | .05 | 30 |
| 2.70 | 2.55 | 2.47 | 2.39 | 2.30 | 2.25 | 2.21 | 2.13 | 2.11 | 2.07 | 2.03 | 2.01 | .01 | |
| 1.92 | 1.84 | 1.79 | 1.74 | 1.69 | 1.66 | 1.64 | 1.59 | 1.58 | 1.55 | 1.53 | 1.51 | .05 | 40 |
| 2.52 | 2.37 | 2.29 | 2.20 | 2.11 | 2.06 | 2.02 | 1.94 | 1.92 | 1.87 | 1.83 | 1.80 | .01 | |
| 1.84 | 1.75 | 1.70 | 1.65 | 1.59 | 1.56 | 1.53 | 1.48 | 1.47 | 1.44 | 1.41 | 1.39 | .05 | 60 |
| 2.35 | 2.20 | 2.12 | 2.03 | 1.94 | 1.88 | 1.84 | 1.75 | 1.73 | 1.68 | 1.63 | 1.60 | .01 | |
| 1.75 | 1.66 | 1.61 | 1.55 | 1.50 | 1.46 | 1.43 | 1.37 | 1.35 | 1.32 | 1.28 | 1.25 | .05 | 120 |
| 2.19 | 2.03 | 1.95 | 1.86 | 1.76 | 1.70 | 1.66 | 1.56 | 1.53 | 1.48 | 1.42 | 1.38 | .01 | |
| 1.72 | 1.62 | 1.57 | 1.52 | 1.46 | 1.41 | 1.39 | 1.32 | 1.29 | 1.26 | 1.22 | 1.19 | .05 | 200 |
| 2.13 | 1.97 | 1.89 | 1.79 | 1.69 | 1.63 | 1.58 | 1.48 | 1.44 | 1.39 | 1.33 | 1.28 | .01 | |
| 1.67 | 1.57 | 1.52 | 1.46 | 1.39 | 1.35 | 1.32 | 1.24 | 1.22 | 1.17 | 1.11 | 1.00 | .05 | ∞ |
| 2.04 | 1.88 | 1.79 | 1.70 | 1.59 | 1.52 | 1.47 | 1.36 | 1.32 | 1.25 | 1.15 | 1.00 | .01 | |

SOURCE: Lehman, R. S. (1995). *Statistics in the Behavioral Sciences: A Conceptual Introduction*. Pacific Grove, CA: Brooks/Cole Publishing. Reprinted by permission of the author.

## TABLE A.6 Studentized Range Statistic

| Error df (df within) | α | 2 | 3 | 4 | 5 | 6 | 7 | 8 | 9 | 10 | 11 |
|---|---|---|---|---|---|---|---|---|---|---|---|
| | | | | | | *k* = Number of Means or Number of Steps Between Ordered Means | | | | | |
| 5 | .05 | 3.64 | 4.60 | 5.22 | 5.67 | 6.03 | 6.33 | 6.58 | 6.80 | 6.99 | 7.17 |
| | .01 | 5.70 | 6.98 | 7.80 | 8.42 | 8.91 | 9.32 | 9.67 | 9.97 | 10.24 | 10.48 |
| 6 | .05 | 3.46 | 4.34 | 4.90 | 5.30 | 5.63 | 5.90 | 6.12 | 6.32 | 6.49 | 6.65 |
| | .01 | 5.24 | 6.33 | 7.03 | 7.56 | 7.97 | 8.32 | 8.61 | 8.87 | 9.10 | 9.30 |
| 7 | .05 | 3.34 | 4.16 | 4.68 | 5.06 | 5.36 | 5.61 | 5.82 | 6.00 | 6.16 | 6.30 |
| | .01 | 4.95 | 5.92 | 6.54 | 7.01 | 7.37 | 7.68 | 7.94 | 8.17 | 8.37 | 8.55 |
| 8 | .05 | 3.26 | 4.04 | 4.53 | 4.89 | 5.17 | 5.40 | 5.60 | 5.77 | 5.92 | 6.05 |
| | .01 | 4.75 | 5.64 | 6.20 | 6.62 | 6.96 | 7.24 | 7.47 | 7.68 | 7.86 | 8.03 |
| 9 | .05 | 3.20 | 3.95 | 4.41 | 4.76 | 5.02 | 5.24 | 5.43 | 5.59 | 5.74 | 5.87 |
| | .01 | 4.60 | 5.43 | 5.96 | 6.35 | 6.66 | 6.91 | 7.13 | 7.33 | 7.49 | 7.65 |
| 10 | .05 | 3.15 | 3.88 | 4.33 | 4.65 | 4.91 | 5.12 | 5.30 | 5.46 | 5.60 | 5.72 |
| | .01 | 4.48 | 5.27 | 5.77 | 6.14 | 6.43 | 6.67 | 6.87 | 7.05 | 7.21 | 7.36 |
| 11 | .05 | 3.11 | 3.82 | 4.26 | 4.57 | 4.82 | 5.03 | 5.20 | 5.35 | 5.49 | 5.61 |
| | .01 | 4.39 | 5.15 | 5.62 | 5.97 | 6.25 | 6.48 | 6.67 | 6.84 | 6.99 | 7.13 |
| 12 | .05 | 3.08 | 3.77 | 4.20 | 4.51 | 4.75 | 4.95 | 5.12 | 5.27 | 5.39 | 5.51 |
| | .01 | 4.32 | 5.05 | 5.50 | 5.84 | 6.10 | 6.32 | 6.51 | 6.67 | 6.81 | 6.94 |
| 13 | .05 | 3.06 | 3.73 | 4.15 | 4.45 | 4.69 | 4.88 | 5.05 | 5.19 | 5.32 | 5.43 |
| | .01 | 4.26 | 4.96 | 5.40 | 5.73 | 5.98 | 6.19 | 6.37 | 6.53 | 6.67 | 6.79 |
| 14 | .05 | 3.03 | 3.70 | 4.11 | 4.41 | 4.64 | 4.83 | 4.99 | 5.13 | 5.25 | 5.36 |
| | .01 | 4.21 | 4.89 | 5.32 | 5.63 | 5.88 | 6.08 | 6.26 | 6.41 | 6.54 | 6.66 |
| 15 | .05 | 3.01 | 3.67 | 4.08 | 4.37 | 4.59 | 4.78 | 4.94 | 5.08 | 5.20 | 5.31 |
| | .01 | 4.17 | 4.84 | 5.25 | 5.56 | 5.80 | 5.99 | 6.16 | 6.31 | 6.44 | 6.55 |
| 16 | .05 | 3.00 | 3.65 | 4.05 | 4.33 | 4.56 | 4.74 | 4.90 | 5.03 | 5.15 | 5.26 |
| | .01 | 4.13 | 4.79 | 5.19 | 5.49 | 5.72 | 5.92 | 6.08 | 6.22 | 6.35 | 6.46 |
| 17 | .05 | 2.98 | 3.63 | 4.02 | 4.30 | 4.52 | 4.70 | 4.86 | 4.99 | 5.11 | 5.21 |
| | .01 | 4.10 | 4.74 | 5.14 | 5.43 | 5.66 | 5.85 | 6.01 | 6.15 | 6.27 | 6.38 |
| 18 | .05 | 2.97 | 3.61 | 4.00 | 4.28 | 4.49 | 4.67 | 4.82 | 4.96 | 5.07 | 5.17 |
| | .01 | 4.07 | 4.70 | 5.09 | 5.38 | 5.60 | 5.79 | 5.94 | 6.08 | 6.20 | 6.31 |
| 19 | .05 | 2.96 | 3.59 | 3.98 | 4.25 | 4.47 | 4.65 | 4.79 | 4.92 | 5.04 | 5.14 |
| | .01 | 4.05 | 4.67 | 5.05 | 5.33 | 5.55 | 5.73 | 5.89 | 6.02 | 6.14 | 6.25 |
| 20 | .05 | 2.95 | 3.58 | 3.96 | 4.23 | 4.45 | 4.62 | 4.77 | 4.90 | 5.01 | 5.11 |
| | .01 | 4.02 | 4.64 | 5.02 | 5.29 | 5.51 | 5.69 | 5.84 | 5.97 | 6.09 | 6.19 |
| 24 | .05 | 2.92 | 3.53 | 3.90 | 4.17 | 4.37 | 4.54 | 4.68 | 4.81 | 4.92 | 5.01 |
| | .01 | 3.96 | 4.55 | 4.91 | 5.17 | 5.37 | 5.54 | 5.69 | 5.81 | 5.92 | 6.02 |
| 30 | .05 | 2.89 | 3.49 | 3.85 | 4.10 | 4.30 | 4.46 | 4.60 | 4.72 | 4.82 | 4.92 |
| | .01 | 3.89 | 4.45 | 4.80 | 5.05 | 5.24 | 5.40 | 5.54 | 5.65 | 5.76 | 5.85 |
| 40 | .05 | 2.86 | 3.44 | 3.79 | 4.04 | 4.23 | 4.39 | 4.52 | 4.63 | 4.73 | 4.82 |
| | .01 | 3.82 | 4.37 | 4.70 | 4.93 | 5.11 | 5.26 | 5.39 | 5.50 | 5.60 | 5.69 |
| 60 | .05 | 2.83 | 3.40 | 3.74 | 3.98 | 4.16 | 4.31 | 4.44 | 4.55 | 4.65 | 4.73 |
| | .01 | 3.76 | 4.28 | 4.59 | 4.82 | 4.99 | 5.13 | 5.25 | 5.36 | 5.45 | 5.53 |
| 120 | .05 | 2.80 | 3.36 | 3.68 | 3.92 | 4.10 | 4.24 | 4.36 | 4.47 | 4.56 | 4.64 |
| | .01 | 3.70 | 4.20 | 4.50 | 4.71 | 4.87 | 5.01 | 5.12 | 5.21 | 5.30 | 5.37 |
| ∞ | .05 | 2.77 | 3.31 | 3.63 | 3.86 | 4.03 | 4.17 | 4.29 | 4.39 | 4.47 | 4.55 |
| | .01 | 3.64 | 4.12 | 4.40 | 4.60 | 4.76 | 4.88 | 4.99 | 5.08 | 5.16 | 5.23 |

*(continued)*

**TABLE A.6** **Studentized Range Statistic** *(continued)*

*k* = Number of Means or Number of Steps Between Ordered Means

| 12 | 13 | 14 | 15 | 16 | 17 | 18 | 19 | 20 | α | Error df (df within) |
|---|---|---|---|---|---|---|---|---|---|---|
| 7.32 | 7.47 | 7.60 | 7.72 | 7.83 | 7.93 | 8.03 | 8.12 | 8.21 | .05 | 5 |
| 10.70 | 10.89 | 11.08 | 11.24 | 11.40 | 11.55 | 11.68 | 11.81 | 11.93 | .01 | |
| 6.79 | 6.92 | 7.03 | 7.14 | 7.24 | 7.34 | 7.43 | 7.51 | 7.59 | .05 | 6 |
| 9.48 | 9.65 | 9.81 | 9.95 | 10.08 | 10.21 | 10.32 | 10.43 | 10.54 | .01 | |
| 6.43 | 6.55 | 6.66 | 6.76 | 6.85 | 6.94 | 7.02 | 7.10 | 7.17 | .05 | 7 |
| 8.71 | 8.86 | 9.00 | 9.12 | 9.24 | 9.35 | 9.46 | 9.55 | 9.65 | .01 | |
| 6.18 | 6.29 | 6.39 | 6.48 | 6.57 | 6.65 | 6.73 | 6.80 | 6.87 | .05 | 8 |
| 8.18 | 8.31 | 8.44 | 8.55 | 8.66 | 8.76 | 8.85 | 8.94 | 9.03 | .01 | |
| 5.98 | 6.09 | 6.19 | 6.28 | 6.36 | 6.44 | 6.51 | 6.58 | 6.64 | .05 | 9 |
| 7.78 | 7.91 | 8.03 | 8.13 | 8.23 | 8.33 | 8.41 | 8.49 | 8.57 | .01 | |
| 5.83 | 5.93 | 6.03 | 6.11 | 6.19 | 6.27 | 6.34 | 6.40 | 6.47 | .05 | 10 |
| 7.49 | 7.60 | 7.71 | 7.81 | 7.91 | 7.99 | 8.08 | 8.15 | 8.23 | .01 | |
| 5.71 | 5.81 | 5.90 | 5.98 | 6.06 | 6.13 | 6.20 | 6.27 | 6.33 | .05 | 11 |
| 7.25 | 7.36 | 7.46 | 7.56 | 7.65 | 7.73 | 7.81 | 7.88 | 7.95 | .01 | |
| 5.61 | 5.71 | 5.80 | 5.88 | 5.95 | 6.02 | 6.09 | 6.15 | 6.21 | .05 | 12 |
| 7.06 | 7.17 | 7.26 | 7.36 | 7.44 | 7.52 | 7.59 | 7.66 | 7.73 | .01 | |
| 5.53 | 5.63 | 5.71 | 5.79 | 5.86 | 5.93 | 5.99 | 6.05 | 6.11 | .05 | 13 |
| 6.90 | 7.01 | 7.10 | 7.19 | 7.27 | 7.35 | 7.42 | 7.48 | 7.55 | .01 | |
| 5.46 | 5.55 | 5.64 | 5.71 | 5.79 | 5.85 | 5.91 | 5.97 | 6.03 | .05 | 14 |
| 6.77 | 6.87 | 6.96 | 7.05 | 7.13 | 7.20 | 7.27 | 7.33 | 7.39 | .01 | |
| 5.40 | 5.49 | 5.57 | 5.65 | 5.72 | 5.78 | 5.85 | 5.90 | 5.96 | .05 | 15 |
| 6.66 | 6.76 | 6.84 | 6.93 | 7.00 | 7.07 | 7.14 | 7.20 | 7.26 | .01 | |
| 5.35 | 5.44 | 5.52 | 5.59 | 5.66 | 5.73 | 5.79 | 5.84 | 5.90 | .05 | 16 |
| 6.56 | 6.66 | 6.74 | 6.82 | 6.90 | 6.97 | 7.03 | 7.09 | 7.15 | .01 | |
| 5.31 | 5.39 | 5.47 | 5.54 | 5.61 | 5.67 | 5.73 | 5.79 | 5.84 | .05 | 17 |
| 6.48 | 6.57 | 6.66 | 6.73 | 6.81 | 6.87 | 6.94 | 7.00 | 7.05 | .01 | |
| 5.27 | 5.35 | 5.43 | 5.50 | 5.57 | 5.63 | 5.69 | 5.74 | 5.79 | .05 | 18 |
| 6.41 | 6.50 | 6.58 | 6.65 | 6.73 | 6.79 | 6.85 | 6.91 | 6.97 | .01 | |
| 5.23 | 5.31 | 5.39 | 5.46 | 5.53 | 5.59 | 5.65 | 5.70 | 5.75 | .05 | 19 |
| 6.34 | 6.43 | 6.51 | 6.58 | 6.65 | 6.72 | 6.78 | 6.84 | 6.89 | .01 | |
| 5.20 | 5.28 | 5.36 | 5.43 | 5.49 | 5.55 | 5.61 | 5.66 | 5.71 | .05 | 20 |
| 6.28 | 6.37 | 6.45 | 6.52 | 6.59 | 6.65 | 6.71 | 6.77 | 6.82 | .01 | |
| 5.10 | 5.18 | 5.25 | 5.32 | 5.38 | 5.44 | 5.49 | 5.55 | 5.59 | .05 | 24 |
| 6.11 | 6.19 | 6.26 | 6.33 | 6.39 | 6.45 | 6.51 | 6.56 | 6.61 | .01 | |
| 5.00 | 5.08 | 5.15 | 5.21 | 5.27 | 5.33 | 5.38 | 5.43 | 5.47 | .05 | 30 |
| 5.93 | 6.01 | 6.08 | 6.14 | 6.20 | 6.26 | 6.31 | 6.36 | 6.41 | .01 | |
| 4.90 | 4.98 | 5.04 | 5.11 | 5.16 | 5.22 | 5.27 | 5.31 | 5.36 | .05 | 40 |
| 5.76 | 5.83 | 5.90 | 5.96 | 6.02 | 6.07 | 6.12 | 6.16 | 6.21 | .01 | |
| 4.81 | 4.88 | 4.94 | 5.00 | 5.06 | 5.11 | 5.15 | 5.20 | 5.24 | .05 | 60 |
| 5.60 | 5.67 | 5.73 | 5.78 | 5.84 | 5.89 | 5.93 | 5.97 | 6.01 | .01 | |
| 4.71 | 4.78 | 4.84 | 4.90 | 4.95 | 5.00 | 5.04 | 5.09 | 5.13 | .05 | 120 |
| 5.44 | 5.50 | 5.56 | 5.61 | 5.66 | 5.71 | 5.75 | 5.79 | 5.83 | .01 | |
| 4.62 | 4.68 | 4.74 | 4.80 | 4.85 | 4.89 | 4.93 | 4.97 | 5.01 | .05 | ∞ |
| 5.29 | 5.35 | 5.40 | 5.45 | 5.49 | 5.54 | 5.57 | 5.61 | 5.65 | .01 | |

Source: Abridged from Table 29 in E. S. Pearson and H. O. Hartley, eds. *Biometrika Tables for Statisticians*, 3rd ed., 1966, Vol. 1, pp. 176–177. Reprinted by permission of the Biometrika Trustees and the author.

Table A.7    Critical Values for the $\chi^2$ Distribution

| df | .10 | .05 | .025 | .01 | .005 |
|---|---|---|---|---|---|
| 1 | 2.706 | 3.841 | 5.024 | 6.635 | 7.879 |
| 2 | 4.605 | 5.992 | 7.378 | 9.210 | 10.597 |
| 3 | 6.251 | 7.815 | 9.348 | 11.345 | 12.838 |
| 4 | 7.779 | 9.488 | 11.143 | 13.277 | 14.860 |
| 5 | 9.236 | 11.071 | 12.833 | 15.086 | 16.750 |
| 6 | 10.645 | 12.592 | 14.449 | 16.812 | 18.548 |
| 7 | 12.017 | 14.067 | 16.013 | 18.475 | 20.278 |
| 8 | 13.362 | 15.507 | 17.535 | 20.090 | 21.955 |
| 9 | 14.684 | 16.919 | 19.023 | 21.666 | 23.589 |
| 10 | 15.987 | 18.307 | 20.483 | 23.209 | 25.188 |
| 11 | 17.275 | 19.675 | 21.920 | 24.725 | 26.757 |
| 12 | 18.549 | 21.026 | 23.337 | 26.217 | 28.300 |
| 13 | 19.812 | 22.362 | 24.736 | 27.688 | 29.819 |
| 14 | 21.064 | 23.685 | 26.119 | 29.141 | 31.319 |
| 15 | 22.307 | 24.996 | 27.488 | 30.578 | 32.801 |
| 16 | 23.542 | 26.296 | 28.845 | 32.000 | 34.267 |
| 17 | 24.769 | 27.587 | 30.191 | 33.409 | 35.718 |
| 18 | 25.989 | 28.869 | 31.526 | 34.805 | 37.156 |
| 19 | 27.204 | 30.144 | 32.852 | 36.191 | 38.582 |
| 20 | 28.412 | 31.410 | 34.170 | 37.566 | 39.997 |
| 21 | 29.615 | 32.671 | 35.479 | 38.932 | 41.401 |
| 22 | 30.813 | 33.925 | 36.781 | 40.290 | 42.796 |
| 23 | 32.007 | 35.172 | 38.076 | 41.638 | 44.181 |
| 24 | 33.196 | 36.415 | 39.364 | 42.980 | 45.559 |
| 25 | 34.382 | 37.653 | 40.647 | 44.314 | 46.929 |
| 26 | 35.563 | 38.885 | 41.923 | 45.642 | 48.290 |
| 27 | 36.741 | 40.113 | 43.195 | 46.963 | 49.645 |
| 28 | 37.916 | 41.337 | 44.461 | 48.278 | 50.994 |
| 29 | 39.087 | 42.557 | 45.722 | 49.588 | 52.336 |
| 30 | 40.256 | 43.773 | 46.979 | 50.892 | 53.672 |
| 40 | 51.805 | 55.759 | 59.342 | 63.691 | 66.767 |
| 50 | 63.167 | 67.505 | 71.420 | 76.154 | 79.490 |
| 60 | 74.397 | 79.082 | 83.298 | 88.381 | 91.955 |
| 70 | 85.527 | 90.531 | 95.023 | 100.424 | 104.213 |

SOURCE: Lehman, R. S. (1995). *Statistics in the Behavioral Sciences: A Conceptual Introduction*. Pacific Grove, CA: Brooks/Cole Publishing. Reprinted by permission of the author.

## TABLE A.8 Critical Values for W (Wilcoxon Rank-Sum Test)

### $N_1 = 1$

| $N_2$ | 0.001 | 0.005 | 0.010 | 0.025 | 0.05 | 0.10 | $2\overline{W}$ |
|---|---|---|---|---|---|---|---|
| 2 | | | | | | | 4 |
| 3 | | | | | | | 5 |
| 4 | | | | | | | 6 |
| 5 | | | | | | | 7 |
| 6 | | | | | | | 8 |
| 7 | | | | | | | 9 |
| 8 | | | | | | — | 10 |
| 9 | | | | | | 1 | 11 |
| 10 | | | | | | 1 | 12 |
| 11 | | | | | | 1 | 13 |
| 12 | | | | | | 1 | 14 |
| 13 | | | | | | 1 | 15 |
| 14 | | | | | | 1 | 16 |
| 15 | | | | | | 1 | 17 |
| 16 | | | | | | 1 | 18 |
| 17 | | | | | | 1 | 19 |
| 18 | | | | | — | 1 | 20 |
| 19 | | | | | 1 | 2 | 21 |
| 20 | | | | | 1 | 2 | 22 |
| 21 | | | | | 1 | 2 | 23 |
| 22 | | | | | 1 | 2 | 24 |
| 23 | | | | | 1 | 2 | 25 |
| 24 | | | | | 1 | 2 | 26 |
| 25 | — | — | — | — | 1 | 2 | 27 |

### $N_1 = 2$

| 0.001 | 0.005 | 0.010 | 0.025 | 0.05 | 0.10 | $2\overline{W}$ | $N_2$ |
|---|---|---|---|---|---|---|---|
| | | | | | — | 10 | 2 |
| | | | | | 3 | 12 | 3 |
| | | | | — | 3 | 14 | 4 |
| | | | | 3 | 4 | 16 | 5 |
| | | | | 3 | 4 | 18 | 6 |
| | | | — | 3 | 4 | 20 | 7 |
| | | | 3 | 4 | 5 | 22 | 8 |
| | | | 3 | 4 | 5 | 24 | 9 |
| | | | 3 | 4 | 6 | 26 | 10 |
| | | | 3 | 4 | 6 | 28 | 11 |
| | | — | 4 | 5 | 7 | 30 | 12 |
| | | 3 | 4 | 5 | 7 | 32 | 13 |
| | | 3 | 4 | 6 | 8 | 34 | 14 |
| | | 3 | 4 | 6 | 8 | 36 | 15 |
| | | 3 | 4 | 6 | 8 | 38 | 16 |
| | | 3 | 5 | 6 | 9 | 40 | 17 |
| | — | 3 | 5 | 7 | 9 | 42 | 18 |
| | 3 | 4 | 5 | 7 | 10 | 44 | 19 |
| | 3 | 4 | 5 | 7 | 10 | 46 | 20 |
| | 3 | 4 | 6 | 8 | 11 | 48 | 21 |
| | 3 | 4 | 6 | 8 | 11 | 50 | 22 |
| | 3 | 4 | 6 | 8 | 12 | 52 | 23 |
| | 3 | 4 | 6 | 9 | 12 | 54 | 24 |
| — | 3 | 4 | 6 | 9 | 12 | 56 | 25 |

### $N_1 = 3$

| $N_2$ | 0.001 | 0.005 | 0.010 | 0.025 | 0.05 | 0.10 | $2\overline{W}$ |
|---|---|---|---|---|---|---|---|
| 3 | | | | | 6 | 7 | 21 |
| 4 | | | | — | 6 | 7 | 24 |
| 5 | | | | 6 | 7 | 8 | 27 |
| 6 | | | — | 7 | 8 | 9 | 30 |
| 7 | | | 6 | 7 | 8 | 10 | 33 |
| 8 | | — | 6 | 8 | 9 | 11 | 36 |
| 9 | | 6 | 7 | 8 | 10 | 11 | 39 |
| 10 | | 6 | 7 | 9 | 10 | 12 | 42 |
| 11 | | 6 | 7 | 9 | 11 | 13 | 45 |
| 12 | | 7 | 8 | 10 | 11 | 14 | 48 |
| 13 | | 7 | 8 | 10 | 12 | 15 | 51 |
| 14 | | 7 | 8 | 11 | 13 | 16 | 54 |
| 15 | | 8 | 9 | 11 | 13 | 16 | 57 |
| 16 | — | 8 | 9 | 12 | 14 | 17 | 60 |
| 17 | 6 | 8 | 10 | 12 | 15 | 18 | 63 |
| 18 | 6 | 8 | 10 | 13 | 15 | 19 | 66 |
| 19 | 6 | 9 | 10 | 13 | 15 | 20 | 69 |
| 20 | 6 | 9 | 11 | 14 | 17 | 21 | 72 |
| 21 | 7 | 9 | 11 | 14 | 17 | 21 | 75 |
| 22 | 7 | 10 | 12 | 15 | 18 | 22 | 78 |
| 23 | 7 | 10 | 12 | 15 | 19 | 23 | 81 |
| 24 | 7 | 10 | 12 | 16 | 19 | 24 | 84 |
| 25 | 7 | 11 | 13 | 16 | 20 | 25 | 87 |

### $N_1 = 4$

| 0.001 | 0.005 | 0.010 | 0.025 | 0.05 | 0.10 | $2\overline{W}$ | $N_2$ |
|---|---|---|---|---|---|---|---|
| | | — | 10 | 11 | 13 | 36 | 4 |
| | — | 10 | 11 | 12 | 14 | 40 | 5 |
| | 10 | 11 | 12 | 13 | 15 | 44 | 6 |
| | 10 | 11 | 13 | 14 | 16 | 48 | 7 |
| | 11 | 12 | 14 | 15 | 17 | 52 | 8 |
| — | 11 | 13 | 14 | 16 | 19 | 56 | 9 |
| 10 | 12 | 13 | 15 | 17 | 20 | 60 | 10 |
| 10 | 12 | 14 | 16 | 18 | 21 | 64 | 11 |
| 10 | 13 | 15 | 17 | 19 | 22 | 68 | 12 |
| 11 | 13 | 15 | 18 | 20 | 23 | 72 | 13 |
| 11 | 14 | 16 | 19 | 21 | 25 | 76 | 14 |
| 11 | 15 | 17 | 20 | 22 | 26 | 80 | 15 |
| 12 | 15 | 17 | 21 | 24 | 27 | 84 | 16 |
| 12 | 16 | 18 | 21 | 25 | 28 | 88 | 17 |
| 13 | 16 | 19 | 22 | 26 | 30 | 92 | 18 |
| 13 | 17 | 19 | 23 | 27 | 31 | 96 | 19 |
| 13 | 18 | 20 | 24 | 28 | 32 | 100 | 20 |
| 14 | 18 | 21 | 25 | 29 | 33 | 104 | 21 |
| 14 | 19 | 21 | 26 | 30 | 35 | 108 | 22 |
| 14 | 19 | 22 | 27 | 31 | 36 | 112 | 23 |
| 15 | 20 | 23 | 27 | 32 | 38 | 116 | 24 |
| 15 | 20 | 23 | 28 | 33 | 38 | 120 | 25 |

(continued)

## TABLE A.8 Critical Values for W (Wilcoxon Rank-Sum Test) (continued)

| | $N_1 = 5$ | | | | | | | | $N_1 = 6$ | | | | | | | |
| $N_2$ | 0.001 | 0.005 | 0.010 | 0.025 | 0.05 | 0.10 | $2\overline{W}$ | 0.001 | 0.005 | 0.010 | 0.025 | 0.05 | 0.10 | $2\overline{W}$ | $N_2$ |
|---|---|---|---|---|---|---|---|---|---|---|---|---|---|---|---|
| 5 | | 15 | 16 | 17 | 19 | 20 | 55 | | | | | | | | |
| 6 | | 16 | 17 | 18 | 20 | 22 | 60 | — | 23 | 24 | 26 | 28 | 30 | 78 | 6 |
| 7 | — | 16 | 18 | 20 | 21 | 23 | 65 | 21 | 24 | 25 | 27 | 29 | 32 | 84 | 7 |
| 8 | 15 | 17 | 19 | 21 | 23 | 25 | 70 | 22 | 25 | 27 | 29 | 31 | 34 | 90 | 8 |
| 9 | 16 | 18 | 20 | 22 | 24 | 27 | 75 | 23 | 26 | 23 | 31 | 33 | 36 | 96 | 9 |
| 10 | 16 | 19 | 21 | 23 | 26 | 28 | 80 | 24 | 27 | 29 | 32 | 35 | 38 | 102 | 10 |
| 11 | 17 | 20 | 22 | 24 | 27 | 30 | 85 | 25 | 28 | 30 | 34 | 37 | 40 | 108 | 11 |
| 12 | 17 | 21 | 23 | 26 | 28 | 32 | 90 | 25 | 30 | 32 | 35 | 38 | 42 | 114 | 12 |
| 13 | 18 | 22 | 24 | 27 | 30 | 33 | 95 | 26 | 31 | 33 | 37 | 40 | 44 | 120 | 13 |
| 14 | 18 | 22 | 25 | 28 | 31 | 35 | 100 | 27 | 32 | 34 | 38 | 42 | 46 | 126 | 14 |
| 15 | 19 | 23 | 26 | 29 | 33 | 37 | 105 | 28 | 33 | 36 | 40 | 44 | 48 | 132 | 15 |
| 16 | 20 | 24 | 27 | 30 | 34 | 38 | 110 | 29 | 34 | 37 | 42 | 46 | 50 | 138 | 16 |
| 17 | 20 | 25 | 28 | 32 | 35 | 40 | 115 | 30 | 36 | 39 | 43 | 47 | 52 | 144 | 17 |
| 18 | 21 | 26 | 29 | 33 | 37 | 42 | 120 | 31 | 37 | 40 | 45 | 49 | 55 | 150 | 18 |
| 19 | 22 | 27 | 30 | 34 | 38 | 43 | 125 | 32 | 38 | 41 | 46 | 51 | 57 | 156 | 19 |
| 20 | 22 | 28 | 31 | 35 | 40 | 45 | 130 | 33 | 39 | 43 | 48 | 53 | 59 | 162 | 20 |
| 21 | 23 | 29 | 32 | 37 | 41 | 47 | 135 | 33 | 40 | 44 | 50 | 55 | 61 | 168 | 21 |
| 22 | 23 | 29 | 33 | 38 | 43 | 48 | 140 | 34 | 42 | 45 | 51 | 57 | 63 | 174 | 22 |
| 23 | 24 | 30 | 34 | 39 | 44 | 50 | 145 | 35 | 43 | 47 | 53 | 58 | 65 | 180 | 23 |
| 24 | 25 | 31 | 35 | 40 | 45 | 51 | 150 | 36 | 44 | 48 | 54 | 60 | 67 | 186 | 24 |
| 25 | 25 | 32 | 36 | 42 | 47 | 53 | 155 | 37 | 45 | 50 | 56 | 62 | 69 | 192 | 25 |

| | $N_1 = 7$ | | | | | | | | $N_1 = 8$ | | | | | | | |
| $N_2$ | 0.001 | 0.005 | 0.010 | 0.025 | 0.05 | 0.10 | $2\overline{W}$ | 0.001 | 0.005 | 0.010 | 0.025 | 0.05 | 0.10 | $2\overline{W}$ | $N_2$ |
|---|---|---|---|---|---|---|---|---|---|---|---|---|---|---|---|
| 7 | 29 | 32 | 34 | 36 | 39 | 41 | 105 | | | | | | | | |
| 8 | 30 | 34 | 35 | 38 | 41 | 44 | 112 | 40 | 43 | 45 | 49 | 51 | 55 | 136 | 8 |
| 9 | 31 | 35 | 37 | 40 | 43 | 46 | 119 | 41 | 45 | 47 | 51 | 54 | 58 | 144 | 9 |
| 10 | 33 | 37 | 39 | 42 | 45 | 49 | 126 | 42 | 47 | 49 | 53 | 56 | 60 | 152 | 10 |
| 11 | 34 | 38 | 40 | 44 | 47 | 51 | 133 | 44 | 49 | 51 | 55 | 59 | 63 | 160 | 11 |
| 12 | 35 | 40 | 42 | 46 | 49 | 54 | 140 | 45 | 51 | 53 | 58 | 62 | 66 | 168 | 12 |
| 13 | 36 | 41 | 44 | 48 | 52 | 56 | 147 | 47 | 53 | 56 | 60 | 64 | 69 | 176 | 13 |
| 14 | 37 | 43 | 45 | 50 | 54 | 59 | 154 | 48 | 54 | 58 | 62 | 67 | 72 | 184 | 14 |
| 15 | 38 | 44 | 47 | 52 | 56 | 61 | 161 | 50 | 56 | 60 | 65 | 69 | 75 | 192 | 15 |
| 16 | 39 | 46 | 49 | 54 | 58 | 64 | 168 | 51 | 58 | 62 | 67 | 72 | 78 | 200 | 16 |
| 17 | 41 | 47 | 51 | 56 | 61 | 66 | 175 | 53 | 60 | 64 | 70 | 75 | 81 | 208 | 17 |
| 18 | 42 | 49 | 32 | 58 | 63 | 69 | 182 | 54 | 62 | 66 | 72 | 77 | 84 | 216 | 18 |
| 19 | 43 | 50 | 54 | 60 | 65 | 71 | 189 | 56 | 64 | 68 | 74 | 80 | 87 | 224 | 19 |
| 20 | 44 | 52 | 56 | 62 | 67 | 74 | 196 | 57 | 66 | 70 | 77 | 83 | 90 | 232 | 20 |
| 21 | 46 | 53 | 58 | 64 | 69 | 76 | 203 | 59 | 68 | 72 | 79 | 33 | 92 | 240 | 21 |
| 22 | 47 | 55 | 59 | 66 | 72 | 79 | 210 | 60 | 70 | 74 | 81 | 88 | 95 | 248 | 22 |
| 23 | 48 | 57 | 61 | 68 | 74 | 81 | 217 | 62 | 71 | 76 | 84 | 90 | 98 | 256 | 23 |
| 24 | 49 | 58 | 63 | 70 | 76 | 84 | 224 | 64 | 73 | 78 | 86 | 93 | 101 | 264 | 24 |
| 25 | 50 | 60 | 64 | 72 | 78 | 86 | 231 | 65 | 75 | 81 | 89 | 96 | 104 | 272 | 25 |

| | $N_1 = 9$ | | | | | | | | $N_1 = 10$ | | | | | | | |
| $N_2$ | 0.001 | 0.005 | 0.010 | 0.025 | 0.05 | 0.10 | $2\overline{W}$ | 0.001 | 0.005 | 0.010 | 0.025 | 0.05 | 0.10 | $2\overline{W}$ | $N_2$ |
|---|---|---|---|---|---|---|---|---|---|---|---|---|---|---|---|
| 9 | 52 | 56 | 59 | 62 | 66 | 70 | 171 | | | | | | | | |
| 10 | 53 | 58 | 61 | 65 | 69 | 73 | 180 | 65 | 71 | 74 | 78 | 82 | 87 | 210 | 10 |
| 11 | 55 | 61 | 63 | 68 | 72 | 76 | 189 | 67 | 73 | 77 | 81 | 86 | 91 | 220 | 11 |
| 12 | 57 | 63 | 66 | 71 | 75 | 80 | 198 | 69 | 76 | 79 | 84 | 89 | 94 | 230 | 12 |

(continued)

## TABLE A.8  Critical Values for $W$ (Wilcoxon Rank-Sum Test) (continued)

| | $N_1 = 9$ | | | | | | | $N_1 = 10$ | | | | | | | |
|---|---|---|---|---|---|---|---|---|---|---|---|---|---|---|---|
| $N_2$ | 0.001 | 0.005 | 0.010 | 0.025 | 0.05 | 0.10 | $2\overline{W}$ | 0.001 | 0.005 | 0.010 | 0.025 | 0.05 | 0.10 | $2\overline{W}$ | $N_2$ |
| 13 | 59 | 65 | 68 | 73 | 78 | 83 | 207 | 72 | 79 | 82 | 88 | 92 | 98 | 240 | 13 |
| 14 | 60 | 67 | 71 | 76 | 81 | 86 | 216 | 74 | 81 | 85 | 91 | 96 | 102 | 250 | 14 |
| 15 | 62 | 69 | 73 | 79 | 84 | 90 | 225 | 76 | 84 | 88 | 94 | 99 | 106 | 260 | 15 |
| 16 | 64 | 72 | 76 | 82 | 87 | 93 | 234 | 78 | 86 | 91 | 97 | 103 | 109 | 270 | 16 |
| 17 | 66 | 74 | 78 | 84 | 90 | 97 | 243 | 80 | 89 | 93 | 100 | 106 | 113 | 280 | 17 |
| 18 | 68 | 76 | 81 | 87 | 93 | 100 | 252 | 82 | 92 | 96 | 103 | 110 | 117 | 290 | 18 |
| 19 | 70 | 78 | 83 | 90 | 96 | 103 | 261 | 84 | 94 | 99 | 107 | 113 | 121 | 300 | 19 |
| 20 | 71 | 81 | 85 | 93 | 99 | 107 | 270 | 87 | 97 | 102 | 110 | 117 | 125 | 310 | 20 |
| 21 | 73 | 83 | 88 | 95 | 102 | 110 | 279 | 89 | 99 | 105 | 113 | 120 | 128 | 320 | 21 |
| 22 | 75 | 85 | 90 | 98 | 105 | 113 | 288 | 91 | 102 | 108 | 116 | 123 | 132 | 330 | 22 |
| 23 | 77 | 88 | 93 | 101 | 108 | 117 | 297 | 93 | 105 | 110 | 119 | 127 | 136 | 340 | 23 |
| 24 | 79 | 90 | 95 | 104 | 111 | 120 | 306 | 95 | 107 | 113 | 122 | 130 | 140 | 350 | 24 |
| 25 | 81 | 92 | 98 | 107 | 114 | 123 | 315 | 98 | 110 | 116 | 126 | 134 | 144 | 360 | 25 |

| | $N_1 = 11$ | | | | | | | $N_1 = 12$ | | | | | | | |
|---|---|---|---|---|---|---|---|---|---|---|---|---|---|---|---|
| $N_2$ | 0.001 | 0.005 | 0.010 | 0.025 | 0.05 | 0.10 | $2\overline{W}$ | 0.001 | 0.005 | 0.010 | 0.025 | 0.05 | 0.10 | $2\overline{W}$ | $N_2$ |
| 11 | 81 | 87 | 91 | 96 | 100 | 106 | 253 | | | | | | | | |
| 12 | 83 | 90 | 94 | 99 | 104 | 110 | 264 | 98 | 105 | 109 | 115 | 120 | 127 | 300 | 12 |
| 13 | 86 | 93 | 97 | 103 | 108 | 114 | 275 | 101 | 109 | 113 | 119 | 125 | 131 | 312 | 13 |
| 14 | 88 | 96 | 100 | 106 | 112 | 118 | 286 | 103 | 112 | 116 | 123 | 129 | 136 | 324 | 14 |
| 15 | 90 | 99 | 103 | 110 | 116 | 123 | 297 | 106 | 115 | 120 | 127 | 133 | 141 | 336 | 15 |
| 16 | 93 | 102 | 107 | 113 | 120 | 127 | 308 | 109 | 119 | 124 | 131 | 138 | 145 | 348 | 16 |
| 17 | 95 | 105 | 110 | 117 | 123 | 131 | 319 | 112 | 122 | 127 | 135 | 142 | 150 | 360 | 17 |
| 18 | 98 | 108 | 113 | 121 | 127 | 135 | 330 | 115 | 125 | 131 | 139 | 146 | 155 | 372 | 18 |
| 19 | 100 | 111 | 116 | 124 | 131 | 139 | 341 | 118 | 129 | 134 | 143 | 150 | 159 | 384 | 19 |
| 20 | 103 | 114 | 119 | 128 | 135 | 144 | 352 | 120 | 132 | 138 | 147 | 155 | 164 | 396 | 20 |
| 21 | 106 | 117 | 123 | 131 | 139 | 148 | 363 | 123 | 136 | 142 | 151 | 159 | 169 | 408 | 21 |
| 22 | 108 | 120 | 126 | 135 | 143 | 152 | 374 | 126 | 139 | 145 | 155 | 163 | 173 | 420 | 22 |
| 23 | 111 | 123 | 129 | 139 | 147 | 156 | 385 | 129 | 142 | 149 | 159 | 168 | 178 | 432 | 23 |
| 24 | 113 | 126 | 132 | 142 | 151 | 161 | 396 | 132 | 146 | 153 | 163 | 172 | 183 | 444 | 24 |
| 25 | 116 | 129 | 136 | 146 | 155 | 165 | 407 | 135 | 149 | 156 | 167 | 176 | 187 | 456 | 25 |

| | $N_1 = 13$ | | | | | | | $N_1 = 14$ | | | | | | | |
|---|---|---|---|---|---|---|---|---|---|---|---|---|---|---|---|
| $N_2$ | 0.001 | 0.005 | 0.010 | 0.025 | 0.05 | 0.10 | $2\overline{W}$ | 0.001 | 0.005 | 0.010 | 0.025 | 0.05 | 0.10 | $2\overline{W}$ | $N_2$ |
| 13 | 117 | 125 | 130 | 136 | 142 | 149 | 351 | | | | | | | | |
| 14 | 120 | 129 | 134 | 141 | 147 | 154 | 364 | 137 | 147 | 152 | 160 | 166 | 174 | 406 | 14 |
| 15 | 123 | 133 | 138 | 145 | 152 | 159 | 377 | 141 | 151 | 156 | 164 | 171 | 179 | 420 | 15 |
| 16 | 126 | 136 | 142 | 150 | 156 | 165 | 390 | 144 | 155 | 161 | 169 | 176 | 185 | 434 | 16 |
| 17 | 129 | 140 | 146 | 154 | 161 | 170 | 403 | 148 | 159 | 165 | 174 | 182 | 190 | 448 | 17 |
| 18 | 133 | 144 | 150 | 158 | 166 | 175 | 416 | 151 | 163 | 170 | 179 | 187 | 196 | 462 | 18 |
| 19 | 136 | 148 | 154 | 163 | 171 | 180 | 429 | 155 | 168 | 174 | 183 | 192 | 202 | 476 | 19 |
| 20 | 139 | 151 | 158 | 167 | 175 | 185 | 442 | 159 | 172 | 178 | 188 | 197 | 207 | 490 | 20 |
| 21 | 142 | 155 | 162 | 171 | 180 | 190 | 455 | 162 | 176 | 183 | 193 | 202 | 213 | 504 | 21 |
| 22 | 145 | 159 | 166 | 176 | 185 | 195 | 468 | 166 | 180 | 187 | 198 | 207 | 218 | 518 | 22 |
| 23 | 149 | 163 | 170 | 180 | 189 | 200 | 481 | 169 | 184 | 192 | 203 | 212 | 224 | 532 | 23 |
| 24 | 152 | 166 | 174 | 185 | 194 | 205 | 494 | 173 | 188 | 196 | 207 | 218 | 229 | 546 | 24 |
| 25 | 155 | 170 | 178 | 189 | 199 | 211 | 507 | 177 | 192 | 200 | 212 | 223 | 235 | 560 | 25 |

| | $N_1 = 15$ | | | | | | | $N_1 = 16$ | | | | | | | |
|---|---|---|---|---|---|---|---|---|---|---|---|---|---|---|---|
| $N_2$ | 0.001 | 0.005 | 0.010 | 0.025 | 0.05 | 0.10 | $2\overline{W}$ | 0.001 | 0.005 | 0.010 | 0.025 | 0.05 | 0.10 | $2\overline{W}$ | $N_2$ |
| 15 | 160 | 171 | 176 | 184 | 192 | 200 | 465 | | | | | | | | |
| 16 | 163 | 175 | 181 | 190 | 197 | 206 | 480 | 184 | 196 | 202 | 211 | 219 | 229 | 528 | 16 |

(continued)

## TABLE A.8   Critical Values for $W$ (Wilcoxon Rank-Sum Test) (*continued*)

| | $N_1 = 15$ | | | | | | | $N_1 = 16$ | | | | | | | |
|---|---|---|---|---|---|---|---|---|---|---|---|---|---|---|---|
| $N_2$ | 0.001 | 0.005 | 0.010 | 0.025 | 0.05 | 0.10 | $2\overline{W}$ | 0.001 | 0.005 | 0.010 | 0.025 | 0.05 | 0.10 | $2\overline{W}$ | $N_2$ |
| 17 | 167 | 180 | 186 | 195 | 203 | 212 | 495 | 188 | 201 | 207 | 217 | 225 | 235 | 544 | 17 |
| 18 | 171 | 184 | 190 | 200 | 208 | 218 | 510 | 192 | 206 | 212 | 222 | 231 | 242 | 560 | 18 |
| 19 | 175 | 189 | 195 | 205 | 214 | 224 | 525 | 196 | 210 | 213 | 228 | 237 | 248 | 576 | 19 |
| 20 | 179 | 193 | 200 | 210 | 220 | 230 | 540 | 201 | 215 | 223 | 234 | 243 | 255 | 592 | 20 |
| 21 | 183 | 198 | 205 | 216 | 225 | 236 | 555 | 205 | 220 | 228 | 239 | 249 | 261 | 608 | 21 |
| 22 | 187 | 202 | 210 | 221 | 231 | 242 | 370 | 209 | 225 | 233 | 245 | 255 | 267 | 624 | 22 |
| 23 | 191 | 207 | 214 | 226 | 236 | 248 | 585 | 214 | 230 | 238 | 251 | 261 | 274 | 640 | 23 |
| 24 | 195 | 211 | 219 | 231 | 242 | 254 | 600 | 218 | 235 | 244 | 256 | 267 | 280 | 656 | 24 |
| 25 | 199 | 216 | 224 | 237 | 248 | 260 | 615 | 222 | 240 | 249 | 262 | 273 | 287 | 672 | 25 |

| | $N_1 = 17$ | | | | | | | $N_1 = 18$ | | | | | | | |
|---|---|---|---|---|---|---|---|---|---|---|---|---|---|---|---|
| $N_2$ | 0.001 | 0.005 | 0.010 | 0.025 | 0.05 | 0.10 | $2\overline{W}$ | 0.001 | 0.005 | 0.010 | 0.025 | 0.05 | 0.10 | $2\overline{W}$ | $N_2$ |
| 17 | 210 | 223 | 230 | 240 | 249 | 259 | 595 | | | | | | | | |
| 18 | 214 | 228 | 235 | 246 | 255 | 266 | 612 | 237 | 252 | 259 | 270 | 280 | 291 | 666 | 18 |
| 19 | 219 | 234 | 241 | 252 | 262 | 273 | 629 | 242 | 258 | 265 | 277 | 287 | 299 | 684 | 19 |
| 20 | 223 | 239 | 246 | 258 | 268 | 280 | 646 | 247 | 263 | 271 | 283 | 294 | 306 | 702 | 20 |
| 21 | 228 | 244 | 252 | 264 | 274 | 287 | 663 | 252 | 269 | 277 | 290 | 301 | 313 | 720 | 21 |
| 22 | 233 | 249 | 258 | 270 | 281 | 294 | 680 | 257 | 275 | 283 | 296 | 307 | 321 | 738 | 22 |
| 23 | 238 | 255 | 263 | 276 | 287 | 300 | 697 | 262 | 280 | 289 | 303 | 314 | 328 | 756 | 23 |
| 24 | 242 | 260 | 269 | 282 | 294 | 307 | 714 | 267 | 286 | 295 | 309 | 321 | 335 | 774 | 24 |
| 25 | 247 | 265 | 275 | 288 | 300 | 314 | 731 | 273 | 292 | 301 | 316 | 323 | 343 | 792 | 25 |

| | $N_1 = 19$ | | | | | | | $N_1 = 20$ | | | | | | | |
|---|---|---|---|---|---|---|---|---|---|---|---|---|---|---|---|
| $N_2$ | 0.001 | 0.005 | 0.010 | 0.025 | 0.05 | 0.10 | $2\overline{W}$ | 0.001 | 0.005 | 0.010 | 0.025 | 0.05 | 0.10 | $2\overline{W}$ | $N_2$ |
| 19 | 267 | 283 | 291 | 303 | 313 | 325 | 741 | | | | | | | | |
| 20 | 272 | 239 | 297 | 309 | 320 | 333 | 760 | 298 | 315 | 324 | 337 | 348 | 361 | 820 | 20 |
| 21 | 277 | 295 | 303 | 316 | 328 | 341 | 779 | 304 | 322 | 331 | 344 | 356 | 370 | 840 | 21 |
| 22 | 283 | 301 | 310 | 323 | 335 | 349 | 798 | 309 | 328 | 337 | 351 | 364 | 378 | 860 | 22 |
| 23 | 288 | 307 | 316 | 330 | 342 | 357 | 817 | 315 | 335 | 344 | 359 | 371 | 386 | 880 | 23 |
| 24 | 294 | 313 | 323 | 337 | 350 | 364 | 836 | 321 | 341 | 351 | 366 | 379 | 394 | 900 | 24 |
| 25 | 299 | 319 | 329 | 344 | 357 | 372 | 855 | 327 | 348 | 358 | 373 | 387 | 403 | 920 | 25 |

| | $N_1 = 21$ | | | | | | | $N_1 = 22$ | | | | | | | |
|---|---|---|---|---|---|---|---|---|---|---|---|---|---|---|---|
| $N_2$ | 0.001 | 0.005 | 0.010 | 0.025 | 0.05 | 0.10 | $2\overline{W}$ | 0.001 | 0.005 | 0.010 | 0.025 | 0.05 | 0.10 | $2\overline{W}$ | $N_2$ |
| 21 | 331 | 349 | 359 | 373 | 385 | 399 | 903 | | | | | | | | |
| 22 | 337 | 356 | 366 | 381 | 393 | 408 | 924 | 365 | 386 | 396 | 411 | 424 | 439 | 990 | 22 |
| 23 | 343 | 363 | 373 | 388 | 401 | 417 | 945 | 372 | 393 | 403 | 419 | 432 | 448 | 1012 | 23 |
| 24 | 349 | 370 | 381 | 396 | 410 | 425 | 966 | 379 | 400 | 411 | 427 | 441 | 457 | 1034 | 24 |
| 25 | 356 | 377 | 388 | 404 | 418 | 434 | 987 | 385 | 408 | 419 | 435 | 450 | 467 | 1056 | 25 |

| | $N_1 = 23$ | | | | | | | $N_1 = 24$ | | | | | | | |
|---|---|---|---|---|---|---|---|---|---|---|---|---|---|---|---|
| $N_2$ | 0.001 | 0.005 | 0.010 | 0.025 | 0.05 | 0.10 | $2\overline{W}$ | 0.001 | 0.005 | 0.010 | 0.025 | 0.05 | 0.10 | $2\overline{W}$ | $N_2$ |
| 23 | 402 | 424 | 434 | 451 | 465 | 481 | 1081 | | | | | | | | |
| 24 | 409 | 431 | 443 | 459 | 474 | 491 | 1104 | 440 | 464 | 475 | 492 | 507 | 525 | 1176 | 24 |
| 25 | 416 | 439 | 451 | 468 | 483 | 500 | 1127 | 448 | 472 | 484 | 501 | 517 | 535 | 1200 | 25 |

| | $N_1 = 25$ | | | | | | |
|---|---|---|---|---|---|---|---|
| $N_2$ | 0.001 | 0.005 | 0.010 | 0.025 | 0.05 | 0.10 | $2\overline{W}$ |
| 25 | 480 | 505 | 517 | 536 | 552 | 570 | 1275 |

**TABLE A.9   Critical Values for the Wilcoxon Matched-Pairs Signed-Ranks *T* Test***

| No. of Pairs N | α Levels for a One-Tailed Test .05 | .025 | .01 | .005 | No. of Pairs N | α Levels for a One-Tailed Test .05 | .025 | .01 | .005 |
|---|---|---|---|---|---|---|---|---|---|
| | α Levels for a Two-Tailed Test .10 | .05 | .02 | .01 | | α Levels for a Two-Tailed Test .10 | .05 | .02 | .01 |
| 5 | 0 | — | — | — | 28 | 130 | 116 | 101 | 91 |
| 6 | 2 | 0 | — | — | 29 | 140 | 126 | 110 | 100 |
| 7 | 3 | 2 | 0 | — | 30 | 151 | 137 | 120 | 109 |
| 8 | 5 | 3 | 1 | 0 | 31 | 163 | 147 | 130 | 118 |
| 9 | 8 | 5 | 3 | 1 | 32 | 175 | 159 | 140 | 128 |
| 10 | 10 | 8 | 5 | 3 | 33 | 187 | 170 | 151 | 138 |
| 11 | 13 | 10 | 7 | 5 | 34 | 200 | 182 | 162 | 148 |
| 12 | 17 | 13 | 9 | 7 | 35 | 213 | 195 | 173 | 159 |
| 13 | 21 | 17 | 12 | 9 | 36 | 227 | 208 | 185 | 171 |
| 14 | 25 | 21 | 15 | 12 | 37 | 241 | 221 | 198 | 182 |
| 15 | 30 | 25 | 19 | 15 | 38 | 256 | 235 | 211 | 194 |
| 16 | 35 | 29 | 23 | 19 | 39 | 271 | 249 | 224 | 207 |
| 17 | 41 | 34 | 27 | 23 | 40 | 286 | 264 | 238 | 220 |
| 18 | 47 | 40 | 32 | 27 | 41 | 302 | 279 | 252 | 233 |
| 19 | 53 | 46 | 37 | 32 | 42 | 319 | 294 | 266 | 247 |
| 20 | 60 | 52 | 43 | 37 | 43 | 336 | 310 | 281 | 261 |
| 21 | 67 | 58 | 49 | 42 | 44 | 353 | 327 | 296 | 276 |
| 22 | 75 | 65 | 55 | 48 | 45 | 371 | 343 | 312 | 291 |
| 23 | 83 | 73 | 62 | 54 | 46 | 389 | 361 | 328 | 307 |
| 24 | 91 | 81 | 69 | 61 | 47 | 407 | 378 | 345 | 322 |
| 25 | 100 | 89 | 76 | 68 | 48 | 426 | 396 | 362 | 339 |
| 26 | 110 | 98 | 84 | 75 | 49 | 446 | 415 | 379 | 355 |
| 27 | 119 | 107 | 92 | 83 | 50 | 466 | 434 | 397 | 373 |

*To be significant, the *T* obtained from the data must be equal to or less than the value shown in the table.
Sᴏᴜʀᴄᴇ: Kirk, R. E. (1984). *Elementary Statistics* (2nd ed.). Pacific Grove, CA: Brooks/Cole Publishing.

# B Computational Formulas for ANOVAs

**ALTERNATIVE TABLE 10.5**   ANOVA summary table using computational formulas

| SOURCE | df | SS | MS | F |
|---|---|---|---|---|
| Between groups | $k - 1$ | $\sum\left[\dfrac{\left(\sum X_g\right)^2}{n_g}\right] - \dfrac{\left(\sum X\right)^2}{N}$ | $\dfrac{SS_b}{df_b}$ | $\dfrac{MS_b}{MS_w}$ |
| Within groups | $N - k$ | $\sum\left[\sum X_g^2 - \dfrac{\left(\sum X_g\right)^2}{n_g}\right]$ | $\dfrac{SS_w}{df_w}$ | |
| Total | $N - 1$ | $\sum X^2 - \dfrac{\left(\sum X\right)^2}{N}$ | | |

**ALTERNATIVE TABLE 10.13**   Repeated measures ANOVA summary table using computational formulas

| SOURCE | df | SS | MS | F |
|---|---|---|---|---|
| Participant | $n - 1$ | $\sum\left[\dfrac{\left(\sum X_P\right)^2}{k}\right] - \dfrac{\left(\sum X\right)^2}{N}$ | $\dfrac{SS_P}{df_P}$ | |
| Between | $k - 1$ | $\sum\left[\dfrac{\left(\sum X_t\right)^2}{n_t}\right] - \dfrac{\left(\sum X\right)^2}{N}$ | $\dfrac{SS_b}{df_b}$ | $\dfrac{MS_b}{MS_e}$ |
| Error | $(k - 1)(n - 1)$ | $\sum X^2 - \sum\left[\dfrac{\left(\sum X_P\right)^2}{k}\right] - \sum\left[\dfrac{\left(\sum X_t\right)^2}{n_t}\right] + \dfrac{\left(\sum X\right)^2}{N}$ | $\dfrac{SS_e}{df_e}$ | |
| Total | $N - 1$ | $\sum X^2 - \dfrac{\left(\sum X\right)^2}{N}$ | | |

**ALTERNATIVE TABLE 11.8  Two-way randomized ANOVA summary table using computational formulas**

| SOURCE | df | SS | MS | F |
|---|---|---|---|---|
| Factor A | $A - 1$ | $\sum\left[\dfrac{(\sum X_A)^2}{n_A}\right] - \dfrac{(\sum X)^2}{N}$ | $\dfrac{SS_A}{df_A}$ | $\dfrac{MS_A}{MS_{Error}}$ |
| Factor B | $B - 1$ | $\sum\left[\dfrac{(\sum X_B)^2}{n_B}\right] - \dfrac{(\sum X)^2}{N}$ | $\dfrac{SS_B}{df_B}$ | $\dfrac{MS_B}{MS_{Error}}$ |
| A × B | $(A - 1)(B - 1)$ | $\sum\left[\dfrac{(\sum X_C)^2}{n_C}\right] - \dfrac{(\sum X)^2}{N} - SS_A - SS_B$ | $\dfrac{SS_{A \times B}}{df_{A \times B}}$ | $\dfrac{MS_{A \times B}}{MS_{Error}}$ |
| Error | $AB(n - 1)$ | $\sum X^2 - \sum\left[\dfrac{(\sum X_C)^2}{n_C}\right]$ | $\dfrac{SS_{Error}}{df_{Error}}$ | |
| Total | $N - 1$ | $\sum X^2 - \dfrac{(\sum X)^2}{N}$ | | |

# Answers to Odd-Numbered Chapter Exercises

## Chapter 1

1. Answers will vary. Here are some examples.

   *Superstition and Intuition*
   Breaking a mirror leads to 7 years of bad luck.
   A black cat crossing your path signifies bad luck.
   I have a feeling that something bad is going to happen on my trip next week.

   *Authority*
   You read in the newspaper that more Americans are overweight now than 10 years ago.
   You recently saw a TV commercial for a new diet product that was endorsed by a very slim soap opera star.

   *Tenacity*
   You have heard the SlimFast slogan so many times that you believe it must be true.

   *Rationalism*
   SUVs use more gas and spew more emissions than many other vehicles. Because emissions contribute significantly to air pollution, those who drive SUVs must be less concerned about polluting the environment.

   *Empiricism*
   I have observed that using note cards can be an effective means of studying for an exam.
   I have observed that using note cards can be an ineffective means of studying for an exam.

   *Science*
   Studies have shown that smoking has been linked to lung disease.
   Studies have shown that elaborative rehearsal leads to better retention than rote rehearsal.

3. Many scientists view being called a skeptic as a compliment because it means that they do not blindly accept findings and information. Being a skeptic means that they need data to support an idea and that they insist on proper testing procedures when the data are collected. Being a skeptic also means applying three criteria that help define science: systematic empiricism, public verification, and solvable problems.

5. Research methods are equally important to all areas of psychology because all that we know about a discipline is gained through research. For those planning to pursue careers in clinical/counseling psychology, knowledge of research methods is important in order to determine whether a particular counseling method or drug is an effective treatment.

7. a. The independent variable is the amount of caffeine.
   b. The dependent variable is the anxiety level.
   c. The control group receives no caffeine, whereas the experimental group receives caffeine.
   d. The independent variable is manipulated.

## Chapter 2

1. There is no correct answer to this question. It requires library work.

3. When participants in a study are classified as "at risk," this means that there is the potential for them to be under some emotional or physical risk. Participants "at minimal risk" are at no more risk than would be encountered in daily life or during the performance of routine physical or psychological examinations or tests.

5. Researchers must consider how informed consent works with children. It should be obtained from the legal guardian for all participants under 18 years of age. However, if the child is old enough to understand language, the researcher should also try to inform the child about the study. The researcher also needs to be particularly sensitive to whether or not the child feels comfortable exercising the rights provided through the informed consent.

## Chapter 3

1. Alternative c is an operational definition of depression.
3. c. +.83. Although this is not the strongest correlation coefficient, it is the strongest positive correlation. It therefore is the best measure of reliability.
5. If the observers disagreed 32 times out of 75, then they agreed 43 times out of 75. Thus, the interrater reliability is 43/75 = .57. Because the interrater reliability is moderate, I would recommend that the librarians use these data with caution. In other words, there may be a problem with either the measuring instrument or the individuals using the instrument, and therefore the data are not terribly reliable.

## Chapter 4

1. This research might best be conducted using some form of naturalistic observation. It would probably be best to use a disguised type of observation, either nonparticipant or participant. Thus, the researcher could have data collectors stationed at all of the locations of interest. These individuals either could be hidden or could appear to be part of the natural environment. In either situation, drivers would not notice that data were being collected. If the data recorders were hidden, they could use a checklist . However, if the data recorders were disguised participants, then a narrative record might be best so that drivers would not notice they were being observed. Thus, the person collecting data could either use a hidden tape recorder or communicate with another individual by cell phone. The concerns would be those already indicated.
3. a. This is a loaded question because of the phrases *capitalist bankers* and *such high interest*

*rates.* A better question would be "Do you believe bankers charge appropriate interest rates on credit card balances?"
   b. The problem with this question is in the alternatives. Students who charged an amount between the alternatives (say, $450) would not know which alternative to choose.
   c. This is a leading question. The phrase *Most Americans believe* leads the respondent to agree with the question. A better question would be "Do you believe that a credit card is a necessity?"

## Chapter 5

1.

| Speed | f | rf |
|-------|-----|------|
| 62 | 1 | .05 |
| 64 | 3 | .15 |
| 65 | 4 | .20 |
| 67 | 3 | .15 |
| 68 | 2 | .10 |
| 70 | 2 | .10 |
| 72 | 1 | .05 |
| 73 | 1 | .05 |
| 76 | 1 | .05 |
| 79 | 1 | .05 |
| 80 | 1 | .05 |
| | 20 | 1.00 |

3. Either a histogram or a frequency polygon could be used to graph these data. Because of the continuous nature of the speed data, a frequency polygon might be more appropriate. Both a histogram and a frequency polygon of the data are shown here.

5. a. $\bar{X} = 7.3$
   Median = 8.5
   Mode = 11
   b. $\bar{X} = 4.83$
   Median = 5
   Mode = 5
   c. $\bar{X} = 6.17$
   Median = 6.5
   Mode = 3, 8
   d. $\bar{X} = 5.5$
   Median = 6
   Mode = 6
7. a. $z = +2.57$; proportion of cars that cost an equal amount or more $= .0051$
   b. $z = -2.0$; proportion of cars that cost an equal amount or more $= .9772$
   c. $z = +2.0$; percentile rank $= 97.72$
   d. $z = -3.14$; percentile rank $= 0.08$
   e. $z = -3.14$, $z = +2.0$; proportion between $= .4992 + .4772 = .9764$
   f. 16th percentile converts to a $z$-score of $-0.99$; $-0.99(3,500) + 23,000 = \$19,535$
9.

| | X | z-Score | Percentile Rank |
|---|---|---|---|
| Ken | 73.00 | −0.22 | 41.29 |
| Drew | 88.95 | +1.55 | 93.94 |
| Cecil | 83.28 | +0.92 | 82.00 |

# Chapter 6

1. The first problem is with the correlation coefficient that was calculated. Correlation coefficients can vary between $-1.0$ and $+1.0$; they cannot be greater than $\pm 1.0$. Thus, the calculated correlation coefficient is incorrect. Second, correlation does not mean causation. Thus, observing a correlation between exercise and health does not mean we can conclude that exercise causes better health — they are simply related.

3. We would expect the correlation between GRE scores and graduate school GPAs to be much lower than that between SAT scores and undergraduate GPAs because both GRE scores and graduate school GPAs are restricted in range.

5. IQ with psychology exam scores: $r = .553$, $r^2 = 30.6\%$
   IQ with statistics exam scores: $r = .682$, $r^2 = 46.5\%$
   Psychology exam scores with statistics exam scores: $r = .626$, $r^2 = 39.2\%$
   All of the correlation coefficients are of moderate strength, with the correlation between IQ scores and statistics exam scores being the strongest and accounting for the most variability.

# Chapter 7

1. $H_0$: $\mu_{\text{freshmen}} \le \mu_{\text{all other classes}}$
   $H_a$: $\mu_{\text{freshmen}} > \mu_{\text{all other classes}}$
   This is a one-tailed test.
3. $H_0$: $\mu_{\text{family size now}} \le \mu_{\text{family size in previous decade}}$
   $H_a$: $\mu_{\text{family size now}} > \mu_{\text{family size in previous decade}}$
   This is a one-tailed test.
5. a. Type I error
   b. Type II error
   c. Type I error
   d. Type II error
7. a. This is a one-tailed test.
   b. $H_0$: $\mu_{\text{private HS}} \le \mu_{\text{HS in general}}$
      $H_a$: $\mu_{\text{private HS}} > \mu_{\text{HS in general}}$
   c. $z_{\text{obt}} = 2.37$
   d. $z_{\text{cv}} = \pm 1.645$ (one-tailed critical value)
   e. Reject $H_0$. High school students at private high schools score significantly higher on the SAT.
9. The $t$ distributions are a family of symmetrical distributions that differ for each sample size. Therefore, $t_{\text{cv}}$ changes for samples of different sizes. We must compute the degrees of freedom in order to determine $t_{\text{cv}}$.
11. a. This is a one-tailed test.
    b. $H_0$: $\mu_{\text{headphones}} \ge \mu_{\text{no headphones}}$
       $H_a$: $\mu_{\text{headphones}} < \mu_{\text{no headphones}}$
    c. $t_{\text{obt}} = -3.37$
    d. $t_{\text{cv}} = -1.796$
    e. Reject $H_0$. Those who listen to music via headphones score significantly lower on a hearing test.

# Chapter 8

1. This is a between-participants design. If participants are randomly assigned to one of the two conditions, then different participants are used in each condition.

3. It is possible that there was a ceiling effect. In other words, the test was so easy that everyone in the class did well (performed at the top). In this case, the test was not sensitive enough to detect differences in knowledge of biology.

5. A Latin square design allows a researcher to utilize a form of incomplete counterbalancing. Thus, with designs that have several conditions, the researcher uses as many orders as there are conditions. For example, in a design with four conditions, the researcher uses 4 orders rather than the 24 orders that would be necessary if complete counterbalancing were used. This means that the researcher can still counterbalance the study without the counterbalancing procedure becoming too difficult.

7. These are all examples of developmental designs — designs in which age is the manipulated variable. With cross-sectional designs, individuals of different ages are studied at the same time, whereas with longitudinal designs, the same people are studied over many years or decades. A sequential design is a combined cross-sectional and longitudinal design. A researcher begins with participants of different ages (a cross-sectional design) and tests or measures them. Then, either months or years later, the research retests or measures the same individuals (a longitudinal design).

# Chapter 9

1. a. An independent-samples $t$ test should be used.
   b. $H_0$: $\mu_{females} = \mu_{males}$
      $H_a$: $\mu_{females} \neq \mu_{males}$
   c. $t(12) = -0.79$, not significant
   d. Fail to reject $H_0$. There are no significant differences in the amount of study time per week for females versus males.
   e. Not necessary
   f. Not necessary

3. a. A correlated-groups $t$ test should be used.
   b. $H_0$: $\mu_{before} \geq \mu_{after}$
      $H_a$: $\mu_{before} < \mu_{after}$
   c. $t(5) = 6.70$, $p < .005$
   d. Reject $H_0$. Participating in sports leads to significantly higher self-esteem scores.
   e. $d = 2.73$. This is a large effect size.

f.

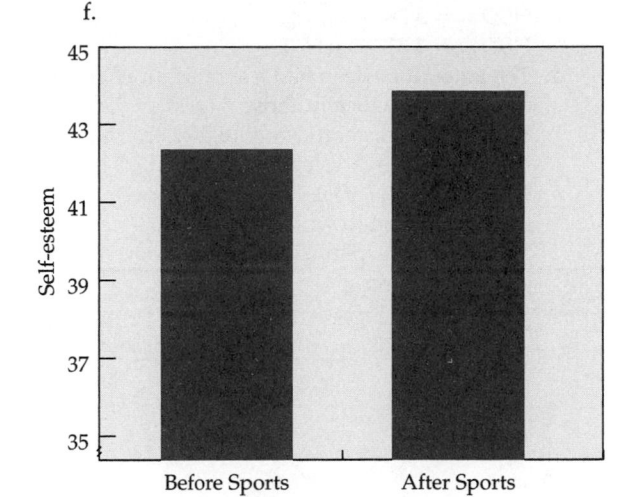

# Chapter 10

1. Conducting a study with three or more levels of the independent variable allows a researcher to compare more than two kinds of treatment in one study, to compare two or more kinds of treatment with a control group, and to compare a placebo group with both the control and experimental groups.

3. Between-groups variance is the variance attributable to both systematic variance and error variance. Systematic variance may be due either to the effects of the independent variable or to confounds. Error variance may be due to chance, sampling error, or individual differences. Within-groups variance is always due to error variance (once again due to chance, sampling error, or individual differences).

5. If $H_0$ is true, then there is no effect of the independent variable and thus no systematic variance. The $F$-ratio is error variance divided by error variance and should be equal or close to 1. If $H_a$ is supported, then there is systematic variance in addition to error variance in the numerator, and therefore the $F$-ratio will be greater than 1.

7. Eta-squared tells us how much of the variability in the dependent variable can be attributed to the independent variable.

9. a.

| Source | df | SS | MS | F |
|---|---|---|---|---|
| Between groups | 3 | 187.75 | 62.58 | 18.14 |
| Within groups | 16 | 55.20 | 3.45 | |
| Total | 19 | 242.95 | | |

b. Yes, $F(3, 16) = 18.14$, $p < .01$.

c. $HSD_{.05} = 3.36$
$HSD_{.01} = 4.31$

d. The amount of sleep had a significant effect on creativity. Specifically, those who slept for 6 or 8 hours scored significantly higher on creativity than those who slept for either 2 or 4 hours.

e. The effect size ($\eta^2$) is 77%. Thus, knowing the sleep condition to which participants were assigned can explain 77% of the variability in creativity scores.

f.

11. a.

| Source | df | SS | MS | F |
|---|---|---|---|---|
| Between groups | 2 | 4,689.27 | 2,344.64 | 0.77 |
| Within groups | 27 | 82,604.20 | 3,059.41 | |
| Total | 29 | 87,293.47 | | |

b. No, $F(2, 27) = 0.77$, not significant.

c. Not necessary

d. The level of exercise did not affect stress level. There was, however, a very large amount of error variance.

e. The effect size ($\eta^2$) is 5%. Knowing the exercise condition to which a participant was assigned does not account for much of the variability in stress scores.

f.

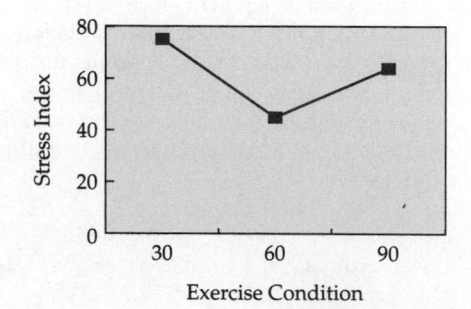

13. a.

| Source | df | SS | MS | F |
|---|---|---|---|---|
| Participant | 6 | 16.27 | 2.71 | |
| Between | 2 | 25.81 | 12.91 | 31.49 |
| Error | 12 | 4.87 | 0.41 | |
| Total | 20 | 46.95 | | |

b. Yes, $F(2, 12) = 31.49$, $p < .01$.

c. $HSD_{.05} = 0.905$
$HSD_{.01} = 1.21$

d. The amount of time practiced significantly affects the accuracy of signal detection. Based on post hoc tests, all group means differ significantly from each other at the .01 alpha level. That is, the group means indicate that as practice increased, signal detection improved.

e. The effect size ($\eta^2$) is 55%. Knowing the amount of time that an individual practiced can account for 55% of the variability in signal detection scores.

f.

15. a.

| Source | df | SS | MS | F |
|---|---|---|---|---|
| Participant | 14 | 136.96 | 9.78 | |
| Between | 2 | 3,350.96 | 1,675.48 | 94.02 |
| Error | 28 | 499.03 | 17.82 | |
| Total | 44 | 3,986.95 | | |

b. Yes, $F(2, 28) = 94.02$, $p < .01$.

c. $HSD_{.05} = 3.85$
$HSD_{.01} = 4.96$

d. The type of study significantly affected exam score. Specifically, the 6-day spaced condition led to higher exam scores than either the 3-day spaced or the massed condition, and the 3-day spaced condition led to better scores than the massed condition.

e. The effect size ($\eta^2$) is 84%. Thus, knowing the type of study used can account for 84% of the variability in exam scores.

f.

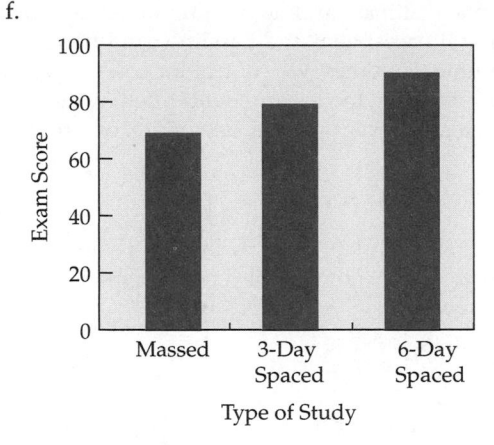

Chapter 11

1. One advantage is that manipulating more than one independent variable allows us to assess how the variables interact, called an interaction effect. In addition, because in the real world behavior is usually contingent on more than one variable, designing experiments with more than one variable allows researchers to simulate a real-world setting more effectively.

3. This is a 3 × 2 × 2 design (or a 2 × 2 × 3). The independent variable Number of Hours has three levels, the independent variable Shallow/Deep Processing has two levels, and the independent variable Group/Individual study has two levels.

5. A 2 × 6 factorial design has two independent variables. Therefore, there is the possibility for two main effects — one for each variable — and one interaction between them.

7.

Experiment 1

Experiment 2

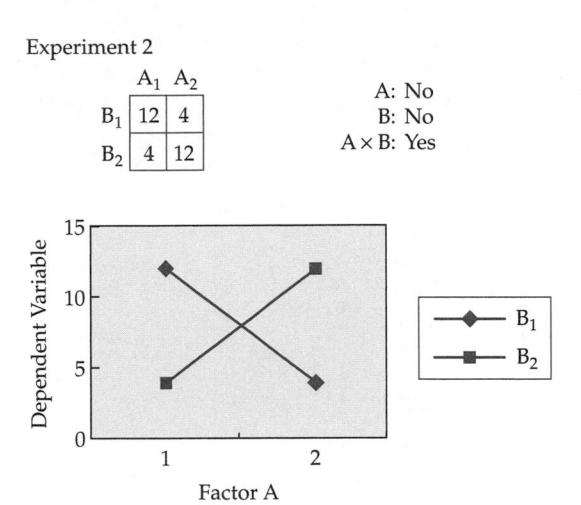

9. No, one of the variables has only two levels. If the F-ratio for that main effect is significant, it means that there were significant differences between those two groups and Tukey's post hoc test is not necessary. However, it is necessary to compute Tukey's post hoc test for the main effect of the variable with six levels. In this case, the F-ratio tells us only that there is a significant difference between two of the groups, and we need to determine how many of the groups differ significantly from each other.

11. a.

| Source | df | SS | MS | F |
|--------|-----|--------|--------|-------|
| Gender | 1 | 0.167 | 0.167 | 0.095 |
| Pizza Brand | 1 | 6.00 | 6.00 | 3.43 |
| Gender × Pizza | 1 | 130.67 | 130.67 | 74.67 |
| Error | 20 | 35.00 | 1.75 | |
| Total | 23 | 171.83 | | |

Note: If calculated by hand, your SS scores may vary slightly due to rounding.

b. The only significant F-ratio is for the interaction, $F(1, 20) = 74.67$, $p < .01$.

c. There is no significant effect of gender on pizza preference. There is no significant effect of pizza brand on pizza preference. There is a significant interaction effect: The males prefer the low-fat pizza over the regular pizza, whereas the females prefer the regular over the low-fat.

d. The effect size ($\eta^2$) is only .09% for gender (gender accounts for less than .1% of the variability in preference scores) and 3.5% for pizza brand. However, the effect size is 76% for the interaction, meaning that the interaction of gender and pizza brand accounts for 76% of the variability in preference scores.

e. Because the variable Gender is not continuous, a bar graph is appropriate. However, because most students find it easier to interpret interactions with a line graph, this type of graph is also provided and may be used.

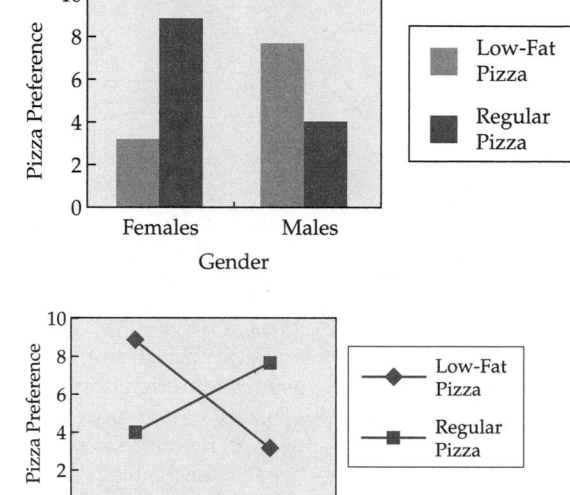

## Chapter 12

1. A true experimental design uses a manipulated independent variable. A quasi-experimental design may have no independent variable (only one group was used and given the treatment) or a nonmanipulated independent variable (although two groups were used, they came to the study already differing, or they chose to participate or not participate in some treatment). Thus, although we can infer a causal relationship based on data from a true experimental design, we cannot do so based on data collected from a quasi-experimental design.

3. The researcher should use a single-group posttest-only design, in which each quiz given across the semester serves as a posttest measure. Because she has no comparison group, this type of study would have limitations.

5. First, the researcher may want information on only the single participant being studied. Second, single-case designs allow for easier replication because only one additional participant is needed rather than another group of participants. Third, single-case research minimizes the error variance that results from indvidual differences in group designs.

7. In a multiple-baseline design, rather than reversing the treatment and baseline conditions numerous times, we control for confounds by introducing the treatment at different times across different people, behaviors, or situations.

## Chapter 13

1. It is appropriate to use a chi-square test when the data are nominal and no parameters are known.

3. a. $\chi^2_{obt} = 8.94$
   b. $df = 1$
   c. $\chi^2_{cv} = 3.841$
   d. The number of students who go on to college from the teacher's high school is significantly greater than the number in the general population.

5. a. The Wilcoxon rank-sum test should be used.
   b. $H_0$: $Md_{no\ service} = Md_{service}$
      $H_a$: $Md_{no\ service} < Md_{service}$
   c. $W(n_{1\ =\ 6}, n_{2\ =\ 6}) = 23.5, p < .01$
   d. Yes, reject $H_0$. Students who completed community service had significantly higher maturity scores.

7. a. The Wilcoxon matched-pairs signed-ranks $T$ test should be used.
   b. $H_0$: $Md_{red\ sauce} = Md_{green\ sauce}$
      $H_a$: $Md_{red\ sauce} > Md_{green\ sauce}$
   c. $T(N = 7) = 3, p = .05$
   d. Fail to reject $H_0$. Taste scores for the two sauces did not differ significantly.

## Chapter 14

1. The title page contains the short title in the top margin (right-justified) along with the page number. The running head is the first line on the title page, followed by the title of the paper (centered), then the author's name (centered), and then the author's affiliation (centered).

3. a. The number 50 should be written out because it begins a sentence. Alternatively, the sentence could be rewritten so that it does not begin with a number.
   b. The proper way to report an $F$-ratio is as follows: $F (1, 12) = 6.54, p < .05$.
   c. The word *data* is plural. Thus, the sentence should read "The data were analyzed using a one-way ANOVA."
   d. The word *while* refers to time and should not be used in this sentence. The sentence should read "One group of participants took the medication, whereas the other group did not."

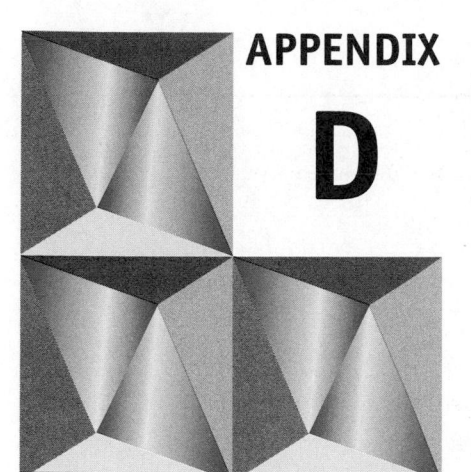

This sample paper by Kim J. Driggers and Tasha Helms was originally published in the *Psi Chi Journal of Undergraduate Research* (2000, Vol. 5, pp. 76–80). This paper is reprinted with permission.

Short title is first two or three meaningful words of title and right justified one-half inch from top of page. Page number appears five spaces after short title. ⟶ Effects of Salary    1

Running head: WILLINGNESS TO DATE

Running head is left justified and provides a short (50 characters or less, including punctuation and spaces) description of the topic of the paper. It is typed in all capital letters.

The Effects of Salary on Willingness to Date

Kim J. Driggers and Tasha Helms

Oklahoma State University

Title, author name(s), and affiliation(s) is (are) centered and double-spaced.

The abstract is typed in block paragraph format and is not more than 120 words long.

Effects of Salary    2

Abstract ←

"Abstract" is centered at the top of page 2.

The purpose of the present experiment was to test the role of salary in date selection by men and women. Male and female college students ($N = 150$) viewed pictures of the opposite sex and rated the target's attractiveness and their own willingness to date the target. Varied among 3 conditions was the level of salary (i.e., $20,000, $60,000, and $100,000) listed. Statistical analyses yielded support for the hypothesis that as the target's salary increased, a participant's willingness to date the target would also increase. That is, as salary increased, both men's and women's willingness to date a target increased. We also found a significant main effect for the sex of participants; as salary increased, women's willingness to date a person increased significantly more than men's willingness.

*OVERVIEW, ALL OF PAPER,*
*NOT AN INTRO*

The title of the paper appears at the top of page 3, centered. The introduction begins on the next line.

### The Effects of Salary on Willingness to Date

To properly review current research in the area of date selection, it is first necessary to highlight theories that form the foundations upon which this research was built. Scientists have studied human mate selection for over a century. Darwin (1871) proposed that physical attractiveness and survival attributes were the essence of mate selection (a.k.a. *natural selection).* Many anthropologists and biologists have explained the factors of physical attractiveness and socioeconomic status (SES) on the basis of evolutionary principles. Often when selecting a mate, one's instinct is a driving factor. Men, according to sociobiologists, search for the most attractive woman to mate with in order to ensure reproductive success (Buss, 1987). Men thus must use physical appearance or related factors (e.g., age and health) to predict the fertility and genes of a woman. To men, mating with a highly attractive woman ensures that their offspring will have a "good" (i.e., viable) genetic makeup. Yet the suggested pattern for women is somewhat different. In terms of evolution, women are more selective than men in their mate selection. Women have more potential risks when choosing a mate (e.g., pregnancy, childbirth, child rearing) and thus concentrate more on a man's ability to provide for her and her offspring (Townsend & Levy, 1990b); hence commitment and the man's ability to offer resources are important factors when it comes to a woman's selection of a man.

Social psychologists explain these differences in mate selection as a social exchange between the sexes (Rusbult, 1980). Scientists have found

In-text citation: Author's name is followed by date in parentheses.

End-of-sentence citation: Author's name and date are both in parentheses.

Use an ampersand (&) when authors' names are in parentheses.

the exchange of a man's security for an attractive woman is the basis of
mate selection (Rusbult, 1980). Elder (1969) found that men's personal
prestige ratings increased when they were paired with an attractive
woman. However, ratings of women in Elder's study were based on
physical attractiveness only. Therefore, women are exchanging attractiveness for the resources men can provide.

These diverse theories highlight the importance of physical attractiveness and SES. Research (Buss, 1987; Darwin, 1871; Elder, 1969; Rusbult,
1980; Townsend & Levy, 1990b) suggests that physical attractiveness is a
better predictor of mate selection in men, and SES is a better predictor of
mate selection in women. Current studies have also found that both of
these attributes play an integral part in female and male mate selection
(e.g., Buss, 1989; Davis, 1985; Goode, 1996; Hill, Nocks, & Gardner, 1987;
Hudson & Henze, 1969; Joshi & Rai, 1989; Sprecher, 1989; Townsend &
Levy, 1990a, 1990b).

In parentheses, multiple citations are separated by semicolons.

When there are three to five authors, give all authors' names in the first citation; use the first author's name followed by "et al." for subsequent citations. If there are six or more authors, use the "et al." form for first and subsequent citations.

Use "and" when authors' names are part of the text.

Townsend and Levy (1990a) questioned participants regarding
different types of relationships ranging from casual conversation to
dating, sex, and other types of serious relationships. Participants rated
their willingness to engage in these types of relationships based on a slide
photograph of a person (face and torso were depicted in the picture).
Results indicated that men and women were more likely to engage in all
types of relationships when a person was physically attractive. Sprecher
(1989), on the other hand, presented only a description of a person (e.g.,

occupation, salary, favorite color) as the stimulus. Sprecher also found that physical attractiveness played an important factor, even in the absence of visual stimuli.

Other current studies have noted SES as an important predictor of interpersonal attraction. SES includes factors such as career, salary, and the attitudes and behaviors attributed to the concerned person (Joshi & Rai, 1989). Research indicates SES is an important element among both sexes in terms of date selection (Bell, 1976; Goode, 1996; Hill et al., 1987; Townsend & Levy, 1990b). For example, Hill et al. (1987) found that attractiveness ratings by both men and women of an unattractive target of the opposite sex increased as their SES increased. Although important to both sexes, SES is even more important to women than to men in terms of date selection (Bell, 1976; Buss, 1987; Goode, 1996; Hill et al., 1987; Nevid, 1984; Townsend & Levy, 1990a, 1990b). Nevid (1984) asked participants to rate personal qualities (e.g., appearance, career, etc.) in terms of their degree of importance in determining their choice of a romantic partner. No visual stimuli were used when the participant determined the order of importance of qualities. Results indicated that women rated SES higher (i.e., as more important) than men in their ranking of importance qualities. Townsend and Levy (1990a, 1990b) asked men and women how willing they were to enter into relationships after presenting them with a picture and description of a person. They found that SES was a better predictor for women than men when deciding whether or not to enter a serious relationship.

When there are three to five authors, use the first author's name followed by "et al." for subsequent citations.

The previously mentioned studies have evaluated the importance of SES in combination with other attributes. Moreover, SES typically has been studied as a global construct, it has never been broken down into its counterparts (i.e., career, salary, attitudes, and behaviors) for evaluation. What are the effects of salary alone on mate selection? How important is salary alone in the overall effect of SES? The present study examined the significance of salary on willingness to date. In order to eliminate the influence of physical attractiveness on ratings, the pictures used in the present study were considered low in physical attractiveness. The independent variable was the salary associated with the photo (three levels: $20,000, $60,000, and $100,000). The dependent variable was the participant's willingness to date a person. The primary hypothesis was that the participant's willingness to date a person would increase as the target's salary increases. Based on previous research, we hypothesized that this relation would be stronger for women.

## Method

*The Method section begins right after the introduction ends, not on a new page. The word "Method" is centered.*

### Participants

*Subsection headings are typed, in italics, flush on the left margin. Subsection headings stand alone on a line.*

The participants in this study consisted of 150 college students (75 men, 75 women) attending a large midwestern university. The average age of participants was 21 years. The ethnic background of participants varied, with 71% of the sampling being Caucasian, 14% Asian American, 8% African American, and 7% Native American. Researchers accessed participants from the college library, dormitories, the student union, and laundry facilities. In these facilities, researchers accessed 55 participants at student organizational meetings, 75 participants at the university library, and the remaining 20 participants in the mezzanines of the dormitories. Only three participants approached refused to participate. Participants were assigned to conditions ($n = 50$ each condition) based on the order in which they were approached by the experimenters.

*Materials*

The materials for the present study consisted of two pictures (one man, one woman) with a short description posted below each picture, and a questionnaire packet (i.e., informed consent sheet, short description of study, and questionnaire). A pretesting group of 20 students selected the pictures used in this experiment. The pretest group selected the most unattractive male and female picture out of 30 different photographs. The male and female pictures the pretest group selected most often as unattractive were used in this study to control for attractiveness. The pictures focused on the faces and upper torso of a Caucasian man and a Caucasian woman separately, both dressed in casual clothes. Included in the short description paired with the picture was the person's age (i.e., 24), occupation (i.e., business field), pets (i.e., none), and marital status (i.e., single), with the only manipulated variable being salary. The salary values were $20,000, $60,000, and $100,000. The short descriptions were the same for both the female and male conditions.

The seven questions in the survey measured the participant's perception of the target's attractiveness and popularity and the participant's willingness to date the target individual. These questions were based on a 7-point Likert scale with the anchors being 1 *(not willing)* and 7 *(extremely willing).* The focus question in this study was "How willing would you be to go on a date with this person?" The other questions were fillers to distract the participant from determining the true purpose of the research.

*Procedure*

The three salary levels defined the three conditions for both the male and female groups. Each participant experienced only one of the three conditions, receiving a picture of the opposite sex. Each condition utilized the same female and male picture.

One researcher was present for each individual participant. The two researchers were 20-year-old Caucasian women of the same height, stature, eye color, and hair color. Each researcher individually tested 75 participants. The researchers told the participants that the purpose of the study was to assess individuals' perceptions. Once the participant finished reading the brief description of the study and signed the informed consent, the experimenter presented the participant with a picture that included one of the short descriptions below it. Participants were allotted 1 min to look at the picture, but they generally looked at it for 30 s or less. After reading the description of the person and observing the picture, the participant responded to the questionnaire. Once completed, the questionnaire and picture were gathered, and the participant was debriefed.

As with the Method section, the Results section does not begin on a new page. The heading is centered.

Tables and figures must be referred to in the text.

When statistical significance tests are presented, the name of the symbol for the test (e.g., *F, t, r*) is italicized. It is followed by the degrees of freedom in parentheses, the test score, and the p value.

The Discussion section follows immediately after the Results section, not on a new page.

## Results

The scores of the focus question (willingness to date), in each condition, were analyzed to determine any significant differences that might exist between conditions and sex. There was a significant increase in willingness to date across salary levels for both men and women (see Figure 1). Effects of sex and salary level were analyzed using a two-way analysis of variance (ANOVA). A main effect for sex was found to be significant, $F(1, 150) = 4.58$, $p < .05$, with women ($M = 3.27$, $SD = 2.07$) receiving higher ratings than men ($M = 2.97$, $SD = 1.68$). A main effect for salary level was significant, $F(1, 150) = 294.96$, $p < .01$, with scores increasing as salary increased. An interaction between sex and condition was also significant, $F(2, 150) = 5.40$, $p < .01$. Subsequent analyses indicated that men and women did not differ at the two lower salary levels; however, the willingness scores of the women were significantly higher than those of the men for the highest ($100,000) salary level $t(48) = 3.213$, $p < .05$.

## Discussion

The purpose of this study was to examine the significance of salary on date selection preferences, while holding status and attractiveness constant. The first hypothesis was that participants' willingness to date a person would increase as the target's salary increased. We also hypothesized that this relationship would be stronger for women. The data supported both hypotheses. Participants' willingness-to-date ratings increased as salary increased, and women were more willing than men to engage in a dating relationship, at least at the highest salary level.

Although evolutionary principles were not tested in this experiment, the results do overlap with findings based on these principles. Evolutionists have found that in terms of mate selection, women hold SES as a more important element than men. Thus, a woman may seek out a mate that has high SES in order to ensure support for her family (Townsend & Levy, 1990b). These results support these evolutionary principles in that women's willingness-to-date ratings did increase significantly more than men's ratings as salary increased. One contradictory result of the present study to these principles is that men's ratings also increased as salary increased, although not as much as women's. A possible explanation may be that this finding is due to an environmental influence because in today's society SES is an important attribute to both men and women (Bell, 1976; Goode, 1996; Hill et al., 1987; Townsend & Levy, 1990b). Thus evolutionary principles may explain the significant difference in men and women's willingness ratings, whereas environmental influences might account for the significant importance overall of SES to both men and women.

The findings presented in this study were not consistent with social psychology theories of mate selection. A common view is that mate selection is a social exchange between the man and the woman (i.e., man's security in exchange for an attractive woman; Rusbult, 1980). If this social exchange theory played a significant part in mate selection, men's ratings of the women would have been consistent across conditions because there was no change in attractiveness.

Although past studies (Goode, 1996; Hill et al., 1987; Joshi & Rai, 1989; Sprecher, 1989; Townsend & Levy, 1990b) have tested the role of physical attractiveness and other attributes combined, this study isolated the influence of salary. SES was found to be a significant factor in these past studies when combined with other attributes. After isolating salary as a single variable to be tested in date selection, the present findings were similar to past studies that combined salary with other attributes (Goode, 1996; Hill et al., 1987; Joshi & Rai, 1989; Sprecher, 1989; Townsend & Levy, 1990b).

This study was a partial replication of Townsend and Levy's study (1990b). The present study used the same format of questions (i.e., willingness to engage in specific relationships based on a Likert scale response), similar stimuli (i.e., pictures), and also similar methods of analysis. Their results indicated that SES in combination with other attributes (e.g., appearance, personality characteristics, etc.) was an important predictor of date selection in both men and women, but more so for women. This study supported past evidence when identifying the differences between men and women in the role of salary in date selection (Bell, 1976; Buss, 1987; Goode, 1996; Hill et al., 1987; Nevid, 1984; Townsend & Levy, 1990a).

Although the present findings support past research, the design involved a sample of college students whose responses were to hypothetical relationships with hypothetical partners, in only one region of the

United States. A replication of this study with a sample encompassing a larger region or multiple regions would help to further support this hypothesis for the purpose of generalization to a more diverse population. Also, personal SES factors of the participants might influence ratings of the target. Controlling for this variable in future studies would broaden the knowledge of this attribute in date selection.

Other methods need to be developed to continue to test the role of SES in date selection. Showing a video of a person or having a person-to-person interaction are suggestions for future stimuli to further test this hypothesis. Future studies could also evaluate the impact of the participants' personal SES in their selections of romantic partners. If a participant has a high income, how important is that attribute to that person when selecting a date? Another future study might also investigate the importance of salary among lesbian and gay male relationships.

The Reference section begins on a new page and is typed in a hanging indent format. References are alphabetized according to the last name of the first author.

Effects of Salary    13

## References

The word "References" is centered at the top of the page.

Bell, Q. (1976). *On human finery.* New York: Schocken Books.

Format for a reference to a book.

Buss, D. M. (1987). Sex differences in human mate selection criteria: An evolutionary perspective. In C. B. Crawford, M. Smith, & D. Krebs (Eds.), *Sociobiology and psychology: Ideas, issues and applications* (pp. 335–352). Hillsdale, NJ: Erlbaum.

Format for a reference from an edited book.

Buss, D. M. (1989). Sex differences in human mate preferences: Evolutionary hypotheses tested in 37 cultures. *The Behavioral and Brain Sciences, 12,* 1–49.

Format for a reference from a journal.

Darwin, C. (1871). *The descent of man, and selection in relation to sex.* London: John Murray.

Davis, K. (1985). The meaning and significance of marriage in contemporary society. In K. Davis (Ed.), *Contemporary marriage: Comparative perspectives on a changing institution* (pp. 1–21). New York: Russell Sage.

Elder, G. H., Jr. (1969). Appearance and education in marriage mobility. *American Sociological Review, 34,* 519–533.

Goode, E. (1996). Gender and courtship entitlement: Responses to personal ads. *Sex Roles, 34,* 141–169.

Hill, E. M., Nocks, E. S., & Gardner, L. (1987). Physical attractiveness: Manipulation by physique and status displays. *Ethology and Sociobiology, 8,* 143–154.

Hudson, J. W., & Henze, L. F. (1969). Campus values in mate selection: A replication. *Journal of Marriage and the Family, 31,* 772–775.

Joshi, K., & Rai, S. N. (1989). Effect of physical attractiveness and social status upon interpersonal attraction. *Psychological Studies, 34,* 193–197.

Nevid, J. S. (1984). Sex differences in factors of romantic attraction. *Sex Roles, 11,* 401–411.

Rusbult, C. E. (1980). Commitment and satisfaction in romantic associations: A test of the investment model. *Journal of Experimental Social Psychology, 16,* 172–186.

Sprecher, S. (1989). The importance to males and females of physical attractiveness, earning potential, and expressiveness in initial attraction. *Sex Roles, 21,* 591–607.

Townsend, J. M., & Levy, G. D. (1990a). Effects of potential partners' costume and physical attractiveness on sexuality and partner selection. *Journal of Psychology, 124,* 371–389.

Townsend, J. M., & Levy, G. D. (1990b). Effects of potential partners' physical attractiveness and socioeconomic status on sexuality and partner selection. *Archives of Sexual Behavior, 19,* 149–164.

Figure Caption

*Figure 1.* Mean rating of male and female participants for each condition ($20,000 $60,000, $100,000) on focus question ("How willing would you be to go on a date with this person?").

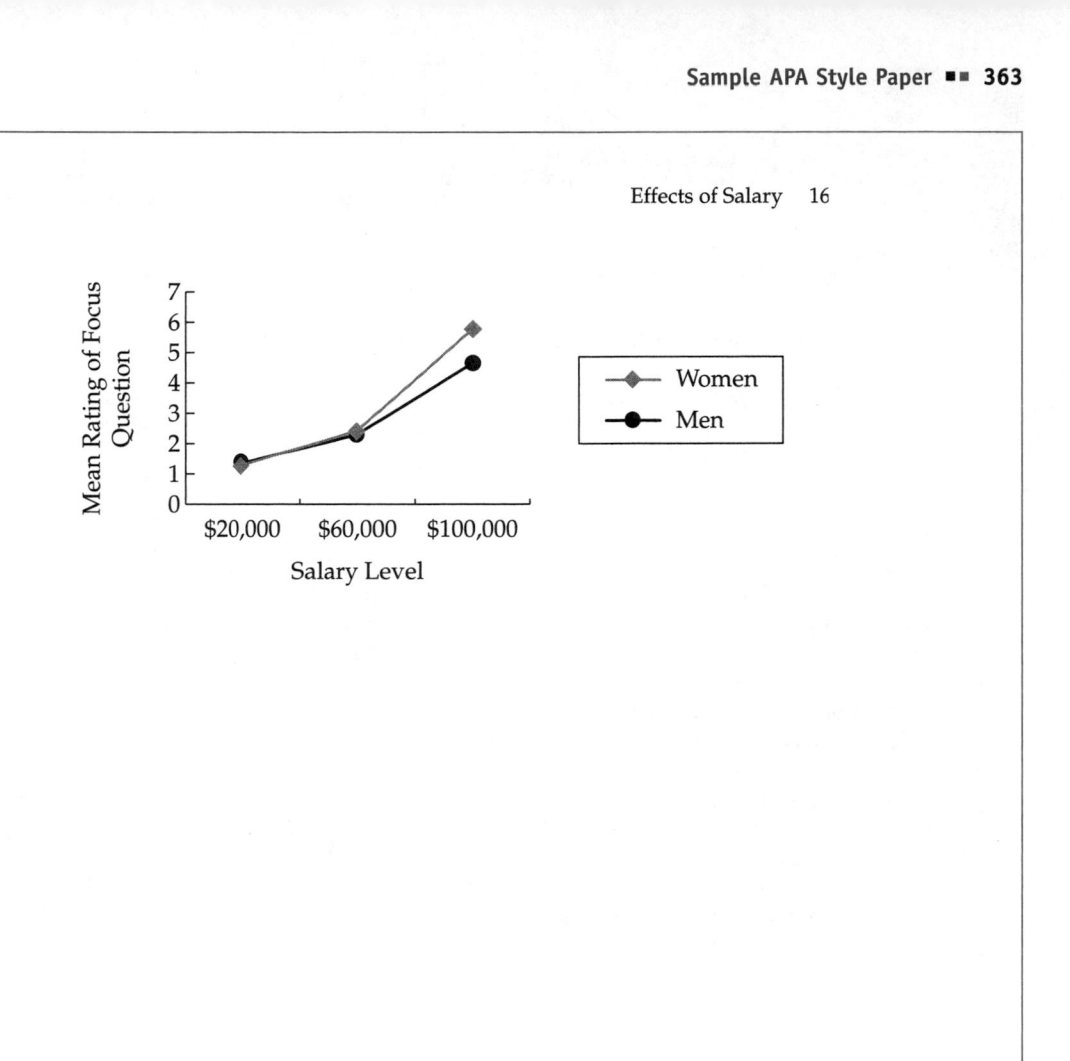

# References

Ainsworth, M. D. S., & Bell, S. M. (1970). Attachment, exploration, and separation: Illustrated by the behavior of one-year-olds in a strange situation. *Child Development, 41,* 49–67.

American Psychological Association. (2002). Ethical principles of psychologists and code of conduct. *American Psychologist, 57,* 1060–1073.

American Psychological Association. (1996). *Guidelines for ethical conduct in the care and use of animals.* Washington, DC: Author.

American Psychological Association. (2001a). *Publication manual of the American Psychological Association* (5th ed.). Washington, DC: Author.

American Psychological Association. (2001b). *Thesaurus of psychological index terms* (9th ed.). Washington, DC: Author.

Anastasi, A., & Urbina, S. (1997). *Psychological testing* (7th ed.). Upper Saddle River, NJ: Prentice Hall.

Aron, A., & Aron, E. N. (1999). *Statistics for psychology* (2nd ed.). Upper Saddle River, NJ: Prentice Hall.

Aronson, E., & Carlsmith, J. M. (1968). Experimentation in social psychology. In G. Lindzey & E. Aronson (Eds.), *Handbook of social psychology* (2nd ed., pp. 1–79). Reading, MA: Addison-Wesley.

Bolt, M. (1998). *Instructor's resources* to accompany David G. Myers, *Psychology* (5th ed.). New York: Worth.

Bratton, R. L., Montero, D. P., Adams, K. S., Novas, M. A., McKay, R. C., Hall, L. J., Goust, J. G., Mueller, M. B., O'Brien, P. C., Atkinson, E. J., & Maurer, M. S. (2002). Effect of "ionized" wrist bracelets on musculoskeletal pain: A randomized, double-blind, placebo-controlled trial. *Mayo Clinic Proceedings, 77,* 1164–1168.

Campbell, D. T. (1969). Reforms as experiments. *American Psychologist, 24,* 409–429.

Campbell, D. T., & Stanley, J. C. (1963). *Experimental and quasi-experimental designs for research.* Boston: Houghton Mifflin.

Cohen, J. (1988). *Statistical power analysis for the behavioral sciences.* Hillsdale, NJ: Erlbaum.

Cohen, J. (1992). A power primer. *Psychological Bulletin, 112,* 155–159.

Cowles, M. (1989). *Statistics in psychology: An historical perspective.* Hillsdale, NJ: Erlbaum.

Cozby, P. C. (2001). *Methods in behavioral research* (7th ed.). Mountain View, CA: Mayfield.

Dillman, D. A. (1978). *Mail and telephone surveys: The total design method.* New York: Wiley.

Erdos, P. L. (1983). *Professional mail surveys.* Malabar, FL: Robert E. Krieger.

Gilovich, T. (1991). *How we know what isn't so: The fallibility of human reason in everyday life.* New York: Free Press.

Goldstein, W. M., & Goldstein, I. (1978). *How we know: An exploration of the scientific process.* New York: Plenum.

Gould, S. J. (1985, June). The median isn't the message. *Discover, 6*(6), 40–42.

Griggs, R. A., & Cox, J. R. (1982). The elusive thematic-materials effect in Wason's selection task. *British Journal of Psychology, 73,* 407–420.

Groves, R. M., & Kahn, R. L. (1979). *Surveys by telephone: A national comparison with personal interviews.* New York: Academic Press.

Hall, R. V., Axelrod, S., Foundopoulos, M., Shellman, J., Campbell, R. A., & Cranston, S. S. (1971). The effective use of punishment to modify behavior in the classroom. *Educational Technology, 11*(4), 24–26. Reprinted in K. D. O'Leary & S. O'Leary (Eds.). (1972). *Classroom management: The successful use of behavior modification.* New York: Pergamon.

Hinkle, D. E., Wiersma, W., & Jurs, S. G. (1988). *Applied statistics for the behavioral sciences* (2nd ed.). Boston: Houghton Mifflin.

Hite, S. (1987). *Women and love: A cultural revolution in progress.* New York: Knopf.

Jones, J. H. (1981). *Bad blood: The Tuskegee syphilis experiment.* New York: Free Press.

Jones, J. L. (1995). *Understanding psychological science.* New York: HarperCollins.

Keppel, G. (1991). *Design and analysis: A researcher's handbook.* (3rd ed.) Engelwood Cliffs, NJ, Prentice Hall.

Kerlinger, F. N. (1986). *Foundations of behavioral research* (4th ed.). New York: Holt, Rinehart & Winston.

Kranzler, G., & Moursund, J. (1995). *Statistics for the terrified.* Englewood Cliffs, NJ: Prentice Hall.

Leary, M. R. (2001). *Introduction to behavioral research methods* (3rd ed.). Needham Heights, MA: Allyn & Bacon.

Li, C. (1975). *Path analysis: A primer.* Pacific Grove, CA: Boxwood Press.

Likert, R. (1932). A technique for the measurement of attitudes. *Archives of Psychology, 19,* 44–53.

Messer, W., Griggs, R. A., & Jackson, S. L. (1999). A national survey of undergraduate psychology degree options and major requirements. *Teaching of Psychology, 26,* 164–171.

Milgram, S. (1963). Behavioral study of obedience. *Journal of Abnormal and Social Psychology, 67,* 371–378.

Milgram, S. (1974). *Obedience to authority.* New York: Harper & Row.

Milgram, S. (1977). Ethical issues in the study of obedience. In S. Milgram (Ed.), *The individual in a social world* (pp. 188–199). Reading, MA: Addison-Wesley.

Mitchell, M., & Jolley, J. (2001). *Research design explained* (4th ed.). Fort Worth, TX: Harcourt.

Olson, R. K., & Forsberg, H. (1993). Disabled and normal readers' eye movements in reading and nonreading tasks. In D. M. Willows, R. Kruk, & E. Corcos (Eds.), *Visual processes in reading and reading disabilities* (pp. 377–391). Hillsdale, NJ: Erlbaum.

Paul, G. L. (1966). *Insight vs. desensitization in psychotherapy.* Stanford, CA: Stanford University Press.

Paul, G. L. (1967). Insight vs. desensitization in psychotherapy two years after termination. *Journal of Consulting Psychology, 31,* 333–348.

Peters, W. S. (1987). *Counting for something: Statistical principles and personalities.* New York: Springer-Verlag.

Pfungst, O. (1911). *Clever Hans (the horse of Mr. von Osten): A contribution to experimental, anima, and human psychology* (C. L. Rahn, Trans.). New York: Holt, Rinehart & Winston. (Republished 1965.)

Rewey, K. L., June, J. A., Weiser, A., & Davis, S. F. (2000). "Is this REALLY APA format?" A presubmission checklist for the *PSI CHI Journal of Undergraduate Research, PSI CHI Journal of Undergraduate Research, 5,* 87–89.

Rosenhan, D. C. (1973). On being sane in insane places. *Science, 179,* 250–258.

Salkind, N. J. (1997). *Exploring research* (3rd ed.). Upper Saddle River, NJ: Prentice Hall.

Schweigert, W. A. (1994). *Research methods & statistics for psychology.* Pacific Grove, CA: Brooks/Cole.

Sidman, M. (1960). *Tactics of scientific research.* New York: Basic Books.

Stanovich, K. E. (2001). *How to think straight about psychology* (6th ed.). Boston: Allyn & Bacon.

Stigler, S. M. (1986). *The history of statistics.* Cambridge, MA: Belknap Press.

Tankard, J., Jr. (1984). *The statistical pioneers.* Cambridge, MA: Schenkman.

U.S. Department of Health and Human Services. (1981, January 26). Final regulations amending basic HHS policy for the protection of human subjects. *Federal Register, 46,* 16.

Wallis, C. (1987, October 12). Back off, buddy. *Time,* pp. 68–73.

Williams, T. M. (Ed.). (1986). *The impact of television: A natural experiment in three communities.* Orlando, FL: Academic Press.

Zimbardo, P. G. (1972). Pathology of imprisonment. *Transaction/Society, 9,* 4–8.

# Glossary

**ABA reversal design** A single-case design in which baseline measures are taken, the independent variable is introduced and measures are taken, and the independent variable is then removed and baseline measures taken again.

**ABAB reversal design** A design in which baseline and independent variable conditions are reversed twice.

**absolute zero** A property of measurement in which assigning a score of zero indicates an absence of the variable being measured.

**action checklist** A tally sheet used to note the presence or absence of behaviors.

**alternate-forms reliability** A reliability coefficient determined by assessing the degree of relationship between scores on two equivalent tests.

**alternative explanation** The idea that it is possible that some other, uncontrolled, extraneous variable may be responsible for the observed relationship

**alternative hypothesis (H$_a$), or research hypothesis (H$_1$)** The hypothesis that the researcher wants to support, predicting that a significant difference exists between the groups being compared.

**ANOVA (analysis of variance)** An inferential statistical test for comparing the means of three or more groups.

**applied research** The study of psychological issues that have practical significance and potential solutions.

**archival method** A descriptive research method that involves describing data that existed before the time of the study.

**average deviation** An alternative measure of variation that, like the standard deviation, indicates the average difference between the scores in a distribution and the mean of the distribution.

**bar graph** A graphical representation of a frequency distribution in which vertical bars are centered above each category along the $x$-axis and are separated from each other by a space, indicating that the levels of the variable represent discrete categories.

**basic research** The study of psychological issues in order to seek knowledge for its own sake.

**behavioral measures** Measures taken by carefully observing and recording behavior.

**between-groups sum of squares** The sum of the squared deviations of each group's mean from the grand mean, multiplied by the number of participants in each group.

**between-groups variance** An estimate of the effect of the independent variable *and* error variance.

**between-participants design** An experiment in which different participants are assigned to each group.

**Bonferoni adjustment** Setting a more stringent alpha level for multiple tests in order to minimize Type I errors.

**case study method** An in-depth study of one or more individuals.

**causality** The assumption that a correlation indicates a causal relationship between the two variables.

**ceiling effect** A limitation of the measuring instrument that decreases its ability to differentiate between scores at the top of the scale.

**checklist** A tally sheet on which the researcher records attributes of the participants and whether particular behaviors were observed.

**chi-square ($\chi^2$) goodness-of-fit test** A nonparametric inferential procedure that determines how well an observed frequency distribution fits an expected distribution.

**chi-square ($\chi^2$) test for independence** A nonparametric inferential test used when frequency data for two or more samples have been collected to determine how well an observed breakdown of people over various categories fits some expected breakdown.

**class interval frequency distribution** A table in which the scores are grouped into intervals and listed along with the frequency of scores in each interval.

**closed-ended questions** Questions for which participants choose from a limited number of alternatives.

**cluster sampling** A sampling technique in which clusters of participants that represent the population are used.

**coefficient of determination ($r^2$)** A measure of the proportion of the variance in one variable that is accounted for by another variable; calculated by squaring the correlation coefficient.

**Cohen's *d*** An inferential statistic for measuring effect size.

**college sophomore problem** The problem of external validity that results from using mainly college sophomores as participants in research studies.

**conceptual replication** A study based on another study that uses different methods, a different manipulation, or a different measure.

**confound** An uncontrolled extraneous variable or flaw in an experiment.

**construct validity** The degree to which a measuring instrument accurately measures a theoretical construct or trait that it is designed to measure.

**content validity** The extent to which a measuring instrument covers a representative sample of the domain of behaviors to be measured.

**continuous variables** Variables that usually fall along a continuum and allow for fractional amounts.

**control** Manipulating the independent variable in an experiment or any other extraneous variables that could affect the results of a study.

**control group** The group of participants that does not receive any level of the independent variable and serves as the baseline in a study.

**convenience sampling** A sampling technique in which participants are obtained wherever they can be found and typically wherever is convenient for the researcher.

**correlated-groups design** An experimental design in which the participants in the experimental and control groups are related in some way.

**correlated-groups *t* test** A parametric inferential test used to compare the means of two related (within- or matched-participants) samples.

**correlation coefficient** A measure of the degree of relationship between two sets of scores. It can vary between $-1.00$ and $+1.00$.

**correlational method** A type of nonexperimental research method that assesses the degree of relationship between two variables.

**counterbalancing** A mechanism for controlling order effects either by including all orders of treatment presentation or by randomly determining the order for each participant.

**criterion validity** The extent to which a measuring instrument accurately predicts behavior or ability in a given area.

**critical value** The value of a test statistic that marks the edge of the region of rejection in a sampling distribution, where values equal to it or beyond it fall in the region of rejection.

**cross-sectional design** A type of developmental design in which participants of different ages are studied at the same time.

**debriefing** Providing information about the true purpose of a study as soon after the completion of data collection as possible.

**deception** Lying to participants concerning the true nature of a study because knowing the true nature of the study might affect their performance.

**degrees of freedom (*df*)** The number of scores in a sample that are free to vary.

**demographic questions** Questions that ask for basic information, such as age, gender, ethnicity, or income.

**dependent variable** The variable in a study that is measured by the researcher.

**description** A depiction or account of a behavior gained through careful observation.

**descriptive statistics** Numerical measures that describe a distribution by providing information on the central tendency of the distribution, the width of the distribution, and the shape of the distribution.

**difference scores**   Scores representing the difference between participants' performance in one condition and their performance in a second condition.

**diffusion of treatment**   A threat to internal validity in which observed changes in the behaviors or responses of participants may be due to information received from other participants in the study.

**directionality**   The inference made with respect to the direction of a causal relationship between two variables.

**discrete variables**   Variables that usually consist of whole number units or categories and are made up of chunks or units that are detached and distinct from one another.

**disguised observation**   Studies in which the participants are unaware that the researcher is observing their behavior.

**double-barreled question**   A question that asks more than one thing.

**double-blind experiment**   An experimental procedure in which neither the experimenter nor the participant knows the condition to which each participant has been assigned.

**ecological validity**   The extent to which an experimental situation can be generalized to natural settings and behaviors.

**effect size**   The proportion of variance in the dependent variable that is accounted for by the manipulation of the independent variable(s).

**equal unit size**   A property of measurement in which a difference of 1 is the same amount throughout the entire scale.

**error variance**   The amount of variability among the scores caused by chance or uncontrolled variables.

**estimated standard error of the mean**   An estimate of the standard deviation of the sampling distribution.

**eta-squared ($\eta^2$)**   An inferential statistic for measuring effect size with an ANOVA.

**exact replication**   Repeating a study using the same means of manipulating and measuring the variables as in the original study.

**expectancy effects**   The influence of the experimenter's expectations on the outcome of the study.

**expected frequency**   The frequency expected in a category if the sample data represent the population.

**experimental group**   The group of participants that receives some level of the independent variable.

**experimental method**   A research method that allows a researcher to establish a cause-and-effect relationship through manipulation of a variable and control of the situation.

**experimenter effect**   A threat to internal validity in which the experimenter, consciously or unconsciously, affects the results of the study.

**explanation**   Identifying the causes that determine when and why a behavior occurs.

**external validity**   The extent to which the results of an experiment can be generalized.

**F-ratio**   The ratio of between-groups variance to within-groups variance.

**face validity**   The extent to which a measuring instrument appears valid on its surface.

**factorial design**   A design with more than one independent variable.

**factorial notation**   The notation that indicates how many independent variables are used in a study and how many levels are used for each variable.

**floor effect**   A limitation of the measuring instrument that decreases its ability to differentiate between scores at the bottom of the scale.

**frequency distribution**   A table in which all of the scores are listed along with the frequency with which each occurs.

**frequency polygon**   A line graph of the frequencies of individual scores.

**grand mean**   The mean performance across all participants in a study.

**histogram**   A graphical representation of a frequency distribution in which vertical bars centered above scores on the x-axis touch each other to indicate that the scores on the variable represent continuous quantities.

**history effect**   A threat to internal validity in which an outside event that is not a part of the manipulation of the experiment could be responsible for the results.

**hypothesis**   A prediction regarding the outcome of a study, often involving the relationship between two variables.

**hypothesis testing**   The process of determining whether a hypothesis is supported by the results of a research study.

**identity**   A property of measurement in which objects that are different receive different scores.

**independent variable**   The variable in a study that is manipulated by the researcher.

**independent-groups *t* test**  A parametric inferential test for comparing sample means of two independent groups of scores.

**inferential statistics**  Procedures for drawing conclusions about a population based on data collected from a sample.

**informed consent form**  A form given to individuals before they participate in a study to inform them of the general nature of the study and to obtain their consent to participate.

**Institutional Review Board (IRB)**  A committee charged with evaluating research projects in which human participants are used.

**instrumentation effect**  A threat to internal validity in which changes in the dependent variable may be due to changes in the measuring device.

**interaction effect**  The effect of each independent variable across the levels of the other independent variable.

**internal validity**  The extent to which the results of an experiment can be attributed to the manipulation of the independent variable rather than to some confounding variable.

**interrater reliability**  A reliability coefficient that assesses the agreement of observations made by two or more raters or judges.

**interval scale**  A scale in which the units of measurement (intervals) between the numbers on the scale are all equal in size.

**interviewer bias**  The tendency for the person asking the questions to bias the participants' answers.

**knowledge via authority**  Knowledge gained from those viewed as authority figures.

**knowledge via empiricism**  Knowledge gained through objective observation of organisms and events in the real world.

**knowledge via intuition**  Knowledge gained without being consciously aware of its source.

**knowledge via rationalism**  Knowledge gained through logical reasoning.

**knowledge via science**  Knowledge gained through a combination of empirical methods and logical reasoning.

**knowledge via superstition**  Knowledge that is based on subjective feelings, belief in chance, or belief in magic events.

**knowledge via tenacity**  Knowledge gained from repeated ideas and stubbornly clung to despite evidence to the contrary.

**kurtosis**  How flat or peaked a normal distribution is.

**laboratory observation**  Observing the behavior of humans or other animals in a more contrived and controlled situation, usually the laboratory.

**Latin square**  A counterbalancing technique to control for order effects without using all possible orders.

**leading question**  A question that sways the respondent to answer in a desired manner.

**leptokurtic**  Normal curves that are tall and thin, with only a few scores in the middle of the distribution having a high frequency.

**Likert rating scale**  A type of numerical rating scale developed by Rensis Likert in 1932.

**loaded question**  A question that includes nonneutral or emotionally laden terms.

**longitudinal design**  A type of developmental design in which the same participants are studied repeatedly over time as they age.

**magnitude**  (1) A property of measurement in which the ordering of numbers reflects the ordering of the variable; (2) an indication of the strength of the relationship between two variables.

**mail survey**  A written survey that is self-administered.

**main effect**  An effect of a single independent variable.

**matched-participants design**  A type of correlated-groups design in which participants are matched between conditions on variable(s) that the researcher believes is (are) relevant to the study.

**maturation effect**  A threat to internal validity in which naturally occurring changes within the participants could be responsible for the observed results.

**mean**  A measure of central tendency; the arithmetic average of a distribution.

**mean square**  An estimate of either variance between groups or variance within groups.

**measure of central tendency**  A number that characterizes the "middleness" of an entire distribution.

**measure of variation**  A number that indicates the degree to which scores are either clustered or spread out in a distribution.

**median**  A measure of central tendency; the middle score in a distribution after the scores have been arranged from highest to lowest or lowest to highest.

**mesokurtic**  Normal curves that have peaks of medium height and distributions that are moderate in breadth.

**mode**  A measure of central tendency; the score in a distribution that occurs with the greatest frequency.

**mortality (attrition)**  A threat to internal validity in which differential dropout rates may be observed in the experimental and control groups, leading to inequality between the groups.

**multiple-baseline design**  A single-case or small-*n* design in which the effect of introducing the independent variable is assessed over multiple participants, behaviors, or situations.

**multiple-baseline design across behaviors**  A single-case design in which measures are taken at baseline and after the introduction of the independent variable at different times across multiple behaviors.

**multiple-baseline design across participants**  A small-*n* design in which measures are taken at baseline and after the introduction of the independent variable at different times across multiple participants.

**multiple-baseline design across situations**  A single-case design in which measures are taken at baseline and after the introduction of the independent variable at different times across multiple situations.

**multiple-group time-series design**  A design in which a series of measures are taken on two or more groups both before and after a treatment.

**narrative records**  Full narrative descriptions of a participant's behavior.

**naturalistic observation**  Observing the behavior of humans or other animals in their natural habitat.

**negative correlation**  An inverse relationship between two variables in which an increase in one variable is related to a decrease in the other, and vice versa.

**negative relationship**  An inverse relationship between two variables in which an increase in one variable is accompanied by a decrease in the other variable.

**negatively skewed distribution**  A distribution in which the peak is to the right of the center point and the tail extends toward the left, or in the negative direction.

**nominal scale**  A scale in which objects or individuals are assigned to categories that have no numerical properties.

**nonequivalent control group posttest-only design**  A design in which at least two nonequivalent groups are given a treatment and then a posttest measure.

**nonequivalent control group pretest-posttest design**  A design in which at least two nonequivalent groups are given a pretest, then a treatment, and then a posttest measure.

**nonmanipulated independent variable**  The independent variable in a quasi-experimental design in which participants are not randomly assigned to conditions, but rather come to the study as members of each condition.

**nonparametric test**  A statistical test that does not involve the use of any population parameters—$\mu$ and $\sigma$ are not needed, and the underlying distribution does not have to be normal.

**nonparticipant observation**  Studies in which the researcher does not participate in the situation in which the research participants are involved.

**nonprobability sampling**  A sampling technique in which the individual members of the population do not have an equal likelihood of being selected to be a member of the sample.

**normal curve**  A symmetrical, bell-shaped frequency polygon representing a normal distribution.

**normal distribution**  A theoretical frequency distribution that has certain special characteristics.

**null hypothesis ($H_0$)**  The hypothesis predicting that no difference exists between the groups being compared.

**observational method**  Making observations of human or other animal behavior.

**observed frequency**  The frequency with which participants fall into a category.

**one-tailed hypothesis (directional hypothesis)**  An alternative hypothesis in which the researcher predicts the direction of the expected difference between the groups.

**one-way randomized ANOVA**  An inferential statistical test for comparing the means of three or more groups using a between-participants design and one independent variable.

**one-way repeated measures ANOVA**  An inferential statistical test for comparing the means of three or more groups using a correlated-groups design and one independent variable.

**open-ended questions**  Questions for which participants formulate their own responses.

**operational definition**  A definition of a variable in terms of the operations (activities) a researcher uses to measure or manipulate it.

**order effects**  A problem for within-participants designs in which the order of the conditions has an effect on the dependent variable.

**ordinal scale** A scale in which objects or individuals are categorized and the categories form a rank order along a continuum.

**parametric test** A statistical test that involves making assumptions about estimates of population characteristics, or parameters.

**partial correlation** A correlational technique that involves measuring three variables and then statistically removing the effect of the third variable from the correlation of the remaining two variables.

**partially open-ended questions** Closed-ended questions with an open-ended "Other" option.

**participant effect** A threat to internal validity in which the participant, consciously or unconsciously, affects the results of the study.

**participant observation** Studies in which the researcher actively participates in the situation in which the research participants are involved.

**participant (subject) variable** A characteristic inherent in the participants that cannot be changed.

**Pearson product-moment correlation coefficient (Pearson's r)** The most commonly used correlation coefficient when both variables are measured on an interval or ratio scale.

**percentile rank** A score that indicates the percentage of people who scored at or below a given raw score.

**person-who argument** Arguing that a well-established statistical trend is invalid because we know a "person who" went against the trend.

**personal interview** A survey in which the questions are asked face-to-face.

**phi coefficient** (1) The correlation coefficient used when both measured variables are dichotomous and nominal; (2) an inferential test used to determine effect size for a chi-square test.

**physical measures** Measures of bodily activity (such as pulse or blood pressure) that may be taken with a piece of equipment.

**placebo** An inert substance that participants believe is a treatment.

**placebo group** A group or condition in which participants believe they are receiving treatment but are not.

**platykurtic** Normal curves that are short and more dispersed (broader).

**point-biserial correlation coefficient** The correlation coefficient used when one of the variables is measured on a dichotomous nominal scale and the other is measured on an interval or ratio scale.

**population** All of the people about whom a study is meant to generalize.

**positive correlation** A direct relationship between two variables in which an increase in one is related to an increase in the other, and a decrease in one is related to a decrease in the other.

**positive relationship** A relationship between two variables in which an increase in one variable is accompanied by an increase in the other variable.

**positively skewed distribution** A distribution in which the peak is to the left of the center point and the tail extends toward the right, or in the positive direction.

**post hoc test** When used with an ANOVA, a means of comparing all possible pairs of groups to determine which ones differ significantly from each other.

**posttest-only control group design** An experimental design in which the dependent variable is measured after the manipulation of the independent variable.

**prediction** Identifying the factors that indicate when an event or events will occur.

**pretest/posttest control group design** An experimental design in which the dependent variable is measured both before and after manipulation of the independent variable.

**principle of falsifiability** The idea that a scientific theory must be stated in such a way that it is possible to refute or disconfirm it.

**probability** The expected relative frequency of a particular outcome.

**probability sampling** A sampling technique in which each member of the population has an equal likelihood of being selected to be part of the sample

**pseudoscience** Claims that appear to be scientific but that actually violate the criteria of science.

**public verification** Presenting research to the public so that it can be observed, replicated, criticized, and tested.

**qualitative variable** A categorical variable for which each value represents a discrete category.

**quantitative variable** A variable for which the scores represent a change in quantity.

**quasi-experimental method** Research that compares naturally occurring groups of individuals; the variable of interest cannot be manipulated.

**quota sampling** A sampling technique that involves ensuring that the sample is like the population on certain characteristics but uses convenience sampling to obtain the participants.

**random assignment** Assigning participants to conditions in such a way that every participant has an equal probability of being placed in any condition.

**random sample** A sample achieved through random selection.

**random selection** A method of generating a random sample in which each member of the population is equally likely to be chosen as part of the sample.

**range** A measure of variation; the difference between the lowest and the highest scores in a distribution.

**rating scale** A numerical scale on which survey respondents indicate the direction and strength of their response.

**ratio scale** A scale in which, in addition to order and equal units of measurement, there is an absolute zero that indicates an absence of the variable being measured.

**reactivity** A possible reaction by participants in which they act unnaturally because they know they are being observed.

**regression analysis** A procedure that allows us to predict an individual's score on one variable based on knowing one or more other variables.

**regression line** The best-fitting straight line drawn through the center of a scatterplot that indicates the relationship between the variables.

**regression to the mean** A threat to internal validity in which extreme scores, upon retesting, tend to be less extreme, moving toward the mean.

**reliability** An indication of the consistency or stability of a measuring instrument.

**representative sample** A sample that is like the population.

**response bias** The tendency to consistently give the same answer to almost all of the items on a survey.

**restrictive range** A variable that is truncated and does not vary enough.

**reversal design** A single-case design in which the independent variable is introduced and removed one or more times.

**sample** The group of people who participate in a study.

**sampling bias** A tendency for one group to be over-represented in a sample.

**sampling distribution** A distribution of sample means based on random samples of a fixed size from a population.

**scatterplot** A figure that graphically represents the relationship between two variables.

**self-report measures** Usually questionnaires or interviews that measure how people report that they act, think, or feel.

**sequential design** A developmental design that is a combination of the cross-sectional and longitudinal designs.

**single-blind experiment** An experimental procedure in which participants do not know the condition to which they have been assigned.

**single-case design** A design in which only one participant is used.

**single-group design** A research study in which there is only one group of participants.

**single-group posttest-only design** A design in which a single group of participants is given a treatment and then tested.

**single-group pretest/posttest design** A design in which a single group of participants takes a pretest, then receives some treatment, and then takes a posttest measure.

**single-group time-series design** A design in which a single group of participants is measured repeatedly before and after a treatment.

**skeptic** A person who questions the validity, authenticity, or truth of something purporting to be factual.

**small-*n* design** A design in which only a few participants are studied.

**socially desirable response** A response that is given because a respondent believes it is deemed appropriate by society.

**solvable problems** Questions that are potentially answerable by means of currently available research techniques.

**Spearman's rank-order correlation coefficient** The correlation coefficient used when one or more of the variables is measured on an ordinal (ranking) scale.

**split-half reliability** A reliability coefficient determined by correlating scores on one half of a measure with scores on the other half of the measure.

**standard deviation** A measure of variation; the average difference between the scores in the distribution and the mean or central point of the distribution, or more precisely, the square root of the average squared deviation from the mean.

**standard error of the difference between means** The standard deviation of the sampling distribution of differences between the means of independent samples in a two-sample experiment.

**standard error of the difference scores** The standard deviation of the sampling distribution of mean differences between dependent samples in a two-group experiment.

**standard error of the mean** The standard deviation of the sampling distribution.

**standard normal distribution** A normal distribution with a mean of 0 and a standard deviation of 1.

**static checklist** A tally sheet on which attributes that will not change are recorded.

**statistical power** The ability to find significant differences when they truly exist.

**statistical significance** An observed difference between two descriptive statistics (such as means) that is unlikely to have occurred by chance.

**stratified random sampling** A sampling technique designed to ensure that subgroups or strata are fairly represented.

**Student's *t* distribution** A set of distributions that, although symmetrical and bell-shaped, are not normally distributed.

**sum of squares error** The sum of the squared deviations of each score from its group (cell) mean; the within-groups sum of squares in a factorial design.

**sum of squares factor A** The sum of the squared deviation scores of each group mean for factor A minus the grand mean times the number of scores in each factor A condition.

**sum of squares factor B** The sum of the squared deviation scores of each group mean for factor B minus the grand mean times the number of scores in each factor B condition.

**sum of squares interaction** The sum of the squared difference of each condition mean minus the grand mean times the number of scores in each condition. $SS_A$ and $SS_B$ are then subtracted from this sum.

**survey method** Questioning individuals on a topic or topics and then describing their responses.

**systematic empiricism** Making observations in a systematic manner in order to test hypotheses and refute or develop a theory.

**systematic replication** A study that varies from an original study in one systematic way—for example, by using a different number or type of participants, a different setting, or more levels of the independent variable.

***t* test** A parametric inferential statistical test of the null hypothesis for a single sample where the population variance is not known.

**telephone survey** A survey in which the questions are read to participants over the telephone.

**test** A measurement instrument used to assess individual differences in various content areas.

**testing effect** A threat to internal validity in which repeated testing leads to better or worse scores.

**test/retest reliability** A reliability coefficient determined by assessing the degree of relationship between scores on the same test administered on two different occasions.

**theory** An organized system of assumptions and principles that attempts to explain certain phenomena and how they are related.

**third-variable problem** The problem of a correlation between two variables being dependent on another (third) variable.

**total sum of squares** The sum of the squared deviations of each score from the grand mean.

**Tukey's honestly significant difference (HSD)** A post hoc test used with ANOVAs for making all pairwise comparisons when conditions have equal *n*.

**two-tailed hypothesis (nondirectional hypothesis)** An alternative hypothesis in which the researcher predicts that the groups being compared differ, but does not predict the direction of the difference.

**Type I error** An error in hypothesis testing in which the null hypothesis is rejected when it is true.

**Type II error** An error in hypothesis testing in which there is a failure to reject the null hypothesis when it is false.

**undisguised observation** Studies in which the participants are aware that the researcher is observing their behavior.

**validity** A measure of the truthfulness of a measuring instrument; indicates whether the instrument measures what it claims to measure.

**variable** An event or behavior that has at least two values.

**variance** The standard deviation squared.

**Wilcoxon matched-pairs signed-rank *T* test**  A nonparametric inferential test for comparing the sample medians of two dependent or related groups of scores.

**Wilcoxon rank-sum test**  A nonparametric inferential test for comparing the sample medians of two independent groups of scores.

**within-groups sum of squares**  The sum of the squared deviations of each score from its group mean.

**within-groups variance**  The variance within each condition; an estimate of the population error variance.

**within-participants design**  A type of correlated-groups design in which the same participants are used in each condition.

**z-score (standard score)**  A number that indicates how many standard deviation units a raw score is from the mean of a distribution.

**z test**  A parametric inferential statistical test of the null hypothesis for a single sample where the population variance is known.

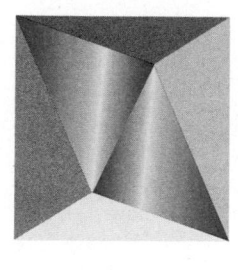

# Index

## TO THE OWNER OF THIS BOOK:

I hope that you have found *Research Methods and Statistics: A Critical Thinking Approach,* Second Edition, useful. So that this book can be improved in a future edition, would you take the time to complete this sheet and return it? Thank you.

School and address:_____

Department:_____

Instructor's name:_____

1. What I like most about this book is:_____

_____

_____

2. What I like least about this book is:

_____

_____

3. My general reaction to this book is:

_____

_____

4. The name of the course in which I used this book is:

_____

5. Were all of the chapters of the book assigned for you to read?_____

   If not, which ones weren't?_____

6. In the space below, or on a separate sheet of paper, please write specific suggestions for improving this book and anything else you'd care to share about your experience in using this book.

_____

_____

_____

**THOMSON**

**WADSWORTH** ™

# BUSINESS REPLY MAIL
FIRST-CLASS MAIL    PERMIT NO. 102    MONTEREY CA

POSTAGE WILL BE PAID BY ADDRESSEE

Attn:  Psychology, Vicki Knight, Publisher

Wadsworth/Thomson Learning
60 Garden Ct  Ste 205
Monterey CA  93940-9967

FOLD HERE

OPTIONAL:

Your name:_____ Date: _____

May we quote you, either in promotion for *Research Methods and Statistics:
A Critical Thinking Approach,* Second Edition, or in future publishing ventures?

Yes: _____   No: _____

Sincerely yours,

*Sherri L. Jackson*